# ULTIMATE TEEN BOOK GUIDE

Editors **Daniel Hahn & Leonie Flynn**
Associate Editor **Susan Reuben**

**A & C Black • London**

*As always, to L.M.H. Also to my father, mother and uncle,
who shared with me their love of books – LF*

First published 2006 by
A & C Black Publishers Ltd
38 Soho Square, London, W1D 3HB

www.acblack.com
www.ultimatebookguide.com

Text copyright © 2006 Daniel Hahn, Leonie Flynn and Susan Reuben
Pages 438–439 constitute an extension of this copyright page

ISBN  0-7136-7330-3
ISBN  978-0-7136-7330-2

A CIP catalogue for this book is available from the British Library.

A & C Black uses paper produced with elemental chlorine-free
pulp, harvested from managed sustained forests.

Printed and bound by Page Bros. (Norwich) Ltd, UK.

# Contents

# Introduction
## by David Almond

Books. There they are lined up on shelves or stacked on a table. There they are wrapped in their jackets, lines of neat print on nicely bound pages. They look like such orderly, static things. Then you, the reader, come along. You open the book jacket, and it can be like opening the gates into an unknown city, or opening the lid on a treasure chest. You read the first word and you're off on a journey of exploration and discovery. When you find your own best books, which might be nothing like the best books for other readers, a kind of magic occurs. The language and the story and your own imagination blend and react and fizz with life and possibility. Sometimes it's like the book was written just for you, as if it's been waiting just for you, its perfect reader. It doesn't always happen, of course. Sometimes a book will fall flat for you. What's all the fuss about? you'll ask. But then you'll find another one that excites you, that speaks clearly to you, that sets up weird resonances in you. It goes on happening all through your life. It's happening to me now, this week, as I read Yukio Mishima's *The Sailor Who Fell from Grace with the Sea*. Why have I waited till now to read this wonderful book? Because I've been reading other books, of course.

Reading is a lifelong adventure. Mishima's is just the latest in a long line of books that have gripped me. Other recent highlights include Sarah Waters' hypnotic narratives, and the novels of Ha Jin. In my teenage years? Two out-of-print books: *The Grey Pilot* by Angus MacVicar that took me from my Tyneside home to flee through the Western Isles with Bonny Prince Charlie;

and *The Adventures of Turkey* by Ray Harris that allowed me to share the adventures of a Huckleberry Finn-ish Australian lad. Then John Wyndham's marvellous *The Day of the Triffids* (UTBG 96) followed quickly by his *The Chrysalids* (UTBG 77), *The Midwich Cuckoos*, *The Kraken Wakes*, as I discovered the excitement of exploring an author's whole oeuvre for the first time. Next an astonishing book called *The Third Eye* by the ex-Tibetan monk T. Lobsang Rampa. For a time I felt that I was Lobsang in some weird way. Then he turned out to be a bloke from Essex. Did I care? Not a bit. His book had worked its magic on me. The 'hoax' was just another part of that magic. Then Hemingway came along. I remember pulling out a collection of his short stories from the library shelf, opening the book, reading the first line of a story called 'A Clean, Well-Lighted Place', a story in which hardly anything seems to happen, but which set up resonances inside me that have never stopped. Then Stevie Smith's poems, and Sylvia Plath's, and Kafka, and so it went on and so it goes on.

The wonderful book that you're holding in your hands now is a kind of traveller's guide. It points you to many sidetracks and highlights and landmarks that other travellers have found worth visiting. Many of them will be as exciting to you as they were to the folk who recommend them. Others might not be. The world of books is almost limitless. As you travel, you'll hit upon your own best books, the books that have a particular fascination and excitement for you. You'll keep moving on, free to roam and explore and discover at will…

David Almond

# How to Use This Book

You'll find that the majority of this book is self-explanatory, and we hope you'll find it easy to use. But here's a bit of help just in case…

Most of *The Ultimate Teen Book Guide* is made up of book recommendations. Our team of contributors has recommended over 700 books for you, so there's bound to be stuff you'll like, whatever your tastes. The book recommendations are listed alphabetically by title, and they work like this:

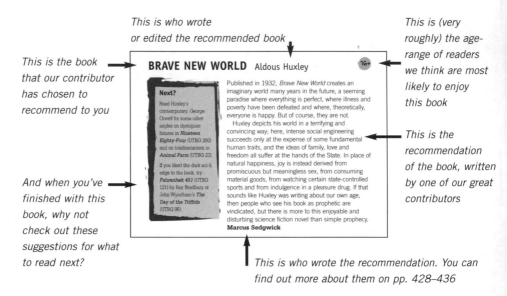

*This is who wrote or edited the recommended book*

*This is (very roughly) the age-range of readers we think are most likely to enjoy this book*

*This is the book that our contributor has chosen to recommend to you*

**BRAVE NEW WORLD** Aldous Huxley 16+

**Next?**

Read Huxley's contemporary, George Orwell for some other angles on dystopian futures in *Nineteen Eighty-Four* (UTBG 260) and on totalitarianism in *Animal Farm* (UTBG 23).

If you liked the dark sci-fi edge to the book, try *Fahrenheit 451* (UTBG 121) by Ray Bradbury or John Wyndham's *The Day of the Triffids* (UTBG 96).

Published in 1932, *Brave New World* creates an imaginary world many years in the future, a seeming paradise where everything is perfect, where illness and poverty have been defeated and where, theoretically, everyone is happy. But of course, they are not.

Huxley depicts his world in a terrifying and convincing way; here, intense social engineering succeeds only at the expense of some fundamental human traits, and the ideas of family, love and freedom all suffer at the hands of the State. In place of natural happiness, joy is instead derived from promiscuous but meaningless sex, from consuming material goods, from watching certain state-controlled sports and from indulgence in a pleasure drug. If that sounds like Huxley was writing about our own age, then people who see his book as prophetic are vindicated, but there is more to this enjoyable and disturbing science fiction novel than simple prophecy.
**Marcus Sedgwick**

*This is the recommendation of the book, written by one of our great contributors*

*And when you've finished with this book, why not check out these suggestions for what to read next?*

*This is who wrote the recommendation. You can find out more about them on pp. 428–436*

The Next? box gives you ideas of what you might like to read once you've finished the recommended book. It might include other books by the same author, or books which are funny / exciting / inspiring / terrifying in the same way as the book you've just finished, or which deal with a similar subject in a different way. The letters UTBG mean the book to read next has a recommendation in *The Ultimate Teen Book Guide* too, which you can find on the page indicated. For example, if you see…

For another powerful tale of fighting racial prejudice in the American South, read Harper Lee's classic *To Kill a Mockingbird* (UTBG 375).

…then you can turn to p. 375 to read about *To Kill a Mockingbird* and decide whether it might be just the book for you.

There are also 13 short features on particular types of book – on fantasy, on historical fiction, on books about love and sex, on horror stories, on sci-fi, etc. If you have a favourite genre of book, you'll find lots of good suggestions about what to read here. Or if you fancy trying something in a genre you don't know much about ('Hmm, I've never really read much fantasy...') the features will give you a good idea of where to start. You'll find a list of these features on p. 3.

The features are all written by experts in the field – usually people who write that kind of book themselves (Catherine Fisher on fantasy, Bali Rai on race, Kevin Brooks on stories about characters going off the rails, K.K. Beck on detective stories). If you want a short and snappy title to start off with – something not too challenging, that will grip you from the first line – Pete Johnson has some great suggestions for you on p. 418. And next to them you'll find lists of relevant titles, most of which you can read about elsewhere in *The Ultimate Teen Book Guide*.

Finally, you'll come across reviews by winners of our schools' competition, the results of our nationwide teen readers' poll (for which, full details of every book can be found on our website: www.ultimatebookguide.com), and all sorts of other bits and pieces...

# About the Editors

Since editing *The Ultimate Book Guide* in 2004, **DANIEL HAHN** has curated two exhibitions, lived in Germany, edited a book about the Globe Theatre, translated quite a lot and started writing a new book (as well as putting together this second *UBG*). He's also done little bits of teaching, organised a couple of charity fund-raisers, and, you know, other things like that. As you can see, he's still got no intention of getting a proper job.

**LEONIE FLYNN** lives surrounded by boxes. Usually she lives surrounded by books, but moving has put paid to that. When not writing, staring at boxes or being heartlessly cruel to young boys (she's a librarian at a school) she attempts to read every book she reads about and to write every story she imagines. Actually, she fails at both, but still manages to remain remarkably cheerful.

**SUSAN REUBEN** is senior publisher at Egmont Books. Four days before *The Ultimate Teen Book Guide* was due to be delivered to the publishers she delivered her first child: Isaac Harry. Any errors and omissions in this volume may be blamed on that. When not feeding her baby, Susan enjoys sleeping.

# 1066 AND ALL THAT

**12+**

## W.C. Sellar and R.J. Yeatman

This wickedly funny skit on British history, written by a teacher and an ad man in 1930, is every bit as effective today. It's not just the puns on names, so bad they're positively brilliant (the Egberts, Ethelwulfs and Ethelbalds become Eggberd, Eggbreth and Eggfroth). It's not just the wry recognition that the grand old tales are mostly bunk, and the great old triumphs (a.k.a. the massacre of other civilisations) look a little different now. It's not even the fake test papers ('Why do you picture John of Gaunt as a rather emaciated grandee?'). No – it's the fact that truth really is stranger than fiction, and that this is the kind of 'nonsense' that actually makes more and more sense, the more you know about history.

**Sarah Gristwood**

### Next?

For the same off-beat humour, try the classic school story *Down With Skool!* (UTBG 110).

Or George Mikes' guide to being British, *How to Be an Alien*.

Watch *Blackadder* on TV, especially series two and three – and read the scripts; they're hilarious, too.

# THE 13½ LIVES OF CAPTAIN BLUEBEAR

**14+**

## Walter Moers

### Next?

Someone else who writes extraordinary fantasy is Terry Pratchett; try *The Colour of Magic*.

*Life of Pi* (UTBG 218) is a strange story involving a lifeboat, a hyena, a monkey, a tiger and a boy.

A whole life encapsulated in one book? Try Raymond Briggs' *Ethel and Ernest* (UTBG 118).

'People usually start life by being born. Not me, though.'

From the first page you are catapulted into a world that is just so refreshingly *different*: full of Hobgoblins, Minipirates, a headless Bollogg, a Bolloggless head, Nocturnomaths and many other weird and wonderful creatures (including, of course, blue bears).

This book covers Bluebear's adventures starting with his rescue from a dreaded whirlpool, as a baby floating in a nutshell, through 12 eventful lives, to his final half-life 'at peace', and holds you entranced throughout.

Not only does this book cater for many genres, from sci-fi to romance, but it also travels at such a fast-moving pace that you will sail through it like a jet-propelled sponge through a sea of information.

**Samuel Mortimer (aged 11)**

# 52 PICK-UP Elmore Leonard

The difficulty with an author like Elmore Leonard is he's written so many books – all, by and large, never less than very good – that it's almost too hard to choose which one to point to and say 'that's the one you should read!'. In the end I plumped for *52 Pick-up* for no particular reason except that I read it ages ago and still clearly remember it. Like every Leonard book, this one is tightly plotted, has razor-sharp dialogue and comes with a real sting in the tail; it's a thriller, it's about blackmail and revenge and it's very cool.

People often look down on crime fiction as being somehow less than literature, but this book has style, class and a great story. What more could you want?

**Graham Marks**

### Next?

The films *Get Shorty* and *Jackie Brown* were both based on books by Elmore Leonard – why not read the originals?

Lots of films have been made of Raymond Chandler's books too; try *The Big Sleep* (UTBG 40) or *Farewell, My Lovely*.

Carl Hiaasen's books are also set in Florida; try *Hoot* (UTBG 175) or *Tourist Season* (UTBG 377).

And have a look at our feature on detective fiction on pp. 104–105.

# 84 CHARING CROSS ROAD Helene Hanff

### Next?

Helene Hanff's *The Duchess of Bloomsbury Street* is a sequel to *84 Charing Cross Road*. *Apple of My Eye* is about her native New York and *Q's Legacy* is about her education in English literature.

Anne Fadiman's *Ex Libris* charts a lifelong love affair with books.

*A Particular Friendship* by Dirk Bogarde charts another friendship between two people who never met.

*84 Charing Cross Road* is a collection of letters exchanged between down-to-earth New York writer Helene Hanff and London bookseller Frank Doel between 1949 and 1969. Miss Hanff, who had a passion for obscure and out-of-print books, initially wrote to Marks & Co, a bookshop at 84 Charing Cross Road, with a list of second-hand books she would like, if they could supply them, so long as they didn't cost more than $5 each. Mr Doel replied, saying that they had managed to find some of the items on her list and were sending them on, with an invoice.

Thus a wonderful correspondence and a 20-year association began. Rereading a few of the letters today I was captivated all over again – this is one of the most delightful books ever published.

**Michael Lawrence**

# 87th PRECINCT series   Ed McBain

I wish I'd known Ed McBain's **87th Precinct** series of police procedural mysteries when I was a teenager. They're short and beautifully written with tight plots, sharp social detail and vivid characters. There are more than 50 of them, written over as many years. The quality dipped a little halfway through, but the late ones show him back on top form, which is unusual for a long-running series.

Each title is set in a fictionalised version of New York with multiple storylines and recurring characters like detectives Steve Carella, Meyer Meyer and Fat Ollie Weeks. They're carefully researched and shot through with world-weary attitude. Many crime writers have borrowed from McBain (as have loads of TV cop shows), but nobody did it better.

**David Belbin**

> ## Next?
>
> Start the series with the early ones: *Cop Hater* or *The Mugger*.
>
> More detective stories? Try a British version with the **Inspector Morse** books (UTBG 191) by Colin Dexter, starting with *Last Bus to Woodstock* or the great Agatha Christie; try *Murder on the Orient Express*.
>
> One of the great classic detective writers is Dashiel Hammett; try *The Maltese Falcon* or *The Glass Key*, both of which are tautly plotted and totally brilliant.

# ABARAT   Clive Barker

Candy Quackenbush lives in Chickentown, USA, the most boring place in the world. But Candy has a destiny. Fate is leading her to an extraordinary land: the Abarat, a great archipelago where each island sits at a different hour of the day. There she must fight the evil that is overtaking the islands, helped and hindered by a cast of bizarre allies and enemies.

Barker's imagination is astonishing, and he leaves most other writers in the dust. *Abarat* is a dizzying ride for children and adults alike. It is sometimes scary, sometimes funny, but always enthralling. If you thought fantasy was all about wizards and elves and fairies, read *Abarat* and find out what real fantasy feels like.

**Chris Wooding**

> ## Next?
>
> If you liked this, read the sequel: *Abarat: Days Of Magic, Nights Of War*.
>
> If you're fond of tales about children escaping the boring, everyday world try C.S. Lewis' *The Chronicles of Narnia*.
>
> Or for a creepier take on the same theme, check out Neil Gaiman's *Coraline* (UTBG 83). Brrr.

# THE ABORTION

16+

## Richard Brautigan

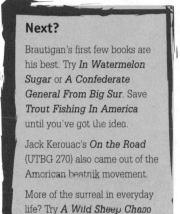

**Next?**

Brautigan's first few books are his best. Try *In Watermelon Sugar* or *A Confederate General From Big Sur*. Save *Trout Fishing In America* until you've got the idea.

Jack Kerouac's *On the Road* (UTBG 270) also came out of the American beatnik movement.

More of the surreal in everyday life? Try *A Wild Sheep Chase* (UTBG 413).

Brautigan's writing looks simple. It isn't. His novels can be sad, funny, wise, silly, innocent and strange. He was a big literary success for a decade or so. Then he wasn't. He killed himself in 1984. Recently his books are being brought back into print. As they should be.

*The Abortion* starts out as a piece about a library where people deposit their unpublished books. Vida brings one that is about why she hates her body. She and the unworldly librarian fall in love. Vida gets pregnant and has an illegal abortion. Might not sound like a lot goes on, but this is one of Brautigan's more heavily plotted books. It's a good introduction to his work, which is as much about moments as it is about story.

**David Belbin**

# ABOUT A BOY Nick Hornby

14+

This should really be called *About Two Boys*: it tells of 36-year-old big-kid Will whose independent income means he doesn't have to work and he owns all the latest state-of-the-art gadgets; his main ambition is to sleep with as many women as possible, with no ties. Into this emotionally barren existence stumbles Marcus (12), a vegetarian hippy with the dress sense of a middle-aged geography teacher, thanks to his depressive mother. Bullied at school, he craves a father figure and imagines Will ideal for the role. Unfortunately, Will disagrees and resents this geeky kid impinging on his life and (God forbid!) feelings.

Somehow, though, their lives become intertwined, and each learns something important from the other: Will teaches Marcus about popular culture and how to be hip, and in turn learns from Marcus how to be grown-up.

Witty, cynical and touching – seriously cool stuff!

**Catherine Robinson**

**Next?**

All Nick Hornby's books are worth reading. Try *High Fidelity* (UTBG 167) or *Fever Pitch* (UTBG 128).

*Man and Boy* (UTBG 234) also deals with a grown man facing up to his emotional responsibilities – sounds heavy, but it's oh so readable!

# ACROSS THE NIGHTINGALE FLOOR

## Lian Hearn

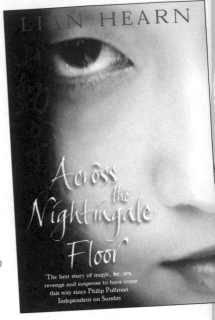

*Across the Nightingale Floor* is the first book in the **Tales of the Otori** trilogy, which interweaves two gripping plots. The first is about a boy torn between three great powers: the Tribe, a clan of highly disciplined, mercenary assassins who are equipped with mystical gifts; the Otori, the honourable warrior clan of his adopted father Shigeru; and the Hidden, a group of highly persecuted pacifists (his mother being one) who believe that their one God will guide them through life. Then there is the tale of Kaede, whose mythical beauty and power mean she is used as a pawn by her captors, who keep her as a political prisoner.

This captivating book is fantastic from cover to cover, combining an incredible plot with intense descriptions and fantastically crafted characters.
**Oscar Dub (aged 13)**

'The best story of magic, lies, sex, revenge and suspense to have come this way since Philip Pullman'
Independent on Sunday

### Next?

There are two sequels: *Grass for His Pillow* and *Brilliance of the Moon*, which continue the story of Takeo and Kaede.

If this makes you wonder about Japanese society, try Katherine Paterson's *Puppet Master*.

Another gripping adventure starts with Mary Renault's *The King Must Die* (UTBG 208).

Catherine Jinks' *Pagan's Crusade* (UTBG 283), set in the 12th century at the time of the Crusades, is just as exciting – and gory!

Or try a classic adventure such as Alexandre Dumas' *The Count of Monte Cristo*.

From its opening, in which a young boy wanders back from a carefree afternoon spent picking mushrooms to find a massacre going on in his village, this story grips the reader and refuses to let go until the very last word. It's an extraordinarily powerful and highly original fantasy packed with scenes of haunting beauty and horrifying violence. In a world where warring clans vie for supremacy while hidden strings are pulled by the mysterious Tribe, the boy Takeo must make a painful choice between power, love and revenge.

This is fantasy at its most sophisticated – but it's not for the squeamish.
**Brian Keaney**

# THE ADVENTURES OF TOM SAWYER

## Mark Twain

### Next?

Sequels? *Tom Sawyer Abroad* is a comic follow-up in which Tom, Huck and Jim go to Africa in a balloon. Or try *Tom Sawyer Detective*, an ingenious murder-mystery.

For something more challenging – the great *Huckleberry Finn* (UTBG 181).

Another journey afloat? *Life of Pi* (UTBG 218).

Mark Twain tells us early on that Tom Sawyer 'was not the model boy of the village. He knew the model boy very well, though, and loathed him', which tells us everything we need to know about his hero, a fast-talking boy who can even persuade his friends that painting a fence is fun. Destined always to disappoint his Aunt Polly, and never to live up to the standards of his half-brother Sid or his cousin Mary, he skips school to go swimming, fishing or to spend time with his friend Huckleberry Finn, son of the town drunkard. When Tom and Huck witness the aftermath of the murder of Horse Williams, their adventures suddenly become a lot less innocent.

The first of Twain's novels concerning these characters, this book captures exactly what it's like to be on the cusp of adulthood.

**Matt Thorne**

# AFTER THE FIRST DEATH   Robert Cormier

Terrorists have hijacked a school bus and are threatening to blow it up. Among them is Milo, a teenager who has known nothing but war and believes only in violence. Kate is the bus driver. 17 years old, she fears that she doesn't have the strength to look after the children suddenly in her charge. Unknown to both, the General in charge of the effort to resolve the crisis is sending his 15-year-old son to the terrorists as a show of good faith. All are, in their own ways, morally and politically innocent, and Cormier shows how innocence can have terrifying and deadly consequences.

Fifteen years after I first read it, *After the First Death* still has the power to make me gasp. Complex and multilayered, it yields new meanings and fresh insights on every rereading.

**Graham Gardner**

### Next?

All of Cormier's books are dark adventures in reading. Try *Heroes* (UTBG 166).

*The Defender* (UTBG 100) is about how terrorism changes everyone's lives.

*The Song of an Innocent Bystander* (UTBG 348) is about a girl taken hostage.

# AGAINST THE DAY

12+

## Michael Cronin

**Next?**

This is a trilogy. The next volume is *Through the Night*, which continues the story of the Resistance.

For a World War II adventure based on real history, read *The Machine-Gunners* (UTBG 229) by Robert Westall.

Keith Roberts' *Pavane* is another alternative history; the story of a Britain defeated by the Spanish Armada.

It's 1940 and the Nazis have invaded Britain. They expect the British citizens to settle down happily under their rule, putting up portraits of Hitler in their homes and honouring his birthday.

But Frank has lost his father to the war and he's not going to just accept the new order of things. And soon he starts to realise that he's not alone – there's a group of people determined to resist the Nazis, who'll risk their lives to help overthrow the regime.

This is a scary look at what Britain might have been like if history had turned out very differently – and it's a gripping adventure story, too.

**Susan Reuben**

# AIRBORN   Kenneth Oppel

12+

Matt Cruse is a cabin boy aboard the luxury airship, *Aurora*. Matt has called this airship home for three years. He has a good chance of being promoted to a junior sailmaker. That is, until a girl called Kate de Vries arrives on board. She is fired by a mysterious quest and they soon become good friends.

However, one night, in the middle of the ocean, they are attacked by deadly Sky Pirates. The ship crash-lands on a strange island and Matt and Kate are thrown into adventures beyond imagining, and the mystery unfurls…

I loved this book. It was like a jigsaw, every page like a piece, fitting together to make a superb adventure which was full of humour.

**Edward Fry (aged 12)**

**Next?**

The sequel, *Skybreaker*, in which Matt encounters a ghost ship and lost treasure.

Or try the exciting *Mortal Engines* (UTBG 250) by Philip Reeve, which has cities on wheels and more airships!

Or for sailing ships, cut-throats and savages, try Geraldine McCaughrean's *Plundering Paradise* or Elizabeth Laird's *Secrets of the Fearless*.

# AL CAPONE DOES MY SHIRTS

## Gennifer Choldenko

Moose Flanagan's family move to Alcatraz where his dad is to be a guard of the infamous inmates at the famous prison there. Life is tough at first and his family are all so tied up with looking after the every need of his mentally ill (probably autistic) sister that they've no time or energy left to give a thought to how Moose is settling in. Angry, he goes out to find new friends and adventures of his own. This enjoyable and exciting insight into the imagined life and times of gangster Al Capone packs a huge emotional punch.

**Eileen Armstrong**

### Next?

Choldenko's *Notes from a Liar and Her Dog* tells of a girl trying to come to terms with her adoption with the help of her tiny Chihuahua and a chicken-drawing best friend, Harrison.

Theresa Breslin's *Prisoner in Alcatraz* offers another compelling insight into conditions in the infamous prison.

Other books bringing historical people and places to life include *Stratford Boys* by Jan Mark (playwright William Shakespeare), and *Fleshmarket* (UTBG 131) (surgeon Dr Knox).

# ALANNA: THE FIRST ADVENTURE

## Tamora Pierce

### Next?

This is the first part of the **Song of the Lioness** quartet. Alanna's quest to become a knight continues in *In the Hand of the Goddess*.

If you want a story where the heroine chooses to be a wizard, try *So You Want To Be A Wizard* by Diane Duane.

And if you want a longer story with castles, knights and magic, try *Magician* by Raymond E. Feist.

Alanna wants to be a knight, but is supposed to become a magician. Her twin brother Thom wants to be a magician, but is supposed to become a knight. So they decide to swap places. The only catch is that to become a knight Alanna has to pretend to be a boy. But keeping her true identity secret and dealing with the harsh routine of knightly training turn out to be the least of Alanna's problems – there's a conspiracy in the royal castle, and Alanna's friendship with Prince Jonathan is going to drag her into the middle of it! Alanna is one of the most likeable heroines you'll ever find in a story – good-hearted, adventurous, and brave.

**Benedict Jacka**

# THE ALCHEMIST  Paulo Coelho

14+

## Next?

Paulo Coelho has written many other books about searching for meaning; try *The Pilgrimage*.

Other stories to make you think? *Jonathan Livingstone Seagull* (UTBG 198) or *Zen and the Art of Motorcycle Maintenance* by Robert M. Pirsig, which really does have something to do with both the things in its title.

If you prefer a more philosophical bent, try Jostein Gaarder's *Sophie's World* (UTBG 348).

This is, on the face of it, a simple fable about Santiago, an Andalusian shepherd boy, and his search for treasure. But the more you read this wonderful story, the more you begin to see in its pages. The book describes Santiago's journey from Spain to Tangiers and on into the deserts of Egypt, where he meets the mysterious alchemist. With his mentor's help, Santiago begins to listen to The Soul Of The World and learns that the treasure he seeks is right under his nose.

This is a brilliant story that asks us to believe in our dreams and listen to our hearts. Coelho is a master storyteller and this is a masterful tale. Remember all that glitters is not gold and prepare to be enchanted. This novel really does live up to the hype.

**Bali Rai**

# THE ALCHEMIST'S APPRENTICE

12+

## Kate Thompson

Since his mother died, Jack has been apprenticed to a blacksmith. But – frankly – he's not very good at it. So one day, having crashed his master's cart, Jack decides to run away. He leaves London, heading south, and soon finds himself at the house of Jonathan Barnstable. Barnstable, it seems, is an alchemist, secretly working away at the mysteries of how to create gold…

And this Mr Barnstable – tall and extraordinary, with white hair and piercing blue eyes – invites Jack to be his apprentice. Under his guidance, Jack learns the secrets of the alchemist's art, and a lot more besides. But this is just the beginning of his adventure…

Full of 18th-century atmosphere, with a likeable hero in Jack and a fascinating character in the mysterious Barnstable, this is an enthralling read.

**Daniel Hahn**

## Next?

Go on to read more Kate Thompson – maybe try her **Missing Link** series next, or her latest, *The New Policeman*.

Or try Alan Garner's *The Owl Service* (which Kate Thompson has recommended on p. 281).

Or how about some Leon Garfield? Read *Smith* first.

# ALCHEMY Margaret Mahy

14+

Roland has it all – he's going out with the sexiest girl in the school, he's effortlessly clever, he's a natural leader. But then things start to go bizarrely awry – his teacher catches him shoplifting, and uses this knowledge to blackmail him into making friends with a girl in his class he normally wouldn't be seen dead talking to.

Then when Roland goes to the girl's house, he enters a disturbing world where nothing in the rooms ever changes, and there's a peculiar presence at the top of the stairs that is definitely not human.

*Alchemy* combines a seriously sinister story of the supernatural with all the normal concerns of a boy on the verge of adulthood – and the result is gripping, quite scary and life-affirming, too.

**Susan Reuben**

## Next?

For another Margaret Mahy ghost story, try the award-winning *The Changeover* (UTBG 69). Or for a Mahy book set entirely in this world, try *Memory*.

Caroline Pitcher's *Mine* (UTBG 246) is also about a teenager encountering the supernatural.

For classic ghost stories, try those by Algernon Blackwood, or M.R. James (UTBG 144).

For something funnier, but still about the supernatural, how about *The Henry Game* (UTBG 166)?

# THE ALDOUS LEXICON Michael Lawrence

12+

## Next?

In *The Homeward Bounders* by Diana Wynne Jones, a boy from the 19th century is forced to wander from world to world, trying to get home again.

*The House on the Strand* by Daphne du Maurier and *Traveller in Time* by Alison Uttley are both about going back in time.

*Piggies* by Nick Gifford presents an alternative view of 21st-century life – one where vampires rule.

I've come close to death at least three times – which means that in alternate realities I've died at least three times… Running flat out in the woods at home and coming to a teetering halt on the edge of a sheer drop that I didn't know was there, is a moment that still haunts me! So what are those alternate worlds – the ones without me – like?

This is a concept that Michael Lawrence sets out to explore in his trilogy, **The Aldous Lexicon**. Alaric Underwood's mother has a 50/50 chance of survival after a train crash. In this world she dies – in an alternate reality she lives. When Alaric finds a way to cross between these two worlds he finds himself having to rethink everything he ever knew about space and time.

**Laura Hutchings**

# ALEX RIDER series Anthony Horowitz

Alex Rider is certainly no ordinary teen. While most kids worry about spots and homework, Alex has a far bigger priority – saving the world! At the mere age of 14 and after the mysterious death of his uncle, he is thrown into the dangerous world of espionage. He quickly learns the tricks of the trade and, armed with an array of amazing (and well-disguised) gadgets, he is sent on his first mission: to the lavish mansion of millionaire Herod Sayle.

If that whets your appetite, Alex's adventures don't stop there. They span over six incredible books (to date), each more exciting and gripping than the last. The characters are unique and believable, the plots are inventive and the scrapes Alex gets himself into are absolutely brilliant. It's definitely recommendable to anyone with a thirst for espionage and mystery.

**Gareth Smith (aged 14)**

### Next?

The **Alex Rider** books in sequence are: *Stormbreaker* (UTBG 356), *Point Blanc*, *Skeleton Key*, *Eagle Strike*, *Scorpia*, *Ark Angel*.

More hair-raising escapes, gadgets and dastardly villains? Try Chris Ryan's **Alpha Force** series, beginning with *Survival* and *Rat-Catcher* (UTBG 304).

Anthony also writes of the paranormal. His new series, **The Power of Five**, begins with *Raven's Gate* (UTBG 305).

# ALICE series Susan Juby

As a big fan of novels featuring funny teen 'diarists', I was delighted to discover Susan Juby's **Alice** series. 16-year-old Alice MacLeod lives in tiny Smithers, British Colombia, where she has been home-schooled since the age of six, after having made the grave mistake of arriving at first grade dressed in a hobbit costume. When the first book in the series opens, Alice is going back to school hoping that this time she'll fit in. Alas, however, her hobbit days are still vividly remembered by her fellow Smithers teens, and Alice is not exactly welcomed with open arms. Between her thrift-shop wardrobe and her aspirations of becoming a novelist, Alice has no hope of ever going 'mainstream'!

Alice MacLeod is the Canadian answer to Sue Townsend's hilarious **Adrian Mole** series and, like Adrian, I hope she'll be around for a very long time.

**Meg Cabot**

### Next?

The second book of the series, *I'm Alice (Beauty Queen?)*.

Another girl who dresses kind of different? Try Dyan Sheldon's *Confessions of a Teenage Drama Queen* (UTBG 82).

Or, of course, try the very funny **Adrian Mole** series (UTBG 324).

# ALL AMERICAN GIRL  Meg Cabot

**Next?**

There is a sequel! *All American Girl: Ready or Not*. Cabot's books all make ordinary characters take on extraordinary roles – a chaperone to a drop-dead-gorgeous star in *Teen Idol*, the heir to the throne in the *Princess Diaries* (UTBG 299), a ghosthunter in the **Mediator** series and a specially gifted crime solver in the **Missing** series.

*Ella Enchanted* by Gail Carson Levine takes a new twist on the most famous princess story of all: *Cinderella*.

Sam is an ordinary teenager who dresses in black and tries hard to be different. She has an extraordinary talent for drawing celebs, and loves music. She's also fallen for her perfect cheerleader older sister's boyfriend, Jack. Skiving her art class one day, Sam ends up saving the President's life outside a record shop, in a completely believable and inventive plot twist. Suddenly she is catapulted into fame and life in the spotlight as Teen Ambassador to the UN – which isn't as easy as it sounds. Luckily, the President's son David is on hand to help her out.

This is an exciting, action-packed teen rom-com with realistic and riveting Top 10 Lists of Everything separating the chapters, and a totally American flavour.

**David Gardner (aged 16)**

# ALL QUIET ON THE WESTERN FRONT
## Erich Maria Remarque

First published in Germany in 1929, later banned by the Nazis, this is the classic anti-war novel. All the horrors of the trenches are here: the sheer terror of shellfire, rats, lice, hand-to-hand combat with sharpened spades, and how it feels to be trapped in a shell hole with a man you've just killed.

But it's as much about youth as it is about war. There's a lyrical quality to the quieter scenes, such as the visit to see a wounded comrade in hospital, melancholy trips home on leave, night swimming in a French river, and a brief romantic interlude with a local girl. The final chapter is as moving as it is cathartic: a fitting epitaph for a lost generation.

**Thomas Bloor**

**Next?**

For more fiction set during World War I try *Strange Meeting* (UTBG 358), the story of an intense friendship set against the run-up to the fateful Somme offensive.

Robert Graves' *Goodbye To All That* (UTBG 153) is a riveting autobiography of life in the trenches.

For a female perspective on the war see Vera Brittain's *Testament of Youth*.

# ALL THE PRETTY HORSES Cormac McCarthy

**16+**

**Next?**

*The Crossing* and *Cities of the Plain* complete **The Border** trilogy.

It is claimed that McCarthy's prose style is similar to William Faulkner's. Try *As I Lay Dying* and see for yourself.

*Brokeback Mountain* by Annie Proulx is a slim but powerful book about the West and growing up; it's also in the collection *Close Range: Wyoming Stories.*

Or try Ernest Hemingway's *The Snows of Kilimanjaro*.

This is the first of a trilogy about the border country between America and Mexico, a land where cowboys ride hard, love deep and hurt so much it almost kills them. I had never read a Western when I picked up this book and for me it is Hemingway on horseback, along with the most poetic and heartbreaking descriptions of landscape and inhabiting it that I know. Even if you are the most couch-potato person on earth you will find your mind riding with Cormac McCarthy, and it is a journey no one should miss.

**Raffaella Barker**

# THE AMAZING MAURICE AND HIS EDUCATED RODENTS Terry Pratchett

**12+**

Smart, sharp, wickedly funny and very fast-moving sums up this, Terry Pratchett's first book for younger readers set in the fabulous Discworld universe. The story itself is loosely based on the traditional tale of 'The Pied Piper of Hamelin'. The Amazing Maurice of the title is a streetwise tomcat, always on the look-out for the perfect scam. He even has his own 'plague' of educated rats, who travel ahead to 'infest' a given town. Maurice then arrives with a 'stupid-looking kid' who plays a pipe, and the townspeople pay him to persuade the boy to charm the rats away. A nice little earner all round. It usually works like magic, but oh dear, not this time… Evil awaits…

**Chris d'Lacey**

**Next?**

Terry Pratchett is one of the most prolific authors around. So, good news: there are LOTS of other Discworld books to read; try *The Colour of Magic*. Need I say more?

OK, I will. For a fun-packed trip round our universe why not try *The Hitchhiker's Guide to the Galaxy* (UTBG 171) by Douglas Adams.

For a different sort of humour try Philip Ridley's *Mighty Fizz Chilla*.

# THE AMULET OF SAMARKAND
## Jonathan Stroud

12+

In a modern-day London controlled by magicians, Simon Lovelace is a master magician who possesses the fabled Amulet of Samarkand. Nathaniel is a young magician's apprentice with a rather precocious talent, who summons the querulous 5000-year-old djinni, Bartimaeus, to relieve him of it.

What starts out as a smallish act of revenge eventually leads to a largish web of intrigue, murder and rebellion. The plot is thrilling enough, but much of the story (including hilarious footnotes) is told by Bartimaeus himself in such a quirky and cranky fashion that it makes it very hard indeed to put down. In fact, I challenge you not to want to read straight through all three books (this is the first of a trilogy) without stopping.

**Chris d'Lacey**

> **Next?**
>
> *The Golem's Eye* and *Ptolemy's Gate* complete the **Bartimaeus** trilogy.
>
> Or take a sideways step into high fantasy with Garth Nix's *Sabriel* (UTBG 316) and its sequels.
>
> Or for different settings with a strangely realistic touch try Mary Hoffman's *Stravaganza: City of Masks*.

# AND THE ASS SAW THE ANGEL  Nick Cave

 16+

> **Next?**
>
> *The Sound and the Fury* by William Faulkner, the wise ol' grandaddy of Southern Gothic literature.
>
> Or *Wise Blood* by Flannery O'Connor, in which a soldier returns to his evangelical Deep South community.
>
> Or what about vampires in New Orleans? Try Anne Rice's lush, erotic and darkly weird *Interview with the Vampire* (UTBG 191).

As a musician, Nick Cave is a legend – from the howling punk sound of his first band, The Birthday Party, to the simmering brew of gospel, blues and rock cooked up by his long-running outfit, The Bad Seeds. Throughout, Nick sings about love, religion and murder, all of which wash up in this lyrical, mad-eyed masterpiece of a novel.

The story is told by a mute and inbred boy called Euchrid Eucrow, who is sinking slowly in quicksand. Despite his looming death, he retraces the tragic story of his life growing up in a plantation community – and it reads like a mangled version of the Old Testament. From biblical downpours to braying mules, crazy preachers, liquored-up crones and lynch mobs, it'll set your imagination ablaze.

**Matt Whyman**

# ANGELA'S ASHES
## Frank McCourt

When Frank McCourt was four years old, his parents took him back from America to live in Ireland. You might think that the story of his childhood, from poverty in New York to absolute poverty in the back lanes of rain-sodden Limerick, would make for depressing reading. In fact, due to the beauty of the writing and the wry humour that worms its way through even the bleakest of scenarios, it's a wonderful, life-enhancing read. Although many of the characters in the book are not so lucky, Frank's is a story of survival of body and spirit against all the odds. A deeply moving, powerful and unforgettable book.

**Malachy Doyle**

### Next?

There are plenty of other Irish coming-of-age stories to get your teeth into. *Paddy Clarke Ha Ha Ha* (UTBG 282) by Roddy Doyle is another book to make you laugh and cry.

Or try *Twenty Years a-Growing* by Maurice O'Sullivan, and *Reading in the Dark* by Seamus Deane.

# ANGUS, THONGS AND FULL-FRONTAL SNOGGING  Louise Rennison

### Next?

Next in the series is *It's OK, I'm Wearing Really Big Knickers...*

Ros Asquith also writes about the perils of boys (and girls) in *Love, Fifteen* (UTBG 226) and *I Was a Teenage Worrier* (UTBG 184).

A slightly less funny take on the whole kissing thing is *The Serious Kiss* (UTBG 330).

I read this book when I was tired and fed up. I bought it at a station bookstall to read on the train. Three minutes later, the train was clattering out of London, and I was already smiling. Two hours later, when I arrived back home in leafy Gloucestershire, I was grinning from ear to ear. It's about the daily life of Georgia Nicolson (a lovable teenage rogue), her beloved cat Angus and the human males in her universe who offer much in the way of aggravation.

One of Georgia's many issues is: if she ever gets up close and personal with the boy of her dreams, how will she cope with the challenging business of snogging? Luckily for Georgia, there's a boy in the neighbourhood who's prepared to give girls private lessons in the sacred art. Although he doesn't charge, it still sure beats a paper round. Sheer entertainment from cover to cover. Laughs guaranteed.

**Sue Limb**

# ANIMAL FARM George Orwell

14+

## Next?

Orwell will make you think about the world. Try the equally alarming *Nineteen Eighty-Four* (UTBG 260).

For a dystopian world that's real, not fantasy, *One Day in the Life of Ivan Denisovich* (UTBG 271).

Sometimes it's easier to see something clearly by stepping aside from it. Pigs on a farm, for instance, or mice in a concentration camp. To some, the Holocaust may not seem a suitable subject for comics, but the allegory *Maus* (UTBG 239) proves them wrong. The Jews are mice, the Germans, cats.

The animals at Manor Farm are unhappy with their lot: their drunken master is letting the farm go to ruin and they're all starving, so they stage a revolution to take over. To begin with everything seems rosy – the animals all work overtime, and everyone's belly is full of food. But it doesn't take long for the pigs to decide that because of their intelligence, they are superior to the stupid chickens and the workhorse Boxer.

A simple animal story? Yes, but this is also an allegory of the Russian Revolution and the society it created. As the pigs famously say, 'All animals are equal, but some animals are more equal than others'. This is a rare kind of book that works as both a political satire and as a great read.

**Julia Bell**

# ANITA AND ME Meera Syal

14+

Meena is nine and growing up fast. She lives with her Punjabi family in a small, otherwise all-white, mining village on the edge of Wolverhampton. She longs to be someone, to run with the pack and be accepted – not because of her colour, but because she wants to be seen as an equal among her peer group. She lies and steals – and idolises the feisty, brassy, blonde Anita, whom Meena's parents worry is leading her astray.

At first, despite their Indian dress, food and Diwali celebrations, Meena and her family seem to fit into the village. But in one searing moment the scales fall from her eyes when Sam Lowbridge, the Bad Boy of the village whom she has always secretly admired, sneers about 'darkies' and 'wogs'. Nothing will feel the same again.

**Jamila Gavin**

## Next?

Another Meera Syal? Try *Life Isn't All Ha Ha Hee Hee*: three friends, three weddings, three stories.

A book that will also make you look differently at racism, Malorie Blackman's *Noughts and Crosses* (UTBG 267) and its sequels.

Bali Rai's *Rani and Sukh* (UTBG 303) is a modern-day 'Romeo and Juliet' story.

# ANNA KARENINA

14+

## Leo Tolstoy

I first read *Anna Karenina* when I was 13 and although it is a very long book with a complicated plot, I was transfixed by it. I think it is the best story about the different kinds of love between men and women that has ever been written – and when I was 13, this was a subject that fascinated me. Anna herself is a real, living woman, with a real woman's virtues and failings, and her life forms the main thread of the narrative. But through the other characters, the book also gives us a living picture of a society quite different from ours that miraculously becomes as real to us as our own.

**Nina Bawden**

### Next?

If this has given you a taste for huge, heart-rending novels, try Tolstoy's epic, *War and Peace* (UTBG 398), or *Dr Zhivago* (UTBG 108) by Boris Pasternak.

There's lots of doomed love from French novelists too – try Gustave Flaubert's unbeatable *Madame Bovary*.

Or for something epic and English, try George Eliot's *Middlemarch*, a magnificent, all-encompassing novel of society and yet individuals, too.

# ANOTHER ROADSIDE ATTRACTION

## Tom Robbins

### Next?

What else should you read after this, but another Tom Robbins! Try *Villa Incognito*.

There are no other authors quite the same, but try John Irving and his *A Prayer for Owen Meany* (UTBG 293).

Many graphic novels have a surreal quality to them; try *Jimmy Corrigan* (UTBG 197) or Neil Gaiman's **The Sandman** series (UTBG 320).

For some writers, language is just this great big box of tricks to have fun and play with. True, reading that sort of thing can be amusing for a while, but it can often be like going to a party and not being allowed to join in. And then there's Tom Robbins, who has the most fun with language of any writer I know; as he says, 'if little else, the brain is an educational toy'.

*Another Roadside Attraction*, written in 1971, was his first novel and 30 years later he's only published a total of eight books. It has an astonishing cast of memorable characters and is about all kinds of things, including flea circuses, religion and the possible end of Western civilization.

**Graham Marks**

# ANTHEM FOR DOOMED YOUTH

## Ed. Jon Stallworthy

'Too terrible to remember, too important to forget', the poetry of the World War I never fails to stir up a yearning outrage that such things happened, were allowed to happen. The 12 poets included here are both the chroniclers of war and its casualties: many died in the trenches.

Starting with Brooke's romantic idealism, progressing to Sassoon's savage, bitter railing, the book pays homage to less well-known poets too, with biographies and portraits, photographs of the battlefields and reproductions of the manuscripts. But it has nothing of the 'school project' about it. It's a window on the senselessness and horror of war. And it bites at the heart like the rat in Roseburg's 'Break of Day', scurrying through the mud to feast on the dead.

**Geraldine McCaughrean**

### Next?

Pat Barker's *Regeneration* (UTBG 309) is a fictional account of Sassoon and Owen's time at a hospital for the 'mentally unstable'.

One of the most famous war novels of recent years is Sebastian Faulks' *Birdsong* (UTBG 43).

Field-Marshall Lord Wavell assembled an anthology of all the poems he memorised over the course of his life – it's called *Other Men's Flowers*.

# AN ANTHROPOLOGIST ON MARS

## Oliver Sacks

### Next?

Others by Oliver Sacks: *The Man Who Mistook His Wife for a Hat* or *Awakenings*.

You might also like an astonishing book on human memory by A.L. Luria called *The Mind of a Mnemonist*.

Nicola Morgan's *Mondays Are Red* (UTBG 248) is about a boy whose senses are muddled by synaesthesia.

Sometimes truth is stranger than fiction. Who'd believe a story about an artist who wakes up in hospital after an auto accident and discovers to his horror that he can only see in black and white? Or the account of a woman who keeps hearing strange songs on a radio, only to find the music is inside her own head? Or a man with violent tics and mannerisms who becomes a surgeon? Or a 14-year-old boy who can't speak but can take a quick look at a palace and draw it perfectly from memory? Oliver Sacks introduces us to these people. And because he didn't just study them, but lived with them, you get a real glimpse into their minds.

**Caroline Lawrence**

# APOCALYPSE

## Tim Bowler

When Kit and his family survive a dramatic boating accident, they are lucky to get washed up on a small island. Unfortunately it doesn't provide the sanctuary they need. The inhabitants are openly hostile and they soon realise their lives are in great danger. What is more disturbing is that Kit starts to notice the presence of a strange, naked man with a birthmark on his face, just like his. In his ensuing struggle to stay alive and make sense of what is happening around him, Kit finds himself dealing with far more than he'd bargained for.

If you enjoy books that are rich in atmosphere, with nail-biting plots, you will love *Apocalypse*. Tim Bowler has written a wonderful, haunting book that kept me on the edge of my seat as events careered towards its thrilling conclusion.

**Susila Baybars**

---

### Next?

Tim Bowler's books are all edgy; try *Stormchasers* about a boy trying to save his kidnapped sister or *River Boy* (UTBG 310).

*Darkhenge* (UTBG 94) is another dark adventure about the blurring of the real and the imagined.

Or for a very different shipwreck – Daniel Defoe's *Robinson Crusoe*! OK, it's a classic, but a rip-roaring read nonetheless!

---

## The Ultimate Teen Readers' Poll

### YOUR FAVOURITE AUTHOR

1 **Jacqueline Wilson**

2 **J.K. Rowling**

3 **Anthony Horowitz**

4 **Roald Dahl**

5 **Lemony Snicket**

6 **J.R.R. Tolkien**

7 **Malorie Blackman**

8 **Darren Shan**

9 **Philip Pullman**

10 **Meg Cabot**

# ARABELLA Georgette Heyer

**Next?**

Heyer's *The Unknown Ajax* is a warm and refreshingly realistic romance; *The Grand Sophy* is sheer sparkling fun.

You might also try one of her witty detective stories, like *Duplicate Death* or *No Wind of Blame.*

And of course, anyone who likes Heyer's romances should be reading the real thing – Jane Austen's *Pride and Prejudice* (UTBG 294).

*Arabella* was the first Georgette Heyer I ever read – the first of very many. I fell in love with the humour, the elegant prose and the amazingly accurate period detail that set Heyer's above other historical romances.

*Arabella* is the Cinderella story of an impoverished Yorkshire girl who comes to London and meets the wealthy Mr Beaumaris – but his pride and her prejudice show signs of getting in the way of their romance. Today, several decades on, I might prefer one of Heyer's more sophisticated stories: something like *The Nonesuch*, or *The Foundling*. But *Arabella* is still one of the great Regency romances; sweet as an ice-cream sundae, but never, ever sickly.

**Sarah Gristwood**

# ARCHER'S GOON
## Diana Wynne Jones

Archer sends his goon to collect the two thousand that Quentin Sykes owes him. Only the 'two thousand' is words, not money, and Sykes is an English lecturer and writer. His children, Howard and Anthea (known universally as Awful), become fascinated by the Goon and by what on earth their father is doing for Archer.

Gradually we discover that the town in which the Sykes family live is governed by seven megalomaniac wizard siblings, two of whom are women. Archer is one of this family, but who is his goon and what has happened to the youngest brother, Venturus?

The complex plot gets weirder and weirder towards the end – only Diana Wynne Jones could carry this off!

**Mary Hoffman**

**Next?**

Other titles by Wynne Jones include *Howl's Moving Castle* (UTBG 180), *Fire and Hemlock* (UTBG 128), and *Eight Days of Luke.*

Debi Glion's *Pure Dead Magic* has some of the same exuberance, especially with names.

Or for a more serious magic book, read Michael Lawrence's **The Aldous Lexicon** trilogy (UTBG 17).

# ARE YOU DAVE GORMAN?

**14+**

## Dave Gorman and Danny Wallace

### Next?

*Dave Gorman's Googlewhack Adventure* is different because Gorman spends the first half of it trying to avoid getting involved in another bet on the grounds that he's too old for that sort of thing and wants to write a novel instead.

*Frost on My Moustache* (UTBG 141) by Tim Moore is another hilarious tale of unheroic travelling.

Dave and Danny are flatmates who, with too much time on their hands and alcohol in their systems, set out to find 54 other people called Dave Gorman (that's one for every card in a pack including the jokers but not the card explaining the rules of bridge). Danny's reluctance to get involved in this adventure is clear from the start and increases as his relationship with his girlfriend suffers and he and Dave clock up some 25,000 miles of travelling. In this great book, Dave's bizarre dedication to his ridiculous task is matched only by the bemusement of the other Dave Gormans he meets.

**Anthony Reuben**

# ARE YOU EXPERIENCED?

**16+**

## William Sutcliffe

When Dave and his girlfriend Liz can't manage to adjust their seatbacks on the flight to India, you know the holiday that follows won't be all plain sailing. (And this is on the first page of the novel.) The ideals that they set out with prove not to be very idealistic, and the realities all too real for these cushy teens. Dave's naïve, deadpan narrative will have you shaking with laughter and wondering why any of us bother to get out of bed in the morning, let alone embrace the universality of the world and travel. If you are contemplating travel in your gap year, read this book. If you simply feel your horizons need widening, read it too. You'll realise you're not as inadequate as you thought.

**Jon Appleton**

### Next?

Paranoia among narrators kept William Sutcliffe going for three novels: try the extremely funny *New Boy* (UTBG 258), his first.

Alex Garland's *The Beach* (UTBG 34) is another captivating book of adventuring abroad.

There's more backpacking in *Lone in Luka* by Gill Harvey which tells of a gap year love affair, and *I is Someone Else* by Patrick Cooper.

# ARTEMIS FOWL  Eoin Colfer

*Artemis Fowl* is one of those books that is able to combine magic, adventure and humour into one roller-coaster read. Artemis Fowl – a 12-year-old boy with a girl's name! – is on a quest to find fairy gold. He plans to kidnap Captain Holly Short of the LEPrecon unit and get the gold as ransom. But he doesn't realise what he's getting into… From Bio-bombs to tri-barrelled blasters, Artemis is in great danger.

You'll meet many interesting and hilarious characters: Mulch Diggums, a smelly dwarf on the run from the authorities; 20-foot trolls with the capacity to kill anything they think is edible; and one of my favourites, Artemis' bodyguard Butler.

Eoin Colfer keeps you spellbound and even manages to involve the reader in a bit of code breaking… Intrigued? Well, there is only one way to find out more… Read the book!

**Benjamin Cuffin-Munday (aged 11)**

### Next?

The sequels are: *The Arctic Incident*, *The Eternity Code* and *The Opal Deception*. There's also a World Book Day special, *The Seventh Dwarf*, which is well worth hunting out, and has a story which fits in between books one and two.

*Faerie Wars* and its sequels by Herbie Brennan are a slightly more serious take on fairies.

Or for something else action-packed, try Robert Muchamore's *The Recruit* (UTBG 307).

# ARTHUR: THE SEEING STONE

## Kevin Crossley-Holland

### Next?

For a completely different take on Arthurian legend, try *The Once and Future King* (UTBG 270), or Susan Cooper's **The Dark Is Rising** series (UTBG 93).

Or, for a marvellous interpretation of how Merlin might have been, try Mary Stewart's *The Crystal Cave* (UTBG 87).

Set in the Welsh Marches in 1199, this is the tale of Arthur de Caldicot who discovers his namesake, the legendary boy-king Arthur, in his 'seeing stone'. In a time of transition between one century and another, one king and another, between childhood and manhood, the 'between places … tremble like far horizons' and all certainties and loyalties are brought into question.

Bullied by his older brother Serle and supported by his friend Gatty, Arthur increasingly identifies with the boy-king as he unravels the true nature of his quest, while the enigmatic figure of Merlin moves effortlessly between one dimension and another. A dense, absorbing tale told in a beautiful, spare style.

**Livi Michael**

# AT SWIM-TWO-BIRDS   Flann O'Brien

**Next?**

Flann O'Brien's *The Poor Mouth* is another satire on Irish life.

Or read *The Crock of Gold* by James Stephens, another Celtic fantasy and satire.

Or if you are feeling especially adventurous, try *Finnegans Wake* by James Joyce.

I first read this as an undergraduate and even now it can reduce me to tears of mirth. The book is a brilliant farce, satire and send-up of different aspects of Irish life, including the Catholic Church and Celtic heroes… But it's also poking fun at literature, and in particular the novel. The narrator believes that stories should have several beginnings and endings and sets out to write such a book. The descriptions of lodging with his hideous uncle and his drunken friends are hilarious. This book is full of crazy fantasy and characters such as the Pooka, the Good Fairy and Orlick Trellis. It's a sort of Celtic Goon humour. Not for the faint-hearted but very rewarding.

**Anne Flaherty**

# AT THE SIGN OF THE SUGARED PLUM

## Mary Hooper

Summer 1665, and Hannah journeys to London to work in her sister's confectionery shop, The Sugared Plum. She never receives the letter forbidding her visit, as plague threatens the city; once there, she cannot return. 'At home in Chertsey, life had been peaceful… Here though, now, there was a bitter, heart-stopping danger in each day.' As more people die, the bustling city that first intoxicated Hannah becomes increasingly gruesome, and the sisters are forced into action to save just one life from the carnage.

It is the details – of clothes, smells, foods, plague-symptoms (nasty!), mass burials – that bring this novel to life. Hannah's curious and determined viewpoint really draws you into this absorbing historical story, and parts of her plague-ridden London are recognisable today.

**Helen Simmons**

**Next?**

Mary Hooper's written more about Hannah in *Petals from the Ashes*.

If you like historical fiction, *No Shame, No Fear* (UTBG 261) by Ann Turnbull is well worth a read; the story is set in the 17th century and follows the fate of two lovers divided by religion.

*A Parcel of Patterns* by Jill Paton Walsh is another gripping novel about the plague, based on the true story of the Derbyshire village of Eyam, where villagers imposed quarantine on themselves to stop disease spreading.

# ATONEMENT Ian McEwan

 14+

**Next?**

None of Ian McEwan's books are easy reads, but you might want to try two others he's written: *Enduring Love* and *The Cement Garden* (UTBG 69).

You might also like *The Wasp Factory* (UTBG 400) by Iain Banks.

I guess I started reading 'grown-up' fiction when I had gone through my own stack of books and the library was closed. I picked up something my mother had left on the coffee table and discovered a new world, complete with naughty bits. I was hooked.

*Atonement* is a novel I would have gobbled up back then. The story starts in 1935 when 13-year-old Briony witnesses a moment that she's not quite old enough to understand, between her older sister and a young man. Her interpretation of this moment leads us into a world of secrets, lies and unbearable damage.

The book spans a lifetime and the ending is one you'll probably read at least twice.

**Sara Nickerson**

# AUTOMATED ALICE

14+

## Jeff Noon

In 1860, Alice, frustrated by being unable to complete a jigsaw, follows her aunt's riddle-ranting parrot into the workings of a clock, which transports them forward in time. One hundred and thirty years later Alice finds herself in a surreal world populated by all manner of the eccentric, electric and eclectic.

Accompanied by her now turbo-charged doll Celia (an anagrammed, automated Alice), she stumbles upon the gruesome jigsaw murders for which they are framed by the sly Civil Serpents. Alice soon discovers that in order to return home she must retrieve the missing jigsaw pieces. But can Alice – both automated and alive – get home before the villains get them? A chaotically creative, ingeniously invented psychedelic plot. Think Carroll's words laced with LSD!

**Felicity-Rose Barrow (aged 16)**

**Next?**

Another book that takes Alice as its starting point is *The Looking Glass Wars* (UTBG 222).

Jasper Fforde plays around with classic works of literature in *The Eyre Affair* (UTBG 120).

The disturbing *Feed* (UTBG 127) by M.T. Anderson shows a future world where everyone's brain is directly linked to the Internet.

The original *Alice's Adventures in Wonderland* by Lewis Caroll is still loved by both adults and children today. Take a tumble down the rabbit hole!

# BAD ALICE  Jean Ure

**Next?**

Jean Ure's teenage novels are many: *See You Thursday*, which begins the relationship between Marianne and a blind musician, Abe, is highly recommended; *One Green Leaf*, *The Other Side of the Fence* and *Plague* are also outstanding.

And read Lewis Carroll's *Alice's Adventures in Wonderland* – excellent whatever your age.

Unusually for a teenage book, this cleverly crafted novel features characters younger than its likely readers. Duffy, staying with his grandmother, befriends Alice, the strange, withdrawn girl who hides in a burrow in a neighbouring garden. Duffy's grandmother can't speak highly enough of Alice's adoptive father, Norman, a key figure in the local church. But when Duffy reads Alice's poems – brilliant, darkly suggestive parodies of 'The Walrus and the Carpenter', 'Jabberwocky' and other *Alice in Wonderland* poems – he realises that the supposedly saintly Norman is mistreating her, and she urgently needs help.

Ingenious and thoroughly engrossing, *Bad Alice* involves the reader by making us feel the powerlessness of a child controlled by a persuasive adult.

**Linda Newbery**

# BALZAC AND THE LITTLE CHINESE SEAMSTRESS  Dai Sijie

This book should be full of anguish, but it's uplifting rather than tragic. It's about two Chinese students who, during China's Cultural Revolution, are forced to work as manual labourers in a remote and extremely primitive area. Their misery is relieved in the most unlikely way – by the discovery of a chest full of novels by Balzac. Such books were banned at the time so the students have to keep their treasure secret, but they can't help sharing the stories with the gorgeous little local seamstress, with whom they both fall in love. This novel is funny, sad, but never solemn, and it gave me an unforgettable picture of China during one of the greatest upheavals in its history.

**Elizabeth Laird**

**Next?**

If you want to read more about the appalling realities of life in 20th-century China, read *Wild Swans* (UTBG 414) by Jung Chang.

*Tulku* (UTBG 385) is about love and friendship amidst the horrors of China's Boxer Rebellion.

*Fahrenheit 451* (UTBG 121) is a very different, and horrifying, story: a look at a future where books are banned.

# BARREL FEVER David Sedaris

## Next?

*Are You Dave Gorman?* (UTBG 28) by, um, Dave Gorman, is a wacky story of everyday madness, as is *Round Ireland With a Fridge* (yes, it is about exactly that) (UTBG 313).

Bill Bryson can make the most commonplace hilarious; try *Notes from a Small Island* (UTBG 266).

This is a collection of really funny short stories and essays in which David Sedaris accidentally swallows Mike Tyson's false teeth, finds squirrel tails in the crisper compartment of his fridge, and watches his dad hit his sister with a bag full of frozen chicken wings after her boyfriend has accidentally set the sofa on fire. Yes, it's a book about normal life, in which the author makes us realise what a thoroughly weird species we are. In the final and funniest essay, 'The Santa Land Diaries', David becomes an elf called Crumpet, working at a big New York department store. There, along with 49 other elves, he poses for photos with children, telling them that Santa will burgle their houses if they don't behave. But be warned! This book is a bit rude (no, a lot rude actually!), something that is obviously guaranteed to put at least 95 per cent of teenagers off reading it. So that's a relief!

**Michael Cox**

# BE MORE CHILL Ned Vizzini

Definitely not a book to be left lying around for your aged grandma to pick up, *Be More Chill* is both very funny and surprisingly realistic.

Jeremy is the biggest geek in high school. Desperately in love with the beautiful Christine, he can't even bring himself to talk to her – but then a friend tells him about 'squips'.

Squips are nano-technology quantum computers, small enough to swallow. Once you have one lodged in your brain it takes over, tells you who to talk to (and how), what clothes to wear – in short, how to be the coolest dude around.

Unfortunately, there's always user error to mess things up!

If you enjoy this book, Ned Vizzini suggests Googling 'squip' – it's a strange world out there on the Net!

**Laura Hutchings**

## Next?

*Hex* (UTBG 167) by Rhiannon Lassiter is a sci-fi thriller, set in the future, which explores the idea of humans being able to interface with computers.

A much more serious book about peer pressure and victimisation is Robert Cormier's *The Chocolate War* (UTBG 75).

If you want more Ned Vizzini, try his *Teen Angst? Naaah... A Quasi-autobiography*, which is exactly what it says it is about!

# THE BEACH Alex Garland

Imagine you're on holiday, backpacking somewhere exotic. You check into a cheap and crummy hotel. There you meet a man who calls himself Daffy (as in Duck), who tells you about a secret place he knows – a secluded beach, almost inaccessible, beautiful and unspoilt, where a young community lives in paradise. Sounds tempting, doesn't it?

So Richard decides to set off to find this heavenly spot, and when he does find it, well, it's just too good to be true. Too good, perhaps, to last…

Alex Garland's first novel was an instant bestseller – there was a period when every time you sat down on a bus or train, the person sitting next to you would be reading it. And it was a worthy success – it's an enthralling tale, sometimes enchanting and sometimes very dark and savage. And the ending, well… Many people didn't think it worked, but I thought it was amazing – read it and judge for yourself!

**Daniel Hahn**

### Next?

Alex Garland's *The Tesseract* is more sophisticated than *The Beach* – a better book, though a harder one.

*Lord of the Flies* (UTBG 223) – the classic story of a paradise that quickly becomes a living hell.

More stories about backpacking? Try *Are You Experienced?* (UTBG 28) or John Harris' disturbing *The Backpacker*.

# BEAU GESTE P.C. Wren

### Next?

A lot of people don't know that there are two sequels – *Beau Sabreur* and *Beau Ideal*.

If you enjoy this kind of historical novel, try D.K. Broster's *The Flight of the Heron* or A.E. Mason's *The Four Feathers*.

Or for another story involving a missing jewel: *The Moonstone* (UTBG 250).

At 13 I wanted desperately to join the French Foreign Legion. The newspapers said that legionnaires were the scum of the earth – but I knew differently. *Beau Geste* was the book responsible for my inside information and I read it over and over again.

When the fabulous Blue Water sapphire is stolen, suspicion immediately falls upon Michael Geste, who mysteriously disappears only hours after it vanishes. Protesting their brother's innocence, John and Digby Geste follow Michael into the French Foreign Legion in an attempt to solve the puzzle of the missing jewel.

What follows next is the most marvellous, heartbreaking adventure. They really don't write books like this any more and the world is poorer for that.

**Laura Hutchings**

# BEAUTY Robin McKinley

 12+

## Next?

More Robin McKinley? Try *Spindle's End* (UTBG 350).

Kate Petty and Caroline Castle's collection *Tales of Beauty and Cruelty* are based on old tales by Hans Christian Andersen.

Patricia McKillip also delves into fairy tale to create magical worlds. Read *Winter Rose*, a dark story of love, murder and obsession.

Or try *The Tower Room* (UTBG 378), part of the **Happy Ever After** series, which retells the tales of 'Rapunzel', 'Sleeping Beauty' and 'Snow White'.

We all know the story of 'Beauty and the Beast': in order to save her father, Beauty, the unselfish heroine, goes to live in the house of the Beast, only to find her self-sacrifice eventually rewarded. So far, so fairy tale.

Robin McKinley's poetic retelling sticks close to the established story (though in this book Beauty's older sisters are very much more sympathetic than in the original tale) and the growth of Beauty's true love for the Beast is satisfying, as are her trials and suffering en route. (The luxury that surrounds her in the Beast's castle may help.) The story is focused on the heroine's crises and responses, and will be particularly enjoyed by readers like me with a taste for tales in which real life blends into fantasy.

**Margaret Mahy**

# THE BEET FIELDS Gary Paulsen

14+

The boy – we never learn his name – runs away from an abusive home, leaving everything behind. It's time to grow up, fast. He takes the first job he finds, hoeing beets on the prairie farms of North Dakota, working in fields so vast they stretch from horizon to horizon. He moves on to driving a tractor, is robbed of his hard-earned wages by a corrupt cop and finally joins a carnival – a travelling fair. In one summer he becomes a man – first work, first wages, first woman – and learns a lot about people, from the illegal immigrant Mexican workers in the beet fields to the geeks and shills of the carnival. Short, punchy, easy to read, hard to forget.

**Jan Mark**

## Next?

*Hatchet* (UTBG 163), also by Gary Paulsen, is also about a boy learning to survive, this time alone in the wilderness; there are sequels, too.

For more about the kind of life Paulsen is describing, try *Of Mice and Men* (UTBG 268) and *The Grapes of Wrath* by John Steinbeck, set about 20 years earlier.

A stranger tale of labouring outside? Try *Holes* (UTBG 173) by Louis Sachar.

# THE BELGARIAD David Eddings

## Next?

Try the **Mallorean** series, another epic by David Eddings.

*Sword of Shannara* by Terry Brooks and *The Magician* by Raymond E. Feist are epic fantasy stories that will keep you absorbed for hours.

For something set in a fantasy world but somehow much more real, try Robin Hobb's **Farseer** trilogy (UTBG 124).

I read the five books of **The Belgariad** more times than I can recall when I was a teenager. I was a big fantasy fan, and these were some of the best fantasy books I'd ever read. The story of a young, seemingly ordinary boy, who gets swept away from his village and involved in the world of wizards and kings, it lacks the imaginative scope of Tolkien, but it's fun, exciting, intriguing fantasy in which the characters are as important as the quest and magical elements. Easy to read and great to share, this was one of the most popular series of books at my school, appealing even to those who didn't read fantasy. Immerse yourself and enjoy!

**Darren Shan**

# THE BELL Iris Murdoch

I can't overemphasise the impact of reading *The Bell* aged 16. It kick-started a chain reaction and I did not stop reading Iris Murdoch until about ten books and a year later when I came up for air. Iris Murdoch is a must for anybody seriously interested in human relationships, beliefs, beauty, darkness and extraordinarily powerful writing.

Be prepared to enter into a world that is immediately riveting, disturbing and totally adult. Dora is the wife of handsome, powerful, but brutal older man, Paul; she tries to leave him but finds she cannot. Instead, she joins him at a strange 'spiritual' community deep in the English countryside. Against a seething backdrop of summer heat, there is far more that goes on than meets the eye. Who is in love with whom? Who believes in what? And will they find the great bell that legend says has lain buried for years in the great lake?

**Rebecca Swift**

## Next?

Another Iris Murdoch? Try *Henry and Cato* or *The Unicorn*.

Murdoch's husband John Bayley wrote a tender portrait of their life together and her final years with Alzheimer's – *Iris*.

Another story set against summer heat and a turmoil of emotions is Ian McEwan's *Atonement* (UTBG 31).

*Frost in May* (UTBG 141) by Antonia White depicts the claustrophobic world of a convent school.

# THE BELL JAR Sylvia Plath

Sylvia Plath is perhaps better known for her poetry and for being the wife of Ted Hughes, but her only novel, *The Bell Jar*, is undoubtedly one of the greatest of modern novels. It's about Esther Greenwood, a 19-year-old girl who suffers a mental breakdown. We watch her gradually becoming disconnected from the world around her while she's working in New York on a magazine, then witness her descent as she returns home to the Boston suburbs, and see her behaviour becoming increasingly erratic until she is finally admitted to a mental hospital. As dark as *The Bell Jar* is, it's shot through with an unforgettable lyrical beauty. It's a demanding and harrowing read – a real classic.

**Sherry Ashworth**

### Next?

*The Catcher in the Rye* (UTBG 66) by J.D. Salinger is about a boy in the grip of a breakdown.

Mark Haddon's *The Curious Incident of the Dog in the Night-time* (UTBG 89) is a first-person narrative about an autistic boy.

Or there's *Cut* (UTBG 90) by Patricia McCormick, about the treatment of a self-harmer in the US...

---

# BELOVED Toni Morrison

### Next?

There are some great African-American women writers: try Alice Walker's *The Color Purple* (UTBG 80) or Maya Angelou's *I Know Why the Caged Bird Sings* (UTBG 183).

Toni Morrison's other books are all good too. Try *The Bluest Eye* or *Jazz*.

Another writer who makes you understand the most powerful of emotions is Gabriel García Márquez; try *Love in the Time of Cholera* (UTBG 227) or *One Hundred Years of Solitude* (UTBG 273).

*Beloved* is the story of Sethe, a woman haunted by a terrible decision she took back in her past – to slit the throat of her baby girl rather than give her up to slavery.

This deeply powerful novel taps veins of history, folkloric tradition and memory. In often beautiful prose, Morrison conjures up pain and suffering, guilt and torment, love and sacrifice. This author is at her best when writing about feelings, about yearnings and about the human spirit. And *Beloved* is full of these ingredients. It's a huge-hearted, tragic story that tugs constantly at your emotions.

**Neil Arksey**

# FANTASY

## by Catherine Fisher

Fantasy is a wide field. Or if you like, a
dark wood. Somewhere in its depths
tangle ghost stories and sci-fi and legends
and psychological archetypes. But all of
them grew from the seeds of myth.

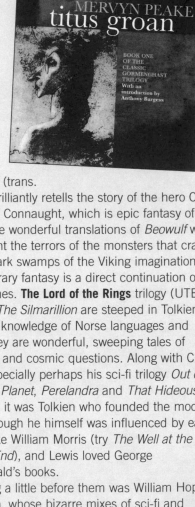

Like many readers, I first ventured into
fantasy through fairy tale, reading
Japanese and Russian and Scandinavian
versions of tales where girls defeat
witches and third sons kill dragons,
and then found they led to myth: to
the wild and crazy tales of Wales and
Ireland – you can find some of these
in *The Mabinogion* translated by Jones
and Jones, or *Early Irish Myths and Sagas* (trans.
J. Gantz). In *The Tain*, Thomas Kinsella brilliantly retells the story of the hero Cu
Chulain's lone stand against the armies of Connaught, which is epic fantasy of the
best kind, up there with Homer, and in the wonderful translations of *Beowulf* we
can confront the terrors of the monsters that crawl
from the dark swamps of the Viking imagination.

Most literary fantasy is a direct continuation of
these themes. **The Lord of the Rings** trilogy (UTBG
224) and *The Silmarillion* are steeped in Tolkien's
enormous knowledge of Norse languages and
stories; they are wonderful, sweeping tales of
adventure and cosmic questions. Along with C.S.
Lewis (especially perhaps his sci-fi trilogy *Out of
the Silent Planet*, *Perelandra* and *That Hideous
Strength*), it was Tolkien who founded the modern
genre, though he himself was influenced by early
writers like William Morris (try *The Well at the
World's End*), and Lewis loved George
MacDonald's books.

Writing a little before them was William Hope
Hodgson, whose bizarre mixes of sci-fi and
fantasy are now cult classics. Look out for *The
House on the Borderland* and the amazing
*Night Land*, which is sometimes so bad it's
unreadable, and yet its nightmare landscapes

are breathtakingly brilliant.

A contemporary of Tolkien's was E.R. Edison, mostly known now for *The Worm Ouroboros*. If you're not afraid of flamboyant costumes, endless names, fantastic swordplay and a very mannered style, you might love this. I do, though it's not for everyone.

A writer who built his own creations on these and other foundations was Mervyn Peake, whose superb **Gormenghast** trilogy (UTBG 154) have to be on anyone's list of great imaginative achievements. The endless ramifications, corridors, halls and towers of Gormenghast castle are mirrored throughout later films and trilogies, album covers and comics.

In children's fiction in the 1960s fantasy really took off too, especially in the books of Susan Cooper and the brilliantly gifted Alan Garner, whose style grew more clipped and taut with each novel, culminating in two of the best young adult books ever, *The Owl Service* (UTBG 281), with its terrifying loop of relived Celtic myth, and *Red Shift* (UTBG 307), a complex triple-time story that really moves up a gear into an almost unbearable intensity. Garner's later books have been for adults, but I'd recommend his most recent, *Thursbitch*.

Fantasy these days is immensely popular. Look out for *Mythago Wood* and its sequels by the admirable Robert Holdstock, or the wonderful, teeming **Majipoor Chronicles** of Robert Silverberg. And then, in another part of the wood, there's Philip Pullman, Terry Pratchett, Tanith Lee, Diana Wynne Jones, all excellent. Keep exploring.

## A few favourite series:

**The Earthsea** quartet by Ursula le Guin

**The Dragonriders of Pern** by Anne McCaffrey

**The Black Magician** trilogy by Trudi Canavan

**The Farseer** trilogy by Robin Hobb

**The Belgariad** by David Eddings

## Time-slip stories:

*Follow Me Down* by Julie Hearn

*The Sterkarm Handshake* by Susan Price

*A Wrinkle in Time* by Madeleine L'Engle

## Travelling to other worlds:

*Abarat* by Clive Barker

**The Aldous Lexicon** trilogy by Michael Lawrence

*The Dark Lord of Derkholm* by Diana Wynne Jones

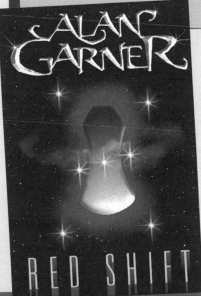

# BEYOND THE DEEPWOODS

## Paul Stewart and Chris Riddell

**12+**

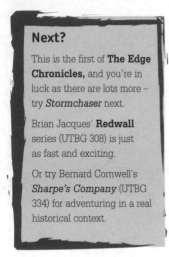

**Next?**

This is the first of **The Edge Chronicles,** and you're in luck as there are lots more – try *Stormchaser* next.

Brian Jacques' **Redwall** series (UTBG 308) is just as fast and exciting.

Or try Bernard Cornwell's *Sharpe's Company* (UTBG 334) for adventuring in a real historical context.

I found this book almost impossible to put down. It features a teenage boy named Twig. Twig is the son of a sky pirate – though he doesn't realise it. As a baby he was left on the outskirts of a woodtroll village, and is brought up by them. Being weak, he is bullied, and comes home with bumps and scars. Then one day, he's finally told by his 'mother' of his origins.

The book is about how Twig spends a year wandering the Deepwoods. Along the way he finds friendship, danger and fear. He also stumbles upon his father, Cloud Wolf, who then abandons him again and Twig finds the most feared creature in all the Deepwoods... I loved this intriguing and exciting book – and the detailed illustrations are amazing!

**Andrew Barakat (aged 12)**

# THE BIG SLEEP Raymond Chandler

**14+**

*The Big Sleep* tells the story of the quick-thinking, fast-talking American private eye, Philip Marlowe. He becomes involved in the affairs of the Sternwood family after he's asked by the old dying General Sternwood to deal with the blackmail of his younger daughter Carmen.

Philip Marlowe is cool, smooth and everything an American private eye should be. The girls seem to like him too, seeing as both the Sternwood daughters fall for his charms early on in the book.

This is a fantastic story filled with overwhelming description and laden with twists and great one-liners: 'She looked as if she'd been poured into the dress and someone forgot to say whoa.' 'It was a blonde. A blonde to make a bishop kick a hole in a stained glass window.' 'He looked as inconspicuous as a tarantula on a slice of angel cake.'

**Raffaella Barker**

**Next?**

How about some spies? Try the **James Bond** books (UTBG 194), starting with *Casino Royale*.

All the other Raymond Chandler's are must-reads. Try *The Long Goodbye* next.

More hard-boiled detective novels? Read Dashiell Hammett, starting with *The Maltese Falcon* or *The Glass Key*. Both Chandler and Hammett had most of their books made into great films!

# BILGEWATER

## Jane Gardam

Marigold Green is the daughter of Bill, the headmaster of a boys' boarding school in Yorkshire, and her nickname, Bilgewater, is a corruption of 'Bill's daughter'. She perceives herself as ugly and awkward and, because she is also motherless, is well aware that she is searching for love and friendship. When Grace Gathering arrives at the school, everything changes. Grace and Marigold were friends in their early childhood and Grace, with her cloud of wondrous hair, appears almost like an angel in the austere surroundings of the school.

The story is told in the first person by Marigold, and Gardam's sure touch brings every character to life; she's particularly good at catching the endearing eccentricity of teachers. Because the novel begins with the narrator being interviewed for a place at Cambridge, we know that Marigold has achieved some academic success... But at what cost? And will she fulfil her potential? A marvellously rich and elegantly written book.

**Adèle Geras**

### Next?

Jane Gardam writes poignantly of an isolated life in *Crusoe's Daughter*.

A story of growing up out of synch with your surroundings: *Anita and Me* (UTBG 23) by Meera Syal.

Or try a book about what it takes to fit in: *Chocolat* (UTBG 74) by Joanne Harris.

## The Ultimate Teen Readers' Poll

### BOOK YOU COULDN'T PUT DOWN

1 **Harry Potter series**

2 **Alex Rider series**

3 **A Series of Unfortunate Events**

4 **The Lord of the Rings trilogy**

5 **The Saga of Darren Shan**

6 **His Dark Materials trilogy**

7 **The Diamond Girls**

8 **A Child Called 'It'**

9 **Girl, 15 (Charming But Insane)**

10 **Holes**

# BINDI BABES  Narinder Dhami

Amber (Ambajit), Jazz (Jasvinder) and Geena
are sisters. They live with their dad as their
mum is dead. They have a pretty cool life,
they're popular, even the teachers like them
and the only things they hate are people pitying
them, or trying to control their lives. After all,
everything's fine, isn't it? They have great
clothes, fun friends, lots of freedom and, best of
all, each other. But then their bossy, interfering
unmarried aunt comes over from India and the
fun can't last. She makes them go to bed early
and won't let them eat junk food. What's to be
done? Hmm, how about an arranged marriage?
Matchmaking begins and, well, things get
complicated – and very funny.

Fast-paced, full of Bollywood sparkle, serious
fun, and girls you'll really sympathise with!

**Leonie Flynn**

### Next?

Read the sequels: next is
*Bollywood Babes*, in which a
faded actress plays havoc with
their lives.

The **Mates, Dates...** series
(UTBG 238) by Cathy Hopkins
is about three friends, boys,
parents and everything girly.

Or what about something a little
tougher about being Asian in
Britain today? Try the series of
linked short stories in *Dominoes*
by Bali Rai.

# THE BIRDS ON THE TREES  Nina Bawden

### Next?

Try *The Fifth Child* by Doris
Lessing, in which four contented
siblings struggle with the family's
latest addition.

Another Nina Bawden? Try
*Circles of Deceit*, a story of
fidelity and forgery.

Another boy who has problems
with life is the hero of *The
Curious Incident of the Dog in
the Night-time* (UTBG 89), or try
the disturbing *I'm the King of
the Castle* (UTBG 188).

If you are interested in the dark and
complex things that go on behind the polite,
bright surface of everyday life, Nina Bawden
is the writer for you. She writes grippingly
about what ordinary families suffer in an
everyday kind of way. In *The Birds on the
Trees* you will meet Toby, who is different.
Adored by his younger sister Lucy, he
bemuses his parents and others around
him. Does Toby have a 'problem', or doesn't
he? Is he ill in some way or just a normal,
rebellious, intelligent boy? Intensity,
emotion, darkness and light are perfectly
communicated, making you think about how
a good book is actually written – as well as
about the particular delicate, uneasy world
that this one is trying to explore.

**Rebecca Swift**

# BIRDSONG Sebastian Faulks

## Next?

After this big, demanding read, how about a first-hand perspective on the Great War. *Memoirs of an Infantry Officer* by Siegfried Sassoon (UTBG 241) is incomparable.

For a good historian's overview try any of Lyn MacDonald's books. *Somme* and *1915: The Death of Hope* are particularly good.

Two more of Sebastian Faulks' books you should try are *Charlotte Grey*, set in World War II, and *The Fatal Englishman*, about some real-life casualties of war.

*Birdsong* is one of the most powerful novels I've ever read. It is a love story, and a deeply moving one at that, and it's also a story about discovering the past, but first and foremost it's a story of war. Stephen Wraysford falls in love with a French woman, loses her, and is sent back to France as a lieutenant in the early stages of World War I. The horrors of that war – the endless mud, the unspeakable waste of life, the heroism, the despair – can rarely have been as clearly conveyed. This is an unforgettable book and I urge you to read it.

**Malachy Doyle**

# BITTER FRUIT Brian Keaney

We all say things we regret – we lose our temper with our friends, our siblings, our parents, then patch things up the next day. But just imagine if you never saw them again, if the next day they died, suddenly. 'I hate you!' Rebecca shouts at her father – and these will be the last words she says to him.

*Bitter Fruit* is the stunning story of Rebecca's grief and guilt, and how she struggles to cope with them. She will learn to rebuild her life and her friendships, but it's not easy. Keaney pulls no punches – his book is tough and clear-sighted; though moving, it's never over-sentimental, and the writing's fantastic, too.

**Daniel Hahn**

## Next?

Try Brian Keaney's *Family Secrets*, about a girl who has never met her father, or his most recent book, *Jacob's Ladder*, a powerfully original take on families, dealing with bereavement, and death itself. Or maybe the very different *Falling For Joshua*, about a girl with a secret.

There aren't many authors who can write about death without getting overly sentimental or horribly depressing; one of the best such books, though, is Gabrielle Zevin's startling *Elsewhere* (UTBG 114), but be warned – it couldn't be less like *Bitter Fruit*!

# THE BLACK MAGICIAN trilogy

14+

## Trudi Canavan

### Next?

The **Song of the Lioness** quartet (UTBG 15) about a girl's quest to become a knight.

*Dream Merchant* by Isobel Hoving is a magnificent fantasy (with the most gorgeous cover!).

Terry Brooks' *Sword of Shannara* starts another epic fantasy series.

In Imardin, magicians of the Guild gather yearly for the Purge of vagrants, miscreants and street urchins from the city. As the gathered mob is herded, a young slum girl called Sonea throws a stone filled with her anger. To the surprise of everyone present, the stone breaks the shield of the magicians and knocks one unconscious. As the situation develops, the Guild's worst fear is realised. A desperate race starts to find Sonea before her uncontrolled power obliterates her and the whole city. Filled with magic and conspiracy, this is one trilogy that cannot be missed.

**Gary Chow (aged 17)**

# BLAME MY BRAIN

14+

## Nicola Morgan

So, you like to sleep late, you get cranky with parents / teachers / whoever, you want to try everything that adults tell you that you shouldn't and you sometimes think that life is pretty pointless. Well, guess what – you're normal! Even scientists think so.

This book is all about you. Well, actually it's about your brain and all the changes it's going through. If you ever wanted to know why you do certain stuff – read this. It's funny, cool and amazingly interesting (as well as being great ammunition the next time someone moans about you). With polls, quizzes, sections on drugs, alcohol, depression, eating disorders, sex, gender, hormones and self-harm, this books tells life like it is, and is something every teen – and their parents – should read.

**Leonie Flynn**

### Next?

Nicola Morgan writes brilliant fiction too – try *Mondays are Red* (UTBG 248), about synaesthesia, or *Sleepwalking* (UTBG 345), about a future world where ideas are forbidden and emotions regulated – and what happens to some teenagers who don't conform.

She also has more books about how to cope with being you; try *The Leaving Home Survival Guide*.

Or Matt Whyman's *XY: A Toolkit for Life*.

# BLANKETS  Craig Thompson

Growing up is never easy. Especially if you live in a fundamentalist Christian household, your younger brother wets the bed you share, and you secretly want to be an artist in a world where art is considered the work of the devil. Well, there's always winter Church camp. Except that only the rich kids can afford ski passes and Craig, the hero of this stunningly drawn 'illustrated novel', hasn't even got enough money for a day one. Then he falls in love for the first time, with the fascinating Raina, and everything changes. But his troubles are only just beginning. Craig Thompson takes us on a moving journey of discovery: about love, friendship, and the importance of a good blanket.

**Ariel Kahn**

### Next?

*Goodbye Chunky Rice* by Craig Thompson deals with the close friendship between two unlikely animals.

Marjane Satrapi's *Persepolis* (UTBG 286) is another amazing graphic novel.

*Oranges Are Not the Only Fruit* (UTBG 275) by Jeanette Winterson is a love story set in a deeply religious community.

*A Portrait of the Artist as a Young Man* (UTBG 291) by James Joyce shows the way an artist develops, falls in love, and comes to terms with his past.

# BLINDED BY THE LIGHT
## Sherry Ashworth

### Next?

Elinor is one of The Chosen, which some would call a cult; but will she stay with her community after a chance meeting with an outsider boy? Read *Forbidden* (UTBG 134) by Judy Waite.

In *Going for Stone* (UTBG 150) by Philip Gross, Nick runs away from home and gets mixed up with a group that aren't quite what they seem.

Robert Swindells' *Abomination* is about the consequences of blind belief.

Recovering from glandular fever, 18-year-old Joe feels lonely and bored. A chance encounter on a train with Kate and Nick draws him into the community of the 'White Ones'. On a weekend visit to their secluded retreat, Joe meets more of their community, including Bea. These people are happy, their lives have purpose, they have everything Joe wants, but…

This is a cleverly crafted, difficult-to-put-down story that explores the extraordinary power that a cult can have to suck people in and then entrap them.

**Yvonne Coppard**

# THE BLOOD STONE  Jamila Gavin

**12+**

This is the tale of Filippo Veroneo, born in Venice in the 14th century, who journeys in search of his father, missing since just before his birth. He travels from Venice to Afghanistan, carrying a ransom – the invaluable jewel, the Ocean of the Moon – sewn into his head for safe-keeping. Love, loyalty, betrayal and cruelty are fundamental to Filippo's world, and there is risk on every page. This great epic is fabulous and atmospheric and gives us tastes of worlds long since gone, including that of the great Moghul court in Agra, home of the Taj Mahal. It is a huge adventure, a compelling journey, as rich and desirable as the jewel that is its title.
**Wendy Cooling**

### Next?

Jamila Gavin's **Coram Boy** (UTBG 84) tells the story of two boys, one a rescued slave, the other the illegitimate son of the heir to a great estate.

Or try her trilogy, beginning with **The Wheel of Surya**, which tells a gripping story of war and peace.

For another journey of challenge, adventure and survival, read Michael Morpurgo's **Kensuke's Kingdom**, a story of a shipwreck.

# BLOODTIDE  Melvin Burgess

**14+**

### Next?

If you enjoyed **Bloodtide**, try the sequel, **Bloodsong**, or another of Melvin's searing novels, such as **Junk** (UTBG 202) (about drug abuse).

Robert Cormier is another author who doesn't pull any punches; try **Heroes** (UTBG 166).

Or for something else that's woven from Norse myth (and is even more violent than **Bloodtide**!), try Neil Gaiman's **American Gods**.

This extraordinary book. This extraordinary, extraordinary book. For more than a year after reading it I was still preoccupied by its images and characters.

*Bloodtide* is a retelling of an old Norse myth, the 'Volsunga Saga', set in a future London where normal society has broken down into two fiercely rival gangs, the Volsons and the Conors. The book is about their struggle for power, but as in all the old myths Fate plays a part, the gods pick their favourites, and a 14-year-old girl and her brothers are left to pick up the pieces of it all.

I'm not going to pretend for a minute that *Bloodtide* is a book for everyone. It is deeply violent in places – so much so that at one point I put the book down (and then picked it up again. I had to pick it up again). It is magnificently well written, but it is brutal. If you want a story that will grip your heart, take you to places other books have never taken you, and leave you *changed*, then take a deep breath and let *Bloodtide* eat its way into your soul.
**Cliff McNish**

# BLUE  Sue Mayfield

 14+

## Next?

Sue Mayfield has written other excellent real-life novels for teenagers; try *Reckless* (UTBG 306), a story about a teenage pregnancy, but with a twist.

If you're interested in reading more about bullying, have a look at *Feather Boy* (UTBG 126) or *Run, Zan, Run* by Catherine MacPhail.

For other stories told in interesting ways, try Aidan Chambers' *Dance on My Grave* (UTBG 91) or the hilarious *The Secret Diary of Adrian Mole Aged 13 ¾* (UTBG 324).

*Blue* is a novel about bullying – and it's terrifyingly realistic. It's set in a recognisable world of GCSEs and school plays; the characters are everyday teenagers.

Anna Goldsmith is just that bit brighter and better looking than some other girls, and this has won her the dislike of Hayley Parkin. Hayley's campaign to unsettle Anna is unrelenting, and all the more effective as it's low-key and persistent. The story is told partly by Melanie Blackwood, a girl caught in the middle, partly by entries in Anna's diary, and partly through the thoughts of Anna's parents. *Blue* is a must-read book for anyone who wants to get wise to the techniques of bullies

**Sherry Ashworth**

# BLUE MOON  Julia Green

14+

Mia is only 15, and her mother left her when she was a small child. *Blue Moon* tells the story of what happens when Mia discovers she is pregnant – her disbelief, her denial, the trauma of letting her father know and all the decisions that have to be made after that point. The novel is realistic and sensitively told. The ending is utterly convincing. Not only do you journey with Mia through the most difficult months of her life, but also discover how the ripples caused by a pregnancy travel much further than you might expect – it's not just Mia, but her family, her boyfriend, her friends and even some strangers on a barge who are caught up in this compelling drama.

**Sherry Ashworth**

## Next?

There's a sequel to *Blue Moon* – *Baby Blue* – which you must read if you want to find out what happens to Mia next.

Other novels about teenage pregnancy include *Dear Nobody* (UTBG 99) and the terrifying *Roxy's Baby* (UTBG 314).

Also try *Cut* (UTBG 90) by Patricia McCormick for another tale of a teenage girl coming to terms with herself.

# THE BODY IN THE LIBRARY Agatha Christie

### Next?

Definitely more Miss Marple – *The 4:50 from Paddington* is another favourite of mine.

Dorothy L. Sayers wrote classy murder mysteries. My favourite is *Murder Must Advertise*, but they're all worth a read.

For another series of (altogether different) books from the same sort of time as Agatha Christie's mysteries, with classy country houses aplenty, try the **Jeeves** stories (UTBG 196) by P.G. Wodehouse.

I think this is my favourite Miss Marple story. In it, Agatha Christie takes a conventional detective-story opening (body in library) and adds layer upon layer of intrigue, with twists and red herrings. Just enough to make you feel marvellously clever and smug for working out whodunit all on your own, and then marvellously stupid when it turns out that you got it altogether wrong, and of course Miss Marple has got it right.

She's a lovely old thing, Miss Marple, apparently quite harmless (meaning that suspects routinely let down their guard in her presence), but at the same time harbouring no happy, optimistic faith in human nature whatsoever; she is a delightful, prim old cynic. And in this story, as in them all, she shines.

**Daniel Hahn**

# BONJOUR TRISTESSE Françoise Sagan 14+

Cécile is a precocious 17-year-old who lives a hedonistic life in the French Riviera with her father, Raymond. The pair drive fast cars, pursue love affairs and sunbathe. But when Raymond decides to marry Anne, Cécile is filled with jealousy and indignation, terrified that her amoral pleasures will be curtailed. She cooks up a plan to prevent the marriage, with unexpectedly tragic consequences. *Bonjour Tristesse* is Sagan's first novel, written at the age of 18, when having failed her exams at the Sorbonne she decided to write instead. It is brief, deceptively simple and utterly compulsive.

**Francesca Lewis**

### Next?

*A Summer Bird-Cage* (UTBG 362) by Margaret Drabble or *The Rachel Papers* (UTBG 301) by Martin Amis. (Both also first novels, incidentally.)

Other books that take place in the summer and convey the season's heat, moral ambiguity and subsequent loss of innocence (or at least acquisition of knowledge) are *The Cement Garden* (UTBG 69) and *The Greengage Summer* (UTBG 157).

Find another feisty, French female narrator in Colette's **Claudine** stories, beginning with *Claudine At School* (UTBG 78).

# BORN CONFUSED Tanuja Desai Hidier

 14+

### Next?

You might also like Bali Rai's novels; try *(Un)arranged Marriage* (UTBG 388). Or read his feature on race in young-adult literature on pp. 392–393.

For sheer exuberance, *Anita and Me* (UTBG 23) by Meera Syal is another great account of growing up in an Indian family in another country – this time Britain.

Or for a poetic look at life in Kerala, try Arundhati Roy's *The God of Small Things*.

*Born Confused* is a big, technicolour novel, swirling with the music, smells and images of two continents. Dimple's 17th birthday present from best friend Gwyn is a fake ID. But for Dimple, identity is complicated: she's an ABCD – American Born Confused Desi. Should she date a 'suitable – Indian – boy' or follow Gwyn, dating American college boys? And when the 'suitable boy' isn't the loser she'd thought and Gwyn embraces Indian-ness to snare him – then what?

Dimple discovers 'you have to get lost to get found': in getting lost, she comes to understand more about her parents' history, about India and about friendship. I love Dimple's unsureness, her devotion to her camera and her sound heart, in this funny / sad quest for belonging.

**Helen Simmons**

# BOWS AGAINST THE BARONS

12+

## Geoffrey Trease

This is the Robin Hood legend given the *Spartacus* treatment. Written in 1934, *Bows Against the Barons* was Trease's first book, and is set in his own native Nottingham. It combines his childhood love of the ripping yarn with a fierce hatred of injustice. From the moment that the young hero Dickon shoots one of the King's deer and has to flee to join the outlaws of Sherwood Forest, he is propelled into a pacy and exciting adventure story. There are night-time raids and climactic battles. The novel is unsentimental and the ending stubbornly resists the temptation to serve up some facile 'happily ever after'.

*Bows Against the Barons* launched Trease on a writing career that produced over 100 novels and made him a seminal author of historical fiction for young people.

**Alan Gibbons**

### Next?

*Cue for Treason* (UTBG 88) is an adventure set in Elizabethan England and even manages to involve Shakespeare.

Another classic writer of historical novels is Rosemary Sutcliff. Try *The Eagle of the Ninth*, set in Roman Britain.

# BOY2GIRL  Terence Blacker

 12+

### Next?

For a boy and girl switching bodies, try Michael Lawrence's **The Aldous Lexicon** trilogy (UTBG 17).

More Terence Blacker? Try *The Angel Factory*, about a seemingly perfect world that is actually dark and treacherous.

Pete Johnson's *Faking It* (UTBG 123) is about a boy pretending a gorgeous girl in a photo is his girlfriend – what happens when the real girl turns up?

In most stories involving the theme 'distant orphan cousin arrives', the cousin is often a wimp or a nerd. But Sam Lopez, who comes to live with his English cousin Matthew, is smelly, rude and full of brassy confidence. And he also has a certain glamour: he is from California, after all.

Matthew and his mates impose an amazing initiation test on Sam. He has to attend school dressed as a girl. Astonishingly, he is very convincing… But I'll leave you to discover the delicious sequence of events.

'This book will make you laugh – or your money back,' it says on the cover. But this is not an easy way to make a fast buck, unfortunately. To avoid laughing at Terence Blacker's book you'd have to be clinically dead.

**Sue Limb**

# THE BOY IN THE BURNING HOUSE

 14+

## Tim Wynne-Jones

Jim Hawkins is just beginning to get over the disappearance of his dad, now presumed dead. So when wild Ruth Rose appears with her crazy theories about what happened to him, accusing Father Fisher, the beyond-reproach local priest, Jim doesn't want to know. But he can't ignore a niggling doubt – what if Ruth Rose is right? Their urgent investigation takes them back to the events of a generation earlier, when a wayward local boy died in a fire no one has yet been able to explain…

Consistently engaging and beautifully crafted, this is a real read-in-one-sitting book.

**Daniel Hahn**

### Next?

*Storm* (UTBG 356) by Suzanne Fisher Staples brings together an unsolved crime and a powerful and unusual friendship.

Or for another exciting and engaging American adventure, Mark Twain's fantastic *Huckleberry Finn* (UTBG 181).

Or try the classic *Treasure Island* (UTBG 379), for a great adventure starring another Jim Hawkins!

# THE BOY IN THE STRIPED PYJAMAS
## John Boyne

I've got a real problem here. You see, I'm not meant to give anything away about this book, as finding out the 'secret' is part of its excitement, but this is a book you finish and then want to talk about to everyone, and I want to share it, too! So, all right, here goes…

*The Boy in the Striped Pyjamas* is different, exciting, and one of the saddest and most terrifying stories I've read. It's also told in such a simple way that you start off thinking, 'Hey! This is a book for kids!' But it isn't. It's powerfully strong stuff, and reading it is a bit like discovering Grimm's fairy tales when you're old enough to see through all the prettiness to the horror underneath – it's unsettling, thought-provoking, and utterly amazing.

**Leonie Flynn**

### Next?

Most read-ons would give the secret away, so you'll have to look out for a certain sort of book. Otherwise, try the stories of the Brothers Grimm or Perrault and be amazed at how different they are from how you remember.

Something else just as shocking? Try *Private Peaceful* (UTBG 300).

# BOY KILLS MAN  Matt Whyman

Based not on a true story exactly, but on the genuine existence of child assassins in modern day Colombia, *Boy Kills Man* is a short, powerful book that thrills, but also emotionally engages, the reader.

The book follows the life of Shorty, a young teenage boy who gets sucked into the underworld of life in the city: a world where the drug lords use children to kill their rivals, since a loophole in Colombian law means they are exempt from prosecution for murder. Desperate for money, but more desperate to prove himself to his peers and his family, Shorty quickly finds himself in way over his head.

This is a book with a troubling ending and no easy answers, but that is its power – it is unashamedly honest and brutal, and at the same time does not sensationalise its material.

**Marcus Sedgwick**

### Next?

Matt Whyman's *The Wild* is about two brothers growing up in Kazakhstan. Bringing in mental illness, destitution and the remains of the nuclear arms race, this is a powerful, unsettling story.

*Keeper* (UTBG 205) by Mal Peet is also partially set in South America.

For another sort of child killer – just as distressing – read Anne Cassidy's gripping *Looking for JJ* (UTBG 222).

# BOY MEETS BOY David Levithan

Paul doesn't have a problem being gay – he's lived with the knowledge since his kindergarten teacher declared it. Loads of his friends are gay, too. But that doesn't make forming new relationships easy. Especially when the ex who dumps him wants him back and Noah, his new beau, finds out. Keeping old friendships alive is just as hard – everyone around Paul is freaking, it seems, and pretty soon he's freaking himself. It's time to get a grip and get the guy he wants. But there's so much more to this wonderfully funny book than that. Sometimes the characters seem over the top but everything about this book is true to life.

**Jon Appleton**

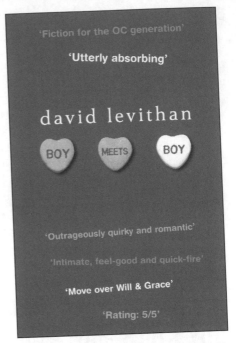

'Fiction for the OC generation'

'Utterly absorbing'

david levithan

BOY MEETS BOY

'Outrageously quirky and romantic'

'Intimate, feel-good and quick-fire'

'Move over Will & Grace'

'Rating: 5/5'

## Next?

Read this and you'll shriek at other gay novels, 'Lighten up!', but for something not a million miles away, try Paul Magrs' *Strange Boy* (UTBG 358).

Aidan Chambers writes of a gay romance in *Dance on My Grave* (UTBG 91), though in fact all his novels deal in some way with sexuality.

*Freak the Mighty* by Rodman Philbrick isn't a 'gay' novel, but it features another unique and memorable main character.

For another warm and funny love story, try Meg Cabot's *All American Girl* (UTBG 19).

# A FEW CHILDHOODS YOU WOULDN'T WANT FOR YOURSELF

*Angela's Ashes* by Frank McCourt

*Chinese Cinderella* by Adeline Yen Mah

*Wild Swans* by Jung Chang

*The Hard Man of the Swings* by Jeanne Willis

*A Child Called 'It'* by Dave Pelzer

*Frost in May* by Antonia White

*This Boy's Life* by Tobias Wolff

# BOY SOLDIER   Andy McNab and Robert Rigby

If there's anyone who knows about the thrills and perils of the SAS it's Andy McNab. And now he's drawn on his own experience to co-author this nail-bitingly exciting story of Danny Watts and his quest for his grandfather Fergus (a disgraced former SAS officer). As you read of the dangers that Danny and Fergus face together, you'll quickly learn the SAS jargon and techniques, and that'll help this extraordinary tale feel real and immediate. (Which in turn will make it even more exciting, and more nerve-racking, as the dangers Danny faces will seem pretty real and immediate too!)

Fast-paced, smart and engaging, let's hope Andy McNab and Robert Rigby are planning to bring us many more great books like it!

**Daniel Hahn**

### Next?

There's a sequel: *Payback*.

Read about the teenagers training to be secret agents in A.J. Butcher's **Spy High** series (UTBG 350).

Or for the greatest super-spy of all – in his teenage years – try *SilverFin* (UTBG 340), Charlie Higson's first tale of a teenage James Bond.

For another extraordinary reconciliation between grandson and wayward grandfather – but treated as differently as you can imagine – read David Grossman's beautiful and witty *The Zigzag Kid* (UTBG 426).

# BRAT FARRAR   Josephine Tey   14+

### Next?

More Josephine Tey? Try *The Franchise Affair*, about a girl accusing two old ladies of kidnap and *The Daughter of Time* in which a convalescing detective tries to solve the mystery of the Princes in the Tower.

For modern mysteries set in the world of horses, Dick Francis' thrillers cannot be beaten. Try *Whip Hand* (UTBG 410) to start with.

You get two books for the price of one with *Brat Farrar*, and it's this unique combination that makes it the best mystery story that I've ever read.

The premise is simple: Patrick Ashby, heir to a considerable fortune, disappears when he is 13. For eight years his family believe that he committed suicide but then, just weeks before his twin's coming-of-age, Pat turns up again. Everyone is happy to see him and accepts that he is who he says he is – everyone except his supplanted twin, Simon.

What really happened to Patrick is, of course, the mystery, but this book also serves as a time machine. When you read it, you are transported back to the 1940s and a way of life that has vanished forever.

**Laura Hutchings**

# BRAVE NEW WORLD Aldous Huxley

**Next?**

Read Huxley's contemporary, George Orwell, for some other angles on dystopian futures in *Nineteen Eighty-Four* (UTBG 260) and on totalitarianism in *Animal Farm* (UTBG 23).

If you liked the dark sci-fi edge to the book, try: *Fahrenheit 451* (UTBG 121) by Ray Bradbury or John Wyndham's *The Day of the Triffids* (UTBG 96).

Published in 1932, *Brave New World* creates an imaginary world many years in the future, a seeming paradise where everything is perfect, where illness and poverty have been defeated and where, theoretically, everyone is happy. But of course, they are not.

Huxley depicts his world in a terrifying and convincing way; here, intense social engineering succeeds only at the expense of some fundamental human traits, and the ideas of family, love and freedom all suffer at the hands of the State. In place of natural happiness, joy is instead derived from promiscuous but meaningless sex, from consuming material goods, from watching certain state-controlled sports and from indulgence in a pleasure drug. If that sounds like Huxley was writing about our own age, then people who see his book as prophetic are vindicated, but there is more to this enjoyable and disturbing science fiction novel than simple prophecy.

**Marcus Sedgwick**

# THE BREADWINNER Deborah Ellis

Four days after her father's arrest, food runs out for Parvana's family. Though Taliban rule absolutely forbids women to leave the house alone, Parvana has no option but to take the risk, disguising herself as a boy and dodging the deadly landmines in an attempt to save her family from starvation.

Using the imagined life-story of a young Afghan teenager, Ellis clearly conveys the brutality and fear of Taliban rule, and brings the human stories behind the headlines to life in a way that is far more hard-hitting and emotionally striking than any TV news report. A brave, timely and topical book – continued in the equally eye-opening *Parvana's Journey* in which Parvana flees across war-torn Afghanistan in search of her father.

**Eileen Armstrong**

**Next?**

The sequel, *Mud City*, takes up the story of one of Parvana's friends.

Ellis' *The Heaven Shop* (UTBG 165) tells the story of AIDS-stricken families in Malawi through the eyes of one young girl.

*Persepolis: The Story of a Childhood* (UTBG 286) tells of one girl's experience of life in Iran.

# BREAKFAST AT TIFFANY'S

## Truman Capote

**Next?**

You'll find another seductive and amoral heroine in *Bonjour Tristesse* (UTBG 48); but beware, you may find it a more shocking read.

The eponymous heroine of *Zuleika Dobson* by Max Beerbohm is another young woman finding her place in the world.

One of the greatest of barbed wits belonged to an American woman called Dorothy Parker. Read her in *The Collected Dorothy Parker*.

Holly Golighty is a Carrie Bradshaw in waiting. Today she would write a column about her adventures in the captivating city of New York, meeting her equally successful friends for brunch and buying herself presents at Tiffany's. Half a century ago, young women who wanted to reinvent themselves needed to do it through men. Capote's short novel is less frothy than the Audrey Hepburn film. Holly's barbed wit barely masks her insecurity; her casual racism and shallowness is jarring to a modern reader. But it's hard not to become smitten with her as the narrator does, and even when you fall out of love with her, you still wish her well.

**Geraldine Brennan**

# BREAKTIME   Aidan Chambers

This is the first in a ground-breaking sequence of six novels by Aidan Chambers, all of which look at physical and emotional experiences – and how we understand and talk about them. All that sounds pretty heavy, but Chambers introduces lots of jokes and playfulness that remind us that experiences are only as real as the language we use to describe them. Several things happen in this book over the course of the holiday period that Ditto is recording – he's been dared to keep a record by his schoolmate Morgan – culminating in, for Ditto, the ultimate experience: his first sexual encounter, with a girl called Helen. Or is it? When it was first published, this book caused a stir for its explicit description of sex; it remains a bold and thought-provoking read today.

**Jon Appleton**

**Next?**

The sequence continues with *Dance on My Grave* (UTBG 91), *Now I Know*, *The Toll Bridge* (UTBG 376), *Postcards from No Man's Land* (UTBG 292) and *This Is All*.

When characters keep diaries and records in fiction, all kinds of unexpected things are revealed. Jan Mark's *The Hillingdon Fox* is one of my all-time favourites.

Or try Jean Ure's *Get a Life*, about a boy who discovers secrets about his brother's sexuality.

# BRIDESHEAD REVISITED

## Evelyn Waugh

Oh man! Describing why I like *Brideshead* in 120 words is a bit like trying to sum up *The Bible* in one sentence. Saying it's about a doomed aristocratic Catholic family isn't, methinks, going to make you want to rush out and buy it. But it's about so much more – it's a great love story; it's a heart-rending tale of loss and rejection; it's a great sweeping narrative that takes in pre-war Oxford, Venice, Paris and Morocco and a large cast of brilliantly drawn characters; it deals with religion and morality, guilt, repression and pain; it's dark, complex, powerful, evocative, poetic, compelling, sumptuous, passionate, moving, at times extremely funny, and ultimately tragic. In short, it's a masterpiece and I totally love it!

**Catherine Robinson**

### Next?

*The Great Gatsby* (UTBG 156) by F. Scott Fitzgerald is also a classic tale of glittering wealth, love, unhappiness and loneliness.

Another novel with a pre-war setting which deals with changing attitudes towards class is E.M. Forster's *Howard's End*.

For those on a Waugh path (!), try *Decline and Fall* or *Vile Bodies* – both very different, dark satires.

# BRIDGE TO TERABITHIA

## Katherine Paterson

### Next?

*Anne of Green Gables* (and sequels) by L.M. Montgomery; set on Prince Edward Island, Canada, the stories show how close rural life can be, as does Karen Wallace's *Raspberries on the Yangtze* (UTBG 304).

Or try *The Secret Garden* (UTBG 325) by Frances Hodgson Burnett – in which a lonely boy and girl find redemption in a magical place.

*Walk Two Moons* (UTBG 396) by Sharon Creech is another stunning American story about coming to terms with tragedy.

Jess doesn't really have any friends until new girl Leslie comes to his rural school. Leslie is rich and lives in a big house and her parents don't even own a television. Like Jess, Leslie is an outsider. Together they create a magical kingdom – Terabithia – down by the creek; as King and Queen of Terabithia they can make a world just as they want it to be. Life is perfect ... until tragedy strikes.

A moving and insightful book about friendship, death and creativity.

**Ann Jungman**

# BRIDGET JONES'S DIARY
## Helen Fielding

Bridget is in her 30s and worried. Although she has a good job, a home of her own and many good friends, she is single and, more than anything, she wants a boyfriend. But the men in her life seem to be too standoffish or too untrustworthy to fit the bill. Her family teases her for being alone and she worries endlessly about how much she weighs, drinks and smokes. Only her closest friends can make her see that life is not so bad after all. Written as a diary, this sweet and very funny book takes us through a year of Bridget's life, as she searches for love, happiness and the perfect diet while dodging unsuitable men, annoying parents and the dreaded 'smug marrieds'.

**Marianne Taylor**

### Next?

*Bridget Jones: the Edge of Reason*, the next instalment of Bridget's chaotic life.

*Does My Bum Look Big in This*? (UTBG 108) by Arabella Weir is another light-hearted tale of the struggles of a singleton.

Want the male perspective? Try Nick Hornby's *High Fidelity* (UTBG 167).

# BRIGHTON ROCK Graham Greene

### Next?

Graham Greene's short stories are wonderfully various, as are his novels, try: *Our Man in Havana* (UTBG 278) or *The End of the Affair*.

The **Maigret** books (UTBG 230) by Georges Simenon, featuring the bumbling inspector, have a cast of crooks and seedy thugs and a similar feel to *Brighton Rock*.

For another story of murder with a powerful setting, this time pre-war London, try *Hangover Square* by Patrick Hamilton (UTBG 160).

Over 40 years ago the first page of *Brighton Rock* made me want to be a writer. It's an opening to die for... and somebody does. Graham Greene's story walks out of Brighton station and straight off the page; it intrigues and appals you, and then goes on haunting the streets of your imagination for the rest of your life. Its characters, their desperate lives, the busy seafront and dark alleys of the dangerous town where Good and Evil are in relentless pursuit of one another stay with you forever. Because, like all the very best books, *Brighton Rock* lives on long after you've turned the last page. Join the crowd on the promenade and you'll see what I mean.

**Michael Cronin**

# THE BROMELIAD trilogy

## Terry Pratchett

**12+**

For the Nomes in the Store there is no day and night, no sun and rain. All these things are just old myths – just like 'the Outside'. However, all that changes when a group of Nomes from the Outside arrive…

In *Truckers*, the Nomes capture a truck, and escape in it before their home, the Store, is demolished. In *Diggers*, the Nomes try to survive in the Quarry – but this becomes a nightmare, especially when the humans intervene… In *Wings*, three Nomes try to get to America to find a spacecraft to take them home, using the Thing (a micro-computer) as a guide.

This gripping fantasy adventure is full of humour, misunderstanding and deeper meaning too – strongly recommended!

**Samuel Mortimer (aged 11)**

### Next?

More Pratchett of course. Try the **Johnny Maxwell** series, beginning with *Only You Can Save Mankind*; or one of his **Discworld** books – *Monstrous Regiment* (UTBG 103) is a good place to start.

For another fantasy that'll make you laugh, read Paul Stewart and Chris Riddell's *Muddle Earth*; or **The Edge Chronicles**, beginning with *Beyond the Deepwoods* (UTBG 40).

Or for more confusion involving a spacecraft, try Andrew Norris' *Aquila*.

# BROTHER OF THE MORE FAMOUS JACK

## Barbara Trapido

 **16+**

### Next?

The Goldman family saga continues in *The Travelling Hornplayer*.

If you love Katherine's voice (and you will) your next port of call simply has to be the brilliant *A Long Way from Verona* (UTBG 221).

William Sutcliffe's *New Boy* (UTBG 258) manages to say a lot about being Jewish in London, while being very funny.

This brilliant comedy is published as an adult book that casts a cool yet affectionate eye over the vulnerability of adolescence, and I can't think of a more perfect time to read it (whether you're male or female) than at the age of 16. Katherine's induction to the sprawling, fractious Jewish Goldman family begins with her meeting patriarchal Jacob for a university interview in north London. A bond is formed, and it deepens over the years: there's love (maternal, paternal, filial, sexual) and lust and pain and betrayal, and I promise you won't put the book down till the end. Just read this fabulous comedy and love it, as I did.

**Jon Appleton**

# BROTHERS Ted van Lieshout

**Next?**

Paul Magrs' *Strange Boy* (UTBG 358) is set in the north-east of England and deals with sexuality.

If you're interested in the treatment of bereavement in *Brothers*, try Brian Keaney's *Bitter Fruit* (UTBG 43).

Or *Skin* by A.M. Vrettos, about a boy learning his sister's dark secrets.

Warning – this is an immensely moving novel. It begins when teenage Luke finds his younger brother Marius' diary – Marius died six months ago. Luke is reluctant at first to start reading it, but begins to write his own diary in it, in which he struggles with his feelings about losing his brother and his growing knowledge that he's gay. When he finally starts to read Marius' entries, he discovers exactly what it is he and his brother had in common and why their relationship will always be meaningful. This is a novel about the big stuff – sexuality, bereavement – but this Dutch author writes with a real lightness of touch. The book will draw you in from the start.

**Sherry Ashworth**

# THE BUDDHA OF SUBURBIA
## Hanif Kureishi

Karim Amir lives in the South London suburbs with his English mother and Indian father. Restless and easily bored, he's desperate to escape and experience life. The book follows his escapades through 1970s London – where he finds himself mixing with every social circle, from the punk scene to the theatre world.

Karim ends up in many of the positions we all find ourselves in in life (and some we almost certainly don't). The unexpected ways in which he deals with these situations are hilarious, yet at the same time painfully honest and genuinely moving. Karim's narrative has a wonderfully fresh and self-mocking tone – however great his dilemmas get he's never going to take life too seriously. But this isn't a book to read if you're easily offended (or if you're looking for a real insight into Eastern philosophy!).

**Katie Jennings**

**Next?**

If you want to know more about how teenage boys think, read *The Rachel Papers* (UTBG 301) by Martin Amis.

*Generation X* (UTBG 143) by Douglas Coupland has more pop culture, or you might like his *Girlfriend in a Coma* (UTBG 147), at least for the Smiths references…

Alan Warner's brilliant too; try *Morvern Callar*, about a girl's search for her identity in Ibiza, or *The Sopranos*, a very funny story of bad girls on a school choir trip.

# THE BURNING CITY   Ariel and Joaquin Dorfman   12+

### Next?

*Refugees* by Catherine Stein is an imaginative response to the events of 9/11. Art Spiegelman's *In the Shadow of No Towers* boldly tries to make sense of that terrible day in comic-strip form.

*Divided City* (UTBG 106) is another story of tensions in a city.

The classic American coming-of-age story is, of course, *The Catcher in the Rye* (UTBG 66) by J.D. Salinger.

Carl Hiaasen is another adult author who has started writing for younger readers too – try *Hoot* (UTBG 175).

In the summer before the tragic events of September 11th, 2001, Heller Highland has just turned 16 and he's the star employee of Soft Tidings, a courier service delivering personal messages all over the city. Heller specialises in bad news, cycling at breakneck speed through Manhattan's crowded streets to deliver sad tidings with a detached sensitivity born of a supreme confidence in his own invulnerability. Nothing can touch him. But suddenly in the course of three or four days, Heller experiences his own loss and suffering and learns the hard way about what is important in life. This is a filmic and fast-moving contemporary fable about the coming of age of a boy, a city and a nation.

**Kathryn Ross**

# THE BUTTERFLY TATTOO   Philip Pullman   14+

Sometimes we have to make choices in ignorance, and our choices may turn out to be wrong... *The Butterfly Tattoo* was written some years before the vast, worldwide success of **His Dark Materials** trilogy. It is, for me, Pullman's most interesting novel – tragic, morally complex and disturbing, it throws up the themes of ignorance versus experience that recur in the trilogy, but deals with them in a different way.

From the startling first sentence – 'Chris Marshall met the girl he was going to kill on a warm night in early June' – you have a sense of doom. 17-year-old Chris becomes obsessed with beautiful, elusive Jenny, and thus embroiled in a morally ambiguous world he does not understand. Chris finds comfort at the end, but for the reader, who knows otherwise, there is none. You'll read it in one sitting: it's unputdownable.

**Patricia Elliott**

### Next?

Ruth Rendell, writing as Barbara Vine, writes dark, psychological thrillers with the same compulsive quality. Try *A Fatal Inversion*.

Patricia Highsmith's books are full of moral ambiguity. Try *The Talented Mr Ripley* (UTBG 364).

*Useful Idiots* (UTBG 391) is a powerful thriller set in the future, as is Neil Arksey's *As Good as Dead in Downtown*.

# THE CALL OF THE WILD Jack London

**Next?**

Jack London wrote amazingly about animals; try another of his classics, *White Fang*. Or *The Sea-Wolf* is different but just as good.

*Roll of Thunder, Hear My Cry* (UTBG 311) by Mildred D. Taylor is about humans being cruel to humans.

Another book that's set in the wild American landscape is J. Fenimore Cooper's *The Last of the Mohicans*.

This is a book about appalling animal cruelty. Buck is kidnapped from his home and taken to the wild north of Canada. Beaten, clubbed and whipped until he obeys, he is harnessed to a sledge with eight other dogs and forced to pull his new owners and their belongings across rock and snow in their search for gold. He learns to fight for his place in the pack, to survive the cruelty of man, dog and nature, and eventually finds a new pride in himself. But things get worse and worse for Buck, until it seems that a happy ending is impossible – or is it?

**Leonie Flynn**

# CALLING A DEAD MAN
## Gillian Cross

A sick man with no memory awakes in a snowy Siberian wood. All he knows is that something has happened that is too terrible to recall. Meanwhile, far away, a family obliterates every trace of an adored son; a gangster organisation senses a threat to its security; and a bereft lover sets out into the unknown with only the slenderest of hopes to support her.

*Calling a Dead Man* takes place after the fall of Communism, when criminal organisations, the Mafiya, are moving in to make as much profit as possible in the resulting power vacuum. We see a frozen world of small, valiant people, some acting with extraordinary generosity and heroism in the face of death, cruelty and relentless poverty.

This is an amazing book, not just for being a taut thriller in an exotic setting, but for describing huge emotions in a barren landscape, and portraying the Siberian people with insight and compassion.

**Sally Prue**

**Next?**

Gillian Cross has written another thriller about a criminal organisation in *Tightrope*.

A brilliant thriller set around the cold war is John le Carré's *The Spy Who Came in from the Cold* (UTBG 351).

A true story of Russia, Communism and Siberia is *One Day in the Life of Ivan Denisovich* by Alexander Solzhenitsyn (UTBG 271).

# CAN YOU KEEP A SECRET?
## Sandra Glover

The last thing on earth Karen wants is to hang out with compulsive liar Zoe, let alone hear the appalling secret that she's pregnant. When a baby is found abandoned nearby some months later Zoe 'confesses' that her secret was an attention-seeking lie – or was it? The reader, like Karen, struggles to separate fact from fiction. But the secret meant more to Karen than Zoe realises, for Karen herself was found abandoned and adopted as a baby and must now face up to her own secret past.

   Glover is one of the most versatile writers around and this is one of her most intricate, involving, read-it-in-one-sitting books.

**Eileen Armstrong**

### Next?

*You* by Sandra Glover offers a slightly different take on the theme of the childkiller.

Glover's *Spiked* is a suspense-filled thriller about Debra, who was abducted after her drink was spiked at a post-GCSE celebration party.

*Midnight* by Jacqueline Wilson looks at adoption through the eyes of Violet, whose brother has just learnt that he was adopted.

# CANDY Kevin Brooks

### Next?

Read Kevin Brooks' other books; *Martyn Pig* (UTBG 236), *Lucas* (UTBG 228) or *Kissing the Rain* (UTBG 209).

*Skarrs* (UTBG 342) deals with similar issues and is just as hard-hitting.

*Boy Kills Man* (UTBG 51) by Matt Whyman also depicts a boy in an extreme and dangerous situation.

London Zoo, one of the settings for *Candy*, also features in another, quite different, book – Russell Hoban's *Turtle Diary* (UTBG 386).

Kevin Brooks pushes his characters into situations you hope will never happen to you: extreme situations, but ones you will believe in absolutely. Candy is a beautiful girl, trapped in heroin addiction and prostitution – and Joe Beck, bass guitarist and genuine good guy, falls madly in love with her. Iggy, Candy's utterly terrifying pimp / drug-dealer, is not happy, and when Iggy is not happy, violence is inevitable.

   This is a story about lack of control, whether because of drugs, or love, or pure chance, or because of the adults who run the world that teenagers have to live in. Lock your door when you read this dark, dangerous and utterly gripping book – you will not want to be interrupted.

**Nicola Morgan**

# CANNERY ROW / SWEET THURSDAY

## John Steinbeck

**Next?**

John Steinbeck's most famous books are *The Grapes of Wrath* and *East of Eden*, but you might like to try some more of his lesser-known stuff. My favourites are *The Wayward Bus* and *Travels with Charley*.

Another writer who deals in misfits is Flannery O'Connor. Try *A Good Man Is Hard to Find*.

These two short books make up a beautifully written portrait of a group of people living on the margins of society. Set in a rundown Californian fishing town in the 1940s, both are based around a community of characters who exist on the edges of life – idlers, tramps, low-lifes, wasters.

There isn't much of a plot in these novels – the stories are more like a jigsaw of relationships and events – but the characters are so fascinating, and the writing so hypnotically good, that they don't need a plot.

Although both books can be read independently, the characters are first introduced in *Cannery Row*, so it's probably a good idea to start there.

**Kevin Brooks**

# CAPTAIN CORELLI'S MANDOLIN

## Louis de Bernières

Dr Iannis practices medicine on the beautiful island of Cephalonia, and with the help of his daughter Pelagia he lives a simple but fulfilling life. Following the invasion of Greece by the Italians things are still not too bad, as the captain of the Italian garrison is the cultured Antonio Corelli, who adores music and playing his mandolin. But then Corelli and Pelagia fall in love, although she is engaged to the local fisherman Mandras, and the couple become caught up in the intrigues and atrocities of war, where friends become enemies and even those they trust the most turn against them.

This book is not just about love but also about how lives are affected by war. At times hilarious, at other times heartbreaking, it is one of my favourite books ever. I think everyone should read it!

**Ileana Antonopoulou**

**Next?**

More de Bernières? Try *The War of Don Emmanuel's Nether Parts*.

For another novel that deals graphically with war (and love), try *Birdsong* (UTBG 43) by Sebastian Faulks.

Or what about *For Whom the Bell Tolls* by Ernest Hemingway?

# CARWASH   Lesley Howarth

14+

I really enjoyed this story about a group of teenagers in a village in Cornwall and the events of one hot summer which leave everyone changed in some way. It's funny, and real, and convincing in every detail. I love the way the story is narrated by different characters: it starts with Luke who runs his own carwashing business in the village, and then moves to Sylvie Bickle ('Bix') who spends most of her time up a tree watching what everyone else is up to. Her sister Liv also plays a central role in the story, as does Luke's brother Danny. Liv likes writing and is on the lookout for material for her stories, but the most dramatic and significant thing is actually happening to her...

You really get to know these characters and live that summer along with them... Brilliant!
**Julia Green**

**Next?**

Try other novels by the same author: *Ultraviolet* (UTBG 387) is set in a world trying to re-create itself after nuclear war. *Drive* is about a boy pulled towards crime.

You might like to try **Lucas** (UTBG 228), by Kevin Brooks – a much harsher, sadder story about peer pressure.

Or *LBD: It's a Girl Thing* (UTBG 216) by Grace Dent, a light, funny, perceptive look at teenage life.

# CAT AMONG THE PIGEONS
## Agatha Christie

12+

**Next?**

Other great detective stories? Try Dorothy L. Sayers' **Gaudy Night** (set in a women's college) or Margery Allingham's **Sweet Danger**.

Ngaio Marsh and Patricia Wentworth are other brilliant female writers from the same period; look out for any of their books – they're all worth a read.

There are two distinct pleasures in reading an Agatha Christie – and the whodunnit is only one of them. The other is the particular period flavour of the worlds she creates. *Cat Among the Pigeons* is set in a famous girls' boarding school (much more convincing than the ones in school stories), where the games mistress gets shot, the groundsman comes from the security services, and one of the pupils carries a whiff of Middle Eastern mystery. Enter Christie's great Belgian detective Hercule Poirot... Though in this particular book, he plays more of a walk-on part than in other novels, like *Murder on the Orient Express*, where he's very much the centre of the show.
**Sarah Gristwood**

# CATALYST  Laurie Halse Anderson

14+

**Next?**

More by the same author? Try
*Speak*.

For another emotional and
intelligent ride through
adolescence, try *The Moth Diaries*
(UTBG 251) by Rachel Klein.

*What the Birds See* (UTBG 407)
by Sonya Hartnett is a painfully
wonderful book with a similar feel,
though it's less direct and raw.

*You Don't Know Me* (UTBG 425)
by David Klass is about a boy pushed
to the edge by his stepfather.

Kate is brilliant and seems in control of
everything; everyone expects her to succeed.
The fact that she seems to have taken her
dead mother's place so brilliantly makes
everyone believe that she is fine. But inside,
she is losing control, and carries unbearable
burdens. When a truly shocking event
occurs, will this tip her over the edge or
save her?

  If this is one of the most painful books I
have ever read, why am I recommending it?
Perhaps because it captures so perfectly
some of the pain of growing up. Parents
should read it too – then they'll think twice
before putting their sons and daughters
under the intense pressure that Kate
Malone faces.

**Nicola Morgan**

# CATCH-22  Joseph Heller

16+

When I was a teenager, reading *Catch-22*
by Joseph Heller changed the way I thought
about life, and it changed the way I thought
about books. It made me see, for the first
time, that war is a kind of insanity. And
it made me realise that a book could
be funny and intensely serious at the
same time. The book's anti-hero, Yossarian,
is an American fighter pilot stationed in
Italy during World War II, desperate to be
excused from flying more missions and
to escape the madness of a situation
where every kind of military double-think
and capitalist excess seems to thrive.
The book has fantastic comic energy
and builds towards a triumphant
surprise ending.

**Jonathan Coe**

**Next?**

Yossarian and friends reappear in
*Closing Time*, where this time the
enemy is death itself.

A scathing look at the contemporary
world, particularly America, is *Dude,
Where's My Country?* by Michael
Moore.

Jonathan Coe's own novel, *What a
Carve Up!*, is great satire and a
stark black comedy about murder
(and other things).

Read our feature on cult books on
pp. 264–265 for more inspiration.

# THE CATCHER IN THE RYE

## J.D. Salinger

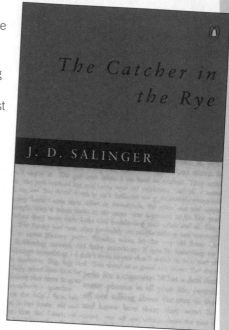

After being thrown out of his fourth expensive boarding school, Holden Caulfield puts time on hold and spends two disastrous days in New York before facing his parents. Heading for a mental and physical breakdown, his favourite word is 'phony' which describes just about everyone he meets and anything he doesn't like; and yet he desperately wants to fit in somewhere, have friends, figure out his future. The people he most admires are children like his little sister. He imagines himself being a 'catcher', someone who can get between them and danger, always haunted by the memory of his brother who died young, the one he couldn't save.

All teen novels are descended from this one, and yet it isn't a teen novel, just a book about one unhappy 16-year-old, and millions have identified with him.

**Jan Mark**

## Next?

Another 16-year-old who deals with a crisis rather differently is the hero of Gary Paulsen's *The Beet Fields* (UTBG 35).

*Billy Liar* by Keith Waterhouse is an account of a teenager in northern England getting himself into every kind of trouble and trying to blag his way out of it.

For more Salinger try *For Esmé – with Love and Squalor* (UTBG 134), his collection of short stories about youth and childhood.

I was 19 and not enjoying my first year at university when I first met Holden Caulfield, the 16-year-old protagonist of *The Catcher in the Rye*. Holden is having a bad time too – we soon discover he is about to flunk out of yet another school, and doesn't know what to do with his life. So he sets out for a weekend in New York before going home to his parents.

Holden is trapped between childhood and maturity, desperate to grow up but afraid of it too, and disgusted by the 'phony' way adults behave. He is also the original teen and one of the great characters of literature. His story is both funny and very moving. Most of us have a Holden Caulfield moment at some time – and I know he helped me with mine.

**Tony Bradman**

# CAT'S CRADLE Kurt Vonnegut

This story is told by a man who is planning a book about the day the first atomic bomb was dropped on Japan. In the course of his researches he meets Newt Hoenikker, son of Dr Felix Hoenikker, 'father of the bomb', which leads him to a small Caribbean island where he comes into contact with a brand-new religion based on lies, falls in love, and becomes president. He also learns about Ice-9, a substance created by Dr Hoenikker which, when brought into contact with water, instantly freezes it and spreads – endlessly.

Kurt Vonnegut is one of the easiest writers to read, and often one of the funniest, but he also puts a very individual spin on the most serious subjects. Everyone should give Vonnegut a try. Even if you don't like the way he writes, you'll have to admit he's an original.
**Michael Lawrence**

> ### Next?
>
> For a look at what the world might be like before and after The Bomb, read Raymond Briggs' graphic novel, *When the Wind Blows* (UTBG 409).
>
> The spine-chilling *Why Weeps the Brogan*? (UTBG 412) is set in a world that's been destroyed.
>
> More Vonnegut? He lived through the bombing of Dresden and wrote about it in *Slaughterhouse 5* (UTBG 345). There's also *The Sirens of Titan* (UTBG 341), *Breakfast of Champions* and many more. All are weird and wonderfully brain expanding

# CAT'S EYE Margaret Atwood

> ### Next?
>
> If you enjoyed the theme of art and what it says about life, read *To The Lighthouse* by Virginia Woolf.
>
> If the theme of bullying and its effects interested you, try *I'm the King of the Castle* (UTBG 188) by Susan Hill.
>
> If it's the adult's view of the child they once were that you enjoyed, try *The Go-Between* (UTBG 150) by L.P. Hartley.

As a successful artist, Elaine Risley returns to Toronto where she grew up, for an exhibition. Elaine's paintings have been inspired by her own experiences, and the truths she splashes on her canvases aren't ones that her former friends are ready for. In order to move on with her adult life, Elaine is forced to confront her past and to relive the bullying she endured at the hands of her fascinating and manipulative friend Cordelia.

*Cat's Eye* is a brilliant and absorbing novel about art, about the nature of time, about friendship, and about how the child you were will always be a part of the adult you become.
**Antonia Honeywell**

# CAUGHT IN THE CROSSFIRE

## Alan Gibbons

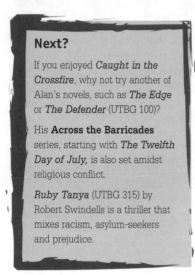

### Next?

If you enjoyed *Caught in the Crossfire*, why not try another of Alan's novels, such as *The Edge* or *The Defender* (UTBG 100)?

His **Across the Barricades** series, starting with *The Twelfth Day of July,* is also set amidst religious conflict.

*Ruby Tanya* (UTBG 315) by Robert Swindells is a thriller that mixes racism, asylum-seekers and prejudice.

The Patriotic League, an extreme right-wing racist party, wants to claim white Britain back, and the events of September 11th give them the perfect excuse to stir up trouble in the north of England. Caught in the crossfire of mounting violence are six teenagers: two Irish lads looking for trouble; a Muslim brother and sister; and Mike and Liam, brothers taking different sides, one of whom is heading for a terrible fate.

Alan Gibbons is a brilliant writer, and this book is typically fast-paced, compulsive and frighteningly relevant. As one teenager wrote recently about it: 'It was just so sensitive, emotional and real… I will never be able to forget this book.'

**Cliff McNish**

# CAUSE CELEB  Helen Fielding

Helen Fielding's massively successful **Bridget Jones** books can't have passed you by – even if you only know them through the films. This book came out a good three years before Bridget, and is even funnier. It's about a disillusioned TV journalist who tries to escape the shallowness of media life and a broken heart by dropping everything to work in a refugee camp in Africa. When famine strikes, she uses her old skills to set up a celebrity TV fundraiser.

Fielding lampoons the vanity of it all, and some of her most savage portraits of stars with their hearts on their sleeves have been proved true in the years since the book was written. It's a laugh – but it makes a very serious point.

**Eleanor Updale**

### Next?

*Bridget Jones's Diary* (UTBG 57) and its sequel, both by Helen Fielding.

If you like the way Fielding playfully dismembers media-centred London life, try *The Best a Man Can Get* by John O'Farrell.

Then move on to anything by Nick Hornby: *About a Boy* (UTBG 11) is a great place to start.

# THE CEMENT GARDEN  Ian McEwan

As a teenager, I was not a reader. I had always been a TV and computer games kid. Then, aged 16, I was given Ian McEwan's *The Cement Garden*. I was gripped, and I still remember the feeling of staying up late into the night, in my own private pool of bedside light, reading and reading, unable to contemplate sleep until I had got to the end of the book. From that moment on, I was transformed from a TV watcher into a reader, and possibly even into a writer.

The story is dark, gory, weird, twisted, funny, and contains sex, bad language, masturbation, gender-bending and the improvised burial of parents. It's a sort of *Lord of the Flies* of the family, with a suburban house standing in for the desert island. Your English teacher could get into serious trouble for giving you this kind of book…

**William Sutcliffe**

### Next?

'A *Lord of the Flies* of the family'? So read *Lord of the Flies* (UTBG 223) and see what you think.

Or Joy Nicholson's *The Tribes of Palos Verdes*, a Californian take on family meltdown as viewed by teenagers.

*The Rachel Papers* (UTBG 301) is a dazzling first novel from Martin Amis, a literary giant.

Or for another disturbing tale of twisted adolescence, read *The Wasp Factory* (UTBG 400).

# THE CHANGEOVER  Margaret Mahy

Apart from the fact that she sometimes has 'premonitions' and suspects that Sorensen Carlisle, a senior boy whom she secretly fancies, might be a witch, Laura Chant is an ordinary 14-year-old. She does well at school and helps her divorcee mum to look after her little brother, Jacko. Then one day a vile man called Carmody Braque brands his evil image on the back of Jacko's hand and from that moment the toddler starts to shrivel and fade. Braque is feeding like a vampire on Jacko's youth. In desperation, Laura turns to Sorensen Carlisle for help and discovers that to defeat Carmody Braque she herself must become a witch too. Sorensen is a terrific character, dangerous and sexy, yet curiously vulnerable, and Laura (along with many readers!) finds herself falling for his enigmatic charms. Mahy makes the extraordinary utterly believable in this supernatural romance.

**Kathryn Ross**

### Next?

In *Poison* by Chris Wooding, the heroine sets out to rescue her little sister when she is abducted by evil Phaeries.

And in Catherine MacPhail's chilling *Another Me* a young girl's life is gradually taken over by someone her own age; someone who looks just like her…

# A CHILD CALLED 'IT'  Dave Pelzer

This is a true story. As a child, Dave Pelzer was brutally beaten, emotionally tortured and starved by his unpredictable, unstable, alcoholic mother, while his fireman father, who had 'broad shoulders and forearms that would make any muscle man proud', did nothing but watch. No longer considered a son but a slave, no longer a boy but an 'it', he slept in an old army cot in the basement, dressed in smelly rags, and when he was allowed the luxury of food it was scraps from the dogs' bowls.

What singled Dave out from his two brothers? Perhaps it was that his voice just carried farther than others. He had to learn to play his mother's games – every humiliation a victory as it meant he had survived yet another day.

Told from the child's point of view, this is a heartbreaking yet heartwarming tale of courageous endurance, of one child's dream of finding a family to love and care for him, to call him their son.

**Elena Gregoriou**

### Next?

Read the sequels: *The Lost Boy* and *A Man Named Dave*.

Dave's brother Richard B. Pelzer has written his own account of their childhood in *A Brother's Journey*.

Other writers have been brave enough to tell of their own terrible childhoods. Augusten Burroughs survived life with an alcoholic father; read his memoir *Running with Scissors*.

Or for the fictional account of the aftermath of brutality try *The Lovely Bones* (UTBG 228) by Alice Sebold.

## BEING DIFFERENT

*Midget* by Tim Bowler

*Face* by Benjamin Zephaniah

*Mondays Are Red* by Nicola Morgan

*The Curious Incident of the Dog in the Night-time* by Mark Haddon

*Wheels* by Catherine MacPhail

*Paralysed* by Sherry Ashworth

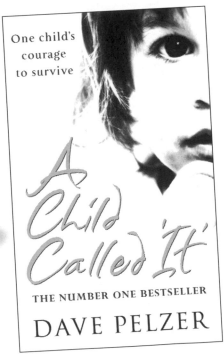

One child's courage to survive

*A Child Called It*

THE NUMBER ONE BESTSELLER

DAVE PELZER

# CHILD X Lee Weatherly

**Next?**

More Lee Weatherly? Try *Missing Abby*, about a girl whose friend goes missing.

Jules performs in a stage version of *Northern Lights* – so read the first part of Pullman's **His Dark Materials** trilogy (UTBG 170).

For another girl finding strength to cope with adversity, read *Lola Rose* (UTBG 219).

When Jules' dad leaves home, things are bad enough. He takes all his possessions, but leaves behind his favourite photo of Jules. Why? What has she done? And why are the newspapers suddenly hounding Jules and her mother? Why are they all trying to get pictures?

As she uncovers the long-buried secret that has torn her world apart, Jules is forced to question everything she has taken for granted about herself and the people closest to her. Lee Weatherly really helps us feel what Jules is going through – one of the worst nightmares of any child's life.

**Yvonne Coppard**

# CHILDREN OF THE DUST
## Louise Lawrence

A perfect day. Blue skies, and swallows nesting. 'But the first bombs had fallen, the headmaster said, and a full-scale nuclear attack was imminent.'

A terrifying beginning to a truly terrifying book. Part I, at any rate, describing as it does in agonising detail how Sarah and her family barricade themselves in the kitchen, while outside the deadly dust clouds gather and the nuclear night closes in.

Parts II and III are inevitably less gripping, but make compulsive reading nonetheless, as the scattered remnants of the population claw their way to a kind of coping.

*Children of the Dust* is written as a book of hope, of belief in humanity's power to renew itself; and therein perhaps lies a weakness, for the brave new world arises with somewhat implausible speed from the ashes, and might even be said to put across the dangerous message: whatever ghastly things we do, we can survive.

For all that, this is undeniably a very, very powerful book.

**Jean Ure**

**Next?**

Can a cartoon ever be as harrowing as a novel? Read *When the Wind Blows* (UTBG 409) by Raymond Briggs and believe it.

For other stories of fictional wars and their aftermath, try *Brother in the Land* by Robert Swindells, *How I Live Now* (UTBG 179) or *Z for Zachariah* (UTBG 426).

# PINK LIT by Cathy Hopkins

In the current marketing trend (or obsession) to brand and pigeon-hole, pink lit has emerged as the 10- to 16-year-old equivalent of adult chick lit. The books are recognisable by their bright-coloured 'girlie' covers. Pink lit is frothy and humorous, with a twist of escapism, whilst also managing to deal with serious(-ish) contemporary teenage girl preoccupations: chiefly, relationships (especially with the opposite sex), maddening or embarrassing parents, school life and friends, and questions such as 'How do boys tick?', 'Where do I fit in?' or 'Where is my life heading?'

These books have become incredibly popular because the characters and situations are instantly recognisable and easy to identify with. They are realistic enough, but not threateningly over-gritty or grim. There is romance without sexually transmitted diseases; embarrassing parents without extreme poverty or distressing abuse. Pink lit books are light and easy reading. They have a wide appeal, being read voraciously by literate teen bookworms, by boys (in secret) who want to get a handle on what goes on in girls' minds and by many who claim normally not to read anything more than the cornflake packet.

Pink lit is often dismissed by critics as trivial or facile, probably because of its lighthearted approach. But I think the reviewers miss the point. As well as providing a bit of welcome leisurely escapism, pink lit also provides a chance to explore some of the problems that beset teenagers at an often wretched and difficult time in their lives.

I've written two series which fit into the pink-lit genre: **Mates, Dates...** (UTBG

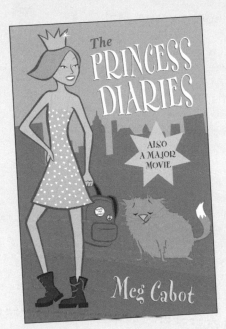

**Other pink lit books you can read about in the *UTBG*:**

*The Sisterhood of the Travelling Pants* by Ann Brashares

*The Princess Diaries* by Meg Cabot

*Teen Idol* by Meg Cabot

*Girl, 15 (Charming But Insane)* by Sue Limb

The **Georgia Nicolson** series (*Angus, Thongs and Full-frontal Snogging*, etc) by Louise Rennison

**Girls in Love** series by Jacqueline Wilson

*I Was a Teenage Drama Queen* by Dyan Sheldon

*The Secret Dreamworld of a Shopaholic* by Sophie Kinsella

*Does My Bum Look Big in This?* by Arabella Weir

238), which is set in North London, and **Truth, Dare…**, set in Cornwall. There is the usual mix of romance, family, school life, and questions such as 'Is there a God?' or 'What am I going to do with my life?' But the main thread that runs through these books is the importance and affirmation of friendship. My publisher has coined a sub-genre, calling them friend lit.

I find my writing very rewarding for two reasons in particular. It is great to know that my stories are popular not just in the UK, but all over the world: the series have been sold in 21 countries. And I love to get e-mails from my readers. The most gratifying thing for me is to hear how I have turned someone on to reading. This sort of message is fairly typical: 'I hated reading, but then I picked up your books and it was like reading about my own life.' Score.

# CHINESE CINDERELLA  Adeline Yen Mah

**12+**

### Next?

There is a sequel: *Chinese Cinderella and the Secret Dragon Society*. These books tell of her childhood; if you want to know what happened next read *Falling Leaves*, written for adults.

If you find yourself interested in Chinese traditions and spirituality, read Yen Mah's *Watching the Tree*.

Or for a record of the dark days in Holland when being Jewish was a crime, read Anne Frank's *The Diary of a Young Girl* (UTBG 102).

This isn't a fairy story; it's a true story, an autobiography. When Adeline was born in China, she was named Jun-ling. Shortly afterwards her mother died, and baby Adeline was blamed. Her family thought her unlucky, and wished she had been the one who'd died. All of them, especially her stepmother, treated her with contempt. Her 'fairy godmother', an aunt who loved her, protected her as much as she could, but that wasn't much. Despite all the ill-treatment, Adeline's story is inspiring. She doesn't fight back – sometimes you wish she would – but she doesn't give up either, and now she's a doctor and businesswoman and writer, free of her cruel family. If you like learning about different lives and different cultures, you'll love this.

**Julia Jarman**

# CHOCOLAT  Joanne Harris

**14+**

Life in the tiny French village of Lansquenet-sous-Tannes is turned upside-down when two strangers arrive, and almost overnight open a shop selling the most delicious chocolates imaginable. At first, many of the villagers are suspicious of the glamorous Vianne and her little girl Anouk, but they soon realise that the newcomers have a knack for finding out people's problems and working out solutions to them, and generally making life better. Only the village priest remains unfriendly – he doesn't trust Vianne or her seductive chocolates and thinks she may be a witch.

*Chocolat* is a lovely, richly detailed story, full of enchanting characters, magical moments and, above all, mouth-watering chocolate!

**Marianne Taylor**

### Next?

*Blackberry Wine* – magical realism and sumptuous settings from the same author.

For another story where food plays an important role, try *Like Water for Chocolate* by Laura Esquivel.

For another story of a stranger, try *Lucas* (UTBG 228) by Kevin Brooks.

Food and seduction? In Anthony Capella's *The Food of Love* Tommaso pretends to be a chef in order to seduce Laura, but it's really his friend Bruno who's doing all the cooking...

# THE CHOCOLATE WAR

## Robert Cormier

Archie Costello is the mastermind behind the Vigils, the secret society that rules Trinity High School, forcing boys to undertake Assignments such as booby-trapping classrooms and baiting teachers. Leon is the corrupt priest who plans to be Headmaster of Trinity. He ignores the Vigils unless they get in his way – or can be of use to him. Jerry is the new boy at Trinity, wanting nothing more than a quiet life, until the Vigils select him for an Assignment and he decides to rebel. When his rebellion threatens both Archie's and Leon's authority, Jerry discovers that he is powerless in the face of the forces they bring down on him.

This is a book like no other: savage, violent, but with moments of strange beauty. Why is it called *The Chocolate War*? Read it and find out.

**Graham Gardner**

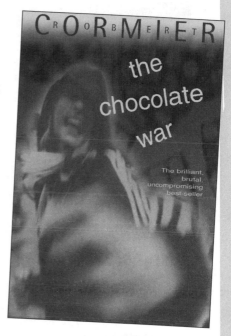

CORMIER

the chocolate war

The brilliant, brutal, uncompromising best-seller

### Next?

If you like dangerous, uncompromising novels, you'll enjoy Robert Cormier's other books, such as *I Am the Cheese* (UTBG 182).

Or try Kevin Brooks' (in my opinion most brilliant) book, *Candy* (UTBG 62).

Or for a really biting read, Catherine Forde's *Skarrs* (UTBG 342).

S.E. Hinton's *The Outsiders* (UTBG 280) is another no-holds-barred story of the strengths and weaknesses of gangs and groups.

For me, *The Chocolate War* is the perfect example of teenage fiction. Actually, it's a perfect example of fiction. It was published in 1974, after being rejected by seven publishers as too dark, too complicated, too downbeat, too violent. It's set in a Catholic boys' high school, which Cormier called a 'metaphor for the world', a school riddled with corruption, bullying, and rigid systems that depend on frightened obedience. On another level, the book is about what happens when a boy refuses to sell chocolates for the annual chocolate sale. And continues to refuse. The book is shot through with scenes that leave you reeling with questions; questions like 'Is this what humans can do to each other?' Read a newspaper and you'll have to say 'yes'.

**Nicola Morgan**

# CHRISTINE Stephen King

16+

## Next?

*Carrie*, King's first novel, follows the torment of teenager Carrie White.

*The Shining*, King's most literary novel, is a tale of madness, isolation and writer's block.

James Herbert and Clive Barker are both British writers of the most chilling horror stories, but they have quite different approaches – if you like being scared witless, try them both!

Stephen King writes the best horror stories, and *Christine* is the most enjoyable of his early books. Arnie Cunningham is a bit of a nerd, but his friend Dennis finds him more interesting than their cooler classmates. Christine is a classic car, a '58 Plymouth Fury that 17-year-old Arnie buys for $250 from a weird old man called Roland D. LeBay. From the moment Arnie buys Christine, Dennis senses something malevolent about her; a suspicion only confirmed when LeBay's brother tells Dennis that LeBay's daughter died, and his wife committed suicide, in the car. As Arnie becomes increasingly obsessed with Christine, Dennis realises his friend's love for the car is going to lead to death and destruction, but he's powerless to stop it.

**Matt Thorne**

# A CHRISTMAS CAROL Charles Dickens

12+

It is Christmas Eve. Bitterly cold. Snow underfoot. Ebenezer Scrooge, a hard-hearted old miser, makes his way home through the narrow, gas-lit streets of London. What does he think of the season of goodwill? 'Christmas! Bah! Humbug!'

But Scrooge was not always such a bitter skinflint. As a boy he was good-hearted. What happened to change him? That night four ghosts visit his cold, bare house and he is taken on a journey to Christmases past, present and future. Scrooge is terrified…

This is a wonderful story, well-nigh perfect, and worthy of its place (after *The Bible*) as the best-known Christmas story in the world.

**Alan Temperley**

## Next?

*The Bible*, if only for Luke 2 and Matthew 2 – the origins of that Christmas story.

*Oliver Twist*, the story of another great Dickensian creation: Fagin, and his gang of boys.

Or what about the story of a ragged young pickpocket in the back streets of 18th-century London: *Smith* by Leon Garfield?

For a bit more of a challenge, read about another great literary miser in *Silas Marner* (UTBG 339).

# THE CHRYSALIDS  John Wyndham

The world has changed. Many generations after Tribulation (a cataclysmic nuclear war), young David Strorm lives in Waknuk, a farming settlement in Labrador. Life is basic, with horses and oil lamps. Nearby is the Fringe, a wilderness where mutants live. Beyond that lie the Badlands, earth blasted and turned to glass. Waknuk is ruled by a stern religion. Mutant animals are offences to God and ritually slaughtered. Human mutants are Blasphemies and driven out. But though visibly normal, David, son of the fiercely righteous Joseph Strorm, is himself a Blasphemy; he can talk to other children, miles off, in his thoughts.

This is a terrific, fast-moving story, packed with ideas. I loved it as a teenager and I love it now.
**Alan Temperley**

### Next?

Even if you're not a sci-fi buff, you'll find that John Wyndham writes great stories; try *The Midwich Cuckoos* or *The Day of the Triffids* (UTBG 96).

You might also enjoy the **Changes** trilogy by Peter Dickinson.

Or Rhiannon Lassiter's **Hex** trilogy (UTBG 167), about the next generation of humans.

# CIDER WITH ROSIE
## Laurie Lee

### Next?

Laurie Lee's life adventures continue in *As I Walked Out One Midsummer Morning* and *A Moment of War*.

Another excellent 'rites of passage' novel is *The Serious Kiss* (UTBG 330).

As is *Pool Boy* by Michael Simmons, in which a boy from an affluent family is suddenly forced to face the harsh realities of living 'on the other side of the tracks'.

Laurie Lee paints a vivid and fascinating portrait of growing up in an English countryside that has disappeared. With a poor but close-knit family as his backdrop, Laurie uncovers people and places around him that are brimming over with intrigue and delight.

His honest prose and evocative imagery stimulate each of the reader's senses as he takes you on a journey from his first experiences of school, through a murder in the locality, to the alluring yet powerful Rosie.

Above all, *Cider with Rosie*'s true magic lies in the way it captures a snapshot of a young boy's life where the possibilities are unlimited and the future is for the taking.
**Jonny Zucker**

# CLAUDINE AT SCHOOL  Colette

Claudine is an attractive, headstrong and precocious adolescent who lives with her unworldly father in the village of Montigny. This, the first novel in Colette's **Claudine** series, is about her mischievous and disruptive behaviour at school. Claudine is bright enough to cruise by on little work, so devotes much energy to battling with her formidable headmistress for the amorous attention of the pretty, golden-eyed classroom assistant Aimée. This witty novel is packed with flirting, bullying and the petty horrors of taking exams.

**Francesca Lewis**

### Next?

*Claudine Married* is the next one in the series. And look out for Colette's story of *Gigi* (UTBG 145), a girl destined to be a courtesan.

In *The Prime of Miss Jean Brodie* (UTBG 295) Muriel Spark breathes life into a band of schoolgirls and their teacher.

If you're a sybarite who enjoys Colette's descriptions of beautiful clothes and objects, try *The Picture of Dorian Gray* (UTBG 287) by Oscar Wilde.

# CLAY  David Almond

### Next?

For a classic tale of learning to animate lifeless matter, read Mary Shelley's *Frankenstein* (UTBG 139). Or for a rather less alarming tale of a boy's relationship with a great inexplicable giant, Ted Hughes' *The Iron Man*.

If you fancy another David Almond, try *Secret Heart* or *Kit's Wilderness* (UTBG 211).

For a story of two people locked in a power struggle that just gets darker and darker, Susan Hill's *I'm the King of the Castle* (UTBG 188).

Stephen Rose, the odd boy with a tragic past, has just arrived at Felling. Stephen Rose, who forms stunning, life-like figures in clay. Local boy Davie soon learns just how remarkable Stephen Rose is; but is his gift a force of good, or of evil?

As always, David Almond paints a world we seem to recognise; but as we read on we realise that we recognise it only in part, we see only its surface. For around us there are always things that we don't see or understand – things hidden in shadows, spirits of the past, powers we can't explain. Throughout his books, these inexplicable things emerge in ways that are sometimes beautiful, sometimes terrifying, but always haunting.

This is a book of secret magic, of faith and doubt, of death and life (no less). And it's one of Almond's best, I think. And if you knew how highly I rate all his work, you'd know just what praise that is.

**Daniel Hahn**

# A CLOCKWORK ORANGE  Anthony Burgess

## Next?

If you like the macabre and bizarre, enter the world of 16-year-old Frank in Iain Banks' *The Wasp Factory* (UTBG 400).

Or if it's shock and a great story that turn you on, try Ian McEwan's first novel, *The Cement Garden* (UTBG 69).

Another group of antisocial friends appear in *Trainspotting* (UTBG 379) by Irvine Welsh.

Want to know more about cult books? Read the feature on pp. 264–265.

I was coerced into reading this story of tolchocking ultraviolence and rape by my 16-year-old son. I thought my feminist soul would hate it. Wrong. It's Burgess' extraordinary achievement to make you empathise with his appalling hero, Alex. Using Nadsat, a brilliant invented language that borrows from Slavic, Burgess contrives to make you into one of Alex's 'droogs'. It's a big book, dangerous, one that grapples with choice and morality. All the more extraordinary for that fact that Burgess wrote it after an attack on his wife which resulted in her miscarrying their child. He might have written it from the perspective of the victim, but instead he writes as the aggressor. I horrorshow wish I'd read it as a teenager.

**Nicky Singer**

# COLD COMFORT FARM  Stella Gibbons

Stella Gibbons's first novel, *Cold Comfort Farm*, published in 1932, remains fresh, relevant and witty today.

Flora Poste, 20, newly orphaned, with no property and only £100 a year, has to decide which relatives to live with. She plumps for the Starkadders on their farm in Howling, Sussex. There she finds an extraordinary collection of individuals, locked into age-old family feuds, stirring lumpy porridge and washing dishes with a thorn stick. At their centre sits Aunt Ada Doom, malevolent, brooding and implacable, haunted by the 'something nasty in the woodshed' she saw as a child and refusing to leave her room.

Flora is determined to create order out of chaos, to inject sanity into the madness, in a novel that is sheer delight from beginning to end.

**Valerie Mendes**

## Next?

Try one of the types of novel that Stella Gibbons is satirising, like Mary Webb's *Precious Bane*.

Or another comic novel, such as *Miss Pettigrew Lives for a Day* by Winifred Watson, in which timid Miss Pettigrew goes to work for a nightclub singer and learns to enjoy life.

Sophie Kinsella's frothy *The Undomestic Goddess* takes another sophisticated urbanite and drops her in the country.

# THE COLDITZ STORY P.R. Reid

 12+

Colditz Castle was the German maximum-security prison for Allied prisoners of war captured in World War II. The castle was built on a vertical cliff, the guards outnumbered the prisoners at all times, and barbed wire and floodlights were everywhere. Colditz was supposed to be inescapable. But the English, Dutch, French, and Polish POWs were undaunted. Out of stolen material, they created tools, disguises, electrical systems and tunnelling equipment; from outside the castle they smuggled in maps, money, civilian clothes and even radio sets in preparation for escape.

I love this book because of how amazingly resourceful the prisoners are: starting from nothing they manage to get the better of their captors not once, but dozens of times.

**Benedict Jacka**

> **Next?**
>
> Patrick Reid wrote a sequel, *The Latter Days at Colditz*.
>
> *The Great Escape* is another very good WWII escape story, written by Paul Brickhill, who also wrote *The Dam Busters*, the story of the RAF's bouncing bombs.

# THE COLOR PURPLE Alice Walker

16+

> **Next?**
>
> Tashi (from *The Color Purple*) gets her own story told in *Possessing the Secret of Joy* – another dark and heart-wrenching story.
>
> Or try reading Grace Nichols' poetry, which manages to be sharp and funny while dealing with issues such as oppression, slavery and self-image.
>
> Another classic African-American novel is *Beloved* (UTBG 37).

This unforgettable tale about Celie, a black woman growing up and living in the American South, must have touched more lives than just about any other book I know.

Raped by the man she believes to be her father, Celie twice falls pregnant and each time has to give up her child for adoption. This awfulness is just the beginning of a long journey through suffering so heartbreaking that on more than one occasion the reader is left wondering how Celie can possibly carry on. But carry on she does. Inspired and loved by the stunning *femme fatale* blues singer Shug Avery, Celie realises for the first time that she doesn't have to put up with the appalling treatment meted out to her by men. And so her life begins to change.

Walker's story is deeply intimate, and her characters so complex, well-rounded and deftly drawn you feel they could walk right off the page.

**Neil Arksey**

# COME CLEAN  Terri Paddock

This story makes you want to howl with rage. 15-year-old Justine is sent to a residential rehabilitation centre, for misdemeanours so minor that it has to be a joke. But it's no laughing matter. The management humiliate and abuse their inmates – sometimes sexually – as effectively as any police state.

*Come Clean* has pace and depth, alternating scenes from the present with memories from the past. The writing is crisp and immediate and shocking, and the sense of powerlessness is conveyed in the detail. The images stayed with me for a long time after I'd finished it. Things like this happen all over the world, all the time, usually for political reasons. This is an introduction to injustice.
**Elizabeth Kay**

### Next?

*Noodlehead* by Jonathan Kebbe (UTBG 261) is also about being put into a 'rehabilitation centre', and is just as thought-provoking.

*The Serious Kiss* (UTBG 330) is another portrait of alcoholism and its terrible consequences.

*Big Mouth and Ugly Girl* by Joyce Carol Oates is about injustice and unlikely friendship.

# COMING UP FOR AIR

## George Orwell

### Next?

More George Orwell: *Keep the Aspidistra Flying*, *Nineteen Eighty-Four* (UTBG 260) or *Animal Farm* (UTBG 23).

H.E. Bates writes lyrically of both the countryside and war; try *The Darling Buds of May* for bucolic humour, or *Fair Stood the Wind for France* for wartime tragic romance.

H.G. Wells' *The History of Mr Polly* is another book about an ordinary man just trying to cope with life.

World War II is imminent. People are fearful but – for now – still going about their daily lives. George Bowling, a middle-aged insurance salesman with a wife and two children, is one such. As the story opens, George is about to set off into town to collect his new false teeth. Later, walking along a busy street (rather pleased with his brand-new smile), his mind is suddenly full of his childhood home in the country, and a longing to see it again. To go back there, away from the hustle and bustle of the city and the threat of war, would be like coming up for air, he thinks. So without a word to his wife, he visits the country town he knew as a boy. What he finds when he gets there, and what he learns about himself and the world he lives in, make up the bulk of this excellent novel.
**Michael Lawrence**

# COMPLETE SHORT STORIES J.G. Ballard

**16+**

Deranged aviators haunt the overgrown runways and gantries of an abandoned Cape Canaveral; the body of a drowned giant washes up on a beach; inhabitants of perfect suburbs succumb to strange psychological states; and in the skies above the desert resort of Vermilion Sands, airborne sculptors carve the clouds into portraits of an insane heiress…

J.G. Ballard's compelling stories balance on a knife-edge between science fiction and surrealism. Some deliver a nightmarish twist; others, almost plotless, return obsessively to the same dream-like landscapes – abandoned testing grounds, empty swimming pools, mysterious deserts. No one else writes like Mr Ballard, and beneath his luminous, metallic prose lie wry humour and a profound humanity. Once read, never forgotten.

**Philip Reeve**

> ### Next?
>
> J.G. Ballard is the author of many novels; try *Empire of the Sun* (UTBG 114), based on his childhood in a Japanese internment camp; or *Hello America*, about a band of future explorers returning to a United States abandoned after catastrophic climate change.
>
> Ray Bradbury is another astonishing writer of short stories. Try *The Illustrated Man*, which influenced many later writers.

# CONFESSIONS OF A TEENAGE DRAMA QUEEN Dyan Sheldon

**12+**

For Lola, the whole world is a stage and she's the star of the show. Funny, daft, infuriating, kind, totally over the top, Lola (whose real name is Mary) tells the story of her new life after her parents separate and she and her twin sisters are moved to New Jersey and a new school.

Wearing clothes to match her mood (velvet capes are the least of it) Lola makes friends and seriously annoys the most popular girl in the school by winning the coveted lead role in the school play. Then her most favourite band, Sidartha, break up and the story spins back to New York as Lola and Ella meet rock gods and more police than should ever be strictly necessary. Fun? You bet.

**Leonie Flynn**

> ### Next?
>
> There is a sequel, *My Perfect Life*, which tells more about Ella and Lola, this time from Ella's point of view.
>
> Another Lola trying to deal with a new life is Lola Rose in Jacqueline Wilson's book of the same name (UTBG 219).
>
> And don't forget to read our pink lit feature on pp. 72–73 for lots more good read-ons.

# CONSIDER PHLEBAS Iain M. Banks

 16+

## Next?

*Consider Phlebas* is part of a sequence of novels about the Culture. Try *Use of Weapons* or *Excession* next.

Just to prove his genius, Banks also writes contemporary novels. Look for books under the name Iain Banks (the M is only used for his sci-fi). Try *Complicity* first.

Someone else with as vivid an imagination is Michael Marshall Smith; try *Only Forward* (UTBG 273).

Horza is a hero, except he's fighting for the wrong side. Which side is that? The one that's losing, of course. From the opening scenes where Horza faces a death that seems impossible to get out of, through a series of complex, terrifying and brutal adventures, this novel drags you through it, your hand over your eyes, half afraid that something awful will happen any minute. And most often it does.

This is a universe where space ships are sentient and where aliens are truly alien. Bringing in issues of faith, tolerance and morality, it still manages to be one of the most exciting books I've read. There are some writers whose imaginations seem too huge to belong to one person, and Iain M. Banks is just such a writer.

**Leonie Flynn**

# CORALINE Neil Gaiman

 12+

Coraline lives in just part of a big old house with her mum and dad and a clutch of eccentric neighbours. One day when she's bored, she opens a door she's never opened before and goes into a parallel universe. It's much more exciting in there! The food is delicious, her bedroom captivating, the toys magical – and there are a new Mum and Dad who love her very much and want her to stay. At first it all seems very cosy, but then stranger and stranger things start to happen.

Neil Gaiman writes in a matter-of-fact, non-sensational way, and this only serves to enhance the strange and haunting quality of his tale… I can still see the deeply creepy 'other mother' with her shiny, black button eyes…

**Mary Hooper**

## Next?

Neil Gaiman writes adult horror, graphic novels and kids' books! Try *The Wolves in the Walls* (UTBG 417), a picture book written with long-time collaborator, Dave McKean.

Robert Westall writes disturbing, scary stories – read *The Scarecrows* (UTBG 320) and try and work out what's real and what's imagined.

And you should also read Lewis Caroll's *Alice's Adventures in Wonderland*!

# CORAM BOY  Jamila Gavin

### Next?

There are many great stories set around this period in history – try Leon Garfield's *Smith* or *Black Jack*.

For something about slavery, try Rosemary Sutcliff's *The Outcast* set in the ancient world, or Gary Paulsen's *Nightjohn* set in America. Both very different, but both pack a strong emotional punch.

Captain Thomas Coram was a philantropist who opened a hospital for abandoned children in the mid-18th century. This book tells the tale of Otis Gardiner, who purported to collect children for Coram's hospital, but actually murdered them, neglected them or sold them as slaves. The sordid story of Gardiner and his simpleton son is set alongside the tale of a young woman who falls in love with an aristocrat and then, sadly, comes to need Gardiner's services. It's a densely embroidered story constrasting rich and poor and city and countryside, and is crammed with detail. This is real edge-of-the-seat stuff, the plot carefully woven and the characters fascinating, and I defy you to finish it without a tear in your eye.

**Mary Hooper**

# CORBENIC  Catherine Fisher

Since he was six, Cal has spent a miserable childhood in Bangor with his mother who is schizophrenic and an alcoholic. He is offered a new life with his uncle Trevor in Chepstow and tries to leave the past behind. On the way he falls asleep on the train and gets off at the wrong station, Corbenic, where he is directed to the Castle Hotel. He finds himself at the castle of the Fisher King, and from then the novel intertwines the Arthurian myth of the Grail and Cal's own journey to find self-knowledge and peace of mind. It's an exciting and moving story with a contemporary theme, a sense of place, the mystery of legend and strong characterisation.

**Brenda Marshall**

### Next?

Another wonderful Catherine Fisher is *Darkhenge* (UTBG 94) about a boy trying to save his sister.

For more Arthurian legends try *Arthur: The Seeing Stone* (UTBG 29).

Want something scary? Try Margaret Mahy's book about change, romance and danger: *The Changeover* (UTBG 69).

For another book about escaping a tough real world through fantasy, read *Jake's Tower* (UTBG 193).

Or try Christine Morton-Shaw's *The Riddles of Epsilon*, a sinister book about a mystery from the past.

# COUNTING STARS David Almond

This is an autobiographical collection of short stories about the childhood of my favourite author. Many of the stories in here were written before any of Almond's novels were published, so reading *Counting Stars* feels like peering into the author's heart and soul to learn what makes him tick.

I love the way Almond writes. He never wastes a word, only tells you about things that matter, and from the first page of this book you know the centre of his universe is family, living and dead. Sisters. Brother. Mam. Dad. It's hard to write about how much you love and cherish and miss people without being schmaltzy and sentimental, but Almond does this brilliantly throughout *Counting Stars*. It's a wonderful book about the important things in life: love, loss, childhood… But so is everything Almond writes.

**Catherine Forde**

> **Next?**
>
> Now go away and read all of David Almond's other books. *All* of them.
>
> If you liked the childhood reality that these stories are based on, try Laurie Lee's memoir *Cider with Rosie* (UTBG 77).
>
> Or read another author's autobiography, such as Michael Lawrence's *Milking the Novelty*.

# CRAZY Benjamin Lebert

> **Next?**
>
> *The Old Man and the Sea* (UTBG 269) – if you've read *Crazy* you'll know why.
>
> *The Catcher in the Rye* (UTBG 66) – another troubled teenager goes AWOL in the city.
>
> Troy reads Stephen King's terrifying *Misery*, but I reckon you should try King's *The Body* instead. Like *Crazy* it's about the bonds of friendship, and a tale of discovery.

Benjamin is 16 and starting at a new school – his fifth. He keeps failing maths, and he's not very good at German; he's 'different', too, partially paralysed down his left side, and finds it hard to fit in.

But this time Benjamin settles quickly into a group of friends. There are five of them: Janosch (the ringleader), Fat Felix and Skinny Felix, Florian a.k.a. Girl, and silent Troy. Benjamin fits right in. After all, none of his friends are really 'normal' either – and anyway, who is?

*Crazy* is an engagingly told story of a few months in the lives of a group of friends – they get drunk, get laid, get into trouble and get on each other's nerves. They talk for hours about profound things like life and death, and they complain about school food, teachers, rules – in fact school in general, but you know they'll miss it when the time comes to leave. And when the book ends you'll be sorry to leave them, too.

**Daniel Hahn**

# CRIME AND PUNISHMENT Fyodor Dostoyevsky

Don't be scared off by the weighty title and this novel's reputation as a Great Work of Russian Literature; this is a gripping read right from the start – a psychological / crime thriller as unputdownable as any bestseller.

Rashkolnikov is an intelligent, proud and embittered young man, living in poverty in St Petersburg. To escape his desperate situation, he plans a robbery and murder. His intended victim is a vile old pawnbroker, whom he feels society will be better off without. He rationalises the murder to himself and is confident that he will be able to get away with it. The reality of the deed is very different…

The inner world of Rashkolnikov is at the heart of the story. Dostoyevsky takes us deep into the nightmare of Rashkolnikov's conscience as he confronts the horror of what he's done.

**Katie Jennings**

### Next?

For a gripping tale of murder and guilt, there's nothing better than Shakespeare's *Macbeth*.

For something shorter by Dostoyevsky, but still full of atmosphere and energy, try his *Notes from Underground*.

For high drama, this time in France, try Émile Zola's *Thérèse Raquin* (UTBG 370).

Or Patrick Suskind's quite extraordinary tale of an extraordinary man, *Perfume* (UTBG 285).

# THE CRY OF THE ICEMARK Stuart Hill

### Next?

For other battle-filled books try Adèle Geras' *Troy* (UTBG 382), her magnificent account of the fall of the legendary city; or *Warrior Girl* (UTBG 399) by Pauline Chandler, a reworking of the true story of Jeanne, the teenage girl who led France against the English in medieval times.

For another Norse-based epic full of battles and really good names, try *Sea of Trolls* (UTBG 322) by Nancy Farmer.

If you like fantasies on an epic scale, with desperate battles against invincible armies, you can't go wrong with *The Cry of the Icemark*. Thirrin Freer Strong-in-the-Arm Lindenshield, Wildcat of the North, Monarch of the Icemark, earns every one of her titles before she has been queen for a year. At the start of the book she's eager for battle with the mighty Polypontian army bent on conquering the world; by its end, she's a seasoned warrior, bloodied and battle-scarred, understanding loss and pain as well as the euphoria of victory. She's also become an astute politician, holding together an unlikely alliance of Greek-style archers and lancers, vampires and werewolves, gigantic white leopards and her own army of the Icemark.

**Gill Vickery**

# THE CRYSTAL CAVE Mary Stewart

## Next?

The series continues with *The Hollow Hills* and *The Last Enchantment*.

*The Mists of Avalon* by Marion Zimmer Bradley is the Arthurian legend told by the women involved. There are sequels, too.

Or you could try the original – Thomas Malory's *Le Morte d'Arthur*.

Catherine Jinks' own **Pagan** books (UTBG 283) recreate the past with just as much realism.

Meet the historical Merlin – or the closest you'll ever get to him! He's not so much a magician as a seer, and his gift is more of a burden than a blessing. A thinker surrounded by fighters, and an illegitimate outcast to boot, he's condemned to a life of rejection and isolation. Yet he battles on single-handedly to ensure that his nephew, Arthur, is born and raised to fulfil the prophecies that plague poor Merlin like a recurring headache.

These fabulous novels are not only drenched in utterly convincing detail about post-Roman Britain and the Gaelic culture, but also introduce one of the wisest, loneliest, most convincing heroes you'll ever encounter. Even readers who aren't fantasy fans will enjoy them.

**Catherine Jinks**

# THE CRYSTAL SINGER
## Anne McCaffrey

Killashandra is a music student with her heart set on becoming a high-ranking oper singer… until the day she learns her voice contains a fatal flaw which means she can never be a top performer. Not content to be second best, she walks away from her old life and is recruited by the 'Crystal Singers', who use their voices to mine crystal from the beautiful but dangerous planet of Ballybran. Killashandra seizes the chance to realise her ambitions, but discovers she must change in more ways than one before she can finally sing crystal.

This is one of the few books on my shelf I reread regularly, getting as much enjoyment out of Killashandra's determined character now as I did the first time.

**Katherine Roberts**

## Next?

Don't miss the sequels, *Killashandra* and *Crystal Line*.

Or Anne's **Dragonriders** series (UTBG 111), set on Pern, where people ride – and fight – on the backs of telepathic dragons. The first of these is *Dragonflight*.

Or my own **Echorium** sequence, beginning with *Song Quest*.

# CUE FOR TREASON Geoffrey Trease

12+

This was my all-time favourite book when I was a child. It's a swashbuckling historical novel set in Tudor times. It has everything – spies, actors, escapes over mountains, treason, and even romance. Real historical characters have walk-on parts. You'll meet Queen Elizabeth I, Shakespeare and Sir Walter Raleigh, among others. Through it all, like a silken weave, are wonderful descriptions of the countryside of England in the days before industrial cities and roaring motorways scarred the landscape; a time when the air was clear, and Kensington was a village miles away from London.

**Elizabeth Laird**

**Next?**

There are some brilliant historical novels out there. Try *King of Shadows* by Susan Cooper, *Moonfleet* by J. Meade Faulkner or *Jamaica Inn* (UTBG 194).

Leon Garfield has written many wonderful stories set in the past. Try *Jack Holborn*, about a search for an African diamond.

# THE CUP OF THE WORLD / THE WIDOW AND THE KING

14+

## John Dickinson

**Next?**

For a recreation of the real Middle Ages, try Kevin Crossley-Holland's **Arthur** trilogy; set in the 13th century; it begins with *Arthur: The Seeing Stone* (UTBG 29).

*The Sterkarm Handshake* (UTBG 354) and *A Sterkarm Kiss* by Susan Price combine sci-fi with the violent history of the Scottish border country.

*The Princess Bride* (UTBG 298) by William Goldman is a mad, exhilarating fairy tale for adults (and anyone else), set in a time that never was or could have been.

Phaedra runs away from a dynastic marriage to join the man who has wooed her by means of 'undercraft'. Other people mistakenly call this witchcraft, and there is a fearful price to pay for practising it. Everything else in these two wonderful novels is entirely human as the players in a power game struggle for control over whole kingdoms, over other people or simply over their own lives, never knowing that someone else is manipulating their every move. Phaedra, discovering how she has been used, learns to play the game herself; and her son, as he grows up, finally brings it all to a conclusion. Set in an imaginary but intensely real medieval country, the story is just as relevant to the times we live in.

**Jan Mark**

# THE CURIOUS INCIDENT OF THE DOG IN THE NIGHT-TIME

## Mark Haddon

14+

One of the most amazing things about a good book is that it can take you inside the mind of a completely different person. Mark Haddon does exactly that in this utterly gripping mystery story. The main character of this book is a 14-year-old autistic boy whose 'voice' rang utterly true to me. Christopher loves the mysteries of Sherlock Holmes, because he often has to rely on clues to know how the people around him are feeling. When he discovers a murdered dog on his neighbour's lawn, he decides to solve the mystery using the deductive methods of his idol.

**Caroline Lawrence**

MARK HADDON

THE CURIOUS INCIDENT OF THE DOG IN THE NIGHT-TIME

WINNER
WHITBREAD BOOK OF THE YEAR
GUARDIAN CHILDREN'S FICTION PRIZE

### Next?

Try other stories of people who see the world in a different way, like those collected by Oliver Sacks in *The Man Who Mistook His Wife for a Hat*.

In *Mondays Are Red* (UTBG 248) Luke's senses are scrambled after he wakes from a coma.

To find out where Christopher gets his methods – and where Haddon got his title – read the **Sherlock Holmes** stories (UTBG 336).

*Al Capone Does My Shirts* (UTBG 15) charts life growing up with an autistic sister on Alcatraz at the time of Al Capone.

It's always great to read exciting books about magic and faraway lands filled with mystical creatures, but every now and then a great book comes along which despite the absence of all things fantastical still has the power to amaze you. This is one of them. It follows teenager Christopher Boone as he grows up with a condition called Asperger's; we are introduced to his strange world and how he copes within it. You see, Christopher is brilliant at maths but can't understand simple human emotions such as fear and confusion. One night Christopher finds his neighbour's dog Wellington brutally murdered in the garden, and so begins his quest to find the killer.

Despite dealing with some serious issues, this story is told in a light and witty style, and as it progresses the characters really feel alive.

**Gareth Smith (aged 14)**

# CUT Patricia McCormick

14+

## Next?

Famous novels about teenagers suffering breakdowns? Try *The Catcher in the Rye* (UTBG 66) by J.D. Salinger or *The Bell Jar* (UTBG 37) by Sylvia Plath, both complex and challenging – but worth it!

*Disconnected* (UTBG 103) by Sherry Ashworth is about a girl who suffers burn-out and stops working at school.

*Massive* (UTBG 237) by Julia Bell treats the subject of eating disorders with care and compassion.

*Cut* is a sensitive treatment of the subject of self-harm. The heroine, Callie, who tells the story, has been cutting herself and is admitted to Sea Pines – or Sick Minds as she calls it. Callie used to be a keen runner until her obsession led her to withdraw from the world completely, to the point where she chooses not to talk anymore – not even to the people who are trying to help her. But as she gets to know the other girls at Sick Minds – anorexics, drug addicts, other self-harmers – she begins to come out of her self-imposed isolation. Reading about Callie's struggle to want to get better is moving, absorbing – and realistic, too.

**Sherry Ashworth**

# THE DA VINCI CODE Dan Brown

14+

This book has topped the bestseller lists for ages. Why? Well, the story revolves around a truly astonishing secret that challenges the very basis of the world's most deeply held Christian beliefs. This secret has been protected for centuries by a hidden society which is still active today. It's wildly controversial and stirs up ferocious, even muderous, passions…

This is a real blockbuster page-turner, with an endless series of cliff-hangers that catapult you through chapter after chapter.

The book begins with a murder, and the body is weirdly arranged to resemble a famous drawing by the old master Leonardo da Vinci. Perhaps da Vinci actually belonged to one of those secret societies. Maybe more of his paintings contain hidden signs and symbols, messages we must try to decode…

You get the picture. I don't normally read thrillers, but this one's like a movie in your head: dark, mysterious and compelling.

**Sue Limb**

## Next?

*The Holy Blood and the Holy Grail* by Michel Baigent (et al) is a real-life investigation into the same mysteries.

Another novel to explore the 'did Jesus really die on the cross?' theory is Nikos Kazantzakis' *Last Temptation*.

*Pompeii* by Robert Harris is a fast-paced thriller that will leave you gasping for breath! As will more Dan Brown. Start with *Deception Point*.

# DAISY MILLER   Henry James

14+

## Next?

For another Henry James, this time with more substance, move on to his *Portrait of a Lady*.

For more turn-of-the-century innocent young ladies travelling around Europe, try E.M. Forster – *A Room with a View* (UTBG 312) or *Where Angels Fear to Tread*. After James' prose you'll find him an easy read!

Or for another dark sort of love story, read *Ethan Frome* (UTBG 117), by James' close friend Edith Wharton.

Winterbourne is a good-natured but rather idle young American man, with not much to do with his life but drift from one European town to another, visiting friends and enjoying 'Society'. But at Vevey he meets Daisy Miller, and he is quite changed.

He's never met anyone like Daisy. She's both so smart and so naïve, totally innocent and yet an incorrigible flirt. And she's tremendously pretty. Winterbourne can't stop thinking about her.

I think Henry James is one of the greatest of all novelists, and *Daisy Miller* is just the way to meet him first. This is only the slimmest of novels – a novella, really – but in the hundred or so pages, James creates a portrait of a character (and a society she can't help being at odds with) that is perfectly poised and thoroughly enchanting.

**Daniel Hahn**

# DANCE ON MY GRAVE   Aidan Chambers

14+

In my opinion, this is the best novel from one of the most provocative authors writing for teenagers today. 16-year-old Hal Robinson is caught 'interfering' with the grave of the recently deceased Barry Gorman. In his own words, and with the aid of extracts from diaries, newspaper clippings and even homework essays, Hal unravels the sweet-sour roller coaster of events leading to his peculiar behaviour and subsequent arrest. The story of an unforgettable summer, packed with lust, obsession and death, told in a remarkably clever and unusual way. Chambers writes it like it is, and his characters are real and raw. This book will challenge your ideas about love, life, sex and literature…

**Noga Applebaum**

## Next?

This is one of six novels for teenagers called the **Dance** sequence. If you liked it, try *Postcards from No Man's Land* (UTBG 292) next.

*Johnny My Friend* by Peter Pohl is admittedly a little hard to find, but if you come across a copy – grab it! It's a beautifully written novel about a relationship revolving around a dark secret.

For a quite different story of teen sexuality, read David Levithan's lovely *Boy Meets Boy* (UTBG 52).

# DANDELION WINE  Ray Bradbury

**14+**

Ray Bradbury is a master of short stories. Whether they're about ghosts, Martians, his childhood, Mexico, Ireland, or a thousand other subjects, he can tell a great story using a minimum of words. For this book, he wove several tales together to create arguably his best novel. It's the tale of a young boy and his adventures one magical, mysterious summer. Funny, scary, but above all *warm*. This is a book that leaves you with a smile on your face; a book that you're truly sorry to put down. Bradbury has been one of my biggest influences, and if you read this book, then one of mine, you'll find shades of the master in just about everything I write.
**Darren Shan**

### Next?

Try some of Bradbury's sci-fi: *The Martian Chronicles* or *Fahrenheit 451* (UTBG 121).

Or the short-story collections of Clive Barker, *The Books of Blood*, which are just as scary and gory as they sound.

Or something by Darren Shan – the horrifically gruesome *Lord Loss* (UTBG 223) or *Cirque du Freak* in which the hero's name is... Darren Shan!

# THE DARK BENEATH
## Alan Gibbons

**14+**

### Next?

Anything by Alan Gibbons is worth a read. Try *The Edge* or *Caught in the Crossfire* (UTBG 68).

*Boy Kills Man* (UTBG 51) by Matt Whyman is a brutal book about child assassins.

Or read *Fugitives* by Alex Shearer, in which a prank goes seriously wrong.

Or try something by Bali Rai. Most of his novels are about fitting (and not fitting) in, like *(Un)arranged Marriage* (UTBG 388).

Issue novels, when they're done well, are worth their weight in gold. Authors who get them right are worth even more. Alan Gibbons is one such author. Imogen, 16 and having finished school, is looking forward to summer. But when her path crosses those of three very different refugees, things start to go wrong.

This is a very dark, tension-packed read, with strong characters. You are drawn in from the first page and the story never lets you go. Prepare to think differently about what a refugee actually is, as the author takes you on an often-harrowing journey beneath the fabric of normality. A brilliant book by a brilliant author.
**Bali Rai**

# THE DARK GROUND Gillian Cross

Gillian Cross' novels always grip you in a stranglehold from the very first page. Her writing is compelling, direct and thought-provoking. This, the extraordinary first book of a trilogy, is no exception. Part thriller, part fable, it made me look at the world in a totally different way.

Robert regains consciousness, after what he supposes is a plane crash, to find himself alone in thick jungle. There is no sign of his family or any other survivors. For some days he struggles to say alive. And then he becomes aware that someone – or something – is watching him...

I daren't write more for fear of giving away the original and ambitious idea behind this novel. All I can say is *read it*!

**Patricia Elliott**

**Next?**

Some questions are left unanswered in this book – so read the sequel, *The Black Room*.

*Calling A Dead Man* (UTBG 61) is another gripping thriller by Gillian Cross.

William Golding's great classic, *Lord of the Flies* (UTBG 223), also shows human behaviour under extreme conditions, as does Tim Bowler's chilling *Apocalypse* (UTBG 26).

# THE DARK IS RISING series
## Susan Cooper

**Next?**

The full order is *Over Sea, Under Stone*, *The Dark Is Rising*, *Greenwitch*, *The Grey King* and *Silver on the Tree*.

Try Alan Garner's brilliant *The Owl Service* (UTBG 281), or Mary Stewart's **Merlin** books, beginning with *The Crystal Cave* (UTBG 87).

*The Various* by Steve Augarde is a sprawling magical fantasy. Or try Catherine Fisher's own books. Start with **The Book of the Crow** series or *The Glass Tower*, a collection of some of her short, intense and unsettling novels.

Moving from the fairly unsophisticated treasure hunt of *Over Sea, Under Stone* to the wonderful final battle under the midsummer tree in *Silver on the Tree*, this quintet of novels is a classic fantasy series. Cooper's books grow in depth and allusion as the reader journeys through them; they move from Cornwall to Wales, and the quest to possess the Grail becomes a cosmic war between the powers of light and darkness, fought through Celtic myth and the archetypes of the Arthurian legend. Cooper is good at atmosphere and brooding landscapes, and these books are a gripping read.

**Catherine Fisher**

# THE DARK LORD OF DERKHOLM

12+

## Diana Wynne Jones

Where teenaged Blade lives, they re-enact 'Dark Lord'-type fantasies for tourists from another world. This year, the Oracle puts Blade's father in charge. And suddenly everything turns dangerous. Why? For one thing, the wizards, the magic, the dragons, demons, griffins and flying pigs are all real; and Blade's father is the last wizard anyone would have chosen to run things. When Blade and his siblings get drafted in to help, they have to grow up rather quickly.

A very exciting book full of elegant magic, but also touching as the pressures and tensions act on Blade's family. Oh, and I should add: while Blade and his parents are human, his siblings have feathers and wings – they're griffins, and they're delightful!

**Rosemary Cass-Beggs**

### Next?

There's a sequel, *The Year of the Griffin*, in which a griffin daughter and her classmates (accidentally) transform their shoddy university into a centre of excellence.

You should also look for Diana Wynne Jones' *Hexwood* (puzzling at first, but deeply satisfying).

And try Mercedes Lackey's **Valdemar** series, where the horses have strange powers! Start with *Take a Thief*, about a pickpocket chosen to become a Herald.

# DARKHENGE  Catherine Fisher

14+

### Next?

*Corbenic* (UTBG 84) by Catherine Fisher also weaves legend into the fabric of today, and is equally exciting and mysterious.

Or try *The Mabinogion* itself – a series of Welsh legends that you'll find surprisingly familiar. Read the version lyrically translated by Lady Charlotte Guest.

Alan Garner also writes books full of mystery and magic; try one of his stories based on Welsh legend, *The Owl Service* (UTBG 281).

Catherine Fisher is a magician of a writer. Imagine a world where a woman can turn into a bird, and the bird's skin be made into a magic bag that is full when the tide is high, and empty when the tide is low. Where a man can live many lives, each of them hunted because he stole wisdom from a goddess' well.

When Rob sees a bird turn into a hare and the hare into a fish and the fish into a man, he has to believe what he sees. Doesn't he? The man is a druid, and together he and Rob walk through a world of pain and loss, in an adventure that is a skein of legend, a taste of *The Mabinogion* and a terrifying look at the power of jealousy and dreams.

**Leonie Flynn**

# DAUGHTERS OF JERUSALEM

16+

## Charlotte Mendelson

The dysfunctional Lux family lives in Oxford. Victor Lux is a professor, desperate to win the prestigious annual Spenser lecture. His wife Jean is tempted by extramarital advances while their daughters, Eve and Phoebe, are locked in a vicious battle of mutual dislike. Eve is academic but can seemingly do nothing right; Phoebe, the wild, spoilt and needy one, is Jean's favourite, to Eve's increasing resentment. This simmering cauldron of dissatisfaction threatens to boil over in spectacular fashion when a predatory don, Victor's rival from way back, arrives in town and shows an unsavoury interest in the neglected Eve. Dramatic revenge-wreaking and revelations result. Mendelson is both erudite and accessible in this delicious black comedy of frustration in a rarefied setting.

**Francesca Lewis**

### Next?

Move on to Charlotte Mendelson's first novel, *Love in Idleness*, the witty story of newly graduated Anna Raine's struggle to cope with London life.

If novels set in academia appeal to you, try *Foreign Affairs* by Alison Lurie and *The Secret History* (UTBG 326) by Donna Tartt.

For more on sibling rivalry and relationships between sisters, try *A Summer Bird-Cage* (UTBG 362) by Margaret Drabble.

## The Ultimate Teen Readers' Poll

### BOOK YOU'VE READ OVER AND OVER

1 **Harry Potter series**

2 **Girls in Love series**

3 **The Lord of the Rings trilogy**

4 **The Saga of Darren Shan**

5 **His Dark Materials trilogy**

6 **Holes**

7 **Double Act**

8 **A Series of Unfortunate Events**

9 **The Princess Diaries series**

10 **Of Mice and Men**

# THE DAY OF THE JACKAL
## Frederick Forsyth

14+

In 1963, a young English assassin is hired by a secretive group to kill the French president at a public parade. This assassin's codename is The Jackal, and the account of his bid to stay ahead of the detective on his trail makes for gripping thriller writing. The book is hailed as a classic of the genre, and rightly so. The suspense never lets up, but the detail makes it so convincing. Often research can weigh a novel down, but here it fuels the story. Famously, Forsyth begins with a criminal masterclass on how to acquire a foolproof false identity. So long as you harbour no plans to follow in the footsteps of the story's anti-hero, you won't fail to be rewarded by this compelling read.

**Matt Whyman**

### Next?

More Forsyth? Try *The Dogs of War*, about a group of mercenaries.

*Jarhead (A soldier's story of modern war)* by Anthony Swofford, the true story of a Gulf War sniper, is packed with military knowledge.

Or for another nail-biting thriller, try Robert Ludlum's *The Bourne Identity*.

# THE DAY OF THE TRIFFIDS
## John Wyndham

14+

### Next?

More Wyndham? Try *The Kraken Wakes* first.

*The War of the Worlds* (UTBG 398) is another classic science-fiction story that's still just as effective as when it was first written.

*Hatchet* (UTBG 163) by Gary Paulsen is the story of a boy on his own, without any resources at all.

Or what about people fighting off other dangerous creatures? Try *Jurassic Park* (UTBG 203).

A mysterious comet fills the sky with green shooting stars, and the next day everyone who has seen them is struck blind. William Masen is one of the few who can still see. Now he has to survive, but it won't be easy. There are triffids – walking poisonous plants – to deal with. And other humans, who want to rebuild the world their own way…

Nowadays there are a lot of 'post-apocalypse' books and movies, in which some disaster strikes the entire planet, leaving only a handful of people alive; but *The Day of the Triffids*, written more than 50 years ago, is the original and still the best. You'll worry about staring at shooting stars for years to come…

**Benedict Jacka**

# DAZ 4 ZOE  Robert Swindells

14+

*Daz 4 Zoe* resembles a futuristic *Romeo and Juliet* in that its main characters are 'star-crossed lovers'. Yes, it's love at first sight, but how will Zoe and Daz manage to see each other? Zoe is a Subby (a member of the well-off suburban classes) and Daz a Chippy (living in poverty in the inner city), so they're forbidden to meet. But neither will be told what to do, and both face enormous risks in breaking the rules of this strictly divided society. The story is told alternately by Zoe and Daz, and you'll have to get used to Daz's unusual spelling (as he's had only very basic schooling, unlike middle-class Zoe), as well as learning new vocabulary. But it's well worth the effort to find out whether Swindells' lovers manage to defy the system and earn themselves a happier ending than Shakespeare's doomed lovers.

**Linda Newbery**

### Next?

More love against the odds? Try Malorie Blackman's *Noughts and Crosses* (UTBG 267), which turns racism on its head.

For another novel that looks at rival gangs, try *The Outsiders* (UTBG 280) by S.E. Hinton.

Jill Paton Walsh's *Fireweed* (UTBG 131), set in London during the Blitz, involves the meeting of a boy and a girl from different social classes.

# DEAD FAMOUS  Ben Elton

16+

There's been a gruesome murder on 'Peeping Tom' – a (barely) disguised version of *Big Brother*. With scores of TV cameras in the house and the nation watching the contestants' every move, you would think this would be impossible – and yet no one knows who did it!

This is a truly riveting modern-day detective story, and at the same time it's a fantastic pastiche of *Big Brother*, the characters beautifully parodied with their inane conversations and egocentricity.

Elton sends up the whole cult of reality TV whilst cleverly sucking you into its addictive world, almost as if you were watching one of the shows themselves. It's a must for all *Big Brother* lovers and for all *Big Brother* haters.

**Susan Reuben**

### Next?

Ben Elton's novels all combine a gripping plot with a political or social agenda. Try *High Society* about drug culture, or *Popcorn* about movie violence.

For another cool detective story, this time futuristic and quite peculiar, try Michael Marshall Smith's *Only Forward* (UTBG 273) which will make you laugh, bite your nails and scratch your head – often all at once.

# DEAD NEGATIVE Nick Manns

**14+**

Nick Manns writes gripping and intelligent political thrillers, set in the deceptively normal worlds of home and school. Elliott is haunted by visions of his dead photographer father, who may have been killed for 'shooting the truth' in the Bosnian conflict. When two men from the Bosnian Embassy turn up to examine his father's photographs, claiming they are hunting down war criminals for their murder of Muslims, Elliott is not sure whether to trust them. At school, meanwhile, racist thugs are bullying his Sikh friend Jaspreet.

Written in short, terse sentences, this powerful novel makes you think about the roots of racism here and abroad, and the courage required to stand up for what you believe to be right and true.

**Patricia Elliott**

### Next?

Linda Newbery's *Sisterland* (UTBG 342) and Bernard Ashley's *Little Soldier* both deal with different aspects of racism and the conflict it causes.

And if you've enjoyed this, don't miss Nick Manns' new thriller, *Fallout*, about a government nuclear cover-up.

For another boy on a quest to find his father, read Joan Lingard's *Tell the Moon to Come Out*.

# DEADKIDSONGS Toby Litt

**16+**

At first, Andrew, Peter, Paul and Matthew seem just like the Famous Five (or rather, Four). They are Gang – not the Gang, just Gang – and they play war games in an English village, prizing Gang loyalty above everything. But the easy bit ends there. Real soldiers fight enemies, and for Gang, most of the adults around them are enemies. Gang wages a dark and brutal war that is far from being a game, especially as the only place that it makes sense is in Gang's head. *deadkidsongs* is a disturbing story about the horrific consequences of confusing fantasy and reality, and about how even adults only see what they want to see, no matter what terrible reality is staring them in the face.

**Antonia Honeywell**

### Next?

Toby Litt likes to experiment with different styles and types of story, so you'll find each book quite different from the others. Try *Beatniks* or *Corpsing* next and see what you think.

If you're fascinated by the bleak portrayal of human nature, try *Lord of the Flies* (UTBG 223) or *Heart of Darkness* (UTBG 164).

If you like the way Toby Litt writes about children, try *Cat's Eye* (UTBG 67) by Margaret Atwood.

If you want to read a novel about a real war, try *Regeneration* (UTBG 309) and its sequels by Pat Barker.

# DEAR NOBODY  Berlie Doherty

14+

*Dear Nobody* is a novel about a teenage pregnancy, but it's so much more than that.

Helen and Chris are in love, and when Helen falls pregnant, each of them wants to do the best they can, despite their fears. But will they stay together under the pressure? Their parents aren't much help. Both Helen and Chris come from homes where there are family secrets, and the unborn baby prompts the couple to explore their own pasts. The story is told partly by Chris, and partly through the letters Helen writes to her unborn baby, the 'Dear Nobody' of the title.

This is a very moving and lyrical account of what it means inadvertently to start a new life.

**Sherry Ashworth**

### Next?

Berlie Doherty is the author of many excellent novels for young adults; both *The Snake-Stone* and *Tough Luck* are very good.

If you're interested in teenage pregnancy, move on to *Blue Moon* (UTBG 47) by Julia Green and *Reckless* (UTBG 306) by Sue Mayfield.

Or take a look at our feature on love, sex and relationships on pp. 168–169 for more suggestions.

# DEATH AND THE PENGUIN
## Andrey Kurkov

16+

### Next?

*Life of Pi* (UTBG 218) is another bizarre animal / human story, this one a tale of survival.

How about more Kurkov? Try *The General's Thumb*, which features a tortoise.

Something else truly surreal? Try Franz Kafka's superb *Metamorphosis*.

Or perhaps the literary surrealism of *The Eyre Affair* (UTBG 120) and its sequel.

It may sound a bit odd and pretentious to recommend a bit of Ukrainian fiction. But who cares? This surreal, black comedy is fantastic.

Viktor is a writer who lives in an apartment in Kiev. His flatmate is a penguin called Misha, who flip-flops round the apartment eating frozen fish. Viktor manages to get himself tangled up in a world of crime and intrigue. He has to keep a step ahead to stay alive.

Andrey Kurkov creates a surreal, deadpan world, in which it seems perfectly natural for a man and a penguin to be friends. It's a real disappointment when you finish the book and find that the real world is a lot more boring and down-to-earth…

**James Reynolds**

# DEEP SECRET  Berlie Doherty

**12+**

*Deep Secret* is based on the flooding of a valley in the Peak District in the 1930s, to create Ladybower Reservoir. What would it be like to live in a village destined to be drowned? The inhabitants of Birchen are faced with the loss of all they know – their farmland, the graves of relatives in the churchyard, the magnificent Hall. But first there's tragedy when Grace, one of twins, slips and is drowned in the stream. Madeleine, her double, pretends she was the twin who died, and takes on Grace's identity; only blind Seth knows the truth.

Multiple viewpoints show us the effects of forthcoming change on a range of characters, all of them strongly individualised. This is a moving, memorable story with a wonderful evocation of time and place.

**Linda Newbery**

### Next?

Try *Dear Nobody* (UTBG 99) or *Holly Starcross* by the prolific and consistently good Berlie Doherty.

*Saskia's Journey* by Theresa Breslin and *A Pattern of Roses* by K.M. Peyton both combine past and present in intriguing ways.

# THE DEFENDER  Alan Gibbons

**12+**

### Next?

If you enjoy this you'll love almost anything by this author. My favourite Gibbons title is *The Edge*, a story of family violence, escape and growing-up. *Caught in the Crossfire* (UTBG 68), written in response to the Oldham race riots, is also a terrific and provocative read.

For another look at politics, this time the war with Iraq, read *Peace Weavers* (UTBG 284) by Julia Jarman.

Or moving to the States there's Christopher Paul Curtis' *The Watsons Go to Birmingham*, a family story that takes us to the American South in the darkest days of racial prejudice.

A father and son go on the run in this fast-paced thriller. Kenny Kincaid's past as a Loyalist paramilitary in violent and troubled Ireland catches up with him years later, and he must flee for his life. He must also reveal to his son, Ian, a past that he could never have imagined – one of murder and robbery and betrayal of friends. The 'friends' are out of jail and they want the man and the money; they want revenge. But the police too are on the heels of Kenny and Ian as this dramatic story, based on real politics, unfolds. As well as the drama there's a moving story of a family torn apart by violence and bloodshed.

This is a book that simply can't be put down, a book that packs a real punch.

**Wendy Cooling**

# DESIRE LINES  Jack Gantos

14+

This is that rare thing, a novel without heroes, or indeed anyone you can really like, but it is not without the power to involve and keep you reading. Walker is gutless, easily preyed upon, and in the end corrupted and treacherous. When a fundamentalist preacher comes to Walker's small Florida town, the preacher's boy, a bigoted zealot like his father, starts a rumour that Walker is gay in order to make him 'out' any 'ho-mo-sexuals' in his school. A bullying and vicious gang of boys also get hold of Walker and involve him in their delinquencies. Walker, caught between the devil and the deep, finally betrays two girls whom he's spied on in the woods making love.

Gantos is a powerful writer who is here challenging his readers' loyalty and integrity as much as the preacher's boy challenges Walker's.

**Lynne Reid Banks**

## Next?

Another novel that challenges our idea – and society's – about what makes a hero: Robert Cormier's *Heroes* (UTBG 166).

Jack Gantos has also written a memoir about his time in prison, *Hole in My Life* (UTBG 172), though it is a harsh, uncompromising read.

Aidan Chambers' *Postcards from No Man's Land* (UTBG 292) is also about making choices.

# THE DIAMOND GIRLS  Jacqueline Wilson

12+

I love Jacqueline Wilson's books – she is one of my favourite authors because she deals with issues we can all relate to. In this book, we meet Dixie, her sisters – Jude, Martine and Rochelle – and Sue, their pregnant mum. Dixie is happy but wishes they didn't live in a poky flat on an estate where no one has their own space. When her mum announces they are moving to a dream house with lots of bedrooms and a large garden, Dixie thinks her wish has come true.

But all is not as it seems – what is wrong with the new house and the baby? Mum has a secret – and Dixie is determined to find it out.

**Florence Eastoe (aged 13)**

## Next?

More Jacqueline Wilson? Try *Lola Rose* (UTBG 219).

Or Ann Brashares' *The Sisterhood of the Travelling Pants* (UTBG 341), about a group of friends during one hot summer.

Can you ever be too young to fall in love? And what if the boy you love has a deep secret? Read Jean Ure's *Love Is Forever*.

Or Pauline Fisk's *The Mrs Marriage Project* about a girl determined to be married as soon as possible!

# DIARY OF A NOBODY

14+

## George and Weedon Grossmith

### Next?

For some more humour that has stood the test of time, try *Three Men in a Boat* (UTBG 372) by Jerome K. Jerome.

Or *The History of Mr Polly* by H.G. Wells, the story of another Everyman and his quest for happiness.

Or try the modern (and teenage) equivalent – *The Secret Diary of Adrian Mole Aged 13 ¾* (UTBG 324).

This surely must be the first spoof diary: before the teen-angst diaries, before the **Princess Diaries** – before, even, **Adrian Mole**. Adrian, actually, has a lot in common with poor old Mr Pooter, the writer of this diary... Both are stoical, humourless, think highly of themselves and, hilariously, fail time and again to see themselves as others see them. Pooter is a social bumbler who desperately wants to rise in society but who inevitably slips on a piece of cabbage along the way. The language of the book is somewhat archaic, but this only adds to the delicious irony of it all. It's wonderfully reassuring to think that the Victorians laughed at Pooter just as we laugh at him – we can't be so different from them then, can we?

**Mary Hooper**

# THE DIARY OF A YOUNG GIRL  Anne Frank

Anne Frank, a Jewish girl living in Amsterdam, was 13 when she began her diary in June 1942. The city was under German occupation. With her family and friends, she hid in a secret annexe of a house. She was 15 when she made her last entry in the diary on 1 August 1944. On 4 August, the eight people in hiding were caught and sent to Auschwitz concentration camp; from there she and her sister Margot were sent to the Belsen camp where they both died the following spring, a month before the camp was liberated. Telling us everything about her life, from her boredom and fear to her feelings about herself, boys and the future, Anne's remarkable diaries were found scattered all over the floor of the annexe after the police left. Luckily for us, as this is probably the most moving war diary ever written. Unmissable.

**James Riordan**

### Next?

*The Boy in the Striped Pyjamas* (UTBG 51) is the story of an innocent in wartime.

*Surviving Hitler* by Andrea Warren is a book about life in a concentration camp.

*Hitler's Canary* by Sandi Toksvig is based on Sandi's own family in Denmark who hid Jews during World War II.

Ian Serraillier's *The Silver Sword* is another classic novel about the war.

# DISCONNECTED  Sherry Ashworth

Sixth form can be a daunting experience for many students. The pressure to do well in the exams that have such an enormous impact on your future could prove more than some people can handle. Catherine is one of these people. Always a straight-A student, she suddenly loses her way. Not sure what she wants to do with her life, and unable to deal with the high expectations of her parents and teachers, she simply gives up. Her grades plummet and she starts drinking heavily. Catherine relates her own journey towards self-discovery in an honest, realistic way, addressing each section of the book to one of the significant people in her life. A hard-hitting novel about things that they may not teach you in school.

**Noga Applebaum**

## Next?

Another Sherry Ashworth? Her book *Paralysed* deals with an accident and its aftermath.

Melinda, the narrator of *Speak* by Laurie Halse Anderson, also has a hard time at a high school in America.

*The Catcher in the Rye* (UTBG 66) by J.D. Salinger is an amazing novel narrated by the unforgettable Holden Caulfield, a cynical, troubled teenager who has been expelled from school and has an opinion about everything.

# DISCWORLD: MONSTROUS REGIMENT

## Terry Pratchett

The old ballad 'Sweet Polly Oliver' is a splendidly sentimental tale, but by the time Pratchett has done with it, the result is blackly witty and scathing. It's also a thrilling read.

We meet Polly in the act of cutting off her long golden hair – she is signing up with the Borogravia army disguised as a boy. But as Polly soon learns, things in the army are not all they seem. Not being a patriot, the fact that her country is losing the war does not much bother her. Finding herself on the front line does, since no one expects her regiment to survive.

Pratchett delights in building tension then releasing it in tour-de-force action sequences. The motley regiment is full of startling characters, and the real revelations are saved up for the end.

**Geraldine McCaughrean**

## Next?

Terry Pratchett has fortunately written loads, including more **Discworld** books; read *The Colour of Magic* next.

Or try Robert Rankin for offbeat, mad humour – and wacky titles such as *The Hollow Chocolate Bunnies of the Apocalypse*.

# DETECTIVE STORIES
## by K.K. Beck

There are many reasons to read detective novels. First of all, you are pretty much guaranteed that things will happen and the plot will move along. That's because, with very few exceptions, a crime has already been, or is about to be, committed and must be solved. So the characters cannot just sit around. They are forced into action, which makes for a plot-driven, engaging read. And, because the criminals are still at large, and presumably don't want to be caught, the detectives are often in jeopardy as they go about their work. This means that the reader can enjoy the suspense of knowing the characters are in danger.

There's also something very satisfying about seeing a crime solved, getting everything properly sorted out, and making sure the guilty are exposed and presumably punished. If only justice always prevailed in real life! Plus, the reader can detect along with the characters. In classic, old-school detective fiction, the clues are usually arranged hiding in plain sight. The author's goal in these kinds of books is to get the reader to say 'Of course! Why didn't I see that?!' Agatha Christie is famous for these sorts of stories. In *The Secret Adversary*, two friends recently returned to London from World War I start their own detective agency, trace a girl named Jane Finn who has disappeared with a packet of important government papers, and foil a plot to take over the world. Agatha Christie was also, of course, the creator of the great sleuths Miss Marple and Hercule Poirot. You can read more about them on p. 48 and p. 64.

There are all kinds of detectives, from amateurs who accidentally stumble on to a crime to hardened private eyes and police

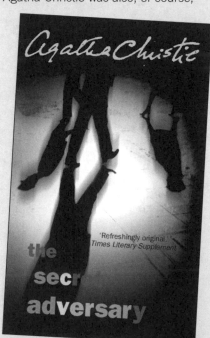

'Refreshingly original.'
*Times Literary Supplement*

the secret adversary

### Some teen spies and soldiers:

**Alex Rider** series by Anthony Horowitz

*SilverFin* by Charlie Higson

*Boy Soldier* by Andy McNab

**Alpha Force** series by Chris Ryan

*To Be a Ninja* by Benedict Jacka

*The Recruit* by Robert Muchamore

**Spy High** series by A.J. Butcher

A PHILIP MARLOWE MYSTERY

RAYMOND CHANDLER

THE BIG SLEEP

INTRODUCTION BY IAN RANKIN

detectives. Because detective stories often feature the same detective in multiple books, after a little dabbling in the field it's easy to find the ones you know you'll enjoy. One of the first and best amateur detectives is Sherlock Holmes. *A Study in Scarlet* is the first Holmes mystery, but you needn't start there. Try *The Hound of the Baskervilles* or any of the 56 short stories (UTBG 336). There's a reason Holmes and his sidekick Dr Watson have lasted so long.

Detective novels can be hard-boiled – violent and action-packed tales of guns and gangsters. Think of Raymond Chandler's *The Big Sleep* (UTBG 40). They can be soft-boiled – gentle stories of pale corpses found neatly on the hearthrug in the vicarage in a quiet village – like Dorothy L. Sayers' **Lord Peter Wimsey** books (UTBG 225). Or anything in between.

Detective novels can also take the reader on interesting journeys to exotic settings and different time periods. Some were written long in the past (traditionally, experts date the beginning of the form back to 1841 and Edgar Allan Poe's short story 'Murders in the Rue Morgue', featuring an eccentric Paris detective called Auguste Dupin), and many of those written more recently are set in historic periods; some of the best are Lindsey Davis' **Falco** stories (set in the year AD 79), which start with *The Silver Pigs*.

Many different sorts of books can fall under the banner of detective fiction. You could try *I'm Not Scared* by Niccolò Ammaniti (UTBG 188), scary, gripping and beautifully written; or Mark Haddon's funny, moving, fascinating *The Curious Incident of the Dog in the Night-time* (UTBG 89); or the deliciously creepy *Strangers on a Train* by Patricia Highsmith (UTBG 359); or *The No. 1 Ladies' Detective Agency* (UTBG 268), the first book in Alexander McCall Smith's popular **Precious Ramotswe** series; or Lee Child's page-turner *Killing Floor*, which begins with drifter Jack Reacher suddenly being arrested for murder…

> **Some older, rather more hard-boiled (or lightly simmered) detectives:**
>
> *52 Pick-up* by Elmore Leonard
>
> *Tourist Season* by Carl Hiaasen
>
> *The Big Sleep* by Raymond Chandler
>
> **87th Precinct** series by Ed McBain
>
> *One for the Money* by Janet Evanovich

# DIVIDED CITY Theresa Breslin

14+

May in Glasgow means the marching season and the start of the Orange Walks. Graham, a Protestant, is like any other boy, turning his back on the protests in favour of playing football with his Catholic friend Joe and following the fortunes of Rangers. Witnessing a racist attack on a Muslim asylum-seeker draws both boys into the rivalries which are tearing their poverty-ridden society apart, pitting neighbour against neighbour and even friends and families against each other.

A bold and brave book about religious, racial, social and political bigotry which shows how sectarianism can be overcome. It can't help but make you see the world differently.

**Eileen Armstrong**

> **Next?**
>
> Breslin's *Remembrance* (UTBG 309) details the lives of five young people drawn into the horrors of World War I.
>
> Other stories tackling small-minded bigotry, sectarian tensions and politically provoked violence include Alan Gibbons' powerful *Caught in the Crossfire* (UTBG 68) and Joan Lingard's **Kevin and Sadie** series.
>
> Malorie Blackman turns racism on its head in the breathtakingly original and hugely thought-provoking *Noughts and Crosses* (UTBG 267) and its sequels, *Knife Edge* and *Checkmate*.

# DIZZY Cathy Cassidy

12+

> **Next?**
>
> Rachel Cohn's *The Steps*, set in the US and Australia, looks at life in a dysfunctional but very happy family.
>
> *Heaven Eyes* by David Almond and *You Can't Kiss It Better* by Diane Hendry are both excellent glimpses into the lives of looked-after children – while Hendry's is very realistic, Almond's has a more magical edge.

Birthdays for Dizzy are extra-special because each brings a gift from the ditzy mum who abandoned her as a baby to travel the world – a rainbow stripy hat, a ragdoll, a pink jewelled necklace, an exotic dreamcatcher. The best present of all comes on her 12th birthday when her mum turns up in person to whisk her off for the summer into a very different life – on the road, under canvas and at festivals – meeting up with some colourful characters along the way, in places Dizzy has never even dreamed of. Suddenly she is forced to rethink her life with her dad and the values she's always accepted, and do some growing up of her own.

Not just another pink and girly book, this one is essential teen reading. Sparkling with warmth, humanity and hope, it will make you laugh and cry.

**Eileen Armstrong**

# DO ANDROIDS DREAM OF ELECTRIC SHEEP? Philip K. Dick

16+

When I was about ten or eleven I outgrew Nancy Drew and fell in love with science fiction. I discovered the sci-fi ABC: Asimov, Bradbury and Clarke, but it wasn't till I was over 30 that I discovered D – Philip K. Dick. This book was made into a brilliant film called *Blade Runner*. The book is quite different, though it is still about bounty hunter Rick Deckard, and set in a dystopian future. The thing I love most about Philip K. Dick is something I don't get excited about in any other author: his *ideas*. But be warned. He was a strange Californian who used to play with his daughters' Barbie dolls.

**Caroline Lawrence**

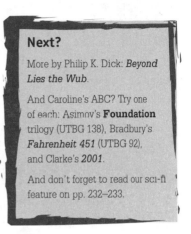

**Next?**

More by Philip K. Dick: *Beyond Lies the Wub*.

And Caroline's ABC? Try one of each: Asimov's **Foundation** trilogy (UTBG 138), Bradbury's *Fahrenheit 451* (UTBG 92), and Clarke's *2001*.

And don't forget to read our sci-fi feature on pp. 232–233.

# DR JEKYLL AND MR HYDE
## Robert Louis Stevenson

14+

**Next?**

You could try some of Stevenson's more obscure and mature fiction, such as *The Dynamiters*.

Or another picture of downright nastiness in humans, *The Wasp Factory* (UTBG 400).

If you want another classic horror story, you just have to try Mary Shelley's *Frankenstein* (UTBG 139).

This short novel by the author of *Treasure Island* and *Kidnapped* is an altogether more sophisticated story, but drips with the darkness to be found in the best of his writing.

Piece by piece unfolds the story of Dr Jekyll, a respectable London medical man, and Mr Hyde, an unsettling and plainly evil man who seems to have become an acquaintance of the doctor's, much to the horror of his friends. You may already know the secret of the connection between the two men, because this story became so famous that its title has become proverbial, but if you do not, then you are lucky enough to get to read this story as its Victorian audience would have done. To contemporary reviewers the book was weird and shocking, and I think it still is, as it speaks of the potentially horrific nature of humankind, as well as its more noble aspects.

**Marcus Sedgwick**

# DR ZHIVAGO  Boris Pasternak

16+

Boris Pasternak was a poet and novelist who fell out with the Soviet dictator Stalin, so he was unable to publish any works in Russia after 1933. He had to have his greatest work smuggled abroad: *Dr Zhivago* was published in 1957 in Italy. This is a thrilling if challenging read, encompassing half a century of Russian history: the excitement of revolution and civil war, the labour camps to which Zhivago's love is confined. Whose side would you have been on? That was the question that the gentle, aristocratic doctor, Yuri Zhivago, has to answer about himself.

**James Riordan**

**Next?**

Another great Russian classic is Tolstoy's *War and Peace* (UTBG 398).

If you fancy reading more about the Russian Revolution, try Mikhail Sholokhov's *And Quiet Flows the Don*.

For an epic account of another country's revolution, this time China, try *Wild Swans* (UTBG 414).

# DOES MY BUM LOOK BIG IN THIS?
## Arabella Weir

14+

This is the diary of Jacqueline M. Pane, your average 30-something manic singleton who obsesses over every detail and scrutinises every possible meaning of every little word.

Naturally, Jacqueline's life is dominated by food and tormented by exercise, and her love life is troubled. Her flat is small but at least work is good; she is the Senior Conference Organiser for the Pellet Corporation, the largest computer and parts supplier in England (but does 'Senior' mean old? Hmm…).

She can get irritating at times as her insecurities are simply neurotic but then you can't help liking her when she does something caring such as doing a big shop at Sainsbury's because she's heard the supermarket's profits are down!

Read this book for a chuckle, and for some great advice on leaving the room without anyone seeing the size of your bum!

**Elena Gregoriou**

**Next?**

*The Secret Dreamworld of a Shopaholic* (UTBG 325) is about life, the universe and shopping. Oh, and it's also very funny.

Or how about another Arabella Weir? Try *Onwards and Upwards*, the story of three 20-something friends.

If you're looking for another heroine who is completely likeable in spite of her (many) flaws, try *Rachel's Holiday* (UTBG 302).

# DOING IT  Melvin Burgess

**Next?**

If you liked reading about navigating the strange waters of relationships, Nick Hornby's *High Fidelity* (UTBG 167) has the same mixture of humour and honesty.

And *The Catcher in the Rye* (UTBG 66) is on the same theme, if English lessons didn't ruin that one for you!

*Junk* (UTBG 202), also by Melvin Burgess, is about the treacherously easy slide into heroin addiction.

This is a story about sex. The main characters (three 17-year-old boys and their girlfriends) spend 330 pages talking, fantasizing, worrying, planning and thinking about sex. Oh, yes, and doing it. There's a lot of doing it. There are things in this book you wouldn't want your mother to read, and I wasn't sure I should be reading it myself.

But this is Melvin Burgess writing, so you know he's going to be ruthlessly honest as well as laugh-out-loud funny, and that in the end he's going to burrow his way down to the truth. And when he does, the truth is wonderfully liberating.

It's an excellent book. Why not ask your parents to give it you for Xmas? No, seriously. Go on, I dare you…

**Andrew Norriss**

# DON'T LET'S GO TO THE DOGS TONIGHT

## Alexandra Fuller

I bought this for my son when he was just back from two incredible weeks in Zambia staying with a school friend. He read it in one hungry gulp and wanted to know if the author had written any more. This is a painful memoir of growing up in Zimbabwe and Zambia and every page screams with the sufferings of change and the grief of not changing. The raw ferocity of Africa takes you by the throat and the complexity of trying to exist and bring up a family in such an environment is brilliantly evoked and humbling to read. But it is also a story about being a child, and the honesty dazzles.

**Raffaella Barker**

**Next?**

*Scribbling the Cat: Travels With an African Soldier*, about Alexandra's journey across battlefields with a veteran of the Rhodesian war, is the sequel.

*Chanda's Secret* by Allan Stratton, also about growing up in an Africa torn apart by disease, and the importance of allowing the processes of change to take place.

*A Long Walk to Freedom* is the memoir of Nelson Mandela, one of the people who made change in South Africa happen.

# DOWN WITH SKOOL!
## G. Willans and R. Searle

I know exactly where I was standing when my friend Eve first showed me this book. With its amazing cartoons and misspelt ramblings about a boys' boarding school, it was, and remains, one of the funniest reads ever. Our Hero Molesworth 1 (brother of Molesworth 2) leads us through the characters and manners of St Custard's in a private language, interspersed with blots. Why did Eve and I – two teenage girls at a 1960s day school – roar with laughter at a book written in 1953? Because schools, and people, don't really change. In fact, with education becoming ever more earnest, I suspect that modern children may laugh even louder. We all love Molesworth. In fact, while we're reading we are Molesworth. Very odd. But a work of pure genius nonetheless.
**Eleanor Updale**

### Next?

There are sequels: *How to be Topp*, *Whizz for Atomms* and *Back in the Jug Agane* (collected in one volume as *Molesworth*).

**Harry Potter** contains a dim reflection of it: in *How to be Topp*, Molesworth writes a play called 'The Hogwarts'!

The same anarchic spirit can be found in *1066 and All That* (UTBG 8) by W.C. Sellar and R.J. Yeatman.

# DRACULA   Bram Stoker

### Next?

More Gothic fiction? Try *Carmilla* by Sheridan Le Fanu or Stevenson's *Dr Jekyll and Mr Hyde* (UTBG 107).

Modern vampires abound; try the **Night World** series (UTBG 259) by L.J. Smith.

Or what about a Gothic parody in Jane Austen's *Northanger Abbey* (UTBG 262)?

Bram Stoker wrote many novels and short stories, but he is best known for one extraordinary book, which if not actually originating a genre, has become the undisputed foundation of not just vampire fiction but the gothic in general.

I won't waste time expounding the intricacies of the plot here, but simply implore you to forget almost any film version you may have seen (with the possible exception of 1922's *Nosferatu*) and delight in discovering the slow beauty of the original book. Quite adventurous stylistically for its time, it uses several different narratives which weave together to create a momentum that by the end of the book is simply unstoppable. A true masterpiece.
**Marcus Sedgwick**

# THE DRAGONRIDERS OF PERN series

## Anne McCaffrey

The first three books about the planet Pern tell the story of the huge, fire-breathing dragons who defend their world against the periodic fall of deadly spores from a neighbouring planet. But dragons cannot do this alone – riders have to guide them in battle. As soon as they hatch, the green, blue, brown and bronze dragonets bond with boys, and the golden queens with girls, to become their lifelong soulmates. Lessa, one of the Dragonriders, impresses Ramoth, the last surviving queen, and together they risk everything to save their planet. By the third book, Jaxom, the boy lord of Ruatha, accidentally impresses a small, unique white dragon with extraordinary abilities who is destined to help Pern in a way no one dreams possible.

**Gill Vickery**

### Next?

Anne McCaffrey has worked out the science of Pern (an acronym of Planet Earthlike Resources Negligible) so if you like hard-science sci-fi, you will enjoy reading about the colonising of the planet and the creation of dragons from the native fire lizards in *Dragonsdawn*.

Or try **The Black Magician** trilogy (UTBG 44) (dragonless fantasy), or Robin Hobb's **Assassins** trilogy (heavily dragonsome fantasy).

# DRAMA QUEEN Chloë Rayban

### Next?

For another story of teenage angst, but this time with an unexpected regal twist, try *The Princess Diaries* (UTBG 299).

*11 o'clock Chocolate Cake* by Caroline Pitcher is about the life and loves of M. and the dramas that happen on the school bus.

*The Broken Bridge* by Philip Pullman is a more sober, but equally riveting, story about an adopted girl searching for her real mother.

Jessica's life is crammed with people whose love lives need sorting out. Mum and Dad have split up, but the divorce hasn't come through yet so surely there's still hope. Best-friend Clare has fallen for the dweeby boy downstairs – but how to get them together? And most intriguing of all is a marriage proposal she receives in the post by accident – but who's it from, and who was it really intended for?

Fortunately she's thought of a fail-safe matchmaking formula so she'll know who's destined to belong together: For example, his perfect teeth but sticky-out ears = her long legs but bitten nails: Match!

Apply it each time and you can't go wrong... can you?

**Susan Reuben**

# THE DUD AVOCADO  Elaine Dundy

**Next?**

Try *Mariana* by Monica Dickens, about another girl encountering life and love.

For another surprising and risqué modern classic – Hanif Kureishi's *The Buddha of Suburbia* (UTBG 59).

You might like Kathy Lette and Gabrielle Curley's account of growing up as surfer chicks in Australia, *Puberty Blues*.

For more coming-of-age stories, read our feature on pp. 296–297.

'I am totally incomprehensible to everyone including myself…'

These are the words of Sally Jay Gorce – a heroine you will never forget. Sally has come as if on fire from a quiet upbringing in America to Paris, capital of Europe, romance and exploration. Once there, she positively flings herself into life. *The Dud Avocado* is as original and funny as its title. From the first line, readers of this novel should hold on to their hats as Elaine Dundy takes you on a ride that is racy, sexy, risqué and hilarious. It's a rites-of-passage novel that is increasingly recognised as a classic of its time, and it's a joyous, intelligent, must-read romp from beginning to end. But be warned, this novel is definitely not for children.

**Rebecca Swift**

# DUNE  Frank Herbert

Dune is a desert planet inhabited by enormous sand-worms which produce a mind-altering substance called 'melange'. This and water are the most precious commodities. The story describes the battle for supremacy between the Atreides family and their enemies, most notably the fantastically spooky Bene Gesserit sisterhood, which is dedicated to harnessing the pure power of thought and so dispensing with science and technology. But it becomes clear that in the course of learning to control their environment and their own fateful vulnerability, the inhabitants cannot do without either technology or mysticism.

If you love travelling in alien worlds, then this book is a must – a science-fiction epic of grandeur and complexity, realised in intricate detail.

**Livi Michael**

**Next?**

Any of the *Dune* sequels – there are six books in total.

Robert Heinlein's *Stranger in a Strange Land* is a classic science-fiction epic that calls into question both religious and political beliefs.

Ursula Le Guin's *The Dispossessed* contrasts the stories of two planets, each with political and ecological problems to solve.

# DUSK  Susan Gates

12+

Curtis is a lab assistant at a secret military research base. He feeds the overly aggressive rats, including the mutated General who is supposed to have human intelligence, although Curtis strongly doubts this. But there's one door he isn't allowed to enter. Behind this door is a creature who shrieks and cries, who eats microwave-defrosted mice and who can demand dinner in a little girl's voice. Behind this door is Dusk. Only once does Curtis dare to break the rules, but once is enough, because when the door is opened, things spiral beyond anyone's control. Dusk's terrifying existence is powerfully described as this fast-paced sci-fi novel explores the boundaries between human and animal and the ethics of genetic engineering.

**Noga Applebaum**

## Next?

*Eva* by Peter Dickinson also examines the relationship between humans and animals, through the eyes of a girl whose brain has been transplanted into a chimp's body.

*Bloodtide* (UTBG 46) is another novel looking at genetic hybrids, though it's much darker.

The ethics of cloning are explored in many books. Some suggestions are *House of the Scorpion* (UTBG 178), *Sharp North* (UTBG 333) and *Unique* (UTBG 390).

# THE ECLIPSE OF THE CENTURY  Jan Mark

## Next?

Another Jan Mark? Try *Useful Idiots* (UTBG 391), about a world where the seas have risen and what's left of civilisation is a dystopian nightmare.

Douglas Coupland's *Girlfriend in a Coma* (UTBG 147) is another novel dealing with the (possible) end of the world.

Or try *The Blue Hawk* by Peter Dickinson, about a world controlled by priests and a boy who commits sacrilege.

Keith's near-death experience brings him not to the gates of heaven but to Qantoum, a city in 'the armpit of Asia', which has been all but forgotten by the rest of the world. After his recovery, he makes his way there and finds himself taking part in an extraordinary drama that is destined to conclude 'beneath a black sun, at the end of a thousand years'.

A must-read for anyone of 14 and upwards who is interested in imaginative fiction. This book reaches the parts of the mind that other books don't. Reading it is a bit like participating in a vivid dream and, as though the dream were your own, the characters and events will remain with you for a long, long time.

**Kate Thompson**

# ELSEWHERE Gabrielle Zevin

14+

## Next?

Of the various other beyond-the-grave stories, I'm a fan of Alex Shearer's *The Great Blue Yonder*, too (UTBG 155).

Towards the end of *Elsewhere*, Owen reads to Liz from *Tuck Everlasting* by Natalie Babbitt, another beautiful tale of endless life. Try it.

For the redemptive powers of another world, try *Corbenic* (UTBG 84).

While crossing the road (and not looking both ways), Liz is hit by a car. She is now dead. *Elsewhere* is the story – in her words – of what happens next.

I can't count the number of stories I've read that have been narrated from beyond the grave. Dozens, probably. But this one is special. This is not like any book I've ever read. The world beyond death is so well imagined and so consistent it feels totally realistic – which is a strange thing to say about a book about the afterlife, I know… But that's how it is – the dream-like elements of the tale are blended with what feels like absolutely stone-cold reality and clarity; and throughout, Zevin's writing is impeccable.

*Elsewhere* is full of character and warmth; it's a book about death, but more than that it's about life. It's an uplifting story about how Liz lives hers, and about how to live yours, too.

**Daniel Hahn**

# EMPIRE OF THE SUN J.G. Ballard

14+

In 1942, at the age of 12, J.G. Ballard was interned in a Japanese prisoner-of-war camp in Shanghai. This powerful, moving novel is based on his own experiences, and gives us a real insight into the horrors of war. Jim, the 11-year-old narrator, is separated from his parents when the Japanese invade Shanghai, and spends weeks living alone until he is captured. Over the next four years, malnutrition, violence and death become everyday facts of life to Jim, whose survival instinct draws him into some sort of rapport with his Japanese guards whom, despite their cruelty, he admires for keeping the inmates secure from the chaos outside. Jim's incomprehension of war, plus his utter determination to survive and to be reunited with his parents, makes for an unforgettable piece of writing.

**Malachy Doyle**

## Next?

Some of the most powerful books about war are memoirs such as *The Diary of a Young Girl* (UTBG 102) and Livia Bitton-Jackson's *I Have Lived for a Thousand Years*.

For a fictional account of life under the Japanese, read Martin Booth's *Music on the Bamboo Radio*.

*Wild Swans* (UTBG 414) tells of one family's struggle to live through China's recent history.

# EMPTY WORLD John Christopher

14+

**Next?**

More post-apocalypse? Try either *Children of the Dust* (UTBG 71) by Louise Lawrence or *Brother in the Land* by Robert Swindells.

*I Am Legend* by Richard Matheson is about the last human left on planet Earth.

Or try more John Christopher; *The Guardians* is about a terrible future where the country is divided into the County and the Conurb.

Have you ever wondered what you'd do if almost everyone on earth died and there were only you and a few other people left on the planet? Written in 1977, this is an enduring vision of just that post-apocalyptic world.

Neil Miller is left to fend for himself after a virulent plague wipes out most of the population. He walks to London where he meets other survivors including Lucy and the psychotic Billie. It's the kind of book that makes you wonder how you'd manage in an empty world, and although breaking into supermarkets and having no adults around sounds fun, Neil's battle with a crushing sense of being alone is the most moving element of this haunting novel.

**Julia Bell**

# ENDER'S GAME Orson Scott Card

12+

Set in the medium-term future, a group of children and teenagers are being trained in Battle School to fight an extraterrestrial race of insect-like beings. Each child is specially chosen: they are the brightest in the world, they are the most adaptable; together, working in teams, the army commanders believe that they will come up with new ways of fighting that no adult could ever conceive.

And they do: or, rather, Ender does. Ender Wiggin. This is the story of his personal struggle, put under constant, relentless pressure, to become the next military commander. It is a brilliant book, believable, full of thrilling battles, unusual aliens and well-crafted characters, but in the end what you remember is Ender. You'll grow to love Ender Wiggin.

**Cliff McNish**

**Next?**

You can go straight on to the sequel, *Speaker for the Dead*. Or, if you can't bear to leave the Battle School (like me), read about them all over again, but from the perspective of the character Bean, in *Ender's Shadow*.

For another great series about training to live and fight in space, try *Midshipman's Hope* (UTBG 244) by David Feintuch.

Or what about being a cadet on an airship? Try Kenneth Oppel's *Airborn* (UTBG 14).

# ERAGON  Christopher Paolini

**12+**

A hunter, quietly creeping through the undergrowth. A boy, orphaned when only a baby. Eragon, the dragon rider, legacy of a legend.

Christopher Paolini has successfully woven a beautiful tale of such magic and wonder it makes readers hurry frantically to the last pages. The touching story of Eragon, a young farm boy whose life is drastically changed the day he finds a dragon's egg, has enticed many people to pick it up so that they too can be part of the intimate bond between boy and dragon. Paolini takes you far away to his mysterious world of Alagaësia where the land's future lies heavily on the shoulders of a young boy, and follows his quest as he makes new friends and encounters new dangers.

I would recommend this book to anyone who enjoys a good read that they can curl up with and be transported to a whole different universe.

**Shazia Mirza (aged 15)**
**Dixons City Technology College**

### Next?

If you enjoyed *Eragon*, the next book in the **Inheritance** trilogy is *Eldest*.

Also try *The Cry of the Icemark* (UTBG 86) by Stuart Hill.

Another great series of dragon books (though very different!) starts with Chris d'Lacey's *The Fire Within*.

The Sunday Times bestseller

*Eragon* is the first part of the **Inheritance** trilogy. It follows the tale of a boy, Eragon, who discovers a dragon's egg near his home. When strange figures come to look for the newly hatched dragon, his home is destroyed and he embarks on a quest to seek revenge and discover his heritage as a mythical dragon rider. Along the way he befriends Brom the storyteller, magical elves and the mysterious Murtagh.

*Eragon* is very fast-paced, without a single boring moment. It is well written, and emotions are wonderfully conveyed. *Eragon*'s world of Alagaësia is described so well that it seems almost real.

**Eleanor Milnes-Smith (aged 13)**

# ESCAPE   Kate Cann

Kate Cann writes about first love and early sexual relationships. Her great strength lies in handling all this without following the fashion of making it nasty or predatory. But she doesn't sanitise it either, and you'll probably recognise the worries and preoccupations of her characters. This book follows a girl through her gap year – from the nightmare of nannying for a neurotic American mother, to the jealous torment of a romance on the road and at the beach. The main character, Rowan, finds her attitudes and plans reshaped by her experiences.

Escape is packaged in quite a girly way, aimed by the publisher at the 'holiday reads' market, but it's way above the 'teen trash' level.

**Eleanor Updale**

> **Next?**
>
> More Kate Cann on love and relationships? Try *Diving In*.
>
> William Sutcliffe's *Are You Experienced?* (UTBG 28) is another story of travelling and sex.
>
> Why not try a look at the way young sex and life decisions have been handled in the past? Look at *Georgy Girl* by Margaret Forster or *The L-Shaped Room* (UTBG 211) by Lynne Reid Banks.

# ETHAN FROME   Edith Wharton

16+

> **Next?**
>
> Read Wharton's *Summer* – she nicknamed it 'Hot Ethan'. Her very different, but equally powerful novel of repressed sexuality is *The Age of Innocence*.
>
> Another excellent short novel set in 19th-century America is Henry James' *Washington Square*.
>
> There are many wonderful tragic love stories out there; try Gustave Flaubert's *Madame Bovary*.

This little book is one of the saddest love stories you'll ever read. Ethan, a lonely farmer in 19th-century Massachusetts, has married his older cousin Zena for company. But she has quickly turned into a miserable, complaining hypochondriac.

When a young woman, Mattie Silver, comes to live with them, Ethan finds himself fascinated by her energy and joyfulness. A kind, inarticulate man, he hardly admits to himself his real feelings for Mattie, as he walks her home from a dance through starlit snows. Chance allows them one night together in the isolated farmhouse.

It's a passionate love story. We know from the outset it will end tragically, but the cruel twist will still take you by surprise.

**Jane Darcy**

# ETHEL AND ERNEST  Raymond Briggs

This is Raymond Briggs' beautiful, candid and moving illustrated account of his parents' married life. Ernest, a milkman, cheekily courts Ethel, a lady's maid. They marry in 1930, and stay together in the same house until they die within months of each other in 1971.

As well as a loving biography, the book is an illustrated social history of what used to be called The Respectable Working Class. During this middle span of the 20th century, the mangle in the back yard gives way to the laundrette, the bike gives way to the car, Hitler and Stalin come and go, ordinary people acquire telephones and television, the Welfare State is born. And so (with difficulty) is Raymond, who later horrifies his parents by going off to art school. ('That lot's all long hair, drink and nude women,' Ernest tells Ethel, wistfully.) There's nothing rose-tinted here. Briggs doesn't flinch from relating and drawing his parents' deaths, either, and it makes you gasp.

**Mal Peet**

### Next?

Search out all of Raymond Briggs' books, from the upsetting **When the Wind Blows** (UTBG 409) to the altogether gross **Fungus the Bogeyman**, to the pathos of **The Snowman**. Read them and weep – from sadness or laughter.

If you learn anything from **Ethel and Ernest**, it's that even the most ordinary people are extraordinary. Read Berlie Doherty's **Granny Was a Buffer Girl** – more 'ordinary' family memories.

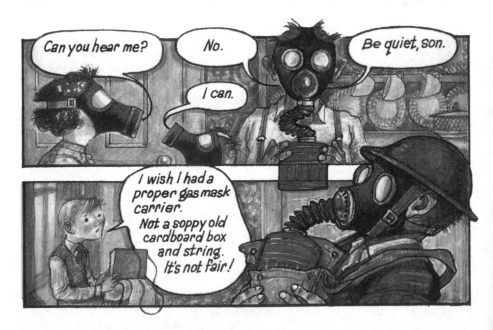

# AN EVIL CRADLING  Brian Keenan

**Next?**

An interesting comparison is John McCarthy's account of the same awful years, *Some Other Rainbow* – see which one you prefer.

*Between Extremes* is Keenan and McCarthy's account of their journey through South America.

Another man who endured terrible times is Nelson Mandela. Read his story in *A Long Walk to Freedom*.

For a tale of lost youth – including the story of a promising journalist killed before his time – read Sebastian Faulks' *The Fatal Englishman*.

What do you do if it's 1985, you're a teacher from Belfast, and you want a change of scene? You probably don't move to Beirut, where the Lebanese civil war is raging.

Well, Brian Keenan did. And guess what happened? He got kidnapped. He spent the next four years as a hostage, kept in blindfold and chains, with no contact with the outside world.

*An Evil Cradling* is Keenan's story. It's about pain, fear and madness. But it's also about the friendship he makes with his fellow hostage John McCarthy.

Keenan is an astounding, exhilarating writer. If you're ever going to be marooned on a desert island – take this book. It'll show you how to cope.

**James Reynolds**

# EXILE AND THE KINGDOM  Albert Camus

I read four of Camus' novels in my late teens, plus the six stories in this slim volume. I found the novels a bit hard going, but I really liked these stories. As a fairly unworldly lad struggling to write my first serious fiction, I was impressed by the directness of the language (albeit in translation from the French). I found the writing crisp and clean, never fussy. Every word seemed to count, and there was a feeling of detachment that appealed to me. You got the impression (well, I did) that if one of the characters died the author would not be among the mourners. Don't bother with *Exile and the Kingdom* if you want rollicking adventure or laughs. But if you want a taste of genuinely good writing, give it a try.

**Michael Lawrence**

**Next?**

The most accessible of Camus' novels, *The Outsider* (UTBG 280).

Unfussy writing in short stories – Raymond Carver is best of all; get hold of *Where I'm Calling From*.

Franz Kafka also has a fondness for writing rather bleak stories; try *Metamorphosis and Other Stories*.

# EXODUS Julie Bertagna

14+

**Next?**

*Ultraviolet* (UTBG 387) is also set in a future damaged environment.

*Watership Down* (UTBG 402) describes another kind of community looking for a safe haven, only this time they are wild rabbits!

*Bloodtide* (UTBG 46) is another excellent sci-fi novel inspired by a myth.

2099 – the ice caps have melted due to environmental damage and Britain is covered in water. Mara watches as the waters slowly rise around Wing, her island home, threatening to swallow everything she has ever known. Cooped up due to violent storms, Mara escapes into the Weave, a virtual-reality cyberspace, now in ruins as civilisation has disintegrated and communities have lost touch. A chance virtual encounter sends Mara's community on a treacherous journey to find shelter in New Mungo, a sky-city erected on the site of today's Glasgow; they are unaware of the cruel fate that awaits them there.

This fascinating futuristic sci-fi quest-adventure, inspired by the Glaswegian coat of arms, raises crucial questions about the consequences of the way we live our life today.

**Noga Applebaum**

# THE EYRE AFFAIR
## Jasper Fforde

16+

When the publishers came to publicising this, Jasper Fforde's first book, they didn't spend their money on advertising. They just sent out free copies saying 'READ IT'. So how can I hope to describe it if they couldn't?

Well, if you're into literature you'll get the joke. Picture 'grammarcites' that eat the punctuation out of sentences. Picture Heathcliff from *Wuthering Heights* meeting Miss Havisham from *Great Expectations* at an anger-management session. Picture Jane Eyre kidnapped out of *Jane Eyre*. Picture darning narrative loopholes. Picture critical analysis of *The Flopsy Bunnies*, quotes from nonexistent books, Prose Portals that let fugitives hide out inside *Hamlet*. It's Douglas-Adams-meets-*Pagemaster*. It defies the laws of time, place, probability, boredom and sanity… Oh, and it's a sort of ongoing crime novel with a great heroine. Beyond all that, all I can say is 'READ IT'.

**Geraldine McCaughrean**

**Next?**

The **Thursday Next** series continues with *Lost in a Good Book*.

*Is Heathcliff a Murderer?* by John Sutherland is literary detection – this time for real.

More irreverent humour can be found in *Good Omens* (UTBG 152), where this time the target is religion.

# FACE Benjamin Zephaniah

This is the story of a teenage boy named Martin Turner.

After a night out, Martin and his friends are walking home when two older boys offer them a lift. The fateful journey ends in disaster. The police chase them and the car overturns and catches fire. Martin is taken to hospital with serious facial burns.

The book goes on to tell how people deal with Martin's disfigurement. Life moves on and Martin forges new friendships and goals.

This book is very realistic and I think we can all relate to the characters. I have certainly gained sympathy for people who suffer any injuries and I think I am a better human being for having read it. I couldn't put this book down.

**Jamie Caplan (aged 11)**

## Next?

Benjamin Zephaniah has written several hard-hitting books that deal with real-life situations. Check out *Gangsta Rap* and *Refugee Boy* (UTBG 308).

For a book that explores racism in an imaginative and surprising way, try Malorie Blackman's *Noughts and Crosses* (UTBG 267).

Finally, for the best book I know about being different, you have to read Rodman Philbrick's *Freak the Mighty*.

# FAHRENHEIT 451 Ray Bradbury

This is the story of a world where books are forbidden, a world where free thought is firmly discouraged, where people feel closer to television characters than to their spouses or children or friends. It's a world where firemen like Guy Montag aren't employed to put out fires but to start them – to track down people who have secretly been hoarding books, and burn their houses down. All for the public good, of course.

This is no fantasy world, though, but our own, some years in the future. *Fahrenheit 451* takes a chilling look at where we might be going, and does so with imagination and momentum and often-brilliant writing. Bradbury has said that he writes 'at the top of my lungs' – and in this book you can't help but listen to his warning.

**Daniel Hahn**

## Next?

Classic dystopian novels include *Brave New World* (UTBG 54) and *Nineteen Eighty-Four* (UTBG 260), another tale of a man standing up against the system.

If you like Bradbury, try his magical *Dandelion Wine* (UTBG 92).

Or try reading about the formative years of a real revolutionary hero in Che Guevara's *The Motorcycle Diaries* (UTBG 251).

# FAKE K.K. Beck  14+

Daniel is a troublemaker who can't be controlled and needs some discipline – or so his stepfather Carl reckons. So Daniel finds himself dragged out of bed, thrown in the back of a car by a couple of muscle-bound 'counsellors', and heading out to a camp in the desert for a spell of intense therapy for uncooperative teenagers. On the way, he gets to share the ride with Keith, a foul-mouthed trailer-trash misfit who shakes off their guards and steals the car. He is just about to dump his unwanted passenger when he hears about Daniel's plan to find his real father Richard, who might just have plenty of cash to spend on a long-lost son…

*Fake* is a book full of deceptions, and just about everyone seems to have something to hide. K.K. Beck's style is mature, gritty and genuinely cool. The text reads like the script of a cult TV series, overlapping the characters' movements and thoughts with a precisely timed pace and then pulling everything together for a sharp and satisfying ending.

**Tim Rose**

### Next?

Another K.K. Beck? *Snitch* is about two kids paid to spy on their friends.

*Noodlehead* (UTBG 261) by Jonathan Kebbe is about a boy locked up in a centre for disruptive kids.

For another story of an unusual – and parasitic – friendship, try Anne Fine's *The Tulip Touch* (UTBG 384), or William Sutcliffe's *Bad Influence*.

## The Ultimate Teen Readers' Poll

# CHARACTER MOST LIKE YOU

1 **Tracy Beaker (The Story of Tracy Beaker)**

2 **Harry Potter**

3 **Hermione Granger (Harry Potter series)**

4 **Ellie (Girls in Love series)**

5 **Alex Rider (Alex Rider series)**

6 **Ron Weasley (Harry Potter series)**

7 **Darren Shan (The Saga of Darren Shan)**

8 **Ashley (Two of a Kind series)**

9 **Klaus Baudelaire (A Series of Unfortunate Events)**

10 **Megan (Secret Meeting)**

# FAKING IT  Pete Johnson

**12+**

## Next?

Gripping anti-bullying stories by Pete Johnson include *The Protectors* and *Avenger*, or try the funnier *Cool Boffin*.

Another book which shows a boys'-eye-view of relationships is *(Un)arranged Marriage* (UTBG 388) by Bali Rai.

*The Edge* and *The Lost Boys' Appreciation Society* by Alan Gibbons show that boys can have feelings, too.

15-year-old Will has plenty of friends who are girls, but no 'girlfriend', so in a desperate bid to improve his street cred he makes one up, with the help of his best friend, Barney. Basing his dream girl on his stepmum's drop-dead-gorgeous, aspiring-actress niece ensures his popularity explodes – but sooner or later she's going to have to put in an appearance or his cover will be blown.

The story's diary form makes Will seem like one of your friends and draws you in. Well-meaning, willy and woefully disaster-prone, he's one of the best teenagers ever brought to life in a novel, by an author whose understanding of what makes teenagers tick is second to none. Just the book for when you need cheering up or to make you feel you're not alone!

**Eileen Armstrong**

# FALLING 4 MANDY  Chris d'Lacey

**12+**

Danny is the school's ace football player and he hates cheating. So what can he do when his best mate Billy starts diving and they start winning even more. Life is further complicated by the glorious Marcia (who is a year older and actually seems to like him), the opposition's mysterious star striker, a girl called Mandy, and a little sister who makes MI5 look like amateurs. Not to mention the fact that Danny keeps throwing up in the most inappropriate places (his family may never use their phone again) and let's be honest, his life is in turmoil.

How can Danny stop Billy cheating – and work out what girls really want? Quite frankly, will Danny ever enjoy a peaceful game again? I promise you, you'll want to know, even if you hate football!

**Leonie Flynn**

## Next?

Chris d'Lacey has also written some books that aren't about football. Try *Fly, Cherokee, Fly*, or *Horace* (UTBG 176).

Another writer who seems to tap straight into the whole family / friends / life thing, and make it all amusing, is Pete Johnson. Try *Rescuing Dad*.

Or what about more football? Try Neil Arksey's futuristic *Playing on the Edge*, or his *MacB*.

# FAR FROM THE MADDING CROWD

## Thomas Hardy

### Next?

Thomas Hardy wrote loads, so if you like his style you can try his others, such as *Tess of the D'Urbervilles* (UTBG 369).

If you like striking heroines, also try Daphne du Maurier's *Rebecca* (UTBG 306).

Or go back a couple of centuries to *Vanity Fair* (UTBG 395) by William M. Thackeray.

Bathsheba Everdene was one of the first romantic heroines of my teenage years. Beautiful, self-possessed, clever, independent – and somehow both grown-up and still growing up. The story follows Bathsheba as she makes choices (plenty of which she gets wrong) about how to live her life. While her story is not short of suffering, compared to plenty of other Hardy novels it is a bundle of laughs, and has all the advantages of an excellent costume drama combined with the perennial dilemma of how to find Mr Right – or whether such a thing as 'Mr Right' really exists.

**Philippa Milnes-Smith**

# THE FARSEER trilogy

## Robin Hobb

Do you want books you can immerse yourself in? Where the created world is so perfect, so real, that you feel you are there, breathing the strange scents, walking in distant alleyways? Then look no further than these amazing books.

Fitz is the bastard son of a prince. He grows up with nothing. Apprenticed to the king's master spy and assassin, Fitz can kill in hundreds of ways and is an adept spy. He also learns (sometimes painfully) about his own magics, the Skill that comes from his father, and the Wit, a forbidden and reviled beast-magic.

With only two friends, a Wolf, Night-eyes, who he is Wit-bonded to, and the strange boy who is the king's fool, Fitz has to survive. He has to – for fate has plans for him. Plans that will lead him into desperate danger.

**Leonie Flynn**

### Next?

This trilogy consists of: *Assassin's Apprentice*, *Royal Assassin* and *Assassin's Quest*. There is a further sequence, the **Tawny Man** trilogy.

If you find Robin Hobb addictive there is another series set in the same world, with some of the same characters, the **Liveship Traders** trilogy.

Another epic that feels real is Frank Herbert's *Dune* (UTBG 112) and its sequels.

# FAT BOY SWIM   Catherine Forde

A brilliant, gripping book about 'fatso' Jimmy Kelly. He's endlessly tormented and bullied because of his size, he's useless at PE, and school in general is a nightmare. But at home, in the kitchen, he can really shine and be himself, with his enviable talent for creating truly fantastic food.

Over the summer, however, things change for Jimmy in all sorts of ways. Being forced into serious swimming leads to self-discovery plus the unearthing of family secrets. There's the challenge of the Swimathon. And he gets together with Ellie. It's an absorbing tale with totally believable characters and the turmoil of Jimmy's life is beautifully depicted. For anyone whose heart sinks at the thought of games lessons, the first chapter captures to perfection the horror of school football while the descriptions of Jimmy's cooking will have you drooling and desperate to try some tablet, the Scottish version of fudge.

**Nick Sharratt**

### Next?

*Dark Waters* by Catherine MacPhail is another read set in Scotland, and is a gritty thriller.

*Girls Under Pressure* by Jacqueline Wilson tackles weight issues seen from a female perspective, as does *Massive* (UTBG 237).

The hero of Kevin Brooks' *Kissing the Rain* (UTBG 209) is another boy bullied for being fat.

## SCHOOLS' COMPETITION WINNER

**1st**

# FAT KID RULES THE WORLD
## K.L. Going

Have you ever felt alone in the world? That you are the one person who doesn't quite fit in? If the answer is yes, read this book. If the answer is no, read it anyway.

Troy knows he could never fit in. He is hugely, morbidly obese, and thinks he has no real future. Just as he's about to throw himself in front of a train and save himself further pain, his life is saved by a homeless punk by the name of Curt McCrae. At first, Troy is in awe of the guitar genius, a legend at his school. Then, slowly, a strange and unstable friendship develops between the pair. Troy's life is about to change dramatically: Curt wants him to be the drummer in his new band! Great, except Troy can't play the drums...

This is a book for anyone who escapes reality through music. Read it, and be alone no more. Misfits unite!

**Zoe Holder (aged 16)**
**Devonport High School for Girls**

# FATHERLAND

14+

## Robert Harris

This is a rare thing, a thriller that makes you think. Set in 1964, in a world in which Germany won World War II and Hitler is still alive and celebrating his 75th birthday, it concerns Xavier March, a Berlin policeman who starts off investigating a murder and ends up uncovering a deep, dark secret that puts his life at risk.

Aside from the great plot, there's also all the detail of how life would be different: like if Edward and Mrs Simpson had become king and queen of England. Written in a taut, spare style, this is a true thriller. You need to keep reading, to find out what's happening – and if March will survive.

**Leonie Flynn**

### Next?

Robert Harris has a talent for taking the past and making it real. Try *Pompeii* about the eruption of Vesuvius; or *Enigma*, about the code-breakers of Bletchley Park.

Someone else who writes terrific thrillers is Dan Brown; try *The Da Vinci Code* (UTBG 90).

Or try a thriller set in 1930s Berlin: Philip Kerr's *Berlin Noir* is bleak, dark and very exciting.

# FEATHER BOY  Nicky Singer

12+

### Next?

Another Nicky Singer? Try *Doll* and *The Innocent's Story* (UTBG 190).

Other books about a journey of self-discovery are *The Shell House* (UTBG 335) and *Postcards from No Man's Land* (UTBG 292).

For other stories about bullying, try *Kissing the Rain* by Kevin Brooks (UTBG 209) or *Fat Boy Swim* by Catherine Forde (UTBG 125).

Robert Noble has a hard time at school; nicknamed Norbert Nobottle by his classmates, his chief tormentor is a boy called Niker who is full of the casual self-confidence that Robert lacks.

But then Robert's life changes when he meets an old lady with a tragic past. She lost her son years back, when he fell out of the top window of their flat. The old lady is dying, and on her request, Robert finds himself going back to the abandoned building where the disaster took place. This is the beginning of a journey that gives him a whole new sense of purpose – although ultimately he discovers that life does not always have simple answers.

**Susan Reuben**

# FEED M.T. Anderson

14+

Imagine a world in which everyone has a live Internet feed hard-wired into their brains, and is online all the time. The teenage hero of *Feed*, Titus, has grown up barraged with advertising, information and e-mail chat that all come into his head with the speed of mental telepathy. He's completely content until the day he meets Violet, an eccentric girl who wonders what it might be like to live without the Feed. Her questions awaken in Titus a curiosity and intellect he never knew he had. But they both discover, with tragic consequences, that it's not so easy to free themselves. The novel is both science fiction and contemporary satire; it's a technological and environmental cautionary tale; it's a moving love story. It's told with astonishing energy and inventiveness and is nothing short of a masterpiece.

**Kenneth Oppel**

### Next?

Another M.T. Anderson? Try *Thirsty*, about a boy who gets very thirsty – for blood.

*Hex* (UTBG 167) by Rhiannon Lassiter is about kids who can access computers with their thoughts and who are outlaws because of it.

*Sleepwalking* (UTBG 345) by Nicola Morgan is about waking up to the reality of a controlled life.

# FESTIVAL David Belbin

14+

### Next?

Also by David Belbin, *The Last Virgin* is about six girls, six boys, sex and growing up.

*One Night* by Margaret Wild is a novel in verse that charts the highs and lows of a relationship.

Or try the outrageous *Are You Experienced?* (UTBG 28) by William Sutcliffe, which exposes the seamier side of backpacking.

Or try Esther Freud's *Hideous Kinky*, about two sisters living with their hippy mother in Morocco.

Leila is a teenage girl who goes to Glastonbury with three friends. Although the story shifts between points of view, successfully weaving together the various narrative threads to build dramatic tension, Leila remains the central focus of the book. Her adventures, including a sexual encounter, are sensitively handled by Belbin in a completely believable manner.

The anarchic festival atmosphere, the unexpected meetings, the surprising moments, the ease with which friends get lost, lose track of time, and lose themselves are all captured in this book. It is well-written, perfectly paced and sprinkled with light touches of humour, and the plot kept me interested right through to the end.

**Neil Arksey**

# FEVER PITCH  Nick Hornby

When this book came out, I thought it had been specifically written for me! It tracks one man's life passage as seen through the prism of Arsenal football club. Everything in his world is inexorably linked with the fortunes of his favourite team. For the football fan, it strikes a tremendously deep chord. For the non-football fan, it is a brilliant invitation inside the mind of an obsessive fan's allegiance to his club. It's funny, clever, thoughtful and fresh.

*Fever Pitch* started a stampede of books that plot people's lives in tandem with their most cherished cultural icons, be they in sport, music, art, etc. But in my view it remains the original and best.

**Jonny Zucker**

> ### Next?
>
> More Nick Hornby? Try *Long Way Down* or *High Fidelity* (UTBG 167).
>
> For great football novels, try the superbly atmospheric, rainforest-based *Keeper* (UTBG 205) by Mal Peet.
>
> Football players' memoirs include David Beckham: *My Side*, and *Off The Record* by Michael Owen. Both are very reader-friendly and each offers fascinating looks behind the scenes of today's world of soccer megastars.

# FIRE AND HEMLOCK

## Diana Wynne Jones

12+

A photograph that 19-year-old student Polly has had since childhood now looks different from how she remembered: where are the horse and the figures that once ran among burning cornfields? Fragments of long-suppressed memories begin to force themselves into Polly's consciousness and she realises that her recollection of the events of the past five years is false. The truth has something to do with an evil, ageless woman and a gifted musician, Tom Lynn, who was once the most important person in her life. How – and why – has she forgotten him? Polly searches for the truth in one of Diana Wynne Jones' most fiendishly complex plots.

**Gill Vickery**

> ### Next?
>
> Another of Diana Wynne Jones' wonderful novels where memory plays tricks and time is turned upside-down is *Hexwood*.
>
> If you like books based on myths and legends, try Catherine Fisher's novels: *The Lammas Field*, also based on the ballad of 'Thomas the Rhymer', or *Corbenic* (UTBG 84), based on the legend of the Holy Grail.
>
> Sarah Singleton's *Century* is about two sisters who one day realise they have no recollection of their mother, or her death.

# FIRE FROM HEAVEN  Mary Renault

You think you have a dysfunctional family? Try Alexander's… His mum hates his dad (but is kind of kinky for snakes), his dad hates his mum and has loads of girlfriends (no, Mum does not approve). Oh, and Alexander? He has ambitions. BIG ambitions (they didn't call him The Great for nothing!).

This is a true story. It tells of Alexander in all his god-like, insane glory, and of his lovers – both male and female. If you've ever thought history boring, read this. For here a legend steps off the page and becomes human: flawed, imperfect, yet utterly wonderful. In fact, be careful, for you might fall in love. I did.

**Leonie Flynn**

### Next?

There are two sequels; next is *The Persian Boy*, Alexander's story told by Bagoas, a Persian eunuch who becomes his lover.

If you want to read a non-fiction account of Alexander the Great, try Robin Lane Fox's biography. Or Mary Renault's own book about him, *The Nature of Alexander*.

Or how about another great portrayal of history that makes it real? Try Robert Graves' *I, Claudius*.

# FIREDRAKE'S EYE  Patricia Finney

### Next?

If you enjoyed the Elizabethan language but get enough Shakespeare at school, try reading Christopher Marlowe's play *Dr Faustus*.

If you enjoyed the intrigue and complications of the spy story, try John le Carré's *Tinker, Tailor, Soldier, Spy* or *The Spy Who Came in from the Cold* (UTBG 351).

If you were intrigued by the role of the madman in this story, move on to *Dracula* (UTBG 110).

We're in the squalid underworld of 16th-century London and someone is trying to assassinate Queen Elizabeth I. Fortunately, Walsingham and Cecil (like many of the characters in this novel, they're people who really lived at the time) are running a secret service to thwart such attempts. The world of the novel is violent and chaotic, the narrator is a madman, and Patricia Finney includes Elizabethan phrases and grammar, so you feel as though you really are lost in history. You're swept along by the complicated and exciting story – it's about spies, about being an outsider in your own world and about what life at the time must really have been like. It's a challenging, seriously gripping read.

**Antonia Honeywell**

# THE FIRE-EATERS David Almond

This memorable story starts with Bobby's first encounter with the fire-eater, McNulty, on a particular Sunday in late summer 1962: 'It was like my heart stopped beating and the world stopped turning'. Bobby and his friends Ailsa (from a sea-coaling family), Daniel (newly moved to the area) and Joseph are living under the shadow of the Cuban missile crisis: World War III might start at any moment. The world is at the edge of the abyss. There are other scary things happening too: Bobby's dad, a shipyard worker, is sick, and Bobby is starting secondary school.

Darkness, inhumanity and war threaten life and love and family throughout the story, and for me make this book seem particularly relevant now. As with Almond's other novels, the writing is beautifully honed and polished, and at the novel's heart, holding back the darkness, are strong, tender friendships and family bonds, and a sense that the world is truly an amazing place. Wonderful.

**Julia Green**

### Next?

Try David Almond's *Clay* (UTBG 78), about belief, friendship and evil.

You might also like *Thursday's Child* (UTBG 373) by Sonya Hartnett, another extraordinary and original writer.

Or what about another book that shows how hope can triumph over the darkest of circumstances? Try Elizabeth Laird's *Jake's Tower* (UTBG 193).

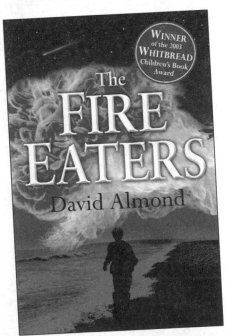

WINNER of the 2003 WHITBREAD Children's Book Award

The FIRE EATERS
David Almond

## THE BOMB

*Cat's Cradle*
by Kurt Vonnegut

*Slaughterhouse 5*
by Kurt Vonnegut

*Why Weeps the Brogan?*
by Hugh Scott

*When the Wind Blows*
by Raymond Briggs

*Children of the Dust*
by Louise Lawrence

*Z for Zachariah*
by Robert O'Brien

# FIREWEED   Jill Paton Walsh

### Next?

Another Jill Paton Walsh worth seeking out is *The Dolphin Crossing*, about the retreat from Dunkirk.

Try the series by Judith Kerr that begins with *When Hitler Stole Pink Rabbit* and follows the story of Anna and her German family.

Or for another book about a wartime runaway, Robert Westall's *The Kingdom by the Sea* (UTBG 208).

*Fireweed* was first published in 1969. Many Blitz novels have been published since, but this, losing none of its potency, is among the strongest. 15-year-old Bill, on the run from evacuation in Wales, returns to London where he meets another refugee – Julie, whose parents suppose her to have sailed for Canada on the doomed ship *City of Benares*. Teaming up, the two eke out an existence on the streets of London, establishing a domesticity beyond their years when they settle in a cook's basement together with an abandoned child, Dickie. Disillusionment for Bill when he feels betrayed by Julie can't diminish, in hindsight, the intensity of their time together. Wonderful writing brings the dangers and uncertainties of the Blitz vividly to life.

**Linda Newbery**

# FLESHMARKET   Nicola Morgan

This novel transports you immediately – and shockingly – to the raw, rough Edinburgh of the 19th century, where the teenage protagonist (Robbie) is determined on a seemingly futile mission of revenge. As a small boy, he witnessed a brutal operation on his mother at the hands of a renowned surgeon, Dr Knox. Days afterwards, she died. Now Dr Knox has come into Robbie's life once more, and Robbie has to face some hard choices.

Dr Knox is a real historical character, as are the corpse-stealers Burke and Hare, with whose murderous work Robbie becomes involved. The writing is so vivid you can almost taste the reeking fog rising between the tenement buildings of the old city, while you suffer with Robbie and his younger sister in their struggle to survive deprivation and danger.

**Patricia Elliott**

### Next?

Also set in Edinburgh, Robert Louis Stevenson's classic *Dr Jekyll and Mr Hyde* (UTBG 107) is a more difficult read, but equally rewarding.

Try, too, Julie Hearn's *Follow Me Down* (UTBG 133), an extraordinary time-slip novel set in 18th-century and contemporary London.

More atmosphere, Edinburgh and murder? Alison Prince's *Oranges and Murder* is just what you're looking for.

# FLOODLAND  Marcus Sedgwick

'Zoe ran. Harder than she had ever run in her life…'

For such a slim book, *Floodland* packs quite a punch. It's a story set in the not-too-distant future, when global warming has caused the waters to rise and cover large parts of England. Zoe has been stranded on Norwich – now an island, unhappy and inhospitable; her attempts to get away and find her parents land her on Eels island, which is even worse – inhabited by wild children, all under the leadership of the sinister and violent Dooby, who Zoe finds very frightening indeed. Her only friend on Eels island is old William, and he's mad. Isn't he?

This is a story of bravery and resilience, a story about unusual friendships; it's sometimes very dark, but always beautiful, and it grips from the first line.
**Daniel Hahn**

> ### Next?
>
> Read more Marcus Sedgwick. Maybe *The Book of Dead Days* next, or the stunning *Dark Horse*.
>
> Another odd tale of being stranded at sea is Yann Martel's wonderful and peculiar *Life of Pi* (UTBG 218).
>
> William Golding's *Lord of the Flies* (UTBG 223) is another tale of young people abandoned on an island, and the wild things they become.

# FLOWERS IN THE ATTIC

14+

## Virginia Andrews

> ### Next?
>
> Try the sequels, *Petals on the Wind*, *If There Be Thorns* and *Seeds of Yesterday*.
>
> Another story of a girl locked in an attic (or is she?) is Josephine Tey's *The Franchise Affair*.
>
> Or for more Gothic and overheated prose, try Anne Rice's *Interview with the Vampire* (UTBG 191).

Four children in 1970s America have a perfect and happy family life, until their father dies tragically, their mother is left destitute and they go to live with their evil grandparents. There they are locked out of sight 'just for one night' for reasons they don't understand. And the one night turns into weeks, the weeks into months. Food becomes scarce, their treatment increasingly harsh…

This book is genuinely harrowing with some violent and some sexually explicit scenes. It's a story full of high melodrama, and literary it certainly isn't; but if you want a really gripping and engrossing read which won't let you stop thinking about it till you've reached the last page (and probably not even then), it's definitely worth a go.
**Susan Reuben**

# THE FLOWING QUEEN  Kai Meyer

12+

Everyone says that Venice is a magical place, but in Kai Meyer's *The Flowing Queen* this is literally true. To read this book is to enter an alternative universe where the Egyptian Empire is intent on world domination. Only Venice, protected by the mysterious Flowing Queen, can stand against the Pharaoh and his armies. But now Venice is under attack – from enemies within.

This book has everything: orphans and pickpockets; mermaids and talking stone lions; evil councillors and ambassadors from Hell, all of it woven together in an intricate narrative that sweeps you away.

This is hardcore fantasy, and for those of you that enjoy this book, the great news is that there are more to follow.

**Laura Hutchings**

### Next?

If you enjoyed the Venetian setting then try *The Thief Lord* by Cornelia Funke or *Stravaganza: City of Masks* by Mary Hoffman.

For adventure stories involving children who unwittingly become caught up in adult machinations, try Joan Aiken's classic *The Wolves of Willoughby Chase* or Philip Reeve's *Mortal Engines* (UTBG 250).

# FOLLOW ME DOWN  Julie Hearn

14+

### Next?

For more grave-robbers, try Nicola Morgan's *Fleshmarket* (UTBG 131).

If you're interested in the battle between good and evil, try Philip Pullman's **His Dark Materials** trilogy (UTBG 170).

Or if you liked the way Julie Hearn writes, read her *The Merrybegot* (UTBG 242), which is about witches and witchfinders, or *I, Coriander* by Sally Gardner, about a girl straying from our world into that of the fairies.

It sounds like a classic story: Tom and his mum visit his gran in London and adventures happen. But… Tom's recently divorced mother has cancer, his gran is vicious-tongued and rarely seen without a drink in her hand, and neither woman really likes the other. To add to the miseries of Tom's life he starts hearing voices. Voices that lead him down into the cellar … and back in time to a London where freaks are sold by the hour to the curious, and where he meets Astra, the mysterious Changeling Child.

In a story that weaves the past into the present, and blurs the real into the unreal, this stunning work is both horror and history, and makes you think about who exactly the real freaks are.

**Leonie Flynn**

# FOR ESMÉ – WITH LOVE AND SQUALOR

## J.D. Salinger

**14+**

### Next?

*Raise High the Roof Beam, Carpenters / Seymour, an Introduction*, and *Franny and Zooey* (UTBG 139) also by J.D. Salinger, are worth seeking out, as is of course the classic *The Catcher in the Rye* (UTBG 66) if you haven't read it yet.

*The Best Short Stories of Ring Lardner*: if you like short stories, particularly by American writers, this is a brilliant collection.

J.D. Salinger is best known for his classic (and only) novel *The Catcher in the Rye*, but he also wrote some other lesser-known stories which are just as good, if not better. *For Esmé – with Love and Squalor* is a collection of nine short stories, many of which deal with the relationships between children and adults – a theme that Salinger approaches like no other writer. He not only sees things from the children's point of view, but he takes us into their minds and their hearts and shows us the world through their eyes.

These are weirdly wonderful stories – 'A Perfect Day for Bananafish', 'Uncle Wiggily in Connecticut', 'Just Before the War with the Eskimos'. They're funny, sad, tragic, mad… and every one is a perfect gem.

**Kevin Brooks**

# FORBIDDEN Judy Waite

**16+**

Elinor has grown up with The Chosen, following the True Cause. She is especially privileged, as she is destined to be the 'bride' of the cult leader when she reaches her 16th birthday. Elinor is happy to be a part of all that – until she happens to meet an 'outsider' boy. She begins to question what the cult is all about and what she really wants to do with her life. But when she thinks about making a break, Elinor discovers how little freedom she truly has. Can she, will she, break free? This tense and gripping story takes the reader through many a twist and turn to find out.

**Yvonne Coppard**

### Next?

If you like this, you might also like another story set in a cult: *Blinded by the Light* (UTBG 45) by Sherry Ashworth.

Read about a love story between two 'outsiders' in *Naked Without a Hat* (UTBG 255).

Try something else by Judy Waite; *The Next Big Thing* is about a boy discovered singing in his garage who becomes a reluctant superstar.

# FOREVER  Judy Blume

Erica has insight. She knew Katherine liked Michael the moment they met at a New Year's Eve party. Katherine admits the fact to herself, which allows the attraction to develop. Eventually she is sure it is love and not childish infatuation. Michael feels it too and after a few failed attempts, they make love.

Their relationship becomes intense and exclusive. But with their future plans all figured out, the couple have to face up to the fact that their senior year at high school is coming to an end and they will be going to different universities. To make matters worse they both have summer jobs. They put their love to the test with a long separation. For Katherine it's a time to reflect and wonder if their love really is forever...

**Elena Gregoriou**

## Next?

More Judy Blume, of course: *Are You There God? It's Me, Margaret* or *Tiger Eyes*.

For a more-recent take on teenage sex, Melvin Burgess' *Doing It* (UTBG 109).

Other life-changing experiences happen in *Festival* (UTBG 127) and the **Megan** trilogy (UTBG 240).

Or for more books on love and life, read Catherine Robinson's feature on pp. 168–169.

Judy Blume

forever
'a teenage classic'

*Forever* follows the developing relationships of teenage couples and their interaction with the adult world. How do liberal parents deal with the reality of their teenage daughter's long-term and developing sexual relationship?

Until I read this book I thought nothing could shock me. First published in the 1970s, *Forever* talks more graphically about teenage sex than anything I've read that was written since. Of course being shocked is not necessarily a bad thing. The book gives a very realistic insight into the workings of teenage relationships and answers questions young people cannot always ask their parents. Well worth reading.

**Anna Posner (aged 16)**

# GRAPHIC NOVELS
## by Mal Peet

I was in a branch of Waterstone's recently and asked where the graphic novels were. 'We don't keep them any more,' I was told, 'they just get stolen.' It's a small triumph for the form, I suppose, that it encourages reading among the thieving classes; but it's a shame that it gets harder to buy graphics just when it seems that they are beginning to win the struggle for serious critical recognition. Of course there are still diehards who dismiss graphic novels *en masse* as immature or flippant reading matter best suited to young readers reluctant to read 'proper' books.

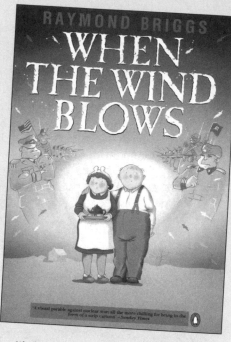

It's true that there's a pretty leaky border between 'comic books' and graphics, and that movie and TV spin-offs and fantasy books (often daringly and beautifully drawn) are predominant. Yet the term 'graphic novel' was coined in 1978 to describe Will Eisner's immensely serious *A Contract with God*, and some of the greatest graphics of the last 20 years have dealt with extremely sombre matters: the Holocaust in Art Spiegelman's two-volume *Maus* (UTBG 239) and Joe Klubert's *Yossel*; the Hiroshima bombing in Keji Nakazawa's two *Barefoot Gen* books; nuclear war in Raymond Briggs' *When the Wind Blows* (UTBG 409); war and ethnic cleansing in Joe Sacco's *Palestine* and *The Fixer: A Story from Sarajevo*.

Indeed, if there is a criticism to be made of the form generally, it would be that graphics tend not towards the lightweight and the comical, but towards the shadowy and the bleak. Even the good old escapist superhero genre has turned darkly ironic; see, for examples, *Batman – The Dark Knight Returns* by Frank Miller, and *Watchmen* (UTBG 401) by Alan Moore and Dave Gibbons.

The fact is, though, that there are now as many genres of graphic as there are of mainstream prose fiction; and in one important respect the graphic is far more challenging and experimental than the prose novel. By combining text, art and the 'grammar' of movies and animation, graphic novelists have devised new, startling and complex narrative techniques which make interesting demands on the reader's verbal and visual literacy. Actually, strip cartoonists have always taken a subversive approach to logical narration; look at collections of Winsor McCay's weird and beautiful *Dreams of the Rarebit Fiend* and *Little Nemo*, and George Herriman's brilliant *Krazy Kat*, which date from the early years of the 20th century and were a major influence on the 'underground' comics of the 1960s and 70s. Contemporary graphic sci-fi / fantasy novelists, such as Bryan Talbot (*The Adventures of Luther Arkwright*) and Neil Gaiman (the extraordinary *Black Orchid*, illustrated by Dave McKean), as well as the ongoing **The Sandman** series (UTBG 320) make it a point of honour to offer few concessions to the reader, weaving together different time frames and points of view to create a 'parallel universes' style of narration which, in a prose novel, would deter all but the most sophisticated readers.

**Some graphic novels you can read about in the *UTBG*:**

*Blankets* by Craig Thompson

*Ethel and Ernest* by Raymond Briggs

*Jimmy Corrigan* by Chris Ware

*Maus* by Art Spiegelman

*Persepolis* by Marjane Satrapi

**The Sandman** series by Neil Gaiman

*V for Vendetta* by Alan Moore

*Watchmen* by Alan Moore and Dave Gibbons

*When the Wind Blows* by Raymond Briggs

# THE FORTUNE TELLER  Alison Prince

14+

### Next?

Peter Dickinson's *The Gift*: Davy Price has inherited the ability to see what others are thinking and learns his family are in danger.

Pauline Fisk's *Telling the Sea*: Nona and her family are on the run from a violent stepfather.

Another Alison Prince? Try *Oranges and Murder*, about a London barrow boy's search for the secret of his real family.

If you are interested in clairvoyants, psychic powers, premonitions and horoscopes, this is a book for you. Mick lives with his sister and his mother. His father died in an accident and Mick tries to support his mother Cathie in her struggle to run a bed and breakfast business. Cathie visits a fortune teller who tells her Mick is going to die. Much of the story is about how Mick and those close to him deal with this premonition. Mick's sister moves out to live with her boyfriend. Cathie meets a new partner and Mick becomes increasingly isolated. The action takes place against the background of the Scottish coastline and a lighthouse, as Mick is compelled to question his destiny.

**Brenda Marshall**

# The FOUNDATION trilogy  Isaac Asimov

14+

The human race has spread across the galaxy to occupy millions of worlds, all ruled from the metal-covered planet Trantor. Only one man, Hari Seldon, realises that the Galactic Empire is in decline. Charting the fall of civilisation by means of the predictive science of Psychohistory, Seldon sets up two secret Foundations 'at opposite ends of the galaxy' to hold it together over the next thousand years. In the course of the trilogy we meet buccaneering mayors, deep-space traders, merchant princes, thieves, mutants, emperors, scheming generals and a host of other colourful characters. Generations and crises come and go, centuries pass, with considerable excitement and a great many surprises and twists. The greatest of all sci-fi epics.

**Michael Lawrence**

### Next?

After completing the trilogy – *Foundation*, *Foundation and Empire* and *Second Foundation* – Asimov wrote more **Foundation** books. *Foundation's Edge* is next.

Asimov also wrote some of the most brilliant sci-fi ever. Try *I, Robot* (UTBG 184), which starts the excellent **Robot** series.

Philip K. Dick's *Do Androids Dream of Electric Sheep?* (UTBG 107) is full of amazing and original ideas.

Another series that spans time and space starts with *Dune* (UTBG 112) by Frank Herbert.

# FRANKENSTEIN  Mary Shelley

14+

If you think that Mary Shelley just played the dutiful wife to her famous poet husband, Percy Bysshe Shelley, think again…

*Frankenstein* started out as a challenge by the great Lord Byron to each of his guests at the Villa Diodati on Lake Geneva: 'Write a horror story.' So Mary sat down to write a book that would have more readers than those of all her poetic contemporaries; it turned out to be one of the most chilling stories ever written. Dr Frankenstein puts pieces of dead bodies together to assemble a creature that he brings to life. The monster escapes and roams the hills and villages around, wreaking havoc. But the monster also gains our sympathy, for within a misshapen body there is a lost soul that craves affection.

**James Riordan**

### Next?

*Angelmonster* by Veronica Bennett is based on this book and Mary Shelley's life.

For another experiment that goes wrong, H.G. Wells' *The Invisible Man*.

Another classic horror story that's still appallingly scary is *Dr Jekyll and Mr Hyde* (UTBG 107).

And read our horror feature on pp. 360–361.

---

# FRANNY AND ZOOEY  J.D. Salinger

16+

### Next?

*The Cheese Monkeys* by Chip Kidd, a novel about a year in art school has some of Salinger's sarcastic humour.

*Studs Lonigan* by James T. Farrell tells of teenage dissatisfaction, but Studs is a harder character than Salinger's whimsical Glass siblings.

For another book about a complex family, and also the trials of growing up, try Colette's *Gigi* (UTBG 145).

For some people, *The Catcher in the Rye* is the only important Salinger book. But his true masterpiece remains incomplete. Since the early 1950s, Salinger has been writing an epic narrative series about a New York family called the Glasses. 'Franny' and 'Zooey' are two of the stories from this sequence, with a sweet simplicity that makes them incredibly enjoyable to read. 'Franny' is a short story about a young female student who meets her boyfriend for dinner, and can't help disagreeing with everything he says; while 'Zooey' is a longer novella, narrated by Buddy Glass, who claims his family hate him writing about them but don't protest because they know he'd burst into tears. All the children in the Glass family are prodigies, appearing on a radio quiz show called 'It's a Wild Child', but when they grow up their problems drive them to depression and suicide.

**Matt Thorne**

# FRENCHMAN'S CREEK Daphne du Maurier

Romance was never quite as passionate or daring as in *Frenchman's Creek*. Prepare to fall in love right along with our heroine Dona; for never was there quite as elusive, romantic or swashbuckling a lover as the pirate known as 'the Frenchman'!

Dona is married, the mother of two, and about to turn 30. She had been the toast of London (of the men at least), but one day, she decides to leave it all and move to her husband's country estate in Cornwall, and her life changes forever. All of Cornwall is desperately trying to capture a French pirate – but who would have thought that his hideout was right in the middle of Dona's estate? And what exactly happens after he offers her a place on his ship? Will Dona choose adventure and love, or stay faithful to her husband and children? You will find yourself holding your breath as the story unfolds…

**Candida Gray**

## Next?

There's more breathless west-country romance in R.D. Blackmore's classic, *Lorna Doone*, or for corsets and passion try *Wuthering Heights* (UTBG 424).

Richard Hughes' *A High Wind in Jamaica* is a story of pirates, unsuitable obsession and adventure.

Daphne du Maurier has written many books, but *Jamaica Inn* (UTBG 194) is the closest you'll find to this.

---

# FRIENDLY FIRE Patrick Gale

## Next?

Hooked? Try two other Gale novels that home in on the truth about childhood: *Rough Music* and *A Sweet Obscurity*.

For a very different boarding-school type story, try Thomas Hughes' classic *Tom Brown's Schooldays*.

Sometimes you can be too sensitive or too protective, as Sophie is. Tom's guilty of this too in the short, sharp *Round Behind the Ice-house* (UTBG 313).

Patrick Gale's recent novels coax you in gently until you find – quite soon – you are pulled into a heady, messy tangle of relationships. We enter *Friendly Fire*, which is set during a 1970s boarding-school adolescence, through the eyes of defensive, pragmatic Sophie, whose parents abandoned her and who's been brought up in a children's home. At Tatham's School she immerses herself in the cold-but-steadfast world of academia, but she cannot evade the complex web of passions that the nearly all-male students spin around them. Her life becomes enriched in unexpected ways, but with that comes the power to threaten the happiness of those closest to her. This book is aptly titled – friendly fire is one of the most dangerous weapons of all.

**Jon Appleton**

# FROST IN MAY Antonia White

**Next?**

There are sequels: *The Lost Traveller*, *The Sugar House* and *Beyond the Glass*.

*Bilgewater* (UTBG 41) is about a girl at an all-boys' school.

Karen Armstrong has written an account of her life as a nun in *Through the Narrow Gate*.

You think your school's tough on you? Read this book. Ten-year-old Nanda is sent to the Convent of the Five Wounds, a boarding school so pious that at night the girls drape their stockings over the rest of their clothes in the shape of a cross. Nanda tries hard to fit in, and this astonishing novel follows her progress until, at 14, disaster and expulsion strike.

Written for adults over 60 years ago, this autobiographical account of a fanatically Roman Catholic schooling will fascinate older readers who can, like Nanda, face a challenge. It also forcefully brings home just what 'faith schooling' can mean, how tightly it can grip, and how long-lasting the effects can be. A salutary eye-opener for today's teenager – and a classic.

**Anne Fine**

# FROST ON MY MOUSTACHE
## Tim Moore

Once it gets started, this is one of the funniest books ever. A hundred and fifty years ago, fearless, swashbuckling Lord Dufferin went off on his derring-do travels, battling with icebergs and polar bears through Iceland and Norway. Modern-day author Tim Moore is a self-confessed 'girl's blouse', and, oozing with derring-don't, he sets off in his footsteps. As Tim watches himself fall so far short of the doughty Victorian in pluck and stamina on the demanding Arctic journey, he gets funnier and funnier. Skip chapter one first time round if you must and start, as does Tim, at 4.30 am in Grimsby, boarding a boat in a Force-8 gale. ('Eat, like, twelve Mars bars,' suggests the taxi driver. 'So you'll have something to chuck up.')

**Anne Fine**

**Next?**

For more crazy men doing heroic (or crazy) things, read *The Worst Journey in the World* (UTBG 422), or *Terra Incognita* (UTBG 368) for a woman's view of ice adventure.

Or less heroic, but as funny as Tim Moore: *Round Ireland with a Fridge* (UTBG 313).

Bill Bryson writes warm and funny travelogues; try *Notes from a Small Island* (UTBG 266).

Or more Tim Moore? Try his hilarious *Do Not Pass Go*.

# THE GARBAGE KING  Elizabeth Laird

14+

## Next?

Elizabeth Laird makes no concessions – all her books are powerful and hard-hitting. Try *Jake's Tower* (UTBG 193) next or *Kiss the Dust* (UTBG 209).

Another book about living on the streets, this time in London: *Stone Cold* (UTBG 355) by Robert Swindells.

For another tale of the strength and importance of friendship and trust, read Keith Gray's *Warehouse* (UTBG 399).

Elizabeth Laird has lived in Ethiopia and from her experience there has crafted this wonderfully true-feeling novel about rich-boy Dani who runs away from his father's ruthless plans for him, and finds himself living on the streets of Addis Ababa among the poorest of the poor. Anyone who has ever tried to imagine everything that makes life safe, happy and comfortable being stripped away, leaving them with nothing but hunger, dirt and danger, should read this book. Amid all the fear and squalor, however, Dani finds a new strength, and the true meaning of friendship, independence and solidarity. A superb and gripping read for anyone who is not afraid of plumbing the depths.

**Lynne Reid Banks**

# A GATHERING LIGHT  Jennifer Donnelly

12+

This wonderful book brilliantly intertwines fiction and reality. Set in a small New England resort town in 1906, it tells the story of Mattie and how her life interacts with that of drowned Grace Brown.

Mattie is torn between her duty to help her father run his farm and to look after her motherless siblings, and her desire to be a writer. When handsome Royal Loomis starts to show an interest, there is an extra reason for Mattie to turn her back on her dreams and stay put. She has in her possession the letters Grace wrote to her lover Chester, and these help Mattie resolve the dilemma about what to do with her own life.

Sympathetic, beautifully written and wonderfully constructed, this is an outstanding read.

**Ann Jungman**

## Next?

For a less air-brushed view of what it was like to be black in early 20th-century America, try *Roll of Thunder, Hear My Cry* (UTBG 311).

*Anne of Green Gables* by L.M. Montgomery shows the toughness of life on a farm and the warmth of small communities.

*Some Other War* by Linda Newbery gives a good picture of country life in England, shown from a working-class viewpoint, before and during World War I. Twins Alice and Jack are changed for ever by the experience of the War.

# GENERATION X Douglas Coupland

16+

### Next?

More Douglas Coupland? Try his *Shampoo Planet*.

*The Lawnmower Celebrity* by Ben Hatch, the sad, funny tale of a teenage boy trying to see the point of it all.

*The Beach* (UTBG 34) by Alex Garland is another book that started as a cult novel – then they made a film of it!

And read our feature on cult books on pp. 264–265.

Dag, Claire and Andy are good friends in their 20s who live in neighbouring bungalows in a quiet American town. Their jobs are dull, they have little money and they see the future as frightening, full of the threat of nuclear bombs and environmental catastrophe. So they escape from all of this by telling one another bizarre, beautiful stories about other worlds where things make more, or sometimes less, sense to them. This is a thoughtful book about friendship, human nature and trying to understand an uncertain world. It is a true 'cult novel', its popularity spread by word of mouth. It is full of new and clever words and terms, like 'McJob' for a low-paid and unimportant job, which are explained in amusing side-notes to the main text.

**Marianne Taylor**

# GEORGIE Malachy Doyle

12+

Georgie lives in a home for disturbed children. He has a terrible secret he won't talk about to anyone. He destroys anything given to him. He rejects anyone who attempts to win his trust.

Then he moves to a new home, where he meets Shannon and Tommo. Shannon is a girl with her own secrets. Tommo is a care worker who won't let Georgie push him away. Together, they help Georgie overcome the nightmares in his past and develop the courage to love again.

*Georgie* is no easy read. At times, it's so honest it's painful. It's also one of the most positive and uplifting books I've ever read.

I'm still not sure about the last chapter, which doesn't quite ring true, but other than that, *Georgie* is utterly believable and totally compelling.

**Graham Gardner**

### Next?

*Disconnected* (UTBG 103) is about a girl escaping life through the solace of alcohol.

*Who Is Jesse Flood?* (UTBG 411) is another great Malachy Doyle, about a boy coming to terms with life and himself.

For another tale of problematic children finding their place, read Sharon Creech's rather more gentle *Ruby Holler* (UTBG 314).

# GETTING RID OF KARENNA
## Helena Pielichaty

Suzanne gets a Saturday job in a hairdresser's and is horrified to discover that Karenna, the bully who made her life miserable in school, is the junior stylist there. All the old, humiliating memories come flooding back. At first Karenna doesn't even recognize Suzanne, but it soon becomes clear neither girl has changed much since they last met. Karenna resents Suzanne being there, butting in on the new life she has carved out for herself since school. Suzanne must overcome the humiliations of the past and find some way to stop Karenna haunting her future.

A real and convincing exploration of the bully-victim relationship.

**Yvonne Coppard**

### Next?

There are numerous books that examine the dynamics of the bully-victim relationship. *Inventing Elliot* (UTBG 192) (Graham Gardner), *The Protectors* (Pete Johnson) and *The Mighty Crashman* (Jerry Spinelli) are among the best.

Robert Cormier's *The Rag and Bone Shop* (UTBG 303) is about a bully whose victim turns on him.

*Stargirl* (UTBG 352) by Jerry Spinelli is a book about what it takes to be popular.

# GHOST STORIES M.R. James

### Next?

Some of the best British ghost stories were written in the early 20th century. Look out for authors like Algernon Blackwood and E.F. Benson. Read Benson's *The Tale of an Empty House* or any collection of short stories.

Susan Hill's *The Woman in Black* (UTBG 420), set at around the same time, is unusual – a ghost story that is a full-length novel.

The living people in these stories are usually learned, respectable types; scholars, clergymen, amateur archaeologists, often nursing a guilty secret, poking about where they ought not to in burial mounds, tombs, churches, libraries. All their learning and respectability cannot protect them from what they disturb. These are not strictly speaking ghosts but crawling, slithering, soft dark things lit only by the occasional glint of sunlight on white bone, trailing cobwebs, mildew, damp musty smells, unspeakable rags of cloth and flesh, bluebottles and fog. You would not want any of them to touch you, but touch is what they do: touch and hang on. After a century the writing may seem a little stately but the stories are thoroughly nasty.

**Jan Mark**

# GIFTS Ursula Le Guin

This is a story of strange countries and magic powers. But nobody in Caspromont can work general, all-purpose magic; instead each family has a traditional 'gift'. Orrec's friend Gry can call creatures to her, but Orrec's family has the gift of 'Undoing', the gift of completely destroying things, a gift so terrible that Orrec must be blindfolded until he can control it. Can Orrec and Gry reach a true understanding of how best to use their gifts? You won't be able to stop reading this book, with its strange sense of foreboding... And maybe it'll make you wonder about any gift you yourself may have...
**Jill Paton Walsh**

## Next?

For more Ursula Le Guin, try *The Dispossessed*.

Then how about Margaret Mahy's *The Changeover* (UTBG 69), Virginia Euwer Wolff's *The Mozart Season*, Mark Haddon's *The Curious Incident of the Dog in the Night-time* (UTBG 89), or Catherine Storr's *Marianne Dreams*? They're all in their different ways about young people with difficult gifts.

Lene Kaaberbol's *The Shamer's Daughter* (UTBG 333) is about a gift that can also be a curse.

# GIGI Colette

16+

Gigi is a teenager, full of defiance, exuberance and obstinacy. Sound familiar? But Gigi is a teenager 100 years ago in the early 1900s.

Gigi belongs to a family whose women essentially all become mistresses, and Gigi's grandmother and great aunt would like her to become the greatest lover of her time. Once her potential is perceived, Gigi is primped and trained more than a 'performing monkey'. She learns all about jewels, table manners and decorum. Her extensive lessons should prepare her to be a perfect mistress, but Gigi has other plans...

*Gigi* is delightful and will capture your heart, but there's a lot to be learned from it too. Think about what it meant to be in the breach between adulthood and childhood a century ago – do you really think things have changed that much?
**Candida Gray**

## Next?

Colette also wrote stories about a schoolgirl called Claudine – saucy, naughty and great reads; start with *Claudine at School* (UTBG 78).

Or her novel *Chéri* about a young man whose life is not all that dissimilar to Gigi's.

*Gigi* was also made into a wonderful film which you should see!

Stories about becoming an adult abound – read our feature on pp. 296–297.

# GIRL, 15 (CHARMING BUT INSANE)

**14+**

## Sue Limb

Limb's novel is a riotous take on Jane Austen's *Emma* and – like *Clueless* before it – is modern, snazzy and very up-to-date. Jess Jordan feels that by comparison to the blonde, beautiful, rich Flora she is hideous, poor and doomed. She spends her time being mesmerised by the fabulously handsome Ben Jones – who is so totally wrong for her.

Jess has been invited to do a stand-up routine at the school show, the one thing she knows she's good at. But the glamorous Flora and her vile band Poisonous Trash threaten to steal the show. Disaster strikes before Jess realises who the man of her dreams really is. It's classic stuff and laugh-out-loud funny.

**John McLay**

> ### Next?
>
> Jess continues her adventures in *Girl (Nearly) 16: Absolute Torture* and there are more novels on the way.
>
> Tui Sutherland's *This Must Be Love* gives a classic Shakespearean tale a modern makeover with witty results.
>
> *Cross Your Heart, Connie Pickles* is quality chick-lit for teens too, penned by adult author Sabine Durrant, or try the hilarious *Angus, Thongs and Full-frontal Snogging* (UTBG 22).
>
> Or read Jacqueline Wilson's books for older readers, such as *Love Lessons*, about a girl falling for her art teacher.

# THE GIRL IN THE ATTIC Valerie Mendes

**12+**

> ### Next?
>
> *Phosphorescence* (UTBG 286) by Raffaella Barker, *Green Fingers* by Paul May and *Zillah and Me* by Helen Dunmore are all gripping reads about girls moving house and making a new start.
>
> *The Wish House* (UTBG 415) by Celia Rees centres on a house that harbours darker, more sinister secrets.

Being dragged off to Cornwall for Christmas by his mum, then being told they're to move there permanently, isn't the best present in the world for 13-year-old Nathan.

Separated from his dad, missing his best friend Tom and his action-packed life in London leads to lots of strops and sulking and a determination never to settle in … until the day he sees a girl painting in the attic of a house they're thinking of buying – a girl who turns out to have a dark family secret Nathan just has to discover.

Mixing mystery, love and contemporary gothic horror, this is a spooky, spine-tingling thriller to read at one sitting.

**Eileen Armstrong**

# GIRL WITH A PEARL EARRING
## Tracy Chevalier

*Girl with a Pearl Earring* is narrated by servant-girl Griet, and simmers with her passion. Griet is a tile maker's daughter, taken to be a maidservant to the great artist Vermeer. With her we are drawn into the Vermeer family house, a small world full of almost unbearable tensions. It is fraught with struggles of class and religion, servants vying for superiority over each other, and rivalries for the affection of a genius who cares only for his painting.

Griet reveals the process of painting as magically as she evokes the mood of the house and its people, and we sense that she herself might have been an artist, had she not been a girl, and of the servant class. I am not sure I like Griet, and I can never predict what she will do next. Yet her narrative is as spellbinding as Vermeer's portraits themselves.

This is a dazzling book with erotic undercurrents. Look out for the ear-piercing scene.

**Caroline Pitcher**

**Next?**

Deborah Moggach's *Tulip Fever* sneaks behind the carefully arranged domestic canvas into a world of betrayal.

*Lady Chatterley's Lover* (UTBG 212) tells the story of a lady and a gamekeeper (aristocratic totty seeks working-class rough).

# GIRLFRIEND IN A COMA  Douglas Coupland

**Next?**

All Douglas Coupland's books are exciting, thought-provoking and well worth a read. Try *Generation X* (UTBG 143) or *Miss Wyoming* next.

Also Irvine Welsh's *Trainspotting* (UTBG 379) for a really hard look at the dark side of drugs.

And for a story from the other side of the coma, Alex Garland's *The Coma*!

This is an immensely hard-hitting but also extraordinarily gripping novel, which starts with Karen, aged 17, losing her virginity to her boyfriend on a ski slope in Vancouver, Canada, and an hour later falling asleep at a house-wrecking party and falling into a coma. The book traces the effect of this and other events on the lives of her friends, who go from bright teenagers to embittered drug- and alcohol-dependent adults. A weird and wonderful read, encompassing drug-induced visions, talking ghosts and even the end of the world as we know it. Basically, and brilliantly, Coupland is telling us to take a long hard look at the way we live our lives, and to do something about it before it's too late.

**Malachy Doyle**

# GIRLS IN LOVE Jacqueline Wilson

This series of books is about three teenage girls who are going through the usual teenage problems. It's full of jealousy, tears, boys and family difficulties. The main character, Ellie, thinks she's fat and boring and is very insecure. Her two best friends are Magda (who is gorgeous and totally boy-mad) and Nadine (who is very cool and striking, though sometimes blunt and rude).

Jacqueline Wilson's books are light and gripping, and I felt I had a real connection with the characters. I would recommend this book to anyone who wants an easy, enjoyable read.

**Rachel Shaw (aged 13)**

### Next?

*Girls Under Pressure*, *Girls Out Late* and *Girls in Tears* continue the series.

Louise Rennison's books are funny and familiar: try *Angus, Thongs and Full-frontal Snogging* (UTBG 22) for starters.

For more friends, families and the tribulations of life in general, read Cathy Hopkins' hilarious **Mates, Dates...** series (UTBG 238).

# GIRLS LIKE YOU: ALEX

## Kate Petty

As the summer holidays get nearer, Holly has the bright idea that each of her friends should throw themselves into a holiday romance and report back at the end of the summer. While the others are excited at the prospect, it's bad news for Alex, a freckly tomboy with four brothers whose track record with boys leaves a lot to be desired. Absolutely certain she'll be the one who doesn't find her summer love, she'd reckoned without the sweet and impossibly nice Paddy...

Crammed with all the problems that matter most – stubborn parents, self-doubt, first love and best-girl friendships – and peopled with characters so lifelike they could be your friends, this is definitely one of those must-reads which will spend more time off the shelf than on it. Just as well it's part of a series.

**Eileen Armstrong**

### Next?

*Summer Heat* brings together four of the **Girls Like You** stories: *Hannah*, *Charlotte*, *Sophie* and *Maddy*.

*The Sisterhood of the Travelling Pants* (UTBG 341) by Ann Brashares and its sequels give the same story idea an American slant.

Other great series about a group of girls include Rosie Rushton's *The Girls* and the **Letters to**... series by Mary Hooper.

# GO AND COME BACK  Joan Abelove

14+

I know this book inside out – that's how many times I've read it. *Go and Come Back* changed me forever.

Alicia is on the brink of marriage when two white women, anthropologists, arrive in her Peruvian village for a year's stay. To Alicia and the others in Poincushmana, the tall blond woman is ugly and the short fat one beautiful. They're not even related to each other. They're friends, a word that doesn't exist in Isabo. The anthropologists ask a million questions and they're incredibly stingy.

Months pass. Alicia adopts a *nawa* (outsider) baby. The rains come and go. Army recruiters come and young men flee. The two white women learn the values of the village. You will, too. You'll see yourself and your life in a new way – and dental floss will never seem the same again!

**Gail Carson Levine**

### Next?

*Shabanu* by Suzanne Fisher Staples is also about a girl on the brink of marriage, this time in the Pakistan desert.

*The Moorchild* by Eloise McGraw is fantasy, but it's also another look at our world with fresh eyes, the eyes of a half-fairy inserted into a human family.

For more outsiders trying to understand an alien culture, read Robert Swindells' *Ruby Tanya* (UTBG 315) or Elizabeth Laird's *Kiss the Dust* (UTBG 209).

# GO ASK ALICE  Anonymous

16+

### Next?

*Streetkid in the City* by Delphine Jamet is another strikingly fresh, real-life account of a tough teenage life.

As is *Junk* (UTBG 202) by Melvin Burgess.

*Come Clean* (UTBG 81) is the story of a girl who tries to use alcohol as a way of escaping her troubles.

Read our feature, 'Off the Rails', on pp. 200–201 for more ideas.

What happens when you're so desperate for acceptance that you'll do just about anything to get it?

This is the real diary of a 15-year-old girl whose name is never revealed. She feels like the odd one out in her well-off, over-achieving family; she's snubbed by the boy she adores; she has problems with her looks, and with the new school that she attends when she moves house. Then a spiked drink at a party changes her life; she plunges into the local drug scene, eventually running away from home and ending up in a psychiatric ward.

Though sad and scary, her story is so painfully honest, vivid and touching that it's hard to put down.

**Catherine Jinks**

# THE GO-BETWEEN L.P. Hartley

**Next?**

*Atonement* (UTBG 31) and *The Remains of the Day* by Kazuo Ishiguro are totally different books, but they do deal with similar subject matter – lost innocence.

Michael Frayn's *Spies* is set during the war and is about two boys convinced one of their mothers is a spy.

Or another L.P. Hartley? Try *The Shrimp and the Anemone*.

What a shame *The Go-Between* is an exam set text! I'm sure it's put some people off, thinking it's somehow 'brainy'. Well, it isn't – but it *is* atmospheric, nostalgic and beautifully written. This tale of class, lust, lies – oh, and cricket – binds you in and doesn't let you go. Set in a country house during the hottest summer on record, at the turn of the last century when men were gentlemen and nothing was ever the lady's fault, it's stuffed full of mystical symbolism (the zodiac, mythology, magic spells) and references to the ever-rising temperature that combine to make you just know something terrible is going to take place…

What does happen is the losing of childhood innocence in a way that affects Leo, the narrator, for the rest of his life. Poignant and ultra-descriptive, this book also happens to contain one of the most famous opening lines in English fiction: 'The past is a foreign country: they do things differently there…'

**Catherine Robinson**

# GOING FOR STONE Philip Gross

Nick runs away after his stepdad hits him. With no money, he lives in squats, sleeping when he can and trying to survive. Then he finds out about the living statues – people who stand in busy streets pretending to be made of stone or metal. Nick tries it himself and finds he's good. Very good. But someone is watching him…

Recruited into a school for statues, Nick meets the brilliant Antonin and the money-man, Dominic, who chooses the best students and sets them up for life. That's the promise. The reality might be something else…

Sharp, unsettling, utterly convincing, this book kept me awake until I'd got to the end. Philip Gross is a genius, creating real characters and a nail-bitingly taut story that'll have you gasping for breath.

**Leonie Flynn**

**Next?**

Another, but very different, Philip Gross; try *The Lastling* (UTBG 215), set in the remote reaches of Tibet.

Another book about the problems of striving for perfection is *Disconnected* (UTBG 103).

Or for something else about fitting in, try *The Passion Flowers* by Nicola Morgan.

# GOLDKEEPER

## Sally Prue

I'm not keen on the title of this book, but don't let that put you off, as the story itself is excellent: very funny indeed and packed with bizarre twists and turns. It spins the yarn of Sebastian, a surprise candidate for the job of high priest's apprentice in the temple of Ora, and his pet rat, Gerald. Not everyone is pleased by Sebastian's apparent good fortune, particularly a certain Mr Meeno (a gangster) and his nephew Horace (who was quite expecting to be chosen himself). The tale darkens as Sebastian and Gerald survive several nasty – and rather unusual – accidents. Is there a plot to get rid of them? Well, of course there is, but that's only the start of their problems…

**Chris d'Lacey**

## Next?

There are not enough really funny books around, but another to try is Alan Temperley's *Harry and the Wrinklies* and *Harry and the Treasure of Eddie Carver*.

If you like this book you'll almost certainly enjoy Jonathan Stroud's *The Amulet of Samarkand* (UTBG 21).

For fast-paced adventure try Eoin Colfer's *Artemis Fowl* (UTBG 29) and its sequels.

For a magical story with an interesting twist on demons, try Sally Prue's first book, *Cold Tom*.

## The Ultimate Teen Readers' Poll

### CHARACTER YOU'D MOST LIKE TO BE

1  **Alex Rider (Alex Rider series)**

2  **Tracy Beaker (The Story of Tracy Beaker)**

3  **Hermione Granger (Harry Potter series)**

4  **Harry Potter**

5  **Mia Thermopolis (The Princess Diaries series)**

6  **Darren Shan (The Saga of Darren Shan)**

7  **Artemis Fowl**

8  **Violet Baudelaire (A Series of Unfortunate Events)**

9  **Legolas (The Lord of the Rings trilogy)**

10 **Ron Weasley (Harry Potter series)**

# GONE WITH THE WIND Margaret Mitchell

**14+**

At the beginning of this book, the heroine Scarlett O'Hara is 16. She is a wilful, flirtatious southern belle from a wealthy Irish-American family. But it is 1861 and Scarlett and her family are soon plunged into the violence and chaos of the American Civil War.

In five years Scarlett loses everything: her home, her family and two husbands. She eventually marries the dashing captain Rhett Butler, a man as passionate and determined as she is. Her troubles have barely begun.

Scarlett does much to invite the reader's disapproval, but her indomitable spirit, her refusal to accept defeat in hopeless situations wins our admiration, and we crave her survival. The book is 1,000 pages long but the protagonists are so lively, and the story so rich in events, it is hard to put down.

**Jenny Nimmo**

### Next?

If you are interested in books set in the American Civil War, *Cold Mountain* by Charles Frazier is a beautifully written novel about a soldier's desperate and dangerous journey home to the woman he loves.

Stephen Crane's *The Red Badge of Courage* vividly depicts the emotions and experiences of a young soldier during the Civil War.

For another romance on an epic scale, try *Katherine* (UTBG 204) by Anya Seton.

# GOOD OMENS

**14+**

## Terry Pratchett and Neil Gaiman

### Next?

If you haven't read Terry Pratchett's **Discworld** series (UTBG 103) then do so at once.

Neil Gaiman's *Neverwhere*, or try the eerie *The Wolves in the Walls* (UTBG 417), a picture book that will make you shiver.

*Good Omens* is parodying *Just William* (UTBG 204); try it and see how.

Terry Pratchett's **Discworld** novels are fabulous. I didn't think he could get any better. Then he got together with Neil Gaiman, the incredibly dark writer of **The Sandman** comics, and the result was *Good Omens*. This book starts out much like the **William** books: small boy playing with his dog in a rural setting. Then it turns out that the little boy is the Antichrist, his dog is the hound of hell and Armageddon is approaching. The story also features a reliable prophet, an angel, a demon, the four horsemen of the apocalypse and the explanation of the satanic origins of the M25 motorway. It's undoubtedly the best book ever written.

**Anthony Reuben**

# GOODBYE TO ALL THAT Robert Graves

14+

## Next?

Siegfried Sassoon also wrote a personal account of the war – *Memoirs of an Infantry Officer* (UTBG 241).

For a fictional, but nearly contemporary, story describing the final breakthrough, try John Buchan's *Mr Standfast*.

*Regeneration* (UTBG 309) by Pat Barker is a novel, but with many real people as characters.

And, of course, the work of the war poets themselves, collected in *Anthem for Doomed Youth* (UTBG 25).

This autobiography covers the first 33 years of poet and author Robert Graves' extraordinary life. He joins the army when he leaves school in 1914 and, for me, this is the best account of the trenches we have. The book, with its matter-of-fact and darkly humorous tone (it is often very funny), reminds me of the old men's stories I heard as a child of something that sounded just like hell. Robert Graves is the most independent-minded of soldiers, and his is an honest, though very personal, story that gives us a glimpse of Siegfried Sassoon, T.E. Lawrence (of Arabia) and Wilfred Owen.

There are lots of World War I novels about the unfairness and butchery of the trenches. Read this wonderful real-life book about a young man determined to be a good soldier, whilst refusing to accept anyone's principles but his own.

**Sally Prue**

# THE GOOSE GIRL Shannon Hale

12+

Anidora-Kiladra Talianna Isilee, Crown Princess of Kilindree, spent the first years of her life listening to her aunt's incredible stories and learning the language of the birds. She feels a failure as a princess: only her father and her horse Falada accept her as she is. Her only friend is her maid … or so she thinks.

When her father dies, Ani inherits the throne, and has to marry the prince of the neighbouring country in order to avoid a war. The plot twists and Ani becomes a goose girl. Falada plays a memorable role as Ani learns to understand herself before she can overcome her enemies. The book is a beautifully written tale of magic, excitement and courage.

**Brenda Marshall**

## Next?

*Grimm's Fairy Tales* by the Brothers Grimm has an earlier version of 'The Goose Girl'.

*Beauty* by Robin McKinley (UTBG 35) is a retelling of the story of 'Beauty and the Beast'.

*The Picture of Dorian Gray* (UTBG 287) is a modern classic tale which will intrigue you and set you thinking about both appearances and consequences.

153

# The GORMENGHAST trilogy   Mervyn Peake

14+

The TV version of **Gormenghast** made me wonder why I'd so loved this book when I first read it. Then I realised TV had bypassed romance in favour of the grotesque.

Titus Groan, with his lilac eyes, heir to a dust-clogged palace, vast but claustrophobic as a tomb – clambers his way out of it through the best piece of world-creation in all literature, to discover a whole other world, sunlit and vibrant. The characters are monstrous but riveting. The rites and rituals that rule palace life are as spectacularly zany as anything in Kafka. To break out of Gormenghast is to escape everything fusty, ancient, suffocating, dull, sterile and pointless… It's about being a teenage rebel, I suppose (though it never occurred to me then).

The trilogy grows stranger as it goes along. Mervyn Peake was a sick man, getting progressively more ill as he completed this *massive* masterpiece. By the time I reached *Titus Alone*, it was all getting a little too strange… But see what you think.

**Geraldine McCaughrean**

## Next?

World-building as complete as this is rare, as is the extraordinary depth of Peake's Gothic imagination. But do try Tolkien (UTBG 172, 224) and see if you agree with Melvin's estimation of his and Peake's respective talents.

Try the strange and eerie creations in *The Illustrated Man* by Ray Bradbury.

T.H. White had his own amazing vision, this time of an Arthurian Britain – read about it in *The Once and Future King* (UTBG 270).

There are an awful lot of fantasy novels out there; maybe you could try something like *Lord Foul's Bane* by Stephen Donaldson.

Or *Neverwhere* by Neil Gaiman.

And see our fantasy feature on pp. 38–39.

Or just go back and reread Lewis Carroll's *Alice's Adventures in Wonderland* – you'll be surprised just how weird it is…

---

When I first read **Gormenghast** by Mervyn Peake I had never come across anything like it in my life. Over 30 years later, I still haven't. How to describe it? It's fantasy in one sense, set in an imaginary time, in the endless, winding castle of Gormenghast and its numberless towers, rooms and passages and uncountable rooms and halls. But you search in vain for wizards and soldiers here. The characters are all unique – bizarre and distorted in one way, but incredibly real and human in others. They have more life in their little fingers than in all Tolkien's hordes.

The prose is gothic and perfect, every sentence ending on exactly the right note. It's a unique invention.

**Melvin Burgess**

# THE GREAT BLUE YONDER  Alex Shearer

## Next?

You may also like Alex Shearer's other books; each one is very different and they are all about unusual people and events. My favourite is *The Speed of the Dark* (UTBG 349).

*Vicky Angel* by Jacqueline Wilson is another intriguing exploration of what might happen after a best friend dies – and a nice easy read.

Or *Elsewhere* (UTBG 114), another book about death, or rather life after death. Thought-provoking, original and beautifully written.

'You sometimes imagine it … being dead and how everyone will be so upset.' But when Harry dies – killed by a lorry – it's harder than he'd imagined. He's desperate to un-say his parting words to his sister: 'You'll be sorry when I'm dead'. Also to say goodbye to his friends, who aren't missing him as he'd envisaged. And someone called Bob Anderson has taken over his life! Slowly, he realises everyone has a different way of accepting his going – and that his arch-enemy Jelly Donkins actually liked him!

In turns funny, sad and hugely thought-provoking, this book about being dead makes you think about how to live better – and reveals where ghosts go in the afternoons!

**Helen Simmons**

# THE GREAT DIVORCE  C.S. Lewis

This book is about a group of people on a coach outing from Hell, visiting Heaven. Most of them, once they've arrived, can't wait to get back.

If you've read C.S. Lewis' **Narnia** books, you've probably realised that the stories were his way of talking about Christianity. This book is a more grown-up version of some of the beliefs he explored there. I read it first when I was 14, have read it a dozen times since, and find something new in it every time. It is seriously clever stuff – and a good story as well – though the language he uses is from the middle of the last century and not always easy.

**Andrew Norriss**

## Next?

You might enjoy *The Screwtape Letters* (UTBG 322), also by C.S. Lewis – advice on temptation from a senior devil to a junior.

And if you're in the mood to ponder the meaning of life, then *Sophie's World* (UTBG 348) is a neat guide to the theories the Big Brains have come up with.

Philip Pullman is an outspoken critic of C.S. Lewis, but you'll find Pullman's rich and allegorical **His Dark Materials** trilogy (UTBG 170) an interesting and satisfying counterpoint to Lewis' work.

# GREAT EXPECTATIONS Charles Dickens

14+

Pip starts off in life as a humble country boy. As we follow him through the years, we encounter escaped convicts, spooky graveyards, unrequited love, and of course the unforgettable Miss Havisham, languishing in her eerie, dust-filled house, still in her bridal gown from years before.

Reading Dickens is like watching the performance of a play given just for you. This was one of the first 'grown-up' books that ever made me cry and laugh out loud too. It frightened and delighted me. It made me realise that those were the things that good books did. It did all the things that Dickens, the consummate actor, the writer with boundless energy and more feelings sometimes than even his enormous heart could contain, loved to do and does better than anyone else.

P.S. Make sure you read the 'Cancelled Conclusion', the alternative ending Dickens discarded, and make up your own mind whether he was right.

**Michael Cronin**

### Next?

A prolonged diet of Dickens can be a little bit rich, so have a break before you start your next meal, and then you might try the wonderful *Nicholas Nickleby*.

*The Moonstone* (UTBG 250), by Dickens' contemporary Wilkie Collins, is a mystery involving a missing jewel and a cast of thousands.

*Jack Maggs* by Peter Carey is the oddly familiar story of a convict returning from Australia to seek justice – and on the way he runs into a certain Mr Charles Dickens.

# THE GREAT GATSBY F. Scott Fitzgerald

14+

### Next?

More American literature – Salinger's *For Esmé – with Love and Squalor* (UTBG 134) or Hemingway's *A Moveable Feast* (UTBG 252).

Also Truman Capote's *Breakfast at Tiffany's* (UTBG 55). Not the same period but something about the yearning strikes the same chords.

A compact but engrossing read, *The Great Gatsby* propels you into a world of fast cars, fancy cocktails and the cool of 1920s America. Through the narrator, Nick Carraway, we meet an array of characters who epitomise the glamour, opulence and wealth of the Jazz Age. Everything revolves around Jay Gatsby and his legendary parties in rich and trendy West Egg. However, Gatsby soon discovers that he can't have it all when he falls in love with Nick's cousin Daisy who, despite her feelings, remains with her adulterous husband Tom.

Fitzgerald immerses us in life in the fast lane, but the pace inevitably burns out and the decadence descends into a gripping and tragic climax…

**Melanie Palmer**

# THE GREAT RAILWAY BAZAAR
## Paul Theroux

Paul Theroux is the doyen of modern travel writing and to my mind this is his best book. A railway odyssey from London's Victoria station to the Trans-Siberian Express, with a cornucopia of journeys in between, including The Mandalay Express from Rangoon, a local Burmese train to Naung-Peng and, in Vietnam during the war, a rattling ride from Saigon to Bien Hoa. Purposeless travel for fun and adventure by a writer with a gift for luminous prose, as well as an eye for the telling detail and a robust sense of humour (not to mention irony). There is acerbic social comment, and plenty of serious stuff there, too.
**Sara Wheeler**

> ### Next?
>
> Move on to Theroux's *The Old Patagonian Express*.
>
> Jenny Diski writes wry and well-observed travelogues that often end up being as much about her as the country she's in. Try *Skating to Antarctica*.
>
> Bill Bryson writes very, very funny books about his travels; the best is definitely the fabulous one about Britain – *Notes from a Small Island* (UTBG 266)

---

# THE GREENGAGE SUMMER
## Rumer Godden

> ### Next?
>
> Read *Le Grand Meaulnes* (UTBG 216) by Alain-Fournier, a fabulous story of coming of age.
>
> Another Rumer Godden? Try the intense novel of suppressed passion, *Black Narcissus*, set in India.
>
> Or for another novel of sexual awakening, try L.P. Hartley's *The Go-Between* (UTBG 150).
>
> And don't miss our feature on books about coming of age on pp. 296–297.

Don't attempt to grow up without reading this book; it has old-fashioned charm, it has the delicious romance of summer and first, unsuitable love, the struggle to cast off the shackles of family and the toppling, incredible sense of being able to follow your instincts even though they are confusing. Set in lush champagne country, the landscape echoes the action as summer shifts from dappled beauty into over-ripe stifling intensity and the children and adults inhabiting Les Oillets break boundaries and grow and change. It is a rites-of-passage novel every bit as lyrical as *Le Grand Meaulnes*.
**Raffaella Barker**

# GULF Robert Westall

**Next?**

More Robert Westall? Try *The Machine-Gunners* (UTBG 229) or *Blitzcat* for very different looks at war.

Other wars? Try the American Civil War, in *The Red Badge of Courage* by Stephen Crane.

Or the Peninsular War in Bernard Cornwell's *Sharpe's Rifles*.

12+

War is a central theme of many of Westall's novels, including the classic *The Machine-Gunners*. In *Gulf*, however, he moves away from World War II, which forms the background of much of his fiction, and chooses a more contemporary conflict. He sets his story against the background of the first Gulf War in the early 1990s. Twelve-year-old Figgis is somehow linked to Latif, a boy caught up in the horror. Figgis' older brother Tom is forced to witness his younger brother's torment as he empathises with Latif's experiences. The whole family is touched by Figgis' troubles and Westall explores family relationships with a sure touch.

Great fiction has the ability to make us see through somebody else's eyes, walk in somebody else's shoes, feel the rhythms of somebody else's life and, in *Gulf*, Westall has produced a great piece of fiction.

**Alan Gibbons**

# GULLIVER Martin Jenkins and Chris Riddell

12+

Why am I recommending that you read a picture-book retelling of a long 18th-century novel? In part because of the genius of the original, Jonathan Swift's brilliant satire *Gulliver's Travels*. Martin Jenkins's retelling loses a lot of the edge and detail of Swift's novel, but the story and the inventiveness and the satire are still there.

But it's mainly for the pictures. Few people can do the things Chris Riddell can with a picture – he's part of a great tradition of English cartoonists who have a great eye for character and a wonderfully precise way with a pen that captures these figures – absurd and pompous or spiky and nasty – with great wit and imagination. The perfect illustrator for Swift, in fact. And of all his work, Riddell's *Gulliver* pictures are my favourites, feeding off Swift's ideas to produce a catalogue of figures that expose all our human follies and frailties for what they are.

**Daniel Hahn**

**Next?**

Try reading *Gulliver's Travels*. If you don't fancy the challenge of the whole book, go straight to the very readable Book IV.

More political satire? Try *Vanity Fair* (UTBG 395).

Chris Riddell collaborated with Paul Stewart on *Muddle Earth* and *Beyond the Deepwoods* (UTBG 40); even if these aren't your type of book, you'll find the illustrations a delight.

# HAMLET
## William Shakespeare

The ghost of your father, the dead king, appears to you, demanding revenge for his murder by your uncle – the same uncle now wearing your father's crown and married to your mother. But is the ghost truly your father's spirit, or a devil in disguise, tempting you to commit the mortal sin? And while you try to decide this you are in danger, because your uncle is suspicious and is planning your death...

I hated Shakespeare at school. I couldn't understand the plays, and was convinced that no one really liked them. People just pretended they did, to seem intelligent. But I wasn't used to reading poetry, and one day realised that I was mentally putting a full stop at the end of each line, chopping the words up into nonsense. So I read 'To be or not to be –' while paying strict attention to the punctuation. A revelation! I was a depressed teenager, and it was as if Shakespeare had put my mood into words – 'How weary, flat, stale and unprofitable seem to me all the uses of this world'.

I read the rest of the play and loved it. The drama, humour and magnificent poetry had been there all along – I'd just been blind to them. Give Bill a chance. He really did write the most amazing stuff.

**Susan Price**

'It has everything – intrigue, romance, politics, violence, revenge, jealousy, wit. It plays itself out on such a grand scale'
KENNETH BRANAGH

*William* SHAKESPEARE

### Next?

More Shakespeare, of course. *Romeo and Juliet* and *A Midsummer Night's Dream* are old favourites. And though it seems odd for us to tell you that you should not read, if you get the chance you really ought to try and see these plays too.

Or if you find reading plays hard, have you read his beautiful *Sonnets*?

Shakespeare is a character in Susan Cooper's *King of Shadows*.

*Dating Hamlet* by Lisa Fiedler tells the story from Ophelia's point of view.

# THE HANDMAID'S TALE
## Margaret Atwood

**Next?**

If you like Margaret Atwood's style, look for her science fiction tale, *Oryx and Crake* or *Cat's Eye* (UTBG 67), her classic of childhood and memory.

Another good mix of science fiction and feminism? Read Ursula Le Guin's *The Dispossessed* and *The Left Hand of Darkness* (UTBG 217).

In some ways this book is really science fiction, but you'll find no spaceships or laser guns here. The story opens in a high-school gymnasium, converted into a dormitory and patrolled by 'aunts' armed with electric cattle prods. It is a frightening near-future scenario, where men have taken away women's independence by the simple method of cutting off their access to money.

The handmaid of the title is a young woman named Offred ('Of Fred'), whose job it is to have babies for Fred's infertile wife. She has no choice in this, because much of the population is infertile following a nuclear disaster. Right from the start we know this is going to be a sinister tale, and it becomes more chilling with every page.

**Katherine Roberts**

# HANGOVER SQUARE  Patrick Hamilton

This has to be one of the most grimly funny books of all time – grim because of Hamilton's evocation of a dark, seedy, miserably anxious London just before the outbreak of World War II. George Harvey Bone is totally caught up in his volatile, ever-changing world, but things get infinitely worse when he pursues the thoroughly awful (but attractive) Netta. Watching Bone slide further and further into dissolute decay makes for compelling reading (and offers a useful warning!). There's not much to enjoy in the milieu of Hamilton's novel, and yet we do care deeply about Bone and his plight in this gripping (sometimes melodramatic) book, published 60 years ago but not forgotten.

**Jon Appleton**

**Next?**

If you enjoyed this, look out for Hamilton's novel sequence, published under the title *Twenty Thousand Streets Under the Sky*.

Irvine Welsh's *Trainspotting* (UTBG 379) could be considered a modern-day version of this book.

William Boyd's *A Good Man in Africa* is another comedy – lighter in tone – about a young man finding himself increasingly adrift in circumstances not entirely of his making.

# HAPPY Keith Gray

Just how much do you want to be a rock star? That's what Will, Danny, Ian and Gavin (a.k.a. 'Happy', the fledgling band of the title) have to discover. And where do their respective loyalties lie, and to whom? Parents, girlfriends, each other? What are they prepared to give up to chase a dream? And can the dream ever become a living, breathing reality?

Told through the eyes of singer / songwriter Will, and lead guitarist Danny, this is a neat, pacy tale about the challenges and difficulties involved in balancing external priorities against internal needs, deciding what in life to keep, what to throw away, and what must be transformed beyond recognition, in order actually to be 'Happy'.

**Chris d'Lacey**

### Next?

Older teens who dream of fronting a band will relate to *Espedair Street*, an adult novel by Iain Banks.

And two of Keith Gray's other books, *Malarkey* (UTBG 234) and *Warehouse* (UTBG 399), deal brilliantly with the trials and tribulations of young-adult life.

For a girl trying to break into the music business, try Jonny Zucker's *One Girl, Two Decks...* (UTBG 272).

*Amy Peppercorn: Starry Eyed and Screaming* by John Brindley is about a girl who becomes a pop star.

# HARD CASH Kate Cann

### Next?

Kate Cann has written many highly popular teen novels – try *Footloose*, about three girls going on holiday together, and *Escape* (UTBG 117).

Another good contemporary teen read is *Carwash* (UTBG 64) by Lesley Howarth.

A series about bring very rich? Try *Gossip Girl* and its sequels by Cecily Von Ziegesar, about a group of New York friends.

Richard Steele is a hard-up art student – and his life is blighted by his lack of cash. In this very funny, highly readable contemporary novel, the author takes a look at what happens when Rich makes some serious money from getting an ad agency interested in his drawings. Suddenly the girl he's been lusting after for ages actually seems interested in him, and he enters a world of trendy adult parties, posh restaurants and designer gear. But is selling his talent the same as selling out? And is Portia, the girl of his dreams, worth the trouble it takes to get her? With her customary light touch, Kate Cann answers these questions and creates a very believable hero in Rich.

**Sherry Ashworth**

# THE HARD MAN OF THE SWINGS

## Jeanne Willis

Young Mick goes through difficult, unsettled times as he's forced to leave his mother, stepfather and beloved little brother, and move in with a father he barely knows. And life with his father's family is complicated; they variously ignore him, scold him and lust after him. So it's no surprise that Mick soon starts getting into fights, and then his troubles get worse, much worse – though I mustn't tell you how...

This story, set in post-World War II Britain, is remarkable, and the character of Mick is too – he's totally realistic, he's positive, he's tough; you'll love him, and you'll worry about him, too. Oh, and the ending of the book – the last few lines – is amazing. It'll just blow you away.

**Daniel Hahn**

> **Next?**
>
> Jeanne Willis has written two other books for older readers: *Rocket Science* and (my own favourite) *Naked Without a Hat* (UTBG 255).
>
> For another story of a boy facing troubles and surviving, somehow, read *Angela's Ashes* (UTBG 22); but this one's true.

# The HARRY POTTER series  J.K. Rowling

> **Next?**
>
> In order they are: *Harry Potter and the Philosopher's Stone*; *HP and the Chamber of Secrets*; *HP and the Prisoner of Azkaban*; *HP and the Goblet of Fire*; *HP and the Order of the Phoenix*; *HP and the Half-Blood Prince*.
>
> More wizards and a wizarding school? Try Ursula Le Guin's *A Wizard of Earthsea* (UTBG 416).
>
> For a classic school story, try Anthony Buckeridge's **Jennings** series.

We first meet Harry as a small baby; his parents are dead and the only family he's got left are his muggle (non-wizard) aunt and uncle, Petunia and Vernon Dursley. Harry has a painful upbringing; he is bullied by his cousin Dudley and forced to live in a dingy cupboard under the stairs.

During his time at Hogwarts School for Witchcraft and Wizardry, Harry develops from a young boy into an adolescent who seems to get moodier by the chapter! But he still has time to save the day, with the help of his loyal friends Ron Weasley and Hermione Granger.

J.K. Rowling has written a colourful masterpiece full of suspense, action and magic. Millions of people have read and loved these books, and I'm sure they'll continue to do so for decades!

**Olivia Armes (aged 14)**

# HATCHET   Gary Paulsen

14-year-old Brian is the sole survivor of a plane crash in the Canadian wilderness. Stranded hundreds of miles from civilisation, he must survive a harsh, unforgiving environment. All he has to help him are his wits and a small hatchet.

At first Brian makes mistake after mistake – one of them almost fatal – as he attempts to build a shelter, find food, protect himself from wild animals and make fire. Then, slowly, he learns to look after himself. As his body and mind adapt to his new life, he undergoes a profound change in outlook and attitude.

*Hatchet* is a gripping story of survival against all odds – of a teenager from the city up against nature in the raw. It is also the story of a boy coming to a new understanding of himself, his abilities and the natural world.

**Graham Gardner**

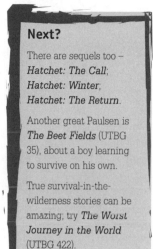

### Next?

There are sequels too – *Hatchet: The Call*; *Hatchet: Winter*; *Hatchet: The Return*.

Another great Paulsen is *The Beet Fields* (UTBG 35), about a boy learning to survive on his own.

True survival-in-the-wilderness stories can be amazing; try *The Worst Journey in the World* (UTBG 422).

---

# THE HAUNTING OF ALAIZABEL CRAY

## Chris Wooding

If you like a macabre, eerie story set in a vividly portrayed cityscape, full of action, with foulsome enemies and ghoulish creatures, then this is the book for you. Hideous things lurk within the labyrinth of the city's Old Quarter, and those who venture out at night are easy prey for the wolves and murderers that stalk the crooked streets, and for creatures far more deadly – the wych-kin. But evil disguised is the deadliest kind of all. Behind the façade of wealth and charity that surrounds the uppermost levels of society lies a terrifying pact with the wych-kin that threatens humankind's very existence. And the key to the conspiracy? The enigmatic Alaizabel Cray.

**Brenda Marshall**

### Next?

Chris Wooding writes dark and atmpospheric novels. Try *The Storm Thief* and *Poison*.

*The Spook's Apprentice* by Joseph Delaney – Thomas Ward is the seventh son of a seventh son so he can do battle with demons and spirits.

Marcus Sedgwick writes wonderfully shady, atmospheric books. Try *The Book of Dead Days*.

# THE HEART IS A LONELY HUNTER

## Carson McCullers

### Next?

More by the same author? Try the *Collected Stories of Carson McCullers*.

*Of Mice and Men* (UTBG 268) – a story of pain and friendship, also set in the Deep South.

For a different sort of cold-and-lonely, in a different America: *The Great Gatsby* (UTBG 156) by F. Scott Fitzgerald.

The Depression still grips McCullers' small town in the Deep South on the eve of World War II, with rumours of fascist activity drifting from Europe. A deaf-mute jeweller's-engraver called Singer takes the pulse of the segregated community through a year, as black and white townsfolk alike tell him their troubles. They are all lonely and desperate, but Singer is lonelier still since his one friend was incarcerated in an asylum – unsatisfactory though that friendship was, as his role of confidant only worked one way. This book is intensely sad, but rewarding for the depiction of human relationships and of people who fail to see that they already have what they need.

**Geraldine Brennan**

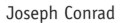

# HEART OF DARKNESS

## Joseph Conrad

Say Joseph Conrad to most people and this is the book that they will think of; between the covers of this slim novel lurks an unforgettable indictment of man.

The premise is simple: Marlowe (the narrator) is employed by a trading company to locate their most effective operative, who is living in the heart of the Congo. The journey that Marlowe undertakes, the man he finds at the end of his travels, and his dawning insight into himself, form the bulk of the narrative.

It's not an easy read, but when Frances Ford Coppola wanted to make a film about the horrors of the Vietnam War and the way in which it had corrupted good men, this was the book that he turned to.

**Laura Hutchings**

### Next?

*Lord Jim* has always been my favourite Conrad novel – not only is Marlowe again the narrator but it also shares the theme of a man discovering essential truths about himself.

If you want to know how this turn-of-the-19th-century novel could be adapted for Hollywood, read Michael Herr's book, *Dispatches*, and then watch *Apocalypse Now* to see how the two books were melded into a cinematic masterpiece.

# A HEARTBREAKING WORK OF STAGGERING GENIUS Dave Eggers

**Next?**

Dave Eggers' subsequent book, *You Shall Know Our Velocity*, is about a crazy road trip.

The original crazy road trip with a friend is Jack Kerouac's *On the Road* (UTBG 270).

*The Zigzag Kid* (UTBG 426) by David Grossman has a 13th birthday go terribly wrong, as the son of a famous detective is whisked away by his arch-enemy on a journey of discovery.

Written on pure joy and adrenaline, this autobiographical book more than lives up to its title, which pokes fun at the things reviewers write. This is all the more amazing considering its subject. The deaths of both parents leave Dave in charge of his younger brother Toph. To help them deal with their grief, he gives Toph the most anarchic education possible, struggling with the demands of suddenly becoming a single teenage parent while also trying to run a magazine and have a love life. A rip-roaring journey into the heart of modern America, dealing with heartbreak with a swagger, this may be the funniest book you ever read. With such a humble author, how could you miss it?

**Ariel Kahn**

# THE HEAVEN SHOP Deborah Ellis

Binti is a rising star of the most popular radio soap in Malawi and loves nothing more than helping her father in the Heaven Shop, where they make coffins to 'take you more quickly to heaven'. When her father falls victim to the AIDS virus, as her mother did too, Binti is split up from her brother and the sister who finds that 'men will give you money if you are nice to them'. Refusing to give up, Binti sets out to look for her grandmother and finds a new way to fight back…

Powerful and poignant, this is an original and ultimately hopeful story that highlights the individuals caught up in a global tragedy on a massive scale. Overflowing with strength and courage and raw, raw humanity, it reveals appalling ignorance and prejudice and packs a powerful punch.

**Eileen Armstrong**

**Next?**

More Ellis? Try *The Breadwinner* (UTBG 54).

*The Garbage King* (UTBG 142) tells the story of street children on the streets of Addis Ababa; while *A Little Piece of Ground* (UTBG 219) offers an astonishing insight into the Palestinian conflict.

*No Turning Back* by Beverley Naidoo also lets the reader into the reality of life as part of a gang of street children struggling to survive, this time in South Africa.

# THE HENRY GAME  Susan Davis

In this wickedly funny trilogy, Abbie and her friend Lauren are ordinary girls living in an ordinary town… Until they find themselves haunted by three very determined ghosts.

Randy King Henry VIII is after their heads in the first book, and gorgeously snobbish poet Lord Byron is after their hearts in the third. But the second book – *Delilah and the Dark Stuff* – is my favourite. New girl at school Delilah (who claims she can cure Lauren's eczema and solve Abbie's love life into the bargain) raises the ghost of the Witchfinder General – NOT a good idea when you are a modern witch! With the sinister witchfinder after the girls' souls, this book contains some seriously spooky scenes.

**Katherine Roberts**

> **Next?**
>
> The rest of the series? After *Delilah* comes *Mad, Bad and Totally Dangerous*.
>
> Or check out the books based on the TV series *Charmed*, about a trio of modern-day witches living in San Francisco.
>
> Meg Cabot's **Mediator** series, about a girl who can see ghosts – and falls in love with one!
>
> For more fiction in the world of Henry VIII, try *The Other Boleyn Girl* (UTBG 276).

# HEROES  Robert Cormier

> **Next?**
>
> More Cormier? Try *After the First Death* (UTBG 13) and *The Chocolate War* (UTBG 75).
>
> More books about war – although World War I in this case – are *Private Peaceful* (UTBG 300) by Michael Morpurgo and *Lord of the Nutcracker Men* by Iain Lawrence.
>
> Slightly more challenging war novels are *Strange Meeting* (UTBG 358) by Susan Hill and *All Quiet on the Western Front* (UTBG 19) by Erich Maria Remarque.

Two men, both with medals for bravery, both survivors of World War II – but one comes home to Frenchtown to kill the other. Why?

Prompted by the 50th anniversary celebrations of D-Day, Cormier wrote this book to express his ideas about heroism. Larry and Francis are inextricably linked by their involvement with Nicole Renard, but guilt and the desire for revenge, rather than love, are the forces that really drive this narrative.

I've never read a Cormier novel that didn't make me think long and hard about the subject matter – and this book is no exception. Personally, I find it hard not to feel sorry for Francis, but you'll have to make up your own mind about him!

**Laura Hutchings**

# HEX  Rhiannon Lassiter

Have you ever sat in front of a computer and really, really wanted to be able to just mesh with it – to make it do exactly what you want? Well, thanks to a mutant gene, that's what Raven can do. Trouble is, the government don't approve of Hexes, and if they found her, she'd be dead – or worse, used as a lab-rat for experimentation. But Raven's clever and, with her brother, Wraith, she's hunting for their sister who's a prisoner somewhere in the city.

Set far into the future, this is totally credible sci-fi. But Raven, Wraith and the people they meet are all like you and me – just with cooler hardware and more amazing abilities!

**Leonie Flynn**

### Next?

There are two sequels – *Hex: Shadows* and *Hex: Ghosts*.

Or try a different Rhiannon Lassiter: the **Borderland** trilogy is about a group of friends who accidentally wreak havoc when they travel into a parallel universe; the second and third volumes are about their efforts to put everything right.

For more utterly real sci-fi; try Diana Wynne Jones' *The Dark Lord of Derkholm* (UTBG 94).

# HIGH FIDELITY  Nick Hornby

### Next?

More Nick Hornby? Try *About a Boy* (UTBG 11) or *Fever Pitch* (UTBG 128); or the wonderful history of his own musical passions, *31 Songs*.

Or for another tale of men refusing to grow up, try Tony Parsons' *Man and Boy* (UTBG 234).

*Doing It* (UTBG 109) by Melvin Burgess is another hard-hitting novel about male obsession – this time the sexual obsessions of teenage boys.

Or for another very funny look at young men; try *The Liar* (UTBG 218) by Stephen Fry.

A great read, this. It's about a guy who's trying to come to terms with having just been dumped by his girlfriend. When he's not thinking about sex, which he is almost constantly, he's thinking about music (he works in a second-hand record shop). It's about male obsessions and it's one of the funniest (and saddest, and truest) books I've ever read. If you're female and you want to find out why men are like they are, read it. If you're male, read it and find yourself laughing and cringing, all at the same time. It clues into the mind of just about every teenage boy I've ever known, except that our hero – and this is what makes it even funnier and even sadder – is actually 35 years old.

**Malachy Doyle**

# LOVE, SEX AND RELATIONSHIPS – where it's all at

## by Catherine Robinson

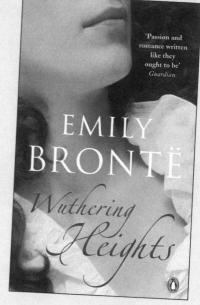

'Passion and romance written like they ought to be'
*Guardian*

EMILY BRONTË
*Wuthering Heights*

When I was growing up – when dinosaurs roamed the land – there were no books for teenagers. Strange, but true. For a keen reader, there was nothing to bridge the gap between kiddies' books and fiction for adults. Oh sure, there were books which appealed, either because of their style or subject matter or both (some of which feature in this guide) but there was nothing specifically aimed at teens, which dealt with the complex yet oh-so-common issues and concerns that make up your average teenager's life.

If ever there is a time in your life when you could do with some reassurance that you're not alone, that whatever you're currently going through, there is, amazingly enough, somebody else out there who's been through exactly the same thing, it's when you're in your teenage years. (Fiction can be hugely comforting for this, in a way that all the self-help books in the world, for all their practical worthiness, simply cannot.) And what is the one topic that, almost without exception, unites us all? That begins to grab us at that age, and continues to be a subject of huge interest and enjoyment, concern and anxiety until we are old and grey? Yup, you've guessed (although the title of this essay may well have given you a bit of a clue) – I'm talking about lurve. Sex. Relationships. Whatever you want to call it, whatever your own particular experience, it's somehow enormously soothing to read a book that strikes a chord, that makes you break off in the middle of a sentence and stare into the middle distance and nod and think: 'Yes, that's *just* how it feels.' Which is not to say, of course, that this only happens in books with this subject matter, only that it is a genre that seems to me to be particularly relevant to teenage readers.

## Doomed lovers:

*Anna Karenina* by Leo Tolstoy

*Noughts and Crosses* by Malorie Blackman

*Wuthering Heights* by Emily Brontë

*Madame Bovary* by Gustave Flaubert

**His Dark Materials** trilogy by Philip Pullman

*The Romance of Tristan and Iseult* retold by Joseph Bédier

Don't get me wrong – I don't want to make any naff claims that I write love'n'relationship books 'to help people' (if I wanted to do that I'd have become a doctor, or a teacher, or something – if only I'd had the brains!). No – the main reason I'm that most curious of beasts, a Teen Author, is because I am blessed, or possibly cursed, with almost total recall of how it felt to be growing up amidst a sea of confusion, raging hormones and adults who just didn't understand what it was like to be me, and when I began to write it just felt right to reflect some of those feelings in the kind of books I'd have grabbed off the shelves had they been around in my own teenage years.

Things have moved on a lot since then, of course – even since I started. Now, practically anything goes. I remember when Judy Blume's *Forever* (UTBG 135) first came out, to teachers' and librarians' apoplexy – it was the first teen book that dealt with the ins and outs (if you'll pardon the phrase) of sex in a realistic, wholly honest and, I have to say, ultimately unromantic way. Now the likes of Melvin Burgess have pushed the envelope just about as far as it can be pushed, and *Forever* seems pretty tame by comparison (though it's still a great read).

And good on them, I say. Why should teenagers be fobbed off with junior Mills & Boon that paints everything in a rosy glow? Let's tell it like it is, and let the readers decide! That's what I shall carry on doing, at any rate. Because, let's face it, it's all just so *fascinating*...!

MELVIN BURGESS

Doing It

*do you remember the first time?*

'Comically toe-curling ... funny, honest and touching'
Observer

# HIS DARK MATERIALS trilogy Philip Pullman 12+

Philip Pullman manages to make you believe a fantasy novel is real with his clever wit and suspenseful endings. This is a series of three stunning books (*Northern Lights*, *The Subtle Knife* and *The Amber Spyglass*), each one better than the last.

A young girl, Lyra, is drawn into a fantastic adventure when her friend Roger disappears under mysterious circumstances. She soon finds out that Mrs Coulter and her evil friends are after her, for some purpose she must discover for herself. An expedition to the North turns into a flight for her life. And now she's started there's no way of turning back…

Be warned … once you've started you won't want to be interrupted.

**Hattie Grylls (aged 12)**

### Next?

More Philip Pullman? Some of his best are the historical **Sally Lockhart** books, starting with *The Ruby in the Smoke* (UTBG 319).

*The Speed of the Dark* (UTBG 349) by Alex Shearer is an atmospheric novel about sculptures that come to life – one of them is of a polar bear.

If you're interested in the debate on religion, try C.S. Lewis' *Screwtape Letters* (UTBG 322).

Or **The Lord of the Rings** trilogy (UTBG 224) by J.R.R. Tolkien or **The Chronicles of Narnia** by C.S. Lewis for more classic fantasy.

If like me you're not a huge fan of fantasy, don't be put off reading this trilogy. Philip Pullman is one of the finest storytellers and once you've been sucked into the intriguing world of *Northern Lights* you'll not want to stop till you've read all three volumes.

Grounding his fictional world in the hauntingly familiar, Pullman weaves reality and imagination with a masterful touch. There are witches, angels, talking polar bears and other much stranger creatures. There is also Oxford and London. Canal boats and cowboys. Milton and cutting-edge science.

Since the publication of **His Dark Materials**, Pullman has famously attacked C.S. Lewis for the religious subtext of his **Narnia** stories. I, for one, read Lewis as a child and remained totally oblivious to any religious message. I have grown up to be a lying, cheating, gambler addicted to Turkish delight, a cannibal, and a devout non-believer to boot. If Lewis was out to Christianise young minds, he failed. Pullman, on the other hand, in his crusade against organised religion, stuffs his trilogy full of imaginary beings and figures from Christian mythology. Despite his intentions, I'd wager that Lyra's adventures will lead far more young readers to religion than **Narnia** ever did. Oh, the irony.

The **His Dark Materials** trilogy cannot be praised enough. Read it and marvel!

**Neil Arksey**

# THE HITCHHIKER'S GUIDE TO THE GALAXY  Douglas Adams

**12+**

Arthur Dent is an ordinary Earth bloke having a very bad day when his old mate Ford Prefect reveals he's not really an Earthling. Ford, it turns out, is a roving reporter from a distant planet, on Earth to compile an entry for a travel guide to the galaxy. But unfortunately that entry will now be redundant as the planet Earth is about to be demolished…

It's a brilliant start to a hilarious book *The Hitchhiker's Guide to the Galaxy* is a subversive and zany jaunt through space, poking fun along the way at all manner of familiar earthly institutions – science and science fiction, bureaucrats, alcohol, gadgets, geeks, jargon, philosophy and pomposity, to name but a few. The surreal universe Adams creates for his travellers is filled with the ridiculous and the absurd. The adventures of our two heroes are comic to the end.

Tragically, Adams died in his 40s; but thankfully he left us not just *The Hitchhiker's Guide…* but also the rest of the great 'trilogy of five' that it begins.

Do not leave the planet without it.

**Neil Arksey**

> ### Next?
>
> The rest of the 'trilogy', continuing with *The Restaurant at the End of the Universe*.
>
> There's nothing really like *Hitchhiker*, but try *Good Omens* (UTBG 152) in which a devil and an angel conspire to prevent the apocalypse – from London.
>
> Or anything by Philip K. Dick. Try *Do Androids Dream of Electric Sheep?* (UTBG 107).

## PHILOSOPHY 101

*The Alchemist* by Paulo Coelho

*Jonathan Livingstone Seagull* by Richard Bach

*Siddhartha* by Hermann Hesse

*The Screwtape Letters* by C.S. Lewis

*Sophie's World* by Jostein Gaarder

THE HITCHHIKER'S GUIDE TO THE GALAXY
*Douglas Adams*
The Multimillion International Bestseller

# THE HOBBIT J.R.R. Tolkien

*The Hobbit* is a prelude to **The Lord of the Rings** trilogy. Since it was written in 1937, this classic tale has delighted generations of readers throughout the world. Bilbo Baggins is a friendly hobbit who is content with his quiet life. One day he receives some strange visitors: a wizard called Gandalf and a band of dwarves. He joins them on a dangerous and exciting quest to raid the treasure hoard of Smaug the dragon. At first Bilbo is nervous and uncertain. He worries about getting back home. As the journey progresses he encounters elves, goblins and trolls and finds himself surprised by his own enthusiasm. Life will never be the same again.

**Brenda Marshall**

### Next?

**The Lord of the Rings** trilogy (UTBG 224) – Tolkien at his greatest.

Diana Wynne Jones creates worlds that seem as real as our own (and often weave in and out of ours too). Try *The Merlin Conspiracy*.

*Eragon* (UTBG 116) is another quest-with-a-dragon book.

Or try Lloyd Alexander's **Chronicles of Prydain**, starting with *The Book of Three*, and find out about Taran, the heroic pig-keeper!

# HOLE IN MY LIFE Jack Gantos

### Next?

Jack interprets his life through the books he reads. Try Jack Kerouac's *On the Road* (UTBG 270) for the road trip of a lifetime. Or *The House of the Dead* by Dostoyevsky, which tells of the author's own imprisonment.

Or try another novel that spins around drugs – *Trainspotting* (UTBG 379) by Irvine Welsh, though it's a much harder read.

Jack Gantos has also written the disturbing *Desire Lines* (UTBG 101).

Jack Gantos is a normal kid; he's lazy, bored, constantly stoned and not really sure what he wants to do, though he kind of thinks he wants to write. Which means college. Which in America means money – something he doesn't have. Then one day a guy offers him a way to make ten grand. All he has to do is help sail a boat to New York, and not care that there is over 900 kg of hash hidden in the bows. Great? No way…

Caught and sent to prison, he does time surrounded by violence, rape and misery. Somehow though he still wants to write – and that need alone is what saves him. This a true story that reads like a thriller – one full of brutality and steeped in drug culture. Read and be shocked – I promise it'll put you off smuggling for life.

**Leonie Flynn**

# HOLES   Louis Sachar

'Unmistakably powerful'
Philip Pullman, The Guardian

Stanley Yelnats IV is an 11-year-old boy wrongly accused of stealing a pair of trainers. Stanley serves his punishment at Camp Green Lake (where there is no lake), where in the unbearable heat he is made to dig holes: a five feet x five feet hole each day, starting at 4:30 every morning!

During breaks in the digging the reader is introduced to such characters as Kissin' Kate Barlow, an avenging outlaw; Madame Zeroni, a gypsy fortune teller and of course Stanley Yelnats, a palindrome in himself! It is Stanley's destiny to be the fourth generation to fall foul of Madame Zeroni's curse.

Will Stanley and his new-found friends unravel the mystery of Camp Green Lake and lift the terrible curse that has been laid upon his family?

**Benjamin Cuffin-Munday (aged 11)**

Set in America, this story starts with poor and luckless Stanley Yelnats being sent to Camp Green Lake, a correction facility for wayward boys. Upon arrival he is told his punishment will be to dig a hole five feet wide and five feet deep, every day in the scorching heat, for the next 18 months. Anything he finds must be handed over to the Warden, no questions asked. It all sounds straightforward, but is anything but.

Louis Sachar has woven the cleverest of plots around characters with fabulous names such as Armpit, Mr Sir and Kissin' Kate Barlow. In a nutshell, *Holes* is one of the best children's books I have ever read – and I've read a lot of them!

**Helena Pielichaty**

### Next?

More Sachar? *Small Steps* continues the story of Armpit and X-Ray a year after they've left Camp Green Lake.

Or try *The Boy Who Lost His Face*, about a boy bowing to peer pressure, with dramatic consequences…

Or the slim-but-great *Stanley Yelnats' Survival Guide to Camp Green Lake*.

Or the darker, sadder, *Milkweed* (UTBG 244) by Jerry Spinelli.

Or the totally charming *Millions* (UTBG 245) by Frank Cottrell Boyce, in which a lot of money comes into the hands of a boy obsessed by saints.

# HOMBRE Elmore Leonard

I've always loved reading Westerns, and this is my all-time favourite. John Russell has lived with the Apaches since he was six years old, but now he's back in the white man's world. It's an ugly world – full of prejudice, greed and exploitation – but John Russell walks through it all with pride and silence. And when things begin to go wrong, he does what has to be done.

That's what this book is all about: doing what has to be done, regardless of the consequences. It's a thrilling read – tough and uncompromising – and when you get to the end, you'll wish that you could live your life like the man they called Hombre.

**Kevin Brooks**

### Next?

*Valdez is Coming*, another great western by Elmore Leonard.

Some more fantastic Westerns (if you've never tried them, give them a go; they're better than you think!): *Shane* by Jack Schaffer; *Lonesome Dove* (UTBG 220) by Larry McMurtry and anything by J.T. Edson (check out your library!).

Or what about Elmore Leonard writing crime? Try *52 Pick-up* (UTBG 9) or any of his books at all!

# HOMECOMING Cynthia Voigt

### Next?

The story continues with *Dicey's Song*, *A Solitary Blue*, *The Runner*, *Sons from Afar* and *Seventeen Against the Dealer*.

*Johnnie's Blitz* (UTBG 197) by Bernard Ashley is the story of a wartime search for family.

*Journey to Jo'burg* by Beverley Naidoo is about two children travelling across South Africa to find their mother.

Another group of children coping without adults are those in *How I Live Now* (UTBG 179).

What would you do if your mother left you in charge of three younger siblings and just disappeared? Dicey does a great job. Having decided that the family should stay together, she avoids the police and sets off across America… When they discover that they have a grandmother in Maryland, they wonder whether maybe she will give them a home. Full of hope they set off to find her. Will their Gran take them in?

A wonderful picture of a family and the rich, complex web of American society, full of interesting and sympathetic characters and a really exciting plot. Dicey, James, Maybeth and Will make terrific travelling companions.

**Ann Jungman**

# HOOT  Carl Hiaasen

12+

This is a conservation story with a difference. It carries a powerful eco-message, but it's hilariously funny too and packed with quirky characters and crazy situations. Roy Eberhardt has recently moved to Florida; he's bright, resourceful and used to being the new kid in town. Roy soon makes friends with Mullet Fingers – a boy who lives on the fringes of society – and his stepsister Beatrice, and he finds himself caught up in their campaign to save a colony of rare owls. The tiny birds live in burrows on land that's earmarked to be the site of yet another Mother Paula's All American Pancake House. The three unlikely allies take up their cause against a corrupt adult establishment, in a lively story with plenty of suspense, wit and great good humour.

**Kathryn Ross**

### Next?

More Carl Hiaasen? Try *Flush*.

If you like Hiaasen's humorous, off-beat characters, try Jonathan Kebbe's *The Bottle-top King*.

If you want to know the real story behind the fast-food industry, read *Fast Food Nation* by Eric Schlosser – it could put you off burgers for life!

Move on to an adult Hiaasen – *Tourist Season* (UTBG 377) is a good place to start.

# HOPE WAS HERE  Joan Bauer

14+

A book to touch all the emotions as the narrator, Hope, tells the story of her life – and her hopes. There's a gentle thread of humour throughout the book, centred in a sleepy Wisconsin town. 16-year-old Hope works in the local diner with her wonderful cooking aunt Addie and other great characters. She's soon caught up in the intricacies of small-town politics as she helps her sick boss campaign against the corrupt mayor standing for re-election. A joy to read as it swings between cooking, serving, eating and politics – there's a good deal of love interest too and moments of anxiety over Hope's unreliable mum.

**Wendy Cooling**

### Next?

More Bauer? Try *Squashed*, an extraordinary story of first love – and of a girl who is determined to grow the biggest pumpkin in the world. Or *Rules of the Road*, about a drive from Chicago to Texas – though it's about the rules of life, really.

Look for Joan O'Neill's books, always full of truth as well as telling strong family stories. Start with *Daisy Chain War*, the first of a quartet of books that follow the life of an Irish family.

Meg Rosoff's *How I Live Now* (UTBG 179) is another special story of love and war, one told in a strong, distinctive voice that demands to be heard – or read.

# HORACE

12+

## Chris d'Lacey

Joel is driven to distraction by his hard-up, always-arguing family and unfathomable first-ever girlfriend. Looking for something to draw for his art project, he comes across an old teddy bear in a skip at a charity shop. But this is no ordinary bear and it gets him into more trouble than it's worth; and as Joel discovers after an antique evaluation at school, it's worth an awful lot! Is the bear the answer to all Joel's problems? Teddy bears being arrested, ice cream, broken legs, unspeakably annoying family members … seemingly random and ridiculous elements for a story, but d'Lacey weaves them all together into a hilariously funny and hugely readable tale we really believe in. It shouldn't work but it does!

**Eileen Armstrong**

### Next?

More Chris d'Lacey? Try *Falling 4 Mandy* (UTBG 123) or *Fly, Cherokee, Fly* which focuses on beating the bullies.

*Rhino Boy* by John Brindley tells the story of a school bully who wakes up one day to find a rhino horn on his head and finds out for himself how his victims feel.

Jack Gantos' **Joey Pigza** books take a hilarious look at a boy who finds it difficult to fit in at school.

Something just as funny? Try Sally Prue's *Goldkeeper* (UTBG 151).

## The Ultimate Teen Readers' Poll

# CHARACTER WHO'D BE THE BEST BOYFRIEND

1 **Harry Potter**

2 **Ron Weasley (Harry Potter series)**

3 **Russell (Girls in Love series)**

4 **Alex Rider (Alex Rider series)**

5 **Michael Moscovitz (The Princess Diaries series)**

6 **Legolas (The Lord of the Rings trilogy)**

7 **Draco Malfoy (Harry Potter series)**

8 **Ty (Heartland series)**

9 **Klaus Baudelaire (A Series of Unfortunate Events)**

10 **Biscuits (Buried Alive!)**

# THE HOURS Michael Cunningham

*The Hours* is an uplifting novel about death. Because it's about death, it's also about life – three lives. Virginia Woolf, in the 1920s, struggles against suicidal depression and writes her novel, *Mrs Dalloway*. In the 1940s, Mrs Brown, suffocated by domestic bliss, longs only for the time to read. And in the 1990s, Clarissa organises a party for Richard, who is dying of AIDS.

It's intriguing to discover the connections between the characters, and the story is fascinating. For me, though, the novel's beauty lies in the way the various protagonists discover the difference between the choices they would like to make for the sake of the people they love, and the choices they must make for themselves.

**Antonia Honeywell**

### Next?

If you liked the lyrical, poetic writing, try Michael Cunningham's *Home at the End of the World*.

If you felt sympathy for Mrs Brown, try *The Lovely Bones* (UTBG 228) or *Mrs Dalloway* itself.

If you like the way the innermost thoughts of the characters form the story, try *Hotel World* by Ali Smith.

# THE HOUSE IN NORHAM GARDENS
## Penelope Lively

### Next?

More Penelope Lively? Try *Oleander, Jacaranda: A Childhood Perceived*, about her experience of growing up in Egypt, or *A House Unlocked*, about the history of her family's house in Somerset.

Another story about one house is Daphne du Maurier's *House on the Strand*.

Penelope Lively's speciality, both in her books for adults and in those for children, is to describe how the past affects the present and how the people in the present deal with such things as memory and history. In this beautifully written and moving novel, Clare goes to live with two ageing aunts in the house of the title. The aunts are described so well that you feel you know them as intimately as Clare does, and if ever a book showed how powerful and intelligent old ladies can be, this is it.

Clare discovers an ancient woodcarving in the attic, and becomes involved with the people who made it long ago and those who brought it back to Oxford. This is a ghost story of sorts, and a wonderful addition to the literature of growing up and finding out about who you are and how your life follows on from the lives of those who came before you.

**Adèle Geras**

# THE HOUSE OF SLEEP Jonathan Coe

 16+

**Next?**

Try some more Jonathan Coe: *What a Carve Up!* and *The Rotters' Club* are particularly good, though if you like this one, try them all!

*Time for Bed* by David Baddiel is about one man's battle with insomnia.

*Life of Pi* (UTBG 218) by Yann Martel is a completely different, but equally quirky and entertaining read.

Sarah has an alarming tendency to fall asleep suddenly, with no warning, at any time of day. Terry swears that he hasn't slept at all for years, and spends his nights watching movies. And Gregory Dudden studies sleep as a science, gradually coming to see it as a disease that must be eradicated at all costs.

A group of students are all linked by their obsession with sleep, and though they drift apart when they leave college, this same obsession brings them together again a decade later.

This very odd subject for a novel results in a read which is touching, gripping, sometimes shocking and occasionally properly, laugh-out-loud funny. I became a Jonathan Coe fan from practically the first page.

**Susan Reuben**

# HOUSE OF THE SCORPION

14+

## Nancy Farmer

Opium is a country that was once Mexico – and its only crop is field upon field of white opium poppies. Matteo grows up hidden away, but some secrets cannot be kept forever, and one day the outside world comes crashing in and Matt's life changes dramatically. Whether caged as an animal or pampered as a pet, Matt finally realises that in order to survive he has to escape. But if he leaves Opium, could worse await him outside?

**Next?**

Nancy Farmer is amazing – read the very different *Sea of Trolls* (UTBG 322) next.

Another fast, gripping story, set in the future, where the hero battles for survival is *Ender's Game* (UTBG 115) by Orson Scott Card.

For something else that explores the ethics of cloning, try *Unique* (UTBG 390) by Alison Allen-Gray.

Thought-provoking, brilliantly told, with characters you feel for and situations that leave you chewing your fingers in anxiety, this book is amazing. With drug culture gone crazy, cloning and slavery, this book is extreme, full of gory detail and packed with suspense. Will Matt survive? And when he finds out what is planned for him, will he even want to?

**Leonie Flynn**

# HOUSE OF THE SPIRITS  Isabel Allende

Clara, destined to become the larger-than-life mother figure, is a sparky and spirited girl, gifted with telepathic abilities, who delights in making objects move and predicting the future. Falling mute on the mysterious death of her beautiful sister, Clara speaks again only to tell of her imminent wedding to the husband she has foreseen, the dark and brooding Esteban, once her sister's fiancé. He builds her a magnificent house which becomes home to their children, grandchildren and an assortment of colourful characters from the neighbourhood. Allende's magical realism, poetic prose and vivid pictures of a country and its people are widely acclaimed, but her real achievement here is in making the reader feel as much a part of the Trueba family as they do of their own.

**Eileen Armstrong**

### Next?

Other equally compelling stories by Allende include *City of Beasts*, an exciting adventure about 15-year-old Alexander, who joins his grandmother on a dangerous expedition deep into the heart of the Amazon rainforest. *Daughter of Fortune* has a more historic feel, charting the life of the courageous and unconventional Chilean Eliza, caught up in the gold rush to California.

Eva Ibbotson's *Journey to the River Sea* (UTBG 199) is an easier but equally riveting adventure read with a similar Amazonian flavour.

# HOW I LIVE NOW  Meg Rosoff

### Next?

*The Fire-Eaters* (UTBG 130), set during the Cuban missile crisis, similarly shows both the wonder and fear that life holds.

For a story of a real girl caught up in a real war, read Anne Frank's *The Diary of a Young Girl* (UTBG 102).

Something with (for me) the same feel (though utterly different) is *I Capture the Castle* (UTBG 183).

Teenage Daisy is sent to England to stay with her aunt, two male cousins and their little sister. The aunt goes abroad, leaving them 'home alone' on the farm. For a short while, Daisy lives in blissful limbo without adult rules, without anyone telling her she's too young for sex with cousin Edmond – a psychic bond even the war can't break. Then a bomb goes off in London. Britain is under attack. And, as the enemy closes in, Daisy and her cousins are forced to survive in a terrifying world they no longer recognise.

*How I Live Now* has a brilliant plot, it's beautifully written, and is all the more scary since 9/11.

(Damn, I wish I'd written it!)

**Jeanne Willis**

# HOW TO DISAPPEAR COMPLETELY AND NEVER BE FOUND  Sara Nickerson

A 12-year-old girl's father drowns; her mother becomes a chain-smoking, chain-sleeping recluse and won't tell the girl anything about her father's death – or even if he had wanted to die.

There's a constant atmosphere of menace in this riveting story, as the girl – Margaret – runs away to an island to investigate what happened to her father. His story becomes inextricably linked with a series of anonymous, hand-painted comic books that appear in the town library every day. And when the comic-book stories start to show Margaret herself in dire peril, she realises she has entered a far more dangerous world than she could have imagined.

Elements of the graphic novel are interspersed with this story, turning an excellent adventure yarn into something really original, and giving it a superbly spooky edge.

**Susan Reuben**

> **Next?**
>
> *Walk Two Moons* (UTBG 396) by Sharon Creech and *The Broken Bridge* by Philip Pullman are both about investigating mysteries surrounding your parents.
>
> *Child X* (UTBG 71) throws its heroine into a different type of family mystery.
>
> A starter graphic novel? Try something in the **TokyoPop** series, where you'll find something for everyone.

# HOWL'S MOVING CASTLE  Diana Wynne Jones

> **Next?**
>
> There is a sequel, *Castle in the Air*.
>
> Other books with a similar flavour are Annie Dalton's *Out of the Ordinary* and Geraldine McCaughrean's *A Pack of Lies*.
>
> Moving cities appear in Philip Reeve's dazzlingly imaginative *Mortal Engines* (UTBG 250).

Sophie is the oldest of three sisters in a world where fairy-tale conventions hold sway, and she never expects to be the one who finds fortune. So she is not really surprised when the Witch of the Waste puts her under an age spell. For most of the book Sophie becomes the aged crone of traditional stories, but it doesn't stop her being the heroine, and the only person who has any control over Wizard Howl.

It was a boy on a school visit who suggested that Wynne Jones could write a book about a moving castle, and Wynne Jones has interpreted the idea with characteristic quirkiness. The four doors of the castle each open on a different place, one of which is in Wales, where Howl becomes known as 'Howell', a local rugby player.

**Mary Hoffman**

# HUCKLEBERRY FINN Mark Twain

### Next?

*The Further Adventures of Huckleberry Finn* by Greg Matthews. Written in 1983, this sequel takes Twain's characters and uses them in a much darker Western that nevertheless manages the near-impossible task of capturing the spirit of Twain's original – one warning: it's much more adult.

For modern stories of the American West, read Annie Proulx's *Close Range*.

Or for another classic tale of the ills of slavery, Harriet Beecher Stowe's *Uncle Tom's Cabin*.

Scared that his drunken father might pursue him for the money he discovered with Tom Sawyer, Huckleberry Finn signs his fortune over to Judge Thatcher; but this doesn't stop his dad from dragging him off to an old cabin and beating him every day. Huck escapes to Jackson's Island where he meets his friend Jim, a runaway slave. Leading the townspeople to believe Jim has murdered Huck for his money, the two of them set sail on the Mississippi, beginning a series of adventures that are far more elaborate, amusing and exciting than those in *The Adventures of Tom Sawyer*. Considered one of the best sequels ever, and a great novel in every respect, this is a must-read.

**Matt Thorne**

# HUNTER'S HEART Julia Green

Fourteen-year-old Simon Piper lives on the Cornish coast with his mum and little sister. They're new to the area. Across the road from Simon lives 16-year-old Leah who decides to manipulate him for her amusement. He is to be her 'summer project'. Told from alternate points of view, Leah and Simon reveal their frustrations with life in their own unique ways. Authentic teenage angst and wild emotions rage on every page and both Leah and Simon are powerfully portrayed. This book is about many things – love, jealousy, obsession and growing up – and is in the immensely likeable 'one of those summers where everything changed' formats that make it a delight to read.

**John McLay**

### Next?

*Blue Moon* (UTBG 47) is Julia Green's earlier novel about growing up – this time from a girl's point of view.

Another rites-of-passage summer story can be found in *Carwash* (UTBG 64). Or how about Sue Mayfield's *Reckless* (UTBG 306)?

John Green's *Looking For Alaska* is a tough but absorbing look at how an American college girl dominates the lives of some of her fellow students.

For lighter relief, but similar poignancy, try *Stargirl* (UTBG 352).

# I AM DAVID   Anne Holm

12+

David is a young prisoner. He is undernourished, has very little experience with 'people' and knows nothing of the big and dangerous world outside the camp.

Late one night, the only friendly guard helps him escape. With few resources and only a little money, David goes in search of his family. He encounters many people, some friendly and some less friendly; all the while knowing that the enemy might catch up with him…

This story touched me in a way that is hard to describe. It brought me to tears at some points, both happy and sad. It's a book about one small boy's outlook on life, how he makes the most of having very little, and it's incredibly moving. Don't be surprised if you're reduced to tears while reading it too.

**David Bard (aged 12)**

## Next?

Another boy trying to find a way home is the hero of Ian Serraillier's *The Silver Sword*.

Donna Jo Napoli's *Stones in Water* is about a group of Italian boys taken captive during the war and forced into being slave labourers far away from home.

Or for a Holocaust story that'll make you weep, read Jerry Spinelli's *Milkweed* (UTBG 244).

Or try the simply told yet horrifying *The Boy in the Striped Pyjamas* (UTBG 51) by John Boyne.

# I AM THE CHEESE   Robert Cormier

14+

Robert Cormier was a brilliant American writer – I deliberately haven't read all his books, because I would hate to feel there were no more left to read. I'm not really a risk-taker but reading his books is the sort of risk-taking I can cope with: you don't know what Cormier is going to do with you and his books take you to the edge of fear and emotion. This is definitely the most powerful one I've read. It's a simple story – Adam Farmer is on a journey, on his bike, delivering a package for his father. But all is not as it seems and the truth is clever, surprising and deeply moving. And as for the ending…

**Nicola Morgan**

## Next?

Obviously, any Robert Cormier books. Try *The Chocolate War* (UTBG 75), *The Rag and Bone Shop* (UTBG 303) and *Heroes* (UTBG 166).

And try *Malarkey* (UTBG 234) by Keith Gray, about a school where nothing is quite as it should be.

*Kit's Wilderness* (UTBG 211) is eerier, and like all David Almond's books, dark and amazing. Like Cormier he takes risks – and thank goodness for us he does!

# I CAPTURE THE CASTLE  Dodie Smith

This book sparkles and bubbles like vintage champagne. Generations of readers have loved it as teenagers, and gone on loving it throughout the years. It captivates from its very first line: 'I write this sitting in the kitchen sink.' Who could resist?

Seventeen-year-old Cassandra is practising her writing skills by keeping a diary. Through her eyes – sometimes naïve, sometimes knowing – we follow the lives of her eccentric family as they struggle to survive, in genteel poverty, amidst the ruins of an ancient castle. With the arrival of two brothers from America, love with all its complications enters Cassandra's life and nothing will ever be quite the same again. We share her awakening to the joys and pains of unrequited passion, right through to the unexpected ending.

Funny, romantic, witty, charming, *I Capture the Castle* is a total delight from beginning to end.
**Jean Ure**

### Next?

*The Pursuit of Love* and *Love in a Cold Climate* (UTBG 226) by Nancy Mitford are set against the same sort of background, and are both wonderfully humorous and warm.

Or something set during World War II (but written much more recently) that captures the life of one family: **The Cazalet Chronicles**, starting with *The Light Years,* by Elizabeth Jane Howard.

---

# I KNOW WHY THE CAGED BIRD SINGS
## Maya Angelou

### Next?

Next in the series is *Gather Together in My Name*.

If you enjoyed reading about the experience of being a black American, try *The Color Purple* (UTBG 80).

For an actual account of being a slave, read *The Narrative of the Life of Frederick Douglass*.

*I Know Why the Caged Bird Sings* is the autobiography of a young black girl struggling against the brutal racial discrimination of America in the 1930s and 1940s. But it's also the story of a woman finding herself in the experiences of her childhood and celebrating the people she loves, especially her beloved older brother and her fierce-but-brilliant grandmother. Even though she's caged by segregation and injustice, Maya still sings of hope and self-respect. Cruel things happen (and at times, this isn't the easiest book to read), but she never presents herself or her family as victims. This fascinating life story is blisteringly honest but never bitter, and that's what makes it so difficult to put down.
**Antonia Honeywell**

# I, ROBOT  Isaac Asimov

This is a collection of short stories by one of the masters of sci-fi – the man who invented the idea of robots as we know them today. Originally published in 'pulp' magazines in the 1940s, most of them take the form of an 'interview' with Susan Calvin, founder of US Robotics, who is looking back over the development of robots in her lifetime and discussing the problems the manufacturers faced along the way.

Asimov had a fantastic imagination and, although the language is a tad dated, these are truly great stories. One of them was recently used as the basis for a movie of the same name. They're immensely readable and filled with that sense of what it would be like to live in a world served by intelligent machines.

**Andrew Norriss**

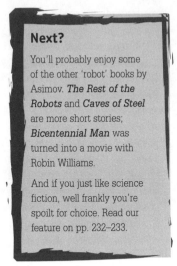

**Next?**

You'll probably enjoy some of the other 'robot' books by Asimov. *The Rest of the Robots* and *Caves of Steel* are more short stories; *Bicentennial Man* was turned into a movie with Robin Williams.

And if you just like science fiction, well frankly you're spoilt for choice. Read our feature on pp. 232–233.

# I WAS A TEENAGE WORRIER

## Ros Asquith

**Next?**

Sneak a look at Matt Whyman's *XY* and *XY100*, which present the boy facts in a stylishly packaged user's manual.

How about the fictional *Girl, 15 (Charming But Insane)* (UTBG 146) by Sue Limb?

And to find out more about the changes going on in your head, read *Blame My Brain* (UTBG 44).

Letty Chubb is a 15-year-old Bridget Jones in the making and this is her compulsively readable, cringe-makingly realistic diary crammed full of really fascinating stuff about everything from food fads to families, school to spots, clothes to contraception. No problem is left unexplored and her sound factual advice is livened up by a riot of laugh-out-loud funny illustrations.

The original and still the best of the crop of teenage diaries, it's 'speling and gramar' mistake-ridden, which adds to the fun, making it the 'ultimate teenage handbook'. It's also the heartstring-tugging and hilarious story of Letty's love for Daniel and the trials and tribulations of life in the eccentric Chubb family. Definitely one to share with your friends again and again!

**Eileen Armstrong**

# THE ICE ROAD   Jaap ter Haar

14+

If you read Nicola Morgan's feature on pp. 328–329, you'll see that she defines good historical fiction as writing that 'makes you feel the cold'. This book does just that. Boris is living in Leningrad in 1942, during that city's appalling siege in which 700,000 people died. For 150 pages you'll be there, too. You will feel cold and hungry, just as Boris does, you will despair at the death and desolation that surrounds him, and you will be entranced, utterly elated at every little sign of hope. You will fear for the health of Boris' ailing mother, delight in the company of his best friend Nadia; and when a death comes it will hit you hard. But don't be put off if it sounds grim – you'll come away from this book sober, certainly, but Boris' generosity and courage will make you stronger too, and full of admiration and hope.
**Daniel Hahn**

> **Next?**
>
> Mary Renault's *The Last of the Wine* (UTBG 213) is set around the siege of Athens during the Peloponnesian War, and is just as harrowing.
>
> Or try something else cold and Russian – *One Day in the Life of Ivan Denisovich* (UTBG 271), or Slavomir Rawicz's *The Long Walk* (UTBG 221).
>
> Another novel that shows the despair of war is Helen Dunmore's *The Siege*.

# IF ONLY THEY COULD TALK

12+

## James Herriot

> **Next?**
>
> James Herriot wrote six more books in the same series, of which the next is *It Shouldn't Happen To A Vet*.
>
> Another very funny story about animals and people is *My Family and Other Animals* (UTBG 254) by Gerald Durrell.
>
> And if you just want a pure animal story, without any humans around, you can't do better than *Watership Down* (UTBG 402).

James Herriot is a vet in the Yorkshire Dales, and this is the first collection of stories about the strange creatures (animal and human) he meets. Look out for the psychotic pig, the sliding seat, the flying chickens, the wailing labrador, the story of the lightning strike, the great pig disaster, James' wonderfully inconsistent partner Siegfried, and his younger brother Tristan. Some of the stories are of triumph, some of failure, and others are just really, really embarrassing, but all are incredibly funny. If you like animals, you'll love this book. I guarantee it.
**Benedict Jacka**

# IF YOU COME SOFTLY Jacqueline Woodson

This love story has a touch of *Romeo and Juliet* about it, and it is gentle, heart-wrenching and unforgettable. The growing love between two 15-year-olds – a black boy and a white girl – is threatened by prejudice, but never defeated by it. Ellie and Miah have a very special relationship, something apart from the rest of the world, so why can't the rest of the world see it like that? It takes an act of fate to change the story, and you will be aching for a happy ending. Although set in America, this is a universal tale that should appeal to young people everywhere.
**Wendy Cooling**

### Next?

Malorie Blackman looks at black / white relationships (with a twist) in *Noughts and Crosses* (UTBG 267).

Bali Rai's *Rani & Sukh* (UTBG 303) looks at the 'Romeo and Juliet' theme too, but this time the young lovers come from feuding Indian families.

My all-time favourite story of first love is *I Capture the Castle* (UTBG 183), a very different but equally compelling story – it was the first book that gave me some idea of what adult love was about.

# THE ILLUSTRATED MUM

## Jacqueline Wilson

### Next?

More Jacqueline Wilson? Try *The Diamond Girls* (UTBG 101), about sisters fending for themselves while Mum has a baby – and what happens when Mum and baby come home.

Anne Fine also writes about families and friends in crisis; try *The Tulip Touch* (UTBG 384).

Or for a light-hearted look at life, try Meg Cabot's *The Princess Diaries* (UTBG 299).

Two sisters, Star and Dolphin, have a mother who is romantic, tattooed and clinically crazy. From the first page, this story exudes apprehension. It subsequently moves through a series of nightmarish domestic crises to a hopeful end, though that initial apprehension is not totally dismissed. Love will continue to strengthen the two young heroines as they sustain their deeply confused 'illustrated' mum, but we know their hard times are not yet over. The story is not only concerned with eccentric events, but also with the way in which vulnerable Star and Dol move towards maturity and strength.

This story somehow manages to deal with a frightening family situation without becoming too depressing; and like anything by Jacqueline Wilson, it is compulsive reading.
**Margaret Mahy**

# THE ILIAD and THE ODYSSEY   Homer

*The Iliad*, generally thought to have been completed around 750 BC, is the story of a great war between the Greeks and the Trojans that broke out after Paris, son of King Priam of Troy, ran off with Helen, beautiful young wife of Menelaus, King of Sparta in Greece. The Greeks gathered a massive army and set sail in 'a thousand black ships' to lay siege to the city of Troy – a siege that lasted for ten full years.

It's a story full of rivalry, jealousy, heroism and love, plus a fair whack of meddling from the dear old gods.

*The Odyssey* is the story of Odysseus, one of the Greek warriors of *The Iliad*, sailing home at the conclusion of the siege of Troy. But what a time he has getting there! The journey takes him a further decade to complete because so much happens on the way. Among other diversions, Odysseus and his crew are held captive by a one-eyed giant (the Cyclops), visit the land of the dead, and battle a man-eating sea monster and a ship-swallowing whirlpool. Odysseus also falls for the odd temptress, which slows him down a bit. What happens when he eventually makes it back is worth waiting for.

These two books are not always an easy read, but once you have read them, these heroes, adversaries and adventures will stay with you for life. (I mean that in a good way.)

**Michael Lawrence**

## Next?

Homer's books are available in many translations, some in verse, some in prose. There is a really accessible modern version by Robert Fagles.

Christopher Logue's *War Music* is a segment of the story retold in modern language and verse.

In Adèle Geras' *Troy* (UTBG 382) the story of the siege is told from the point of view of the women involved.

# I'M NOT SCARED Niccolò Ammaniti

## Next?

Robert Cormier writes about the dark side of human nature; try *The Chocolate War* (UTBG 75) or *I Am the Cheese* (UTBG 182).

*Thursday's Child* (UTBG 373) by Sonya Hartnett is another claustrophobic novel.

Another exquisite book about death: Alice Sebold's *The Lovely Bones* (UTBG 228).

And read our detective stories feature on pp. 104–105.

It is the scorching summer of 1978. A hideous discovery in a ruined farmhouse deep in the Italian countryside tears nine-year-old Michele Amitrano's childhood apart in this dark, claustrophobic novel. The sense that something terrible is about to happen grips you from its opening sentence and keeps you turning the pages. (And in my case flicking them back to find the clues I'd missed first time round.)

So be warned: this story will haunt you. Guaranteed. It's a chiller, a thriller, a horror, and a heartbreaking study of the evil and cruelty that can lurk in the hearts of those you love and trust more than anyone. Oh, and like all the best stories, it's beautifully written and there is final redemption. But at what a price!

**Catherine Forde**

# I'M THE KING OF THE CASTLE
## Susan Hill

Six years after an unhappy marriage and his wife's death, Joseph Hooper advertises for a housekeeper. Into his life come Helena Kingshaw and her fatherless son, Charles. Hooper's son Edmund throws Charles a note: 'I didn't want you to come here.' The feeling is mutual.

What follows is a brilliant and disturbing story about – as Susan Hill says – 'cruelty and the power of evil … a victim and a tormentor … isolation and the lack of love'.

As the balance of power shifts to and fro between Edmund and Charles, we begin to fear the worst. The ending is brutal and terrifying. Read the novel and be afraid. Be very afraid.

**Valerie Mendes**

## Next?

Try Susan Hill's *The Woman in Black* (UTBG 420) for another terrifying read.

Or Henry James' perplexing and scary *The Turn of the Screw* (UTBG 386).

For another book about the power one young person can have over another, try Anne Fine's *The Tulip Touch* (UTBG 384).

# IN THE SHADOW OF THE ARK
## Anne Provoost

**14+**

According to the *Old Testament*, God sent a flood to wipe out mankind but spared one righteous man, Noah, and his family. Re Jana, a shipwright's daughter, forms a relationship with Ham, Noah's youngest son, and when the flood comes she is hidden aboard the Ark, where she sees the terrible story unfold as Noah tries to carry out God's instructions to the letter. What kind of a man builds a great ship, packs it with animals and leaves his fellow humans to drown? What kind of man employs a huge workforce to build it, allowing the workers to believe that they are earning a place on it before abandoning them? What kind of a god would tell them to do it?

**Jan Mark**

### Next?

Because of global warming, writers are beginning to think hard about floods. *Not the End of the World* (UTBG 263) is also about what might have happened aboard Noah's Ark, as is David Maine's *The Flood*.

Another look at the possible truths behind myths and legend are Mary Renault's novels about the Greek hero Theseus: *The King Must Die* (UTBG 208) and *The Bull from the Sea*.

*Floodland* by Marcus Sedgwick (UTBG 132) is also about a flood, but this time not Noah's!

# THE INHERITORS William Golding

**16+**

### Next?

Golding wrote many books, the best of them set in the past. *The Scorpion God* comprises three novellas that give an unusual interpretation of historic and prehistoric events. Or leap forward in time and read *The Spire*, about the building of a medieval cathedral.

*The Kin* (UTBG 207) is another novel about early humans.

This book was written 100 years after the first Neanderthal skull was discovered. Even so, little was known about these early humans and they were generally thought to be more ape than man; this was the first attempt to think of them as people. They use fire but cannot make it; they scavenge but do not hunt; they have a little speech but find it difficult to share ideas; and when the new people come with their canoes and weapons they have no way of defending themselves. From what we've learned since, the end of the Neanderthalers was probably not like this, and it is still not certain if they actually did die out as Golding hints, but it is still a moving, very human story.

**Jan Mark**

# INNOCENT BLOOD P.D. James

### Next?

P.D. James has been called the Queen of Crime – but so has Ruth Rendell! Try Ruth's *A Sight for Sore Eyes* (UTBG 338) or *A Fatal Inversion* (Ruth writing as Barbara Vine) and decide for yourself.

Another mystery in which no one is quite as they seem is Patricia Highsmith's chilling *The Talented Mr Ripley* (UTBG 364).

For more crime and mystery, turn to our detective stories feature on pp. 104–105.

With all the confidence of her new freedom as an adult and aided by a new law passed by the government, 18-year-old Philippa Palfrey sets out to find the birth mother who gave her up for adoption as a small child. She discovers that her parents were the infamous Ductons, guilty of murdering a child. Philippa confidently thinks she can rebuild a life with her mother, who is due for release from jail – she even eschews older, established relationships in preparation. But is Philippa truly equipped to operate in a murky new world – and is she truly naïve enough to think she can 'own' her mother exclusively? A brilliant thriller about innocence and guilt, from a master storyteller.

**Jon Appleton**

# THE INNOCENT'S STORY Nicky Singer

14+

The first thing that has to be said about this book is it's a brave book to have written. Our narrator Cassina has recently been killed in a suicide bombing, and her disembodied spirit hangs around in the brains of her parents and her killer, listening to their thoughts. But the book's bravery isn't just because of the subject matter – suicide bombs, religious extremism, death – but also in the narrative techniques Nicky Singer uses to tell the story. The idea of having a dead spirit floating around visiting other people's brains is hard to pull off – but in *The Innocent's Story* it's done with imagination and confidence. As a reader you'll quickly forget the device and start relishing the details of the story. And (without saying too much) the ending is extraordinary. My friends and I have had long discussions about whether it works or not – see what you think.

**Daniel Hahn**

### Next?

For more Nicky Singer, read her award-winning *Feather Boy* (UTBG 126) next.

Malorie Blackman's *Checkmate*, the third book in her **Noughts and Crosses** series (UTBG 267), is also about the makings of a suicide bomber.

The most imaginative and enchanting story of the afterlife that I've read is Gabrielle Zevin's debut novel, *Elsewhere* (UTBG 114).

# INSPECTOR MORSE books Colin Dexter

## Next?

Arthur Conan Doyle's *The Hound of the Baskervilles* (UTBG 336) – Sherlock Holmes is one of the all-time great literary detectives.

Agatha Christie's Miss Marple – try *The 4:50 from Paddington* or *The Body in the Library* (UTBG 48).

Or a wonderful story that involves solving a crime, this one set in the past – *A Gathering Light* (UTBG 142) by Jennifer Donnelly.

John Thaw's TV portrayal of Chief Inspector Morse has helped to popularise the novels of Colin Dexter. Morse is intelligent, well-read, a lover of Wagner, a swiller of ale and solver of crossword puzzles. Together with his faithful partner Sergeant Lewis, an honest egg-and-chip-loving Geordie, he unravels a succession of crimes based around Oxford. The books are well written with plenty of twists and red herrings. My favourite is *The Dead of Jericho*, in which the corpse discovered is Anne, one of Morse's ex-girlfriends. Apparently it is suicide, but Morse digs beneath the world of publishing and the bridge society in Oxford to get at the truth behind the tragedy. It is an intriguing page-turner.

**Brenda Marshall**

# INTERVIEW WITH THE VAMPIRE

## Anne Rice

In a dingy room a boy listens to a despairing vampire tell his story. While a tape spools on he hears of centuries of life, of love and passion, of the enigmatic and captivating Lestat, the beautiful vampire child Claudia, and above all of Louis, the one cursed with hating his own life and its eternal craving for blood.

Lush, compelling, horribly beautiful, this macabre, gruesome and exquisite book is steeped in the erotic, the sensual and the perverse. Though there had been vampire books before it, and there have been many since, this is the one that started a cult and made Anne Rice into the heroine of black-clad teens across the world.

**Leonie Flynn**

## Next?

The **Vampire Chronicles** continue with *The Vampire Lestat* and *The Queen of the Damned*, both of which are amazing. (The series goes on, but the later stories are not quite as good.)

Or try Holly Black's *Tithe* and *Valiant* for all-out sex, drugs and faeries.

A really different take on vampires is Joss Whedon's TV series, *Buffy the Vampire Slayer*. There are some great tie-in novels; try any of them, or those about the *Buffy* spin-off, *Angel*.

# INVENTING ELLIOT  Graham Gardner

14+

Maybe at the new school everything will be different. Nobody knows Elliot there; nobody knows anything about him – so he can be whoever he wants to be, right? Well, yes, but…

Scratch the surface and you'll see that Holminster High is really run not by the teachers but by a powerful and sinister group of older students called The Guardians. And The Guardians want Elliot. Joining them will allow him to belong, but to what exactly? The Guardians aren't a warm and friendly social club; they're cold and clever and manipulative. And they're used to getting what they want. Is Elliot strong enough to resist?

The first page will grab you, and then won't let go; Gardner keeps the momentum and tension up right to the thrilling closing sentence. It's a gripping, often-terrifying, book – a great piece of spare and powerful writing.

**Daniel Hahn**

## Next?

*Inventing Elliot* was inspired by Orwell's *Nineteen Eighty-Four*, the book from which Graham Gardner took his epigraph. So read *Nineteen Eighty-Four* (UTBG 260) next.

For another heroic individual standing up against the gang that rules his school, read Robert Cormier's classic *The Chocolate War* (UTBG 75).

# IS ANYBODY THERE?  Jean Ure

12+

## Next?

Another Jean Ure? Try *Sugar and Spice*. A new girl at school finally means that nerdy Ruth has a best friend, but what is she really like?

Another girl who is psychic and has to live with the consequences involved is *When Lightning Strikes*, the first of Meg Cabot's **Missing** series.

Or try Marcus Sedgwick's *The Foreshadowing*, in which Sasha tries to use her psychic powers to save the lives of her brothers in the trenches.

Would you like to have a mum who was a medium? That is, someone who could predict the future. Sounds fun, doesn't it? But what if you took after her and you were psychic, too? And what if your friends expected you to use your powers when you didn't want to?

Jean Ure's book starts off in the most compelling way, with the narrator Joanna telling of how she did that one thing that everyone always tells you not to do: get into a car with someone you don't know. The tension goes on from here and you won't be able to read fast enough to find out what happens. A story of friendship, of growing up and something more besides…

**Mary Hooper**

# IVANHOE  Sir Walter Scott

**14+**

## Next?

Charles Dickens' story *A Tale of Two Cities* (UTBG 364), set at the time of the French Revolution, is also about love and hatred and is just as exciting as *Ivanhoe*.

Alexandre Dumas was influenced by Sir Walter Scott; try *The Three Musketeers* (though try and forgot the films!) or the classic *The Man in the Iron Mask*.

Walter Scott wrote many books, mostly set in his native Scotland; try *The Pirate* or the wild adventure that is *Rob Roy*.

In an England torn apart by civil war, where Saxons battle Normans, Wilfred of Ivanhoe returns from the Crusades. Disinherited by his scheming father he battles for his name, his country, his life and his love, Rowena. From the deadly games of jousting, to witch trials, near death and rescue and healing by the black-eyed, beautiful Jew Rebecca, *Ivanhoe*'s story is fast, furious and compelling. And in Brian de Bois Gilbert it also has one of the best villains ever.

This is a story of hatred and conflict, of Christians, Jews, Muslims, families and kings. It is also about the healing power of compassion and the enduring strength of love. In weaving all the threads together Scott spins a tale that has become a true legend.

**Leonie Flynn**

# JAKE'S TOWER  Elizabeth Laird

**12+**

Jake can't believe that his mother won't leave her violent partner. So he constructs an imaginary tower – a place where he can escape the violence and fear pervading their home.

When things finally spin out of control, Jake and his mum wind up with a grandmother he's never known. As old resentments and bitterness froth to the surface of their lives, Jake discovers an entirely new world. It is here that previously accepted truths are shattered and his mythical father becomes a wonderful reality.

Subtle yet dramatic, it's a stark, painful novel at times, but it also stands as a beacon of hope – as powerful as Jake's tower itself.

**Jonny Zucker**

## Next?

Another Elizabeth Laird? Try *Kiss the Dust* (UTBG 209) about the trials of a Kurdish refugee family or *The Garbage King* (UTBG 142), a powerful tale about street children.

*Fat Boy Swim* (UTBG 125) has a bullied hero empowered in a way he never expected.

*Freak The Mighty* by Rodman Philbrick contains protagonists who find the strength to overcome incredible adversity.

# JAMAICA INN  Daphne du Maurier

Mary Yellen couldn't possibly have imagined the wild and twisted adventure she would embark on after she moved into Jamaica Inn. She quickly realises that it's no ordinary inn, since there are no guests staying there, and before long she starts to hear mysterious visitors who come and go in the dead of the night... Uncle Joss, a monstrous hulk and brute of a man, is not really her uncle, but rather her half-witted, terrified aunt Patience's husband. But Mary isn't scared of Uncle Joss, and is not about to leave her aunt alone in his clutches, and so she chooses to stay at the Inn. In doing so, she is swept up in all its dark secrets.

Your hair may be on end before you finish *Jamaica Inn*; if you enjoy a good suspenseful romance, this one won't disappoint you.

**Candida Gray**

### Next?

You'll find another terrific romance in Georgette Heyer's *These Old Shades* (UTBG 370).

More Daphne du Maurier? Try *My Cousin Rachel*, about love, doubt and murder.

Robert Goddard's *Set in Stone* is about grief and a mysterious old house.

# The JAMES BOND books  Ian Fleming

16+

When I was about 12, and a pupil at a boys' boarding school in Berkshire, we all read the **Saint** books avidly. The author, Leslie Charteris, was our hero and we all wanted to be just like his hero Simon Templar, the Saint himself.

But then one day a man named Ian Fleming wrote a book called *Casino Royale*, about a super-spy with a licence to kill. Almost overnight, every one of us boys dropped the **Saint** and picked up **James Bond**. The Fleming books weren't better written than the Charteris books and Bond's adventures weren't more exciting than Templar's; but they contained a treasure trove of meticulous and rather grown-up detail – Walther PPK pistols and supercharged Bentley cars, vodka martinis ('shaken, not stirred') and gambling dens and shadowy Soviet organisations which went in for really *horrible* torture. Lastly, but most importantly, Ian Fleming wrote about beautiful girls with wonderful names who did a whole lot more than just kiss the hero fleetingly on the lips. With that sort of competition, poor old Simon Templar didn't stand a chance.

**Ian Ogilvy**

### Next?

If you like James Bond, try the detailed and realistic books by Tom Clancy. Start with *Patriot Games*.

Curious about Bond's back-story? Try the brilliant *SilverFin* (UTBG 340).

For more spies but a slightly tougher read, try John le Carré's *The Spy Who Came in from the Cold* (UTBG 351).

# JANE EYRE Charlotte Brontë

 12+

## Next?

Mr Rochester's early life is imagined in *The Wide Sargasso Sea* (UTBG 413).

Charlotte's sisters wrote of love and passion too. Try *Wuthering Heights* (UTBG 424) (Emily) or *Agnes Grey* (Anne).

Mrs Gaskell knew Charlotte Brontë; her *Life of Charlotte Brontë* is a warm, fascinating study.

*Jane Eyre* caused a real stushie – a storm of protest – when it was first published. Politicians, press and churches wanted it pulped. It was too dangerous, too depressing, full of controversial 'issues' and revolutionary ideas that had no place in a novel read by impressionable young people. In fact, it was cutting-edge stuff, a roaring success with the young readership who were supposedly threatened by it.

Having survived a grim and loveless childhood, Jane ventures into the world on her own, still a teenager, and falls in love with her rich employer. But this man has a dark secret…

This story of a young character's ultimate survival in a brutal world has resonated with generation after generation – and it's still gripping stuff for readers today.

**Julie Bertagna**

# JEANNIE OF WHITE PEAK FARM

Berlie Doherty

 12+

I love this book. It tells the story of human beings in their own wide landscape of hills and sky. This same Derbyshire landscape has driven many of my own novels in the time I have lived here.

Jeannie lives on an isolated farm 'in the soft folding hills of Derbyshire… Nothing ever seemed to change there'. Yet over four years the life of each member of Jeannie's family *does* change – violently. Jeannie tells us in her truthful teenage way the stories of her gran, her sisters, her mother and brother, their triumphs and tragedies. Brooding over the family like the dark hillside is the character least willing to face change or the outside world: Jeannie's implacable father. Jeannie herself grows up during the time span of the story. She learns to recognise not only the warmth and beauty in her life, but also the cruelty and unhappiness.

**Caroline Pitcher**

## Next?

Another by Berlie Doherty? Try *Deep Secret* (UTBG 100), about the Barnes family and their secrets…

*A Parcel of Patterns* by Jill Paton Walsh is also set during the plague.

If you hanker after vivid landscape and passion, read the classic *Wuthering Heights* (UTBG 424).

# The JEEVES stories

## P.G. Wodehouse

12+

P.G. Wodehouse wrote dozens of novels and short stories about Jeeves, and they almost all have the same basic plot. Likeable upper-class twit Bertie Wooster gets himself into some sort of pickle; his efforts to put things right only make it worse, and in the end his super-capable manservant Jeeves exerts his mighty brain to save the day. But in P.G. Wodehouse's hands the formula never stales, and the fact that the world of gentleman's clubs and country-house parties he writes about is so dated that it feels like fantasy doesn't matter either. The writing is fresh and chatty, the jokes are funny and the plotting is brilliant. The short stories in particular are perfect little pieces of comic engineering, and wonderfully entertaining.

**Philip Reeve**

### Next?

P.G. Wodehouse's many **Blandings** stories are every bit as good as the **Jeeves** ones.

Or for something from the same era that is equally funny, yet also much deeper and darker, try Stella Gibbons' *Cold Comfort Farm* (UTBG 79).

Margery Allingham's detective stories also have a delightful relationship between a rich man and his butler; start with *Mystery Mile*.

# JEMIMA J  Jane Green

14+

### Next?

Other books by Jane Green you will enjoy: *Mr Maybe* and *Bookends*.

There's a whole world of must-read chic lit out there; read our feature on pp. 72–73.

*Tales of the City* (UTBG 365) and its sequels by Armistead Maupin are unputdownable, quick to read and full of characters to fall in love with.

Reading *Jemima J* is as satisfying as a Sunday afternoon on the sofa with a box of Maltesers. A deliciously compulsive read, it tells the story of Jemima Jones' transformation from overweight and lonely reporter for the *Kilburn Herald* to size 10, sought-after, glamorous feature writer and international jet-setter. This is a totally feel-good book that has you laughing, crying and falling in love along with Jemima. There are some positive messages too: about dieting, best friends, fashion and learning to love yourself. Plus some hints about surviving long-haul transatlantic flights that I have found invaluable!

**Abigail Anderson**

# JIMMY CORRIGAN, THE SMARTEST KID ON EARTH Chris Ware

 14+

**Next?**

Chris Ware has also written *Quimby the Mouse*, about a love / hate relationship between a cat and mouse.

*Jar of Fools* by Jason Lutes has a magician searching for his disappeared father.

*Postcards from No Man's Land* (UTBG 292) by Aidan Chambers interweaves the story of a boy with the shocking truth he discovers about his grandfather who fought in World War II.

If you thought that comics were just about superheroes, think again. Chris Ware is probably the greatest comic artist working today and this novel about three generations of the Corrigan family is both moving and beautiful. Two men, grandfather and grandson, both named Jimmy Corrigan, and living in Chicago a hundred years apart from each other, are abandoned by their fathers. Both lead lonely, difficult childhoods and spend their lives searching for love and family in a fumbling, sometimes tragic way. The story shuttles back and forth between them; in the past, one is abandoned as a child, while in the present, his adult grandson is contacted out of the blue by his father and makes a fateful journey to meet him.

**Ariel Kahn**

# JOHNNIE'S BLITZ Bernard Ashley

12+

Johnnie thinks he's hard enough. After running away from Approved School he heads home, only to find London torn apart by Hitler's bombing raids and everything he knew gone. Forced into going on the run again, he meets up with his cousin, Tommy, and his simple-minded child-bride Bren, who's got a baby girl who isn't her own.

Together they skip London and head for a gypsy camp. But Bren starts to hurt the baby, and Johnnie knows he has to do something. So he heads off again, trying to get the baby home.

Dark, unheroic, so real the pages almost taste of fear and distress, this is a stunning re-creation of a time too often glamorised in stories. There's no glamour here, just a cracking story and a boy who you really want to get away.

**Leonie Flynn**

**Next?**

More Bernard Ashley? Try *The Trouble With Donovan Croft* (UTBG 381), or *A Kind of Wild Justice*, about another boy on his own, trying to deal with a violent gang.

Robert Westall's *The Kingdom by the Sea* (UTBG 208) is about a boy on the run.

*Creepers* by Keith Grey is an exciting, gritty thriller about what you'll do for your friends.

# JONATHAN LIVINGSTONE SEAGULL

## Richard Bach

> ### Next?
>
> Try *Wind, Sand and Stars* by Antoine de St Exupéry, who was also an aviator.
>
> More Richard Bach? Try *Illusions*.
>
> Or Paulo Coelho's road-trip of self-discovery, *The Alchemist* (UTBG 16).
>
> Or for a novel that explores what it is to be human, Hermann Hesse's *Siddhartha* (UTBG 338).

This book was a massive bestseller on publication and has retained its iconic status. It is one of those rare, utterly simple stories that achieve the enduring quality of myth.

Dedicated to 'the real Jonathan Livingston Seagull who lives within us all', the book tells the tale of a bird who is expelled from his flock for trying to do so much more than fly. Outcast and alone, he learns that 'boredom and fear and anger are the reasons a gull's life is so short', and discovers the compassion he needs to return to the flock.

The book is enhanced by the close and detailed observations of nature and flight. Because Richard Bach was an aviator as well as an author, the aeronautical detail is exact. A powerful tale of freedom and transcendence that speaks to us all.

**Livi Michael**

# JONATHAN STRANGE AND MR NORRELL

## Susannah Clarke

Strange by name and strange by nature, this huge book looks at first glance like a historical novel, complete with old-fashioned spellings and elaborate footnotes. But start reading and you find yourself drawn into a fantasy 19th century where magic works and lost roads lead into the wild and dangerous realms of the mysterious Raven King... The complex story revolves around the rivalry between two magicians: the reclusive Mr Norris and his rebellious pupil Jonathan Strange. It has been compared to **Harry Potter** but it is far better than that; Ms Clarke's magic seems rooted in a deep love of British landscape and folklore, and her intensely visual writing make this the most fully realised imaginary world since Tolkien's.

**Philip Reeve**

> ### Next?
>
> Try Charles Dickens' vast and brilliant *Bleak House*.
>
> Something more modern? Glen David Gold's *Carter Beats the Devil* relates the rivalry between two very different magicians...
>
> Or for much more British myth and legend, introduce yourself to Merlin in *The Once and Future King* (UTBG 270).

# JOURNEY TO THE RIVER SEA

## Eva Ibbotson

This is classic storytelling! The heroine Maia has been tragically orphaned. Word comes that she has an uncle and aunt who are willing to adopt her; only snag is that they live on the Amazon in South America. But Maia is a plucky girl, always keen to see the best in everything. While her school mates fear she could be eaten by crocodiles or poisoned by snakes, she sets off with excitement at the prospect of seeing this magnificent river and all the wonderful plants and animals which live in the forest. Best of all, she looks forward to meeting her cousins – the twins, Beatrice and Gwendolyn. But when she arrives, the family aren't nearly as welcoming as she'd hoped.

Underneath the almost fairy-tale atmosphere of bad people and hapless children is the power of the human spirit to overcome adversity. And there is such a sense of fun in the brilliant way Ibbotson allows her plot to twist and turn right to the bitter, and wonderful, end.

**Jamila Gavin**

### Next?

Another Eva Ibbotson? Try *The Star of Kazan*, about an orphan girl in Vienna.

Karen Wallace's *Raspberries on the Yangtze* (UTBG 304) for a wonderful evocation of both a place and sibling rivalries / friendships.

Or Jamila's vivid story of growing up in India, *The Wheel of Surya*.

## The Ultimate Teen Readers' Poll

## CHARACTER WHO'D BE THE BEST GIRLFRIEND

1 **Hermione Granger (Harry Potter series)**

2 **Lyra (His Dark Materials trilogy)**

3 **Mia Thermopolis (The Princess Diaries series)**

4 **Sabina (Alex Rider series)**

5 **Tracy Beaker (The Story of Tracy Beaker)**

6 **Alice (Alice in Wonderland)**

7 **Lucy (The Chronicles of Narnia)**

8 **Lizzie Maguire**

9 **Eowin (The Lord of the Rings trilogy)**

10 **Pandora (Adrian Mole series)**

# OFF THE RAILS

## by Kevin Brooks

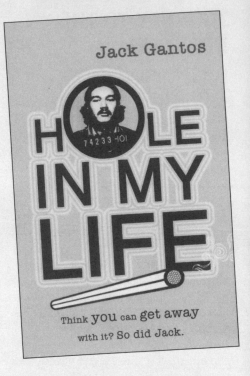

Jack Gantos

H**O**LE IN MY LIFE

Think **you** can get **away** with it? So did Jack.

The first book I read that really grabbed hold of me and took me away to another world was *The Catcher in the Rye* by J.D. Salinger. I read it when I was about 14. My English teacher just gave it to me one day and said: 'See what you think of that.' He was one of those crazy English teachers who actually encourage you to read stuff you don't have to read for school. He was also fond of throwing chairs at people, but that's by the by. Anyway, I read *The Catcher in the Rye* and I loved it, and I've never forgotten it. You can read more about this classic story on p. 66, but basically it's about a teenage boy called Holden Caulfield who goes a bit crazy and runs away from school, and then his life starts spiralling out of control. *That* was the part that really grabbed me – the spiralling-out-of-control part – and ever since then I've always been drawn to reading (and writing) books about people whose lives go off the rails.

It's not a uniquely teenage experience – there are plenty of books about adults losing control of their lives – but in the teenage world the dividing line between order and chaos is so much more fragile than in the adult world, which makes it a perfect setting for journeys into chaos and confusion. When we're growing up, everything is unsettled – our lives, our emotions, our relationships – and so it doesn't take much to step over the line and become lost in the spiral.

That's how it was for me, anyway.

In fact, that's *still* how it is for me!

Which is where the fascination comes from, I suppose. I like to read about stuff that *could* happen to me, but probably – and hopefully – won't, because it allows me to experience all the fears and the thrills and the confusion of going off the rails without actually doing it myself.

All books, of course, work on lots of different levels – which is part of what makes reading so great – and this kind of story is no different. Take *Peace Like a River* (UTBG 284) by Leif Enger, for example. Yes, it tells the story of a young boy whose life suddenly changes when his older brother kills a man and goes on the run, and, yes, it's all about that spiralling journey into an unknown world – but there's so much more to it than that. There's tragedy, poetry, mystery. There's stuff to make you think. There's beautiful language, unforgettable characters, a compulsive story… Basically, there's everything you could ever wish for in a book.

Another brilliant story about stepping over the line is *Skarrs* (UTBG 342) by Catherine Forde. Again, the book is chock-full of all sorts of other things too, but one of the central themes is how the main character, Danny, struggles with his conscience as he gets drawn into a world which he knows is wrong for him, but he finds very hard to resist. It's this kind of struggle, this inner conflict, that takes us right inside the character's mind, and once we're in there, that's when the story becomes real. We're living it. We're there. It's happening to us. Great stuff.

A final example, this time an intriguing mixture of fiction and reality, is *Hole in My Life* (UTBG 172) by Jack Gantos. This book tells the true story of what happened to the writer Jack Gantos when he was convicted of smuggling drugs as a young man. We learn about his somewhat chaotic early life, his constant struggle to find himself, and his time in prison, where he finally began to do what he'd always wanted to do – write books. It's an amazing story, and I suppose one of the most fascinating things about it is that the wonderful books that Jack Gantos now writes are often about the kind of young people whose lives are prone to tumbling out of control, just like his did.

Is that a neat ending, or what?

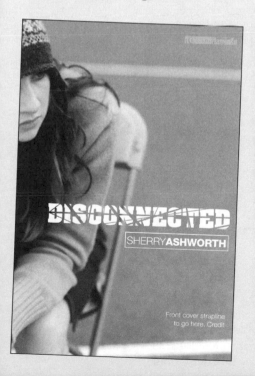

Front cover strapline to go here. Credit

## You might also like to try:

*The Chocolate War* by Robert Cormier

*Junk* by Melvin Burgess

*The Outsiders* by S.E. Hinton

*Desire Lines* by Jack Gantos

*Kerosene* by Chris Wooding

*Candy* by Kevin Brooks

*Disconnected* by Sherry Ashworth

*Trainspotting* by Irvine Welsh

*Go Ask Alice* by Anonymous

*Come Clean* by Terri Paddock

*Tough Guys Don't Dance* by Norman Mailer*

*Junky* by William Burroughs*

*probably not for the younger (or faint-hearted) reader

# JUNK  Melvin Burgess

This is the story of two young people, Gemma and Tar, who fall in love with each other, and with drugs. If you've ever wondered why anyone would be daft enough to stick a needle in their arm and inject heroin, this book will tell you. It charts the downward spiral of Gemma and Tar with a clinical, terrifying precision that lets you see the slide is easier than you'd think. This doesn't make for comfortable reading. The events are real. Many of them are highly unpleasant, and become more so as the book goes on… but by then it's too late: you like and care about the main characters so much you have to keep reading.

**Andrew Norriss**

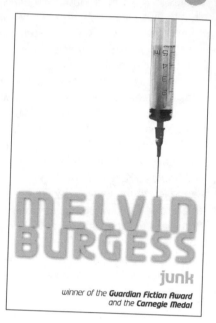

junk

*winner of the **Guardian Fiction Award** and the **Carnegie Medal***

### Next?

If you enjoy reading about tough situations, you could try *I Am the Cheese* (UTBG 182) about a boy caught up in violence and a struggle for power in his American school; or *Blue* (UTBG 47) by Sue Mayfield, in which the heroine is involved in self-harm.

If you like seeing events from different points of view, try *Dear Nobody* (UTBG 99) by Berlie Doherty, or *Caught in the Crossfire* (UTBG 68) by Alan Gibbons. Like *Junk* they're both thoughtful books about people, and not just about 'issues'.

You'll probably enjoy *Doing It* (UTBG 109), also by Melvin Burgess, which looks at sex with the same ruthless honesty.

And if gritty, real-life stories are to your taste, why not try *Stone Cold* (UTBG 355) by Robert Swindells?

Gemma and Tar run away together, escaping from their unhappy, quarrelsome families. They fall in with people who live differently, dress differently and look at the world in a different way. Their new life is exhilarating, like flying – and part of the exhilaration comes from taking drugs.

But *Junk* isn't 'a book about drugs'. It's about *people*. People so real that you're right inside their heads, sharing their excitement and fears, the lies they tell themselves and the hard lessons they learn. The questions all the characters face are: What's real? What's solid enough to last a lifetime?

Finding out takes them through painful and difficult experiences and they don't all come up with the same answers. Not a book for the squeamish, but it's a terrific read.

**Gillian Cross**

# JURASSIC PARK Michael Crichton

When I was about 12 I read *The Lost World* by Sir Arthur Conan Doyle and was entranced by an adventure in which brave men found themselves having to cope with dinosaurs. After all, though dinosaurs have a prehistoric reality, they somehow contrive to be fabulous too. *Jurassic Park* gets off to a scary beginning and is able to call on modern genetics to give a science-fiction credibility to the dinosaurs in this story, but at heart it has a lot in common with Conan Doyle's original fantasy. A park intended to display re-created dinosaurs has been scientifically contrived, but inevitably things go wrong and once again brave men have adventures as they confront prehistoric monsters.

**Margaret Mahy**

## Next?

*The Lost World* by Arthur Conan Doyle has the same premise – though was written much earlier.

Other Michael Crichtons to look out for are *The Andromeda Strain*, which is about the threat of alien bacteria capable of wiping out the human race, or *Sphere*, about a 300-year-old spaceship found on the Pacific Ocean floor.

Or for a fast-paced mystery story, try *The Da Vinci Code* (UTBG 90).

# JUST SIXTEEN Jean Ure

This book is unusual in tackling the subject of teenage pregnancy from the point of view of the young man involved, the father-to-be. It's a very successful attempt on the part of a woman writer to speak as a young man. The voice Ure adopts for Sam seems entirely natural and unforced. Sam falls in love with Priya and when Priya discovers she's pregnant, all sorts of problems, both emotional and social, come to the fore. It would be a shame to spoil readers' pleasure by giving away the ending, but the book describes the dilemmas of being in love and in difficulty most engagingly. Priya, who's only there in the dialogue and in what Sam tells us about her, is as present in the story as Sam is. The matter of her ethnic origin is dealt with honestly and without sensationalism.

This is an often funny and enjoyable book, but also one that might help many young people who face similar problems.

**Adèle Geras**

## Next?

*The Opposite of Chocolate* (UTBG 274) is about an unwanted pregnancy and the choices and problems it brings.

Another book about sex and trusting your partner is *Tin Grin* (UTBG 374).

More Jean Ure? *Is Anybody There?* (UTBG 192) is about what it's like to be psychic and *Get a Life* is about sexual confusion and friendship.

# The JUST WILLIAM series

## Richmal Crompton

12+

Has there ever been a funnier, messier, more anarchic, more exuberant, more moody, more golden-hearted, more human example of our species than William Brown? Has there ever been a more unlikely author to have created him than Richmal Crompton, genteel and sober Latin and Classics mistress at a posh London school for young ladies? Has there ever been a series of novels that gave us more fun as kids and that we're less likely to grow out of, no matter how sophisticated and worldly we become later in life?

If there has, please let me know because I've read all the **William** books about 20 times each.

*Just William* is a good one to start with, and if you like it there are 37 more.

**Morris Gleitzman**

### Next?

Richmal Crompton's William has a companion in crime on most bookcases – **Jennings** by Anthony Buckeridge.

For books that take a hilarious look at what school used to be like, read *Down with Skool!* (UTBG 110) and its sequels.

Probably the funniest boy you'll find in more recent books is Sue Townsend's **Adrian Mole** (UTBG 324).

# KATHERINE  Anya Seton

14+

This was the first historical novel I ever read, and it took me over completely, luring me into a medieval world of lust and intrigue. When I was at school, the only way you could get away with reading anything even a little bit sexy was to have it wrapped up in a historical package, and I'm sure my teachers must have thought I was more interested in the court of Edward III than Katherine's love affair with his son, Prince John, which is at the heart of the book. Having said that, this book did get me into reading about the past, and I ended up studying history at university, so perhaps the teachers knew what they were doing after all!

**Eleanor Updale**

### Next?

Many books mix historical fact with fiction. Josephine Tey wrote a book called *The Daughter of Time* about the Princes in the Tower.

*The Other Boleyn Girl* (UTBG 276) by Philippa Gregory tells the story of Anne Boleyn's sister, Mary, who was another of Henry VIII's mistresses.

And for a light touch with both humour and romance read Georgette Heyer, who wrote almost exclusively about the Georgian / Regency period. Try *These Old Shades* (UTBG 370).

# KEEPER  Mal Peet

Don't be put off this book if you don't like football – it will still captivate you. *Keeper* tells the life story of El Gato – the Cat – the world's greatest goalkeeper. During an interview with journalist Paul Faustino, El Gato reveals how he, an impoverished boy from the South American rainforest, became the iconic figure Faustino reveres. As the interview progresses, El Gato reveals how the mysterious figure he calls 'The Keeper' taught him almost everything about goalkeeping from a makeshift goalmouth in the heart of the rainforest. Peet's story is as original as it is gripping, building up tension as skilfully as any penalty shoot-out. Once you've read this book, I guarantee you will never watch a goalkeeper in the same way again.

**Helena Pielichaty**

### Next?

This was Mal Peet's first; his second, very different, novel is *Tamar* (UTBG 367).

In *Match of Death* by James Riordan, football becomes a sideline to much darker and more dangerous issues in World War II.

Eva Ibbotson's *Journey to the River Sea* (UTBG 199) is set in an unspoiled rainforest in South America.

# KEEPING THE MOON

## Sarah Dessen

### Next?

To be honest, I haven't read anything like it, but for some reason which I can't explain, these books come to mind as ones you might also enjoy: *A Gathering Light* (UTBG 142) by Jennifer Donnelly, *The Fire-Eaters* (UTBG 130) by David Almond, *Starseeker* (UTBG 352) or *Apocalypse* (UTBG 26) by Tim Bowler and *The Shell House* (UTBG 335) by Linda Newbery.

This is a book about fitting in, not fitting in, and being yourself. It's not a rip-roaring adventure, but the power is in the utterly wonderful characterisation (every single character is beautifully drawn and fascinating) and the mood. It feels like a drifty book, a summer's dream of a book, a growing-up book; poignant, gentle and lovely, but nevertheless with decent pace. I read it in America and it's very American – I love lots of American young adult fiction for its controlled intensity and bravery. This doesn't have a particularly teenage voice, because it is quiet and the characters are a little older, but I do think it speaks genuinely to teenagers. Adults will definitely enjoy eavesdropping.

**Nicola Morgan**

# A KESTREL FOR A KNAVE
## Barry Hines

**Next?**

Chris d'Lacey's *Fly, Cherokee, Fly* is about a boy finding an injured racing pigeon and trying to heal her. And there's a sequel, *Pawnee Warrior*.

Melvin Burgess is well known for hard-hitting social realism; *Kite* is less gritty than some, but is still a very real account of a boy raising a bird of prey – not a good idea when your father is a gamekeeper.

Billy Casper is about to leave school with no job skills and no prospects. His life is hard and lean and he is in trouble with everyone, particularly his dangerous older brother, Jud. But there is another side to Billy, which emerges when he is with the hawk that he has nurtured and trained.

The author is so close to his character that we engage with everything that happens to Billy – we feel his pain and humiliation and rage at the frustrations of his life, and we soar with his spirit when he flies the wild and beautiful kestrel. This is a fast, gritty novel that raises important questions about the values of modern society. It was also made into a landmark British film, *Kes*.

**Kate Thompson**

# KIDNAPPED Robert Louis Stevenson

It's the year 1751, and orphaned David Balfour has set out to claim his inheritance from his uncle Ebenezer. But his uncle has other plans, and David finds himself a prisoner on the high seas – until he befriends exiled Jacobite Alan Breck Stewart. Together they escape, but before David can wreak his revenge on Ebenezer, he and Alan are pursued across Scotland by the English, who regard Alan as a dangerous rebel.

You can't get better historical fiction than this. Alan is wonderfully believable, full of flaws, but brave and shrewd and cocky. David is the perfect foil, with his even temper and dogged good sense. The language and attitudes take you straight back in time; you'll find yourself speaking with a Scottish accent after reading this book.

A classic!

**Cathy Jinks**

**Next?**

*The Three Musketeers* and *Twenty Years After* by Alexandre Dumas, for a flawless portrayal of 18th-century action adventure.

Another adventure set in Scotland? Try John Buchan's *The Thirty-Nine Steps* (UTBG 371).

Or for more Jacobites try *The Flight of the Heron* by D.K. Broster, the first in a trilogy about the Stuart uprisings.

# KIM Rudyard Kipling

**Next?**

Kipling was a great writer of short stories, many of them set in India. Try the collections *Plain Tales from the Hills* and *Soldiers Three*.

More undercover (and underground) activities, this time in pre-war Europe, are to be found in Geoffrey Household's *Rogue Male*.

If you want to know more about spies in the Hindu Kush, read *The Great Game: on Secret Service in High Asia* by Peter Hopkirk.

*Kim* reads like a fantasy quest through a fabulous landscape of sweltering plains, snowy passes among towering mountains, roads, trains and cities teeming with people – holy men, soldiers, pilgrims, thieves, spies. But it is not a fantasy; this is 19th-century India, before Partition, and the quest is two-fold: a Buddhist lama seeking a sacred river and a youth involved in 'The Great Game' of espionage between the British Raj and the expansionist Russian Empire across the North-West Frontier. This is old-style spying, with codes, passwords, disguises and secret agents. Some aspects of Kipling can be hard to like these days but in *Kim* he celebrates every race and religion; it's a story as much about tolerance and friendship as it is about adventure.

**Jan Mark**

# THE KIN Peter Dickinson

This epic tale was originally published as four books, each told from the viewpoint of a youngster growing up in Africa at the dawn of humanity. Suth, Noli, Ko and Mana have to face bears, tigers, famine and human enemies on their long and hazardous journey towards adulthood.

The individual stories fit beautifully together, and I especially liked the invented myths between the chapters – such as 'How People Were Made' – which feel as though they have been transcribed from ancient cave walls, even though we have no written records from so long ago. Mixing myth and history with a moving and entertaining story, this is one of those books that lingers in the soul long after the final page has been turned.

**Katherine Roberts**

**Next?**

Another brilliant Peter Dickinson is the fantasy-based *The Ropemaker*.

You might like *Wolf Brother* (UTBG 417), which is set at the time of the first humans and is terrifically exciting.

If you like a bit of romance and are looking for a more adult read, you should enjoy Jean M. Auel's **Earth's Children** sequence, starting with *The Clan of the Cave Bear*.

# THE KING MUST DIE   Mary Renault

14+

Plunged headlong into the colourful world of ancient Greece, you identify so strongly with the hero that you, too, would have sacrificed yourself rather than your honour, and sailed to Crete to dance the dance of death with the bulls. Theseus comes across as a real person: a womaniser and a warrior, thoughtful though not academic, ambitious but not ruthless. When he reaches Knossos and the Labyrinth, he must take part in the dangerous rite of bull-leaping. No one survives for long – but Theseus really *is* made of kingly stuff. This is one of the most exciting books I have ever read; I reread it every few years, and enjoy it just as much each time.

**Elizabeth Kay**

### Next?

The good news is that there's a sequel: *The Bull from the Sea*.

Mary Renault wrote many other books about the ancient world, and they're all worth looking out for, particularly *The Last of the Wine* (UTBG 213) and *Fire From Heaven* (UTBG 129).

Or try some detective stories set in Ancient Rome with Stephen Saylor's **Gordianus the Finder** stories, starting with *The House of the Vestals*.

Or for rip-roaring adventure, try P.C. Wren's books about the Foreign Legion, starting with *Beau Geste* (UTBG 34).

# THE KINGDOM BY THE SEA   Robert Westall

12+

### Next?

Another Westall set in the war? *Blitzcat*. Don't let any prejudice against books with animals put you off – it's brilliant!

For a very different setting and war, try *Across the Nightingale Floor* (UTBG 12) by Lian Hearn.

Another child battling against the world is the hero of Ian Serraillier's *The Silver Sword*.

It's World War II. Harry has got used to air raids, but this one's different: when he comes out of the shelter, his home and family are gone. Grief-stricken, he decides to make a new life on his own. He starts walking, following the coastline and adopting a stray dog along the way.

Away from the death and destruction on Tyneside, he quickly meets new dangers – but also finds beauty and kindness, often in the most unlikely places. He is starting to love and trust again, when a shocking turn of events threatens his hard-won peace and he must find a way of holding onto his hopes and dreams.

Both brutal and beautiful, *The Kingdom By the Sea* is the story of a boy journeying towards independence and finding his place in a new world. I defy any reader not to cry at least once.

**Graham Gardner**

# KISS THE DUST

**12+**

## Elizabeth Laird

Tara's father is involved with the Kurdish rebels under the terrifying regime of Saddam Hussein. The family are forced to flee their home, and eventually they arrive in London as refugees. They have lost everything: their friends and neighbours, their possessions and the community who spoke their language and understood their ways. Set in the time of the first Gulf War in the 1990s, this is the book to read if you want to try and understand what life must be like for refugees and asylum-seekers in our country today.

**Yvonne Coppard**

### Next?

Elizabeth Laird also wrote *Red Sky in the Morning*, about a girl living with the prejudices surrounding her family life with a disabled brother.

*Refugee Boy* (UTBG 308) describes what it's like to be a refugee in Britain today.

*Mud City* by Deborah Ellis is about an Afghan girl's life in a Pakistan refugee camp.

# KISSING THE RAIN

**12+**

## Kevin Brooks

### Next?

If you enjoyed this, try some more Kevin Brooks – the gripping *Martyn Pig* (UTBG 236), the gentler *Lucas* (UTBG 228) or the shocking *Candy* (UTBG 62).

For another story about a boy who's bullied for being overweight, read *Fat Boy Swim* (UTBG 125) by Catherine Forde.

*Grass* by C.Z. Nightingale is the story of a girl who witnesses a racist attack, and the subsequent decisions she is forced to make.

'I shoulda kept my big mouth shut. I DIN'T SEE *NOTHING*, ALL RIGHT?'

Moo Nelson has it really tough. Bullied at school for being fat, his greatest pleasure is standing on a road bridge, staring, staring at the traffic and letting it shut him into a world of his own… Until the day he witnesses a murder from the bridge, and gets deeply involved in another, far more seedy and sinister world where he's forced to make some impossible choices.

Moo narrates his own story at breakneck speed, in a tone that's aggressive and defensive at the same time, so you can just feel what it's like to be inside his head. And it's not a comfortable place to be, I can tell you.

**Susan Reuben**

# THE KITE RIDER

12+

## Geraldine McCaughrean

### Next?

All Geraldine McCaughrean's books are great. Try *Plundering Paradise* for a brilliant, fast-paced story about pirates, or *The White Darkness* for obsession and loneliness.

Try *Lost Horizon* by James Hilton, about finding paradise hidden in the Himalayas.

*Tulku* (UTBG 385) by Peter Dickinson is an extraordinary adventure set in China and Tibet.

Haoyou's father flies up into the clouds and comes back without a soul, his heart having burst with fear 'like a sack of grain'. Now Di Chou, the man who sent his father to his death, wants to marry Haoyou's mother. While escaping from both his grasping uncle Bo and Di Chou, Haoyou is taken on by the Great Miao Je, owner of an exotic circus, and becomes a virtuoso kite rider, seeking his father's spirit in the sky. But Miao Je is on a dark quest of his own.

This is a stunning story of revenge and restoration that will keep you hooked to the final page.

**Livi Michael**

# THE KITE RUNNER

14+

## Khaled Hosseini

I couldn't put this book down once I'd started reading it. There are three things I like in a book: 1) a good story that keeps me gripped; 2) that it's well written / a pleasure to read; and 3) that it gives an insight into another way of life. This book does all three. It is about the value of friendship and family with 1970s Afghanistan as the background and starting point. It is written with such warmth and I came away feeling that I knew more about what had happened over there than I could have gained from watching a hundred in-your-face documentaries. Everyone (and I mean everyone) I have recommended this to has loved it as much as I did!

**Cathy Hopkins**

### Next?

*Memoirs of a Geisha* (UTBG 241) by Arthur Golden also gives a glimpse into another culture and time.

*My Forbidden Face* by Latifa is a searing account of life under the Taliban.

*The Bookseller of Kabul* is Asne Seierstad's story of her time living with a family in Kabul.

# KIT'S WILDERNESS David Almond

**12+**

## Next?

Among David Almond's other books, *The Fire-Eaters* (UTBG 130) is my favourite. It has the same quality of looking at the real, everyday world and seeing something mysterious.

*Red Shift* (UTBG 307) and *The Owl Service* (UTBG 281) do this, too.

If you like David Almond's ability to describe real places, linking past and present, you might enjoy *Sea Room* by Adam Nicolson. It's a non-fiction book about the little islands that his father gave him when he was 21, and I think it's magic.

*Kit's Wilderness* explores 'the desire we have to be terrified, to look into the darkness'. When Kit Watson makes friends with John Askew and Allie Keenan, they play the game called Death, and Kit finds himself drawn into a strange place where the darkness of the past links somehow with the darkness inside his own head and the dark tunnels of the disused mines.

There is danger and cruelty and, in the end, a real death, but the book is full of warmth, too. In Kit's stories and Askew's drawings, in the acting of Allie, 'the good bad ice girl', and in the character of Kit's grandfather, the darkness becomes a source of strength and beauty. It's an extraordinary book. But don't take my word for it. Read it yourself.

**Gillian Cross**

# THE L-SHAPED ROOM Lynne Reid Banks

**16+**

The L-shaped room is at the top of a run-down boarding house in Fulham run by a tyrannical landlady and full of colourful characters – not to mention bedbugs! 27-year-old Jane runs here when her father throws her out after discovering she is pregnant. Jane feels numb, like her life has ended, but gradually she discovers that her life is just beginning. This is one of the most unflinchingly honest and self-aware books I have ever read: it tells you a lot about what it means to grow up, however old you are. Bear in mind that this book was written in 1960 and some of its attitudes towards race, religion, class and sexuality seem to come from another planet; but it's a fascinating look at London two generations ago: how much has changed, how little.

**Abigail Anderson**

## Next?

*Two is Lonely* and *The Backward Shadow* by Lynne Reid Banks complete the trilogy.

*The Dud Avocado* (UTBG 112) and *The Greengage Summer* (UTBG 157) are both about girls coming of age in the mid-20th century.

*The Bell Jar* (UTBG 37) by Sylvia Plath is another honest first-person narrative about a young woman in a crisis.

# LADY CHATTERLEY'S LOVER D.H. Lawrence

*Chatterley* is arguably the most controversial book of the 20th century. What shocked its readers (and those who didn't read it but followed the famous obscenity trial in the newspapers) wasn't the boundary-breaking story of a married aristocratic lady having an affair with a working-class man, a gamekeeper on her estate, but the way the book was written – or more particularly the way the sex scenes were written. The rough, honest, earthiness of the language was unlike anything any respectable person had ever read before. Or at least would admit to having read before. Such language! In print! Outrageous!

And it's great. The whole book – not just those few famous and controversial scenes – is energetic and rough and unfussy, and the characters live and breathe from the first page to the very last. Read it and see what all the fuss was about.

**Daniel Hahn**

### Next?

Another D.H. Lawrence? *Sons and Lovers* is probably the best known; I've always rather liked his short stories, too.

*A Clockwork Orange* (UTBG 79) is in no way like *Lady Chatterley*, except that it too was scandalous when it was first published. See if you're shocked, too.

For another exploration of the tensions in the British class system, read *The Go-Between* (UTBG 150) or E.M. Forster's *Howard's End*.

# THE LAND Mildred D. Taylor

Here is a compelling prequel to Mildred D. Taylor's great *Roll of Thunder, Hear My Cry*. Remember Cassie Logan? This coming-of-age story is told by her grandfather, Paul-Edward, who is born into slavery shortly before the end of the Civil War. His father is a wealthy white landowner. Paul-Edward looks almost white. That complicates relationships with both his white family and black peers. Although he is the son with the greatest feeling for his father's land and horses, he will never inherit them. Injustice, humiliation and betrayal lead him to run away at 14. His determination to make his own way, and realise his dream of acquiring his own land, drives the novel and the reader.

**Beverley Naidoo**

### Next?

*Roll of Thunder, Hear My Cry* (UTBG 311), *Let the Circle be Unbroken* and *The Road to Memphis* are three more instalments in the saga of the Logan family.

A book about slavery – and about what constitutes freedom – is *Nightjohn* by Gary Paulsen, about an escapee who returns to slavery in order to teach reading and writing to his fellow slaves.

# LAST CHANCE TO SEE

## Douglas Adams and Mark Carwardine

**Next?**

If you haven't already, read *The Hitchhiker's Guide to the Galaxy* (UTBG 171). Then read *Dirk Gently's Holistic Detective Agency*.

Bill Bryson is another travel writer who is worried about snakes in Australia in his book *Down Under*.

Mal Peet's *Keeper* (UTBG 205) is partially about the destruction of the rainforest.

Douglas Adams takes the writing style that we all adored in *The Hitchhiker's Guide to the Galaxy* and applies it to a series of trips to see some of Earth's most endangered species. And it works! The descriptions of the creatures themselves are beautifully interwoven with tales of the people who devote their lives to trying to save them. In one part, Adams is going to an area with lots of poisonous snakes so he goes to see an expert on venom. He asks what he should do if he gets bitten by a deadly snake and is told: 'You die, of course. That's what deadly means.'

**Anthony Reuben**

# THE LAST OF THE WINE

16+

## Mary Renault

This book takes place about 2,500 years ago, when Athens was at the height of its glory. Mary Renault takes you into the homes, courtyards, baths and temples of the ancient Greek city. The young hero Alexias is fictional, but he meets real historical figures of his time – Socrates, Plato and Xenophon. He competes in the games, takes a dream cure, fights in wars and falls in love. (Renault deals very sensitively with homosexuality in the ancient world.)

This is one of those rare historical novels that does what all historical novels should: it transports you to another place and time. I read this book as a teenager, and it changed my life.

**Caroline Lawrence**

**Next?**

Read Mary Renault's *Fire From Heaven* (UTBG 129), the first in the **Alexander** trilogy, for a wonderful evocation of the ancient world.

For one of her stories set in the more recent past – World War II – and dealing with love between two men: *The Charioteer*.

Another author who makes history real is Bernard Cornwell. Try his **Grail Quest** series about the Hundred Years War, beginning with *Harlequin*.

# LAST SEEN WEARING TRAINERS
## Rosie Rushton

This book is dedicated to 'Everyone who has been scared by someone they love; and all those with the courage to face their fears'. It presents differing points of view – the narrative is told by Katie, Lydia, Tom and Grace. A mum and her daughter have trouble coping, teenagers try to make sense of their worlds and a secret emerges. A complex web of family relationships unfolds. Lives intertwine and decisions taken years ago create terrifying consequences. The pace is fast, the plot twists and there is real tension. What do people do in the name of love? I know it is a cliché but this is one thriller you really can't put down. Do try it!

**Brenda Marshall**

> **Next?**
>
> More Rosie Rushton? *Just Don't Make A Scene, Mum!* or *What a Week to Get Real*, about four friends coping with boys and life.
>
> *The Illustrated Mum* (UTBG 186), where the children support a mum who's finding it hard to cope.
>
> If you enjoy exploring different sides of a story through multiple narrators, try Steven Herrick's *The Simple Gift* (UTBG 340).

# THE LAST SIEGE Jonathan Stroud

The nearby ruined castle has never interested Emily and Simon – for them it's just a place for tourists. Then one snowy winter, when the castle is locked up, they meet Marcus. His vivid imagination and fascination with the castle's murderous past bring the ruin to life. He persuades them to break in and spend the night there. But the place starts to exert a more powerful grip than any of them could have imagined. And when they feel the castle is under siege, they are prepared to defend it.

Stroud has written a powerful psychological thriller. His depiction of the castle is especially vivid, and as it goes from being a place of refuge to a nightmarish trap, you really feel as though you're there.

**Katie Jennings**

> **Next?**
>
> *Silent Snow, Secret Snow* (UTBG 339) by Adèle Geras, about a family snowed in at a remote house and the secrets and lies that emerge.
>
> More Stroud? Read *The Leap*, about a girl who won't believe that her brother is dead.
>
> Or try Robert Westall's *The Devil on the Road*, about a motorbike rider who takes refuge in a barn with strange symbols carved over the door, and inadvertently triggers a terrifying chain of events that could lead to a girl's death.

# LAST TRAIN FROM KUMMERSDORF

## Leslie Wilson

A superb World War II story told from the viewpoint of the defeated Germans. Hanno is one of Hitler's boy soldiers, sent to stop the inevitable Russian advance. After seeing his twin Wolfgang killed, Hanno joins a stream of refugees fleeing west to surrender to the Allies rather than the avenging Russians.

Hanno has never questioned the Nazi philosophy; it is all he has ever known. However, when he meets up with Effi, whose family have been in the Resistance, he starts to wonder what his dead father got up to in Russia and to doubt the morality of the Nazi cause. The reader can feel the hunger and fear of the refugees, and also the pain of having to make sense of a changing world without a leader and without the certainties that the defeated nation had been used to.

**Ann Jungman**

### Next?

*The Ice Road* (UTBG 185) is about the siege of Leningrad, showing the courage of ordinary people in their struggle to survive.

For a book about more recent refugees, try *Kiss the Dust* (UTBG 209).

Or *Johnnie's Blitz* (UTBG 197): children in the midst of war, this time during the Blitz in London.

# THE LASTLING Philip Gross

### Next?

More Philip Gross? Try *Going for Stone* (UTBG 150), about a boy involved with a strange cult-like group.

If you like stories about intrepid journeys, try Thor Heyerdahl's *Kon Tiki*, which describes his journey across the Pacific; or Captain Scott's diary of his epic journey to the South Pole.

If you like lighter travel writing, you will enjoy Bill Bryson's humorous *Notes from a Small Island* (UTBG 266).

Paris is in the Himalayas on a trek with her uncle and his friends. They meet Tahr, a young Tibetan monk, who reluctantly joins them as his protector has died in an accident. Paris and Tahr are thrown together and each learns something about themselves. As the journey progresses, Paris realises the purpose of her uncle's quest – he and his friends are an exclusive gourmet dining club, dedicated to eating the rarest possible animals. When a young yeti-like creature is discovered, Tahr convinces Paris that they have a duty to protect her, come what may.

The book is full of powerful descriptions of places and feelings. It stimulates the imagination and raises questions about moral and environmental issues. It is also a gripping read!

**Brenda Marshall**

# LBD: IT'S A GIRL THING

## Grace Dent

### Next?

The bambinos are back in *LBD: The Great Escape*. They're a little older but are still determined to go the Astlebury Festival. Somehow.

There's more girl power on display in *Guitar Girl* by Sarra Manning, which is about a teenage girl's rise to rock stardom.

For more about music? Try Graham Marks' *Radio Radio* (UTBG 302) or Jonny Zucker's *One Girl, Two Decks...* (UTBG 272).

14-year-old Ronnie Ripperton and her best friends Claude and Fleur are the feisty trio who call themselves the LBD – *Les Bambinos Dangereuses*. They love boys and music and are all longing to go to a local music festival, which naturally offers great snogging opportunities, and where even the gorgeous Spike Saunders will be playing. When their parents forbid them from going, Claude comes up with the brilliant idea of staging their own charity concert at the school. They start organising auditions, but things start to go awry almost immediately and there's soon drama and excitement to be had all round. Very funny, and totally believable – it's a great summer read.

**John McLay**

# LE GRAND MEAULNES

## Alain-Fournier

A magical novel set in the dreamy hinterland between childhood and adulthood. Augustin Meaulnes, 17 and bursting with energy, if a bit rude, explodes into life at a small rural boarding school in France. Confiding only in his friend François, Meaulnes departs on a journey involving a house in the woods in the dead of night, enchanted revelries, scarlet waistcoats and vagabonding in Paris, all of which slip away from our hero as quickly as they present themselves.

In an apparent blend of fantasy and reality, Alain-Fournier conjures a quest for the unobtainable, at the same time painting a memorable portrait of lost love, and lost youth. Marvellous.

**Sara Wheeler**

### Next?

Sadly, Alain-Fournier died before writing any other books. But why not try *Claudine at School* (UTBG 78) by Colette, another French coming-of-age story?

As is the dark and adult *Bonjour Tristesse* (UTBG 48) by Françoise Sagan.

Read our feature about coming-of-age books on pp. 296–297.

# THE LEFT HAND OF DARKNESS

## Ursula Le Guin

**Next?**

If you liked this book, you'll love *A Wizard of Earthsea* (UTBG 416) about the wizard Ged and the responsibilities of magic; also Le Guin's short stories in *The Wind's Twelve Quarters*, which are superbly imaginative.

Virginia Woolf's *Orlando* (UTBG 276) has a life that spans centuries and crosses the gender divide.

On the glacial planet of Gethen it's always deepest winter. When an ambassador from the Ekumen (a federation of planets) visits, he discovers that the inhabitants live a feudal existence and that they have only one gender, becoming male or female at different times in their lives. In a wonderful story of love and danger and journeying through landscapes of ice, Le Guin plays havoc with our preconceptions of male and female, and imagines how it would be if a person could be both a mother and father. This isn't just an ideas book though – it's a rich, exciting story. Definitely one of the all-time classic fantasies.

**Catherine Fisher**

# LETTERS FROM THE INSIDE

16+

## John Marsden

I can do no better than quote Robert Cormier, who described this book as 'absolutely shattering as it brings to vivid life two teenage girls and then strangles your heart over what happens to their relationship'.

The girls start as strangers writing letters to each other, penpals with secrets and fears which they slowly reveal. But what they reveal will change them in ways they could not have predicted, and their lives become tangled together. You have to concentrate while you are reading, because the whole story is in the letters and you don't quite know what to trust. But the effort will be rewarded, I promise, and you will not forget this book.

**Nicola Morgan**

**Next?**

For a book about secrets and lies and the harm they can do, try E.R. Franks' *Friction*.

You may well enjoy another book by John Marsden, such as *Tomorrow When the War Began*, in which a group of friends return from a camping trip to find their families dead and the world a changed place.

You might also like any of Robert Cormier's dark, edgy books. Start with *Heroes* (UTBG 166).

# THE LIAR  Stephen Fry

16+

### Next?

Stephen Fry has written other novels including *The Stars' Tennis Balls* as well as an exceptional memoir, *Moab Is My Washpot* (UTBG 247).

If you fancy trying an altogether more respectable story of Cambridge life, try E.M. Forster's *Maurice*, or (for real life, not fiction) Clive James' *May Week Was in June*.

I can't think of many books that have made me laugh as much as this one. But try the very funny (though otherwise quite different) Ben Elton. Start with *Popcorn*.

It must be great to be as clever as Stephen Fry. Apart from the various other difficult things he's very good at, he's also managed to write this fantastically funny novel; and what's more he makes the writing and the humour – both light and elegant – seem altogether effortless.

It's the story of the brilliant and decadent Adrian Healey, student at St Matthew's College in Cambridge, who worships toast (pronounced 'taste') almost as much as he worships Hugo Alexander Timothy Cartwright, and who is, frankly, a bit of a tart. There's also a bit of light murder, some spying, and a scene involving lots of brand names that makes me laugh just thinking about it. What more could you want? It's a pleasure to read.

**Daniel Hahn**

# LIFE OF PI  Yann Martel

14+

After the tragic sinking of a cargo ship carrying his family and their zoo, 16-year-old Pi is left shipwrecked. Think things could not get any worse? Add the endless Pacific Ocean, a hyena, a zebra (with a broken leg), a female orang-utan … and a 450-pound Royal Bengal tiger. Well, it's not a normal story.

*Life of Pi* is a captivating novel written from Pi's own point of view as he bobs about in the middle of a never-ending expanse of ocean. It's a story of courage, survival and nerve, with a mixture of suspense, tension, surprise and cleverness. It takes a while to get going, but patience is a virtue as the story culminates in an interesting twist…

**Louise Manning  (aged 14)**

### Next?

Did you like the tale of boy and tiger? Try Rudyard Kipling's *The Jungle Book*. He also wrote another marvellous story about a boy in India, *Kim* (UTBG 207).

If you liked the magical realism, there are many more wonderful books to look out for. Try Isabelle Allende's *House of the Spirits* (UTBG 179), or García Márquez's *Love in the Time of Cholera* (UTBG 227).

# A LITTLE PIECE OF GROUND   Elizabeth Laird

In this story of Arabs under Israeli military occupation, the Palestinians are portrayed as victim-heroes. As someone who – like this author, neither Jew nor Arab – has written books about this terrible conflict, from the Jewish side, I am in a good position to praise this successful attempt to chronicle sympathetically the day-to-day struggles, humiliations and shifts of living under occupation by an enemy. The author doesn't spare us in her tale of the boy in Ramallah whose simple dream is to clear the rubble of war off a patch of ground to make a football pitch. It is a tiny microcosm of courage in the midst of the destruction and misery of war, a powerful token that something like normal life somehow goes on, and love and dreams are kept alive in the hope that some day the occupation will end. For the sake of Elizabeth's Arabs, and my Jews, I can only hope so too.
**Lynne Reid Banks**

> **Next?**
>
> Another Elizabeth Laird? Try *The Garbage King* (UTBG 142).
>
> A Palestinian girl's story is told in Suzanne Fisher Staples' *Shabanu, Daughter of the Wind*.
>
> Or read Lynne's book about Israeli Jews, *One More River*, a 'Romeo and Juliet' story based around life on a kibbutz.

# LOLA ROSE   Jacqueline Wilson

> **Next?**
>
> Wilson has a wonderful way of seeing family living. *The Diamond Girls* (UTBG 101) looks at tough single-parent family life; *Dustbin Baby* stars an adopted child tracing her parents, and *The Illustrated Mum* (UTBG 186) sees two sisters cope with a depressed (tattooed) mum.
>
> Diane Hendry's *You Can't Kiss It Better* is another look at children trying to cope with being adults.
>
> Alan Gibbons' *The Edge* is about a boy and his mother running away from violence.

What would you do if you felt your life was a mess, and there was no way out – but then luck suddenly dealt you a winning card? When Jayni's mum wins the lottery they can finally escape the torture and torment that they face from Jayni's dad, so they move to London to start a new life. That's when Jayni decides to stop being plain old 'Jayni' and becomes 'Lola Rose' instead.

It's a high life, with rich clothes and posh hotels. Then, inevitably, the money runs out, forcing them to move into a grotty flat. Everything seems fine until Lola's mum becomes seriously ill, and Lola has to grow up far too quickly...

A fast-paced, heart-warming must-read; Lola's struggle to come though problem after problem is utterly inspirational.
**David Gardner (aged 16)**

# LONESOME DOVE Larry McMurtry

14+

## Next?

*Dead Man's Walk* is next in the saga.

*Riders of the Purple Sage* by Zane Grey is just about the oldest Western, and in it you'll find some of the ideas that became clichés of the genre (girl disguised as boy; terse, hard-eyed heroes).

Or how about another classic that was made into one of the most famous cowboy films ever, Jack Schaefer's *Shane*.

Whilst reading this book I was thrown from my horse, trampled by stampeding cattle, bitten by rattlesnakes, struck by lightning, battered senseless by hailstorms and washed away in flash floods. And during my quieter moments, I was regularly chased, shot at and beaten up by the toughest and most terrifying bunch of dudes I've ever had the misfortune to get on the wrong side of. However, I enjoyed every second of it, my worst moment coming when I dropped this brilliant adventure story in the bath, causing it to swell up to the size of a dead longhorn steer. And despite the fact that the entire masterpiece about Life in the Old Wild West is a mere 1,000 pages short, at the end of it I found myself yelling: 'More, McMurtry! More! Reach for your pen this minute! You doggone ornery, cotton-pickin' brilliant author, you!'

**Michael Cox**

# THE LONG WALK

## Stephen King / Richard Bachman

Stephen King's the most commercially successful author in the world. But one fine day he got suspicious and wondered if he could repeat his success as an unknown author. To find out he wrote five Bachman books, and *The Long Walk* is the best of them.

The US government has started up a race. One hundred teenage boys are selected for it. But it's no ordinary race. It's a long walk, and once you start you can't stop. If you do, the penalties are terrifying. There can be only one winner. Will it be 15-year-old Ray Garrity, or will he be gunned down like all the others before he can reach the prize?

This is a vintage King. I can honestly say that every teenage boy over the age of 14 I have given *The Long Walk* to has loved this dark and brilliant tale.

**Cliff McNish**

## Next?

More Stephen King? Start with the horror story, *Carrie*, about a girl with psycho-kinetic powers who goes on the rampage in small-town America.

James Herbert writes psychologically adept horror; try *The Rats* or *The Lair*.

# THE LONG WALK  Slavomir Rawicz

**Next?**

*Seven Years in Tibet* by Heinrich Harrer is the story of a man's escape from a prisoner of war camp and his refuge in a monastery in Tibet.

The story of another Siberian prisoner who endures terrible hardship in order to find freedom is told in *As Far As My Feet Will Carry Me* by Josef M. Bauer.

A climbing trip that goes disastrously wrong is recounted in *Touching the Void* (UTBG 377).

This is the most extraordinary escape story one could possibly imagine – and it's all true. The writer, Slavomir Rawicz, was a Polish cavalry officer who was taken prisoner by the Russians during World War II, tortured, and sentenced to 25 years' hard labour in one of the murderous gulags that Stalin set up in Siberia. From a guarded encampment in the middle of hundreds of miles of snowbound forest, he and six fellow captives scrambled under the wire and escaped. They set out on a journey of unimaginable hardship and endurance, crossing the icy wastes of Siberia, the Gobi desert, Inner Mongolia and Tibet before reaching safety and freedom in India. This book had me on the edge of my seat right the way through. Trust me. Your hair will stand on end.

**Elizabeth Laird**

# A LONG WAY FROM VERONA  Jane Gardam

If you want an account of what school was like during the war, if you are curious to see the way some writers become writers, if you like eccentric characters and an accurate depiction of relationships between girls, then this is the book for you. Jessica Vye is an honest and engaging narrator. Her first-person voice is strong and clear and what she has to tell us is fascinating. The book begins with a visiting writer (his appearance at school is most beautifully described), who manages to inspire Jessica to such an extent that she runs after him and thrusts her complete works into his hands as he's leaving for home on the train. He returns her work with a note that says: 'Jessica Vye, you are a writer beyond all possible doubt.' It's hard to tell how autobiographical this book is, but that judgement also applies to Jane Gardam, and it's a pleasure to be in such competent authorial hands.

**Adèle Geras**

**Next?**

A story that weaves books, friendship and rivalries together is *Old School* by Tobias Wolff, set in a US boys' prep school.

Another Jane Gardam? Try *Bilgewater* (UTBG 41), set in an English public school.

Or for an account of a real writer's growing-up, read Penelope Lively's *Oleander Jacaranda*.

# LOOKING FOR JJ   Anne Cassidy

**14+**

Children who murder other children – cases like this make BIG headlines in newspapers. But what is the real story behind the headlines, and what is it like if you are the teenage girl who was convicted of murder, now newly released into the world? What I liked about this brave story is that it makes you really think about the issues, and see things from an unusual perspective.

'JJ' has been given a new identity on her release – she has a job, and a boyfriend and a new life to look forward to – but someone knows who she is, and is looking for her. She has to go on the run yet again. At the same time as these compelling and powerful events are happening, another story is unravelling, about the murder itself: why and how it happened. I found this novel compulsive reading!

**Julia Green**

### Next?

Try other books by Anne Cassidy: *Missing Judy*, about how the loss of a sister affects a family, or *Tough Love*, about the blinkers love puts on truth.

*The Lovely Bones* (UTBG 228) is also based around a crime.

Or for a really dark read about a boy who witnesses his father's murder and discovers a whole new life, Graham Marks' *Zoo* (UTBG 427).

*As If* is Blake Morrison's response to the real-life case of two child killers.

# THE LOOKING GLASS WARS   Frank Beddor

**14+**

Using Lewis Carroll's classic children's story *Alice's Adventures in Wonderland* as his inspiration, Beddor has created a storming, imaginative, bloody tour de force that deserves not to be overlooked.

The author imagines that Alice's Wonderland did indeed exist and that it was not fairy tale after all. Princess Alyss Heart was heir to the throne of Wonderland, but was cruelly usurped when her Aunt Redd stormed Wondertropolis and murdered her parents. Fleeing for her life, Alyss was transported to our world, the world of Charles Dodgson and literary Oxford in the late 19th century. Beddor has pulled off a wonderfully complicated twist of creativity and his ambitious novel is a visual feast that is begging to be made into a film.

**John McLay**

### Next?

Where better to start than with Beddor's inspiration, *Alice's Adventures in Wonderland* and *Through the Looking Glass* by Lewis Carroll?

Stuart Hill's *The Cry of the Icemark* (UTBG 86) involves another princess fighting for her rightful kingdom.

*The Eyre Affair* (UTBG 120) takes characters from famous books and makes them do some awfully strange things…

# LORD LOSS  Darren Shan

14+

Everything goes wrong for Grubbs Grady from the moment he plays a joke on his sister. Though why his family get so uptight about a few rotting rat guts is a mystery – one that gets solved pretty quickly when Lord Loss appears, along with his nightmare companions, Vein and Artery. Demons one and all, they literally tear Grubbs' family apart. Locked into a home for the mentally unstable, Grubbs is just about ready to give up, until one day his long-lost uncle comes to take him home. To peace and quiet? Not likely…

This book is not for the faint-hearted! From the end of chapter one you step into a world of demons – a world that drips with gore, pain, magic, werewolves and bloodcurdling excitement.

**Leonie Flynn**

### Next?

If you haven't read Darren's other books – and you like to be scared witless – do so! Start with *Cirque du Freak* and keep going.

Other bloodthirsty accounts of werewolves can be found in *Wereling* by Stephen Cole or *Flesh and Blood* by Nick Gifford.

Or try one of Darren's own favourites, such as Charles Dickens' thrilling story of the French Revolution, *A Tale of Two Cities* (UTBG 364)

# LORD OF THE FLIES
## William Golding

14+

### Next?

William Golding wrote complex books – try *The Spire*, about the building of a cathedral, or *The Inheritors* (UTBG 189) about the first humans.

*Brave New World* (UTBG 54) is another bleak view of how humanity has evolved.

*Heart of Darkness* (UTBG 164) is about another journey into violence and madness.

*Lord of the Flies* tells the story of a group of young boys stranded without adults on a deserted island after a plane crash. After a promising beginning, the group fragments and very soon descends into savagery. It is brilliant because it gives an idea of what could happen when ordinary boys are left alone.

I could easily identify with the characters and I used to think about my own friends and what character from the book they would be. With such vivid descriptions of the setting it was easy to wonder what might have happened if it had been us left alone on that island…

**Andy McNab**

# THE LORD OF THE RINGS trilogy

## J.R.R. Tolkien

12+

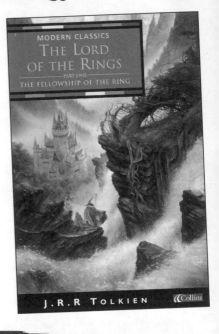

After reading *The Hobbit* and loving it, I thought I should try the trilogy that followed. So I did. For six days I spent my time reading, rereading and losing myself in life in Middle Earth, where the story is set. The trilogy begins with *The Fellowship of the Ring*, following the journey of one hobbit, named Frodo Baggins, who must destroy the One Ring in order to save Middle Earth. Frodo starts off with a fellowship of nine, but by the end of the book the Fellowship has lost four members and the remaining group decide to go their separate ways. Frodo's quest to destroy the Ring is continued in the next two books – *The Two Towers* and *The Return of the King*.

**Florence Eastoe (aged 13)**

Ask six different people why this book is important to them and you'll get six different answers.

For some it's the sheer scale of the story – the epic struggle between Good and Evil that will always be relevant to our own lives. For others it's the Fellowship, the friendship that binds nine disparate individuals and keeps them going through one perilous adventure after another. And then there's Tolkien's creation of an alternate world, complete with its own language and history.

For me, it's always been the realism. The characters may be hobbits and elves and walking trees but I know what they eat, when they sleep and how they feel. When I read this book I believe in it utterly – and that's fantasy at its best.

**Laura Hutchings**

### Next?

If you are one of the many who devoured the appendices at the end of **The Lord of the Rings** then try Tolkien's *The Silmarillion* and *Unfinished Tales*.

Gone are the days when the closest to a fantasy section that bookshops got was science fiction. Now there's almost too much to choose from. My personal favourites are: the novels of Robin Hobb – particularly the **Farseer** trilogy (UTBG 124), Philip Pullman's **His Dark Materials** trilogy (UTBG 170), and last, and perhaps best of all, Katherine Kurtz's **Deryni** novels. Start with *Deryni Rising*.

If you haven't read it already, try *The Hobbit* (UTBG 172) – the story of how the Ring was found.

# The LORD PETER WIMSEY books

## Dorothy L. Sayers

Peter Wimsey is an intellectual, highly sensitive amateur detective with a taste for good wine – and a talent for solving crimes. He appears in around a dozen books, all of them full of strong, quirky characters and ingenious plots. The solutions often depend on his detailed knowledge of subjects like bell-ringing and arsenic poisoning, and the author has an exceedingly characteristic way of weaving obscure quotations into the dialogue. Only one woman can really keep up with Wimsey – and when they meet she's on trial for the murder of her lover.

Don't expect graphic details of sex and violence or serious discussion of current issues. The books are elegant puzzles, written to tantalise and entertain. But they don't trivialise life. Everything is underpinned by Wimsey's curiosity and enjoyment of the world around him, and his commitment to rigorous intellectual honesty.

**Gillian Cross**

> **Next?**
>
> More Wimsey? My favourites are *Strong Poison*, *Gaudy Night* and *Murder Must Advertise*.
>
> You might also enjoy the detective stories of Margery Allingham.
>
> Or the very funny **Jeeves** stories (UTBG 106).

# LOST AND FOUND  Valerie Mendes

> **Next?**
>
> More Valerie Mendes? Try *The Girl in the Attic* (UTBG 146), or her latest, *The Drowning*.
>
> For a beautiful story of falling in love, read *Naked Without a Hat* (UTBG 255).
>
> For a story of finding love, friendships and loss, try *Going for Stone* (UTBG 150).

This book is described on the cover as a 'mystery', but I don't think that's really what it is. Sure, there's a secret waiting to be revealed, and a few gripping chapters of Missing Persons and calling the police and anxious waiting by the phone and chases down the canal bank. But the best bits of the story for me were watching the main character Daniel as he begins to form relationships with Clare and Martin, his new foster parents; with his adopted 'grandmother' Laura; and with the lovely Jade, the new girl over the road with the entrancing singing voice and the rainbow-coloured dress.

Daniel is a wonderfully drawn and sympathetic character, and you can't help wanting things to work for him; the story is enchanting, but never sentimental; and of course there's also all that 'mystery' excitement, too – what more could you want?

**Daniel Hahn**

# LOVE, FIFTEEN  Ros Asquith

This is a heartrending and hard-hitting story about the risks that go hand in hand with falling in love for the first time. Feisty and full of fun, Amy ends up pregnant after a drink too many to console herself over her boyfriend's move to the US. Knowing that a baby doesn't fit into her life plan to hit the big time as a rock star, she has some difficult decisions to make and confides many of her thoughts to her diary. Refreshingly, the focus is on her friends' and family's lives too, and this carefully researched story strikes just the right balance between responsibility and froth. It's sure to hit home.

**Eileen Armstrong**

### Next?

Ros Asquith is best known for *I Was a Teenage Worrier* (UTBG 184) and its sequels featuring the irrepressible Lettie Chubb, a kind of female Adrian Mole with attitude.

Fans of these books will love the coolosity of Louise Rennison's crazy *Angus, Thongs and Full-frontal Snogging* (UTBG 22) (think Bridget Jones as an angst-ridden, lovesick teenager) and devour the Cathy Hopkins **Mates, Dates...** series (UTBG 238).

Or try Sue Limb's books starting with *Girl, 15 (Charming But Insane)* (UTBG 146) starring Jess and her long-suffering mother.

# LOVE IN A COLD CLIMATE  Nancy Mitford

### Next?

*The Pursuit of Love* is the brilliant sequel.

Or for the story told by a different sister (and without the fictional cover story), read *Hons and Rebels* by Jessica Mitford.

Dodie Smith's *I Capture the Castle* (UTBG 183) is the perfect companion to the Mitford books.

This English classic describes, hilariously, the doings of the Radletts, a large, titled family living in a chilly country house in the run-up to World War II. Fanny, the narrator, is a cousin who spends long holidays with the family. They hunt (and are hunted! – Fanny's fierce and eccentric Uncle Matthew delights in setting his bloodhounds on his children in 'child-hunts'), and discuss sex in the 'Hons' Cupboard' – the only warm place in the house. The girls dream of parties in heated mansions, and going to school (banned by Uncle Matthew), and running away, and not being bored any more. As they grow up, all this and much more comes to pass, with the emphasis on Fanny's favourite cousin, Linda, who, as someone truly remarks 'is such an interest in one's life!' Never out of print in over 60 years, this is a must for anyone who wants insights into, and a good laugh at, the upper classes.

**Lynne Reid Banks**

# LOVE IN THE TIME OF CHOLERA

## Gabriel García Márquez

If you long to escape from our everyday world, and would like to travel far away (to South America) and long ago (the start of the 20th century), this book will take you there. You are slowly drawn into a dazzling world of extraordinary detail, and begin to tune in to the life of two young people: Florentino and Fermina (great names, by the way). Their love affair is drawn out over decades, and years and years must pass before it will reach some kind of dream-like resolution.

It's the kind of book you can only read very slowly, allowing one of the great writers of our age to hypnotise you with his evocation of a society that is beautiful and magical but also brutal and primitive. The book is hugely satisfying. I want to read it again NOW. Although, speaking as a hypochondriac, I felt there was maybe a *teeny* bit too much about love and not *quite* enough about cholera.

**Sue Limb**

### Next?

García Márquez has written some of the best-loved books of the past few decades. Try *One Hundred Years of Solitude* (UTBG 273) next.

Something similar, but not similar? A Greek story by an Englishman about an Italian? *Captain Corelli's Mandolin* (UTBG 63) by Louis de Bernières.

Isabelle Allende's usual subtlety is brought to the high adventure of *Zorro*.

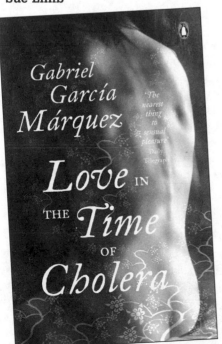

## SIBLINGS

*Round Behind the Ice-House*
by Anne Fine

*The Diamond Girls*
by Jacqueline Wilson

*Brothers* by Ted van Lieshout

*The Cement Garden*
by Ian McEwan

*Ruby Holler*
by Sharon Creech

*Reckless* by Sue Mayfield

*Saffy's Angel*
by Hilary McKay

# THE LOVELY BONES  Alice Sebold

**14+**

This is a startling book. Within a few lines you learn that the narrator is Susie Salmon, a murdered 14-year-old girl. She describes her own grisly murder at the hands of a neighbour. She is in a kind of heaven, a frozen place where she can only watch the life she has left behind. We see the effects of the murder on her mother and father, how it destroys their life together. We also see, with horror, that the murderer is not caught – and there is evidence of other deaths.

There is life after death for Susie but she's in a lonely place. We often read about the loss felt by grieving relatives, but Susie's loss is greater: she has lost everything.

**Anne Cassidy**

### Next?

*Lucky* by Alice Sebold is the account of a traumatic rape and its aftermath.

*The Great Blue Yonder* (UTBG 155) by Alex Shearer is told by a boy from beyond the grave.

Or Ali Smith's beautifully woven *Hotel World*, in which five people at the Global Hotel (one of them a lately dead girl) tell their stories.

Or read one of the most enchanting life-after-death stories, Gabrielle Zevin's *Elsewhere* (UTBG 114).

# LUCAS  Kevin Brooks

**14+**

### Next?

Other books by Kevin Brooks? All of them are worth reading: *Martyn Pig* (UTBG 236), *Kissing the Rain* (UTBG 209) and *Candy* (UTBG 62).

*The Fire-Eaters* (UTBG 130) because this is another powerful story about an outsider, and the nature of fear.

*I Capture the Castle* (UTBG 183) by Dodie Smith: another 'confessional' story told by a girl whose father is a writer, dealing with matters of the heart (wonderful, too!).

Kevin Brooks writes powerful, original stories. *Lucas* is my favourite so far. The main character, Caitlin, tells the story of what happened to her one extraordinary summer, when a mysterious, beautiful boy called Lucas arrived at the island, where she lives with her dad and brother in a close-knit but fearful community. Caitlin's friendship with Lucas helps her to be the person she really is, rather than going along with how most of the other teenagers behave, but that's a really difficult thing to do when you're 15. Lucas, the outsider, becomes a focus for all the fear and hatred the islanders feel about someone 'different' from them, with terrible and tragic consequences. I loved the island setting, the descriptions of the sea and the mudflats and dunes, and the way we are powerfully shown the danger of the 'crowd mentality'. You won't forget this story.

**Julia Green**

# THE MACHINE-GUNNERS Robert Westall

 12+

Chas McGill is a boy living in England during World War II. For him, the war presents an opportunity to collect shrapnel and other military bits and pieces. It's an exciting adventure which he and his friends are all enjoying. But when a German plane crashes, they take its pilot 'hostage' and Chas gets his hands on a real, fully-functioning machine-gun…

A raw, powerful beast of a book, this features some of the most realistic and genuinely likeable characters in all children's fiction. Robert Westall wrote many fine books, but this is far and away his finest, and one of my all-time favourites when I was a teenager. Nil carborundum!

**Darren Shan**

### Next?

The sequel, *Fathom Five*. Chas is now 16, but still finding adventures, this one about a suspected spy.

Or what about a boy in a very different war? Try the **Pagan Chronicles** starting with *Pagan's Crusade* (UTBG 283).

Martin Booth's *Music on the Bamboo Radio* is about a boy who escapes into China after the fall of Hong Kong to the Japanese.

---

# THE MAGIC TOYSHOP
## Angela Carter

14+

### Next?

If you like the poetry of the language and the sense of magic, try *Orlando* (UTBG 276) by Virginia Woolf.

If you like the way Angela Carter uses fairy-tale images, read *The Bloody Chamber*, her collection of short stories.

If you like the way Angela Carter describes the decisions Melanie faces as she grows older, try *The Last September* by Elizabeth Bowen.

15-year-old Melanie secretly slips into the night wearing her mother's wedding dress. The next day she learns that her parents have been killed in an aeroplane crash. She is sent with her little brother and sister to live with their unknown Uncle Philip, the toymaker. Burdened with guilt and responsibility, Melanie has to confront her approaching adulthood in the strange, surreal world she has entered. Surrounding her are an aunt struck dumb on her wedding day, magical mechanical birds, and puppets that are either dream or nightmare but are definitely not toys. Controlling everything is Uncle Philip. Does he see Melanie as a person, or as another puppet he can shape and control? A rich and disturbing novel with no easy answers.

**Antonia Honeywell**

# The MAIGRET books Georges Simenon

I love Maigret. Simenon wrote his **Maigret** detective books at breakneck speed, often in just a few days. Maybe that's why the stories feel so immediate and alive. I love Simenon's sparse and simple prose, his claustrophobic settings, where tensions simmer away and then explode – driving quite ordinary people to violence. I love the way Maigret bumbles about, often just as confused as we are, 'feeling' his way towards a solution. And how he struggles, as we often do, to understand the darker secrets of the human heart and why people behave as they do.

Where to start? Perhaps with *Maigret Goes to School* or *Maigret Goes Home* or *Inspector Cadaver* and, if you get hooked, there are 73 more!
**Susan Gates**

> **Next?**
>
> Simenon without Maigret? Try *Stranger in the House*, *The Mouse* or *The Man Who Watched the Trains Go By*.
>
> For something lighter, try other famous detectives like Chandler's Marlowe in *The Big Sleep* (UTBG 40), Conan Doyle's **Sherlock Holmes** stories (UTBG 336) or Christie's Poirot in *Death on the Nile*. Or the more recent **Inspector Morse** books (UTBG 191).

# MAKE LEMONADE Virginia Euwer Wolff

> **Next?**
>
> There's a follow-up, which is also excellent, called *True Believer*.
>
> The theme of being trapped by life, as an unloved and unwanted daughter, is explored in Adeline Yen Mah's autobiographical *Chinese Cinderella* (UTBG 74).
>
> Or try *Girl in Red* by Gaye Hicyilmaz, in which Frankie is captivated by a Romanian gypsy girl who comes to live close by, but has to deal with the fact that his own mother is leading the fight to get her and her family evicted.

A beautifully written book about LaVaughn, a 14-year-old girl, who is determined to break out of the inner-city poverty of her upbringing and get to college. To raise funds she takes on a regular babysitting job for Jolly, a struggling single mother, but ends up getting drawn deeper and deeper into the seemingly hopeless situation in which Jolly has found herself.

It's a very sensitive, deeply moving but highly readable story, told in the first person without a single wasted word. It explores themes of friendship, family and self-respect; and of young people against all the odds aiming to make something of their lives. Although it deals with the most difficult of issues, this is a book brimming with warmth, humour and hope, and leaves the spirit soaring.
**Malachy Doyle**

# MAKING SENSE

## Nadia Marks

14-year-old Julia is uprooted from her native Cyprus and made to settle with her family in London, without a single word of English and knowing no one. Her attempts to get to grips with the language and the sometimes unfathomable British culture as she makes new friends, finds a boyfriend and starts a new school make for fascinating, and at times very funny, reading.

*Bitter Sweet* continues Julia's story as she falls in love with a boy her parents definitely wouldn't approve of, makes a return visit to see her old friends and family in Cyprus, discovers that her culture shock can never be completely overcome, and learns to live with her new identity, caught between two completely contrasting ways of life.

These insightful and very readable stories with definite girl appeal about making friends, finding love and learning to keep your own identity in a foreign culture are based on the author's own experience.

**Eileen Armstrong**

### Next?

*The Dark Beneath* (UTBG 92) by Alan Gibbons is the story of an asylum-seeker the community won't accept.

*The Other Side of Truth* by Beverley Naidoo (UTBG 277) and *Refugee Boy* by Benjamin Zephaniah (UTBG 308) both offer moving insights into the bewilderment of child refugees living in Britain.

## The Ultimate Teen Readers' Poll

## BOOK YOU DON'T WANT YOUR PARENTS TO KNOW YOU'VE READ

1 **Angus, Thongs and Full-frontal Snogging**

2 **Girls in Love series**

3 **A Child Called 'It'**

4 **Bridget Jones's Diary**

5 **Junk**

6 **How to Cope with Your Parents**

7 **The Kama Sutra**

8 **Bumface**

9 **Forever**

10 **Being Jordan**

# SCIENCE FICTION by Andrew Norriss

I grew up with a comic called *The Eagle*, which had stories on the front page about a pilot in the United Planets Spaceforce called Dan Dare. He had his own spaceship, the *Anastasia*, that could take him anywhere in the galaxy, and I *so* wanted to go with him. His adventures were set far in the future – about the year 2000 as I remember – and I've been hooked on science fiction ever since. They say the genre began with people like Jules Verne and H.G. Wells, but for my money science fiction really started in the 1940s and 1950s, and the three big names that launched it were Isaac Asimov, Robert Heinlein and Arthur C. Clarke. These were the guys, I later discovered, who had inspired the writers of *Dan Dare*. Heinlein wrote stories about humanity colonising the planets and spreading out across the galaxy, much as Americans had conquered the West, but fighting off aliens instead of Indians. Asimov's **Foundation** trilogy (UTBG 138) went even further into the future and described the fall of the first human, stellar empire, while in *2001* Arthur C. Clarke wondered if we hadn't already been visited by aliens in the distant past who might yet return and take humanity on to the next level.

Nobody took these guys seriously as literature, but the ideas they were coming up with were mind-blowing – and they were just the tip of the iceberg. I'll never forget the first time I came across the idea of stargates, in Murray Leinster's *The Wailing Asteroid*. Clifford D. Simak's *The Way Station* was my favourite reread for years, and I still have my dog-eared copy of Theodore Sturgeon's *More than Human*, which suggested that humanity might evolve into gestalts... The ideas went on and on, and the possibilities and the hope seemed endless.

I didn't much like it when science fiction grew up. I knew that writers like Ray Bradbury and Kurt Vonnegurt were seriously clever, but they used sci-fi – in books like *Fahrenheit 451* (UTBG 121) or *Slaughterhouse 5* (UTBG 345) – to show humanity screwing it up on a galactic scale. They were well written, but they weren't what I was looking for.

I wanted the fun stuff, and fortunately it's still around. A lot of it gets written for television these days – for *Star Trek*, *Babylon V* or *Farscape* – but there are still some authors producing ideas that will astound, and describing worlds you wish you could live in. Iain M. Banks would be top of my list. His **Culture** novels – *Consider Phlebas* (UTBG 83) or *Excession* – have the same mind-expanding power as the old days. I liked David Brin's **Uplift** novels, beginning with *Sundiver*, and Jerry Pournelle's **Falkenberg's Legion** stories are rip-roaring sagas where you know the right guys will always win through.

Some of these writers may not be quite what you're looking for, but the good news is that bookshops these days have whole shelves stuffed with sci-fi. All you need to do is dip and pick until you find the stuff that works for you. Good luck in the hunt! And may the Force be with you as you boldly go to infinity and beyond…

## Some classic sci-fi:

*I, Robot* by Isaac Asimov

*Do Androids Dream of Electric Sheep?* by Philip K. Dick

*Starship Troopers* by Robert A. Heinlein

*The Left Hand of Darkness* by Ursula Le Guin

*Ender's Game* by Orson Scott Card

*The Hitchhiker's Guide to the Galaxy* by Douglas Adams

*Dune* by Frank Herbert

*The Day of the Triffids* by John Wyndham

*The War of the Worlds* by H.G. Wells

## Who am I? (cloning etc):

*House of the Scorpion* by Nancy Farmer

*Zoo* by Graham Marks

*Sharp North* by Patrick Cave

*Taylor Five* by Ann Halam

*Unique* by Alison Allen-Gray

H. G. WELLS
THE
WAR
OF THE
WORLDS
NOW A MAJOR MOTION PICTURE

# MALARKEY Keith Gray

12+

**Next?**

*Tom Brown's Schooldays* by Thomas Hughes – you'll see that things have hardly changed in 150 years.

Or try another Keith Gray, such as *Warehouse* (UTBG 399) or *The Fearful* about a boy trying to make sense of what his father wants him to be.

In *Skinny B, Skaz and Me* (UTBG 344) the hero has to deal with gangs and friends who aren't what they seem.

We've all had it: that feeling you get when you're the new kid at school. The feeling that your every move makes you stick out like a sore thumb, when all you want is to blend in.

It's like that for John Malarkey at Brook High, only worse. He's been there for two weeks and already the gang that runs the school has singled him out for special treatment. When somebody steals from a teacher and plants the stolen item in Malarkey's bag, the new boy finds himself on the run from both students and staff, and life becomes seriously hectic.

The situation and setting in *Malarkey* are instantly familiar to me, though it's a very long time since I was at school. It's still a mean old scene, and Keith Gray's got it absolutely spot on.

**Robert Swindells**

# MAN AND BOY Tony Parsons

16+

Finally, a book about sex, love, and marriage from the man's perspective! Harry Silver would appear to have it all. There's the beautiful wife, the adorable son and the high-paid job. But Harry throws it all away in a moment of weakness. Now, quickly approaching 30, he must re-evaluate his life and learn how to be a single dad.

This book is about growing up, becoming a responsible adult and taking a hard look at yourself and your relationships. It is funny and endearing, but also sad at times. Harry's relationship with his own father is one of the highlights of the book and is tackled in a touching way. Tony Parsons manages to deliver a book filled with wonderful characters that is both stimulating and refreshing.

**Ileana Antonopoulou**

**Next?**

If you want to find out what ultimately happens to Harry, why not read the sequel, *Man and Wife*, by the same author?

Nick Hornby's *About a Boy* (UTBG 11) is also about a man who's never really stopped being a teenager.

Blake Morrison's *And When Did you Last See Your Father?* is the author's memories of his father, told with both irritation and great affection.

# THE MAN IN THE HIGH CASTLE

## Philip K. Dick

Philip K. Dick is deservedly a legend among sci-fi writers. Several of his books formed the basis of some great movies, *Blade Runner* among them. With *The Man In The High Castle* he gave an enormous boost to the 'alternative history' genre, in this case the idea that Germany and Japan actually *won* World War II and divided the defeated US between them.

The story is set in 1962 against a background of mounting tension between Japan and a Nazi Germany bent on total world domination, and the destinies of several characters become entangled as the plot is worked out. This strange, haunting book and its Zen-like approach to history and the clash of cultures will resonate in your mind for a very long time.

**Tony Bradman**

### Next?

Other stories that tell of alternate histories are Robert Harris' *Fatherland* (UTBG 126) (Germany won the war and invaded the UK), or Ben Jeapes' *New World Order* (aliens alter the course of the English Civil War).

What about another Philip K. Dick? Try *We Can Remember It For You Wholesale* (UTBG 404).

---

# MANSFIELD PARK Jane Austen

### Next?

*Pride and Prejudice* (UTBG 294) is probably Jane Austen's most famous novel. *Northanger Abbey* (UTBG 262) is wonderful too. Come to think of it, they all are...

For another comedy of manners that's every bit as sharp and telling, read *Vanity Fair* (UTBG 395).

Or try Karen Joy Fowler's modern story of five people who meet every month in *The Jane Austen Book Club*.

This is funny, really very funny, and has excellent dialogue and such honesty from Fanny the heroine that even the most solipsistic teenager could not help but learn something from her. At the beginning the characters are assembled at a country house and planning to perform a play. This device is as brilliant as any psychological workshop for showing the reader a multitude of behaviours that only intensify through the novel. Jane Austen is my favourite English novelist, and although this book is not faultless – I find the ending a little frustrating – it is clever and perceptive. Read it and recognise your friends and yourself, and just hope you are not BB.

**Raffaella Barker**

# MARTYN PIG  Kevin Brooks

What do you do when you're in love with the girl across the street, a girl you think outclasses you in every department? *Martyn Pig* starts from this premise and then gets a good deal darker. Martyn's gloomy, self-deprecating nature makes him the ultimate angst-ridden teen, while his drunken father is the epitome of the boozed-up middle-aged lout.

The first-person narrative illustrates the claustrophobic nature of Martyn's loneliness, trapped inside his own head, yearning for something he believes to be out of his reach. This gritty thriller doesn't flinch away from some grim themes, but Martyn, for all his flaws, is a sympathetic character, and the twist in the tale is both moving and satisfying.

**Thomas Bloor**

### Next?

Brooks excels at putting his characters in the kind of unusual situations you would never want to find yourself in. Try *Lucas* (UTBG 228), or *Bloodline*, a tense thriller told at gunpoint.

*Boy Kills Man* (UTBG 51) also sees young people driven to murder, this time in South America and for very different reasons.

Raymond Chandler's *The Big Sleep* (UTBG 40) contains another poignant and lonely narrative voice, hidden behind the hard-boiled front.

P.D. James' English crime novels, such as *A Taste For Death*, have an air of chilly melancholy to them, which can also be found in *Martyn Pig*.

Did I hate him? Of course I hated him.
But I never meant to kill him.

**KEVIN BROOKS**

Martyn Pig is a boy with a weird name and not much else; not particularly interesting, not wonderfully good-looking and not very popular either. In one week, though, his life is turned upside-down and inside-out, trapping him in a web of lies and deadly events.

Martyn lives with his dad, an alcoholic, and the only thing good in his life is his best friend Alex. She's also his only hope, the only person he can turn to when he does something wrong, very wrong. But was he in fact wrong to do what he did? Is it only wrong if he gets caught? This is a fantastic story, dark and very clever, must-pickupable and unputdownable, which thrills and shocks. Kevin Brooks amazes and provokes. He is without doubt one of the best authors for teenagers... Ever!

**David Gardner (aged 16)**

# MASSIVE  Julia Bell

This brilliant novel is simultaneously funny and utterly tragic. It's about an anorexic mother driving her daughter towards the same condition.

Carmen's mother is obsessed with making her daughter thin and beautiful, but Carmen finds comfort in food ... at first. The real awfulness begins when Carmen herself decides she *would* like to be thin – very thin. Then it's no longer funny.

Parents should read this book. It reveals how we often don't support or understand each other: there are teachers, girls and parents who are ignoring pain when they should be supporting and caring for those in trouble – in the book and in real life. I laughed and cried while reading this book. It is wise and witty and wincingly poignant.

**Nicola Morgan**

### Next?

*The Opposite of Chocolate* (UTBG 274) by Julie Bertagna also shows girls at their most and least supportive of each other and is very moving.

Another book dealing with anorexia is *Second Star to the Right* (UTBG 323).

But for the most devastating book about self-starvation, and the damage girls can do to each other and themselves, you must read *Speak* by Laurie Halse.

---

# MASTER AND COMMANDER
## Patrick O'Brian

### Next?

If you want more about life under sail, try the **Hornblower** books by C.S. Forester.

A classic story of the sea is Herman Melville's epic *Moby-Dick*.

For warfare on land you can't get much better than Cornwell's **Sharpe** books (UTBG 334).

The first in a series of 20 superb novels chronicling the lives and adventures of two unforgettable characters: Jack Aubrey, the dashing sea captain in Nelson's navy – bluff, courageous, magnificently flawed; and his friend, the naval surgeon Stephen Maturin – moody, taciturn, fascinatingly complex. This is historical fiction of the very highest order. Don't worry about the nautical terms. You're in the safest of hands and, besides, these are not just stories about the sea. There are storms, shipwrecks and battles to be sure, but there are also intrigues, affairs, scandals, duels, the murky world of secret intelligence and much more. O'Brian's canvas is huge. These are stories of love and loyalty, humour and humanity, beautifully written and with a sense of the period so powerfully evoked you think you're there.

**Tim Bowler**

# THE MASTER OF BALLANTRAE

**14+**

## Robert Louis Stevenson

### Next?

More Stevenson? *Kidnapped* (UTBG 206) and *Dr Jekyll and Mr Hyde* (UTBG 107) are both fine reads.

Another novel of Scotland, war and friendship: D.K. Broster's *Flight of the Heron*.

Alexandre Dumas wrote some fast, brilliant adventure stories. Try *The Count of Monte Cristo*.

Or for something even more romantic, try *The Prisoner of Zenda* (UTBG 299).

This exciting story, set in 18th-century Scotland, opens at the ancestral home of the Duries of Durisdeer and Ballantrae. Narrated by Mr Mackellar, steward of the estate, it turns upon the intense rivalry between two brothers who could not be less alike. The eldest, James, Master of Ballantrae, is a charming swashbuckler who despises his dour, unadventurous brother Henry. When James is reported killed at the battle of Culloden, Henry assumes his place as head of the household and marries James' betrothed. The story might end there, but James returns from the dead and upsets everything. A rich and moving tale, strong in character and action. Read it by firelight in an old, creaky house for best effect.
**Michael Lawrence**

# MATES, DATES... series Cathy Hopkins

Lucy, Nesta, TJ and Izzie seem as real as the people you meet at school, in the mall, at the market and so on. These four girls come from very different backgrounds, but their mateship bonds them together for life – more so than with boys (although their friendship is strained on more than one occasion *because* of boys). Each book tells the story of a few weeks of change in one of the girls' lives, but we always know what the others are thinking and doing, and most importantly how they all help each other resolve their problems. Frank and funny, moving and thought-provoking, the **Mates, Dates...** series makes for compelling reading about what it's like being a teen today.
**Jon Appleton**

### Next?

More Mates? Try *Mates, Dates and Inflatable Bras* next.

*Girl, 15 (Charming But Insane)* (UTBG 146) also tackles entertainingly what it's like being a teenager today.

Make sure you read Georgia Nicolson's diaries, starting with **Angus, Thongs and Full-frontal Snogging** (UTBG 22).

Ros Asquith is another writer who understands what teenage life is really like. Try *I Was a Teenage Worrier* (UTBG 184) for starters.

# MAUS Art Spiegelman

An extraordinary 'graphic', or comic-book, novel about the Holocaust. In Poland, in the 1940s, Jews hide from the Nazis who are seeking to exterminate them. It's a game of cat-and-mouse, and Spiegelman makes that metaphor the basis of his drawings. The Polish Jews are mice, the Nazis are cats; *Maus* becomes a darkly fascinating version of Beatrix Potter's twee fantasies.

Two narratives run side by side: the story of Spiegelman's parents and their struggle to survive, and an account, set in contemporary America, of Spiegelman's thorny relationship with his ageing and difficult father, Vladek.

At the heart of the book is a painful question. To paraphrase Vladek, addressing his son, the author: 'I survived Hell so that you could be born; why aren't you what I wanted you to be?' It's a question that survivors of tyranny continue to ask and their children still struggle to answer. Maybe a book as good as this is the answer.
**Mal Peet**

THEY TOOK US TO A BUILDING IN A PART OF SRODULA SEPARATED BY WIRES— A GHETTO INSIDE THE GHETTO — AND THERE WE HAD TO SIT AND TO WAIT.

THE COMPLETE

MAUS

WINNER OF THE PULITZER PRIZE

art spiegelman

### Next?

*Persepolis* (UTBG 286) uses pictures to illuminate a dark story – better than any amount of text.

Or for something else about the Holocaust, try either *Stones in Water* by Donna Jo Napoli (about two boys stolen from their homes to be slave workers in Eastern Europe) or *Daniel Half Human* by David Chotjewitz (about how a friendship is torn apart when one boy is found to be half-Jewish).

# MAXIMUM RIDE: THE ANGEL EXPERIMENT  James Patterson

14+

### Next?

Another James Patterson? Mostly he writes for adults, but try *When the Wind Blows*, which has some of the same characters as *Maximum Ride*.

Something with more horror and just as much excitement: Darren Shan's *Lord Loss* (UTBG 223).

Or for a different sort of flying, this time on the backs of dragons, try the **Dragonriders of Pern** series (UTBG 111).

Max is 14; she's a wise-cracking, quick-witted girl. Oh, and she has wings. With two per cent bird DNA, she and her group, or 'flock', are the result of genetic engineering. Light-boned, strong, fast, they live as outcasts from the 'school' that bred them. Until the day the Erasers – half-wolf killing machines – steal away Max's youngest flock member, Angel, and the race to save her from being no more than a lab-rat is on.

This is a book where you dive straight into the action and keep on going. With love and friendship, great villains, and enough thought-provoking back-story to keep you thinking as well as frantically page-turning, this is fast and furious fiction at its best.

**Leonie Flynn**

---

# MEGAN trilogy  Mary Hooper

16+

When I was young there were no books dealing with teenage pregnancy – not, at any rate, for us teenagers. Had the **Megan** trilogy been available then, how we would have devoured it! Our curiosity was boundless, and these books would have satisfied it as no amount of PHSE lectures ever could. There is nothing rose-tinted here: Hooper tells it like it is. No one is sympathetic when Megan discovers she's pregnant. Her family feel disgraced, her boyfriend doesn't want to know, and her best friend is having 'a great time telling everyone my secrets'. Megan is on her own, and adoption seems the only solution.

The first book charts her progress up to the moment of birth when she suddenly says: 'One thing became crystal clear: nothing on earth would make me part with this baby. Nothing.' The two following books show how she copes with being a young mum.

**Jean Ure**

### Next?

More Mary Hooper? Try *Zara*, about psychological game-playing. Or *Holly*, about a girl who finds out that the man she thinks is her father isn't.

For more about sex and babies, read our feature on pp. 168–169.

*Reckless* (UTBG 306) is about a girl who has to deal with her twin brother getting a friend pregnant.

# MEMOIRS OF A GEISHA  Arthur Golden

## Next?

If this starts you off on a quest to find out more about geishas, try Liza Dalby's *Geisha*.

The real-life geisha Arthur Golden interviewed tells her own story in *Geisha of Gion* by Mineko Iwasaki.

To read of the wartime experiences of a Japanese community abroad, try *Snow Falling on Cedars* (UTBG 340).

This was everything I want in a book. Beautifully written, it gives an insight into another time and culture – in this case from 1929 to the post-war years of Japan. It is told from the point of view of Sayuri, a geisha girl.

The closed world of geishas has always fascinated me, from the ritual that dominates every aspect of their days to the intimate details of their personal lives. Part of the appeal of this book was that the author claimed to have got his information from a real geisha who told him her life story. But it is what he has done with what she told him that makes this such a great read – he has woven fact and fiction into a heartbreaking and breathlessly lovely tale.

**Cathy Hopkins**

# MEMOIRS OF AN INFANTRY OFFICER
## Siegfried Sassoon

For years I resisted reading *Memoirs of an Infantry Officer*, knowing that it was a description of Sassoon's experiences of World War I, in the trenches of France in 1916. I could hardly bear to read of the horrors that were to destroy that idyll he had grown up with. But, in due course, read it I did. It didn't disappoint me. I should have known that, despite the brutality overwhelming him, despite the unbearable anguish of loss, and his growing realisation that a 'noble' war had become monstrously evil, the poet in him never ceased to identify beauty, humour and humanity.

### Next?

*Memoirs of a Fox-hunting Man* is the first in this trilogy and *Sherston's Progress* the last.

Sassoon's poems are wonderful, too; try them in an anthology of war poets like *Anthem for Doomed Youth* (UTBG 25).

Amidst the carnage, he could find beauty in a sun setting over a ravaged landscape, or a bird trilling above the rattle of guns. It's a book you can get immersed and lost in, but finally emerge feeling that, just when the world seems completely irredeemable, 'Suddenly everyone burst out singing; and I was filled with such delight as 'prisoned birds must find in freedom…'.

**Jamila Gavin**

# THE MERRYBEGOT Julie Hearn

## Next?

Julie Hearn's first novel, *Follow Me Down* (UTBG 133), is a 'time-slip' set in contemporary London and among the 'monsters' of old Bartholomew Fair.

Try also two other wonderful historical novels about witch hunting: Celia Rees' powerful *Witch Child* (UTBG 415) and Melvin Burgess' *Burning Issy*.

Or try Diana Wynne Jones' *Witch Week*, about a school for children of witches.

Do people only see what they believe they can see? In this rollicking, rumbustious historical novel set in the superstitious West Country during the English Civil War, boundaries are blurred between delusion, illusion, magic and the everyday.

Nell is a Merrybegot, a child conceived on May morning and thus sacred to nature. She is gradually learning her craft so that she can follow her grandmother as cunning woman of the village. But if you are an unconventional, feisty girl in a period of witch hunting, you are surrounded by malice and danger. Characters both human and supernatural romp through the story, which sparkles with audacious humour, yet is touching, too.

**Patricia Elliott**

a child conceived on May morning, believed to have powers of witchery

JULIE HEARN

## AFRICAN-AMERICAN WOMEN TELL IT AS IT IS

*The Color Purple*
by Alice Walker

*Beloved*
by Toni Morrison

*I Know Why the Caged Bird Sings*
by Maya Angelou

*Roll of Thunder, Hear My Cry*
by Mildred D. Taylor

# MIDGET   Tim Bowler

**12+**

15-year-old Midget doesn't have much going for him. He's three-feet tall and trapped inside a puny, twitching body he can't control. He can only communicate in grunts and gestures. And as if this weren't enough, his charismatic and cruel older brother Seb is torturing him, and no one knows. Will Midget find a way to fight back?

This was Tim Bowler's first book and though it is short, interestingly it took him ten years to get right. Time well spent. *Midget* is a masterly study in pace, tension and suspense. Your fingers, turning the pages, burn.

**Cliff McNish**

**Next?**

More Tim Bowler? Try the Carnegie-Medal-winning *River Boy* or *Starseeker* (UTBG 352).

Another story about coming to terms with physical difficulties is *Face* (UTBG 121), about a boy whose life changes after an horrific car crash.

For a more disturbing, more challenging read, try *Stoner and Spaz* by Ron Koertge, about a relationship between two misfits.

# MIDNIGHT IN THE GARDEN OF GOOD AND EVIL   John Berendt

**16+**

**Next?**

There really isn't another book quite like *Midnight in the Garden of Good and Evil* (though there is a film of it, starring Kevin Spacey and Jude Law).

John Steinbeck's *Cannery Row* (UTBG 63) has some of the same flavour.

John Grisham's legal thrillers are set in the similar world of New Orleans and Mississippi – try *The Partner* first.

When this book first came out in America, readers thought it was a novel. But according to Berendt, he really did have the luck to meet this extraordinary cast of characters and to witness the bizarre plot.

It all takes place in the Deep South, in Savannah, where Berendt, a New York journalist, finds himself captivated enough by the place to rent a home there for several months every year. He meets society belles and low-life characters too, like the sleazy lawyer Joe Odom, whose life is one long travelling party. But the real stars are the transvestite black cabaret artist, the Lady Chablis, and the ambiguous millionaire Jim Williams, who is tried four times for the same murder.

Some of the subject matter is very 'adult', but not gratuitously so; the city of Savannah plays a central part in this book, and it's this subject matter that gives the city its decadent character.

**Mary Hoffman**

# MIDSHIPMAN'S HOPE
## David Feintuch

14+

Nicholas Seafort is a trainee officer on an interstellar transport ferrying colonists to a distant world. This is a world guided by moral rigour, where corporal and capital punishments are the norm and God is the highest secular, as well as religious, power (and treason is punished as blasphemy). Introverted, full of self-doubt, Nicholas has to take command after an accident kills all the senior officers. With only the engineer surviving to help him, he has to find a way to save the ship and the colonists, fight aliens, deal with treachery and salve his own troubled conscience.

Fast-paced, sharply characterised, this series makes for compulsive reading. Beware, **Seafort** is addictive!

**Leonie Flynn**

> ### Next?
> There are many more **Seafort** titles, most told by Nicholas himself, though one is told by someone who hates him. *Challenger's Hope*, *Prisoner's Hope* and *Fisherman's Hope* are the next three.
>
> *Ender's Game* (UTBG 115) by Orson Scott Card is also about learning to fight and live in space.
>
> What about books set on a 19th-century sailing ship? Try *Master and Commander* (UTBG 237).

# MILKWEED  Jerry Spinelli

12+

> ### Next?
> For the most famous true account of the Holocaust, read *The Diary of a Young Girl* (UTBG 102).
>
> For a 'based on a true story' account of the Warsaw Ghetto uprising, read *Mila 18* by Leon Uris.
>
> *My Secret Camera: Life in the Lodz Ghetto* by Mendel Grossman and Frank Dabba Smith is full of photos taken in a Polish ghetto, showing what life was like there.

*Milkweed* is an utterly compelling, moving and engrossing story with a main character whose life at the beginning is worse than most of us could imagine, and which deteriorates steadily throughout. It is also a book about the Holocaust.

Misha Pilsudski is a wild little thief without family, home or education. Is he Jew, gypsy or neither? It makes little difference as he is herded into the Warsaw Ghetto with the rest of the boys in his gang and begins to live through the horrors of life there.

Jerry Spinelli has an uncanny ability to plunge right to the heart of a character. Misha whirls you along with his story which, like himself, is endlessly energetic with a spirit that is never crushed.

**Susan Reuben**

# THE MILL ON THE FLOSS

## George Eliot

### Next?

More Eliot – try *Silas Marner* (UTBG 339) next. Or the wonderful (wonderful!) *Middlemarch*.

Of course, if *Middlemarch* doesn't grab you, try a different novel of repressed passion – Wilkie Collins' *No Name*.

Or Virginia Woolf's *A Room of One's Own* (UTBG 312), which is about the role of creative and exciting women in society.

One of George Eliot's most famous and best-loved books, this is the tragic story of Maggie Tulliver and her brother Tom. An intelligent and passionate teenager, Maggie is bored by the stifling and judgmental villagers of St Ogg's. She longs for the love and approval of her brother, who is forced to study. Tom, embarrassed by his sister's passionate nature, ultimately rejects and humiliates her. This isn't an easy book to read, but the portrait of Maggie's conflicted and frustrated character is subtle and moving and gives the reader a real sense of how hard growing up must have been for girls in the 19th century who weren't allowed equal access to education.

**Julia Bell**

# MILLIONS  Frank Cottrell Boyce

I like nothing better than being drawn into a story right from page one and *Millions* does just that. It's about a boy called Damian Cunningham who lives with his older brother Anthony and their widowed father.

Damian is obsessed by the saints and knows all there is to know about each and every one of them, much to the consternation of his teacher and classmates who can't shut him up. Fast-paced, multi-layered and humorous, the plot really takes off when the brothers find a bag of stolen money at the bottom of their garden, with mixed but hilarious consequences.

Read the book first, laugh, cry and enjoy, then go see the film and buy the T-shirt. Then read the book again.

**Helena Pielichaty**

### Next?

*Joey Pigza Swallowed the Key* by Jack Gantos about a boy with ADHD who has the same heart-tugging warmth as Damian.

*Holes* (UTBG 173) by Louis Sachar is another multi-layered, real-life adventure story with an edge.

*Ruby Holler* (UTBG 314) by Sharon Creech – a poignant story of a brother and sister using humour and cunning to overcome life's perils.

*Hoot* (UTBG 175) by Carl Hiaasen. New kid in town overcomes the bullies in an ingenious way.

# MILO'S WOLVES  Jenny Nimmo

Milo is Laura's dad, and he used to be a stuntman. But, after a few too many broken bones, he's now a house-dad while Mum, Mary, works. One day a 'long-lost' brother is brought home. But Laura takes one look at Gwendal and knows he isn't her real brother. Which leaves the question, who (and what) is he?

Gwendal and his new family are watched by the sinister Mr Culfire, and strange grey shapes seem to dog their every move. Milo has to save them all, and he'll need every trick he's ever learned if he and his family are to survive. Achingly poignant on the subject of not belonging, this is also a thrilling and intriguing story full of suspense.

**Leonie Flynn**

### Next?

Jenny Nimmo is always worth reading; try *The Rinaldi Ring*, about a boy haunted by a girl once kept prisoner in the room he now sleeps in; or *Griffin's Castle*, in which the stone animals from Cardiff Castle come to life to help Dinah – though their help may cost more than she imagines.

Another book about someone who might, or might not, be an angel is *Skellig* (UTBG 343) by David Almond.

Another scary and unsettling book about wolves? Try the picture book, *The Wolves in the Walls* (UTBG 417).

---

# MINE  Caroline Pitcher

14+

Shelley feels like nothing belongs to her. Her dad won't let her come to stay for Christmas with him and his new family; her mum loves her little brother best; she's stuck in a remote village with no friends and no one she wants to talk to.

But there are people who want to talk to *her*, whether she likes it or not – two disembodied voices, one on the stairwell and one out by the old mine, who have stories of loneliness to tell that have strange echoes of her own. At first Shelley tries to ignore the voices, but she can't help slowly getting drawn into their increasingly shocking tales.

This is a bleak but compelling story of teenage isolation, with a supernatural element to give it a disturbing twist.

**Susan Reuben**

### Next?

For more Caroline Pitcher, try *11 o'clock Chocolate Cake* or *Cloud Cat*.

For another teen story of the supernatural, read Margaret Mahy's gripping *Alchemy* (UTBG 17).

Or for a story of another girl who finds herself cut off from society, this time through pregnancy, try *Dear Nobody* (UTBG 99).

Or for a girl who talks to ghosts, try Meg Cabot's **Mediator** series.

# MISS SMILLA'S FEELING FOR SNOW

## Peter Høeg

Peter Høeg's novel took the world by storm when it appeared ten years ago. It was a totally unexpected bestseller. It's the story of a Danish woman – by birth a Greenlander, an ice-dweller – who stumbles on a major conspiracy.

The delight is in the detail, and Høeg's minute description of a wintry world is as magical (to those of us from less extreme climates) as anything you'd find on top of the Christmas tree.

The book falls into two distinct halves and some may find the second – when Smilla leaves Copenhagen for the Arctic seas and the heart of the mystery – to be harder going. But the dazzling prose will propel you all the way.

**Sarah Gristwood**

### Next?

More Peter Høeg? Try *Borderliners*, about a group of kids suffering at an experimental school.

Other surprise hits in a similar vein were David Guterson's *Snow Falling on Cedars* (UTBG 346) and Nicholas Evans' *The Horse Whisperer*.

Or Rebecca Wells' wonderful *The Divine Secrets of the Ya Ya Sisterhood* – though this one is strictly for the girls.

# MOAB IS MY WASHPOT Stephen Fry

### Next?

Now read Fry's *The Liar* (UTBG 218).

There are a lot of showbiz autobiographies, but not many are worth reading for any more than gossip. But you could try Pamela Stephenson's very good biography of her husband Billy Connolly, *Billy*.

Like Fry, actor Dirk Bogarde wrote both novels and volumes of memoir, the first of which, *A Postillion Struck by Lightning*, is a wonderful evocation of growing up in the country.

This autobiography covers Fry's first 20 years. If you are a fan of his brand of humour you will love this, but you will also be surprised by it. Stephen Fry is a very complex character and his story makes for fascinating reading. He was a disruptive and rebellious pupil but still managed to get to Cambridge University. He spent time in prison for forging credit card signatures, but somehow comes across as straightforward and honest. He is a talented comedian and yet has battled with depression and suicidal tendencies. Fry writes frankly and with no holds barred about his life, his sexuality and his family, in a book that is by turns witty, poignant, perceptive, sad and very funny.

**Yvonne Coppard**

## MONDAYS ARE RED  Nicola Morgan

14+

Following a near-fatal case of meningitis, Luke discovers that his senses have been strangely altered; he sees music, smells colours and can taste through his fingertips. He has developed a condition called synaesthesia, and the author's dexterity with language allows us to experience the world as richly as Luke does. 'Mondays are red. Sadness has an empty blue smell. And music can taste of anything from banana puree to bat's pee.' But there's a flip side to this sensation-drenched world, and it's Dreeg, a foul creature who has taken up residence in Luke's brain and who persuades him that he can do anything. Ugliness is heightened as well as beauty and in his fight to recover his full health, Luke grows ever more selfish and mean-minded, even putting his family at risk. This is a startlingly original novel and a sensory rollercoaster that will leave you breathless.
**Kathryn Ross**

> ### Next?
>
> No two novels by Nicola Morgan are the same, but all are superbly written. Try *Sleepwalking* (UTBG 345), a chilling vision of a future world where individual thought is outlawed.
>
> The hero of Tim Bowler's *Starseeker* (UTBG 352) is a musical genius who also has synaesthesia.
>
> Two novels that explore the heightened senses of smell and taste to very different effect are Patrick Suskind's *Perfume* (UTBG 285) and *Chocolat* (UTBG 74) by Joanne Harris.

## SCHOOLS' COMPETITION WINNER

=3rd

## MONTMORENCY  Eleanor Updale

*Montmorency* follows the story of rich gentleman Montmorency and his servant, Scarper. Trouble is, they happen to be the same person!

Montmorency is a young thief who has a terrible accident that nearly costs him his life. Instead an inspiring doctor saves him and turns him into a scientific wonder in an age where people in Britain still died from drinking bad water. Montmorency knows he will do anything to maintain a life of dignity. And he knows how to do it: the sewers. He learns to imitate the rich by copying the movements of his friend Lord George Fox-Selwyn, and so he begins a double life – operas and races by day, thefts by night. Soon he has enough money to live the life he wants without criminal behaviour. But when Scarper's life calls, can Montmorency resist?
**Stephen McGruer (aged 14)**
**Boclair Academy**

# MONTMORENCY   Eleanor Updale

Although written for young people, there are no child characters in this witty tale of the rise of Montmorency. His life in Victorian London is a challenge after his body's been put back together by a surgeon and he's spent time in prison. He has a double persona – there's Montmorency the wealthy, upper-class gentleman, who turns into the degenerate servant Scarper, a thief who uses the sewers of London to get in and out of all sorts of places to rob the city's rich. The police are baffled by the wave of mysterious and seemingly unstoppable thefts but Montmorency must always remain on his guard – the smallest mistake could destroy both his lives…

The book is full of intrigue and ingenious plots and is a real page-turner.

**Wendy Cooling**

> ### Next?
>
> *Montmorency* sequels so far are: *Montmorency on the Rocks* and *Montmorency and the Assassins*.
>
> The intrepid and resourceful James Bond would have made quite a good thief, don't you think? Try Charlie Higson's *SilverFin* (UTBG 340), about Bond's first spy case as a teen.
>
> Raffles was the first famous gentleman thief; track down his stories by E.W. Hornung, starting with *Raffles: The Amateur Cracksman*.

# THE MOON RIDERS   Theresa Tomlinson

> ### Next?
>
> For another story about Amazons, you might like to try *The Amazon Temple Quest*, published as part of Katherine Roberts' **Seven Fabulous Wonders** series.
>
> If you are interested in the story of Troy, then try Adèle Geras' *Troy* (UTBG 382).
>
> Or you could seek out a translation of *The Iliad* (UTBG 187) – the epic Greek poem about Achilles' adventures, which Alexander the Great kept under his pillow so he could read about his hero every night!

The legendary Amazon warriors were a tribe of women from what is now Turkey, who lived without men and fought their own battles on horseback. Their culture is seldom explored very deeply, but in this book they are called 'Moon Riders' and dance under the moon, as well as fighting when called upon to do so.

Myrina, a young Moon Rider, rides to the aid of Troy when the city is besieged by the Greeks, which gives us a familiar tale told from a different point of view. The dramatic black cover adds to the atmosphere, and by the end of the book I wanted to leap on a horse and join them!

**Katherine Roberts**

# THE MOONSTONE
## Wilkie Collins

14+

### Next?

Other Wilkie Collins to look for are *The Woman in White* (UTBG 420) and *No Name*.

*Beau Geste* (UTBG 34) is a mystery and adventure that hinges on the theft of the Blue Water sapphire.

Or for a mystery involving an ancient chalice and a curse, try Margery Allingham's *Look to the Lady*, involving her aristocratic sleuth, Albert Campion.

The poet T.S. Eliot described this book as 'the first modern English detective fiction'. When Rachel Verrinder inherits the Moonstone – a huge and cursed yellow diamond stolen generations ago from an Indian shrine – from her distant relation John Herncastle, she has no idea what havoc this gift is about to wreak. We discover that Herncastle, alienated from his family, has bequeathed the stone to Rachel as a form of revenge, and as the events of the novel unfold it becomes almost impossible to put it down. Both this novel and *The Woman in White* were Victorian equivalents of blockbuster bestsellers like *The Da Vinci Code* – hugely popular and read by almost anyone who could read.

**Julia Bell**

# MORTAL ENGINES  Philip Reeve

12+

*Mortal Engines* follows the fortunes of city boy Tom and a disfigured outcast girl, Hester. It's set in a world where gigantic motorised cities roam the earth; a future in which our civilisation is just a fragment of memory and technological advancement has proved flawed and fleeting. The story introduces a host of richly drawn characters as it rushes towards an apocalyptic conclusion.

This is adventure on a grand scale, but Tom and Hester never get lost in the sweep of it all. Reeve is also determined to keep the moral waters murky, challenging preconceptions at every turn.

**Thomas Bloor**

### Next?

The sequel, *Predator's Gold*, is every bit as good, as is the third, *Infernal Devices*, set 16 years on, centering on Tom and Hester's daughter, Wren.

For more sprawling adventure try the Brian Aldiss science-fantasy sequence, the **Helliconia** trilogy.

Different views of how the future might be are found in *Children of the Dust* (UTBG 71) and *Ender's Game* (UTBG 115).

Or what about airships, pirates and huge adventure? Try *Airborn* (UTBG 14).

# THE MOTH DIARIES  Rachel Klein

There is simply nothing else like this book. I could read it again and again. Set in a girls' boarding school in America, it delves deep into the intense world of female adolescence, through the extraordinary eyes of a girl with a 'borderline personality disorder, complicated by depression and psychosis'.

The book is gothic, dangerous, oozing passion, paranoia and blood. Not to mention deaths – several. Is creepy Ernessa merely creepy, or is she a vampire? And is Lucy becoming weak through anorexia, or is her blood being sucked by Ernessa? The ironic tone is perfect, the voice utterly original. It is absolutely my favourite book in the world. Ever. Can you tell?

**Nicola Morgan**

## Next?

Well, as I said, there's nothing like it. But try *Mr Wroe's Virgins* by Jane Rogers, another fascinating look at young women together – written for adults.

And *Catalyst* (UTBG 65) brilliantly depicts the intensity of friendships and of life during adolescence.

Another series about intense emotion, passion and friendship set in a boarding school is Adèle Geras' **Happy Ever After** trilogy, starting with *The Tower Room* (UTBG 378).

---

# THE MOTORCYCLE DIARIES
## Ernesto 'Che' Guevara

You've seen the T-shirts – and you probably know something of the most romantic revolutionary of all time. This is the back-story, the man before he became the myth, in his own words...

Che Guevara was born in Argentina and fought alongside Fidel Castro in the three-year guerrilla war in Cuba. He became Minister for Industry following the victory of the Cuban revolution, but found 'ordinary' life unfulfilling, and went to fight for freedom in the jungles of Bolivia where he was caught and murdered under orders from the US. Written eight years before the Cuban Revolution, these are Che's diaries as he drives a 500cc Norton motorbike across Latin America, with his mate Alberto. Their adventures, written up by Che during and after the journey, make up this wonderful, beautiful and painful book.

**James Riordan**

## Next?

Read his fellow-traveller Alberto Granado's book: *Travelling with Che: The Making of a Revolutionary*; or for the whole life story, read the excellent biography by Jon Lee Anderson.

Or something more political, try Che's own book which explains his politics: *Guerilla Warfare*.

# A MOVEABLE FEAST  Ernest Hemingway

*A Moveable Feast* is a retrospective account of Hemingway's days in Paris as a young man trying to write fiction, mostly in cafés. Some elements of the account might be considered fiction – such as the degree of poverty supposedly experienced by Hemingway and his first wife Hadley – but this is incidental. Although much of the dialogue sounds like a translation from a language the author doesn't speak too well, the book is an exuberant, mostly warm-hearted evocation of Paris in the 1920s, when he hung out with a host of other young writers and artists trying to make their way in the world. Hemingway shot himself in 1961, shortly before his 62nd birthday. This book was published posthumously.

**Michael Lawrence**

### Next?

Michael Lawrence also went to Paris at 21 to write; read about it in his memoir *Milking the Novelty* (you can buy it from his website – www.wordybug.com).

More Hemingway? Try *To Have and Have Not*, a love story set during the Spanish Civil War.

F. Scott Fitzgerald admired Hemingway. Read the jazz-age classic, *The Great Gatsby* (UTBG 156), written while he was in France in the 1920s.

---

# MR MIDSHIPMAN EASY  Captain Marryat

### Next?

If you like the idea of sea warfare, try the Alexander Kent books, starting with *Midshipman Bolitho*, that take his hero through the Napoleonic wars, rising in the ranks to admiral.

Another series of famous sea stories: the **Hornblower** series by C.S. Forester. *Mr Midshipman Hornblower* is first. Like the Kent books, these are all fantastic, and you'll want to zip through the whole lot.

Don't be put off by the rather dated philosophising in this book. It was written in the middle of the 19th century, after all. The author was himself a midshipman in Nelson's navy and rose to be a captain. Many of the dashing escapades he describes are based on real events.

Reading the book, you can understand why the beginning of the 19th century was the heroic age of sail, when boys as young as 12 fought the great sea battles alongside hardened sailors, shinned up the masts in gales to haul in the sails, and stormed the forts on enemy shores to capture their guns. This book is especially dear to me because my great-great-great-grandfather was serving on this very ship. He was 15, and a third-class boy. Fred Marryat was 16 and a junior officer. They can't have been friends, but they must have known each other.

**Elizabeth Laird**

# MURKMERE Patricia Elliott

**Next?**

You might also enjoy the wildly imaginative **Gormenghast** trilogy (UTBG 154).

Garth Nix's *Sabriel* (UTBG 316) is another fantasy novel grounded in a re-imagined historical period, where trenches and barbed wire provide scant protection against the walking dead.

*Jane Eyre* (UTBG 195) by Charlotte Brontë is the classic tale of a troubled master with a dark secret and well worth a read.

Aggie comes to Murkmere Hall and Leah's story begins. Two teenagers of wildly differing character and background meet in turbulent times, setting in motion a chain of dark and richly mysterious events.

*Murkmere* is set in an alternative 18th-century England, ruled by a corrupt élite who lord it over a downtrodden people. There's an oppressive state religion that sees wild birds as objects both of veneration and of terror. This divided society is mirrored in Murkmere Hall, where the reclusive Master, crippled in a mysterious accident, broods in his library while his predatory butler exerts a sinister control over the household.

*Murkmere* blends gothic fantasy with invented history, to create a world as convincing as it is enthralling.

**Thomas Bloor**

# MY BRILLIANT CAREER Miles Franklin

Written in 1895 when the author was 16, the language of *My Brilliant Career* is old-fashioned but vivid. 'Do not fear encountering such trash as descriptions of beautiful sunsets and whisperings of wind,' writes heroine Sybilla, promising the reader stronger stuff. She longs to be a writer, but her life in the Australian bush is drudgery. She loathes and loves her resigned mother, drunken father, pretty younger sister and dirty little brothers. Escape looks unlikely, till rich handsome Harry Beecham offers marriage. Should she accept?

This book has realism, romance and humour, big feelings and big ideas. It captures the longings and conflicts of teenage life – and the even greater frustrations of a century ago – and you may well find it inspiring.

**Julia Jarman**

**Next?**

More Sybilla? Try *My Brilliant Career Goes Bung*.

Jane Austen writes about another world where women escaped drudgery through the right marriage – try *Pride and Prejudice* (UTBG 294) or the match-making *Emma*.

*The Yellow Wallpaper* (UTBG 425) by Charlotte Perkins Gilman is of the period, and tells of a marriage and one woman's breakdown.

# MY DARLING, MY HAMBURGER   Paul Zindel   14+

## Next?

Other books by Paul Zindel are a must: *The Pigman* (UTBG 288), *The Undertaker's Gone Bananas* and *I Never Loved Your Mind*. Nobody else writes quite like him, so you really should read them all!

*Are You There, God? It's Me, Margaret* and *Forever* (UTBG 135) by Judy Blume are great if you enjoy the American context and want to see the world from a girl's perspective.

This isn't *Dawson's Creek*, and it's certainly not *The OC*. It's a no-glamour look at American teen life – losing your virginity and parents / teachers totally missing the point.

This book packs a real emotional punch and – I think I can say this – doesn't have a happy ending. Maggie, Liz, Sean and Dennis are all in their final year at High School, negotiating the world of dating, first love and sex. Just when *is* the right time to stop snogging and suggest going for a hamburger?

The story is told in a mixture of letters, short stories, notes passed in the cafeteria and the usual 'Liz got out of the car' type narrative. It's like having hidden cameras in each of the characters' homes, so you really get to know them.

**Abigail Anderson**

# MY FAMILY AND OTHER ANIMALS   12+
## Gerald Durrell

First published in 1956, this is the autobiography of an English schoolboy whose family moved to the Greek island of Corfu. Gerald Durrell loved animals, and in this laugh-out-loud yarn he recounts the astonished and often-horrified reaction of his mother, two brothers and sister as he ferries home a selection of strange and wonderful insects, birds and beasts (including the odd octopus, toad and glow-worm).

Durrell paints a beguiling portrait of the Ionian landscape and a rural way of life that has since vanished. He explores the island with his dog Roger, gets into scrapes, has adventures and conveys wonderfully to the reader how simple it can be to drink in the exuberance of living. A natural-history classic.

**Sara Wheeler**

## Next?

The series continues with *Birds, Beasts and Relatives,* and there are loads more.

*All Creatures Great and Small* is the first of James Herriot's autobiographical tales about being a vet in Yorkshire.

Gerald Durrell's brother Lawrence also wrote a book about a Mediterranean island – a lyrical evocation of southern Cyprus, *Bitter Lemons*.

# MY SIDE OF THE MOUNTAIN

## Jean George

**Next?**

If you liked the wildlife aspect of this book, try *A Kestrel for a Knave* (UTBG 206).

Other great books about animals and the wilderness are *The Call of the Wild* (UTBG 01) and *White Fang*, both by Jack London.

*Woodsong* by Gary Paulsen is about growing up in northern Minnesota and training sledge dogs for a race.

Some books manage to capture your dreams, and for me this is one of them. It tells the story of a young boy called Sam Gribley who runs away from his cramped New York home to live off the land in the woods of the Catskill mountains. With only himself and his tamed animals for company, Sam spends a lot of time thinking about things that he hasn't really thought about before – life, living, other people, his family – and gradually he begins to find out all about himself. This book's got it all – adventure, escapism, insights and feelings – and it's told in such a wonderfully simple way that you feel as if Sam is talking directly to you.

If you read it, you'll never forget it.

**Kevin Brooks**

# NAKED WITHOUT A HAT

## Jeanne Willis

*Naked Without a Hat* is a story about love and acceptance. Throughout the book an underlying secret waits to be discovered. The story is highly original and the twist at the end is unpredictable. The book touches on modern subjects that have previously been taboo. It exposes people's judgements. It is interesting to see, once you have learnt the secret of the book, if you can reread it without prejudice. I found it to be a highly enjoyable read. I was eager to discover the secret. It was interesting to see the world through the eyes of a young man in love and this story made me, a self-confessed cynic, believe that young love could exist.

**Anna Posner (aged 16)**

**Next?**

Other Jeanne Willis? Try *Rocket Science*, in which a boy finds an alien creature that apparently feels neither fear nor pain, though the book is really about how we deal with difference.

Or the terrifying *The Hard Man of the Swings* (UTBG 162), set in post-war Britain, about a boy dealing with bullying.

*The Shell House* (UTBG 335) is an atmospheric novel of trying to fit in and the problems of first love.

# NARZISS AND GOLDMUND

## Hermann Hesse

A book for 'seekers'! I read this when I was a teenager and loved it. I was going through my 'looking for the answers to the Universe' phase (actually still am, come to think of it…) and I found Hermann Hesse's books a joy as he seemed to be asking similar questions to my own. What is the way to happiness? The pleasure of the flesh or its denial?

In *Narziss and Goldmund*, Hesse creates two very different characters to represent the flesh versus the spirit: Narziss the aesthete, who lives a life of serenity in a monastery, and Goldmund the artist, restless and discontent, who seeks answers through pleasure, art and beauty. Different roads but with the same destination in mind. Reading what they both have learnt at the end is a revelation.

**Cathy Hopkins**

### Next?

*Siddhartha* (UTBG 338) by Hermann Hesse is about another seeker and his path to find knowledge and happiness.

*The Prophet* by Kahlil Gibran is a collection of beautifully written passages about life; from love and work, to death.

*Illusions* by Richard Bach is another cult exploration of why we are.

# THE NATURE OF THE BEAST

## Janni Howker

### Next?

Janni has written two other powerful novels: *Isaac Campion*, which tells the story of a boy's bitter relationship with his father, and *Martin Farrell*, about plunder, robbery and vengeance. There is also a wonderful short-story collection, *Badger on the Barge*.

*Billy Elliot* by Melvin Burgess is set in a northern town during the miners' strike.

A terrifically powerful novel by one of Britain's finest authors. It's set in a northern English mill town and superbly conveys the effects of unemployment, in terms of the pain and the anger it brings on the entire community.

Meanwhile, out on the moors, there's a sheep-killer on the loose and to young Bill Coward, desperate to do something to help, it becomes a symbol of the turmoil in his own life. He decides to track down the creature and kill it, and the tension builds and builds to a truly heart-stopping finale.

This is one of those rare books where the people feel totally real and we're right there with them – in their loss of work, dignity and hope.

**Malachy Doyle**

# NEVER EVER  Helena Pielichaty

12+

Erin is devastated when her dad's business goes bankrupt and the family are forced to move from their posh house to the local council estate; she's away from her friends, sharing a bedroom and, horror of horrors, without a phone! Life goes from bad to worse when she discovers that Mr Popular from school, Liam, lives on the estate too. He's gorgeous and he knows it, *and* he's got a crush on Erin – who can't stand the sight of him.

A family crisis leaves Erin no choice but to beg him for help, but it turns out that he needs *her* help for his best mate Tommo, too. Maybe opposites do attract and they were meant to be together after all…

In a book that fizzes with all the agony and excitement, chaos and confusion of being a teenager, Pielichaty makes you feel your life is normal and underlines the dangers of judging by appearances!

**Eileen Armstrong**

> **Next?**
>
> Other books by Helena Pielichaty include *Getting Rid of Karenna* (UTBG 144), which takes a helpful and hopeful look at bullying; *Jade's Story*, a sensitive and insightful look at the mental breakdown of a parent; and *Vicious Circle*, about a teenage girl and her mother's life of poverty and grotty bedsits.
>
> Cathy Hopkins' **Mates, Dates…** series (UTBG 238) covers similar topics, but is much lighter in tone.

# THE NEVERENDING STORY  Michael Ende

12+

> **Next?**
>
> *The Last Unicorn* by Peter S. Beagle is another book about fantasy itself.
>
> *The Princess Bride* (UTBG 298) by William Goldman is the only other book I know of with the same 'feel'. (I can't put it any more specifically than that!)
>
> For another book that blurs the lines between fantasy and reality, try Alan Garner's *Elidor*.

Bastian Balthazar Bux loves stories – they're a way for him to escape from the school he hates, and the other boys who bully him. So when he finds *The Neverending Story*, he just has to take it away to read.

But *The Neverending Story* is no ordinary book – it's a gateway to Fantasia, where Atreyu the Hunter is on a quest to save the Childlike Empress. As the story unfolds, Bastian realises that he is what Atreyu is searching for, and to save the Empress he will have to enter Fantasia. In Fantasia, Bastian can have everything he's ever wished for, but there's a hidden danger waiting to trap him: while entering Fantasia was hard, leaving it will be all but impossible…

**Benedict Jacka**

# NEW BOY William Sutcliffe

16+

Hysterically funny, deeply cynical and absolutely filthy, this book is every mother's nightmare. Mark makes friends with Barry, the handsome new boy in his class. Actually, first of all he checks him out in the showers, and proceeds to fancy him madly for the course of their friendship. Of course, this doesn't make him gay. Not at all. He even gets to lose his virginity to a girl – who happens to be Barry's sister and looks just like him. Then Mark's brother comes home from university and things start to really get complicated…

As well being about sex, *New Boy* is also about the horrors of school, the homoerotic undercurrents of rugby, the terror of choosing a university and how seriously mad most teachers are.

**Leonie Flynn**

### Next?

Mark thinks that *Le Grand Meaulnes* (UTBG 216) is juvenile and boring – but I think it's amazing. Read it to see who you agree with.

Mark adores *Portnoy's Complaint* (more sex!) and reckons it should replace the school hymn book. It's by Philip Roth, and very funny indeed.

William Sutcliffe has also written a brilliant novel about travelling: *Are You Experienced?* (UTBG 28). Or read his feature on cult books on pp. 264–265 to see the sort of thing he likes to read himself.

# NICOLA AND THE VISCOUNT Meg Cabot

12+

### Next?

Meg Cabot's *Victoria and the Rogue* in which Lady Victoria returns from India or *Avalon High*, about a girl who travels back in time.

Georgette Heyer is the queen of 'Regencies'; try *Powder and Patch*, in which a country bumpkin turns himself into a dandy, just to please a girl.

Nicola adores poetry – why not read some of her favourite poet's, Lord Byron, and see where so many of our ideas of romantic heroes come from.

Straight out of school, Nicola is just like any girl. She loves dresses and shoes, worries about her skin (freckles are just so not in) and desperately wants the cutest guy around to like her. She could be any girl? Right – except Nicola lives in 1808, almost 200 years ago. But, so what if the clothes are different, and the manners slightly more polite – the boys are still the same! So, will it be the 'god', Sebastian, or her best friend's infuriating brother, Nathaniel?

With the lightest of touches on history and a sparkling heroine, this romance, with its whirl of parties and dances, its great clothes and wonderful repartee, is the perfect antidote to any dull day.

**Leonie Flynn**

# THE NIGHT COUNTRY   Stewart O'Nan

This is an adult novel, but its perfectly pitched teen voice, setting and subject matter make it a book that many teen readers will enjoy.

The story is based in familiar territory, a Hallowe'en tragedy in small-town America: three teens are killed in a car accident, one of the passengers lives on severely brain damaged and one escapes unharmed. A year on and the dead have returned to visit the living…

Sad, funny and chilling by turns, this is a highly unusual ghost story. O'Nan takes you through the quiet streets, the hopes, fears, and dreams of suburban America. The story is told from the point of view of the ghosts who have been summoned by the living and whose bitter longing helps to shape the tragedy unfolding before them.

**Celia Rees**

## Next?

Both Stephen King and Peter Straub have been generous with their praise of the book – maybe you should try one of theirs next? Start with King's *The Long Walk* (UTBG 220).

For another American writer who finds the distinctly odd inside the overtly ordinary, try Ray Bradbury's *The Golden Apples of the Sun*.

Also Lois Duncan's *I Know What You Did Last Summer* about a group of teenagers with a secret.

# THE NIGHT WORLD: SECRET VAMPIRE   14+
## L.J. Smith

## Next?

Meg Cabot's **Mediator** series links a 16-year-old girl with the supernatural. If you think your life is hard, just try being in love with a ghost from the past!

Other Meg Cabot books (where does she find the time to write them all?) that are equally unusual are the **Missing** series, about a girl who develops a strange power after she is struck by lightning.

16-year-old Poppy is dying of cancer – it's inoperable and she has only weeks to live. Her best friend James is devastated. He knows that he can save Poppy – but in order to do so he will have to break the most fundamental rules of the Night World and, by so doing, place his own life in danger.

*Secret Vampire* is the first in the incredibly popular **The Night World** series and if you liked *Buffy* or *Charmed* or *Angel* then these are the books for you. Well-written, fast-paced and smart, they take the ordinary world of American teenagers and mix it up with the supernatural.

So beware of that good-looking boy in your class – he could be a vampire in search of his next meal!

**Laura Hutchings**

# NINETEEN EIGHTY-FOUR  George Orwell

14+

It is the future. Britain is ruled by a totalitarian government. The Party demands total obedience; dissent is a crime punished by imprisonment, torture or death. There is no freedom: whoever you are, wherever you are, somebody could be watching you.

Winston Smith works for the Ministry of Truth, fabricating the present and rewriting the past. He does his best to conform – to love The Party and all that it stands for – but dreams of rebellion, revolution and liberation. Captured by the dreaded Thought Police, he is imprisoned and subjected to terrifying interrogation and indoctrination. Can he maintain his freedom of mind and spirit – particularly after he finds out what is inside Room 101?

First published in 1949, George Orwell's novel is as powerful and relevant today as it was more than half a century ago. Utterly convincing, utterly terrifying, it will change the way you look at the world.

**Graham Gardner**

---

### Next?

For another view of a totalitarian future where hope is at a premium try *Fahrenheit 451* (UTBG 121).

For a world where slavery is legal, where to be Jewish is a crime, try *The Man in the High Castle* by Philip K. Dick (UTBG 235).

Something quite different by Orwell? Try *Keep the Aspidistra Flying*.

---

## The Ultimate Teen Readers' Poll

## BOOK YOU'D LIKE MADE INTO A FILM

1 **Alex Rider series**

2 **His Dark Materials trilogy**

3 **The Saga of Darren Shan**

4 **Artemis Fowl**

5 **Inkheart**

6 **Teacher's Pet**

7 **Last Chance**

8 **The Mum-minder**

9 **Skellig**

10 **A Child Called 'It'**

# NO SHAME, NO FEAR  Ann Turnbull

During the 17th century, the Quakers were persecuted for their beliefs and were not allowed to assemble in groups of more than five. Susannah, a Quaker girl whose father is in prison at the start of this novel, falls in love with Will. His father is alderman of a town dead set against this new breed of believer.

Susannah and Will narrate the story in turn, chapter by chapter, and so we have a fascinating overview of the time. Turnbull writes most beautifully and the daily details of life, work, prison and so on are brilliantly depicted. Susannah and Will's emotions could be those of any of us living today and the book will appeal to readers with a taste for a love story that is about much more than just two teenagers falling in love. Boys as well as girls will enjoy it and learn from it in equal measure.

**Adèle Geras**

## Next?

For another story that brings the past vividly back to life, try Nicola Morgan's *Fleshmarket* (UTBG 131).

For more about Quakers, try the World War II novel *Slap Your Sides* by M.E. Kerr, in which a family are imprisoned because they believe that war is wrong.

Or a different sort of historical novel? Try *At the Sign of the Sugared Plum* (UTBG 30) by Mary Hooper, set at the time of the plague.

# NOODLEHEAD  Jonathan Kebbe

Marcus hates being cooped up in school, so he runs away. No doors, no rules – perfect. Except they keep dragging him home. But, after one run too many, when they haul him back from France it's not to his home, but to Dovedale Young Offenders' Institute.

Sharing a room with three no-hopers, his head stuffed with drugs so he can't even think, he finds it worse than school, worse than his nightmares. But Marcus is made of strong stuff, and the day they lock him up is the day the real battle begins as he struggles against drugs, sadists and do-gooders, all in an effort to prove his worth – and his sanity.

**Leonie Flynn**

## Next?

A classic story of juvenile rehabilitation – with a twist – is Louis Sachar's *Holes* (UTBG 173).

K.K. Beck writes a mean adventure story – try *Fake* (UTBG 122), in which two boys escape before they too get locked up.

Or *Zoo* (UTBG 427) by Graham Marks, in which a boy is kidnapped, kills a man while escaping, but then finds he might not be running in the right direction after all.

# NORTHANGER ABBEY  Jane Austen

Catherine leaves her dull village to visit the city of Bath, with its parties and fashionable people. She is daunted at first – but she is not a complete innocent, for she has read all about such exciting places in novels. So she knows very well that, whilst everyday people are kind, honest and respectable, there are also villains in the world who commit dark deeds of hair-raising gore and horror. Distinguishing one from the other, however, proves strangely difficult, and this leads Catherine into all sorts of embarrassments, troubles and dangers.

Northanger Abbey, like all Jane Austen's novels, is a comedy about a girl testing her beliefs about the world and finding love on the way. It's full of marvellous characters and jokes, but at the same time it's very subtle. It's a bit like a whodunnit (it contains what is very nearly a murder mystery), for everyone has their own agenda, and no one is quite as they appear. Or not to the poor heroine, in any case!

**Sally Prue**

## Next?

More Jane Austen? Try *Sense and Sensibility* first.

If you're interested in gothic novels, try the one Catherine is hooked on: *The Mysteries of Udolpho* by Mrs Radcliffe.

For a more modern Gothic novel, read *The Woman in Black* (UTBG 420).

# NOT A PENNY MORE, NOT A PENNY LESS  Jeffrey Archer

## Next?

Jeffrey Archer has written many fast-paced novels including *Kane and Abel*, and several volumes telling of his own experience in prison – *The Prison Diaries*, by FF 8282.

Robert Harris writes exciting page-turners; try *Fatherland* (UTBG 126), which speculates what might have happened had Germany won the war.

*House of Cards* by Michael Dobbs and *The Client* (or indeed anything) by John Grisham are also exciting thrillers.

Four men from very different backgrounds – an aristocrat, a doctor, an art dealer and an academic – are conned into buying shares in Prospecta Oil, which turns out to be a dud company. But agent Harvey Metcalfe picked the wrong victims this time. The four men band together and form elaborate plans to swindle Metcalfe back until they have regained the exact sum of money he took from them – not a penny more, not a penny less.

Jeffrey Archer is not a popular man, having spent time in prison himself for dishonesty, but he knows how to plot a good story and this is his best.

**Yvonne Coppard**

# NOT DRESSED LIKE THAT YOU DON'T

Yvonne Coppard

**Next?**

*Everybody Else Does, Why Can't I?* continues the mother-daughter conflict, as Jennifer gets a boyfriend…

Louise Rennison's hilarious *Angus, Thongs and Full-frontal Snogging* (UTBG 22).

Pete Johnson's *Faking It* (UTBG 123), the diary of a boy who invents himself a girlfriend for want of a real one, will be more appealing to boys.

If Jennifer thinks one thing it can be guaranteed her mum will think the opposite. While Jennifer is worried about fashion, friends, parties and boyfriends, her mum worries about Jennifer's GCSEs and if she'll get good grades. Jennifer writes about her feelings in a diary. What sets Coppard's books apart from other teen-angst books is that her mum is writing a diary too, and by reading their cleverly alternating diary entries we are allowed into their relationship, privileged to see both sides of the all-too-familiar arguments! Everyone who's ever had or been a teenager should read this laugh-out-loud-funny book. Spiky cartoon drawings enhance the humour.

**Eileen Armstrong**

# NOT THE END OF THE WORLD

Geraldine McCaughrean

This is, quite simply, a fantastic book. A retelling of the story of Noah that asks the most profound questions about faith, the relationship of man to animals, and what it might actually be like to be plunged into the 'dark reeking paradise' that is Noah's Ark.

**Next?**

Try John Rowe Townsend's *Noah's Castle* for a different take on the Noah story, or Julie Bertagna's *Exodus* (UTBG 120) for a story about escaping from a flood.

Or a slightly more adult version of the story, *In the Shadow of the Ark* (UTBG 189).

What is it like to leave behind neighbours, your best friend, the rest of your family, to certain death? What is it like when you have to butcher the last of a species that a future world will never know? As everything degenerates into madness, sickness and squalor, it is up to the overlooked member of the family, Timna, the one whose name will not be remembered when the Old Testament version is told, to find a new way in a wholly new world.

This is a small book with many dimensions – an epic, thundering read.

**Livi Michael**

# CULT BOOKS
## by William Sutcliffe

What is a cult book? Is it more than just a book that your granny would hate?

To qualify as a cult book, you have to be popular, but only with the right people. You mustn't be too popular, and your readers must absolutely not be grannies or golfers; they should be tattoo artists or rock stars. *Pride and Prejudice* (UTBG 294) is not a cult book. *The Da Vinci Code* (UTBG 90) certainly isn't a cult book.

Even though it has sold at least a million copies, *Trainspotting* (UTBG 379) is still a cult book, but only because those million readers are mostly under 30, and because the book is exclusively populated by drug addicts, weirdos and psychopaths. *The Beach* (UTBG 34) was once a cult book, but since the Leonardo di Caprio film, it probably doesn't qualify any more. It's hard to define a cult book, but you know one when you see one.

I had always wanted to write one, and first began to think I might have done it when I saw a heap of pirated photocopy editions of *Are You Experienced?* (UTBG 28) for sale near an Indian beach. Although the bookseller was, in effect, robbing me, the strange thing was, I felt more flattered than annoyed. It felt, in some way, like an induction into an exclusive gang.

One of the most important things about cult books is that they don't go away. When I was 18, you just had to read *On The Road* (UTBG 270), *Catch-22* (UTBG 65), *Steppenwolf* and *A Clockwork Orange* (UTBG 79), and that's just as true today. When my son hits that age in another 17 years, I expect he'll probably want to turn to them, too.

'Welsh writes with a skill, wit and compassion that amounts to genius. He is the best thing that has happened to British writing for decades' *SUNDAY TIMES*

**Trainspotting**

**IRVINE WELSH**

'Has all the makings of a cult classic' – Nick Hornby

**The Beach**
ALEX GARLAND

You could say that it's something to do with sex, drugs, travelling or adventure, and there's an element of truth in all those things. These books are all about forbidden or dangerous ways of life. They are culty because they give you intimate contact with people you'd be a little afraid to sit next to on the bus. The characters in these books are bigger, louder, crazier and more reckless than anyone your parents will ever introduce you to.

And that's exactly why these books are so important to read as you enter adulthood. As you begin to chafe at the restrictions of your life in the parental home, these are the books that take you out of your safe little nest and show you all the best, worst, riskiest, brightest and stupidest things that you could possibly do with your life.

At 18, anything is possible, and you have to read these books to find out what 'anything' really means. You'd be dumb to set about emulating the characters in these novels, but if you're intelligent and curious about the world, this is where you turn to find out what the limits are, and what happens if you reach them.

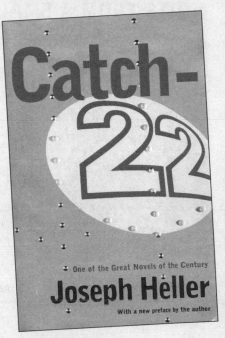

## More cult books you can read about in the *UTBG*:

**The Lord of the Rings** trilogy by J.R.R. Tolkien

**Discworld** series by Terry Pratchett

*The Buddha of Suburbia* by Hanif Kureishi

*Jonathan Livingstone Seagull* by Richard Bach

*Narziss and Goldmund* by Hermann Hesse

*Generation X* by Douglas Coupland

*Interview with the Vampire* by Anne Rice

# NOTES FROM A SMALL ISLAND Bill Bryson

12+

This book should come with a health warning: *Do Not Read on Public Transport or You'll Laugh Out Loud and People Will Think You're a Loony*. Bryson is journeying around Britain on a farewell tour before moving back to the US; on the way he manages to take a wry sideways swipe at the British and their eccentricities both endearing and baffling (he lists Sooty, HP sauce, steam trains and making sandwiches from bread you've sliced yourself among the things he doesn't really get), without ever making you think he holds anything other than great fondness for us all. He's that apparently rare creature, an American who understands irony – just don't get him started on 1960s and 70s UK town planners or you'll regret it…!

**Catherine Robinson**

## Next?

Bill Bryson's *Notes from a Big Country* repeats the same funny formula, this time in the US.

*Round Ireland with a Fridge* (UTBG 313) isn't serious travel writing but it is seriously funny!

The classic round-Britain travelogue is Paul Theroux's *The Kingdom by the Sea*.

*Queenan Country* by Joe Queenan: another American laughing at Britain, but – like Bryson – loving it really.

---

# NOTES ON A SCANDAL Zoë Heller

16+

Sheba is having an affair with a male pupil at her school. The only problem with this is that she's a teacher. Sheba confides in trusted colleague Barbara who is flattered by being party to this secretive tryst.

Barbara starts a journal – tracking the development of Sheba's teacher-pupil relationship along with insights about her own friendship with Sheba. It is through Barbara's eyes that we see Sheba's increasingly complex entanglement with the student.

But as petty rivalry and jealousy ignite Barbara's insecurities, her loyalty and devotion to Sheba slither into acts of spite and revenge. The tale unfolds darkly, with cruel twists that make you wince.

I literally could not put this book down – it's sharp, menacing and totally outstanding.

**Jonny Zucker**

## Next?

Zoë Heller's *Everything You Know* is another exploration of people's weaknesses and strengths. It's about a murderer who discovers his dead daughter's diaries.

*Friction* by E.R. Franks is a tense story based in school, this time about bullying.

*Doing It* (UTBG 109) is about a group of boys and their sex lives (including an affair with a teacher).

# NOUGHTS AND CROSSES  Malorie Blackman

**14+**

### Book One: Noughts and Crosses

Once in a while you discover a mind-blowing, thought-provoking, gut-wrenchingly emotional book that changes your life. Not often, but it does happen, and *Noughts and Crosses* is one such book. If you don't read another book all year, read this and you will never look at issues such as bullying or racism in the same way again.

Malorie Blackman is such a master at creating believable characters you feel you've known them all for years. This means, of course, that when they face pain, danger or tragedy, you share it with them; so grab a box of tissues and a slab of chocolate before you start reading.

The two main characters are Sephy, a Cross (and you'll understand what that means within the first few pages) and Callum, a Nought, who has been Sephy's best mate since childhood. The problem is that in their world Noughts and Crosses don't mix, never mind profess eternal friendship to one another. Their parents, locked in their own worlds of prejudice, tunnel vision and fear, battle to make their children understand the rules they live by.

The wonderful thing about this book is that it shows us all that, in the end, you can and must live by your own conscience and follow your own star. There is no other way.

**Rosie Rushton**

MALORIE
BLACKMAN
Noughts & Crosses
Winner of the Children's Book Award

'Intelligent, emotional and imaginatively wicked'
BENJAMIN ZEPHANIAH

### Book Two: Knife Edge

18-year-old Sephy is alone and terrified – as she gazes down at her new-born daughter. Sephy lives in a world where the ruling Crosses treat the Noughts as second-class citizens. But whilst Sephy is a Cross, the baby's dad was a Nought.

Jude, a Nought terrorist, blames Sephy for what happened to his brother, the father to Sephy's baby. Full of bitterness and hatred, his actions take him to the brink of disaster…

**Louise Manning (aged 14)**

### Next?

When you've read these two, you'll be desperate to read the story's thrilling conclusion in book three: *Checkmate*.

Or for slavery and prejudice in the recent American past, Mildred D. Taylor's *Roll of Thunder, Hear My Cry* (UTBG 311) and the rest of the Logan family saga.

For a story about slavery in Britain, try Philippa Gregory's *A Respectable Trade*.

# THE No.1 LADIES' DETECTIVE AGENCY
## Alexander McCall Smith

12+

This is a humorous first novel of a series of books set in Botswana, Africa. The story follows the doings of the colourfully named Precious Ramotswe as she founds a detective agency.

The book is great fun to read and the author describes the scenes so vividly that it is easy to imagine the landscape, the people and of course the cattle – a subject which everyone refers to regularly during conversation.

So open the cover and pack your Factor 99 sun cream and before you know it you'll be driving along a dusty road called Zebra Drive in a rickety, old, white van, before passing such landmarks as Tlokweng Road Speedy Motors, The Botswana Secretarial College and, of course, The No.1 Ladies' Detective Agency.

**Alexander Carn  (aged 12)**

### Next?

More quirky detective stories? *The Eyre Affair* (UTBG 120) is a harder read, but if you know anything about books it's brilliant.

*Brat Farrar* (UTBG 53) is a very English detective story.

*West with the Night* by Beryl Markham tells of her youth in Kenya and life as a pioneer aviator.

Or the rest of the **Precious Ramotswe** books – there are lots in the series. *Tears of the Giraffe* comes next.

# OF MICE AND MEN  John Steinbeck
14+

### Next?

*Cannery Row* and *Sweet Thursday* (UTBG 63), also by Steinbeck, are tragi-comic stories about the people who live in a poor area of Monterey on the California coast.

Another strange friendship is movingly explored in Ursula Le Guin's *The Left Hand of Darkness* (UTBG 217), a science-fiction novel.

Two migrant workers, Lennie and George, travel from farm to farm. Lennie thinks that they look after each other, but really all the looking-after is done by George: Lennie has the mind of a four-year-old. Trusting, affectionate, he understands nothing of what goes on around him, the hopes and disappointments of adulthood, sexuality, racial prejudice. He does not know that he is a man, dangerously strong, unaware of how he seems to women and to other men. George's whole life is dedicated to caring for his childhood friend who is still a child, until the day comes when something happens that George has always dreaded…

Not a love story, this is one of the greatest stories ever written about love.

**Jan Mark**

# THE OLD MAN AND THE SEA

Ernest Hemingway

## Next?

If you liked this Hemingway, you could try his novel based around his experiences in the Spanish Civil War, *For Whom the Bell Tolls*, or his account of life as a poor writer in Paris in the twenties in *A Moveable Feast* (UTBG 252).

Another epic battle between a man and a fish? *Moby Dick* by Herman Melville (OK, not technically a fish, but you know what we mean).

*The Old Man and the Sea* is really just a long short story, but part of Hemingway's attraction is his ability to convey an emotional world with spare and simple prose.

Santiago is an old fisherman down on his luck. He hasn't caught a fish for 84 days and the other fishermen think he's all washed up. But far out to sea he finally hooks a huge marlin – the largest he has ever hooked – and so ensues a battle between the old man and the fish that lasts not hours, but days.

It may not sound much to build a story on, but this is a powerful book about the hopes and tears that life is founded on, played out through the tired but noble figure of the old man.

**Marcus Sedgwick**

# OLIVIA JOULES AND THE OVERACTIVE IMAGINATION Helen Fielding

Olivia Joules, a sassy, independent and *beautiful* journalist, is desperate for excitement. She's convinced that there's something very dodgy indeed about the suave and sexy Pierre Ferramo whom she meets at a face-cream launch. But is he really as sinister as he appears, or is it just Olivia's overactive imagination at play?

Either way, Olivia is determined to find out what lies behind Pierre's immaculate exterior – in more ways than one! And her trail leads her on an adventure to some of the most glamorous spots in the world.

This is an extremely silly, very entertaining and very fast read for all fans of Bridget Jones, and anyone who fancies the idea of a light, girly thriller.

**Susan Reuben**

## Next?

If you haven't already read *Bridget Jones's Diary* (UTBG 57), it's an absolute must. Or try Helen Fielding's earlier *Cause Celeb* (UTBG 68).

For another chick-lit-meets-detective story, try *One for the Money* (UTBG 272).

Or the massively successful *The No.1 Ladies' Detective Agency* (UTBG 268).

# ON THE ROAD Jack Kerouac

**16+**

### Next?

*Heart of Darkness* (UTBG 164) by Joseph Conrad is a quest into the heart of the African jungle and the human heart.

*One Flew Over the Cuckoo's Nest* by Ken Kesey is about an outsider who takes on the authorities in a mental institution.

*Huckleberry Finn* (UTBG 181) is the original, hilarious road trip, following Huck's adventures with escaped slave Jim.

Join Sal Paradise for the journey of a lifetime across the US in search of love, music, and inspiration. In *On the Road*, Kerouac recasts his own experiences in the company of madman, prophet and con-man Neal Cassady (Dean Moriarty in the novel). They don't know where they're going, only that they have to go, and the faster, the better, in search of the ultimate high, until they cross the border into magical Mexico. Kerouac captures the intense joys and sorrows along the way, in a book that opens the wide spaces of America on the page until you can almost smell them. Once you've read this book, no journey you make will ever be the same.

**Ariel Kahn**

# THE ONCE AND FUTURE KING T.H. White

**12+**

From the magic-infused good humour of the opening chapters, this vivid retelling of the Arthurian legends gradually moves into darker territory. The plot sweeps from the Welsh borders to the Orkneys and to Cornwall, covering the length of the land.

But the drama is painfully human in scale. Witness the Orkney brothers, desperately seeking their mother's attention through a horrifying unicorn hunt, or Lancelot running mad in the forest, or Arthur, alone in his pavilion before the final battle, contemplating the collapse of all his hopes.

This is less a story of good versus evil, more a depiction of idealism set against mankind's innate destructiveness. Though grounded in an alternative medieval Britain, this is still very much a parable for our times.

**Thomas Bloor**

### Next?

More King Arthur? Try the historically accurate *Sword At Sunset* by Rosemary Sutcliff, or her younger trilogy: *The Sword and the Circle*, *The Light Beyond the Forest* and *The Road to Canmlann*. Like most of her books, they are powerful and engrossing.

Marion Zimmer Bradley's *Mists of Avalon* tells the Arthur story through the eyes of the women involved.

Rick Yancey's *The Extraordinary Adventures of Alfred Kropp* is about a plot to steal Excalibur.

# ONCE IN A HOUSE ON FIRE Andrea Ashworth 16+

**Next?**

If you like memoirs and confessional literature, try *Bad Blood* by Lorna Sage, about her strange childhood.

Or *The Bell Jar* (UTBG 37) by Sylvia Plath, one of the most important books written by a woman in the 20th century.

Another evocation of 1970s schooldays can be found in *The Rotters' Club* by Jonathan Coe.

Author Andrea Ashworth's father drowned when she was five. Her sister was three, her mother Lorraine 25. They lived in Manchester and money was tight. Lorraine's film-star looks soon attracted a new man and she fell pregnant with a third daughter. But the girls' new father beat Lorraine and she wore sunglasses all year round to hide her bruises.

Ashworth's memoir recounts her childhood in a house ablaze with violence. She survived and excelled, escaping the heat by winning a place at Oxford. Her memoir is a love story of sorts, and her bright passion for words eclipses the darkness of her subject matter.

**Francesca Lewis**

# ONE DAY IN THE LIFE OF IVAN DENISOVICH Alexander Solzhenitsyn 16+

In Stalin's USSR five million people were locked up in prison camps (called gulags). Most were innocent. You could find yourself imprisoned for a 'wrong' opinion or for being a Baptist. At a whim, sentences were increased by ten years. Countless numbers died.

This novel is an account of a single day in the life of Ivan Denisovich Sukov, imprisoned for escaping from the Germans in World War II. Life in the gulag is harsh: ice 4-cm thick inside the dormitory windows, filthy soup, inadequate clothes, cruelty. Stupidity too: attempting to build a power station when the earth is as hard as granite and concrete freezes in the bucket before it can be used.

Solzhenitsyn, a Nobel Prize winner, was such a prisoner. This short, readable and explosive novel brought the gulag system to the attention of the world.

**Alan Temperley**

**Next?**

*Papillon* by Henri Charrière is an account of life and escape from the 'hell-hole of disease and brutality' that was Devil's Island.

*The Wooden Horse* by Eric Williams is the story of one of the most famous escapes from a German prisoner-of-war camp in World War II.

And *An Evil Cradling* (UTBG 119) by Brian Keenan is the astonishing true story of his kidnapping and survival against the odds.

# ONE FOR THE MONEY Janet Evanovich

When Stephanie Plum loses her job in a lingerie store, she decides to become a bounty hunter. I guess that's what you do if you're born in New Jersey – a place where houses are neat, cars are all-American, guns are big and little girls all want to be Barbie. The hunt for sadistic prize-fighter Benito Ramirez takes her into some dark (and quite gruesome) territory. But things aren't all doom and gloom – the love of Stephanie's life so far has been Rex the hamster, but soon she's torn between cool cop Joe Morelli and Ranger the macho mercenary.

The **Stephanie Plum** series has run to ten books already, and every one of Evanovich's fans wait for another with bated breath.
**Sarah Gristwood**

### Next?

England's answer to Janet Evanovich is Lauren Henderson, whose even more raunchy heroine Sam is the star of books like *Freeze My Margarita*.

Meg O'Brien's *The Daphne Decisions* launched another very modern Miss Marple.

For an historical slant, try Elizabeth Peters' *Crocodile on the Sandback* about Egyptologist Amelia Peabody.

*Olivia Joules and the Overactive Imagination* (UTBG 269) is a take on the female detective heroine.

# ONE GIRL, TWO DECKS, THREE DEGREES OF LOVE Jonny Zucker

### Next?

If you enjoyed reading about Zoe, try *Saffy's Angel* (UTBG 317) about the eccentric Casson family.

And for a teenager who doesn't fit in at all, try *Stargirl* (UTBG 352).

For a tougher, grittier take on getting into the music industry, Benjamin Zephaniah's *Gangsta Rap*.

Zoe Wynch is determined to become a DJ. She spends every spare moment in her room practising on her decks, but everything and everyone seem to be against her dream: her architect mum thinks she should be devoting loads more time to her homework; Rix, the patronising creep down the record store, keeps telling her girls can't possibly be DJs; and at the music station where she works on Saturdays she has to spend her whole time glued to the photocopier. But worst of all, despite calling herself 'DJ Zed' Zoe's never actually had her own gig, and it doesn't look like there's much prospect of her getting one.

This is one sassy heroine whose life, loves and hopes make for great reading, whether or not you're into the music scene.
**Susan Reuben**

# ONE HUNDRED YEARS OF SOLITUDE

## Gabriel García Márquez

Often prize-winning books aren't the classics we are led to believe they are. This novel is. Winner of the 1982 Nobel Prize for Literature, this is a journey into South America, following the fortunes of generations of the Buendia family as they found and then strive to retain the town of Macondo. With its wonderful writing, often-insane characters and a charm that many so-called classics lack, you fall into this story and start to question what is real and what isn't, as flying carpets, women who give birth to iguanas and clouds of yellow flowers escape from the pages. A magical, fantastical book. A real triumph of the imagination. Novels do not come much better than this.

**Bali Rai**

### Next?

García Márquez has written many wonderful books. Try *Love in the Time of Cholera* (UTBG 227) or the haunting *Of Love and Other Demons*.

If you found the South American setting interesting, try anything by Isabel Allende – start with *House of the Spirits* (UTBG 179); or the strange and fairy-tale-like *The Alchemist* (UTBG 16) by Paulo Coelho.

# ONLY FORWARD   Michael Marshall Smith

Stark is our gun-toting, cat-loving hero – a detective with a special talent that no one else alive possesses. He travels within the strange, future city of a thousand neighbourhoods on a seemingly impossible rescue mission, beset at every twist and turn by ever-more bizarre and life-threatening challenges.

This wholly original adventure will linger in the minds of readers not simply because of the whirlwind blur of genres, jokes and violent thrills, but because of its powerful emotional core. You not only want Stark to win, you actually care for him, too.

More poignant than Terry Pratchett, more bloodthirsty than Douglas Adams: get ready for a bumpy ride. I guarantee you will not have read anything like this before.

**Keith Gray**

### Next?

*Spares* by Michael Marshall Smith is a sci-fi / comedy / thriller all wrapped up in one, with just as many weird thrills as his first.

Anything by Douglas Adams, who must have been a huge inspiration for MMS.

And don't forget the original (and perhaps still the best) wise-cracking detective, Philip Marlowe. *The Big Sleep* (UTBG 40) by Raymond Chandler is the first time we meet him.

# OPERATION RED JERICHO

## Joshua Mowll

**12+**

### Next?

For a pirate story that is more than it seems, try Tanith Lee's *Piratica*.

For secret societies of course there is Dan Brown's very popular *The Da Vinci Code* (UTBG 90).

And definitely try Philip Pullman's *The Ruby in the Smoke* and the rest of his **Sally Lockhart** books (UTBG 319).

Mowll takes that cheesy old device, the hidden archive of a secret society, and fills it with zing. The plot is preposterous, the narrative action so incessant that it makes an Indiana Jones adventure look half-asleep, and the book itself is a thing of beauty.

The setting is Shanghai and the South China Seas in 1920. Becca and Douglas McKenzie get involved with the activities of the Honourable Guild of Specialists (founded 1533) in their search for a lost gravitational device of awesome power. They get more than they bargained for: tons of violence and an awful lot of cod science. Beautifully designed, the book features maps, period photos, cut-away diagrams, pencil sketches and ephemera of all sorts. A must for nerdy swashbucklers and swashbuckling nerds.

**Mal Peet**

# THE OPPOSITE OF CHOCOLATE

## Julie Bertagna

**14+**

It's a long hot summer and Sapphire's relationship with her boyfriend Jay ends on the same night that she finds out she's pregnant. Someone is starting fires on the estate where she lives and she watches them burn night after night as her own family implodes with news of her pregnancy.

There are lots of books about teen pregnancy but this tackles the issue in a fresh way. Sapphire's mother wants her to have an abortion. Her father wants her to keep the baby. Her sister wants her to sell it. Sapphire shakes them all off and makes an unusual bond with a lad who is a loner. Together they find out things about each other, taking the novel towards a tragic and unexpected end. Riveting stuff!

**Anne Cassidy**

### Next?

Other books about relationships and pregnancy: the **Megan** trilogy by Mary Hooper (UTBG 240), *Roxy's Baby* by Catherine MacPhail (UTBG 314), or *Dear Nobody* by Berlie Doherty (UTBG 99).

Another Julie Bertagna? Try *Exodus* (UTBG 120), set in a Scotland drowning after global warming.

# THE ORACLE  Catherine Fisher

This, the first title in a compelling trilogy set in an invented yet highly believable Graeco-Egyptian world, drew me immediately into a parched Mediterranean landscape.

Mirany has become the new Bearer of the terrifying scorpion bowl in the service of the Oracle, the mouthpiece of the god. The old Archon has died and Mirany must search for the new god in secrecy, surrounded by treachery and danger. For a girl who has always privately questioned the actual existence of the god, her quest is especially fraught. This is powerful writing, as vivid and full of colour as a painting, yet with concise, intense sentences conveying an almost unbearable sense of danger.

The second book, *The Archon*, is just as gripping, but there are deeper truths to be found, too – about faith, choice and loyalty in these extraordinary, original novels that culminate in the breathtaking *The Scarab*.

**Patricia Elliott**

### Next?

For more absorbing, believable other-worlds, *A Wizard of Earthsea* (UTBG 416) and its sequels are modern classics.

All of Catherine Fisher's novels are brilliant. Try the atmospheric *Darkhenge* (UTBG 94).

In *The Sterkarm Handshake* (UTBG 354) the future clashes with the past in an original time-slip novel.

# ORANGES ARE NOT THE ONLY FRUIT

## Jeanette Winterson

### Next?

*Blankets* (UTBG 45) also describes a boy's struggle to break away from his religious community.

*Sugar Rush* (UTBG 362) explores what happens when Kim falls for her best friend Maria.

In *Candy* (UTBG 62) Joe falls for a mysterious girl who isn't what she seems.

Jeanette doesn't have an easy time of things. Adopted, growing up in a fiercely religious Pentecostal family, she has to endure endless church meetings, and her 'Mam's' conviction that she is actually God's Chosen One. Jeanette is not even sure she believes in God.

As if that weren't enough, she falls in love with a fiery-haired girl from the fishmonger's, and starts having visions of her very own personal orange demon. She has to decide if she is to live up to the expectations of her community, or follow her heart and her visions.

Threaded through this funny, moving, semi-autobiographical story of first love and big ideas are brilliant retellings of fairy tales that comment on the unique, entrancing story.

**Ariel Kahn**

# ORLANDO Virginia Woolf

Virginia Woolf jokingly called *Orlando* 'a biography' – and also 'a writer's holiday'. The title character was based on her own lover Vita Sackville-West, and the book is set in Vita's family home of Knole. The novel follows him / her through a magically long, ever-youthful life, with a sex change from man to woman along the way.

It may sound too bizarre, but Woolf's sheer exuberance and pleasure sweeps you along, from the Elizabethans through the Victorians to Woolf's own day. Racy, rushing prose, so lush you could drown in it, and a loving, intimate knowledge of 400 years of English history.

**Sarah Gristwood**

## Next?

More Virginia Woolf? Try the slim, satisfying and thought-provoking *A Room of One's Own* (UTBG 312).

Other historical novels which are also great classics include *Ivanhoe* (UTBG 193) and *A Tale of Two Cities* (UTBG 364).

For more recent takes on past times, try a Philippa Gregory such as *A Respectable Trade* or, come to that, historical detective stories, like Lindsay Davis' *The Silver Pigs*.

# THE OTHER BOLEYN GIRL Philippa Gregory

## Next?

Gregory's *The Queen's Fool* charts the power struggle between Mary Tudor and her sister Elizabeth, as both try to become Queen of England. *The Virgin's Lover* focuses on the impossible love triangle involving Elizabeth and her married lover Robert Dudley. High drama, intrigue, passion and court politics combine in an unforgettable read. *The Constant Princess* tells the story of Catherine of Aragon.

In *Mary, Bloody Mary* by Caroline Meyer, Mary Tudor, daughter of Henry VIII, tells the story of her childhood.

The riveting story of Anne Boleyn's sister, Mary, who at the age of 13 was first introduced to Henry VIII by her family to further their ambitions at court and was gradually replaced in Henry's affections by Anne.

Gregory creates cold and calculating characters so completely nasty and manipulating that we cannot help but empathise with Mary and enjoy the comeuppance Anne receives after her rise to greatness. The equally fascinating historical detail of daily life at court creates a stunning backdrop to the drama of the characters' relationships, really bringing the history books to life.

**Eileen Armstrong**

# OTHER ECHOES Adèle Geras

**14+**

Flora is a thoughtful sixth-former convalescing after fainting dramatically at her boarding school. Unsettled by a dream of her childhood in Borneo, Flora makes a record of that long-ago time, painstakingly sorting and arranging vivid, sometimes half-remembered memories into a coherent story. *Other Echoes* is a jewel of a book about a teenager looking back at a pivotal time in her life. What could have happened then that makes her feel so compelled to write it down now? The answer is partly young Flora's discovery of who lives in the haunted house on the hill, but mostly it concerns ghostly memories, loss, and the realisation of how cruel life can be even in the midst of beauty.

**Gill Vickery**

### Next?

Another book about growing up abroad is *Oleander, Jacaranda: a Childhood Perceived* by Penelope Lively.

You can learn about the events that provide the background to Flora's story in J.G. Ballard's *Empire of the Sun* (UTBG 114).

For books about going to boarding school, as the older Flora does, read Adèle Geras' wonderful **Happy Ever After** series, beginning with *The Tower Room* (UTBG 378).

---

# THE OTHER SIDE OF TRUTH Beverley Naidoo

**12+**

When Sade and Femi's mother is shot in front of them as punishment for their journalist father's controversial newspaper articles, they see no choice but to trust a female contact to take them to safety in Britain where their uncle lives. The woman, however, takes their money and abandons the children in London. The rest of the book follows Sade and Femi in their increasingly desperate attempts to find their uncle and stay in Britain. Help comes in the unlikely form of a very familiar newsreader.

If you have ever heard other people make negative comments about refugees and secretly agreed with them, then this is a book that you really need to read. I guarantee that it will make you think differently.

**Laura Hutchings**

### Next?

You can see how Sade and Femi get on in the sequel, *Web of Lies*.

Another very powerful book by Beverley Naidoo is *Journey to Jo'burg*, which deals with what life was like under apartheid rule in South Africa.

If you like books that make you think about real-life issues, then try *Noughts and Crosses* (UTBG 267) by Malorie Blackman, *Stone Cold* (UTBG 355) by Robert Swindells, or *Private Peaceful* (UTBG 300) by Michael Morpurgo.

# OUR MAN IN HAVANA Graham Greene

**14+**

Graham Greene specialised in creating and perfecting his own vivid world, inhabited by lonely men, spies and assassins. His heroes are ordinary men who find themselves out of their depth in James Bond-style adventures.

In *Our Man...* Jim Wormald has a humdrum job selling vacuum cleaners in 1950s Cuba. But he needs more money. So he accepts an offer to become an agent of the British Secret Service, which asks him to recruit his own network of agents in Cuba, something Wormald has no idea how to do. So he decides, simply, to make it all up. But his lies soon develop a life of their own. The more Wormald invents, the more dangerous his life becomes.

**James Reynolds**

### Next?

In Graham Greene's *The Comedians*, a hotelier (Mr Brown), a confidence trickster (Mr Jones) and an innocent American (Mr Smith) pass time in Papa Doc's Haiti.

Ernest Hemingway was also fascinated by Cuba. Read *The Old Man and the Sea* (UTBG 269).

Another exciting novel set in Cuba? Read Elmore Leonard's *Cuba Libre*.

Or why not try a novel by a Cuban writer? The dense, eccentric, playful *Three Trapped Tigers* by G. Cabrera Infante is written in a style as unlike Greene as you can imagine.

# OUT OF BOUNDS Beverley Naidoo

**14+**

### Next?

Other books by Beverley Naidoo about South Africa under apartheid include *Journey to Jo'burg*, *Chain of Fire* and *No Turning Back*.

*Cry the Beloved Country* by Alan Paton gives another view of the same times.

*To Kill a Mockingbird* (UTBG 375) is a story of growing up in the racially segregated southern United States.

For 50 years South Africa was ruled by the system of apartheid, the white minority making sure they remained in control by colour-coding the rest of the population and making it progressively harder for them to live, work and get an education. These stories show how the lives of ordinary harmless people were destroyed: families were forced to leave their homes because the neighbourhood was reserved for lighter skins; people were beaten and jailed for having friends of a different colour; a father was separated from his children for being a different shade of brown. First they endured, then they began to fight back, and finally Nelson Mandela was set free to lead them to a new start. Likely to leave you seething in furious disbelief, but it's all true.

**Jan Mark**

# OUT OF THE BLUE  Sue Welford

12+

**Next?**

Carl Hiaasen's *Hoot* (UTBG 175) is another story that mixes human lives with a plan to rescue endangered animals.

Read Matthew Sweeney's beautiful, touching *Fox* about another unlikely friendship between a boy and a fox.

Try more Sue Welford – how about *Waiting for Mermaids*, or *Nowhere to Run*?

Like the character of Kegan? Try *Martyn Pig* (UTBG 236).

Kegan thinks his life couldn't get any worse – his father is an abusive drunk, his mother barely knows he exists, at school he doesn't have any friends (at least, not any he wants) and everybody calls him Rat Boy.

Then it does get worse! A family tragedy, and a threat to the family of foxes he has come to love – the only things that made his life liveable. But matters improve when he befriends odd new-girl Zoë. She makes him take control of his life, fight for what he wants and pursue his dreams.

So much is packed into this slim book – a fine central character, a thought-provoking plot and a lot of emotional punch. It's about things that happen, those moments that surprise and change you – good things and bad things, things that just happen, out of the blue…

**Daniel Hahn**


# OUT OF THE DUST  Karen Hesse

12+

Deservedly, Hesse won the 1997 Newbery Medal with this tight, spare novel. It is written as a series of free-verse poems that depict a year in the Oklahoma Dust Bowl in the 1930s.

The narrator is 14-year-old Billy-Jo, and through her eyes we watch the land giving itself up to the dust storms; dust invades her family's fields, their home, their food, their minds. It is like another character, mercilessly wearing down all hope as the weeks and months progress.

Then a terrible disaster strikes the family: Billy-Jo's mother dies. She and her father blame themselves and each other and can't find a way of talking about it and healing the grief. But there's another character too – music. Like her mother, Billy-Jo is a brilliant pianist. The accident that killed her mother scarred Billy-Jo's hands, and she despairs that she will ever play again. And if she can't, what's left for her?

This is a story about tremendous courage and strength, and the personality of the narrator sings through every line.

**Berlie Doherty**

**Next?**

Something by Berlie Doherty herself? Try *Granny Was a Buffer Girl*.

*The Simple Gift* (UTBG 340) about running away from an alcoholic father, or *Locomotion* by Jacqueline Woodson. Both are told in verse form.

# THE OUTSIDER  Albert Camus

### Next?

*The Outsider* is an underrated colleague of novels like *The Catcher in the Rye* (UTBG 66), which is essential reading.

If you liked Camus' style as a writer, you could try his gripping account of an outbreak of the black death in a modern-day French town – *The Plague*.

For something equally bleak try Franz Kafka's *The Castle* or *Metamorphosis*. Both are surreal yet deeply real.

Written in the first person, *The Outsider* opens with the death of the narrator Meursault's mother. Meursault is a young bachelor in Algiers. Shortly after his mother's funeral, he gets involved in some violence with Arabs in the town, which results in him shooting one of them on the beach later that day. He goes to court, but the court seems to be more interested in his apparent lack of grief for his mother than his killing of the Arab.

Camus was an interesting man – a French Algerian, a philosopher, and a pretty good goalkeeper too. *The Outsider* is a product of the existentialist philosophy that Camus explored – the nature of what it is 'to be', whether life has meaning or not, and by implication questions of how we should exist within the rules of society.

**Marcus Sedgwick**

# THE OUTSIDERS

14+

## S.E. Hinton

Hinton was 17 when she wrote this great novel and it is her most popular book to this day. Set in late 1960s America, it's a story about social divisions and gangs.

According to Ponyboy Curtis there are only two types of people in this world – Greasers and Socs (short for 'socials'). The Socs have it all and they flaunt it to Ponyboy and his mates who come from the wrong side of town. Life is tough if you're a Greaser but the long nights are often livened up when the Socs and the Greasers have a rumble. The problems start when Ponyboy's friend Johnny kills a Soc during yet another fight. Ponyboy feels the death more than he thought he would and begins to question all the things he's ever taken for granted.

**Bali Rai**

### Next?

*Bloodtide* (UTBG 46) by Melvin Burgess is set in a future London ravaged by warring gangs.

*The Brave* by David Klass is about a moral dilemma: join a gang and fit in, or don't and be bullied?

More S.E. Hinton? Try *Rumblefish* (UTBG 315), which has a similar theme.

# THE OWL SERVICE  Alan Garner

12+

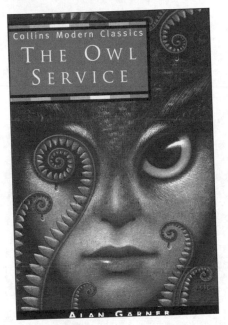

When they find a stack of old plates in the attic, Gwyn and Roger see an abstract, floral pattern, but Alison sees something else. Owls. Strange and sinister things start to happen in the Welsh valley. Gwyn discovers the beginnings of the story in an ancient legend of magic and murder, but its end, it seems, is still to come. Only the gardener, old Huw Halfbacon, will talk about it. But he, surely, is mad…

On its opening page the book draws the reader in to its eerie atmosphere, and from then on the tension never lets up. It has its lighter moments as well, though, and the characters are complex, engaging and often funny. A powerful, unforgettable book, well worthy of its classic status.

**Kate Thompson**

A teenage girl becomes obsessed by the owl patterns on an old dinner service found in a disused attic. At the same time, her stepbrother and the son of their housekeeper become rivals for her affections. What none of them realise is that they are replaying a tragedy that occurred centuries before. As ancient jealousies are translated into fresh hatred, it seems inevitable that they will destroy each other unless they can find a way to overcome terrifying forces they barely comprehend.

*The Owl Service* is a rare and special book that combines mythology and fantasy with social realism. Its real strength comes from the way it shows how good and evil stem from the passions of individual human beings, and how the battle between them takes place in all of us.

**Graham Gardner**

### Next?

Alan Garner has written some of the most amazing books ever! Try the strange and haunting *Red Shift* (UTBG 307) or the vivid excitement of *Elidor*.

Margaret Mahy writes complex, dark and scary books too; try *The Haunting* or *Alchemy* (UTBG 17).

Someone else who mixes the very real and the altogether unworldly is David Almond; try *Skellig* (UTBG 343) first.

Catherine Fisher often weaves Welsh legends into her stories. *Corbenic* (UTBG 84) is a wonderfully atmospheric mystery.

# PADDY CLARKE HA HA HA  Roddy Doyle

14+

Paddy Clarke is a ten-year-old boy growing up on a council estate in Dublin in the late 1960s. His world revolves around his gang, his school and thinking of ways to torture his younger brother Sinbad. In Paddy's world parents argue, teachers whack you and everything is a sin. It's more cutting edge than *Just William* – these kids are one step ahead of the law.

The book is narrated as a diary, and we really feel sympathy for Paddy. He's worried his parents are about to split up. His world is cruel and yet loving – he's confused. The book is funny, but also sad. But beware – it's full of Dublin slang that you may have to work at to understand at first!

**Anne Flaherty**

WINNER OF THE BOOKER PRIZE 1993

# Roddy Doyle
paddy clarke ha ha ha

## Next?

Roddy Doyle's **Barrytown Trilogy**, about the life of the Rabbitte family in Dublin, starts with *The Commitments* and continues with *The Snapper* and *The Van*.

For a look at life in Ireland before the war, read *Angela's Ashes* (UTBG 22) by Frank McCourt.

Jamie O'Neill's marvellous *At Swim, Two Boys* is a story of two Dublin boys at the time of World War I. Or for something rather more brutal, Patrick McCabe's extraordinary and disturbing *Butcher Boy*.

## BREAKING BOUNDARIES

*Doing It* by Melvin Burgess

*Junk* by Melvin Burgess

*Sugar Rush* by Julie Burchill

*Forever* by Judy Blume

*The Cement Garden* by Ian McEwan

# PAGAN'S CRUSADE   Catherine Jinks

This book is set in the 12th century, but don't expect to find any antiquated language – the hero thinks and speaks as if he's around today. Sixteen-year-old Pagan Kidrouk (born in Bethlehem, but not in a stable) is a streetwise, foul-mouthed monastery brat who sees life as a series of opportunities. Usually opportunities that aren't altogether legal. Employed as squire to a Templar knight, Lord Roland, he thinks he'll be escorting pilgrims to the Holy Land, which sounds cushy, but instead of the easy life he ends up in Jerusalem fighting Saladin.

Pagan is a great character, with a sharp wit and sharper tongue. The books chart his relationship with Lord Roland, who eventually becomes both friend and mentor, and his own journey into adulthood. Full of huge battles, brutal violence, and fascinating historical detail, these books are brilliant and should be read by everyone!

**Leonie Flynn**

### Next?

The **Pagan** books continue with *Pagan in Exile*, *Pagan's Vows* and *Pagan's Scribe*.

For another orphan who is befriended by a knight, try *Across the Nightingale Floor* (UTBG 12), though the Japanese setting makes it very different.

Or for something else set in the Middle Ages, try Bernard Cornwell's **Grail Quest** series.

# PAPER FACES   Rachel Anderson

12+

The war is over, but Dot isn't happy – if anything, she's more afraid than before. The end of the war means the looming threat of her father's return – a man who's just a paper face to her from the snapshot in her mother's handbag – and a new life that she can't predict.

This is the tale of one child's life in post-war Britain. The whole story is seen through Dot's young, inexperienced eyes, and you have to deduce for yourself the poverty and semi-neglect in which she lives, with a mother who loves her but is too young and dizzy to try to make a good life for her. It's so beautifully written that I read it slowly to savour every word.

**Susan Reuben**

### Next?

For an autobiographical account of a young girl during World War II, read the famous *The Diary of a Young Girl* (UTBG 102) by Anne Frank.

An excellent story about an evacuee is *Goodnight Mister Tom* by Michelle Magorian.

For an adventurous but also thoughtful and moving tale about a boy's experience in a different time of conflict, read *I Am David* (UTBG 182) by Anne Holm.

# PEACE LIKE A RIVER  Lief Enger

**12+**

## Next?

Read some of Cormac McCarthy's stories – start with *All the Pretty Horses* (UTBG 20).

Charles Frazier's *Cold Mountain* is set during the American Civil War.

Other classic Western novels include *Hombre* (UTBG 174) and *Shane* by Jack Schaefer.

11-year-old Reuben Hand begins life by not breathing for 12 minutes. But by a miracle he survives 'in order to be a witness' to other miracles. Reuben has a poetic younger sister, a brave older brother and a wise father. He suffers from terrible asthma but survives to become the narrator of this funny, tragic and ultimately uplifting story. *Peace Like a River* has elements of *To Kill A Mockingbird*, *Cold Mountain* and Cormac McCarthy's modern Westerns, but it is a masterpiece in its own right. Every sentence is a joy, every thought is fresh, every character believable. Without being preachy or moralising it does what stories are meant to do: it inspires you to live a better life.

**Caroline Lawrence**

# PEACE WEAVERS  Julia Jarman

**14+**

Forced to live with her father on a US airbase while her mother protests against the outbreak of war in Iraq, 16-year-old Hilde gets involved with an archaelogical dig. Unearthing a gold brooch she wonders and dreams about its owner Maethilde, a 16th-century peace weaver, and ponders the parallels in their lives. Drawing strength from Maethilde's heroic efforts and determination, Hilde begins to speak out about the futility of war and the need for peace, trying to influence the political decision-makers around her whose decisions have very real consequences on the lives of the innocent.

This is an intricately woven story for our time that asks big questions about war, morality, politics, responsibility and whether fighting is ever justified. It offers no easy answers but nevertheless radiates hope that through open communication, honesty and more visionary young people like Hilde, peace is possible.

**Eileen Armstrong**

## Next?

Jarman's *Hangman* wraps up cruel school bullying in a haunting time-slip story about World War II, while the spooky *Ghostwriter* packages learning difficulties in a suspenseful thriller.

Elizabeth Laird's *A Little Piece of Ground* (UTBG 219) and Deborah Ellis' *Parvana's Journey* highlight the human face of contemporary warfare and the devastation caused to ordinary lives.

*The Shell House* (UTBG 335) skilfully straddles two time periods: the present and WWI.

# PENNINGTON'S 17th SUMMER K.M. Peyton

## Next?

There's a sequel, called *Beethoven's Medal*.

K.M. Peyton has also written a series of books about horses and families that begins with *Flambards*.

*Cuckoo in the Nest* by Michelle Magorian is about a boy who wants to be an actor.

Try *Skinny B, Skaz and Me* (UTBG 344) by John Singleton, the story of a boy who always seems to be in trouble.

I fell in love with Patrick Pennington more than 30 years ago. Reading the book again, I still think he's one of the most attractive young men in fiction. He comes bounding off the page, a 'fourteen-stone hulk of a boy with shoulders on him like an all-in wrestler and long, reddish-brown hair curling over his collar'. It's the contrast between beauty and (not to put too fine a point on it) mild thuggishness that makes him such a star. That, and the fact that he has a great musical gift and plays the piano brilliantly.

All the way through the novel, you long for him to succeed. You long to help him, set him right, you sympathise with him at every turn and you get to know his school, his parents and friends, and also to share his adventures. You're rooting for him all the way, and his triumphs are even sweeter because he's had to go through a lot to get to them. A superb book which was even better second time around.

**Adèle Geras**

# PERFUME Patrick Suskind

I lent my copy of *Perfume* to my daughter when she was 14. I never got it back. A murder story steeped in sensuality, utterly original and often shocking, it's set in stinking 18th-century Paris and is about a man called Grenouille who has 'the finest nose in Paris and no personal odour'. His ambition is to make the most wonderful perfume in the world – distilled from the scent of murdered girls.

This is a richly written book which will open your eyes (and nose) wide, and you will learn and think and wonder. It's the sort of adult book that teenagers often love – it reaches deep inside you and changes you.

**Nicola Morgan**

## Next?

*Under the Skin* by Michel Faber – hard to say why this came to mind, except that it's also brilliantly bizarre, macabre and sinister, and a book I love.

*Dan Leno and the Limehouse Golem* by Peter Ackroyd is another murder story in a historical setting, and also fast-moving and gripping.

Another book that is both a mystery and a window into another world is Umberto Eco's *The Name of the Rose*, set in a monastery during the Middle Ages.

# PERSEPOLIS: The Story of a Childhood

## Marjane Satrapi

Quite unique! Marjane Satrapi draws in powerful black-and-white comic-strip images. *Persepolis* is her own story about growing up in Iran as the outspoken child of wonderfully open-minded parents. When the Shah is overthrown by the Islamic revolution, a beloved Marxist uncle and friends return from the Shah's barbaric jails. But joy is short-lived. A new religious tyranny takes over. War follows with Iraq. To have a rebel spirit is dangerous, so for her own safety 14-year-old Marjane is sent away to school in Austria.

  *Persepolis 2* follows the lonely story of this witty, sharply honest teenager into young adulthood as 'a Westerner in Iran and an Iranian in the West'. It's powerfully personal, opening our eyes to the politics and human beings behind black veils. I laughed, gasped and cried.

**Beverley Naidoo**

> ### Next?
>
> *Maus* (UTBG 239) about the Holocaust and *In the Shadow of No Towers* from the master graphic artist Art Spiegelman.
>
> Joe Sacco's eyewitness comic book *Palestine* is a heart-stopper.
>
> Or try *The Breadwinner* (UTBG 54), about an Afghan girl trying to save her family from starving.

---

# PHOSPHORESCENCE Raffaella Barker

> ### Next?
>
> In *Tin Grin* (UTBG 374) a girl moves from the city to the country, and meets a boy…
>
> For another story of young people trying to keep their head above water as life threatens to drown them, read *Waving, Not Drowning* (UTBG 402).

Up until the age of 14, Lola's life in Staitheley on the north Norfolk coast is a constant of familiar sights, sounds and smells. Then everything changes. Her parents separate and Lola moves to her mother's native London.

  At first she feels self-conscious amongst her new sophisticated city friends. Following an amazing shopping trip with Mum, her clothes turn out to be 'new but in the wrong way'. Her phone is a different make to those of all the other kids, it's 'much bigger – like the mobile-phone equivalent of being fat'.

  It is Lola's geography project on 'Phosphorescence' which leads to a school trip back to her old home by the sea. In her desperate attempt to fit in with others and the excitement of being with the gorgeous Harry, she ignores all she has ever been taught about the unpredictable nature of the sea, and leads the group into danger…

**Elena Gregoriou**

# PICNIC AT HANGING ROCK   Joan Lindsay

A short and strange novel that purports to recount a genuine mystery from St Valentine's Day 1900 in the Australian bush. The book is so convincing that many people quickly believed this to be the case. In fact it is a work of fiction, but a rather surreal and excellent film version by Peter Weir in 1975 helped to establish this story as an enduring modern myth.

Set in and around a private girls' school in rural Australia, the darkness of the book quickly establishes itself as a day trip by the girls and their teachers to the local picnic site at Hanging Rock turns into a nightmare when four of them go missing. By nightfall the girls still cannot be found, though the alarm has been raised and seemingly every inch of the eerie cliffs has been scorched.

What happened on the rock is never totally explained, which adds to the claustrophobic and sinister atmosphere that the book creates. A timeless gem.

**Marcus Sedgwick**

> **Next?**
>
> For more in an Australian setting, try *My Brilliant Career* (UTBG 253), about a girl hungering for life and love while coping with the outback.
>
> For something spooky and atmospheric, *Rebecca* (UTBG 306).
>
> For another scary story about a school group going astray try *Underworld* (UTBG 380).

# THE PICTURE OF DORIAN GRAY   Oscar Wilde

> **Next?**
>
> *Dr Jekyll and Mr Hyde* (UTBG 107) is also about someone whose hideous alter ego personifies the evil in his soul.
>
> Natalie Babbitt's beautiful novel *Tuck Everlasting* will make you think about the disadvantages of immortality.
>
> For books about swapping bodies, read the terrifying ghost story *The Victorian Chaise Longue* by Marghanita Laski, and the novel *Vice Versa* by F. Anstey.

You will find some of the attitudes in this book – taken for granted in Wilde's time – unacceptable today. The style is also overblown and more florid than you might be used to. But if you can accept these limitations, you will be fascinated by the story of Dorian Gray, who sacrifices his soul for eternal youth and good looks. The corrupting effects of Dorian's lifestyle, however, have to show up somewhere and they are mirrored in his portrait; the more violent and decadent Dorian's actions, the more warped and ugly the painting becomes. Eventually it degenerates into such a hideous parody of Dorian that he destroys it, thus bringing about an unpredictable and terrifying climax to the novel.

**Gill Vickery**

# PIED PIPER  Nevil Shute

14+

Sometimes you dream of finding a treasure trove: jewels or money or a map of a secret island. I found treasure when I rented a furnished flat and found a whole trunk full of novels by Nevil Shute.

*Pied Piper* is about an old man who goes on a fishing trip to France during the first months of the war against Hitler. As the Germans advance he has to try and make his way back to the coast, and safety in Britain – but on the journey he meets more and more people who beg him to take along their children. He ends up with a whole collection of them – French ones, English ones, Dutch ones…

The way the children interact to help each other, and the adventures they encounter on the way, are both touching and exciting. It's a book that breaks down barriers between nationalities and between the old and the young, and I've read it about seven times!

**Eva Ibbotson**

## Next?

Everything by Nevil Shute is good – but *A Town Like Alice* (UTBG 378) is particularly rich and colourful.

*A Little Boy Lost* by Marghanita Laski is about a man's search for his son who has been lost in the war. It has an absolutely brilliant last line!

And Robert Westall's *The Machine-Gunners* (UTBG 229) – a wartime adventure story in which a young boy finds a gun from a crashed bomber and sets up a secret fortress to defend his home town.

# THE PIGMAN  Paul Zindel

14+

## Next?

*The Pigman* is a bit of a one-off, but *Boy Kills Man* (UTBG 51) by Matt Whyman and *Friction* by E.R. Frank both portray situations where someone gets in too deep and everything spirals out of control.

*Girl in a Garden* by Lesley Chamberlain, an adult novel, also has a similar theme though a different and less in-your-face feel.

John and Lorraine are ordinary kids with ordinary names and ordinary lives. The Pigman, or Mr Pignati, is a sad and lonely old man who is somewhere between ordinary and extraordinary. Their friendship with him becomes the catalyst for extraordinarily awful events. On page four you learn that the Pigman eventually dies, but this knowledge does not lessen the impact of the way in which John and Lorraine each tell their stories of the shockingly realistic and ultimately heart-rending events leading up to his death.

This is a story of what happens when simple events spiral out of control. It's also a story of taking responsibility – even if it's too late.

**Nicola Morgan**

# PIRATES! Celia Rees

Boys have had juicy adventure stories forever, while girls have generally had to make do with much tamer stuff. But not always – for Celia Rees writes adventure stories for girls, every bit as juicy as those for boys.

*Pirates!* has scenes set on the docks of 18th-century Bristol, in the turquoise bays and emerald mountains of pirate-haunted Jamaica, and in the jungles of Madagascar. The heroine finds life as a merchant's daughter narrow and unsatisfying; especially when her stepmother decides to make a young lady of her. After her father's death, she's shipped off to Jamaica, and is shocked by the ugly truth about how her family made its money – slavery. She learns that the law tolerates great injustice and cruelty; and she has to join an outlawed pirate crew to find a sort of democracy, and also friendship, loyalty and love.

It's all so exciting and well-told, that you won't even notice the solid knowledge and research that underpins it all. You simply believe that Celia Rees could captain a fast yankee schooner from the Indies to Afric's shore. A wonderful read!

**Susan Price**

### Next?

For another girl pirate, *Piratica* by Tanith Lee is about a girl whose life is not quite what she thinks it is. *Plundering Paradise* by Geraldine McCaughrean is also a tale of pirates, adventure and Madagascar.

And pirates in icy waters? *Sea of Trolls* (UTBG 322) by Nancy Farmer.

For another, altogether different, Celia Rees, try her acclaimed *Witch Child* (UTBG 415).

## ANIMALS

*Redwall* by Brian Jacques

*Watership Down* by Richard Adams

*Animal Farm* by George Orwell

*The Amazing Maurice and His Educated Rodents* by Terry Pratchett

*The Call of the Wild* by Jack London

*Pirates!* Celia Rees

# PLAGUE  Malcolm Rose

**Next?**

Of course there was a real plague in London back in 1665, and you can read about that in *At The Sign Of The Sugared Plum* (UTBG 30) by Mary Hooper.

If you enjoy *Plague*, you're bound to like Malcolm Rose's other thrillers, such as *Clone* and *Transplant*.

In John Wyndham's *The Day of the Triffids* (UTBG 96) the world goes blind – but why?

*Plague* is one of the most exciting – and gruesome – scientific thrillers you'll ever read. It's set in ordinary, everyday Milton Keynes. There, one by one, the inhabitants fall victim to a new strain of a virus that results in a haemorrhagic fever – which means you bleed uncontrollably until you die. As yet there is no cure. It's a race against time to find one, and caught up in the drama are three teenagers – Rev from the good side of town, Lucy his girlfriend from the council estate, and Scott, son of one of the doctors at the hospital.

*Plague* is pacy, nerve-wracking and not for those of a delicate disposition!

**Sherry Ashworth**

# POBBY AND DINGAN  Ben Rice

Are you a fruit-loop if you talk to people who don't exist? Ashmole thinks his sister Kellyanne definitely is, because of her devotion to her invisible friends Pobby and Dingan. But when these friends go missing at their father's opal mine and Kellyanne sinks into a decline, Ashmole has to face the fact that they are utterly real, at least to her – and also that he loves her enough to risk humiliation and even violence to make the folks of Lightning Ridge take Pobby and Dingan seriously.

This short novel paints a memorable word-picture of a small mining community in Australia, and of a family riven by struggles and differences. With Ashmole as catalyst, they all rally round in the crisis of Kellyanne's illness.

Ashmole is a true hero, not least because he is torn between disbelief and belief in his little sister's friends, who in the end can only be seen as the intangible soul, not only of Kellyanne, but of Lightning Ridge itself.

**Lynne Reid Banks**

**Next?**

For another slim, thought-provoking book – this time set in America – read *Tuck Everlasting* by Natalie Babbitt.

For another book about believing in people, *Storm Catchers* by Tim Bowler.

A sometimes chilling story set in an English mining community, David Almond's *Kit's Wilderness* (UTBG 211).

# POLO Jilly Cooper

**Next?**

Jilly Cooper excels at these huge romps of novels; try *Riders* next. Or some of her more-gentle romances, all of which have girls' names, such as *Emily*.

*Vanity Fair* (UTBG 395) is the 19th-century equivalent of Jilly Cooper's work – read it for a superb portrayal of the best social-climbing heroine ever.

When I first read this book the cover said it all – the gold lettering *Polo* and the image of a man's legs in tight, white jodhpurs, with a woman's manicured hand close to his crotch. Reading this again, I noticed the new cover has been slightly toned down (just the jodhpurs now). But the content is still as racy as I remembered.

Polo is a fast-paced, dangerous and exciting sport, played on horses by rich people with double-barrelled names. If this book is to be believed, the players are also pretty interested in sex. Like an upper-class version of *Footballers' Wives*.

You've probably never met selfish, bitchy characters like this before. Beautiful, talented and brally Perdita, who gets on a lot better with horses than with people. Ageing film stars and their toy boys, Argentinians with flashing eyes and wicked tempers. And even Prince Charles makes a couple of appearances.

**Katie Jennings**

# A PORTRAIT OF THE ARTIST AS A YOUNG MAN James Joyce

James Joyce is considered by many to be the greatest writer of the 20th century. This, his first novel, is closely based on his own life, and is an amazingly convincing portrayal of the thoughts and actions of a highly sensitive young man.

The book takes us from the early childhood of Stephen Daedalus, our hero, through to university and a decision to leave Dublin, Ireland, faith and family. Stephen is tormented by religious and sexual guilt, but also changed forever by the idea and experience of beauty. It's not always an easy read, this, but the writing is superb and you may well find it a truly inspirational book, as I did.

**Malachy Doyle**

**Next?**

Some other powerful stories of young men growing up are to be found in *Cider with Rosie* (UTBG 77) and *Le Grand Meaulnes* (UTBG 216).

*Counting Stars* (UTBG 85) by David Almond tells stories of his own youth.

*The Toll Bridge* (UTBG 376) by Aidan Chambers and Robert Westall's *Falling into Glory* are both about the complexities of love.

# POSTCARDS FROM NO MAN'S LAND
## Aidan Chambers

As compelling as all Chambers' novels, this deserves more than one reading. Jacob is in Amsterdam to visit relatives of the family who saved his grandfather, wounded in the Arnhem fighting. His experiences in the present alternate with the memoirs of Geertrui, who rescued and loved his grandfather. Readers will be equally gripped by both stories, and by Jacob's questioning of his identity as he meets the novel's other characters: Daan, Geertrui's angry, charismatic grandson; the fascinating Ton, mistaken for a girl at an attempted pick-up; Hille, an engaging possible girlfriend; and Geertrui herself, now dying of cancer and awaiting euthanasia.

All their stories weave together into a gripping, thought-provoking story.

**Linda Newbery**

### Next?

More Aidan Chambers? Try *Dance on My Grave* (UTBG 91).

At the start of *Postcards...*, Jacob has just visited the Anne Frank House; *The Diary of a Young Girl* (UTBG 102) is essential reading for anyone interested in World War II, Jewish history, or in human courage and resourcefulness.

*Tamar* (UTBG 367) by Mal Peet deals with similar issues – it's also a breathtaking read.

# POWER OF THREE  Diana Wynne Jones

### Next?

*The Homeward Bounders*, also by Diana Wynne Jones, is another mind-tangling story of other worlds.

If you want to try a completely different future world, give Philip Reeve's *Mortal Engines* (UTBG 250) a try.

Or try something by Margaret Mahy – how about *The Changeover* (UTBG 69)?

This is the intricate story – the author specialises in intricate stories – of Gair. His brother and sister both have supernatural gifts. In the beginning Gair, the oldest of the three, feels inadequate and just plain ordinary, and this at a time when his people are being threatened both by the Giants and the Dorig. But Gair, who struggles to become wise, does have a noble part to play on behalf of his magical society. His powerful siblings retreat. Gair exercises power at various levels.

I was well into the story when I found the Giants were not the sort of giants I had originally supposed. Wynne Jones' humour does not detract from the mystery and family drama that make up this complex and entertaining tale.

**Margaret Mahy**

# A PRAYER FOR OWEN MEANY John Irving  14+

I've read all of John Irving's books and rate him amongst my all-time top authors, and this is definitely my favourite novel by him. It's dead funny, totally unpredictable (as all good writing is) and ultimately, gut-wrenchingly tragic. It's about a boy called Owen Meany who 'SHOUTS ALL THE TIME!' and is physically quite little, even when he 'grows up'. Fairly early on in the story Owen accidentally deprives the narrator of his mum during a baseball game, when he clobbers the ball which hits and kills her – this sort of thing always makes for an interesting narrator / character relationship.

After reading this book I was completely convinced I had knocked around with Owen Meany during my own childhood and teenage years but couldn't quite remember where he lived or what school he'd gone to. All I did know was that we'd had some great times together and that he'd been my best pal ever. However, I suspect that most people feel this once they've read this great book.

**Michael Cox**

> ## Next?
>
> More John Irving? *The World According to Garp* (UTBG 421) is another tragic, hilarious book to make you think.
>
> Garrison Keillor is another author who writes about weird characters in rural America. Start with *Lake Wobegon Days*.
>
> Another American youth, but this time a powerful true story – Tobias Wolff's *This Boy's Life* (UTBG 372).

# PREY Michael Crichton  16+

> ## Next?
>
> Philip Kerr's *Gridiron*. If you like *Die Hard*, you'll love this techno-thriller set in a state-of-the-art skyscraper (with a mind of its own).
>
> *The Big Picture* by Douglas Kennedy, another movie for the mind, and a hugely addictive page-turner.
>
> *A Simple Plan* by Scott Smith, in which two brothers find a million bucks, but at what price? So much better than the film adaptation.

People often dismiss books that 'read like a movie'. I have never understood why. I was raised on films, and the hours I spent in front of the silver screen inform my novels today. Michael Crichton knows how to write thrillers that truly play out in your mind's eye. That his novels tend to become major films speaks volumes. *Jurassic Park* may be his most celebrated work, but I think *Prey* is better. There are no dinosaurs in this cautionary tale of technology run wild. The bad guys here are nanobots – microscopic flying machines with an instinct to swarm, that turn on their scientist creators. Read the book now, before the film comes to a cinema near you!

**Matt Whyman**

# PRIDE AND PREJUDICE
## Jane Austen

14+

When I was 13 I found *Pride and Prejudice* and was hooked from the moment I read the opening sentence: 'It is a truth universally acknowledged, that a single man in possession of a good fortune, must be in want of a wife.' The novel, set in the late 18th century, concerns Mr and Mrs Bennet and their five daughters, all of whom, in their mother's eyes, are in need of a good husband, especially one with a fortune. Jane is pretty and sweet-tempered, Kitty and Lydia are frivolous and flirtatious, and poor stolid Mary is dull. Then there is Elizabeth, the heroine at the centre of the story, a spirited young woman well able to stand up to the rather arrogant Darcy when he comes wooing her. The characters are all convincingly and wittily drawn and live on in the memory long after one finishes the book.

**Joan Lingard**

### Next?

More Jane Austen, of course. To compare, try **Persuasion**, a more sombre tale overall but with another cracking hero, Captain Wentworth.

The marriage problem is still around; read about it in Bali Rai's *(Un)arranged Marriage* (UTBG 388).

A woman who sees marriage entirely as a means to her own ends (as in getting very rich) is Becky Sharp in **Vanity Fair** (UTBG 395).

For more Regency romance you can't beat Georgette Heyer; try *Arabella* (UTBG 27).

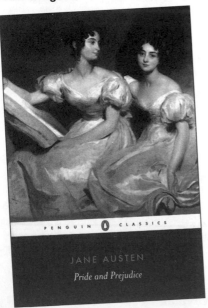

PENGUIN CLASSICS

JANE AUSTEN
*Pride and Prejudice*

I love books that you can read over and over and still find something new to enjoy in them. *Pride and Prejudice* is that kind of a book. The very first time I read it, it was as a romance. I wanted the spirited Elizabeth to marry Darcy. I found his aloofness really sexy. And she turned him down! I could never understand how she could prefer the smarmy Wickham! The next time I read it, I laughed out loud at Mr Collins, cringed at Mrs Bennet and enjoyed the dry wit of her husband.

It is a totally compelling story. There are no surprises. I know exactly what is going to happen, but I never tire of reading this book.

**Catherine MacPhail**

# THE PRIME OF MISS JEAN BRODIE

**14+**

## Muriel Spark

This is an immensely readable and funny book about a group of girls in a select Edinburgh school and their unconventional teacher Miss Brodie. Set in the 1930s just before the outbreak of World War II, it charts the girls' development from the ages of 11 to 18, at Marcia Blaine School where students wear lilac uniforms and hatlessness is an offence. Miss Brodie – who cultivates a small group of students as her elite 'set' – is charismatic and inspirational but ultimately dangerous – not least because of her admiration of fascism and her dubious sexual motives. There is an excellent play based on the novel by Jay Prissori (which I was in, aged 17!) and also a great film starring Maggie Smith.

**Sue Mayfield**

### Next?

*Picnic at Hanging Rock* (UTBG 287) is about a girls' school where things go very wrong during a walk in the country.

More by the great Muriel Spark? Try *The Girls of Slender Means* next.

Iris Murdoch was another writer who wrote exquisitely about relationships; try *The Bell* (UTBG 36) first.

For another book about girls in the 1930s, try *The Pursuit of Love* by Nancy Mitford.

## The Ultimate Teen Readers' Poll

### BEST BOOK ABOUT OTHER WORLDS

1 **Harry Potter series**

2 **The Lord of the Rings trilogy**

3 **His Dark Materials trilogy**

4 **The Chronicles of Narnia**

5 **Kensuke's Kingdom**

6 **Skellig**

7 **Artemis Fowl**

8 **The Edge Chronicles**

9 **Alice in Wonderland**

10 **The Divide**

# COMING OF AGE

## by Matt Whyman

Becoming an adult doesn't require an entry exam. There's no need to go on a training course, or do anything that involves pass or fail. It's just something that happens to everyone at some stage, whether they like it or not.

So how do you graduate to the grown-up world? Is it something to do with your developing body, the way you see your place in the world, or how people relate to you? The truth is everyone has a different experience. For some it can be a slow and subtle transformation, while others might encounter a single event that changes their life forever...

'A fabulous story of sexual fascination – guilt-free, intoxicating and delicious' Melvin Burgess

Ultimately, there is no right or wrong way to go through it. What matters is that you're able to make sense of things, so you can get on with making the most of your life. Which is where books can work wonders...

Whether you're into action, adventure, romance, gritty realism or faraway fantasies, a book works best when it stirs up your heart and mind. A really good one won't end with the full stop either. If a story strikes a chord, it can leave a question mark hanging over your head. You're left to think about what you've just read, and how it relates to your growing sense of identity. It doesn't have to be exclusively about characters on the cusp of adulthood, like the hormone-crazed lads in *Doing It* (UTBG 109) by Melvin Burgess, or the girls in Julie Burchill's *Sugar Rush* (UTBG 362). You might connect with big ideas, like those explored across Philip Pullman's **His Dark Materials** trilogy (UTBG 170) or simply admire the attitude that shines from any tale that grips you. It's all about stirring up emotions, and making you feel alive.

James Herbert wrote my coming-of-age novels of choice. I was addicted to being scared witless as an endless chain of inescapable horror confronted the hero. It might've stopped me from sleeping at night, but the fact that these guys always managed to survive showed me the value of determination. The lovemaking scenes were an added bonus, and frankly I learned more about how to do it from *The Rats*, *The Fog* and *The Survivor* than I did when we covered human reproduction in biology. It may have led me to believe that 'unsafe sex' meant getting under the covers together without first checking the room for zombies and bloodthirsty rodents, but then I learned about life wherever I could get the information.

Nowadays, there are non-fiction books that cover all the subjects I so desperately wanted to know about. They can be a great source of information and advice, especially when it comes to issues we find hard to talk about with friends and family. You might be concerned by personal stuff that's just too embarrassing for words, and so it can come as a revelation when you find what you're looking for on the page. Knowledge, after all, is power.

With clear, balanced information to hand, you can reach decisions with confidence about how to make the most of your life. It beats just hoping for the best and then lying awake worrying at night. Besides, you need that time to enjoy the books that make your world go round.

MEG ROSOFF

How I Live Now

'Magical and utterly faultless'
– Mark Haddon

Shortlisted
ORANGE
AWARD
for new
writers

## Ten books about coming of age:

*This Boy's Life* by Tobias Wolff

*A Boy's Own Story* by Edmund White

*How I Live Now* by Meg Rosoff

*Gigi* by Colette

*The Dud Avocado* by Elaine Dundy

*Empire of the Sun* by J.G. Ballard

*The Rachel Papers* by Martin Amis

*Le Grand Meaulnes* by Alain-Fournier

*The Cement Garden* by Ian McEwan

*The Go-Between* by L.P. Hartley

# THE PRINCESS BRIDE

12+

## William Goldman

You know a book is really good when you remember certain details about reading it: what the weather was like, what colour socks you were wearing. When I plopped myself down on my green vinyl beanbag chair and opened *The Princess Bride*, it was raining and my socks were red. And I don't think I moved for the next six hours because Westley, the handsome farm boy, was risking death (and much worse) for Buttercup, his one true love.

This book is an amazingly fun ride – a cut-to-the-chase story of love, adventure, really good guys and wickedly bad. It's also smart, funny, hard to put down and not just for fantasy lovers.

**Sara Nickerson**

### Next?

A very funny book that satirises all the stories of wizards, elves and poor boys who end up saving the world is Paul Stewart and Chris Riddell's *Muddle Earth*.

*Good Omens* (UTBG 152) is a totally loopy look at the battle between Good and Evil.

Want another funny fantasy story (that's also great for non-fantasy readers)? Try something by Robert Rankin, such as the anarchic *Waiting for Godalming*, about God's other son (Colin) and a private detective hired to investigate God's death.

Or *Blart* by Dominic Barket, about a pig-boy reluctantly dragged into a quest.

Now, I know what you young males are thinking. You're thinking *there's no way I am going into a bookstore and asking for a novel with the words 'princess' and 'bride' in the title*. I know this, because that's what I thought myself many years ago. Some of my more enlightened classmates had read the book and were urging me to get it, but for a while I couldn't get past my machismo. Finally the glowing reviews became too much to ignore, so I asked a friend if I could borrow it. And he said *no, you have to buy this yourself. You have to walk up to the counter and say the words. It's like a badge of courage.*

So I did. I walked in there and said the words. Then I went home and did not eat for eight hours. Instead I devoured Mr Goldman's masterpiece. This is simply the funniest book you will ever read, packed with hilarious one-liners, riotous characters and side-splitting situations. It is also jammed with swordfights, giants, riddles, revenge, magic and torture chambers. The plot is clever, the style is hypnotic and the conclusion is satisfying. William Goldman should be paying me for all the nice things I'm saying. But they're true, all true. Take my word for it, break open the piggy bank, go down to the store and say the words. You will not be disappointed.

Oh yes – there is a princess in the story, who is also a bride.

**Eoin Colfer**

# THE PRINCESS DIARIES  Meg Cabot

### Next?

There are six, so far, in this series – look out for them all. And, of course, all the other Meg Cabot books.

Gail Carson Levine writes totally modern fairy stories, try her *Ella Enchanted*, about a princess gifted at birth with obedience.

*The Sisterhood of the Travelling Pants* (UTBG 341) is about a group of girls like Mia – though none of them are princesses!

Mia's your average American teenager until her dad arrives with a secret that's been hidden since she was born: she's really a princess! But how? Enter 'Grandmère', to turn the 5'9" 'freak' into a beautiful, graceful princess. Soon Mia is being plucked, styled and tutored to within an inch of her life, yet she still can't understand boys! Mia's life is changing, and not necessarily for the better!

I love this book. Any girl will sympathise with Mia's problems and understand her worries. Meg Cabot's way of telling the story through diary entries really works, and you end up knowing Mia, and hoping that she gets her happy ending.

**Issie Darcy (aged 13)**

# THE PRISONER OF ZENDA  Anthony Hope

Rudolf Rassendyl, a rather idle English gentleman, decides to journey to Ruritania to see a distant cousin, whom he's never met, be crowned king. In Ruritania, Rassendyll dozes against a tree before continuing on to the castle. He wakes to voices discussing his striking likeness to the future king (also called Rudolf). That night the two cousins – Rudolf Rassendyl and Rudolf the soon-to-be King of Ruritania – dine together. Early next morning, Rassendyll is woken and told that the future king is out cold – he drank too much the night before – and that he, Rassendyll, must stand in for him at the coronation. But this is only the beginning of the adventure. When the King is abducted by his jealous brother Michael and his ruthless henchman Rupert of Hentzau, Rassendyll is forced to keep up the pretence that he is the King – in the course of which he falls for Princess Flavia, the King's betrothed.

The young reader who loves tales of intrigue, adventure, heroism and villainy (and doesn't mind a spot of love) need look no further...

**Michael Lawrence**

### Next?

...except perhaps afterwards, to the sequel, *Rupert of Hentzau*.

Then try *The Count of Monte Cristo* by Alexandre Dumas which has more impersonated nobles, heroism and romance.

Or try the historical **Sally Lockhart** books (UTBG 319) starting with *The Ruby in the Smoke*.

# PRIVATE PEACEFUL  Michael Morpurgo

**14+**

Nobody has written more classic children's books than Michael Morpurgo – but for me this is his best book yet.

Set against the background of World War I and the shocking fact that over 290 soldiers were unjustly executed for cowardice, it tells the story of two brothers, Charlie and Thomas Peaceful, their life in the English countryside before the war, their recruitment and subsequent fate.

It's a book with an angry heart, but the mood is often gentle, even elegiac. In one chapter, an aeroplane flies over the two brothers. It's a moment of wonder. A defining moment in an English summer. And yet also a harbinger of the horrors to come.

*Private Peaceful* is brilliantly structured, with a twist that took me completely by surprise. It should be read by anyone studying the Great War... In fact by anyone wanting to read a great writer at the top of his form.

**Anthony Horowitz**

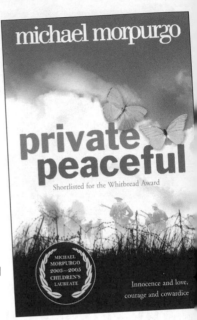

'We hear the shell coming and know from the shriek of it that it will be close, and it is.'

Life in the battlefields of World War I was ghastly and left men with the most horrific memories. Old and young men fought and spent long hours together in the squalid conditions of the trenches.

For young Private Thomas Peaceful it is no different. Patriotic and naïve, he joins up to follow his older brother into war. He soon finds out that war is not what the posters back home said it would be like. Spending many an hour in the trenches he reflects on his childhood and fond countryside memories.

Michael Morpurgo's writing style is amazing and brings the story to life. It leaves you shocked, stunned and sad all at once. A mixture of reflection, romance and a poignant climax make this book a definite must-read.

**Louise Manning (aged 14)**

## Next?

For another simply told but very moving story of the same war, Michael Foreman's *War Boy*.

Or for a slightly harder read about World War I try *When the Guns Fall Silent* (UTBG 409).

Michael Morpurgo writing about a different war? Try *Waiting for Anya*. Or you might like a book he edited of short stories about war: *War: Stories About Conflict*.

A book that shows a terrible side of a different war is Jerry Spinelli's *Milkweed* (UTBG 244).

# A QUESTION OF COURAGE   Marjorie Darke

It is 1912 and Emily Palmer works long hours as a dressmaker. Not only is she expected to hand over most of her meagre wages to her family, but she also has to act as a skivvy for her brothers.

Then she meets Louise Marshall, who introduces her to the suffrage movement. Emily moves to London to become more involved in 'the Cause'. But she soon learns that the times are extremely hostile to women, especially women strong enough to fight for their rights. The suffragettes are jeered at in the streets, manhandled and imprisoned…

This story is a potent reminder of what so many had to do to earn the right to vote (a right that so many today don't bother to exercise!).

**Helen Paiba**

> **Next?**
>
> *A Rose from Blighty* continues Emily's story.
>
> *Remembrance* (UTBG 309) is set during World War I and follows the story of a group of friends.
>
> For another tale of a young woman caught up in the suffrage movement, read Linda Newbery's *Polly's March*.

# THE RACHEL PAPERS   Martin Amis

Charles Highway is turning 20 tomorrow and is making the most of the occasion to put his teenage years into order – to reflect on his romantic conquests (and other rather less important things) and file away his collection of notes…

Charles is implausibly clever and well-read, and a methodical planner of every amorous encounter he has (his *Conquests and Techniques: A Synthesis* is particularly handy for this). But when he meets Rachel, well … OK, so Charles' seduction techniques may work, maybe he will be able to get her to sleep with him – but what then? He soon discovers there are certain things you can't plan…

This dazzling novel was Martin Amis' first, published when he was just 25. It's funny and filthy and the writing is electric, and it boasts a captivating main character you cannot stop listening to. You may not altogether approve of him, but then, they're often the most interesting, aren't they?

**Daniel Hahn**

> **Next?**
>
> Everything that Martin Amis writes is exceptional, though nothing is quite like this. Try *London Fields* next, though it's a bit more of a challenge.
>
> *The Cement Garden* (UTBG 69) is nothing like this book – except, I suppose, that it's about teenagers and sex and is pretty shocking – but it was Ian McEwan's first novel, too.
>
> I don't know another narrative voice like Charles Highway, but for one with seriously powerful narrative energy, read *Vernon God Little* (UTBG 395).

# RACHEL'S HOLIDAY  Marian Keyes

**14+**

## Next?

All Keyes' books have equally sharp insights into love, marriage, divorce, babies, perfect partners (or not!) and female friendship. *Under the Duvet* is a very different collection of short stories and journalistic scribblings.

For another fabulously unsorted heroine try *The Secret Dreamworld of a Shopaholic* (UTBG 325).

And you'll find lots more recommendations in our pink lit feature on pp. 72–73.

One of the funniest so-called 'chick-lit' authors you'll ever find, but she's so much better than that. Keyes' tongue-in-cheek humour, witty one-liners and sparkling dialogue is so real you'll almost hear it, and watch her characters spring out from the pages as you read.

Although the Rachel of the title swears to herself and those around her that she only uses recreational drugs for purely recreational reasons, she nevertheless finds herself at the Cloisters Rehab Clinic 'just in case'. She quickly consoles herself that she's not at all like any of the other mad, bad and loser residents (some of whom are truly hilarious) but soon finds her salvation – and soulmate – in Chris, definitely a 'man with a past'.

Like the purple-wrapped toffee in a box of chocolates, Keyes' fiction always hides something important at the centre. It's as addictive as Rachel's drugs and as moreish as those chocolates.

**Eileen Armstrong**

# RADIO RADIO  Graham Marks

**14+**

It happens almost by accident – the pirate radio station they've been working on has been shut down and as they all sit despondently in Cherrytree Café, Tom makes a casual suggestion, let's 'start our own station and do it our way…'

A casual suggestion, but as it turns out 'Reel FM' will shape their summer holidays, it will make and break friendships, and send Stella, Nick, CC and the others off into their next year changed.

Graham Marks' novel is written as a screenplay – dialogue, set-up shots, camera angles – which may take you a few pages to get used to; but soon you'll find it a really effective way of telling an exciting story with many perspectives in a way that's snappy and engaging.

**Daniel Hahn**

## Next?

Try more Graham Marks – *How It Works* or *Zoo* (UTBG 427).

Read Jonny Zucker's great story of a young life changed by music – *One Girl, Two Decks…* (UTBG 272).

For another group of teenagers whose lives change in a single summer, try *How I Live Now* (UTBG 179) by Meg Rosoff.

# THE RAG AND BONE SHOP
## Robert Cormier

Cormier, whose *The Chocolate War* virtually invented the modern teenage novel, once said that he had to be emotionally involved with the novel he was writing. It shows in everything he produced, his writing probing the dark side of human existence with a scalpel-like intelligence. In *The Rag and Bone Shop,* 12-year-old Jason is interrogated about the murder of Alicia Bartlett. The interview, conducted by a man called Trent, comes to resemble a priest's confessional. *The Rag and Bone Shop* is a compelling psychological thriller. At around 150 pages, it can be read in one sitting and is one of the most convincing young-adult novels ever written. What's more, it concludes with one of the most stunning plot twists you will ever read. Don't miss it!
**Alan Gibbons**

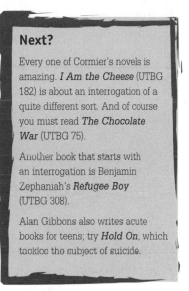

**Next?**

Every one of Cormier's novels is amazing. *I Am the Cheese* (UTBG 182) is about an interrogation of a quite different sort. And of course you must read *The Chocolate War* (UTBG 75).

Another book that starts with an interrogation is Benjamin Zephaniah's *Refugee Boy* (UTBG 308).

Alan Gibbons also writes acute books for teens; try *Hold On*, which tackles the subject of suicide.

# RANI AND SUKH  Bali Rai

Two kids in the same year at school: fit lad, fanciable girl. There's a mutual attraction and they get together, but there's a problem. 'Well, isn't there always?', I hear you ask. Yes, but this one's different.

Rani's and Sukh's parents are from the Punjab, and something happened there, years ago, that neither youngster knows about. It means that to this day, the Sandhu and Bains families – to which the two kids belong – will have nothing to do with each other. No exceptions, even in the face of true love. If the families meet by chance, there's bloodshed.

I found Bali Rai's novel absorbing because the conflicts in it arise from both a clash of cultures and a clash *within* a culture. Exciting stuff.
**Robert Swindells**

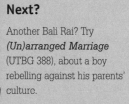

**Next?**

Another Bali Rai? Try *(Un)arranged Marriage* (UTBG 388), about a boy rebelling against his parents' culture.

Or to read about India try Jamila Gavin's *Out of India*, a memoir of her childhood.

*Caught in the Crossfire* (UTBG 68) is about racial tension and prejudice.

# RASPBERRIES ON THE YANGTZE

## Karen Wallace

The brilliant first sentence of this book cannot fail to draw you in. The story seems simple and slow to begin with, but builds up quickly as secrets unfold one by one. Nancy, the narrator, is a nosy young girl growing up in a small town in Quebec, Canada, some decades ago. She spends most of the time horsing around with her brother and friends. A piece of gossip she overhears leads Nancy to investigate the goings-on at the home of the prim and proper Wilkins family, where things are clearly amiss. The story is told in a very funny, but also honest and touching, manner. This short gem of a book is bound to charm your socks off.

**Noga Applebaum**

> ### Next?
>
> Read more about Nancy and her adventures in an English boarding school in the sequel *Climbing a Monkey Puzzle Tree*.
>
> *To Kill a Mockingbird* (UTBG 375) is also a novel told from a point of view of a girl growing up in a small American town during the 1950s.
>
> *Huckleberry Finn* (UTBG 181) is the quintessential novel about growing up in northern America (even if it isn't quite Canada).

# RAT-CATCHER Chris Ryan

> ### Next?
>
> If you haven't read them already, get the **Alex Rider** series by Anthony Horowitz, starting with *Stormbreaker* (UTBG 356).
>
> Another series of great adventures is Robert Muchamore's **Cherub** series, starting with *The Recruit* (UTBG 307).
>
> *To Be a Ninja* (UTBG 374) by Benedict Jacka is about three siblings with a terrifying father who end up training in a secret camp to be ninja.

This is the second in the **Alpha Force** series of books written by Chris Ryan, a former member of the SAS. Alex, Li, Paula, Hex and Amber are undercover agents – the Alpha Squad. They are highly trained in martial arts, code-breaking, computer-hacking and many other skills. The team is on a mission in South America. They hear rumours about a man called the Rat Catcher who has been killing street kids in Ecuador, and decide to investigate. Will they be sufficiently skilled to lead a successful operation? There are useful how-to-be-a-spy tips from Chris Ryan in the back of the book, and the gripping twist-and-turns narrative is always accompanied by a strong sense of realism.

**Brenda Marshall**

# RAVEN'S GATE Anthony Horowitz

**Next?**

If the idea of battling it out with sinister villagers appeals, try *Yaxley's Cat* by Robert Westall.

Or, if you enjoy the idea of a group of people coming together to fight the powers of darkness, then **The Dark Is Rising** series (UTBG 93) by Susan Cooper can't be recommended too highly.

Darren Shan writes scary novels about fighting the powers of evil; try the first in **The Saga of Darren Shan**, *Cirque du Freak*.

What I want to know is how Anthony Horowitz does it?! Does he ever sleep?

Not only do we have the excellent **Alex Rider** books, but now there's his new series: **The Power of Five**.

*Raven's Gate* is the first book and it introduces Matt Freeman, a 14-year-old boy with powers that even he doesn't fully understand. There's a little incident involving robbing a warehouse and Matt finds himself an unwilling part of a new government scheme for young offenders, forced to go and live with a sinister stranger, Mrs Deverill, in a remote village in Yorkshire.

Obviously, nothing is as it seems and soon Matt finds himself up against the powers of darkness, fighting for his life.

**Laura Hutchings**

# THE READER Bernhard Schlink

This extraordinarily original novel bears the stamp of lived experience on every page. A young German man studying in his native city shortly after World War II gets deeply involved with an older woman neighbour. She's a simple bus conductor without social graces, and he's embarrassed to introduce her to his friends and family. This, and not their love affair, makes him deeply guilty, and when she disappears he feels sure it's because of him.

Years later he learns the shattering truth about her wartime past, and a secret even deeper than that which has blighted and deformed her whole life. A profoundly moving story about love, shame and expiation, strongly recommended for serious readers.

**Lynne Reid Banks**

**Next?**

*Sophie's Choice* by William Styron – a heartbreaking story of decisions about love, loss and the Holocaust.

Or *Schindler's Ark*, Thomas Keneally's story (based on a real person and real events) about how many Jews were saved from the Nazis by the heroism of ordinary people.

Another book about how secrets change our worlds is Alan Gibbons' *Blood Pressure*, in which a boy discovers his father's dirty secret.

# REBECCA Daphne du Maurier

12+

Some people find the narrator of this classic romantic mystery, set in 1930s Cornwall, to be wimpy and insipid. And yes, perhaps, compared to today's out-there, kick-butt-style heroines she might seem a touch passive. But I think anyone who's ever felt socially ill at ease, or that they don't really deserve a particular chunk of happiness, or even but-why-does-he / she-love-*me*? – and let's face it, that's pretty much all of us – will readily identify with her.

This haunting, magical, gripping Gothic tale starts as an account of how the narrator met the handsome, brooding and irresistible Maxim de Winter. And it soon becomes apparent that his past holds a dark mystery…

Du Maurier's wonderfully descriptive writing makes this page-turner one of my fave books ever – and if the ending doesn't leave you open-mouthed with disbelief, turning the pages to see if some are missing, I'll eat my PC!

**Catherine Robinson**

> **Next?**
>
> Du Maurier's classic Cornish spine-tingling mystery, *Jamaica Inn* (UTBG 194).
>
> Sally Beauman's *Rebecca's Tale* sets out to fill in some of the gaps, as does *Mrs de Winter* by Susan Hill.
>
> The original tale of inexperienced-young-girl-meets-and-falls-in-love-with-older-man-with-a-secret, *Jane Eyre* (UTBG 195) is a must!

# RECKLESS Sue Mayfield

14+

> **Next?**
>
> More Sue Mayfield? Try *Voices* next.
>
> For the story of another relationship developing, try Margaret Wild's novel in verse, *One Night*.
>
> Or for a young father coming to terms with his new baby, Margaret Bechard's *Hanging on to Max*.

This is the story of twins Rachel and Joshua, and a summer holiday spent camping at Kettlebeck in the Yorkshire Dales. The holiday is glorious – the sun is shining, there's a river to cool off in at the hottest part of the day, and there are lots of fun people their age. And one of them, a girl called Charlie, just happens to be gorgeous… Josh can't help noticing her and, well, it's only a matter of time…

Told partly from Josh's point of view, partly from Rachel's, this engaging book tells the story of the summer, and of its consequences. It begins with Josh arriving at someone's front door and ringing the bell… By the time we return to this scene on the last page of the book Josh and Rachel have come a long way; and because Sue Mayfield's characters are so well-drawn and alive, we feel we've come a long way with them.

**Daniel Hahn**

# THE RECRUIT Robert Muchamore

12+

**Next?**

*The Recruit* is first in the **Cherub** series. Sequels are *Class A*, *Maximum Security*, *The Killing* etc.

Chris Ryan's **Alpha Force** novels are great, fast-paced reads. Try *Rat-Catcher* (UTBG 304).

*Boy Soldier* (UTBG 53) has a great deal of real detail about military life – the author was in the SAS.

To find out about the teen years of the world's most famous spy, James Bond, read *SilverFin* (UTBG 340).

This thriller is a cross between Anthony Horowitz's **Alex Rider** books and the violent Luc Besson film *Nikita*. A 12-year-old yobbo on the verge of becoming a delinquent is 'recruited' by a special branch of the British Secret Service. He undergoes brutal training and at the end of it is sent on his first mission.

The story is never predictable, there are no clear-cut goodies or baddies and it's sometimes violent and crude. But all this just adds to the 'real feel'. If your librarian has sent you off to borrow a book and you can't bear to read a story about elves or princesses or spoiled rich kids who never go to the toilet, try this. You won't regret it.

**Caroline Lawrence**

# RED SHIFT Alan Garner

14+

*Red Shift* is neither a teen novel with pretensions, nor an adult novel in disguise, but one of the very few genuine crossover novels. It was written before such a term was even invented, and was one of the books that made me want to write for teenagers.

Garner writes with spare energy and a narrative mastery that allows him to challenge and question our assumptions as readers. The story moves backwards and forwards in time, and between different characters all linked by their presence in one particular place, Mow Cop in Cheshire. The location has witnessed dark, powerful human emotions that resonate still.

*Red Shift* takes in myth, history, philosophy and astrophysics, and can move seamlessly from bitter love story to a meditation upon the space-time continuum. This one slim volume manages to say far more that is profound than much longer, more ponderous works.

**Celia Rees**

**Next?**

Other novels written by Alan Garner for younger readers: *Elidor*, *The Weirdstone of Brisingamen* (UTBG 406) and *The Owl Service* (UTBG 281). His adult novels include *Sandloper* and *Thursbitch*.

Other books that I would consider to be real crossovers are William Golding's **Lord of the Flies** (UTBG 223) and the novels of Robert Cormier.

# REDWALL Brian Jacques

OK, so you pick up this book and think – animals? How stupid, I'll put it back. But, I promise that if you do, you'll be missing a really good read. *Redwall* is a book full of exciting adventure and heroic battles. It's well written and full of excitement.

Redwall itself is a castle, founded by Martin the Warrior – a powerful and great fighter who appears in the first books of the series. *Redwall* features a descendent of Martin (though he doesn't realise it at first), Mathias, who, through a lot of puzzling and with help of friends, takes up the mighty sword of Martin to defeat his enemy Cluny the Scourge. This is an excellent read and I give the whole series 10/10!

**Andrew Barakat (aged 12)**

## Next?

Brian Jacques' *Castaways of the Flying Dutchman*, about a wrecked ship, a cursed crew and a mute boy who travel the world helping people.

*The Sight* by David Clement-Davies is the story of good and evil in a world of wolves.

Garry Kilworth writes brilliantly about worlds where all the inhabitants are animals: try either *The Silver Claw*, about the mammalian city of Vequince or **The Welkin Weasels** series.

# REFUGEE BOY Benjamin Zephaniah

## Next?

Zephaniah is also a poet and musician whose original work engages with many social issues. Try his poetry collection *Too Black Too Strong*, or *School's Out: Poems Not for School*.

*The Frozen Waterfall* by Gaye Hicyilmaz is another story about immigrants, this time a Turkish family in Sweden.

*Voyage* by Adèle Geras takes place in the early 20th century on a ship filled with Eastern European refugees hoping to start a new life in America.

Where can you go when nobody wants you? This is the dilemma that Alem Kelo faces. His father is Ethiopian, his mother Eritrean, and when these neighbouring countries plunge into a bloody war, Alem and his family are persecuted wherever they go. When Alem's father suggests a short vacation in England, Alem is happy to leave the strife behind. However, he soon discovers his father's true intention. Fearing for their son's life, Alem's parents have decided to leave him behind in England to seek asylum. Through Alem's personal story, Zephaniah uncovers the trials and tribulations that refugees go through in England. The heartlessness of the law is powerfully contrasted with the kindness of the local community that reaches out to Alem to offer him a new home.

**Noga Applebaum**

# REGENERATION  Pat Barker

**16+**

Anyone interested in World War I will love this book. It's set in a mental hospital – at Craiglockhart near Edinburgh – where the poet Siegfried Sassoon is sent for treatment after criticising the war. There, Sassoon meets Wilfred Owen (another young poet) and William Rivers, a psychiatrist charged with 'curing' the mentally disturbed so that they can be sent back to fight again.

It's a great story, and you'll want to keep reading just for that, but along the way it deals with poetry, bravery, friendship, and the central question of whether it is sane to fight. If you're struggling with the War Poets at school, reading this book will make everything fall into place.

**Eleanor Updale**

### Next?

*Regeneration* is part of a trilogy. It continues with *The Eye in the Door* and *The Ghost Road*.

The poems themselves: *Collected Poems of Wilfred Owen* and *War Poems of Siegfried Sassoon*, or the anthology, *Anthem for Doomed Youth* (UTBG 25).

*Testament of Youth* by Vera Brittain is based on her own diaries written while working as a nurse at the battlefront in World War I.

The brilliant *Birdsong* (UTBG 43) brings trench warfare to terrifying life.

# REMEMBRANCE  Theresa Breslin

**12+**

### Next?

Another Theresa Breslin? Try the very different and extremely brutal *Divided City* (UTBG 106).

For a memoir of the time – as easy to read as a novel – try Vera Brittain's *Testament of Youth*.

For a dark, tragic story of life on the front line of the same war, try *Strange Meeting* (UTBG 358).

*Peace Weavers* (UTBG 284) tells two interlocking stories of girls speaking out against war.

It's 1915. Stratharden in Scotland is far from the front, but World War I is nevertheless affecting the lives of five young people. At the village shop, 14-year-old Alex is plotting to join his brother John Malcolm in the trenches. Maggie his sister welcomes the chance to broaden her horizons in a munitions factory. At the Big House, upper-class Charlotte becomes a nurse to 'do her bit', and while her brother Francis argues against the war, Charlotte falls in love with John Malcolm. You turn the pages fearfully. The writer is so honest – you see everything from severed limbs to passionate love – and the characters are so real. Who will live, who die? It's as if they were your family.

**Julia Jarman**

# THE RIDDLE OF THE SANDS

## Erskine Childers

14+

**Next?**

A natural follow-up would be *The Thirty-Nine Steps* (UTBG 371), an adventure novel that in 1935 was made into a classic Hitchcock film.

*Brat Farrar* (UTBG 53) by Josephine Tey involves a mystery about identity.

Or for navigating a way through a different war try Jill Paton Walsh's *The Dolphin Crossing*.

I'm not one for sea stories, but simply can't resist this one. Carruthers, a young Edwardian dandy, is cooped up in London all August by work. Then he's invited by his friend Davies to join him yachting and duck shooting in the Baltic. Carruthers goes; but nothing is as expected. The *Dulcibella* is a 'scrubby little craft', not for pleasure; and there are no ducks. Instead, Davies reveals his suspicions that Germany is secretly preparing for an invasion of England (this is some ten years before the outbreak of World War I in 1914). The springboard would be the Frisian islands that fringe the North Sea coastline. The two friends sail the *Dulcibella* through treacherous tides, shifting sandbanks and blinding fogs to outwit a prospective enemy. There are maps and charts. A breathless read.

**Philippa Pearce**

# RIVER BOY  Tim Bowler

12+

This book – which made me cry – is the story of Jess and her relationship with her unusual and cantankerous grandfather, a painter in the last stage of his life. Jess, her mother and father and gravely ill Grandpa go on holiday to a remote cottage beside a river in the place where Grandpa lived until he was 15. Here, Grandpa struggles to complete a strange painting while Jess, a long-distance swimmer, has a series of mysterious encounters while swimming in the river.

**Next?**

More Tim Bowler? Try *Apocalypse* (UTBG 26).

Another book about grandfathers is Sharon Creech's *Walk Two Moons* (UTBG 396). Or try David Almond's haunting *Kit's Wilderness* (UTBG 211).

Another book that uses a river journey in a symbolic way is Mark Twain's *Huckleberry Finn* (UTBG 181). The writing is nothing like *River Boy*, though!

This is a beautiful, moving, mystical novel that uses the metaphor of rivers and swimming to explore themes of death and fulfilment. Tim Bowler manages to capture deep truths without being sentimental or didactic.

**Sue Mayfield**

# ROLL OF THUNDER, HEAR MY CRY

## Mildred D. Taylor

Set in the violent and aggressively racist American Deep South of the 1930s, *Roll of Thunder...* became an instant classic. The Logans, a black family, are struggling not just to survive, but to make a better life for themselves in a world that is hell-bent on keeping them down in the dirt.

Told from the point of view of Cassie, the Logan's fiercely defiant daughter, this vivid fictional account records the relentless everyday injustices and vicious brutalities that real people suffered in that part of America at the time.

Cassie's stubborn refusal to be cowed by the racists, and the inventiveness and cunning with which she outwits them time and again, are testimony to the brave struggles that helped bring about the Civil Rights movement and transformed that region of the US. *Roll of Thunder...* is unforgettable, deeply moving and, above all, uplifting.

**Neil Arksey**

**Next?**

More Mildred D. Taylor? Try others about the Logan family: *The Story of the Trees* and *The Land* (UTBG 212).

*A Gathering Light* (UTBG 142) is a story of what life was like for black communities in early-20th-century America.

# THE ROMANCE OF TRISTAN AND ISEULT

## Retold by Joseph Bédier

**Next?**

If you fancy another great epic romance, try a version of Thomas Malory's *Morte d'Arthur*, or Shakespeare's *Romeo and Juliet*.

For a more modern (more modern, but still pretty old) doomed love story, you can do no better than *Wuthering Heights* (UTBG 424).

For more fate and passion, read Audrey Niffenegger's *The Time-traveller's Wife*.

'My lords, if you would hear a high tale of love and death...' is how this short, great masterpiece begins. It's one of the most famous stories in the world, and what's striking about the way it's retold by Joseph Bédier is the sense of fatality that hangs over the lovers. The language is simple, forceful and beautiful. (Chapter headings include, for example: The Philtre, Ogrin the Hermit, The Quest for the Lady with the Hair of Gold, Iseult of the White Hands, The Ordeal by Iron.) Only a stone could read it without a sickening sense of rising doom and, towards the end, make sure you keep the tissue box handy.

**Anne Fine**

# A ROOM OF ONE'S OWN Virginia Woolf

16+

### Next?

Fay Weldon's *Letters to Alice on First Reading Jane Austen* is another skilled and funny take on women and writing.

Or, for first-hand experience of the problems to be faced, try the journals of some women writers – Sylvia Plath's, or Katherine Mansfield's maybe.

Virginia Woolf features in Michael Cunningham's wonderful *The Hours* (UTBG 177).

OK, so it's one of the building blocks of feminism. But the real point about Virginia Woolf's essay is the delicately lush writing, the angry imagination, that make reading it a pleasure every inch of the way.

Why – she asked, back in the 1920s – had women been able to tell so little of their own story? Was it because of the stumbling blocks in their way? Imagine that William Shakespeare had had a sister, just as talented as him … what might her fate have been? Some of the conditions Woolf describes may be different now. (In order to write, she said, a woman needs a room of her own 'and five hundred pounds a year'.) But some may feel that the fundamentals have not altered greatly.

**Sarah Gristwood**

# A ROOM WITH A VIEW

## E.M. Forster

14+

With its bright social comedy and its cast of distinctive characters, *A Room with a View* (first published in 1908) is the most accessible of E.M. Forster's novels – and is also an excellent film starring Helena Bonham-Carter as the young, impressionable Lucy Honeychurch.

On the Grand Tour in Italy, Lucy meets passionate George who claims to love her for her very essence – but back at home in Surrey she becomes engaged to the pompous, buttoned-up Cecil. Lucy must defy convention if she's to follow her instincts rather than class expectations. Stuffy Aunt Charlotte, liberated novelist Eleanor Lavish and the kindly Reverend Beebe attempt to guide her – although several of the characters are not what they seem.

**Linda Newbery**

### Next?

For more comedies of manners, try *Pride and Prejudice* (UTBG 294) or *Sense and Sensibility* by Jane Austen.

E.M. Forster's *Collected Short Stories* will introduce you to more of his preoccupations; several, including 'The Machine Stops', have a fantasy element.

Another wonderful, colourful book set in Italy is *Miss Garnet's Angel* by Sally Vickers.

# ROUND BEHIND THE ICE-HOUSE

Anne Fine

**Next?**

More Anne Fine? Try *Up On Cloud Nine* (UTBG 391).

Twins always make fascinating characters in fiction but then so can the closeness of brothers and sisters. One of my favourites is Jill Paton Walsh's *Goldengrove Unleaving*.

There is a close brother-sister relationship at the heart of *Ruby Holler* (UTBG 314) by Sharon Creech.

Until now, twins Tom and Cass have had no secrets from each other. They've documented their every failing in The List – a secret book, hidden in the ice-house on their family's farm, which contains all the complaints adults have made about their changing, fickle childhood ways. All of a sudden, the changes have become harder to describe. Cass is secretive and distanced from Tom as she moves in a more adult world – or maybe a darker world – than the twins are used to. But is it solely that Cass is concealing the truth – or has Tom's naïvety pulled the pair apart? In this short, spare novel, Anne Fine has spun a complex and intense web of relationships.

**Jon Appleton**

# ROUND IRELAND WITH A FRIDGE

Tony Hawks

This was the first of a crop of books in which somebody makes a drunken bet, does something ridiculous and then writes a book about it. In this case, Tony Hawks is bet £100 that he cannot hitch-hike around the circumference of Ireland with a fridge within one calendar month. The premise is clearly very silly. Fortunately, Hawks is an excellent writer and a very funny man, so the fridge just becomes an ice-breaker (if that's possible) in conversations with the many entertaining people he meets on his quest. Highlights include his entry into the Ballyduff Bachelor Festival and his bizarre decision to take the fridge surfing in Sligo.

**Anthony Reuben**

**Next?**

The sequel *Playing the Moldovans at Tennis* is based on an even sillier bet and is just as entertaining.

*McCarthy's Bar* by Pete McCarthy is an Irish travelogue based on a less silly premise.

*Are You Dave Gorman?* (UTBG 28) by Dave Gorman and Danny Wallace is another highlight of the 'making stupid bets while drunk' genre.

# ROXY'S BABY Catherine MacPhail

I made the mistake of starting this brilliant book late one night – a mistake because I then had to stay up to read it all, but also because it then gave me the most appalling nightmares. It's that sort of book…

Roxy is going to have a baby. She won't tell her mum or stepdad or her goody-two-shoes sister – they won't understand. Instead she runs away. Before long she meets the kindly Mr and Mrs Dyce who offer to take her to a home they have set up to look after girls in just her predicament. When she arrives it's beautiful, friendly, safe – it's perfect. Except it's really none of those things. Roxy has a terrible suspicion there's something sinister going on. She's right. And it's worse than the worst thing you can possibly imagine…

**Daniel Hahn**

### Next?

Read more Catherine MacPhail – *Underworld* (UTBG 389), or *Another Me*. Or for another chiller, how about some Stephen King (UTBG 76, 220, 318)?

For a rather less alarming book (but still a powerful one) about a young mother-to-be, read *Blue Moon* (UTBG 47) and its sequel *Baby Blue*.

# RUBY HOLLER Sharon Creech

### Next?

More Sharon Creech? Try *Love that Dog*, a brilliant book told in verse, or *The Wanderer* (UTBG 397), a sea-bound adventure.

*Children of the Oregon Trail* by A. Rutgers van der Loeff focuses on another orphan – John Sager – and his epic journey to the Wild West.

*The Beet Fields* (UTBG 35) has a rural setting – a 16-year-old boy leaves home to forge a new life.

Or for another boy whose life is changed by an elderly person, try Louis Sachar's *The Boy Who Lost His Face*.

The Boxton Creek Home for Children is run by the unpleasant Trepids. Twins Florida and Dallas won't toe the Trepids' line and are consequently on the receiving end of multiple punishments. So they spend their days dreaming of escaping.

The Trepids would love to rid themselves of Florida and Dallas, but every family they've been placed with has returned them to Boxton Creek like an unwanted package.

So when they're sent to spend time with the elderly Tiller and Sairy in Ruby Holler, the twins await their inevitable return to the home. But Tiller and Sairy aren't your average couple and Ruby Holler is a truly wondrous place.

As Florida and Dallas finally enjoy the sweet taste of freedom, their hopes and dreams change radically. It's a very moving, well-paced and clever tale.

**Jonny Zucker**

# RUBY TANYA   Robert Swindells

I'm not usually a great fan of thrillers: few authors can manage to devise an exciting plot and keep the suspense going throughout a whole book – so I almost didn't read this story. The blurb on the back cover looked good: 'highly topical and mesmerizing', but I dithered a while before succumbing. And was it worth it? Absolutely.

The main characters, feisty Ruby Tanya, named by her strongly patriotic father, and the gentle Asra, whose family are seeking asylum in Britain, are well-drawn; and so are all the challenges – prejudice, discrimination, bigotry and even a bomb at their school – that they face to remain friends.

This is a heartwarming, life-affirming, gripping read that shows danger doesn't always come from the direction you'd expect.

**Chris d'Lacey**

### Next?

If you like gritty reads try some of the other great books by Robert Swindells: *Stone Cold* (UTBG 355), *Dosh* or the chilling *Abominator*.

*Martyn Pig* (UTBG 236) by Kevin Brooks also deals engagingly with a character who finds himself trapped in a desperate situation.

Or for a different look at the subject, try *Refugees* by Catherine Stein, which intertwines the story of a New York girl and a boy in Afghanistan around the events of 9/11 or Nicky Singer's *The Innocent's Story* (UTBG 190).

# RUMBLEFISH   S.E. Hinton

### Next?

More S.E. Hinton? Try *That Was Then, This Is Now*, *The Outsiders* (UTBG 280), or her adult novel, *Hawke's Harbour*.

Bali Rai has also written about gangs; try his hard-hitting *The Crew*.

For a girl gang in the 1950s, try Joyce Carol Oates' *Foxfire*.

A rare example of a classic novel becoming a cult film, *Rumblefish* is in my opinion Hinton's greatest work. It centres on Rusty James, a disillusioned tough guy who longs to emulate his absent brother Motorcycle Boy and become a gang-fight legend. But when Motorcycle Boy returns, he's changed and Rusty James doesn't understand him any more. Then Rusty's world begins to fall apart and things take a tragic turn.

This is a hard-hitting, no-nonsense read that takes you right into the heart of Rusty's world. Read the book and try and see the film too, directed by Francis Ford Coppola and starring Mickey Rourke and Matt Dillon. Neither will disappoint you. Brilliant.

**Bali Rai**

# THE RUNAWAY JURY  John Grisham

14+

You know what you're going to get when you open a John Grisham book: a great, clear plot, plenty of suspense, a sympathetic hero and a fair bit of courtroom drama. If you want poetry, go somewhere else; for irresistible, page-turning, must-find-out-what-happens-next narrative, Grisham's your man. And as an ex-lawyer himself, he knows his legal stuff, but never lets the details get in the way of a thrilling story.

*The Runaway Jury* is vintage Grisham and, I think, my favourite. This time the court case in question is a suit against a massive tobacco corporation. It seems that someone is tampering with the jury selection to try and guarantee the sort of verdict Big Tobacco will like. But one of the jurors, Nicholas Easter, has an agenda of his own too. Complications ensue. Great stuff.

**Daniel Hahn**

### Next?

I always find I want a break between Grishams – two in a row and the similarities might be just a little too much. So I'd read something else next... But when you do want to come back to him, go for *The Partner*.

For another legal thriller, a little denser, try Scott Turow's *Presumed Innocent*.

Or José Latour's gripping Miami-based thriller, *Outcast*.

---

# SABRIEL  Garth Nix

12+

### Next?

Of course you'll want to read the sequels: *Lirael* and *Abhorsen*.

Another jaw-dropping fantasy series of great power and imagination: Robin Hobb's **Assassins** trilogy, beginning with *Assassin's Apprentice*.

Garth Nix has also written the **Keys to the Kingdom** series, which starts with *Mister Monday*, about a boy who is supposed to die but instead becomes involved in a battle against evil.

The sun is shining in Ancelstierre. A few yards away, across the border in the Old Kingdom, it's snowing. But that's not surprising because everything is different there. Machinery doesn't work, the dead won't stay in their graves and the magic of the Great Charter, intended to keep the kingdom safe forever, is faltering as blood is shed on ancient stones. Dreadful creatures from beyond the Seventh Gate of Death have been waiting for this moment for centuries. Now their chance has come, and only one person stands against them: Sabriel, a 16-year-old schoolgirl with a terrible destiny.

This is an utterly compelling book, and one that will make you remember why you first enjoyed reading.

**Brian Keaney**

# SABRINA FLUDDE  Pauline Fisk

 12+

**Next?**

Try David Almond's *Skellig* (UTBG 343) for more lyrical magical realism.

Alan Garner's *The Owl Service* (UTBG 281) has Welsh legends and magic combined with darkly atmospheric writing.

**Fire and Hemlock** (UTBG 128) by Diana Wynne Jones is also wonderfully inventive, with a brilliant opening chapter in which a girl gatecrashes a funeral...

*Sabrina Fludde* is a strange and lyrical story that transforms the everyday into the mythological. A girl is washed up on the banks of a river, with no memory of how she got there or who she is. She discovers she is in the ancient market town of Pengwern, but as she wanders its streets nothing is familiar. As she searches for clues to her identity, she finds that her past is entwined with a local legend. But with this knowledge comes danger.

What has stayed with me is the vivid and magical atmosphere of the setting, which is both contemporary – with its shopping malls and graffiti – and steeped in history and legend. The eccentric, misfit characters the free-spirited heroine encounters on her quest are equally memorable – from Phaze II, a homeless boy who lives high in the eaves of a railway bridge, to a boatsman descended from Barbary pirates.

**Katie Jennings**

# SAFFY'S ANGEL  Hilary McKay

12+

Cadmium, Saffron, Indigo and Rose Casson were named by their eccentric artist parents after paint colours. But Saffy discovers that the colour saffron isn't on the paint chart and, shockingly, that Eve Casson is her aunt – not her mother. Suddenly, she no longer belongs. Only a haunting dream of a heat-filled garden and a mysterious angel link her to her past, and thus begins her quest – for the angel and for some deep part of herself.

I love the way McKay balances the sheer ordinariness of family life with its moments of emotional intensity: she perfectly captures why certain things just matter. *Saffy's Angel* is wonderfully funny: this slightly mad but wholly believable family really stay with you. You'll laugh – but also ponder.

**Helen Simmons**

**Next?**

The doings of the Casson family are continued in *Indigo's Star* and *Permanent Rose*.

You might also enjoy E. Nesbit's books about the Bastable Family – *The Treasure Seekers* is the first one. They have a similar, truthful kind of humour.

And don't miss *I Capture the Castle* (UTBG 183), another funny / sad novel about a wholly eccentric family falling in and out of love.

# SALEM'S LOT

## Stephen King

This book changed my life. A modern-day riff on *Dracula*, it follows the downfall of a town besieged by vampires. The beauty of this book is in watching King build up a totally convincing cast and town, then subject them to the horrors of a vampire attack. In the book, vampirism is like a plague, and King details the fallout of such a disaster. I LOVED this. It opened up a whole new world of nightmares to me and, as all horror fans know, nightmares are cool! Like most of King's books, there's stuff in here which isn't suitable for younger readers – so if your parents catch you reading this and kick up a fuss, don't tell them *I* recommended it to you!

**Darren Shan**

### Next?

Try *The Hand of the Devil* by Dean Vincent Carter about a young journalist thrown into a nightmare.

*Dracula* (UTBG 110) by Bram Stoker – the original.

*Weaveworld* (UTBG 405) is another complex and involving horror story.

How would it feel to be the last human on a planet inhabited by ravenous vampires? Try *I Am Legend* by Richard Matheson to find out…

Edgar Allen Poe's stories have frightened readers for over 100 years. Try *Tales of Mystery and Imagination* (UTBG 365).

## The Ultimate Teen Readers' Poll

## BOOK THAT SCARED YOU THE MOST

1 **Harry Potter series**

2 **Goosebumps series**

3 **The Lord of the Rings trilogy**

4 **A Child Called 'It'**

5 **Alex Rider series**

6 **Stone Cold**

7 **Skellig**

8 **The Rats**

9 **Cirque du Freak**

10 **Hannibal**

# The SALLY LOCKHART books Philip Pullman

**Next?**

Anthony Hope's *The Prisoner of Zenda* (UTBG 299) has strange happenings in a Central European country.

For something funnier, Lindsey Davis' **Falco** books, set in Ancient Rome – start with **The Silver Pigs**, which is in fact set in Roman Britain.

The original detective of old London is, of course, Sherlock Holmes (UTBG 336).

The first three novels are exciting mystery-adventures set in Victorian London, starring Sally Lockhart and her friends. Sally is 16 when *The Ruby in the Smoke* begins, desperate to widen the limited horizon before her as an orphaned middle-class Victorian girl of slender means, and to find out who killed her father in the South China Sea.

Her final confrontation with her enemy takes three books to arrive, and on the way through *The Shadow in the North* and *The Tiger in the Well* Philip Pullman leads us everywhere shunned by polite Victorian society: opium dens, séances, music halls, East End missions and socialist gatherings.

In *The Tin Princess*, the focus shifts to Central Europe and the perils of a small kingdom hemmed in by rival powers. Sally makes only brief appearances, but there are two strong new heroines and a sense of the political forces pulling the strings of the story.

**Geraldine Brennan**

# SAMMY AND JULIANA IN HOLLYWOOD
## Benjamin Alire Saenz

*Sammy and Juliana in Hollywood* tells the bleak and beautiful story of Sammy Santos, a Mexican-American teenager growing up not in California's city of dreams, but in a bleak neighbourhood in Las Cruces, New Mexico, in the late 1960s. A loner, Sammy finds all-too-brief happiness with the damaged Juliana, as he struggles to come of age in a time and place riven by racism, poverty and the violence of the Vietnam War.

In language that's sometimes stark, sometimes poetic and always strikingly authentic, Alire Saenz shows us a young man's journey from innocence to experience, and how for Sammy, as for so many others in the summer of '69, love walked hand-in-hand with loss.

**Jennifer Donnelly**

**Next?**

*CrashBoomLove: A Novel in Verse* by Juan Felipe Herrera is about a boy growing up as a migrant worker.

*Fallen Angels* by Walter Dean Myers is about a Harlem teenager who enlists to fight in Vietnam, and his struggle to survive.

# THE SANDMAN series Neil Gaiman

Imagine if death were a Goth punk and she had three strange sisters: Delirium, Despair and Desire; and three brothers: Destiny, Destruction and the mysterious Dream. Blending myth, fantasy and horror with powerful stories of the real world, this 12-volume series changed the face of comics.

Morpheus, the Lord of the Dreaming, is the key to the whole series. At its opening he is the prisoner of a crazy sect who wants the secret of immortality. When he frees himself, he must relearn his powers and reshape his kingdom, discovering new allies – and new enemies. His magical journey will keep you riveted, with narrow escapes, retellings of famous legends that blaze with life, and a shocking, surprising ending.

**Ariel Kahn**

### Next?

Death, one of the best characters in **The Sandman** series, gets two of her own books: *The High Cost of Living* and *The Time of Your Life*.

Alan Moore's **Swamp Thing** series is a modern retelling of 'Beauty and the Beast' with added villains.

Philip Pullman's **His Dark Materials** trilogy (UTBG 170) explores similar themes of myth and religion.

Or try Neil Gaiman writing in collaboration with Terry Pratchett, in *Good Omens* (UTBG 152).

# THE SCARECROWS Robert Westall

### Next?

Robert Westall has written some of the scariest books around. Read *The Watch House* (UTBG 400) about a battle between two ghosts – one benign, the other really not!

Or what about a collection of macabre short stories by great writers? Try *Gothic!* edited by Deborah Noyes.

*Jake's Tower* (UTBG 193) is about a boy cutting himself off from the world.

Simon hates his stepfather, who is unlike his real, dead father in every way imaginable. Angry and lonely, he distances himself from his family at every opportunity. Then he discovers the old water mill. Somehow, it seems to welcome him. Simon spends more and more time there, brooding. But the mill has a violent past, and his rage awakens murderous ghosts. Three scarecrows appear in the field next to his home. No one will admit to putting them there. Every day they get a little closer – until Simon realises that only he has the power to fight off the evil threatening his family.

*The Scarecrows* is a rare book: both scary supernatural thriller and moving family drama. Almost every page taut with menace, it shows how ordinary people can bring evil into being and give it terrifying life.

**Graham Gardner**

# THE SCARLET PIMPERNEL   Baroness Orczy

**12+**

Forget any film versions you've seen of this book and read the real thing. You'll find that the hero Sir Percy Blakeney is younger than he's shown on screen, and built like Arnold Schwarzenegger. Although some of the attitudes and beliefs of the time in which it was written are surprising and even distasteful to us today, the story of dandified young Englishmen forming a secret league dedicated to spiriting away French aristocrats from the shadow of the guillotine during the Reign of Terror is still an exciting one. If you can disregard the unpleasant attitudes, you'll enjoy the novel for its plot and historical background, showing a time when fear and brutality stalked the streets of Paris.

**Gill Vickery**

> ### Next?
>
> For a more realistic and brutal but equally exciting account of the French Revolution, read Leon Garfield's *Revolution*.
>
> A classic novel set in this period is *A Tale of Two Cities* (UTBG 364).
>
> If you enjoy romantic historical fiction about the 18th century, try the novels of Georgette Heyer, such as *These Old Shades* (UTBG 370).
>
> *The Master of Ballantrae* (UTBG 238) is a classic story of brothers, feuds and treachery.

# SCOOP   Evelyn Waugh

**14+**

John Boot, a fashionable novelist, is desperate to be a war reporter. His distant cousin William Boot is blissfully happy writing about badgers on his impoverished country estate. John's famous – William's not. John can write – William can't. John's streetwise – William's scared of London. And because, in Evelyn Waugh's comic novel, everyone knows they're right and no one listens to anyone else, it's William who ends up in a war no one knows is happening, to invent news stories he doesn't understand, to satisfy a media which is only interested in profit. *Scoop*'s a bit dated, but the central cynicism about the way the media manipulates world events is, if anything, more relevant now than it was in 1938 when the novel was published.

**Antonia Honeywell**

> ### Next?
>
> If you liked the satire – the way Evelyn Waugh shows how corrupt the world is by making you laugh – try reading Christopher Brookmyre's *Quite Ugly One Morning*.
>
> If you liked the political comment, try reading Orwell's *Nineteen Eighty-Four* (UTBG 260).
>
> If you liked Mrs Stitch, the ridiculous society hostess, try Anita Loos' *Gentlemen Prefer Blondes*.

# THE SCREWTAPE LETTERS C.S. Lewis

My teacher commended this to me – woeful handicap for any book – but I loved it anyway. Wormwood, a raw recruit in the Infernal Civil Service, is assigned to win a young man's soul by tempting him to stray from the straight and narrow and damn himself. Since the young man is in love, the task shouldn't prove too hard…

The pressures on both are intensified by the setting: wartime London. (Indeed, I'm guessing the book was some kind of spiritual bomb shelter C.S. Lewis built for himself as World War II raged around him.) Wormwood is answerable to his high-ranking uncle, Screwtape – an affectionate and patient teacher. The book takes the form of correspondence, and it is their relationship which sticks in the mind, even more than the will-he-won't-he? progress of the poor sinner. The end is a real gut-wrencher.

Think you know C.S. Lewis? Narnia this ain't.

**Geraldine McCaughrean**

> ### Next?
>
> For another C.S. Lewis, try *The Great Divorce* (UTBG 155) where the inhabitants of Hell take a holiday in Heaven, and find there's no place like home.
>
> *The Alchemist* (UTBG 16) is another tale of finding a spiritual path.
>
> Or what about a classic? Try Jonathan Swift's *Gulliver's Travels*, which shows human nature at its most absurd.

# SEA OF TROLLS Nancy Farmer

> ### Next?
>
> Norse mythology is amazing. Read any version you can find; the stories are dark, cruel and wonderful.
>
> *Beowulf* (try the version translated by Seamus Heaney) is the story of another quest.
>
> Or for more stories based on the same legends, try Catherine Fisher's **The Snow-Walker's Son** trilogy.

Jack is an apprentice bard. He has a hard life, but things go from bad to worse when his village is raided by Vikings and he and his spoiled baby sister are taken as slaves by Olaf One-Brow. He is taken far into the North to the court of Ivar the Boneless and his half-troll queen. After accidentally causing the queen's hair to fall out, Jack finds himself sent on a quest to find Mimir's Well and on his journey finds trolls, dragons, sea monsters, berserkers, battles, a troll-boar called Golden Bristles and a shield maiden who wants to die.

Weaving Norse myth into spellbinding adventure, this is storytelling on a grand scale. I really couldn't put it down, devouring it in one (very long!) sitting, totally unable to do anything but read and read until I knew exactly what was going to happen to Jack.

**Leonie Flynn**

# SECOND FROM LAST IN THE SACK RACE
## David Nobbs

**Next?**

There are two sequels: *Pratt of the Argus* and *The Cucumber Man*.

Tom Sharpe has written some hilarious satirical novels – try *Porterhouse Blue*, about university life.

Try *The Rotters' Club*, also about 1970s youth, by Jonathan Coe himself. He has a very good line in bittersweet humour.

There are plenty of famous coming-of-age stories. This one is less famous; Nobbs was a well-known TV writer in the 1970s and 80s, and British cultural snobbery has probably stopped him from being taken as seriously as his novels deserve. This is perhaps his funniest and saddest book, about a lonely youngster called Henry Pratt who has an unsettled upbringing in Yorkshire before being sent off to a posh boarding school, where he finds himself hopelessly out of depth and surrounded by characters with names like Tosser Pilkington-Brick. The novel's insights into childhood are heartbreakingly truthful, but are also cushioned by warm irony and brilliant comic set-pieces.
**Jonathan Coe**

# SECOND STAR TO THE RIGHT
## Deborah Hautzig

Leslie has the kind of life anyone would like. She has a brilliant best friend, does well at school and gets on great with her mum. But Leslie's not happy. If only she were thin, then life would be perfect, wouldn't it?

She loses her first few pounds by accident, during a spell of flu. It's the break she needs and Leslie starts to diet, seriously, egged on by the 'dictator' inside her. The pounds start dropping off, but getting thinner doesn't make things perfect. What Leslie eats, or doesn't eat, becomes an obsession; it takes over her life and in the end she risks losing everything she cares for most.

This harrowing insight into the mind of a girl with anorexia nervosa is brilliantly observed and utterly compelling.
**Susila Baybars**

**Next?**

For more about eating disorders, try the fictional *Diary of an Anorexic Girl*, by Morgan Menzie, based on the author's own experiences.

*Massive* (UTBG 237) by Julia Bell is about three generations of one family, all with eating disorders.

Or read *Last Seen Wearing Trainers* (UTBG 214), about a girl running away from her alcoholic mother.

# THE SECRET DIARY OF ADRIAN MOLE
## AGED 13¾  Sue Townsend

12+

Adrian is an average teenager. He has typical problems: acne, bullies and a troublesome love life. His parents don't care what he does (while his gran cares too much – worse luck!) and his dog's always getting ill. He looks after a beetroot-sandwich-obsessed senior citizen called Bert Baxter who doesn't appreciate him at all.

*Adrian Mole* is hilarious. It's well written and I found it very true to life. And this is only the first book in a whole series, during which we watch him grow up – he's in his mid-30s in the latest instalment, and still hopeless!

**Max Arevuo (aged 13)**

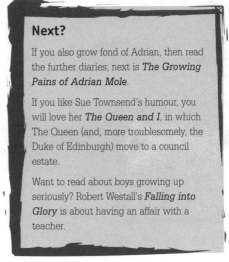

### Next?

If you also grow fond of Adrian, then read the further diaries; next is *The Growing Pains of Adrian Mole*.

If you like Sue Townsend's humour, you will love her *The Queen and I*, in which The Queen (and, more troublesomely, the Duke of Edinburgh) move to a council estate.

Want to read about boys growing up seriously? Robert Westall's *Falling into Glory* is about having an affair with a teacher.

Sue Townsend

the secret diary of

adrian mole aged 13¾

'The funniest book of the year' – Daily Mail

I am very fond of Adrian Mole. In this, his first diary, our hero from Ashby de la Zouch talks frankly and candidly about his life. His days are spent pawing over *Big and Bouncy*, despairing at the behaviour of his wayward parents, trying to control ancient Bert Baxter, agonising about his spots, writing (dreadful) poetry and measuring his 'thing'. Life is difficult for an intellectual such as Adrian.

Adrian's diaries have been essential reading for all our family over the years. The humour is subversive, laugh-out-loud, and sometimes bittersweet. Adrian's distinct voice flows easily on and on … and on. His diaries provide a delightful social history and I look forward to Adrian becoming a pensioner and behaving as unpredictably as ever.

**Caroline Pitcher**

# THE SECRET DREAMWORLD OF A SHOPAHOLIC  Sophie Kinsella

14+

OK, listen up: if there is one book you read this year, it has to be this. You mother would agree with me. This book will tell you everything, I mean everything, that you should NOT do when it comes to money. You see, Becky loves to go shopping. All she has to do is enter a shop and she suddenly finds that she MUST have at least one or two items off the shelves. This would all be fine and dandy if she were unbelievably rich, but she isn't, and nasty little unpaid credit card bills and bank letters start to pile up…

Becky remains unbelievably lovable every step of the way, even when you desperately want to stop her from doing the next unthinkable thing. For money problems lead to lies, and lies to bigger lies… What will happen when Becky promises never to shop again? Or when she lands a job advising people what to do with their money? Or worse yet, when she starts to fall in love?

**Candida Gray**

> **Next?**
>
> There are three sequels; start with *Shopaholic Abroad*.
>
> *Does My Bum Look Big in This?* (UTBG 108) is a funny look at single life.
>
> Jane Green also writes very warm, funny books about being female and (usually) single. Try *Bookends* or *Jemima J* (UTBG 196).

# THE SECRET GARDEN  Frances Hodgson Burnett

> **Next?**
>
> *A Little Princess* also by Frances Hodgson Burnett. Intead of rags to riches, this one is from riches to rags and like *The Secret Garden* is ultimately a triumph-against-the-odds book.
>
> For another almost-tragedy that turns out fine and lovely in the end, try E. Nesbit's *The Railway Children*.
>
> *Ruby Holler* (UTBG 314) by Sharon Creech is about orphan twins finding their place in the world.

This is a timeless story of survival against the odds. It is about a thoroughly cross and opinionated tweenie who is a real pain in the butt, but who is transformed into a decent human being through finding a secret garden that is overgrown and needs a makeover (how modern is that?).

I'm a sucker for Pygmalion-type transformations with a 'before' and 'after' and *The Secret Garden* has a very satisfying transformation. Everyone comes good. Cripples walk again, emotional cripples feel again, a dying garden is brought back to life. Hurrah! It is ultimately a feel-good book, the story of a survivor that inspires and warms the heart. Aaaah…

**Cathy Hopkins**

# THE SECRET HISTORY  Donna Tartt

Richard sees Hampden College as the chance to leave behind his unglamorous past and fashion a new identity. Drawn to an elite group of students, centred around their charismatic classics professor, Richard is captivated by their sophistication, eccentricity, casual affluence and the way they seem to live in a world set apart from the everyday. But as he sets about working his way into their confidence he discovers they have a secret history far darker than his own: one involving blackmail and murder.

This psychological thriller is far more than a whodunnit (we find out the facts on almost the first page). It's not even about whether the murderers are going to get caught. The book's skill lies in the way it makes murder appear rational and justifiable before the event and then hits you with the true horror of its consequences. It may sound like a grim read, but Tartt injects black humour into even the bleakest situations.
**Katie Jennings**

> **Next?**
>
> Another Donna Tartt? Her most-recent book is *The Little Friend*.
>
> For another tale of a crime and its consequences try *Crime and Punishment* (UTBG 86).
>
> F. Scott Fitzgerald's *Tender is the Night* is about secrets among the rich. Evelyn Waugh wrote tellingly about the decadent lives of the rich, too, in *Brideshead Revisited* (UTBG 56).

# SECRETS IN THE FIRE / PLAYING WITH FIRE  Henning Mankell

> **Next?**
>
> Aubrey Flegg's *The Cinnamon Tree* begins with a landmine explosion. Shifting between Africa and Ireland, it is a thriller involving the arms trade.
>
> Peter Dickinson's *A.K.* is a dramatic story about a boy soldier and the terror of war.
>
> For more about AIDS in Africa, read *Chanda's Secret* by Allan Stratton.

Can you imagine losing your legs? That's war. In *Secrets in the Fire*, Sofia steps on a landmine beside the path in a remote region of Mozambique. Henning Mankell has based Sofia on a real girl: a young friend with no legs but an indomitable spirit.

In the sequel *Playing with Fire*, Sofia is envious that her older sister Rosa can laugh and dance with the boys after her hard day's work in the fields. Sofia is too embarrassed by her plastic legs and crutches to join them. But when Rosa falls ill (she has AIDS), it is Sofia who helps both Rosa and her mother to face the harsh truth.

Mankell writes beautifully. Both stories are deeply moving. They might also leave you very angry.
**Beverley Naidoo**

# SEEKER William Nicholson

12+

**Next?**

More William Nicholson? Read **The Wind on Fire** trilogy (UTBG 414).

For power struggles and mysterious tribes, try Marcus Sedgwick's *Dark Horse*.

Or one of my favourites, Susan Cooper's **The Dark Is Rising** series (UTBG 93).

For as long as he can remember, Seeker has wanted to join the Nomana, the mysterious group of powerful 'warriors'. Morning Star and the Wildman want to, too. They all think they understand the Nomana, and ought to be allowed to join. But it's not quite that simple. The Nomana won't accept just anyone…

Will the three of them ever be let in? What's the terrible 'secret weapon' the Nomana are muttering about that's set to destroy them? What happened to Seeker's brother, the heroic Blaze? Where's Morning Star's mother? And what is the source of the Nomana's power?

Many of your questions will be answered in this wonderful book, and for the rest, well, there are sequels on the way. If they're as good as this book, William Nicholson has another classic series on his hands.

**Daniel Hahn**

# A SEPARATE PEACE John Knowles

14+

It's hard to imagine now what it's like growing up in a world truly at war, where you and / or many of your peers may well be dead within a year. That's the situation in which Gene, Phineas and their friends – the class of 1943 at an expensive boys' boarding school in New England – find themselves. But while World War II looms large, and the weight of duty to their country weighs heavily for this 'draft bait', the key battle recounted in *A Separate Peace* is fought closer to home. Gene, the narrator, is an introverted intellectual. His roommate Finny is a popular athlete and a natural leader, who is crippled by an accident which may be Gene's fault. Knowles beautifully captures Gene's tortured brooding and the destructive jealousy that can turn even the closest friends into enemies.

**Terri Paddock**

**Next?**

*Peace Breaks Out* – although not a sequel, John Knowles' later book is set at the same school, where war hero Pete has returned to teach after World War II.

*The Catcher in the Rye* (UTBG 66) – J.D. Salinger's classic portrays another memorable protagonist, Holden Caulfield, whose story begins when he's expelled from an American prep school.

*Lord of the Flies* (UTBG 223) has a more exotic setting, a desert island, but the shipwrecked schoolboys also explore their baser instincts.

# HISTORICAL FICTION
## by Nicola Morgan

So you think history is boring? Just useless facts about dead people? Not relevant to our lives? I admit I probably thought that too. My memories of history lessons at school are not exactly inspirational. Mainly, I remember one teacher making us do press-ups if we got a date wrong and another teacher punctuating her terrifying lessons with cries of 'Henry VIII *never* fiddled with his pencil!' The only thing this taught us was how to clench our stomach muscles so hard that the laughter did not explode. And I can still do press-ups.

All that changed when I found myself writing a historical novel, *Fleshmarket* (UTBG 131). It came about by accident, after I heard a story – a true story – so powerful that the woman in it began to haunt me. The trouble was, I didn't know the history of the time. OK, I knew some dates and facts – that's the easy bit (and the boring bit, to be honest) but I didn't really *know* the past. When I began the research, reading history books, I found I still didn't *know*, not really. Then I found primary sources, original newspapers, the actual paper touched by actual people from the time, and I began to have the inklings of connection. My heart began to beat faster. But I was still outside, looking through a doorway. Only when I began to know my own fictional characters, the characters I pushed through that door, did I properly understand. Only then did I *feel* the past.

That is why historical fiction is very different from a history lesson and why it should never feel like one (especially not like the ones I remember). Non fiction tells you a type of truth – it can tell you the freezing point of water and even how the molecules behave as they freeze, but only fiction can make you feel the cold. The task for a novelist is to make you feel the cold without lecturing you about the

### Costume romances:

*Arabella* by Georgette Heyer

*These Old Shades* by Georgette Heyer

*Nicola and the Viscount* by Meg Cabot

*Frenchman's Creek* by Daphne du Maurier

*Jamaica Inn* by Daphne du Maurier

*Katherine* by Anya Seton

*War and Peace* by Leo Tolstoy

*Gone With the Wind* by Margaret Mitchell

behaviour of molecules, without appearing to teach anything.

Historical fiction *is* relevant to us today: it gives us a reflection of our own times, something we can compare our lives with, sometimes showing how much the world has changed, often showing how little anything changes. The one thing that remains the same, in past, present and future, is human nature, in all its richness and its potential for good and for evil. And really, a historical novel is exactly like any other, just with a different setting. It shows humans behaving like humans, behaving as we always have done and always will.

## Books where the past is real:

*Coram Boy* by Jamila Gavin

*No Shame, No Fear* by Ann Turnbull

*Witch Child* by Celia Rees

*Al Capone Does My Shirts* by Gennifer Choldonko.

*The Ruby in the Smoke* by Philip Pullman

Witch Child
Celia Rees
'A powerful, absorbing and unusual novel' The Bookseller

Birdsong
SEBASTIAN FAULKS
'Magnificent – deeply moving' Sunday Times

## (Great) War stories:

*All Quiet on the Western Front* by Erich Maria Remarque

*Cold Mountain* by Charles Frazier

*Goodbye To All That* by Robert Graves

*Birdsong* by Sebastian Faulks

*Strange Meeting* by Susan Hill

*Regeneration* by Pat Barker

*Remembrance* by Theresa Breslin

*Private Peaceful* by Michael Morpurgo

*Memoirs of an Infantry Officer* by Siegfried Sassoon

# A SERIES OF UNFORTUNATE EVENTS

**12+**

## Lemony Snicket

Become part of the Baudelaire orphans' grim epic as they are pursued by the dastardly and stunningly inept Count Olaf, who wants to get his hands on the Baudelaire family fortune. But these are orphans with many talents: Violet is an inventor who can fashion a solution to almost any problem; Klaus is a bookworm who has read innumerable books on every subject imaginable; and Sunny... well, Sunny likes biting things.

**A Series Of Unfortunate Events** is written for younger children, and goes out of its way to educate the reader as to the meaning of more complicated words. But older readers will still find plenty to enjoy here, whether it is the wonderfully Gothic and drear atmosphere of the books, the novelty of reading a children's story that flatly refuses to give you a happy ending, or simply the ghoulish glee of watching the Baudelaire orphans suffer.

**Chris Wooding**

> **Next?**
>
> You want Gothic? Try one of the best ones: *Frankenstein* (UTBG 139).
>
> If you like seeing children treated awfully, pick up anything by Charles Dickens. *Oliver Twist* will start you off.
>
> Or Philip Ardagh's **Unlikely Exploits** series.

---

# THE SERIOUS KISS  Mary Hogan

**12+**

> **Next?**
>
> Another book about being uprooted into a strange place is *Phosphorescence* (UTBG 286).
>
> Or what about a very different sort of moving away? Try *Wendy* (UTBG 406), which imagines the story of Peter Pan's Wendy Darling.
>
> I can't recommend another Mary Hogan, as she hasn't written anything else yet, but as soon as she does I have no doubt it'll be a wonderful read!

Whether drunk or sober, Libby's dad is a pig. He's also a waster who loses all the family money, meaning they have to move away from everything she knows, out of the city and into a trailer park on the edge of a shabby desert town. White trash lifestyle? Thank you, Dad.

Libby hates it all. Even her old best friend drops her, and the only person prepared to befriend her now is the fat school misfit. In fact, life looks like it might be just about over. But then she meets a boy, and makes friends with some of the weirdest (but coolest) people. So, will her dad stop being a loser? Will her mum stop feeding them take-outs and actually start cooking? And what about that kiss?

**Leonie Flynn**

# SET IN STONE  Linda Newbery

**Next?**

Now try Linda's other books, particularly *The Shell House* (UTBG 335) and *Sisterland* (UTBG 342).

For more secrets and mysteries try *The Woman in White* (UTBG 420) or *The Woman in Black* (UTBG 420).

Another book set amongst a strange family is *Titus Groan,* the first of the **Gormenghast** trilogy (UTBG 154).

Set in Stone begins in 1920, with successful artist Samuel Godwin looking back to his youth and his employment as tutor to the daughters of recent widower, Ernest Farrow. Samuel is intrigued by the ménage he finds at Fourwinds, which includes the enigmatic Charlotte Agnew, companion to the girls. He senses a mystery involving Gideon Waring, sculptor of the magnificent carvings that give the house its name.

Linda Newbery characteristically refuses to compromise, either in narrative complexity, or in subject matter. A shocking secret lies at the heart of the family; no one is quite as Samuel sees them, and nothing is quite as it seems. His shifting perspectives make *Set in Stone* a powerful page-turner, gripping to the end.

**Celia Rees**

# SEVENTH HEAVEN  Alice Hoffman

It is 1959. The oldest member of a small community on Long Island suddenly dies. His wife leaves town, and their empty house on Hemlock Street gradually falls apart. A terrible smell invades the street and a flock of vicious birds arrives to terrorise the neighbourhood. The people wonder if they are being punished. But for what? It has always been a happy and peaceful community.

This sounds like the opening to a horror story, but *Seventh Heaven* is nothing like that. It is the story of ordinary people whose lives, gently explored, become strange and remarkable.

So when 17-year-old Ace begins to fall in love with a ghost, we are not at all surprised, just incredibly moved.

**Jenny Nimmo**

**Next?**

If you like this book, you might enjoy some of Alice Hoffman's other novels; *Turtle Moon*, *The River King* and *Illumination Night* have the same blend of ordinary lives touched by enchantment.

Or you could try Anne Tyler's novels; *The Accidental Tourist* and *Dinner at the Homesick Restaurant* are not only touching, but also enthralling and, sometimes, very funny.

Or how about Carol Shields' *The Stone Diaries*, the story of one woman's life from birth to death.

# THE SHADOW OF THE WIND
## Carlos Ruiz Zafón

This is a beguiling tale full of intrigue and heartbreak. Daniel, the son of a widowed bookseller, who lives with his father above their shop in post-war Barcelona, sets out on a quest to discover the truth about Julian Carax, a mysterious writer whose novel (also called *The Shadow of the Wind*) is at the centre of the mystery. Along the way there are stories within stories, and different narrators take up the tale. Although books and writing are central to this novel, ultimately it is infatuation, young love and heartbreak that weave together the complex plot.

   With a host of fabulous characters and a back story that unfolds through the dark times of the Spanish Civil War, *The Shadow of the Wind* captures the old-world charm of an almost forgotten Barcelona. One minute you're on the edge of your seat, the next you're reaching for the tissues. An enormously readable book

**Neil Arksey**

> **Next?**
>
> *As I Walked Out One Midsummer Morning* is about Laurie Lee's experiences in the same war.
>
> Ernest Hemingway's *For Whom the Bell Tolls* is a classic about the Spanish Civil War.
>
> Another complex and wonderful book: Umberto Eco's *The Name of the Rose*.

# SHADOWMANCER G.P. Taylor

> **Next?**
>
> Another G.P. Taylor? Try *Wormwood*, about an astronomer, a prophecy and an angel whose feathers are plucked one by one.
>
> The most different slant on God and religion imaginable, you have to try Pullman's **His Dark Materials** trilogy (UTBG 170).
>
> Or for more mystery and magic try Trudi Canavan's **The Black Magician** trilogy (UTBG 44).

'It is the song of the deep. They are calling the dead to feast. The Seloth will not stop until the ship is broken on the rocks. They want sacrifice not mercy.'

   It is the 1700s. Thomas, Kate and Raphah are brought together in mysterious ways, and are sent on a mission from God to retake a golden statue (the Keruvim) from the cruel, power-hungry priest Demurral, before he can use it to kill God and control the universe. But there are many complications...

   This is a fast-moving tale of magic, evil, superstition and witchcraft that never fails to keep you in suspense. If you want to be transported into a time where not even life can be taken for granted, you will enjoy this book.

**Samuel Mortimer (aged 11)**

# THE SHAMER'S DAUGHTER

## Lene Kaaberbol

 12+

Dina's mother, the Shamer, is haughtily summoned by Lord Drakan to prove a murderer's guilt. But the man is innocent. So she refuses to testify against him and finds herself, Dina and the 'murderer' caught up in a deadly power game. Dina struggles desperately to save her mother and the accused man from death, and in doing so she begins to come to terms with inheriting her mother's shamer power.

I'm not a regular fantasy reader, but I loved this· filled with tension, the story whips along at a cracking pace and – scary dragons apart – it's set in a very real and tangible world. Dina certainly has guts, and will make you see that the role of the Shamer – teller of truth – isn't for fantasy worlds alone. Exciting and thought-provoking.

**Helen Simmons**

### Next?

Lene Kaaberbol has written a further three books about Dina and her journey to understanding the role of the Shamer: *The Shamer's Signet*, *The Serpent Gift* and *The Shamer's War*.

You might also like *The Giver* and *Gathering Blue* by Lois Lowry, set in a world where everyone is engineered to be the same.

For another exhilarating fantasy, try Clive Barker's *Abarat* (UTBG 10).

# SHARP NORTH   Patrick Cave

 12+

### Next?

The sequel, *Blown Away*, about Adeline, or *House of the Scorpion* (UTBG 178) by Nancy Farmer, another fantastic sci-fi thriller whose protagonists have much in common with Mira.

*Exodus* (UTBG 120) by Julie Bertagna also takes place in a futuristic flooded Britain.

Or how about the different but equally thrilling **The Oracle** trilogy (UTBG 275).

An isolated spot in the Highlands, an unknown woman pursued by grey-clad men, red blood spills on white snow as a young girl accidentally witnesses a murder. This is the atmospheric opening of Cave's gripping sci-fi thriller. Mira's simple existence is shattered by the violent scene, sending her on a long journey to find her true identity. The book is set in a futuristic Britain, a half-drowned country governed by powerful families who would do just about anything to retain their control, including some very unethical experiments. A web of lies and political corruption is slowly closing in on Mira, who must use every resource she has in order to survive.

**Noga Applebaum**

# SHARPE'S COMPANY  Bernard Cornwell

**14+**

**Next?**

You will certainly want to read others **Sharpe** books – I've got 18 on my shelf and Cornwell is still writing them. Chronologically, they start with *Sharpe's Tiger* but the first one he wrote – and one of the best – was *Sharpe's Rifles*.

C.S. Forester's **Hornblower** series is set at sea druing the Napoleonic wars, as is Elizabeth Laird's fast and action-packed *Secrets of the Fearless*.

Sharpe is a soldier in the Peninsular wars – the wars Britain fought in Spain and Portugal against Napoleon in the early 1800s. These were times of great cruelty and great heroism, and Bernard Cornwell describes them better than anyone. His hero is a rough, tough Lieutenant of the 95th Rifles, and the events in which he is involved actually happened. When you read in the book about the 'forlorn hope' and the attack on the great fortress of Badajoz you will be blown away – as were most of the men in the first advance…

*Sharpe's Company* is the third of a wonderful series and possibly my favourite. Cornwell makes you wonder how anyone could think history was boring.

**Andrew Norriss**

# SHE  H. Rider Haggard

**14+**

In my mid-teens I was mightily stirred by H. Rider Haggard's adventure novels, by this one most of all perhaps, partly because of the detailed drawings in my hardback edition of the proud, deliciously bare-breasted Queen Ayesha.

In *She*, Ludwig Horace Holly and his young ward Leo Vincey set sail for Africa to seek the truth behind the death, over 2,000 years earlier, of Kallikrates, an ancestor of Leo's. After hair-raising escapades on the high seas and among cannibals, Holly and Leo are taken to the concealed realm of the great white queen Ayesha (She-Who-Must-Be-Obeyed), who admits to having murdered Kallikrates herself for rejecting her several lifetimes ago. Ayesha has ruled this hidden land for all those centuries, never losing her youth and beauty. Recognising Leo as a true descendant of her lost love, the queen leads him and his guardian on thrilling and dangerous adventures which not all will survive…

**Michael Lawrence**

**Next?**

Another Rider Haggard? There's a sequel, *Ayesha*. Or try the yarn *King Solomon's Mines*.

John Buchan's *Prester John* is also set in the dark heart of Africa.

Or try some of Rudyard Kipling's short stories in *The Man Who Would be King*.

# THE SHELL HOUSE   Linda Newbery

This is a big and complex novel which explores in some depth, and with great honesty and tenderness, the emotional awakening of two young men from different periods of history. One is Greg, a modern teenager, drawn into the past by his involvement in the restoration of a stately home. The other is Edmund, a young soldier, who fought and loved – and subsequently disappeared – in World War I.

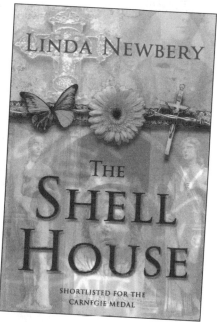

Sexual identity, as revealed through Edmund's sufferings, is one strand of this many-layered novel. Another is the nature of religious belief, as Greg's girlfriend, the aptly named Faith, struggles with the concept of her Christianity. Still another is the need for Greg to discover what he really feels and thinks, and to remain true to his ideals.

An astonishingly wide canvas is covered, ranging across both time and the conflicting emotional landscapes of the two main characters. All in all, a deeply satisfying read.

**Jean Ure**

## Next?

A couple of other books that set the troubles of sexuality against a backdrop of World War I: Jennifer Johnston's *How Many Miles to Babylon?* and Susan Hill's *Strange Meeting* (UTBG 358).

Or for more Linda Newbery, read *Sisterland*, (UTBG 342) which weaves a compelling story around Alzheimer's, sexuality and racism.

Aidan Chambers' *Dance on My Grave* (UTBG 91) also deals with complex issues of sexuality.

## ICE IN BEARDS – VERY COLD PLACES INDEED...

*The Worst Journey in the World* by Apsley Cherry Garrard

*Terra Incognita* by Sara Wheeler

*Frost on My Moustache* by Tim Moore

*Touching the Void* by Joe Simpson

# The SHERLOCK HOLMES stories

## Sir Arthur Conan Doyle

**12+**

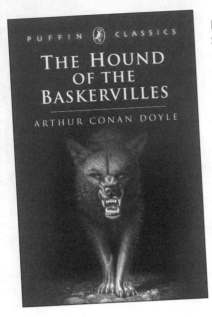

It's impossible to imagine a world without Sherlock Holmes. Sir Arthur Conan Doyle's creation is more famous than many historical figures. The actor / director Orson Welles once described Holmes as 'the greatest man who never lived and who will never die'.

I'd start with the very first story, *A Study in Scarlet*, and then read the first half-dozen or so short stories in order. That way you'll get to know Holmes, his faithful companion Doctor John Watson and the Victorian world they inhabit. After that, you can pick and choose. There are 56 short stories and four short novels, offering an extraordinary mix of pure deduction, adventure and intrigue. Like them, and they will stay with you for ever.

**Philip Ardagh**

I can remember how my heart sank when I opened a big present and found this heavy volume inside. I must have been about 14, and I couldn't imagine anything less enticing. Sometimes that's the best way to approach a book. The thrill of being surprised is wonderful. These four stories: *A Study in Scarlet*, *The Sign of Four*, *The Hound of the Baskervilles* and *The Valley of Fear*, are all you need to get hooked on Holmes and Watson, and their world of crime and mystery. The stories were first published in the late 19th century, and these days there may even be an extra thrill: Holmes is wonderfully politically incorrect. A modern publisher would insist on cleaning up his habits and attitudes before allowing you anywhere near these compelling stories.

**Eleanor Updale**

### Next?

There are heaps more Holmes stories found in: *The Adventures of Sherlock Holmes*; *The Memoirs of Sherlock Holmes*; *The Return of Sherlock Holmes*; *His Last Bow*; *The Casebook of Sherlock Holmes*.

If you want something more modern, go to P.D. James (UTBG 190, 390) Colin Dexter (UTBG 191) or Ruth Rendell (UTBG 338). They all write books where the same detective returns to solve new mysteries.

Or try Dorothy Sayers' **Lord Peter Wimsey** stories (UTBG 225), starting with *Clouds of Witness*.

# SHORT STORIES H.G. Wells

H.G. Wells is the founding father of British science fiction – a brilliant storyteller whose books are full of speculations about the future. Of the short stories, the most famous is 'The Time Machine', in which the hero travels through untold millennia to the very end of the world. Then there's 'The Country of the Blind', where the sighted man is at no advantage, and 'The Man Who Could Work Miracles', who ends up dearly wishing he couldn't. Wells imagines what would happen if the earth stopped revolving, if diamonds could be grown, if a man could see two periods of time at once, if tentacled invaders were to crawl from the sea. Through stories, he explores his theories and beliefs, mixing terrifying fantasy firmly with the world of Edwardian Britain.

**Catherine Fisher**

### Next?

Try Wells' novels. *The War of the Worlds* (UTBG 398) is a classic of alien invasion, and *The Invisible Man* takes the idea of invisibility to its logical limits.

Wells' work inspired William Hope Hodgson's bizarre and brilliant *The Night Land*.

Or try some rather more recent science fiction, such as Arthur C. Clarke's *Childhood's End*, or Isaac Asimov's *I, Robot* (UTBG 184).

Or see our feature and list of great sci-fi reads on pp. 232–233.

# THE SHORT STORIES OF SAKI H.H. Munro

Tobermory the cat is taught human speech and starts repeating in public everything he has overheard in private. A stray child turns out to be a werewolf. Conradin makes a god of his pet ferret and prays for vengeance on his hateful guardian – successfully. Through these very short stories rampage fiendishly inventive children, dictatorial aunts, liars, bored young men who make life hell for other people just to pass the time, and every species of animal from chickens to wolves, usually wreaking havoc of some kind. Often savage, sometimes sad, always witty, these portraits of Edwardian society are like snapshots taken with a camera that has a crack in the lens.

**Jan Mark**

### Next?

Rudyard Kipling was writing many of his short stories at about the same time as Munro. Try *Debits and Credits* or *Limits and Renewals*.

Once you get a taste for short stories it's hard to get enough. Sylvia Townsend Warner wrote some very entertaining and rather strange stories, often tinged with the supernatural, such as those in *One Thing Leading to Another*.

Or try G.K. Chesterton's slightly strange *The Man Who Was Thursday*, about an anarchist and a policeman.

# SIDDHARTHA  Hermann Hesse

14+

Young Siddhartha is loved and admired by everyone, not least the girls of the town, who sigh when he passes. But Siddhartha is not content. He feels that something is missing from his life and, with his faithful friend Govinda, joins a band of wandering holy men. The friends travel and live with the holy men for three years until the day they hear of old Gotama, the wise man known as the Buddha, and go to hear him preach. Govinda is impressed by the Buddha and decides to follow him, but Siddhartha does not want to learn how another man acquired his wisdom: he wants to find his own, by way of his own experiences. And so his real quest begins – a difficult and complicated journey that is fulfilled only in old age.

I loved this book when I first read it, and loved it all over again when I read it some years later – though I confess without experiencing the slightest urge to go on a quest like Siddhartha's…

**Michael Lawrence**

**Next?**

More Hermann Hesse? Try *Narziss and Goldmund* (UTBG 256) or *Steppenwolf*.

Richard Bach also writes about the getting of wisdom – try *Jonathan Livingstone Seagull* (UTBG 198).

Or try the Dalai Lama's *The Art of Happiness: A Handbook for Living*.

# A SIGHT FOR SORE EYES  Ruth Rendell

14+

**Next?**

Although in her 70s, Rendell knows exactly what it's like to be young. Some of her best evocations of youth are found in *Going Wrong* and *The Crocodile Bird*.

P.D. James writes mainly about Inspector Dalgliesh, but why not try one of her books about Cordelia Gray instead? *The Skull Beneath the Skin* is my favourite.

And of course you can turn to our feature on detective stories on pp. 104–105 for more recommendations.

Rendell is my all-time favourite author and this thriller is one of her best. Teddy Brex is born a beautiful, lovable child into a family lacking in love. After her mother's violent murder, Francine Hill is encaged in a strict family setting that permits no room for any emotion but a desperate desire for escape. When the two young adults meet there's an instant attraction. But can a man who's never been loved learn to love? And is it inevitable that ugliness is so corrosive that it sours even the most beautiful subject? These are two questions asked in Ruth Rendell's compulsively readable thriller, which as always spins several threads at once and culminates in a devastating, brilliant end.

**Jon Appleton**

# SILAS MARNER  George Eliot

16+

### Next?

I went on from this to *Tess of the d'Urbervilles* (UTBG 369) by Thomas Hardy (more rural England and dastardly men) and *Jane Eyre* (UTBG 195), the ultimate book of unjust suffering and longing.

One of the themes of *Silas Marner* (though I don't think I realised it at the time) is the dignity of labour. You can get more of that from *Sons and Lovers* by D.H. Lawrence.

Some people do like *Mill on the Floss* (UTBG 245), of course. Try it and see if you are one of them.

This was the first 'posh' book I read outside school. I had heard of George Eliot, and how she was a woman hiding behind a man's name, but I was put off by the size of her books on the library shelves. So I chose the thinnest: *Silas Marner*. It's a great story, set in the early 19th century.

Silas Marner, a weaver, is turned into a reclusive, miserly outsider when falsely accused of theft. Then he is transformed again when he finds and adopts a young girl. This book has everything: tragedy, mystery, and a dissolute, sexy, aristocratic villain. At school, we read Eliot's *The Mill on the Floss* out loud in class. It took weeks. I thought I was going to die of boredom. But *Silas Marner* was fab.

**Eleanor Updale**

# SILENT SNOW, SECRET SNOW
## Adèle Geras

14+

The ideal read for a cold winter's day. Curl up on the sofa with a box of your favourite chocolates within a hand's snatch and ENJOY! All human life is here, with its fancies and foibles and its deep, dark secrets.

Snowed in at the Big House, cut off from the outside world, the Golden Family spend their Christmas loving, hating – laughing, crying – pining for what might have been, planning for what will be. And we as the readers become privy to it all, as we see through the eyes of each character.

Soft is the snow, and silent are the secrets, in this hidden world of the emotions.

**Jean Ure**

### Next?

You can't go wrong with Adèle Geras. Try *Troy* (UTBG 382) next, or *The Tower Room* (UTBG 378), part of the **Happy Ever After** series.

For a very funny and light look at family Christmases (and a nice easy read), try Anne Fine's *The More the Merrier*.

**The Dark Is Rising** series (UTBG 93) is a spooky Christmas read.

# SILVERFIN Charlie Higson

James Bond is 13, and a new boy at Eton. School is bad enough, but then he makes enemies and his holiday in Scotland becomes something less than relaxing. With the help of a beautiful girl and a tough, streetwise kid, Bond survives the attentions of an obsessed millionaire, imprisonment, experimental drugs, torture, perilous escape and coming to terms with the death of seemingly everyone he loves.

This is brilliantly researched and perfectly in keeping with the other Bond stories. From the gruesome opening chapter to the final scenes, this is a rip-roaring adventure, and one that Ian Fleming would surely have approved of. And best of all? This is just the first in a series – I can't wait!

**Leonie Flynn**

### Next?

The sequel, *BloodFever*, of course.

Or one of the original **James Bond** books by Ian Fleming (UTBG 194); try *Dr No* for starters.

Robert Muchamore writes great adventures for his teen heroes. Try *The Recruit* (UTBG 307), first in the **Cherub** series.

Or for another story set in the wilds of Scotland that'll have you chewing your nails, try John Buchan's *The Thirty-Nine Steps* (UTBG 371).

# THE SIMPLE GIFT Steven Herrick

### Next?

*The Simple Gift* reminds me – weirdly I know – of Bunyan's *Pilgrim's Progress*.

And the father-son relationship has echoes of Kevin Brooks' *Martyn Pig* (UTBG 236), although with a happier outcome.

Alan Gibbons' *The Lost Boys' Appreciation Society* is also about finding a home in a harsh world. Or try a futuristic version of the theme, in *As Good As Dead in Downtown* by Neil Arksey.

Written in free verse, this story is told through short, stand-alone poems, each a little masterpiece in its own right. A most unusual novel, it opens with 16-year-old Billy abandoning his loveless home and cruel father to hit the road and live rough. But if you think you're in for a grim, downbeat read, you'll be surprised.

Basically *The Simple Gift* explores goodness and kindness. Despite his background, Billy is a character of fundamental dignity and integrity. He might be down and out, living in an old railway carriage, but his decency enriches the lives of others.

And ultimately in this gritty, uplifting fairy tale for our times, Billy himself trades his past for true friendship and love.

**Catherine Forde**

# THE SIRENS OF TITAN  Kurt Vonnegut

Everyone knows Vonnegut wrote *Slaughterhouse 5*. And yes, it's a brilliant book that must be read. But he wrote a lot of other classics too. This, one of his earliest, is also one of his best. A wickedly funny satire about the meaning (and meaninglessness) of life, it features many of his trademarks – science fiction, time travel, knowledge of the future, man's role in the universe, our ultimate end.

Vonnegut's books can be bleak as well as hilarious – but they'll always make you think. He's not just a brilliant sci-fi writer – he's a great writer full stop. Don't let phrases like 'chrono-synclastic infundibulum' put you off. Vonnegut's books come dressed as sci-fi, but they're always about humans and our struggles to make sense of the world and of life. But be warned: if you read this book, you might never look at *The Bible* in the same light again!

**Darren Shan**

> **Next?**
>
> *Slaughterhouse 5* (UTBG 345) and *Mother Night*, both by Kurt Vonnegut.
>
> *Childhood's End* by Arthur C. Clarke is about what humanity might become, with encouragement from outside.
>
> *The Hitchhiker's Guide to the Galaxy* (UTBG 171) must be the funniest sci-fi novel ever.

# THE SISTERHOOD OF THE TRAVELLING PANTS  Ann Brashares

> **Next?**
>
> Try *Feeling Sorry for Celia* by Jaclyn Moriarty; wry, hilarious and written in the form of letters. Or Carolyn Mackler's *Love and Other Four Letter Words*, about parents separating, moving to New York and love.
>
> And *Sisterhood...* has sequels, too: *Second Summer of the Travelling Pants* is next.
>
> You might then like to try Meg Cabot's *Teen Idol*.

This is the story of one pair of trousers, four very different girls and one very special friendship. Carmen, Lena, Bridget and Tibby are destined to go their own separate ways in the summer but resolve to share their lives by passing the pants (a rather stylish pair of jeans that somehow fits each of them perfectly) from one to the other in turn. The four girls' summer experiences, with all their highs and lows, are woven skilfully together into a satisfying story of friendship and self-discovery.

**Philippa Milnes-Smith**

# SISTERLAND Linda Newbery

**Next?**

Another wonderful Linda Newbery? Try her latest, *Set in Stone* (UTBG 331) or *Lost Boy*.

David Almond's *The Fire-Eaters* (UTBG 130) is another book that manages to make international politics a part of an engaging personal story.

Or for more about the contemporary Middle East, try Elizabeth Laird's *A Little Piece of Ground* (UTBG 219).

This novel covers an enormous amount of ground very well. It's at one and the same time a love story about the relationship of a British girl and a Palestinian boy, a story about memories of World War II, a tale of two sisters and the rivalry between them, and a discussion of racism and contemporary Middle East politics. This makes the book sound worthy, which it emphatically isn't. We are always engaged with the characters and their lives, and the pace ensures that readers will want to keep turning the pages. The relationship between the British girl Hilly and her grandmother, and the role of memory and history in the novel, make it one that's worth rereading. There are no easy answers at the end, but the author strikes a hopeful note in the final pages.

**Adèle Geras**

# SKARRS Catherine Forde

This is a story in two parts; with two voices, two tales to tell. First there's Danny, who's in trouble – all attitude and bravado and paper-thin front, ready to take on anyone, especially when he's with Jakey, the bad boy gone worse who's befriended him.

And then there's his Grampa Dan, who's just died and whom we learn about through the diary he wrote while a prisoner of the Japanese in Burma during World War II.

The two stories dovetail together beautifully in a book which is set in Forde's native Scotland and uses a lot of dialect, but is so well-written you won't need subtitles. *Skarrs* is edgy, page-turning and full of great characters, and I loved it.

**Graham Marks**

**Next?**

Liked the way Catherine Forde writes? Then try her first book *Fat Boy Swim* (UTBG 125), or her latest, *The Drowning Pond*.

Want to know more about what happened to prisoners in Japan during the war? Try James Clavell's *King Rat* or J.G. Ballard's semi-autobiographical *Empire of the Sun* (UTBG 114).

Another book where music plays an important role is Benjamin Zephaniah's *Gangsta Rap*.

# SKELLIG   David Almond

This is one of my favourite books of all time! It's about a boy called Michael, who has just moved to a rather derelict house and whose baby sister is so seriously ill we don't know whether she's going to survive. It's about fear, and sadness, and loss, but also about healing and recovery and love, and tenderness. At the heart of the story is the extraordinary figure of Skellig, whom Michael discovers in the tumbledown garage. At first he seems like a disgusting old man, covered in cobwebs, but bit by bit Michael's (and the reader's) view is transformed.

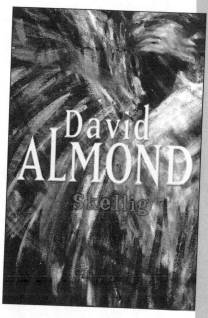

Michael, his friends Leaky and Coot, Mina (a home-educated girl with a special way of seeing things) and Michael's family are all real and totally believable, but this story is also magical and extraordinary. Reading it felt to me like going on an intense, moving journey. I couldn't put it down!

**Julia Green**

With a new house and a new school, Michael has a lot to cope with even without his baby sister falling dangerously ill. With his parents preoccupied with the baby and the doctor always in the house, Michael is left to his own devices, and one day finds a mysterious man – or is it a bird? – or maybe an angel? – in the ramshackle garage at the bottom of the garden. Together with his new friend Mina they take the strange being, with wings and a peculiar liking for flies and Chinese takeaways, to her grandfather's house, and Michael's life changes forever…

Words aren't enough to describe the magic of this book. It's a story about faith and hope, life, love and death – big serious issues – but there's humour too, and it's so well-written you feel you're there with them. Imaginative, inspired, original, full of poetry and emotion, you'll not be able to put it down when you're reading it or put it out of your head when you've finished.

**David Gardner (aged 16)**

### Next?

*A Kestrel for a Knave* (UTBG 206) – a powerful story about the relationship between a boy and a wild bird.

*Coraline* (UTBG 83) is a magic / reality mix with a far darker and more sinister edge, based on a backwards reality, not unlike a creepier version of Lewis Carroll's *Alice's Adventures in Wonderland*.

Other David Almonds to look for include his disturbing look at good and evil, *Clay* (UTBG 78).

Another slightly surreal story about reality not quite being what it seems is Alan Garner's *Elidor*.

# SKINNY B, SKAZ AND ME   John Singleton

12+

## Next?

More John Singleton? Check out his other novel, *Star*.

Another author with a talent for making the everyday world sound special is David Almond. *Kit's Wilderness* (UTBG 211) is particularly unsettling...

For an author who can capture the grim reality of life without losing his sense of humour, try Alan Gibbons' book *The Lost Boys' Appreciation Society*.

14-year-old Lee doesn't like his sister, Skinny. After all, in their house the first rule is: what Skinny wants, Skinny gets. But then Skinny gets sick, and whilst Lee is trying to show that he does care (after all, nothing says I love you so much as hair glitter, right?) life takes a turn for the worse.

Just how Lee gets on the wrong side of the Hoodz5 boys, ends up climbing a death-trap water tower with his best 'friend' Skaz – who literally leaves him hanging – and finds out that the girl he fancies is the daughter of the local crime boss, makes a fast-paced, enjoyable read.

This is a book that tells it how it is and leaves you wishing for more.

**Laura Hutchings**

# SLAKE'S LIMBO   Felice Holman

14+

A great American novel that deserves far greater fame in Britain. Artemis Slake is 'born an orphan at the age of thirteen, small, near-sighted, dreaming, bruised, an outlander in the city of his birth'. Fleeing from constant bullying, he goes underground, literally. He finds a cave in New York's subway system and doesn't go home again. From his hideout, cautiously, he builds a new, almost-independent life, forming delicate relationships with subterranean people who, to his surprise, do not want to hurt him.

The story is free of sentimentality, even of pity, and Holman's writing is wonderful. Somehow it manages to be dense and rich but laid-back at the same time; sometimes it jolts and sparks like a speeding underground train. And it's miraculously compact – a mere 90 pages in my edition. An unmissable masterpiece.

**Mal Peet**

## Next?

More books about running away and the problems it brings? Try Keith Gray's *Runner* and *Warehouse* (UTBG 399) or Steven Herrick's *The Simple Gift* (UTBG 340).

*Underworld* (UTBG 389) is about a group of kids trapped underground and how they survive.

*Fake* (UTBG 122) by K.K. Beck is about two boys running away from a centre for juvenile rehabilitation.

# SLAUGHTERHOUSE 5 Kurt Vonnegut

Kurt Vonnegut lived through the fire-bombing of Dresden in World War II and then spent 20 years trying to find a way to write about it. He finally came up with this – one of the most famous anti-war novels of all time. Billy Pilgrim, with his blue and ivory feet, stumbles through time and space. Billy becomes an optometrist, a private in the US army, a specimen on show in an alien zoo, an innocent, a father, a son, a husband – quite often all at once. People die. A lot of people die. So it goes.

Absurd, tragic and very funny, this is Vonnegut's masterpiece. As a plea for less butchery and less blind obedience to authority, it sears.

**Leonie Flynn**

## Next?

For another war book – that makes you see just how horrible it is – try *Catch-22* (UTBG 65) by Joseph Heller, one of the funniest books written about this subject – and the scariest.

Or for a vision of the future that'll chill you, where knowledge and ideas are forbidden and books are burned, try Ray Bradbury's *Fahrenheit 451* (UTBG 121).

Or maybe you fancy something else by Mr Vonnegut? Try *Breakfast of Champions*, a hilarious, cynical rollercoaster of a novel (in which Kilgore Trout himself appears!).

# SLEEPWALKING Nicola Morgan

## Next?

Nicola's other brilliant books include *Fleshmarket* (UTBG 131), a gory story about early experiments in surgery, and *Mondays Are Red* (UTBG 248), an interesting insight into synaesthesia.

*Blinded by the Light* (UTBG 45) by Sherry Ashworth looks at people being controlled, this time by brainwashing cults. Or try her intriguing exploration of the world of dreams, *The Dream Travellers*.

Wouldn't it be great if everything was just perfect – or would it? Would it really be that good never to have to worry about anything? Is that living? Isn't life all about overcoming problems? Surely if we didn't have to, we'd all be robotic. Or are we already? Are we all really robotic, not in a mechanical sense, but in that from the moment we are born a computer has our lives mapped out for us?

This is the story of four chosen teenagers, the Outsiders, who lie outside a world that is 'perfect' in just this way, and who set off on an adventure to infiltrate the government building that is controlling the minds of the Citizens. This book sounds like sci-fi but also screams adventure thriller with a small dose of real life mixed in. The balance between emotion and adventure is spot on, and the climax is fantastic!

**David Gardner (aged 16)**

# THE SLIGHTLY TRUE STORY OF CEDAR B. HARTLEY

## Martine Murray

What can I say about this book, other than that it's extraordinary? It reads like an Australian Margaret Atwood with an added layer of quirkiness. For starters, Cedar B. Hartley's real name isn't Cedar B. Hartley at all, but Lana Monroe, who as well as telling the story draws weird little pictures with captions such as 'terrapin inside a sock' and 'Oscar in cone shape'. This is a story about being an outsider, growing up and growing friendships with a big dose of acrobatics thrown in for good measure. And then there's Oscar with his brain injury, Kite (who's a bird person) and Stinky the dog. If there's only one book you read from this guide, make it this one!

**Philip Ardagh**

> **Next?**
>
> Hilary McKay's *Dog Friday* is another story of friendship brought about by a lost dog.
>
> Martine Murray is also an illustrator, so why not check out her drawings in *Henrietta* or *A Moose Called Mouse*?
>
> More quirky characters? try *Stargirl* (UTBG 352).

# SNOW FALLING ON CEDARS

## David Guterson

> **Next?**
>
> More Guterson? Try *Our Lady of the Forest*, about a girl who has visions or his collection of stories, *The Country Ahead of Us, the Country Behind*.
>
> For another portrait of a small fishing town, try E. Annie Proulx's *The Shipping News*.
>
> A book that tells of Japan just after the war is *Memoirs of a Geisha* (UTBG 241).

The book is set in 1954 on the island of San Piedro off the coast of Washington. The death of a local white fisherman in suspicious circumstances leads to the arrest of Japanese-American Kabuo Miyamoto, who is charged with his murder. The narration is by the local newspaper editor and one-time boyfriend of the accused's wife. The story then twists and turns and we're treated to flashbacks to the 1940s, following the bombing of Pearl Harbour, when the island's Japanese-Americans were sent to internment camps. The imagery is beautiful and vivid, and the characters rich. The book becomes a courtroom drama, a romance, a murder mystery and an account of the war seen from the side of the 'enemy'. If you've seen the movie don't be put off. This book is priceless.

**Ileana Antonopoulou**

# THE SNOW GOOSE  Paul Gallico

This moving and haunting little story was first published in 1940. It's about the relationship which develops between a lonely older man (Philip Rhyader) and a young girl, Frith, who brings him a wounded snow goose to be healed. Philip, an artist, feels a special connection with the wild birds on the marshes near his home on the east coast: 'his heart was filled with love for wild and hunted things'. It's this same feeling that drives him to take his boat to help rescue the soldiers stranded at Dunkirk, joining many other 'little ships'.

The story is simply and beautifully told. It captures perfectly the remote setting, and the birds, and the feelings of the girl who comes to love the lonely and isolated man.

**Julia Green**

### Next?

The stories in Michael Morpurgo's collection *The White Horse of Zennor* also have a haunting quality and a strong sense of place. (Incidentally Michael is a *Snow Goose* fan, too.)

William Fiennes' *The Snow Geese* is a blend of travel and autobiography as the author follows migrating geese from Arctic Canada to the Gulf of Mexico.

Most of Paul Gallico's novels are now out of print. But do try and hunt out *Thomasina*, about a girl and a cat.

# SOMETHING IN THE AIR

12+

## Jan Mark

### Next?

In the **Quantocks** quartet, Ruth Elwyn Harris tells the stories of the Purcell sisters from World War I to World War II. It begins in 1910 with *The Silent Shore*, which shows how Sarah's idyllic world is shattered by the outbreak of war.

Theresa Breslin writes about the tragic effects that World War I had on young people in *Remembrance* (UTBG 309).

The best books have a feeling about them that lingers long after you've forgotten the details and *Something in the Air* is like this, filled with a sense of loss and sadness that you can't forget. Set just after World War I, the book is about Peggy who begins to hear noises in her head. Is she hearing communications from the dead as her glamorous, bereaved young aunt hopes, or is she going mad? The truth is stranger and more rational. In her quest to discover what is really causing the noises, Peggy finds the way to a future full of possibilities, progress and hope. Peggy refuses to be tied to the past, though she will never forget it.

**Gill Vickery**

# THE SONG OF AN INNOCENT BYSTANDER 16+
## Ian Bone

Imagine that when you are nine years old you are one of the hostages in a siege – a man with a gun holds you and a load of adults who don't know you in a fast-food restaurant because he HATES the company that owns it. Imagine that you survive, and ten years later a journalist wants to interview you. But imagine too that you have worse memories – and guilt – from that horrible event than anyone knows or imagines. Except the strangers who were with you.

This book examines terrible memories, and the reader experiences them with the young girl. Has she been damaged? Can she be healed? It's gripping, sometimes horribly so, but exceptionally real and moving.

**Nicola Morgan**

### Next?

*Looking for JJ* (UTBG 222) is another great book that examines how a terrible event in childhood can have resonances in later life.

*Noughts and Crosses* (UTBG 267) (and sequels) by Malorie Blackman also vividly portray young people dealing with guilt and remorse within a traumatic setting.

*Z for Zachariah* (UTBG 426) by Robert C. O'Brien is about a girl's disturbing encounter with an older man.

# SOPHIE'S WORLD Jostein Gaarder 14+

### Next?

If you want to read more about philosophy, watch out! Many books tend to be a bit stodgy. But anything with the word 'beginner' in the title is usually a safe bet.

*The Bluffer's Guide to Philosophy* is glib, quite rude, very funny and very useful!

Jostein Gaarder has written many books. Try *The Solitaire Mystery*, a philosophical novel with a dwarf.

This amazing book starts with two simple questions: Who are you? and Where does the world come from? When 14-year-old Sophie finds these questions written on pieces of paper in her mailbox one day, her extraordinary journey into the history and mystery of philosophy is only just beginning.

If you thought philosophy was dull and boring, or only for large-brained geniuses – think again! It really is astonishing and fascinating stuff, and it's so fundamental that it relates to everything we do. The story itself is full of suspense and excitement, with plenty of twists and turns, and it'll keep you thinking and guessing right to the end.

**Kevin Brooks**

# THE SPEED OF THE DARK  Alex Shearer

**Next?**

If your appetite for gothic horror is still sharp, there's always *Frankenstein* (UTBG 139).

And of course there's the classic study of the conflict of good and evil in Man's nature, *Dr Jekyll and Mr Hyde* (UTBG 107).

For more dark tales by Alex Shearer read *The Stolen* and *The Lost*. But he also writes brilliant comedy – cheer yourself up with *Bootleg*, about what happens when The Good for You Party tries to improve the nation's health by banning chocolate!

Young Christopher Mallen is fascinated by Ernst Eckmann's miniature sculptures – a salt grain carved into an iceberg complete with penguins, the Empire State Building on the tip of a pencil – each perfect in every detail, but so tiny that they can only be viewed through a powerful microscope. Eckmann is obsessed with Christopher's father Robert Mallen's beautiful girlfriend, a dancer called Poppea, and when he discovers how to miniaturise living tissue, he sees a way not only to possess her, but to take his jealous revenge on Robert. When first Poppea and then Robert Mallen mysteriously disappear, Eckmann takes Christopher in and treats him like a son. It is only when Eckmann dies that Christopher learns the ghastly truth about their disappearance. And there will be many more twists and terrors before we reach the end of this chilling and utterly compelling tale…

**Kathryn Ross**

# SPIGGOT'S QUEST  Garry Kilworth

A college boy called Jack crashes his motorbike and finds himself trapped in a world where all of mankind's myths, legends and fairy tales are frighteningly real. He meets a boggart called Spiggot who has been sent by his father to deliver a suit of golden armour to the King of the Fairies. He is accompanied by Kling, a giant water rat. Spiggot is tempted into wearing the armour himself to do battle with a foe. His quest through Liofwende involves encounters with trolls, goblins, ogres, gnomes and fairies. The fantasy world is vividly brought to life and there is also humour, particularly where the reader shares Jack's perspective on the mythical world.

**Brenda Marshall**

**Next?**

This is the first book in the **Knights of Liofwende** trilogy; next is *Mallmoc's Castle*, then *Boggart and Fen*.

*Faerie Wars* by Herbie Brennan: another book where human and fairy worlds meet.

*Sabriel* (UTBG 316) is the first of a trilogy in which Sabriel has to make a terrifying journey in the hope of rescuing her father.

# SPINDLE'S END  Robin McKinley

**Next?**

Robin McKinley has also retold the story of 'Beauty and the Beast' in her book *Beauty* (UTBG 35).

And if you like complex retellings of traditional tales, try Adèle Geras' *The Tower Room* (UTBG 378). Or Angela Carter's *The Bloody Chamber*, a collection of short stories based on fairy tales.

For more magic with a twist read *Wicked: The Life and Times of the Wicked Witch of the West* by Gregory Maguire, which challenges our notions of good and evil.

**14+**

You might think you know the story of 'Sleeping Beauty' but you don't, not as Robin McKinley tells it. The country in which it takes place so drips with magic that every ordinary household tries to have a fairy on hand to control it.

Katriona's aunt is a fairy, but it is Kat herself who has the adventure, which involves rescuing a certain bewitched baby princess and keeping her in hiding till she comes of age. The last part of the book involves a cunning plan to outwit the wicked witch and becomes very surreal indeed.

Don't be put off by the slow, intense pace at which the story unfolds: you'll find complex magic, romance and masses of atmosphere.

**Mary Hoffman**

# SPY HIGH series  A.J. Butcher

**14+**

Deveraux College is an exclusive boarding school for teenagers with great potential. But not just academic potential – these teens are training to be secret agents. To those enrolled at Deveraux, it's known as Spy High.

Book one of the series introduces six new recruits – Bond Team – and we watch them face the demands of Spy High training, including battles against Stromfeld, a virtual reality megalomaniac villain. And Stromfeld, evil as he is, isn't the toughest challenge that Bond Team will face; there's a real villain out there too, a villain who creates horrific mutant monsters – a villain called Dr Averill Frankenstein.

This isn't a book to read if you're looking for beautifully turned passages of descriptive prose, nor indeed for detailed and sophisticated characterisation; but if you want a gripping story, an easy read with breathless pace, they don't come any better.

**Daniel Hahn**

**Next?**

If you liked this you might want to move straight on to the next in the series: *The Chaos Connection*.

For another very special training school, how about Benedict Jacka's *To Be a Ninja* (UTBG 374)?

Or Chris Ryan's **Alpha Force** series, try *Rat-Catcher* (UTBG 304).

# THE SPY WHO CAME IN FROM THE COLD
## John le Carré

A classic spy story. It's a story of secrets and schemes, betrayals, double agents and triple agents, barbed-wire checkpoints, interrogations. The story twists and turns back on itself, as we try to work out whose side everyone is really on.

British secret agent Leamas is on one final mission to eliminate East German head of counter-espionage Mundt; but it seems that Mundt may really be a double agent for the British. Except he isn't really. Except he is. Is he?

This is a world where you can't trust anyone, can't believe anything they say; Leamas can trust only himself, his girl Liz and his boss Control. But can he really? As he gets closer and closer to the nail-biting finale, the question of who his real friends are will take on the greatest importance imaginable. Seriously gripping stuff.

**Daniel Hahn**

### Next?

For more spies and complicated plots, try Len Deighton's **Hook, Line and Sinker** series; or for another classic le Carré, *Tinker, Tailor, Soldier, Spy*.

For the opposite take on spies – this time heroic and glamorous rather than slightly dark and seedy – try the **James Bond** books (UTBG 194).

A wartime story about boys who take their spying a little too seriously is Michael Frayn's *Spies*.

---

# STAR OF THE SEA   Joseph O'Connor

### Next?

If you like a story of murder at sea, why not try *The False Inspector Dew* by Peter Lovesey?

Herman Melville also wrote about life at sea in *Billy Budd*.

Another Joseph O'Connor? Try the very different *Inishowen*, a black comedy about relationships.

This book tells the stories of the captain and passengers of the *Star of the Sea*, a ship sailing to New York in 1847. Through them, the author examines the misery caused by the Irish potato famine, one of the greatest disasters of the 19th century, which killed as many as one million people and forced another two million to emigrate. We see the issues through the eyes of all levels of society, from the fallen aristocrat eating fine food in first class to the peasants eating gruel below deck, who have had to sell everything they own to pay for their passage. In the background is a deeply political story of social upheaval, but the narrative is strong enough to make it feel like more of a murder-mystery than a historical document.

**Anthony Reuben**

# STARGIRL   Jerry Spinelli

12+

## Next?

Quirky reads are my favourites. I thoroughly recommend *Holes* (UTBG 173) by Louis Sachar, *Joey Pigza Swallowed the Key* by Jack Gantos, and *Saffy's Angel* (UTBG 317) by Hilary McKay.

Another Jerry Spinelli? Try *Milkweed* (UTBG 244).

Or what about a Chris d'Lacey? Try the delightful *Horace* (UTBG 176), about love, families and a very valuable teddy bear.

I recommend *Stargirl*, unreservedly, wherever I go. It's a fabulous, lyrical, magical book about individuality and being different; about being yourself and having the maturity to allow everyone else to be themselves, too. It's also about being one of the herd, peer pressure, and the cautionary tale of what happens when you give in to that force and don't follow your own heart and your own star. Furthermore, it's a joyous story of first love, bittersweet and poignant, full of tension and emotion, beauty and tragedy, thrilling, inspiring, and a homage to non-conformity.

If ever there was a book which should be compulsory 'rite-of-passage' reading for everyone, male and female, from age 12 to age 112, this is the one. Unforgettable.

**Chris d'Lacey**

# STARSEEKER   Tim Bowler

12+

Luke has exceptionally sensitive hearing. He is also, like his dead father, musically talented. Sounds dominate his world: playing the piano, the music in his head, hearing other sounds and being captivated or fascinated by them. One part of what Bowler does so well in this book is to give us an insight into what it might be like to be 'gifted'. But it's also the story of a boy trying to come to terms with his mother's new partner.

## Next?

Tim Bowler writes beautiful and engaging books; try *Apocalypse* (UTBG 26) or *River Boy* (UTBG 310).

*You Don't Know Me* (UTBG 425) is about a boy also trying to deal with his mother's intimidating new partner.

A very different book about being 'gifted' is John Wyndham's *Chocky*. Matthew starts counting in binary code, which is odd; and odder still, who is it that's living inside his head?

Both these elements are cleverly bound together by a gripping thriller plot about Luke's struggle to break free of Skin and Daz, bad boys whose spell he has fallen under. And Bowler evokes so well the awful dilemma of someone who is being intimidated by bullies into carrying out their dirty work for them. Luke is supposed to break into an old lady's house and steal a jewellery box, but the house holds far more treasure than mere jewellery…

**Neil Arksey**

# STARSHIP TROOPERS Robert Heinlein

 14+

**Next?**

You'll certainly enjoy other books by Heinlein. Probably best to start with the early stuff – *Stranger in a Strange Land* and *The Moon is a Harsh Mistress* are both pretty amazing, and he wrote some wonderful short stories, too.

For other great battles in space, read *Ender's Game* (UTBG 115), in which the hero goes through training before being thrown into the realities of war, *Midshipman's Hope* (UTBG 244) or one of Iain M. Banks' sci-fi novels, such as *Consider Phlebas* (UTBG 83).

Robert Heinlein is one of the founding giants of science fiction and if you want to know why, read *Starship Troopers*. Set 5,000 years in the future, on one level this is the story of how John Rico joins the military and learns to defend human civilisation against the alien Bugs. But it is so much more than that. Heinlein spits out more ideas in a page than many writers put in an entire novel. You may not agree with them – Heinlein was very right-wing on some issues – but they are always brilliantly woven into the story, which has rightly become one of the classics of science fiction.

**Andrew Norriss**

# STEALING STACEY Lynne Reid Banks

12+

When Stacey's mum disappears to help her long-absent dad, Gran takes the opportunity to 'kidnap' Stacey and takes her to stay on an outback cattle station. In London, Gran is a wealthy, glamorous woman, but at the station a different person emerges. With her, Stacey gets used to boiling temperatures, creepy-crawlies, an outside dunny, a do-it-yourself shower and in fact a completely different way of life. She is soon raising an orphaned baby kangaroo and getting on well with everyone. But action is needed as she realises Gran has no intention of taking her home.

A great escape story and a warm family tale that moves at a cracking speed.

**Wendy Cooling**

**Next?**

For another charming book with an Australian setting (and this time by an Australian author), read *45 and 47 Stella Street* by Elizabeth Honey.

*Walk Two Moons* (UTBG 396) by Sharon Creech is the story of a girl travelling – and bonding – with her grandparents.

Or for something quite different – but very powerful – by Lynne Reid Banks, track down a copy of *One More River*.

Or how about *My Brilliant Career* (UTBG 253), for a girl's life growing up in the bush?

# THE STERKARM HANDSHAKE

**14+**

## Susan Price

Like all great fantasies, *The Sterkarm Handshake* is simple. Every part clicks into place, making exact sense.

A multinational corporation develops the technology to travel into the past to exploit untapped resources, but fails to take into account the people they will encounter. The time tunnel is situated in the Borders. 21st-century scientists meet 16th-century Sterkarms: a fierce, amoral clan of border raiders who live by stealing and fighting. The Sterkarms think the scientists are elves, so that's all right then...

Susan Price makes use of history, language and myth, setting past and present at angles to act as mirrors, each world illuminating the other. The cultural differences can be very funny, but the implications are ominous and the consequences potentially tragic, not least for lovers Per and Andrea, caught between worlds.

**Celia Rees**

### Next?

Find out what happened next in *The Sterkarm Kiss*. It won't disappoint. Or try Susan Price's other novels including *Ghost Drum*, a fantasy set in a country of frozen wastes.

For those who love classic fantasy based on myth and folk belief, try *A Wizard of Earthsea* (UTBG 416) and its sequels.

## The Ultimate Teen Readers' Poll

## BEST BOOK ABOUT RELATIONSHIPS

1 **Harry Potter series**

2 **Girls in Love series**

3 **Noughts and Crosses**

4 **Romeo and Juliet**

5 **His Dark Materials trilogy**

6 **The Princess Diaries series**

7 **Angus, Thongs and Full-frontal Snogging**

8 **Vicky Angel**

9 **The Time-traveller's Wife**

10 **Skellig**

# STONE COLD  Robert Swindells

**Next?**

For a different take on killing, try Nick Gifford's *Incubus*, in which a boy's father is found guilty of multiple murders.

For gangs, sex, poverty and racism, read Bali Rai's *The Crew*.

All Robert Swindells' books are thought-provoking and brilliant. Try the terrifying *Brother in the Land*.

Driven from home by a drunken, abusive stepfather, teenage Link is forced to live on the streets. In the hands of a less skilful writer this might have just been an 'issues' book about homelessness. And Swindells does indeed detail the grinding misery of sleeping rough, but he is also a master storyteller. The inclusion of a chilling and predatory serial killer adds an extra dimension to the novel. Though passionate, the book isn't in any way preachy. The plot and sub-plot sweep along, drawing the reader towards the satisfyingly unsettling conclusion. This is the novel for which Robert Swindells deservedly won the 1994 Carnegie Medal. It's a terrific read.

**Alan Gibbons**

# THE STONES OF MUNCASTER CATHEDRAL
## Robert Westall

There are actually two long short stories in this book, and while 'Brangwyn Gardens' is a creepy enough tale of the supernatural, it is the title piece, 'The Stones of Muncaster Cathedral', that shines.

Joe Clarke is a steeplejack who has been hired to restore the stonework on the tower of Muncaster Cathedral. Like all steeplejacks he knows that some jobs are unlucky, but there's something different about this one. Right from the start he senses something present in the claustrophobic stones around him; something that turns out to be full of evil intent towards the young boys of the town.

A truly shocking ending awaits as Joe finally discovers the secrets of the tower and its hideous gargoyle.

**Marcus Sedgwick**

**Next?**

This story by Robert Westall is a bit older than some of his others, but you could try *Urn Burial* or *The Scarecrows* (UTBG 320) both of which are deeply scary and unsettling.

Or read **The Dark Tower** sequence by Stephen King, starting with *The Gunslinger*.

If you'd like some more sophisticated horror try H.P. Lovecraft. Read any of his frankly bizarre tales and enjoy!

# STORM  Suzanne Fisher Staples

14+

This is a beautifully written and deeply moving account of two teenagers – a black girl, Tunes, and a white boy, Buck. Tunes' father works for Buck's family's and they have grown up together. But friendship and loyalty are tested when Tunes becomes the suspect in a local murder.

You never doubt for one minute that Tunes has been falsely accused and that the threatened injustice is a result of racism. And any momentary doubts that Buck has are quickly brushed aside. But as the story progresses, with Tunes' young life in the balance, the teenagers' desperate struggle against the blinkered attitudes of local white adults is painful to follow – all the way to its sad and courageously truthful end.

**Neil Arksey**

**Next?**

Something else by the same author? Try *Shiva's Fire*, about a girl in India born with strange abilities and a gift for dance.

Rosa Guy's *The Friends* is about prejudice of all sorts.

For another powerful story of racism, read the classic *To Kill a Mockingbird* (UTBG 375).

Or try Mary Ann Rodman's *Yankee Girl*, about a white girl moving to the Deep South in 1964.

## SCHOOLS' COMPETITION WINNER

=3rd

# STORMBREAKER
## Anthony Horowitz

Have you ever been bored at school and wished you were somewhere else, running from a dozen armed guards who were shooting at you? Alex Rider has. And when his uncle dies in a 'car accident', he investigates and really is thrown into the world of spies and espionage. No sooner does he find out the truth about his uncle's mysterious death, MI6 get hold of him. He is sent to an SAS training camp where he learns the most important rule: survival is everything. Then he is whisked away on his first mission armed only with state-of-the-art technology and a fake identity.

*Stormbreaker* really played with my emotions, which jumped from grief to curiosity, concern to suspense and excitement, and finally to relief; this book is just so hard to put down – and once you've put it down you have to pick it up again! I would recommend this book to everyone I know. Children and adults alike will enjoy it.

**Liam Hallatt (aged 15)**
**Myrtle Springs School**

# STRAIT IS THE GATE André Gide

I read this book in my late teens and just picking it off the shelf again gave me a jolt of almost physical pain. The story concerns Jerome's fierce love for his cousin Alissa, a lofty meeting of souls where Alissa's devotion to 'something higher than herself' allows God, in Jerome's view, to tear off his lover's wings. But in the battle between holy virtue and personal happiness, Jerome himself is, in fact, not without blame. With a similarly sacrificial devotion he allows himself to believe that 'any path, provided it climbed upwards' will lead to his dearest one. And so in just over 128 stark pages the doomed lovers ascend inexorably to a climax that is as bleak as it is compelling.

**Nicky Singer**

## Next?

If you're now yearning for a rather more instinctual sexual awakening, try D.H. Lawrence's *The Virgin and the Gipsy*.

Or for other French views of love and passion, Gustave Flaubert's *Madame Bovary*, or Françoise Sagan's *Bonjour Tristesse* (UTBG 48).

Gide's not an easy writer, but he makes you think. Try *The Immoralist*, about the nature of personal responsibility and the purpose of life.

# THE STRANGE AFFAIR OF ADELAIDE HARRIS Leon Garfield

## Next?

If you liked this, just find more Garfield – anything by Garfield – whose career was a firework display of brilliant storytelling. Look out for *Smith*, *John Diamond* or *Devil-in-the-Fog*.

For more funny historical fiction, try Mark Twain's *A Connecticut Yankee at King Arthur's Court*; or to find out what happened to unwanted babies in another time, *Coram Boy* (UTBG 84).

Joan Aiken wrote great historical adventure – read her *Midnight Is a Place*.

This is one of the funniest school stories ever written. We're in the past – the 18th century. Bostock and Harris, two schoolboy friends, commit a dreadful deed: having been taught the history of ancient Sparta, they decide that they too would like to expose a baby to be either eaten, or else rescued by a wild animal. They start a huge hue and cry among the masters and boys of the school, and the whole thing attracts the attention of a sinister detective, a Mr Raven, whose mind is not black enough to plumb the depths of Bostock and Harris.

This book has an amazing ending – the cheekiest and most appalling you will ever meet.

**Jill Paton Walsh**

# STRANGE BOY  Paul Magrs

14+

### Next?

*Brothers* (UTBG 59) also treats the subject of a boy discovering his true sexuality with delicacy and understanding.

*The Wrong Boy* (UTBG 424) is another funny and recognisable book about troubled adolescence.

Oh, and don't miss Paul Magrs' *Hands Up!*, which is laugh-out-loud funny.

Or *Toast* by Nigel Slater, the true story of the famous chef's childhood.

Growing up is never easy, but for ten-year-old David it's more difficult than for most. His parents' marriage breaks up and he has a bunch of awkward relations to deal with. But luckily David has superpowers – or so he thinks. He also finds he's attracted to John, the older boy down the road.

*Strange Boy* is a delightfully tender, funny and honest account of a childhood spent in the north east of England in the 1970s – and immensely readable. All the characters are sympathetically drawn and you may discover that, as original a creation as David is, you find lots in him to identify with – especially if you've ever felt slightly on the outside of things.

**Sherry Ashworth**

# STRANGE MEETING  Susan Hill

14+

It's 1916, in the midst of World War I (which will be over by Christmas, so they're told). After three months' active service, John Hilliard returns to his family, wounded. Back at the frontline he finds that his battalion has altered drastically – fatally. More changes occur, of which the most significant is meeting David Barton. Barton seems able to articulate a wealth of feeling that Hilliard never knew possible. He writes endless letters back home, describes heartfelt emotions about the brutality of war, and becomes close to Hilliard. Yet Hilliard still feels he does not understand him. Their bond intensifies as death looms ever closer. Compelling and devastating.

**Jon Appleton**

### Next?

One of the most famous books about World War I is the brilliant *All Quiet on the Western Front* (UTBG 19) by Erich Maria Remarque.

Susan Hill wrote a clutch of short, brilliant novels and then stopped, in favour of other kinds of book. Seek out her early books, especially *I'm the King of the Castle* (UTBG 188) and the terrifying *The Woman in Black* (UTBG 420).

Or how about *How Many Miles to Babylon?* by Jennifer Johnston, another bleak book about World War I?

# STRANGERS ON A TRAIN  Patricia Highsmith

**Next?**

Almost everything Highsmith has written is worth reading, particularly *The Tremor Of Forgery* and *The Talented Mr Ripley* (UTBG 364).

How about another book that Hitchcock filmed? Try Robert Bloch's *Psycho*.

Another great crime novel is Dashiol Hammett's *The Glass Key*, with its TB-ridden, gambling, drinking hero.

Two men get talking on a train. Both want somebody murdered. Each needs a perfect alibi. So they agree to swap murders. Or at least one of them – an alcoholic called Bruno who turns out to be a psychopath – thinks they've agreed. So he carries out the murder. Complications arise…

Highsmith's a great suspense novelist, rather than a crime writer, and this novel was ideally suited to become a fine Hitchcock film with a script by Raymond Chandler. I can't easily explain why I'm so drawn to her work, which shows remarkable sympathy for sociopaths, yet little for her own sex. Although American, she was only greatly appreciated in Europe. Her work is dark, laconic, unsettling and almost always gripping.

**David Belbin**

# STRIPES OF THE SIDESTEP WOLF
## Sonya Hartnett

This is a novel to read slowly, taking in the detail of the Australian landscape and wildlife, lingering over Hartnett's striking and original imagery and letting the story work its way quietly into your mind. The story moves between three main characters: 23-year-old Satchel O'Rye, Chelsea Piper, sister of his best friend Leroy, and the wolf of the title. All three are outsiders, all are struggling to survive in a place under threat: a little town which has been bypassed by the new highway, causing businesses to fail and families to move away. Satchel's difficult, complex relationship with his family (and his dog Moke) is very well described. Satchel and Chelsea's developing connection with the 'wolf' becomes the clue to their own survival, and ultimately a symbol of hope.
**Julia Green**

**Next?**

Try *Thursday's Child* (UTBG 373) by the same author and see what an original and challenging writer she is.

She also wrote *Surrender*, a book about friendship, the truth of memory and a dog.

Or try *The Lastling* (UTBG 215), about a social club that eats rare species and a meeting with the yeti.

# HORROR AND GHOST STORIES –
## spooks, crooks and mystery books
### by Hugh Scott

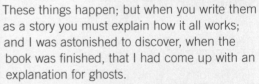

Listen. Weird things happen. I was sitting alone and a pen rose up off the arm of an armchair, then it dropped to the floor. When I was in primary school my best friend passed me on the stairs, and when I got to the playground, he was walking along the pavement.

Other strange events have stirred my imagination; but the main fascination for me is this: if such things can happen, then there is more to life than being born, doing things, and then dying. So I write spooky stories. I love to be involved in puzzles that gradually reveal solutions.

When I wrote *The Place Between*, I was creating a ghost story where somebody walked through walls, and somebody else disappeared before the eyes of startled witnesses.

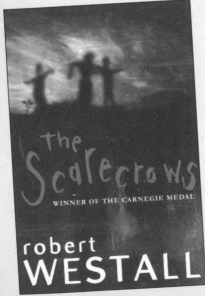

These things happen; but when you write them as a story you must explain how it all works; and I was astonished to discover, when the book was finished, that I had come up with an explanation for ghosts.

And this is what writing (and reading) are about: *discovery*! Finding out what is possible, and occasionally revealing an answer to a great mystery. Aren't we all fascinated by mystery? Isn't every child and adult at least slightly curious about the Loch Ness monster? And flying saucers?

We are always asking questions, and sometimes we find answers. Then we dig into the next mystery, swiftly and keenly, because we love the unknown. If there is no mystery in our lives, we make one by writing or reading the next book, and send the hairs on the back of our necks rising in terror.

Let me tell you this: if you love weird stories, go to your local charity shop and look for volumes of ghost stories. Most of these stories will be old fashioned, like 'The Upper Berth' by F. Marion Crawford, where the storyteller books his passage to sail to America, and finds that his companion in the upper berth is a drowned man, and he himself will be next to go overboard – unless he can find a way of escaping!

Or find perhaps 'The Whistling Room', which is a scream-making tale of a room with a past – and also a horrifying present. My heart almost stopped beating when I was reading this amazing story. It was written by William Hope Hodgson. Some of the scariest stories of ghosts and the macabre were written a while ago – try E.F. Benson's 'The Tale of an Empty House'; the *Ghost Stories* of M.R. James (UTBG 144); Edgar Allan Poe's *The Fall of the House of Usher*, his *Tales of Mystery and Imagination* (UTBG 365); or Algernon Blackwood's *Ancient Sorceries and Other Weird Tales*. H.P. Lovecraft wrote short stories and novellas which take you into other dimensions, leaving you gasping with relief when you remember you are merely reading.

**Books to stop you sleeping at night:**

*Interview with the Vampire* by Anne Rice

*Lord Loss* by Darren Shan

*The Watch House* by Robert Westall

*The Scarecrows* by Robert Westall

*The Rats* by James Herbert

*Alchemy* by Margaret Mahy

*Frankenstein* by Mary Shelley

# SUGAR RUSH Julie Burchill

14+

## Next?

Try Julie's *On Beckham* or read her *Guardian* columns and find out why people either absolutely love her or don't.

*Weetzie Bat* (UTBG 405), part of the **Dangerous Angels** series, is about a group of friends / lovers living in LA.

You'll find a more intense look at falling for another girl in *Oranges are not the Only Fruit* (UTBG 275).

Or for more streetwise girls trying to deal with life, read Catherine Johnson's *Face Value* set in the cut-throat world of modelling.

*Sugar Rush* does exactly what it says on the cover. It's a high-speed, toxic slice of teen life, an emotional melting pot, a story that's so evocative you can smell the perfume, taste the vodka, hear the soundtrack. This is Julie Burchill's first teen novel, although she's been writing (mostly journalism) since punk rock upset the music-biz apple cart back in the 1970s. Her debut follows Kim who, having had to move schools, meets, falls for and has a full-on relationship with Maria, a.k.a. Sugar. The book, which has no pretensions to be anything but as entertaining as possible, is set in Brighton and holds a very honest mirror up to what it's like to be young and in lust.

**Graham Marks**

# A SUMMER BIRD-CAGE Margaret Drabble

 16+

Oxford graduates Sarah and Louise are sisters with a lot in common, but they have never been close. The stunningly beautiful, aloof Louise has just married Stephen, a pretentious but rich novelist, and is living an apparently charmed life in Kensington. Sarah, who has always felt inferior to her glamorous sister, shares a chaotic flat with a friend and has two main preoccupations: what to do with the rest of her life; and why her sister married the odious Stephen in the first place. Gradually Sarah comes to see the truth behind the sophisticated façade of Louise's marriage and the sisters reach an understanding. Drabble's first novel is a fascinating, witty, fast-paced study of high-powered sibling rivalry.

**Francesca Lewis**

## Next?

Other books set at least partly in Oxford are *Brideshead Revisited* (UTBG 56) by Evelyn Waugh and *Daughters of Jerusalem* (UTBG 95) by Charlotte Mendelson.

For more life in London beyond university, try *Saving Agnes* by Rachel Cusk.

*A Summer Bird-Cage* was Drabble's first novel; try either of her next two: *The Garrick Year*, the story of a woman married to an actor, or *The Millstone*, the story of a woman coming to London in the 1960s.

# THE SUMMERHOUSE Alison Prince

Two astounding stories for the price of one – the first about a girl's friendship with a local writer Stan, stuck for ideas. Together with her friends, she and Stan create the second story about a futuristic GM research site that controls the dreams of its employees and creates dogs with dragons' breath… As the girl learns the writer's craft from Stan, so he absorbs the friends' preoccupations – fear of death, foster families and domestic violence.

As their fictional story unfolds, larger preoccupations of genetic modification, second sight and the afterlife are skilfully explored. Richly textured and breathtakingly clever, this is, quite simply, unique.

**Eileen Armstrong**

> **Next?**
>
> Other books by Alison Prince include *Three Blind Eyes*, an exciting murder mystery set in Dickensian London; and *Oranges and Murder*, a historical thriller about the murder of a barrow boy's father set in the early 19th century.
>
> Another aspiring author is the lively Lily Blennerhassett in Elizabeth Cody Kimmel's *Lily B On The Brink Of Cool*.
>
> A troubled girl, who conquers her reading and writing problems to make a very special book to bring her estranged mum home again, is the premise behind Paul May's *Green Fingers*.

# THE SUPERNATURALIST Eoin Colfer

> **Next?**
>
> If you enjoyed this book you will love *The Wish List* and the **Artemis Fowl** series (UTBG 29) by the same author.
>
> For something a little darker – Garth Nix's *Sabriel* (UTBG 316) and its sequels.
>
> If you liked the James-Bond style adventure, try *SilverFin* (UTBG 340) by Charlie Higson, about the young James and his first journey into the world of the spy.

*The Supernaturalist* is an exciting and intriguing book about Cosmo Hill, who lives in Satellite City, the city of the future. But Cosmo is an orphan, stuck in an orphanage where orphans are used to test new products. Statistics say he only has about a year to live – unless he escapes. He succeeds but nearly dies in the process, and is found by the Supernaturalists, a group of youngsters who save people by shooting at the invisible parasites that come to the scene of accidents and suck life from the injured. When the Supernaturalists realise that Cosmo can see the parasites too, they allow him to join their group. I loved this book and its unusual characters and was gripped while reading it.

**Adam Cohen (aged 13)**

# A TALE OF TWO CITIES Charles Dickens

I'd read a few Dickens books, and enjoyed them, but hadn't been blown away. Then I read this and my opinion of him changed completely. This is a masterful, suspenseful novel with more twists than any modern thriller. Set at the time of the French Revolution, the two cities are Paris and London, and the story centres on a few unfortunate individuals who get caught up in the madness of the time. Both epic and personal, this is a book that will take your breath away. Plus, it has maybe the strongest opening and closing lines in all literature! Brooding and incisive, it also boasts some wickedly sly scenes – the revelation of why one character always has dirt under his nails had me howling out loud with laughter! Even if you think you don't like Dickens, read this book!

**Darren Shan**

> ## Next?
>
> More Dickens? Try the very different *Nicholas Nickleby*.
>
> *Fleshmarket* (UTBG 131) by Nicola Morgan brings a cruel, gory and brutal 19th-century Edinburgh to life.
>
> Or for another classic about the French Revolution, Baroness Orczy's *The Scarlet Pimpernel* (UTBG 321).

# THE TALENTED MR RIPLEY Patricia Highsmith

> ## Next?
>
> Patricia Highsmith wrote four sequels to *The Talented Mr Ripley*; they are all good, but the first two, *Ripley Under Ground* and *Ripley's Game*, are the best.
>
> A different Highsmith? Try *Strangers on a Train* (UTBG 359) about planning a perfect murder.
>
> For another story with an anti-hero, try the difficult but amazing *Crime and Punishment* (UTBG 86) by Fyodor Dostoyevsky.

In 1950s Italy a penniless young American named Tom Ripley charms his way into a group of rich, arty expatriates. Tom's envy of his host's carefree life and beautiful possessions propels him into murder, several changes of identity and a tense game of cat-and-mouse as he tries to evade the Italian police and his victim's family. Tom Ripley is a fascinating character: nervy, audacious, imaginative and almost completely amoral. But despite his tendency to bludgeon people to death with blunt instruments he never becomes a mere monster; this brilliant and unsettling book is written in such a way that you sympathise with Tom entirely in both his crimes and his panicky, improvised attempts to cover them up, and the short chapters and constant twists will keep you turning the pages right to the end.

**Philip Reeve**

# TALES OF MYSTERY AND IMAGINATION

## Edgar Allan Poe

My aunt Nancy had a spooky bookcase in a dark corner of the hall, and among the books there was this one.

Now, I loved language when I was a boy; I loved the way words fitted themselves together in my mouth, and I loved finding words I didn't recognise; and in that volume Poe fitted words together with such precision that I was delighted; and as for words I didn't know – well, the stories were stacked with them and made reading his tales not only a journey into mystery, terror and imagination, but into a revelation of new language. Edgar Allan Poe's stories are still published, even though he lived in the early 19th century, and they are still as terrifying! Stories like 'The Black Cat', 'The Gold Bug', 'Hop-Frog' and, oh, so many more. Treat yourself to a good scare. I dare you…

**Hugh Scott**

### Next?

Anything by Algernon Blackwood. Or M.R. James' *Ghost Stories* (UTBG 144).

How about scary stories in pictures? Start with the first volume of **The Sandman** series (UTBG 320) and see how far you dare go…

Or try something of Hugh's: *Why Weeps the Brogan?* (UTBG 412)

# TALES OF THE CITY Armistead Maupin

16+

### Next?

The series is best read in order. *Tales of the City, More Tales of the City, Further Tales of the City, Babycakes, Significant Others, Sure of You.*

Maupin's *Maybe the Moon* and *The Night Listener* are good, too.

Edmund White's trilogy of fictionalised memoirs about growing up gay will be too explicit for some and loved by others; it starts with *A Boy's Own Story*.

I devoured Armistead Maupin's *Tales of the City* on a three-hour bus journey across Crete, then had to wait until I got home before I could read the next in the series. These novels, originally written as a newspaper serial, are compulsive reading: a soap opera about a San Francisco full of promise (and secrets) for gay and straight characters alike. They're insightful and enormous fun, with lots of mysterious twists and aspects that will challenge some readers' prejudices.

The mood gets darker and the writing even better as the series progresses. Maupin only comes a cropper when he sets one novel in the UK – *Babycakes*. (Think of *Friends* set in London and you'll know what I mean.)

**David Belbin**

# TALES OF THE UNEXPECTED Roald Dahl

14+

As well as his famous children's books, Roald Dahl wrote a series of brilliant short stories for adults, many grotesque and with a twist in the tale.

Billy Weaver, 17 years old, stays in a B&B run by a sweet old lady. Her hobby, it turns out, is taxidermy. Who knows Billy is there? His tea tastes a bit funny…

After the death of a crabbed old professor, his brain is kept alive in a laboratory basin. It has one floating eye. His wife, whose life he has made a misery, wishes to take him home…

Mary Maloney, six months pregnant, kills her husband with a frozen leg of lamb then pops it in the oven. Detectives searching for the murder weapon eat it with relish…

Would you risk a bet with a smart, old gentleman? If you win you get his gorgeous Cadillac; if you lose he gets to chop off one of your fingers…

Great fun.

**Alan Temperley**

### Next?

Roald Dahl's children's stories can be enjoyed by anyone. Read *The BFG*, *The Witches* and *Danny, the Champion of the World*.

H.H. Munro (UTBG 337) and O. Henry are two other fine writers of short stories. I am also a fan of the **Rumpole** stories by John Mortimer.

Or if you fancy something more macabre, try Allan Poe's *Tales of Mystery and Imagination* (UTBG 365).

## SCHOOLS' COMPETITION WINNER

=3rd

# TALK OF THE TOWN Ardal O'Hanlon

I was sceptical when I first read *Talk of the Town*, as I believed the concept of a story set in rural Ireland to be quite boring. However Ardal O'Hanlon's television profile prompted me to read it. O'Hanlon's ways of deceiving the reader into believing the book to be a light-hearted one are quite unique. The reader could be forgiven for assuming the book is full of humour and loveable rogue stories told with the innocence of a young mind. What they discover as they delve into the life of this young man is a world of rural claustrophobia and a downward spiral of paranoia, depression and restlessness. *Talk of the Town* also supplies a selection of classic punchlines and laugh-out-loud one-liners to provide the comic relief.

The book is all in all a fantastic read for maturer readers – I beg you to try it, as I feel I am on a one-woman crusade to try and spread the word of its sheer brilliance!

**Siobhan Tully (aged 16)**
**Convent of Jesus and Mary Language College**

# TAMAR  Mal Peet

1944: two young Dutchmen code-named Tamar and Dart, trained in England by the Special Operations Executive, are parachuted into the Occupied Netherlands to organise local resistance groups who are by no means united in their struggle against the invaders. The liberation of Europe is imminent but conditions are desperate, bringing out the worst as well as the best in people.

50 years later, the suicide of Tamar sends his granddaughter in pursuit of her inheritance – not the money he has left her, but a secret of identity enclosed in the events of that last terrible winter of the war. This is not a testosterone-fuelled actioner but a quiet, remorseless account of civilian heroism, of men and women living in continuous fear, driven to unthinkable acts.

**Jan Mark**

## Next?

*Between Silk and Cyanide* by Leo Marks (who appears in *Tamar* very briefly), the true story of World War II secret agents and their wireless codes.

Set in the same period, *Fair Stood the Wind for France* by H.E. Bates tells of a wounded RAF bomber pilot escaping, through occupied France.

*Keeper* (UTBG 205) by Mal Peet is completely different but no less absorbing.

# TAYLOR FIVE: THE STORY OF A CLONE GIRL  Ann Halam

12+

Is a clone a whole human being or just a photocopy of one? Taylor asks herself this question as she grows up at a remote jungle refuge for orang-utans. From an early age she is aware that she was cloned so that her body tissues could be used to develop a cure for a terrible disease. Taylor finds this hard to take and refuses to meet her gene mother, an extraordinary scientist. However, Taylor's world is about to collapse as terrorists invade the refuge and she escapes into the jungle with Uncle, an intelligent orang-utan. This is the start of a treacherous journey, and Taylor experiences fear and loss on the way to discovering her true self. Pain and violence are powerfully described in this action-packed sci-fi novel.

**Noga Applebaum**

## Next?

Try Ann Halam's *Siberian*. Or one of her books written under her real name, Gwyneth Jones.

Many books discuss the ethical dilemma presented by human cloning. Try *House of the Scorpion* (UTBG 178), *Unique* (UTBG 390) or *Sharp North* (UTBG 333).

*How I Live Now* (UTBG 179) is about a girl living in a country under violent occupation.

# TENDER IS THE NIGHT F. Scott Fitzgerald

16+

This had a huge impact on me as a teenager because it is about the fine line we all walk between sanity and madness. I spent months marvelling that the only thing that stopped me driving my car into a brick wall or a knife into the heart of my boyfriend was the fact that I am sane. Dr Dick Diver's affair with Nicole Warren echoes Zelda Fitzgerald's relationship with her psychiatrist and is a compelling examination of moral breakdown, and of how society shuns those it considers weak, whether mentally or morally. And of course it's so beautifully written that it leaves a glimmer in your heart like a diamond necklace…

**Raffaella Barker**

### Next?

Another Fitzgerald? Try *The Beautiful and the Damned* about a wild, rich couple whose lives fall apart when they run out of money.

Another great novel about mental instability is Sylvia Plath's *The Bell Jar* (UTBG 37).

The landmark work on psychoanalysis is Freud's *The Interpretation of Dreams*; but there's also a condensed, more manageable version, the 25-page 'On Dreams', which is fascinating. (You can find it in Peter Gay's *The Freud Reader*.)

# TERRA INCOGNITA

14+

## Sara Wheeler

### Next?

More classic travel writing? Robyn Davidson's *Tracks* (about crossing Australia on a camel), Bruce Chatwin's *Songlines* and Patrick Leigh Fermor's *A Time of Gifts*, about walking across Europe in the 1930s.

The best account of the Scott expedition, by a man who was on it, is *The Worst Journey in the World* (UTBG 422).

This travel book has everything: eye-opening descriptions (Antarctica – the Terra Incognita of the title – is 'intact, complete and larger than my imagination could grasp'); very funny characters, including José who married his Harley Davidson and the penguin experts who can tell individual penguins apart; and there's even a recipe for Antarctic bread-and-butter pudding. The author spent months with polar scientists who are as much a part of her story as are the famous explorers whose lives she recounts. Incidents range from the funny – the seal that unexpectedly pops up through the ice-hole latrine – to the sublime – playing Beethoven's *Fifth* in the virgin landscape.

A warning: you might not think you're interested in Antarctica now, but after this book you will be.

**Jane Darcy**

# TESS OF THE D'URBERVILLES Thomas Hardy  *14+

**Next?**

If you liked this novel by Hardy, then there are many more to choose from – *Under the Greenwood Tree* and *Far From the Madding Crowd* (UTBG 124) are many people's favourites.

Another dark love story set against the backdrop of a wild landscape: Emily Brontë's *Wuthering Heights* (UTBG 424).

*A Gathering Light* (UTBG 142) is also about a girl (in the past) who gets involved in a murder…

Maybe the best-known of Hardy's novels set in his semi-fictional county of Wessex, *Tess of the D'Urbervilles* is both beautiful and sad. The story draws the reader quickly into the life of Tess Durbeyfield, an unassuming servant girl who comes to discover that her true heritage lies with the powerful D'Urberville family. But this is no joyous rags-to-riches story. Tess is a tragic figure, manipulated and misled, and makes a striking heroine for this classic novel of suffering.

The greatest strength of the book is the poetry of Hardy's writing, with which he creates wonderfully dark and mysterious atmospheres. Tess was Hardy's favourite heroine and this is a good place to start reading his work. But be warned! There are no happy endings.

**Marcus Sedgwick**

# THERE'S A BOY IN THE GIRLS' BATHROOM Louis Sachar  12+

No one likes Bradley Chalkers, so when new fifth-grader Jeff offers to sit next to him, you hope this will be the start of a friendship. But life isn't that simple with Bradley. His opening words to Jeff are 'Give me a dollar or I'll spit at you'.

Bradley is so out of control he's sent to the school guidance counsellor, Carla. To his surprise she doesn't criticise him, even when he's discovered in the girls' bathroom. Bradley's big moment comes when one of the girls invites him to her birthday party – his first invitation since that time he sat on someone's birthday cake…

This is a very funny book which might help you to understand why some people behave as they do…

**Jane Darcy**

**Next?**

Other funny and thoughtful books about troublesome boys include Louis Sachar's *Holes* (UTBG 173) and Jerry Spinelli's *The Mighty Crashman*.

A sadder (and harder) book is Cynthia Voigt's *A Solitary Blue*, about a boy torn between his parents. It's one of the **Tillerman** series.

# THÉRÈSE RAQUIN Émile Zola

16+

**Next?**

If you like stories of murder, love and obsession why not try *The Postman Always Rings Twice* by James M. Cain?

The story of Shakespeare's *Macbeth* has its similarities, too.

Guy de Maupassant is another writer of exceptional skill; read *Boule de Suif* or any collection of his short stories.

Passion, murder, ghosts and guilt – what more can a teenage girl ask for in a novel?

Thérèse lives with her sickly husband Camille and his adoring mother. Then Laurent comes into her life, and Thérèse throws herself into adultery, and ultimately the murder of her husband, with complete abandon.

But even Camille's death can't bring them happiness. His drowned ghost haunts them, standing in the shadows of their room night after night, turning their life into a constant nightmare, until in the end their passion turns to hatred.

This is a claustrophobic story steeped in atmosphere. I loved it when I was 15, and I love it now.

**Catherine MacPhail**

# THESE OLD SHADES Georgette Heyer

12+

Justin, the Duke of Avon, is the epitome of 18th-century elegance. But he's also a very dangerous man. When he comes across Leon, the illegitimate teenage son of his greatest enemy, living a rough life in Paris, he takes the boy on as his page, hoping to devise a plan with which to humiliate the boy's father. Soon, however, he discovers that Leon is really a Leonie, and that she may not be illegitimate after all.

Beneath his suave and chilly exterior Justin is really a street fighter, just like Leonie. But unlike Leonie, who's hot-tempered, he believes that revenge is a dish best enjoyed cold. This historical romance matches up two intense and enormously colourful characters in a totally satisfying way.

**Cathy Jinks**

**Next?**

*Devil's Cub* is the sequel to *These Old Shades*, but anything by Georgette Heyer is worth a read, especially *Frederica* and *Arabella* (UTBG 27), which are both Regency romances.

Another girl who dresses as a boy in order to get what she wants is Alanna in the **Song of the Lioness** quartet (UTBG 15).

Meg Cabot also writes Regency romances; try *Victoria and the Rogue*. It's a light-hearted romp that'll make you smile.

# THINGS FALL APART Chinua Achebe

**Next?**

*The Song of Solomon* by Toni Morrison begins with an African folk tale and transforms it into a quest for identity.

For an anti-colonial view, read the masterpiece, **Heart of Darkness** (UTBG 164).

More Achebe? Try **The Arrow of God**, about an Ibo village priest in conflict with the British in 1920s Nigeria.

'Okonkwo was well-known throughout the nine villages and even beyond.' Thus begins *Things Fall Apart*. Okonkwo is a member of the Ibo tribe in an area of Africa now known as Biafra. The story of Okonkwo is in many ways the story of black Africa and its confrontation with white colonialism and Christianity.

When the story opens, Okonkwo has been a champion wrestler for over 20 years. He is famous. He is feared. He is respected by all. His is the world of the rainforest: spirits and drums and unflinching tradition. Into this world comes the white man with his religion and guns and civilised ways. Okonkwo has met the match of his life.

**Jerry Spinelli**

# THE THIRTY-NINE STEPS
## John Buchan

This is a classic thriller – a story of pursuit and escape. The hero, Richard Hannay, bored with his return to life in Britain, finds himself unexpectedly involved in an adventure in which he is hunted not only by the police for a murder he did not commit, but also by a rather more sinister group bent on destroying Britain, and anxious (since he has clues to their identity) to eliminate him. He evades his pursuers with a variety of innovative disguises and hair's-breadth escapes, enriching his story with an account of his moods and responses, and with descriptions of the varying landscapes (especially that of Scotland) which become themselves part of the adventure. Despite certain racist elements (it was written a long time ago), this is a great story told at breakneck pace.

**Margaret Mahy**

**Next?**

There are more Richard Hannay adventures, the most famous of which is **Greenmantle**.

Another classic story that still grips is **Rogue Male** by Geoffrey Household, about one man's plot to assassinate Hitler.

Another adventure that starts with a mistaken identity is **The Prisoner of Zenda** (UTBG 299).

**Tamar** (UTBG 367) is about spies and espionage in World War II and it is a thrilling read.

# THIS BOY'S LIFE  Tobias Wolff

14+

This story begins with ten-year-old Toby and his mother driving from Florida to Utah 'to get away from a man my mother was afraid of and to get rich on uranium'. In Utah it'll all be different – and to prove it Toby changes his name. From now on, we are to call him Jack. He's borrowing the name from Jack London.

Of course, Utah isn't what Jack expected. There's no fortune to be made, and his mother just ends up with another man Jack can't stand, the violent car mechanic Dwight. We watch Jack face those same challenges that we all have to deal with – how to find out who we are, to understand other people, to find our way in the world. In short, we watch him grow up.

Wolff's writing is simple and effective – and it's a true story, too. Ten-year-old Toby grew up to be a very fine writer.

**Daniel Hahn**

> ### Next?
>
> There's a sequel to this – *In Pharaoh's Army* – but I think you should go on to read Wolff's fiction instead. His short stories are very good; his novel, *The Old School*, is stunning.
>
> Jack's brother Geoffrey has also written a memoir – *The Duke of Deception*; read it to find out about the other half of the family…
>
> *The Sea-Wolf* by Jack London is about a literate, civilised man up against a brutal ship's captain.

---

# THREE MEN IN A BOAT  Jerome K. Jerome

14+

> ### Next?
>
> Other hilarious travel books include Pete McCarthy's *McCarthy's Bar* and Bill Bryson's *Neither Here Nor There*.
>
> And don't miss another 19th-century classic, *Diary of a Nobody* (UTBG 102).
>
> Or one of the great American humourists – James Thurber. Anything he wrote, anything at all.

This is a comic classic. Three Victorian young men: the unnamed narrator, George and Harris, together with Montmorency the dog, set off on a leisurely boat trip up the Thames. They've dreamed of picnics on riverbanks, evenings beneath the stars and some comfortable nights at country inns. The reality is somewhat different, as the narrator finds when he accidentally takes an early-morning plunge in the river, or when Harris claims he's been attacked by 32 swans.

Along the way are memories of other mishaps, including the time when Harris said he knew how to get round the maze at Hampton Court (he didn't) and when he tried to sing a funny song without knowing the words. Priceless.

**Jane Darcy**

# THURSDAY'S CHILD  Sonya Hartnett

From the very first sentence, this remarkable book grabs you by the throat: 'Now I would like to tell you about my brother, Tin…'

The narrator is Harper Flute telling of her childhood in rural Australia between the two World Wars when her father, a scarred survivor of World War I, brings his family to live on an almost unsustainable parcel of land during the Great Depression. Tin, Harper's young brother, becomes obsessed with tunnelling beneath the earth, and he is the pivot on which the story turns… *born on a Thursday and so fated to his wanderings…*

This book has an immensely powerful realisation of place, compelling characters, soul-tearing moments, and atmosphere that seeps into your life.

**Theresa Breslin**

> **Next?**
>
> Read about a boy who uses fire as a way of dealing with the pressures in his life in Chris Wooding's *Kerosene*.
>
> *Of Mice and Men* (UTBG 268) by John Steinbeck is a novel of the American Depression.
>
> For a tale of staying alive in the Australian outback, try James Vance Marshall's *Walkabout* (UTBG 396).

---

# TIME BOMB  Nigel Hinton

Four friends experience one final summer of freedom before beginning secondary school. But this is post-war Britain and the bombsite where they play hides a terrible danger.

When Eddie is betrayed by one adult after another, he swears his friends to secrecy and takes his revenge.

You'll find yourself thinking about this story long after you've put the book down. Not only does Nigel Hinton manage to conjure up the ghost of the long, hot summer of August 1949, but he lets you into the lives of Andy and his friends to such an extent that the epilogue comes almost as a body blow.

Unforgettable!

**Laura Hutchings**

> **Next?**
>
> Robert Westall's *The Machine-Gunners* (UTBG 229) is also about a group of friends in the 1940s who hide a wartime secret. But unlike in *Time Bomb,* here Britain is still at war and their secret can talk!
>
> Other highly recommended Robert Westall titles (all of them set in World War II) include *Blitz* (short stories), *Kingdom by the Sea* (UTBG 208) and *Blitzcat*.
>
> Why not try another Nigel Hinton? He is probably best known for *Buddy* but try the excellent *Collision Course*, about a boy who accidentally kills an old lady when he's out joyriding.

# TIN GRIN  Catherine Robinson

**14+**

After the misery of a big city and a violent father, Mattie, her sister and her mum are quite happy living in the country on their own. But then Mum gets herself a new husband, one who comes complete with a son, Geoffrey, an uber-nerd with bad dress sense, spots and braces. Mattie hates him on sight.

Add to the mix the god-like Sam Barker, sex, having to share a room with her messy sister, everyone else pretending that life is great, and Mattie's life becomes a nightmare. Or does it? How often do you read stories centred on people you don't like? Not often. And anyway, you like Mattie, you want her to be happy, to get the boy and banish Tin Grin for ever.

Then, slowly, you start to see the world from other people's point of view...

**Leonie Flynn**

### Next?

In *Phosphorescence* (UTBG 286), Lola moves from the country into the city. Not only is she a country bumpkin but she's never kissed a boy. Will she survive – especially when the school plans a camping trip back to her old village?

More Catherine Robinson? Try *Celia*, about a girl trying to find her real mother, or *Mr Perfect*, about a girl pursued by an older man.

Or read our feature about love 'n' relationship books, on pp. 168–169.

# TO BE A NINJA  Benedict Jacka

**12+**

### Next?

This is Benedict's first, but there is a sequel on its way. Look out for it soon!

Another boy learning Japanese martial arts is the hero of Lian Hearn's *Across the Nightingale Floor* (UTBG 12).

Or try *So Below* by Matt Whyman in which Yoshi takes refuge in the world that exists below London's streets.

Ordinary school can be bad enough, but Ninja school is worse. After all, with one wrong move you could kill someone, so discipline is strict and the training tough. Allandra and Ignis are on the run from their violent, drug-baron father – who still has their brother Michael, who was caught when the other two escaped.

At the secret training camp, Allandra fits in quickly, but Ignis hates the rules – and the bullies. But they learn, grow stronger, become part of a group, making the friends they never had in their old life. But then Allandra is kidnapped, and it's up to Ignis and their friends to save her – and Michael.

Packed with details of ninjitsu training, and all the complications of making friends and dealing with enemies, this manages to be both a thriller and a thought-provoking look at violence.

**Leonie Flynn**

# TO KILL A MOCKINGBIRD
## Harper Lee

14+

Scout was in grammar school when it happened – the thing that rocked her family and divided her sleepy Southern town. She is a patient storyteller, telling of the odd neighbours down the block with their dark history; her life in a single-parent household; the angst of a southern girl who doesn't have it in her to be a lady. And then there's her father, Atticus. If you're looking for father figures, like I was as a teenager, he's your man. This book changed my life and continues to challenge me as a writer and a reader. It introduced me to characters of honour who stood for their ideals despite raging injustice. This is a stunning story about childhood colliding with ignorance and prejudice, and the grace people need to build a better world.
**Joan Bauer**

This is one of those astonishing books that stay with you for ever. Set in the Deep South of America during the Great Depression of the 1930s, it tells the story of Scout and Jem Finch and their father, Atticus, a lawyer who defends a black man wrongly accused of raping a white girl.

On one level, it's a seemingly simple tale about the fears and prejudices of a small-town community, and how one man stands up for what he thinks is right; but within that simplicity there's so much more. It's a story about innocence and growing up, about conscience and courage, about seeing the world for what it is.

Wonderfully told by nine-year-old Scout, *To Kill a Mockingbird* has everything you could ever want in a book: a gripping story, strong emotions, engaging characters and – best of all – that very special feeling of being alive.
**Kevin Brooks**

### Next?

*A Separate Peace* by John Knowles brilliantly brings to life the world of a wartime boarding school.

John Steinbeck's *Of Mice and Men* (UTBG 268) is also set in the American South and is about difference and acceptance.

If you liked the style and subject matter of *To Kill a Mockingbird*, you should enjoy *Peace Like a River* (UTBG 284).

For another stunning book set in 1930s America, try *The Grapes of Wrath* by John Steinbeck.

You'll find a more recent look at false accusation and prejudice in Rosa Guy's *The Disappearance*.

TO KILL A MOCKING-BIRD

*Pulitzer Prize Winner*
*over 30,000,000 sold*

HARPER LEE

# THE TOLL BRIDGE Aidan Chambers

14+

## Next?

Try *Breaktime* (UTBG 55), *Dance on My Grave* (UTBG 91), *Now I Know*, or *Postcards from No Man's Land* (UTBG 292) – each title stands alone, yet is part of Chambers' **Dance** sequence.

Try *You Don't Know Me* (UTBG 425), about a boy and his violent stepfather.

Another boy, another bridge? Try the equally thought-provoking *Kissing the Rain* by Kevin Brooks (UTBG 209).

A very funny look at what it means possibly to be gay can be found in Paul Magrs' *Strange Boy* (UTBG 358).

Aidan Chambers is a wonderful writer – intelligent, provocative, profound. His novels exert a grip that may have you turning the pages too quickly, yet they're always worth rereading and re-rereading. *The Toll Bridge* is probably my favourite. 'Jan' (not his real name) is at a transitory period of his life, symbolised by his taking up residence in a toll-house by a river bridge. Seeking isolation, he finds his privacy invaded by the deeply disturbed Adam, by forthright Tess, and by Gill, the devoted girlfriend who loves him oppressively. There's an utterly compelling intensity to this novel of adolescents in search of purpose, identity and escape.

**Linda Newbery**

# TOMMY GLOVER'S SKETCH OF HEAVEN

16+

## Jane Bailey

Kitty returns as a student teacher to the Gloucestershire village where she was evacuated during World War II and fostered by a couple who, although not actively unkind, showed her little affection. Undaunted, Kitty found companionship elsewhere, forming a devoted bond with Tommy, a boy from the local orphanage. In those days Kitty knew little but learned fast and, sensing the strained relationship between her 'uncle and aunt', asked questions that no one else dared to utter. Her forthright curiosity cut through adult prudery and nasty-mindedness to uncover secrets both sad and dreadful – and almost everyone in that small community had something to hide, including Tommy. Kitty realised too late that she might have exposed one secret too many, that she and Tommy could have sabotaged their own chances of a happy ending.

**Jan Mark**

## Next?

For memories of a real Gloucestershire childhood, *Cider with Rosie* (UTBG 77).

*The Go-Between* (UTBG 150) is another story of an adult returning to visit the scene of traumatic childhood experiences.

Katherine Mansfield wrote short stories based on her childhood in New Zealand.

# TOUCHING THE VOID Joe Simpson

An astounding adventure story, with the extra-special ingredient of being true. Author Joe Simpson and fellow mountaineer Simon Yates tackle one of the highest unclimbed peaks in the Peruvian Andes. They get to the top, but on the way down Joe falls and breaks his leg. Simon, in an astonishing feat of bravery, somehow manages to lower him down, until Joe topples over an edge and is left hanging in space. Simon, tied to him, is being slowly pulled off the mountain and is eventually forced to break the last rule of mountaineering – he cuts the rope. Convinced Joe's dead, Simon descends, but meanwhile Joe, showing quite incredible courage and determination, tries to crawl to safety.

This is a riveting and inspiring read, even if you've never climbed higher than to the top of a stepladder.

**Malachy Doyle**

> **Next?**
>
> More mountaineering? Try *Facing Up* by Bear Grylls, the youngest Briton at the time to have climbed Everest.
>
> Or more by Joe Simpson – try *Dark Shadows Falling*, which reflects on recent mountaineering tragedies.
>
> Or for more snow (but with fewer peaks), Sara Wheeler's *Terra Incognita* (UTBG 368) about Antarctica and the men and women who have had to understand its wilderness.

# TOURIST SEASON Carl Hiaasen

> **Next?**
>
> *Native Tongue* by Carl Hiaasen – more low-life hi-jinks from the Sunshine State. He also writes for younger readers; try *Flush*.
>
> *Me Talk Pretty One Day* by David Sedaris – everyday confessions of an ordinary American who happens to be hugely funny.
>
> Or try an Elmore Leonard – more Florida, more guns. Start with *Rum Punch*.

A critic once wrote that Carl Hiaasen's comedy thrillers are 'better than literature' and I agree wholeheartedly. I read *Tourist Season* after a weighty Russian classic about long winters and thin gruel. To find myself in the sweltering heat of Florida was refreshing, and the anarchy and savage exuberance packed into the story came as a revelation. A native son of the state itself, Hiaasen's novels rage against the destruction and corruption of his beloved environment. In this, his first novel, it's Florida's tourist industry that he picks apart with glee.

Just don't read it in company. You'll laugh and snort and hoot so much that everyone will want you to explain what's so funny.

**Matt Whyman**

# THE TOWER ROOM
Adèle Geras

14+

## Next?

Second in the sequence is *Pictures of the Night*.

Fairy tales make fabulous dark novels: try *Beauty* (UTBG 35) for suppressed passion and exquisite prose.

Or slightly darker than **Happy Ever After**, try *The Magic Toyshop* (UTBG 229).

Think you are too old for fairy tales? Not the kind Adèle Geras writes. In her magical **Happy Ever After** series, she brings well-loved stories such as 'Rapunzel', 'Sleeping Beauty' and 'Snow White' right up to date. Well, not quite – her stories are set in the early 1960s in a boarding-school world of common rooms, prep and tea with Headmistress. But don't let that put you off – the emotions experienced by her three main characters, Megan, Alice and Bella, are bang up-to-date as they fall in and out of love, fear for their lives or grapple with the process of growing up in a world that's becoming far too sheltered for their liking. *The Tower Room* is my favourite of the trilogy; the title refers to the bedroom shared by the three girls at school, a room that feels very safe and secluded until one day when Megan looks out of the window and her life changes forever. And the unexpected ending will leave you desperate to know what happens next…

**Rosie Rushton**

# A TOWN LIKE ALICE  Nevil Shute

14+

This story begins with a solicitor trying to trace a woman who is due to inherit a fortune. When he finds her, Jean Paget turns out to be a simple typist – but like all Shute's 'ordinary' people, Jean is not really ordinary at all. As a prisoner of the Japanese during the war, she saw and did some extraordinary things, and how she decides to spend her money is even more extraordinary.

This is a war story and a love story combined. It moves at a slow and gentle pace, but be patient. It is a brilliant yarn about a woman determined to use all her resources to heal and create, after a period in history that had seen so much hatred and destruction.

**Andrew Norriss**

## Next?

You'll probably enjoy other Nevil Shute books. *Trustee from the Toolroom* (UTBG 383) is one of my favourites; *On The Beach,* about life after a nuclear war, is another.

If you are interested in World War II in the Far East, read **Quartered Safe Out Here** by George Macdonald Fraser. Or for the true story of life in a Japanese POW camp, try *The Railway Man* by Eric Lomax.

# TRAINSPOTTING  Irvine Welsh

**Next?**

More dark Scottish writing? Alan Warner's **Morvern Callar** begins with a girl waking up next to her dead boyfriend (and a great deal of money).

Moving south, Jonathan Coe's **The Rotters' Club** is a bittersweet story of the adolescence of four schoolboys.

Other Irvine Welsh? Try **The Acid House**, a collection of dark short stories.

*Trainspotting* is about a group of drug addicts, the levels to which they'll stoop to get drugs and how drugs dominate their lives. It doesn't glamorise drug taking; in fact quite the reverse, it tell the story of life under the influence – exciting, dangerous, ruinously destructive, all-consuming and ultimately soul-destroying. But it's told in such a gripping way you're ripped along without stopping to make judgements as you go.

This is a roller-coaster, hair-raising, unputdownable read – its energy, vitality and rawness make it so fresh and new. The language, once you've got a handle on it, is so evocative of the lifestyle. It gives you such an immediate sensation of the world the characters inhabit you really feel as if you're right in there with them – which, thankfully, you're not. It's daring, thrilling, frightening and very funny.

**Arabella Weir**

# TREASURE ISLAND  Robert Louis Stevenson

*Treasure Island* is a perfect story of exotic adventure. It starts on homely dry land – but coastal – at the Admiral Benbow pub. The innkeeper's young son, Jim Hawkins, tells the tale and is its daring hero. Mystery, dread and tension build up with the arrival of Blind Pew, *tap-tapping* his way to deliver 'the black spot', a doom of execution, to a double-crossing old shipmate. We realise that these are pirates on the track of treasure. But it's Jim who lays hands on the essential treasure map and, with the local squire and doctor, sets sail. Chief among their rascally crew is one-legged, parrot-on-the-shoulder Long John Silver: he conceals black treachery under geniality and seeming honesty and helpfulness. No wonder there is bloodcurdling action on Treasure Island...

**Philippa Pearce**

**Next?**

If the character of Long John Silver fascinates you, try **Dr Jekyll and Mr Hyde** (UTBG 107), a chilling story of good and evil.

More pirates? What about **girl** pirates? Try **Piratica** by Tanith Lee, about a girl who almost by accident becomes a pirate, or **Pirates!** (UTBG 289) by Celia Rees.

OK, more **boy** pirates? Try Brian Jacques' **Castaways of the Flying Dutchman** or H. Rider Haggard's **King Solomon's Mines**.

# A TREE GROWS IN BROOKLYN

**12+**

## Betty Smith

I don't remember how I came across *A Tree Grows in Brooklyn* but I do remember the deep pleasure of reading it and how the story stayed with me a long time afterwards. The book is set in Brooklyn, New York at the turn of the 20th century. It focuses on Francie Nolan and her younger brother Neeley, taking us through their poverty-stricken but never dull childhood. Guided by their hardworking, determined mother Katie, their handsome but drunkard father Johnny and their wonderful but wanton Aunt Sissy, the children, like the hardy Trees of Heaven growing through the Brooklyn gutters, struggle to reach the sky. Problems are overcome with tough love, tenderness, humour and, in one powerful incident, carbolic acid and a bullet.

**Helena Pielichaty**

### Next?

*My Childhood* by Maxim Gorky – a Russian account of childhood poverty, beautifully and movingly told.

*Angela's Ashes* (UTBG 22) is the story of a poor Irish family.

Or, for a more up-to-date version of the above, try Roddy Doyle's *The Snapper*, in which a modern working-class Irish family get to grips with their teenage daughter's unexpected pregnancy.

# THE TRICKSTERS  Margaret Mahy

**14+**

### Next?

Margaret Mahy's The *Changeover* (UTBG 69) and *Alien in the Family* have a similar mix of beautifully realised characters and magical events.

Alice Hoffman's *Illumination Night* and *The River King* are novels about young people caught in strange situations.

Or *Night Maze* by Annie Dalton, about an orphan boy battling a family curse.

Harry (or Ariadne) is 17, shy, self-conscious (she wears glasses) and a budding writer. She and her large, noisy family are spending the summer by the sea, in a place where almost 90 years ago a boy was drowned. His body was never found.

One hot afternoon, Harry dives under the sea and a hand touches hers. Whose hand? She immediately surfaces and sees a figure on a rock, 'water streaming from every part of him'. And then he is gone. Eventually the ghostly drowned boy becomes real, but in a surprisingly and completely unexpected form. Harry's relationship with this unique character makes for an enchanting and spine-tingling story.

**Jenny Nimmo**

# TROLL FELL  Katherine Langrish

In an unspecified Nordic landscape of fjords and extreme weather, Peer's life has suddenly been turned upside-down. Before the ashes of his father's funeral pyre have even cooled, up turns one of his mean uncles who then drags him off to be kept as a virtual slave in a dilapidated mill. Peer's only solace is in the company of Hilde, a neighbour from a nearby farm – together they uncover Peer's uncles' devilish plot to steal troll treasure from the dark and magical Troll Fell – a course not recommended if one values one's life.

This is a novel that is atmospheric, dramatic, stylish and intensely engaging. It is by turns gritty and bleak, but also magical and uplifting.

**John McLay**

**Next?**

Look out for *Troll Mill*, Katherine Langrish's sequel to her first Scandinavian troll-fest. It has more chilly drama and fantasy.

*Sea of Trolls* (UTBG 322) by Nancy Farmer is a blockbuster of a troll novel, with more dragons and Vikings (and, yes, trolls) than you can shake a stick at. (And have you ever tried shaking a stick at a troll?)

Or Catherine Fisher's **Snow Walker's Son** sequence, which blends Norse myth with adventure.

# THE TROUBLE WITH DONOVAN CROFT
## Bernard Ashley

When Keith Chapman's parents tell him that he is to have a foster brother his own age, Keith holds out high hopes of having someone to play football with and share his games. When his foster brother arrives, however, things don't work out quite as Keith had planned. Donovan turns out to be a deeply troubled boy of West Indian origin, whose way of dealing with the trauma of leaving his parents is to remain silent.

Despite Keith's best efforts to look after him and make him happy, Donovan's misery is deepened by encounters with bullying and racism, often by people who should know better.

This is a deeply moving story that deals with issues that are always relevant in our society.

**Elizabeth McManus**

**Next?**

Try Bernard Ashley's *A Kind of Wild Justice*; or his *Little Soldier*, about a boy transplanted from war-torn Africa to England.

Other powerful books dealing with clashes of cultures include *Out of Bounds* (UTBG 278) by Beverley Naidoo and *The Burning City* (UTBG 60) by Ariel and Joaquin Dorfman.

# THE TROUBLE WITH LICHEN
## John Wyndham

Surely if anyone discovered a strange lichen that could stop people ageing it would be a wonderful thing for humanity? Not if they decide to keep it secret and make millions in the cosmetics business…

John Wyndham was a hugely ingenious writer of science fiction with a sharp eye for satire and how people always seem to mess things up. In our times, obsessed with beauty, celebrity and never growing old, this book is even more powerful than when it was written, and manages to be funny and terrifying all at once. It's not as well known as some of his others, but it's my favourite John Wyndham.
**Catherine Fisher**

### Next?

Wyndham wrote a handful of good books. In *The Midwich Cuckoos* all the children are aliens, and plants take over a world where everyone has been blinded in *The Day of the Triffids* (UTBG 96). And then there's *Chocky*, where a little boy's imaginary friend is not so imaginary…

You might also like Arthur C. Clarke's *The City and the Stars*, or Isaac Asimov's *Caves of Steel*.

Another book that deals with attempts to stop the ageing process is Nancy Farmer's *House of the Scorpion* (UTBG 178).

# TROY  Adèle Geras

### Next?

Something else by Adèle Geras? Try the sequel *Ithaka*, or *Silent Snow, Secret Snow* (UTBG 339), about a family full of secrets and betrayals.

Christopher Logue's *War Music* is a marvellous retelling of *The Iliad* in modern verse. Or for a prose version read Rosemary Sutcliff's *Black Ships Before Troy*.

*No Shame, No Fear* (UTBG 261) is also about forbidden love, this time between a Quaker girl and a rich young man.

You probably know the famous story of Helen of Troy, whose face launched a thousand ships and inspired a bloody battle that lasted for ten long years. If you don't it doesn't matter. Geras tells you what you need to know and more: the inside story, the woman's-eye view, the best bits. Seen for the most part by two sisters, Xanthe and Marpessa, it shows the war affecting the lives of ordinary folk as well as famous. Fittingly it begins in the Blood Room, where Xanthe awaits the wounded from the latest battle – for blood runs through the story. But so does humour, friendship and love. Stories within the great story, all vividly told, will keep you gripped to the end.
**Julia Jarman**

# TRUE GRIT  Charles Portis

'People do not give it credence that a 14-year-old girl could leave home and go off in the wintertime to avenge her father's blood.' So starts one of the best Western novels ever written. Mattie is looking for a man with 'true grit' who will help her hunt down her father's killer. She settles on Rooster Cogburn, a hard-drinking, walrus-moustached cowboy. But really Mattie is the one with 'true grit'.

Roald Dahl said it was the best novel to come his way in a long time, and Donna Tartt writes: 'I cannot think of a novel – any novel – which is so delightful to so many disparate age groups and literary tastes.' In other words: read it. You'll love it.

**Caroline Lawrence**

### Next?

There are many great stories set in the American West. Elmore Leonard's *Hombre* (UTBG 174) is about humanity and heroism. Thomas Eidson's *St Agnes' Stand* is about a man on the run and his meeting with a nun, Sister Agnes.

Or try *All the Pretty Horses* (UTBG 20), a tougher read, but stunning.

Or one of the great American novels, that exciting tale of adventure and friendship, *Huckleberry Finn* (UTBG 181).

# TRUSTEE FROM THE TOOLROOM
## Nevil Shute

Keith Stewart is a toolroom engineer who is not, on the surface, that well qualified to travel to the other side of the world looking for buried treasure on behalf of his ten-year-old niece. But Nevil Shute specialised in stories about ordinary people thrown into extraordinary situations, and Keith copes better than you might imagine.

He sets about his task with a quiet, methodical persistence, discovering himself to have skills and friends of which he was barely aware. And by the time he returns, we can see him as the hero he really is.

I've read every book Nevil Shute wrote, reread them regularly, and this is one of my favourites. A gentle but utterly absorbing story by a master craftsman.

**Andrew Norriss**

### Next?

Another Shute? Try *Pied Piper* (UTBG 288), about an 'ordinary' man again, who gets caught up in trying to rescue a group of children after the invasion of France in 1940. Or *A Town Like Alice* (UTBG 378) set around wartime events.

Graham Greene is another master storyteller. Try *Our Man in Havana* (UTBG 278) for a cynical look at spies.

# TRUTH OR DARE  Celia Rees

14+

**Next?**

Family secrets often provide the heart of great novels. I'd recommend *The Opposite of Chocolate* (UTBG 274) by Julie Bertagna, *The Secret Line* by William Corlett and *Tell Me No Lies* by Malorie Blackman as compelling follow-ups to this one.

*The Curious Incident of the Dog in the Night-time* (UTBG 89) by Mark Haddon has been an extraordinary success, at its centre a character with Asperger's syndrome.

*Worm in the Blood* (UTBG 422) by Thomas Bloor is about a family tainted by an ancient curse.

This engrossing book is essentially a detective novel, but not in the traditional sense. Josh reluctantly accompanies his mother when she goes to care for his ill grandmother. It's a bleak experience, separated from his friends and holed up in a house in which the chill wind of illness seems compounded by an atmosphere of secrets and lies. Gradually, almost unintentionally, Josh begins to ask questions about his surroundings, and about the splinters of family stories which don't quite match up to make sense. He begins to uncover the story of an uncle he believed had died in his teens. The real story is revealed by evidence from the present, and stories of the past – and it is just as tragic, in its way.

**Lindsey Fraser**

# THE TULIP TOUCH  Anne Fine

12+

Natalie is a good girl. Tulip is not. But when their paths cross, the relationship is almost magnetic – Natalie simply can't resist her mesmerising friend. As their story gradually unfolds, we watch, horrified, as Tulip pushes Natalie further towards the point of no return.

Anne Fine doesn't resort to histrionics or drama to tell her stories. The language of each sentence is as clear as a bell. Yet this story, like so many of her others, keeps us wondering long after we've closed the book. That's largely because we become so engrossed in the characters that their realness extends beyond the last page. But it's also because we wonder what we might have done, and how we would have reacted in the same situation.

**Lindsey Fraser**

**Next?**

I'd recommend anything else by Anne Fine, but especially *Goggle Eyes* and *Step by Wicked Step*.

*Big Mouth* and *Ugly Girl* by Joyce Carol Oates and *Noughts and Crosses* (UTBG 267) by Malorie Blackman look in very different ways at the role prejudice can play in people's judgements about other people.

*Kamo's Escape* by Daniel Pennac is another take on the impact one person can make on another.

# TULKU Peter Dickinson

12+

Very occasionally a book comes along that is too big for the pages it is written on, so that it spills right off the edges into a larger-than-life reality of its own. *Tulku* is one such book.

In the Boxer Rebellion, the Christian mission where Theo has been brought up is destroyed and his father killed. While escaping, he meets an intrepid plant collector called Mrs Jones, and her guide, Lung. Their journey is at once a breathtaking adventure story and a spiritual rite of passage. All Theo's rigid beliefs unravel as they penetrate the mysteries of Tibet, and Mrs Jones is transformed from eccentric adventurer to spiritual warrior and mother of the Tulku, or Dalai Lama. There are so many things to love about this vivid novel that I cannot possibly do them all justice. You will have to read it!

**Livi Michael**

### Next?

*She* (UTBG 334) and *Ayesha* by H. Rider Haggard, for more tales of exotic adventure; or *Greenmantle* by John Buchan about adventures in Arabia.

Or for more adult books about spiritual journeys, try *Siddhartha* (UTBG 338) or *Narziss and Goldmund* (UTBG 256) by Hermann Hesse.

Peter Dickinson wrote some amazing books; try *The Kin* (UTBG 207).

# TURBULENCE Jan Mark

12+

### Next?

Clay makes a passing reference to the superb *The Great Gatsby* (UTBG 156) by F. Scott Fitzgerald, and it's worth reading it to see exactly why.

There's no one who writes quite like Jan Mark, so if you like this, seek out more of hers – try *Useful Idiots* (UTBG 391) and *They Do Things Differently There*.

In *The Tricksters* (UTBG 380), Mahy writes brilliantly about people whose sudden presence undermines other people's lives for good.

Jan Mark has written some brilliant books and this is one of her best. Clay (Clare) Winchester narrates what happens when her parents bring home Sandor Harker and his wife Ali for dinner one evening. It's Sandor who shines that night, making everyone feel that they're the most important person in the room. Clay is flattered, but soon everyone she knows falls under Sandor's spell, and their own solid relationships show signs of foundering as a result. Sandor's exhibitionism and his insidious pervasion of Clay's close circle of family and friends make gripping and at times disturbing reading, but the book is infused with Jan Mark's uniquely dark, sometimes laugh-out-loud, humour.

**Jon Appleton**

# THE TURN OF THE SCREW Henry James

This must be one of the most terrifying ghost stories ever written. A young governess, appointed to an Essex country house, becomes instantly devoted to Flora, her young charge. When Flora's brother Miles is sent home from school in disgrace, the two children develop an oddly knowing behaviour that makes the governess deeply uneasy. They are apparently under the malevolent influence of Peter Quint and Miss Jessop, former employees at Bly, both now dead. All the young woman's courage is needed to protect her charges from the silent, watchful pair. Uncertainty about whether the manifestations are real, or only imagined by the children or by the disturbed governess herself, adds to the chilling ambiguity of this unforgettable tale.

**Linda Newbery**

### Next?

Try the ghost stories of M.R. James (UTBG 144) or Edgar Allen Poe's *Tales of Mystery and Imagination* (UTBG 365); or the story of that other famous governess, *Jane Eyre* (UTBG 195) by Charlotte Brontë; or *Wuthering Heights* (UTBG 424) by her sister Emily.

Or *Rebecca* (UTBG 306), the tale of a young girl who finds herself haunted by her husband's beautiful first wife.

Another James? His *Daisy Miller* (UTBG 91) is very different.

# TURTLE DIARY Russell Hoban

William G. works in a bookshop and Neaera H. is a children's writer seeking inspiration for her next book. They lead careful, reserved English lives, but the large sea turtles confined in the aquarium at the London Zoo independently haunt them both.

Through their diaries their stories unfold, revealing tragedy, self-doubt and strange parallels. Keen observers, sensitive and honest, they wonder at the way we humans treat nature, they stand in awe of the turtles' instinct to navigate vast oceans when it seems so hard to navigate their own lives. Then, despite themselves, William G. and Neaera H. become jointly part of 'an event that seemed to want to happen'. This intimate, funny-sad book is quite wonderful. Russell Hoban is an original and a poet.

**Elizabeth Honey**

### Next?

Douglas Adams and Mark Carwardine's *Last Chance to See* (UTBG 213) is a serious book about endangered animals, but it's also extremely funny.

*Hoot* (UTBG 175) manages the tricky task of being both a book about saving wildlife and a wild adventure story.

Another Hoban? Try the complex and wonderful *The Mouse and His Child*. Don't think it's just a book for kids.

# THE TWELFTH DAY OF JULY Joan Lingard

**Next?**

Kevin and Sadie's story continues with *Across the Barricades*.

Other Joan Lingard books include *Tell the Moon to Come Out*, about a boy travelling illegally into Franco's Spain to try and find his missing father; or *Natasha's Will*, which weaves two stories, one an escape from war-torn Russia, the other a search for the escapee's will many years later.

Theresa Breslin's *Divided City* (UTBG 106) is about conflict between Protestants and Catholics.

Belfast in the run up to the 12th of July is a time for parades and celebration for the Protestant community, and a time of fear and resentment among the Catholics. A dare carried out by Kevin, a Catholic, involving entering a Protestant 'no-go' area, triggers a chain reaction of events, both exciting and very dangerous. It leads to an unlikely and somewhat risky friendship between Kevin and Sadie, an attractive, feisty Protestant.

As the action escalates, tempers fly, resulting in an incident that causes both sides to examine the seriousness of their prejudices and bigotry.

The issue of the Troubles is dealt with in a clear and balanced way in this exciting, fast-moving book.

**Elizabeth McManus**

# ULTRAVIOLET Lesley Howarth

Vi lives with her father in a futuristic, damaged world in which the sun's radiation makes it impossible to venture out for most of the year and people live in underground cities. To compensate for the lost outdoors, Vi and her peers play virtual-reality games. Some of these are so sophisticated that players can paste elements from their own lives into the game. Vi becomes restless and 'leaks' outside, dressed in protective fabric that her father invented. Her outdoor adventure seems straightforward at first, but watch out for the twists as this book borrows the narrative structure of a computer game – in other words, there is more than one way for it to be played out! A great book from an unusually imaginative author.

**Noga Applebaum**

**Next?**

Why not try one of Lesley Howarth's other books? *Carwash* (UTBG 64) takes place in a small town, while *Maphead* is the story of an alien trying to make sense of our world.

*Breaktime* (UTBG 55) is another novel that plays around with narrative and blurs the boundary between fact and fiction.

*Sharp North* (UTBG 333) by Patrick Cave also tells the story of a resourceful teenage girl in a world affected by environmental changes.

# (UN)ARRANGED MARRIAGE Bali Rai

Manny is a typically rebellious teenager, rejecting the authority of his violent, drunken 'old man', beaten by his brothers, frustrated by his mother's subservience. Destined for an arranged marriage he hasn't asked for, to a girl he doesn't know or want, he deliberately sets out to make himself the most unmarriageable husband material possible. He's determined to follow his own path through life, but reckons without being tricked into a trip to India by his tradition-bound Punjabi family, that threatens to put an end to his dreams…

Culture clashes, family loyalty, honour, traditional values, taking chances, alienation and identity are all brought sharply into focus through the eyes of a 17-year-old boy. With a sharp ear for contemporary dialogue, a stunning eye for detail and perfect pace, Rai is truly one of the strongest writers around for young people.

**Eileen Armstrong**

> **Next?**
>
> *Rani and Sukh* (UTBG 303) is Bali Rai's take on the 'Romeo and Juliet' story, while *What's Your Problem?* is about racism and violence.
>
> *Walking a Tightrope* is a collection of short stories by some of the UK's best Asian novelists.
>
> *Anita and Me* (UTBG 23) is about growing up in the only Punjabi family in a British mining town.

# UNDER PRESSURE / BAD BOYS

## Tony Bradman

> **Next?**
>
> If you thought these players were competitive, you should read Neil Arksey's *MacB!*. Neil's *Playing on the Edge* is brilliant, too.
>
> For a funnier look at boys' growing pains, try Jeremy Strong's *Stuff*.
>
> Or for more boys behaving badly? Try something very different with Pete Johnson's *The Protectors*.

If you think books are too hard and too boring, try these, especially if you like football. Set in the youth squad of a national football team, the stories are action-packed and totally realistic. Whether it's Craig and his money-grubbing dad; Darren and his desperate need to succeed; or (in the second book) Ben, who really wants to be cool and liked, whatever it takes; or Lee who really just wants to make his own mind up about things without interference, the boys of City FC's training school all have their problems. And that's before they've even set foot on the pitch!

With lots of football, friendship and rivalries, these books are all about a world in which boys are under huge pressure to succeed – and which is far less glamorous than the headlines may make out.

**John McLay**

# UNDERWORLD
## Catherine MacPhail

God, what a scary book this is. You'll get sucked in by the first few harmless pages – school stuff, outsiders, little rivalries – and suddenly find you're in the middle of an appalling nightmare. But by then it's too late. You're hooked.

*Underworld* isn't blood 'n' guts scary – there are no vicious monsters, sharp-fanged Draculas or anything like that – but what it has is much, much worse. It vividly portrays the terror brought by things you can't see, by things hidden in the shadows, when you find that you and your friends are trapped deep underground, in the darkness, and there are noises…

**Daniel Hahn**

## Next?

To see the range of different books Catherine writes, move on from this to *Roxy's Baby* (UTBG 314), or *Another Me*. Quite frankly, try everything she's written as it's all pretty amazing.

*The Watch House* (UTBG 400) by Robert Westall has some of the scariest ghosts ever written about.

Raffaella Barker's *Phosphoresence* (UTBG 286) also has a school trip that goes disastrously wrong.

## The Ultimate Teen Readers' Poll

# BOOK WITH THE MOST EXCITING PLOT

1 **Harry Potter series**

2 **Alex Rider series**

3 **The Lord of the Rings trilogy**

4 **A Series of Unfortunate Events**

5 **His Dark Materials trilogy**

6 **Skellig**

7 **Holes**

8 **Artemis Fowl**

9 **Girls in Love series**

10 **The Saga of Darren Shan**

# UNIQUE Alison Allen-Gray

What might happen if a person was cloned from a sibling who'd died? Dominic is one such boy, but he's nowhere near as clever or talented as his dead brother was. The unbearable weight of expectations now heaped on him by his parents pushes him to the edge. So he sets out to answer a myriad of questions…

It's a journey beset with hazards and dangers as Dominic must make vital decisions in his quest to uncover the truth at the heart of his family's dark secrets.

*Unique* is a perfect mix of sci-fi and science. It's powerful and scary because in the near future, it could well be a description of a new reality.

**Jonny Zucker**

### Next?

Another futuristic story is *As Good as Dead in Downtown* by Neil Arksey.

*Truth or Dare* (UTBG 384) by Celia Rees is another exciting book about dark family secrets.

If you like fast-paced adventure stories why not try *The Burning City* (UTBG 60)? Its plot lunges forward like the main character's hurtling courier bike.

*House of the Scorpion* (UTBG 178) by Nancy Farmer also deals with the subject of cloning, as does *Clone* by Malcolm Rose.

# AN UNSUITABLE JOB FOR A WOMAN
## P.D. James

I read this book in one go on the night before my daughter Catherine was born. She has turned out to be a great fan of detective fiction, and I often wonder whether that last experience in the womb is to blame!

This is the story of Cordelia Gray, tackling the mystery of two apparent suicides: of her partner in a detective agency, and of a 21-year-old Cambridge student. It's a good introduction to the work of P.D. James, one of my favourite murder-mystery writers. Her books always have more to them than just the solution of a puzzle. Stick with them, and her main character, the sleuth and poet Adam Dalgliesh, will become one of your best friends.

**Eleanor Updale**

### Next?

There are plenty more P.D. James books to choose from. Try *Cover Her Face* and *The Skull Beneath the Skin*.

James can be a little gory. If you want something more gentle, go for Dorothy L. Sayers. *The Nine Tailors* is a good place to start.

If you want something more bloody than P.D. James, try Ian Rankin, whose **Rebus** books can be violent. Start with *Knots and Crosses*.

# UP ON CLOUD NINE   Anne Fine

**12+**

### Next?

Sadly you won't find anything else quite like this book! I suppose the closest you'll come are the novels of Sharon Creech. *Walk Two Moons* (UTBG 396) and *The Wanderer,* about a sea journey that helps a girl remember the truth about her past, are particularly recommended.

The theme of friendship is explored in very different ways in *The Tulip Touch* (UTBG 384) by Anne Fine and *Vicky Angel* by Jacqueline Wilson.

When Stolly falls out of a top floor window it's only the jasmine bush that saves him from certain death.

His best friend Ian, spending the day at Stolly's hospital bedside, thinks back over their childhood and gradually begins to understand what Stolly has tried to do and why.

If you've ever wondered what a 'life-affirming' book is then read this one. It's about life (and death) and why some people seem to manage better in this world than others. As far as I'm concerned books don't get any finer than this!

**Laura Hutchings**

# USEFUL IDIOTS   Jan Mark

The year is 2255. Climate change has altered the shape of the world; whole countries and great cities are under water. What's left of Britain is now The Rhine Delta Islands, part of the United States of Europe. Jan Mark's wonderfully imagined new world order depends upon homogeneity; genetically engineered humans lead long and blandly pleasant lives. Anything that encourages non-conformity and individualism is deeply distrusted. Digging up the past to discover one's 'primitive' roots is therefore a dangerous activity, and when a group of archaeologists unearth a rare intact skeleton on 'Aboriginal' land they find themselves in deep trouble.

Part sci-fi, part crime thriller, *Useful Idiots* asks thorny and absorbing questions about what it takes to be an individual in a world submerged in historical and political amnesia.

**Mal Peet**

### Next?

Jan Mark often looks to the future to make us think about the present. Try *Riding Tycho* next, about a girl who discovers that there is more to life than misery and tyranny.

Or Arthur C. Clarke's *2001*, which makes us question everything we know about our origins.

*A Rag, a Bone and a Hank of Hair* by Nicholas Fisk is an early novel on the subject of cloning. Or for another distressing dystopia, try Aldous Huxley's classic *Brave New World* (UTBG 54).

# RACE IN YOUNG-ADULT FICTION by Bali Rai

When I was at school, finding books about ethnic minority characters was like a treasure hunt. I'd start at one end of the school library and search every shelf, scanning the titles for any hint of ethnicity. I'd take the promising novels off the shelf and read the blurb on the back, looking for tell-tale signs, such as Asian names or Caribbean settings. I'd study the covers too, hoping to see an ethnic face. Like most treasure hunts, most of the time I was doomed to failure. All the books seemed to me to be about middle-class white kids from posh families who never swore or worried about money. And mostly they never had non-white friends.

Someone gave me *A Little Princess* by Frances Hodgson Burnett, which did have an Indian character in it, but I didn't like it. And I wasn't Indian. I was British and Asian. Where were all the characters that

reflected my life, at home and at school? Finally I found books by Farrukh Dhondy and Bernard Ashley and I was satisfied for a while. But I read those quickly and when they were gone, there were no more.

Today there are more books about British Asians and Blacks but not as many as there should be. Reading rates amongst young men of Afro-Caribbean and Pakistani / Bengali descent in particular are very low. One of the reasons is that they don't find books that relate to them and their lives. Too often the characters that they do find are like those mobile phone snap-on covers. The colours are different but the underlying component is universal. That's one of the reasons that I write about characters from different backgrounds to the literary norm. To try and represent the 'real' voice of multi-ethnic Britain. As do authors such as

Benjamin Zephaniah, Malorie Blackman, Narinder Dhami and Preethi Nair.

That is not to say that Asian youngsters, for example, should only read about Asian lives. That would be wrong. But they must feel as though their lives are a part of the literary tradition. And many of them do not. That is why race and writing about race is so important. To get non-readers from ethnic minority backgrounds to start reading you need to pull them in. One of the best ways is to give them novels about characters that they can relate to. Real characters whose lives reflect Britain today. Not the middle-class utopia of boating lakes, boarding schools and wizards but the streets of inner-city Britain, which is where the vast majority of ethnic minority kids live.

Once books about such young people become a norm and not a speciality, only then can we start to say that race in Britain is truly represented in fiction. Things are changing from when I did my treasure hunts but I still get young ethnic minority people asking me if I know of other books, like mine, which deal with their lives, their hopes and their dreams. I'll only be happy when they stop asking me that question. And that is still a long way off.

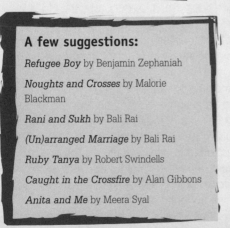

## A few suggestions:

*Refugee Boy* by Benjamin Zephaniah

*Noughts and Crosses* by Malorie Blackman

*Rani and Sukh* by Bali Rai

*(Un)arranged Marriage* by Bali Rai

*Ruby Tanya* by Robert Swindells

*Caught in the Crossfire* by Alan Gibbons

*Anita and Me* by Meera Syal

# V FOR VENDETTA

## Alan Moore (illustrated by David Lloyd)

What if Guy Fawkes had succeeded? This dark, gripping graphic novel blends George Orwell's *Nineteen Eighty-Four* with Robin Hood. The mysterious 'V' is a mask-wearing, Shakespeare-spouting terrorist, committed to bringing down the government in a 21st-century fascist Britain. On the very first page, he succeeds in blowing up the Houses of Parliament; but this is just the beginning of his plans. Evie, a young woman he rescues from a vicious police attack, gradually uncovers more about his extraordinary past. For he is a man betrayed, and he will stop at nothing to bring down those responsible. Evie herself is to play a key role in his schemes, one that no one could have predicted.
**Ariel Kahn**

### Next?

Alan Moore's *Watchmen* (UTBG 401), about the end of superheroes and the beginning of the nuclear age.

*Brave New World* (UTBG 54) by Aldous Huxley explores a genetically engineered future.

*Someone to Run With* by David Grossman has two parallel stories; one about a boy who enters the criminal underworld in Jerusalem to try and return a lost dog, and the moving story of the girl who the dog belongs to.

# THE VACILLATIONS OF POPPY CAREW

14+

## Mary Wesley

### Next?

More Mary Wesley? Start with *The Camomile Lawn*.

*Love in a Cold Climate* (UTBG 226): lots of the same kinds of romantic twists but set 60 years earlier.

*Janice Gentle Gets Sexy* by Mavis Cheek: another funny, unusual love story.

I would happily marry any of the three heroes of this utterly charming book. Don't be put off by the old-fashioned word in the title: 'vacillations'; when I first read the book I was delighted to discover a very modern, funny and romantic story that is full of irresistible characters.

I'd hate to spoil the plot by telling you too much, as there are some great surprises early on, but the whole adventure kicks off with Poppy's boyfriend dumping her for another woman (the posh, beautiful, blonde Venetia who has very cold feet), then her father dying and requesting a very unusual kind of funeral. Poppy begins a whole new life, in which she has to make some choices, not least about those three delicious men…
**Abigail Anderson**

# VANITY FAIR William M. Thackeray

## Next?

To find another book with the breadth and variety of *Vanity Fair*, you'd be best moving on to another Victorian novel – something like *Bleak House* by Charles Dickens.

If it's Thackeray's humour you like, you'll probably also enjoy Jane Austen's *Pride and Prejudice* (UTBG 294).

A modern American novel clearly influenced by *Vanity Fair* is Tom Wolfe's *The Bonfire of the Vanities*, set in 1980s New York.

OK, so *Vanity Fair* is long. And it was written over 150 years ago. But no other novel will repay you so richly for reading it. Why? Because it has everything – humour, drama (it covers the battle of Waterloo), and a fascinating cast of characters, including one of the most memorable ever invented – the classic anti-hero, Becky Sharp.

From the moment she leaves school and throws her copy of Dr Johnson's *Dictionary* out of the carriage window, there are no rules for Becky. She uses her wits, her skilful reading of character and her sly beauty to climb her way to the top of the rotting social pile that is London in the 1830s. But when she gets there, is it worth it? Read the novel and find out!

**Sherry Ashworth**

# VERNON GOD LITTLE D.B.C. Pierre

Just when I start complaining that books don't surprise me any more, along comes one like *Vernon God Little*. And *Vernon God Little* didn't just surprise me – it pretty much knocked me over. I don't know when I've last read a book with the energy, the freshness and fearlessness, the relish, the sheer hurtling momentum of this one.

It's the story of a teenager in a small Texan town, in the wake of a terrible school shooting. The town is Martirio, the barbecue-sauce capital of Texas.

The narrator's voice belongs to Vernon Little – and what a voice it is. Angry and sharp and smart and witty and profane, and with the power to blow away a stolid, cynical seen-it-all-before reader like me. It's a great feeling.

**Daniel Hahn**

## Next?

For another distinctive and off-centre American hero, try John Irving's brilliant *A Prayer for Owen Meany* (UTBG 293).

For a narrative voice that's energetic, captivating (and a little odd), Patrick McCabe's dark and dazzling *Butcher Boy*, though for some of it you'll need a strong stomach.

And if you've not read *The Catcher in the Rye* (UTBG 66), now's your chance. I'd have thought Vernon and Holden would have got along.

# WALK TWO MOONS  Sharon Creech

**12+**

Sal (short for Salamanca) and her father moved a year ago, after her mother left 'in order to clear her heart of all the bad things', and never returned. In this wonderful novel, Sal travels back with her gram and gramps to find her mother, and over the long journey across America to Idaho she tells them the story of her friend Phoebe; at the same time she is revealing another story, about herself. The ending of this story moves me to tears each time I read it.

There are great characters, funny bits, wise sayings: 'Don't judge a man until you've walked two moons in his moccasins'; and most importantly of all, Sal's utterly convincing voice telling the story. I loved this book!

**Julia Green**

### Next?

Other books by Sharon Creech: try *The Wanderer* (UTBG 397), about a yacht journey across the Atlantic; or *Chasing Redbird*.

*To Kill a Mockingbird* (UTBG 375), a wise, wonderful, moving story which is also about seeing from someone else's point of view, and has a strong female narrator.

Joan Bauer is another great American writer; try *Hope Was Here*, about a girl constantly moving from place to place.

# WALKABOUT  James Vance Marshall

**12+**

### Next?

*Hatchet* (UTBG 163) by Gary Paulsen: another exciting story about survival in the wilderness (Canada, this time); or Gillian Cross' *The Dark Ground* (UTBG 93), about a boy alone in a strange jungle.

Sonya Hartnett is a great Australian writer; try *Stripes of the Sidestep Wolf* (UTBG 359).

I read this as a teenager, and loved it then for the descriptions of the Australian landscape – wild and remote, beautiful but also dangerous – as well as for the powerful story of what happens when two children crashland in the middle of the Australian desert. They have no chance of survival: it's thousands of miles to Adelaide, where they were supposed to be going, in intense heat with no food and hardly any water.

And then they meet an Aboriginal boy, who knows everything about survival in this place. Yet the girl is full of fear. Their meeting is also the meeting of two very different cultures, and (without giving too much away) what happens is a tragic mirror of what has happened so often when people misunderstand and fear each other.

*Walkabout* was written back in 1959, and you'll notice some uses of language about race that we consider totally inappropriate today, but don't let that put you off this perceptive and moving story.

**Julia Green**

# WALKING NAKED  Alyssa Brugman

Suicide isn't an easy subject, but *Walking Naked* tackles it head-on with starkly elegant, wry humour. Megan is one of the beautiful people; Perdita is the school outcast. Thrown together in detention, Megan is drawn to Perdita, who is unexpectedly funny, intelligent, uncompromising – and desperate. But when her friends force Megan to take sides, she shuns Perdita – and then must live with the consequences.

Megan's honesty about her own behaviour – of which she's not proud – is painful, but this isn't a grim book. Perdita introduces Megan to poetry, a dialogue which underpins their unorthodox friendship, revealing Perdita's personality and Megan's growing understanding of herself – and of someone utterly different.

**Helen Simmons**

## Next?

Track down *Lucas* (UTBG 228). It's about a mysterious, beautiful outsider who arrives on an island, but for some reason everyone hates him.

*Girl, Interrupted* by Susanna Kaysen deals with the feeling that you don't want to go on with your life. Not as gloomy as it sounds, as it is full of raw humour and hope.

Nick Hornby's funny and sad *A Long Way Down* is about four very different people who become each other's support group.

# THE WANDERER  Sharon Creech

## Next?

*Ruby Holler* (UTBG 314) is also about family and loyalty, but is more quirky and magical.

There is another exciting sea voyage to be found in the pages of Elizabeth Laird's *Secrets of the Fearless*. This one is historical and set aboard a sailing ship.

If you like swashbuckling adventure on the high seas, with some futuristic vampire pirates thrown in, look no further than Justin Somper's **Vampirates** series.

Sophie has persuaded her three uncles and two cousins to let her join them on a trip of a lifetime aboard *The Wanderer* – a 45-foot sailboat which they plan to sail north up the coast from Connecticut, then east across the ocean towards England where Sophie's grandfather is looking forward to a visit from his three sons. 13-year-old Sophie is an orphan, daydreamer and headstrong tomboy, and an absorbing and intriguing main character. During several windswept weeks at sea, Sophie manages to inspire everyone around her despite being on the very brink of coming to terms with her own fractured and half-remembered family history. The author's descriptions of the sea and of Sophie's emotional and physical journeys are first class.

**John McLay**

# WAR AND PEACE Leo Tolstoy

16+

**Next?**

After this massive book you may find yourself hooked on Russian classics. Move on to *Anna Karenina* (UTBG 24) (tragic love story), Dostoyevsky's *Crime and Punishment* (UTBG 86) (tragic, thought-provoking thriller), or Mikhail Lermontov's *Hero of Our Time* (psychological tragedy).

Or for something epic and not tragic at all, Vikram Seth's *A Suitable Boy*, set in India – many families and many classes and many generations (and many pages) – a great and glorious read.

Count Tolstoy served as a military officer in the Crimea, but turned against war and began the pacifist movement of which Gandhi was his most eminent disciple. He is also Russia's greatest novelist. He spent ten years creating his masterpiece, *War and Peace*, an epic (i.e. whopping great) novel about Napoleon's invasion of Russia, seen through the lives of three aristocratic families. Tolstoy himself appears in the novel as the gentle, peaceable, bumbling Pierre Bezukhov.

Don't be put off by the length of the book, or by Uncle Reg's comment that he 'started reading it once, but never finished it'. This is one of the greatest books ever written, so it merits perseverance.

**James Riordan**

# THE WAR OF THE WORLDS

12+

## H.G. Wells

Imagine invaders from Mars arriving at the end of your street! H.G. Wells' science-fiction adventure will have you on the edge of your seat as sinister cylinders rain down from space on South London and slowly unscrew to reveal Martians brandishing heat-rays…

The narrator of this story is one of the first to witness the Martians' war machines – huge tripods – stalking across the scorched heathland near his former home. Meeting up with a fellow survivor, he hides in a house that is hit by a second wave of cylinders. What are the Martians making in their crater? Will our hero be reunited with his wife? Will the Martians and their tripods take over the world? Can humanity – and the Earth – hope to survive? H.G. Wells studied biology, and his answer may take you by surprise!

**Lesley Howarth**

**Next?**

Another sci-fi classic (this time very funny) is *The Hitchhiker's Guide to the Galaxy* (UTBG 171). It too begins with a threat to the future of Earth…

Or for something a bit more guns 'n' battles, try *Starship Troopers* (UTBG 353) by Robert Heinlein.

Or more H.G. Wells? Try *The Invisible Man*.

# WAREHOUSE Keith Gray

14+

The Warehouse is a place where kids go when everything in their lives has fallen apart. Robbie's brother beats him up. Amy has had everything stolen from her. Independently they end up with Canner, the Can Man, the fixer, who helps them to the sanctuary of the Warehouse. Once there we find a twilight society in which the young people try to pull the broken bits of their lives together. We find out about Canner, and then there's King Lem, the boss man who has problems of his own.

The freshness of this story comes in the way it is shaped. Parallel tales are told from the perspective of different characters. It reminds the reader that the Warehouse is a place of many potential stories, not just one.

**Anne Cassidy**

> ### Next?
>
> *Stone Cold* (UTBG 355) by Robert Swindells is about homelessness and *The Simple Gift* (UTBG 340) by Steven Herrick is about running away from home.
>
> Other Keith Gray? Try *The Fearful*, about a father and son trying to come to terms with each other and the past.
>
> *The Lost Boys' Appreciation Society* by Alan Gibbons is about a boy coming to terms with grief.

# WARRIOR GIRL Pauline Chandler

12+

A sweeping and dramatic historical epic which tells the story of Mariane, Joan of Arc's brave and trustworthy friend whose parents have been brutally murdered by the occupying English army. Persuaded to rally to Joan's cause, Mariane had reckoned without those wanting to have an English ruler on the throne, including her scheming and corrupt uncle, Sir Gaston. Mariane is forced to choose between saving herself and saving her country fighting at Joan's side.

Meticulous research, larger-than-life characters from every social class, a fiery heroine, fast pace and a nifty ending make this an unforgettable evocation of 15th-century France which really pulls readers back into the heart of the action.

**Eileen Armstrong**

> ### Next?
>
> *Dark Thread* by Pauline Chandler tells the time-travelling life story of Kate, a young weaver girl.
>
> Period detail as authentic and engrossing as in *Warrior Girl*, this time of Elizabethan everyday life, can be found in *Tread Softly* by Kate Pennington.
>
> Another young girl called upon to play her part in making history is 14-year-old Betsy in Staton Rabin's *Betsy and the Emperor*. Betsy's life on the island of St Helena is irrevocably changed when Napoleon Bonaparte arrives.

# THE WASP FACTORY   Iain Banks

**16+**

### Next?

More Iain Banks? My favourite is *The Crow Road,* which follows young Prentice McHoan as he attempts to make sense of his complex, wildly eccentric, but strangely endearing Scottish family. And Iain's science-fiction novels have a cult following, too.

*O Caledonia* by Elspeth Barker is another surreal and hilarious tale of a dark and troubled adolescent.

And if you've got the taste for well-crafted horror, read Melvin Burgess' *Bloodtide* (UTBG 46), a terrifying and visceral epic of love, betrayal and revenge.

*The Wasp Factory* is not for the squeamish. Banks piles on the horror in graphic detail, BUT it is also extremely well-written, compulsively readable and studded with the author's trademark dark humour. The narrator is Frank Cauldhame, a disturbed and disturbing 16-year-old who lives on a small island with his reclusive father. He lives his life according to a series of bizarre and unpleasant rituals, which usually involve killing something and which bring some kind of twisted order to his troubled world. Frank is obsessed with death; indeed he tells us that he has killed three children. But can we believe anything Frank says when he himself is so clearly deranged? Banks' skill as a writer lies in making the monstrous Frank human and in making us care about him.

**Kathryn Ross**

# THE WATCH HOUSE   Robert Westall

**12+**

My favourite ghost story of all time: not just because it's very spooky, but because it's long enough for you to discover the full history behind the ghost (or ghosts) and the building they haunt. The story centres on the Watch House on top of a cliff, from where the lifeboat men used to look out for ships in distress. Anne comes to live in the cottage next door for the summer as her parents' marriage is in trouble. This unhappy girl becomes a channel for the unhappy ghost; she gets drawn into the world of Victorian Garmouth and discovers a grisly secret. Full of great comic characters as well as scary bits, this book presents interesting theories on what ghosts are and how they work.

**Abigail Anderson**

### Next?

Oscar Wilde's *The Canterville Ghost* is also about a ghost and a little girl – a mix of humour and horror.

Another very spooky haunted house can be found in Susan Hill's chiller *The Woman in Black* (UTBG 420).

More Westall? Something unsettling? Try *The Scarecrows* (UTBG 320).

*The Turn of the Screw* (UTBG 386) by Henry James is one of the scariest stories ever written.

# WATCHMEN  Alan Moore and Dave Gibbons

14+

Don't ever let anyone tell you comics are just for kids. *Watchmen* puts that idea well and truly to rest. Alan Moore is a superb writer, Dave Gibbons a startlingly good artist, and together they serve up one hell of a story that first came out in 1986 as an award-winning 12-issue mini-series and later a graphic novel. OK, so it's almost 20 years old, but the paranoia, the multiple plot lines, the tension and the unique mix of sci-fi, philosophy and conspiracy theories still ring true. Moore writes as densely plotted a storyline as you could wish for, while Gibbons packs more detail, thought and design into a single page than you'll find in most complete comic books.

**Graham Marks**

## Next?

Check out Moore's *The League of Extraordinary Gentlemen*, which is drawn by Kevin O'Neill, and his collaboration with Eddie Campbell, *From Hell*, about Jack the Ripper; both are far better than the movies made from them.

And look out for Frank Miller's great **Batman** story *The Dark Knight Returns*.

In non-graphic terms, why not try the mind-boggling **Catch-22** (UTBG 65).

## DEATH

*Bitter Fruit* by Brian Keaney

*Brothers* by Ted van Lieshout

*Elsewhere* by Gabrielle Zavin

*The Great Blue Yonder* by Alex Shearer

*The Lovely Bones* by Alice Sebold

*River Boy* by Tim Bowler

# WATERSHIP DOWN Richard Adams

**12+**

Something terrible is going to happen to Hazel's home warren. His brother Fiver has foreseen disaster, and Fiver's sixth sense is never wrong. So, along with a handful of companions, Hazel and Fiver set off into the unknown. And so begins a great adventure, in which the small band of rabbits will face every danger imaginable in their search for a new home.

There's no other book like *Watership Down*. It's an animal story, an adventure and an epic all rolled into one. I've read it more than ten times, and each time I find something new.

**Benedict Jacka**

### Next?

*The Incredible Journey* by Sheila Burnford is another story about a group of animals travelling a long way. A nice easy read.

The **Redwall** series (UTBG 308) by Brian Jacques is another group of adventures where all the characters are animals.

Or *Urchin of the Riding Stars*, part of the **Mismantle Chronicles** by M.I. McAllister, about a world where animals are in charge.

If you want something as epic as *Watership Down*, though, your best bet is **The Lord of the Rings** trilogy (UTBG 224).

# WAVING, NOT DROWNING Rosie Rushton

**14+**

There's Jay, trying to look after his forgetful nan while keeping his own troublesome life under control. Fee, whose boyfriend has stopped calling her, whose parents' marriage is falling apart and who might – just maybe – be pregnant. And there's Lyall – angry and hurting and unable to cope with the memories of his sister's death, the guilt and the rage at himself and the world.

Three 16-year-olds, whose stories wind in and out of each other in clever and often surprising ways; I read it gripped in a single sitting, and no doubt you will, too.

*Waving, Not Drowning* is a book about teenagers struggling as their lives spiral out of control, but it's not maudlin or grim – really it's a story of growing confidence, learning to trust and love, finding answers and finding happiness.

**Daniel Hahn**

### Next?

For a story with echoes of Lyall's, read Sue Welford's *Out of the Blue* (UTBG 279).

For a story more like Fee's, try Julia Green's *Blue Moon* (UTBG 47) and the sequel *Baby Blue*.

Or if Jay was the one you found most interesting, try Valerie Mendes' *Lost and Found* (UTBG 225).

For several stories cleverly intertwined, try David Belbin's *Festival* (UTBG 127).

# WAYLANDER
## David Gemmell

The Drenai king is dead – murdered by a ruthless assassin. Enemy troops invade the Drenai lands. Their orders are simple – kill every man, woman and child. Stalked by beast-like men, the great warrior Waylander has to journey alone to the shadow-haunted lands of the Nadir to find the legendary Armour of Bronze to save the kingdom. But can he be trusted? For he is Waylander the Slayer: the traitor who killed the king.

David Gemmell is a British writer who has been writing great sword-and-sorcery fantasy novels for over 20 years, and now has a huge adult and teenage readership. If you like your heroes tough, with frequent explosive action, with war or the threat of it always in the air, then Gemmell's for you.

**Cliff McNish**

### Next?

If you enjoyed *Waylander*, why not try another of Gemmell's **Drenai** novels, such as the equally excellent *Winter Warriors*.

How about some dragons with your sword-and-sorcery? Try Anne McCaffrey's **Dragonriders of Pern** series (UTBG 111), starting with *Dragonflight*.

Or for a doorstop read that will keep you enthralled, *Magician* by Raymond E. Feist.

## The Ultimate Teen Readers' Poll

## BOOK THAT CHANGED YOUR LIFE

1 **Harry Potter series**

2 **A Child Called 'It'**

3 **The Bible**

4 **The Lord of the Rings trilogy**

5 **The Story of Tracy Beaker**

6 **The Diary of A Young Girl**

7 **His Dark Materials trilogy**

8 **Noughts and Crosses**

9 **A Series of Unfortunate Events**

10 **Holes**

# WAYWALKERS  Catherine Webb

**14+**

Catherine Webb was only 16 when she wrote this novel, but it doesn't feel as if it was written by a novice.

The hero, Sam, is a son of Time who harbours an unsuspected alter ego. He leads us through time from World War I horror scenes to the present day, where Scandinavian gods are threatening to unleash Hell. Embarked on a hunt for the keys to stop Armageddon, Sam begins to discover the full extent of his powers…

The narrative moves fast, incorporating enough red herrings to engage the brain – though too many complications and characters if you like your adventures simple. The style is colourful and often funny. The battles, which crop up on a regular basis, are well done. And the climax whets your appetite, supplying just enough to satisfy but leaving you hungry for more – which is where the sequel, *Time Keepers*, comes in…

**Geraldine McCaughrean**

> **Next?**
>
> Catherine Webb writes about the power of dreams in *Mirror Dreams*.
>
> S.E. Hinton also started writing very early indeed – *The Outsiders* (UTBG 280), is another astonishing debut.
>
> More Norse myth? Try Catherine Fisher's *The Snow Walker's Son*.
>
> Christopher Paolini began writing *Eragon* (UTBG 116) when he was 15!

# WE CAN REMEMBER IT FOR YOU WHOLESALE  Philip K. Dick

**16+**

> **Next?**
>
> Books that'll bend your imagination abound from the pen of Philip K. Dick. Try *Do Androids Dream of Electric Sheep?* (UTBG 107) or *The Man in the High Castle* (UTBG 235).
>
> Or what about *Neuromancer* by William Gibson, the book that spawned the whole cyber-punk genre?

A marvellous collection of sci-fi short stories with surreal titles like 'The Electric Ant', 'Your Appointment Will be Yesterday' and 'Cadbury, the Beaver Who Lacked'. The title story was made into the film *Total Recall*. Apart from other films directly based on his stories (*Blade Runner*, *Minority Report* etc) you will see Philip K. Dick's influence in films such as *The Matrix*, *Twelve Monkeys* and *Eternal Sunshine of the Spotless Mind*.

Dick loved to toy with concepts like time travel, memory and identity. For example: a Gulliver-like time traveller finds people are tiny in the past and huge in the future. Why? Because the universe is expanding. Simple, but brilliant.

**Caroline Lawrence**

# WEAVEWORLD  Clive Barker

16+

When one of his father's racing pigeons escapes, Cal chases it to a strange gathering of birds over what looks to be an old carpet thrown out in a back yard. This carpet belongs to Suzanna, who has just inherited it from her grandmother. But in this story of magic and nightmares, nothing is quite what it seems. For the carpet contains another world – Weaveworld – inhabited by people with terrifying powers, who call us 'Cuckoos'.

Stalked by a sinister salesman called Shadwell and Weaveworld refugee Immocolata, Cal and Suzanna are sucked into terrifying adventures a million miles away from Harry Potter and his tame wizard school. This book weaves fantasy with horror into a story that amazed me when I first read it and has continued to delight me ever since.

**Katherine Roberts**

### Next?

You might like Clive Barker's other stories, such as *Imajica*. Or, for an easier read, look for his beautifully illustrated **Abarat** quartet (UTBG 10).

Or for more horror, try James Herbert's *The Rats* – and never look at journeys underground the same way again…

In Ray Bradbury's *The Illustrated Man*, a fairground worker's tattoos come alive and tell their stories.

# WEETZIE BAT

16+

## Francesca Lia Block

### Next?

The rest of the series: *Witch Baby*, *Cherokee Bat and the Goat Guys*, *Missing Angel Juan* and *Baby Be-Bop*. They're all about love, happiness and the struggle to be true to both, and yourself.

Something else fantastical? Try Gabriel García Márquez's *Love in the Time of Cholera* (UTBG 227).

Or for something else about the weirdness that is LA, try Clive Barker's *Coldheart Canyon*.

Weetzie is freaky; she's way too cool for school and hates the kids who walk around blind to the beauty and wonder of Los Angeles. Then she meets Dirk, who's her soulmate, except… he's gay. But what does that matter? Though Dirk needs someone, so they find Duck. And then Weetzie needs someone, too. And all the while there's Slinkster Dog, and the city, and the whole wild brilliance of being alive, really alive.

There are some books you love so passionately that you never want them to end – for me *Weetzie Bat* is one of those. It's not a long book, or written in an arty, fancy sort of way. But it tells the story of Weetzie so beautifully that it makes you feel as if you're dreaming, not reading.

**Leonie Flynn**

# THE WEIRDSTONE OF BRISINGAMEN

## Alan Garner

**Next?**

If you like stories that make your spine tingle, try *The Owl Service* (UTBG 281) by Alan Garner.

And Kate Thompson's *The New Policeman* in which time, music and the world of fairy all blend in an exciting adventure.

Or **The Dark Is Rising** series (UTBG 93) – five books that bring together Arthurian legend and a magnificent battle between good and evil.

Deep underground, a wizard watches over 140 magical knights. But the stone that binds them – the Weirdstone of Brisingamen, 'Firefrost' by name – is lost. Two seemingly ordinary children, Colin and Susan, are the key to finding it again. But they know nothing about their destiny until they are chased across Alderley Edge by dark creatures seeking to pursue and destroy them. The wizard rescues Colin and Susan from the dark creatures, and the fight between good and evil is on!

Long before we first heard of Harry Potter, this story was gripping its readers. It's wonderfully eerie, with great characters.

**Yvonne Coppard**

# WENDY  Karen Wallace

14+

The heroine of this atmospheric novel set in Edwardian times is not just any Wendy, but *the* Wendy – Wendy Darling of J.M. Barrie's *Peter Pan*. The events in the novel happen before the story of *Peter Pan* takes place. We find out all about the Darling family, their neighbours (the awful Cunninghams), life upstairs in the nursery, and life at Rosegrove, where the Darlings spend their summers.

All is not well with Mr and Mrs Darling. Wendy becomes increasingly aware that there are hidden tensions and secrets, and resolves to find out the truth. With a wonderful cast of characters, authentic historical detail and a brilliantly clever twist at the end, *Wendy* is a novel you won't forget.

**Sherry Ashworth**

**Next?**

Karen Wallace has written three other excellent novels: *Raspberries on the Yangtze* (UTBG 304), *Climbing a Monkey Puzzle Tree* and *The Unrivalled Spangles*.

If you're interested in the Edwardian background in *Wendy*, try L.P. Hartley's novel, *The Go-Between* (UTBG 150), though it's quite a challenging read.

Or you could always go away and reread *Peter Pan* by J.M. Barrie; you may find the orginal is darker than you remember.

# THE WERELING  Stephen Cole

**14+**

So you think werewolves are merely creatures of legend? You're sure? Well, Tom is pretty certain too. Until he goes for a walk in the woods and ends up rescued from a near-drowning by the strangest family. For is it really a rescue? Amid secrets and lies, Tom tries to work out what's happening – why his senses are suddenly so acute, why the family want him and why their daughter, Kate, seems so unhappy.

Paced like an episode of *Buffy the Vampire Slayer*, dripping in gore and with characters you really feel for, this book is unnervingly realistic. Together Tom and Kate go on the run, and you'll be urging them on every step of the way, wanting them to be safe. Thank goodness there are sequels!

**Leonie Flynn**

> **Next?**
>
> The sequels are *Wereling II: Prey* and *Wereling III: Resurrection*. Be warned, the series gets scarier and more violent as it goes on.
>
> For something else scary (and even more bloodthirsty), try *Lord Loss* (UTBG 223).
>
> For something else that makes the weird totally real, try *The Night World* (UTBG 259), or *Tithe* by Holly Black.

# WHAT THE BIRDS SEE

**14+**

## Sonya Hartnett

> **Next?**
>
> Another novel by Sonya Hartnett is *Thursday's Child* (UTBG 373), about a family surviving during the Depression of the 1930s.
>
> There are many fine books around by Australian writers. Look for *Wolf on the Fold* by Judith Clarke, about different generations of one family; and *Jinx* by Margaret Wild, a novel told entirely in short poems.
>
> Or try the historical *Pagan's Crusade* (UTBG 283).

Stories about children are not necessarily *for* children. Nine-year-old Adrian, taken from his unstable mother, abandoned by his father, is raised by his gran, who looks after him but never troubles to conceal the fact that she finds him a burden; her own adult children are enough of a headache. But she would be very sorry if something happened to him, especially as the neighbourhood, a quiet Australian suburb, is haunted by the fate of three young children who went missing and were never found. This beautifully written, desperately sad story about a lost child and the unhappy adults who fail him, is also haunted – by a sense of unspoken horror that becomes only too real at the end.

**Jan Mark**

# WHEELS Catherine MacPhail

**12+**

## Next?

Other Catherine MacPhail books are: *Underworld* (UTBG 389), *Roxy's Baby* (UTBG 314), set in a refuge for young pregnant girls, and *Another Me* – a spooky thriller about a girl coming face to face with her double.

*Unique* (UTBG 390) by Alison Allen-Gray is another thrilling thriller, this time about cloning, but packed full of chases, danger and near misses.

*Saffy's Angel* (UTBG 317) by Hilary McKay and *Paralysed* by Sherry Ashworth also look at life in wheels of steel.

How would you feel if your dad was killed in a car accident one night and that same accident left you faced with spending the rest of your life in a wheelchair?

That's exactly what happens to James. But when he is still in hospital recovering, something weird happens. He's sure he sees the other man who was supposedly killed, the man who was driving the car... So how come he's still alive?

MacPhail keeps us in suspense, with a surprise on every page. *Wheels* forces us to think again about how the disabled are treated in society. It shows wheels aren't everything and friendship and determination are stronger than metal. An edge-of-the-seat thriller, which really hooks you from the start.

**David Gardner (aged 16)**

# WHEN ISLA MEETS LUKE MEETS ISLA
## Rhian Tracey

**14+**

Isla meets Luke – girl meets boy (and vice versa). Just like any old fairy tale. But you'll soon see, this is no fairy tale.

There aren't many love / relationship stories I'd recommend equally readily to readers of both sexes, but *When Isla Meets Luke...* is one of them. The fact that the chapters alternate between the two characters' points of view certainly helps; but what really makes it special is a strong and believable story that's sometimes touching but never soppy, and its two altogether lifelike lead characters.

You'll get attached to both Isla and Luke – you'll get frustrated by them, as with real people, but they'll make you laugh, too. You may well find yourself hoping that Rhian Tracey will take the easy road and let them have a fairy-tale ending. Wouldn't that be nice? But Tracey is a far better writer than that.

**Daniel Hahn**

## Next?

The sequel: *Isla and Luke: Make or Break*.

Rhian Tracey has also written *The Bad Girls' Club*, another lively story with multiple narrators.

Other books with multiple narrators are *Lost and Found* (UTBG 225) and *Waving, Not Drowning* (UTBG 402).

# WHEN THE GUNS FALL SILENT

## James Riordan

### Next?

James Riordan writes brilliantly about war. Try *Match of Death*, in which a young team literally have to play for their lives, or *The Prisoner*, where two kids find a wounded German pilot and then have to decide what to do with him.

For one of the best war books of recent years, try the stunning *Private Peaceful* (UTBG 300). It looks a simple read but try it and see what you think.

Rats nesting in corpses, the firing squad for deserters, filth, noise – and the constant danger of death. Welcome to the Western Front in 1914.

Jack lies about his age to enlist – after all, why waste time when everyone says the war'll be over by Christmas? He doesn't want to miss any of the fun. But Jack learns that war isn't anything like he imagines, and instead of fun it's just about as awful as anything can possibly be.

There's no real way for us to know what it was like to be human canon-fodder, but this book has a good try. Sparsely told, with letters and diary entries alongside the narrative, it simply tells the story of one boy's war, complete with terror, love, friendship and loss. Oh, and football, too.

**Leonie Flynn**

# WHEN THE WIND BLOWS Raymond Briggs

James arrives home, his wife greets him. 'Hullo, dear.' 'Hullo, love.' 'Did you have a nice morning, dear?' Peaceful, domestic, altogether unthrilling; gentle, no urgency, no alarm. But soon we see that this tranquillity and this routine are about to be broken. It is 1982, the height of the Cold War, and the Russians are about to drop The Bomb. James and Hilda remember the Second World War; but the Third will be the ultimate; it'll mean complete devastation, thanks to the madness of Mutually Assured Destruction, absolutely *everyone* will die.

And in this stunning graphic novel Briggs doesn't pretend otherwise; there's no last-minute salvation (An antidote! In the nick of time!). Though his story is simple and witty, you should prepare to have your heart broken. And this half-hour read will stay with you forever – I don't know anything like it.

**Daniel Hahn**

### Next?

For another graphic novel dealing with grim themes, move on to *Maus* (UTBG 239) – genius.

*Z for Zachariah* (UTBG 426) is a powerful (and unsettling) story set in a post-nuclear holocaust.

More Raymond Briggs? Try the wonderful (and wonderfully disgusting) *Fungus the Bogeyman*! Meanwhile *Ethel and Ernest* (UTBG 118) also has a gentleness underpinning a strong and moving story...

# WHIP HAND  Dick Francis

**Next?**

The first Sid Halley story is *Odds Against* – it tells how he lost his hand.

John Francome, another ex-jockey, also writes thrillers: start with *Dead Ringer* or *High Flyer*.

Or try Robert Harris; *Fatherland* (UTBG 126) supposes Germany won the war and *Enigma* is about code breaking during World War II.

This thriller is set in and around the world of horse racing.

Sid Halley was champion steeplechase jockey until a fall, and then a sadistic crook, robbed him of half his left arm. Surgeons have fitted him with an electrically operated plastic hand which is rather clumsy. As a consequence he has had to renounce the thrill of riding and has become a private investigator, specialising in the racing world. With his friend Chico, a cheery young judo teacher, Sid is enquiring into a series of mysterious events, principally the poor performance and death of several promising young racehorses. This brings him to the attention of some very nasty criminals. Sid values his courage above all things, and it's sorely tested when a villain threatens to blow off his remaining hand with a shotgun…

**Alan Temperley**

# THE WHISPERING ROAD  Livi Michael

'There's always been Annie', says Joe; but many times he is tempted to abandon her and, for a desperate period, he does give in to that temptation. She is his little sister and they are on the run together from the cruel masters that they have been farmed out to by the workhouse. Their bid for freedom takes them to dangerous places, and they have to live on their wits to survive.

It is a picaresque journey in which one extraordinary situation follows another and characters as strange as the people of dreams or nightmares weave in and out of their lives. The incidents that the children are involved in are as wild and fascinating as the stories Joe tells, and as the visions his sister has.

This is a great, pacy adventure story that works on many levels; it's both a disturbing and a heartwarming read.

**Berlie Doherty**

**Next?**

No one wrote better historical adventure series than Joan Aiken. Read *Go Saddle the Sea*.

*The Cup of the World* (UTBG 88) is an epic adventure set in a fantasy Middle Ages.

Or Frances Hardinge's *Fly by Night* about a girl, a goose and a fabulously reimagined 18th-century England.

# WHITE TEETH   Zadie Smith

16+

*White Teeth* is about two unlikely friends, Archibald Jones and Samad Iqbal, who meet in a tank during World War II. The novel then fast-forwards to 1970s London, where the friends meet again. They both get married, Archie to Clara – the daughter of a Jamaican Jehovah's Witness, and Samad to Alsana. Both men have children and the story twists and winds though seminal years in their lives. Their friendship grows and strengthens as they struggle to adapt to a world neither of them belongs to. This may sound sad, but it isn't. The book is hilarious and tackles the issues of multiculturalism and religion in a touching way. Zadie Smith has produced a novel that is always funny and poignant, but at the same time wise. I loved it and so will you!

**Ileana Antonopoulou**

### Next?

*Brick Lane* By Monica Ali tells a multicultural story of London, too.

More Zadie Smith? Try *The Autograph Man* or *On Beauty*.

*The Buddha of Suburbia* (UTBG 59) is a fabulous book about London, being Asian and sex (of all sorts!).

# WHO IS JESSE FLOOD?
## Malachy Doyle

12+

### Next?

If you enjoyed *Jesse Flood* you might also like to try *Feather Boy* (UTBG 126) by Nicky Singer and *Snow Spider* by Jenny Nimmo, both of which feature boys who feel different and who struggle to find their identity. All three books look at how teenage boys are affected by family events such as divorce or bereavement.

*Fat Boy Swim* (UTBG 125) by Catherine Forde is about a boy who finds a most original way of making a difficult life bearable.

Or Linda Newbery's atmospheric *Lost Boy* about a boy, bubbles, friendship and a secret from the past.

Jesse Flood is different from other kids – he's hopeless at school, sports and talking to girls (though he's a whizz at ping-pong). Jesse lives in his head to shut out the world, and his diary reveals his thoughts on life and love, as well as his embarrassing failures with girls. He describes teenage life in a small town like being in a long tunnel, waiting for the light to shine through. Malachy Doyle shows great sympathy for the pain of being a teenager and the boredom of small-town life, and creates a distinctive character in Jesse Flood.

**Anne Flaherty**

# WHY WEEPS THE BROGAN? Hugh Scott

12+

There are some books that you just can't say a lot about, for fear of spoiling the plot. *Why Weeps the Brogan?* is just such a book. Gilbert and Saxon are brother and sister and they live in a museum. Daily life is a battle against the poisonous spiders that have started to infest the building and there's a monster on the upper levels that they have to feed. And that's about all I can tell you.

This is a novel where everything hinges upon what is revealed in the final page (don't read it first!) and when you've reached that final page you will want to turn around and start at the beginning all over again.

Very clever and totally unforgettable.

**Laura Hutchings**

### Next?

It's a little difficult to suggest reads-ons for this book without giving too much away! *Z for Zachariah* (UTBG 426) by Robert O'Brien, *Brother in the Land* by Robert Swindells and *Children of the Dust* (UTBG 71) by Louise Lawrence have similar survival themes.

You might also enjoy the science-fiction novels of John Wyndham. *The Day of the Triffids* (UTBG 96) is the place to start with these.

# WICCA: BOOK OF SHADOWS

14+

## Cate Tiernan

### Next?

Try some of the tie-in novels to the TV series *Buffy the Vampire Slayer* for more supernatural drama.

Holly Black's *Tithe* is a powerful drama with more magic and supernatural excitement.

*Witch Child* (UTBG 415) is a historical story featuring a teenager accused of being a witch.

*The Merrybegot* (UTBG 242) delves into a period of history when it was unsafe to be different.

This is the first in a long teen series that is both addictive and very spooky. 16-year-old Morgan is smitten when Cal Blaire, who is a real hottie, transfers to her school and throws a party in a huge field to which everybody goes. Around the campfire, he asks them to join him in a Wiccan thanksgiving ritual. Reactions range from curiosity to fear. Most leave but others, including Morgan and best friend Bree, stay. Some are curious about Wicca. Some are attracted to others present and want to stay near them. And some, like Morgan, have more complex motivations. She's an orphan and curious about her origins, and it turns out Wicca might hold all the answers.

**John McLay**

# THE WIDE SARGASSO SEA  Jean Rhys

The Sargasso Sea, mysterious and sluggish, swirls between Europe and the West Indies, its waters choked with seaweed, its floor strewn with shipwrecks. This image of the sea mirrors the confused and dangerous relationships between Britain and the West Indies during the 19th century. Edward Rochester marries Antoinette Cosway, a Creole (white West Indian) for her money, only to find she has none. Once in England Antoinette finds herself renamed Bertha and locked away in a secret annexe. Mad with grief, Bertha burns the house to the ground. This is *Jane Eyre* from the point of view of the Creole woman, sidelined and despised in the original book: the 'madwoman in the attic' has been given a voice at last.

**Gill Vickery**

### Next?

*The Awakening* by Kate Chopin is another account of a woman desperate to escape from the stifling life that's imposed on her.

*The Yellow Wallpaper* (UTBG 425) by Charlotte Perkins Gilman is a brilliant, absolutely terrifying, 'madwoman in the attic' story.

You may also enjoy Andrea Levy's *Small Island*, a modern novel about the Windrush generation arriving in Britain from the West Indies.

Or try Jean Rhys' short stories: *Tigers are Better Looking*.

# A WILD SHEEP CHASE  Haruki Murakami

### Next?

The **Sherlock Holmes** stories (UTBG 336) for more mysteries within mysteries.

Another Murakami? Read *Norwegian Wood*, a novel in two volumes, one red, one green, which became a national obsession in Japan; or the wonderfully surreal *The Wind-up Bird Chronicle*.

Or how about surrealism without the humour? Try Kafka's dark and disturbing *The Trial*.

Murakami is one of those authors you just have to trust. In his books the strange runs parallel with the mundane. Sometimes the two blur, until it's hard to tell the difference. His books read like dreams, and this one is no exception. The hero is quiet, ordinary, but his life, with its endless circular journeys, its despair, is changed when he's hired by Mr Big to find the sheep that changed *his* life. Yes, the title is almost literal! On his quest he meets a girl with the most beautiful ears in the world, talks with the dead, meets a Sheep Man and reads *Sherlock Holmes*. Surreal, darkly comic, utterly engrossing, this is a wonderfully written book that just might change *your* life.

**Leonie Flynn**

# WILD SWANS  Jung Chang

A mind opening and mind-blowing account of three generations of Chinese women living in Maoist China. From the painful practice of binding women's feet so that they could only take dainty steps, to the struggles of the Long March, it is the fascinating and often shocking details that make this true story so gripping. It reads like a novel, and you have to keep reminding yourself that it's not.

The way the Communist authorities imposed control and turned friend against friend and relative against relative is vividly brought to life – but what shines through most of all is the sheer power of individual human will and determination. It's an inspirational book.

**Nicola Morgan**

## Next?

For another true and moving story about the Chinese way of life, try Adeline Yen Mah's *Falling Leaves*.

Jung Chang has followed this up with a biography of the larger-than-life Chinese leader, *Mao: the Unknown Story* (written with her husband Jon Halliday).

Or if you want to read another story of surviving traumatic early years, try *A Child Called 'It'* (UTBG 70) by Dave Pelzer.

# THE WIND ON FIRE trilogy
## William Nicholson

## Next?

William Nicholson wrote the screenplay to the film *Gladiator* and you may notice some similarities to the Manaxas in *Slaves of the Mastery*. His new series begins with *Seeker* (UTBG 327).

Pullman's **His Dark Materials** trilogy (UTBG 170) is also loved by fantasy fans and fantasy haters alike.

This is a fantasy trilogy as full of human truth as it is of adventure, and you may well love it even if fantasy's not usually your thing.

In *The Wind Singer*, the Hath family live in the city of Aramanth, where the whole of life is controlled by exams. Even two-year-olds have to play their part, taking tests that will help decide on their family's future. When Kestrel Hath dares to rebel against the system, she starts off a chain of events that launches her on an epic journey with her twin brother Bowman and their friend Mumpo, their aim to bring love and kindness back into the city.

*Slaves of the Mastery* and *Firesong* are set five years later: the peace of Aramanth is shattered when the entire population is taken as slaves by warrior invaders. The Hath family emerge as true leaders as they struggle to set their people free and to lead them to their homeland.

**Susan Reuben**

# THE WISH HOUSE   Celia Rees

## Next?

Celia Rees is a prolific writer, with many titles in print ranging from *Witch Child* (below), to thrillers set in the present day such as *Truth or Dare* (UTBG 384) and *The Bailey Game*.

Linda Newbery's *Set in Stone* (UTBG 331) also features a striking country house and an impressionable young man who falls under its spell, though with a late-Victorian setting.

Readers who know Celia Rees through her best-selling *Witch Child* or *Sorceress* are likely to be surprised by this more recent coming-of-age novel, set in the 1970s.

On holiday in South Wales with his exceedingly dull parents, Richard is captivated by The Wish House and its unconventional inhabitants, in particular Clio, the beautiful, troubled girl who befriends him, and with whom he has his first sexual experience. Her father, the egotistical artist Jethro Dalton, exerts an autocratic rule over the household; as secrets emerge, Richard realises how thoroughly he has been manipulated.

An enticing feature of this novel is the art-show catalogue preface to each chapter, which Celia Rees has written so skilfully that the reader almost sees the exhibits.

**Linda Newbery**

# WITCH CHILD   Celia Rees

Forget boring historical novels about long-dead people; *Witch Child* is so 'now' and so vivid that you sometimes forget that the heroine Mary lived in the 17th century. Celia Rees is one of those writers with the magical gift of drawing the reader into a relationship with her characters by the end of page one, with the result that homework goes undone, sleep is set aside and a vast amount of chocolate is munched until the adventure comes to an end. Except that in *Witch Child*, it doesn't. So gripping is the writing and so believable the plot that when you reach the final page – and no, I'm not going to tell you just how cleverly executed it is – you simply have to rush out and buy the sequel, *Sorceress*.

## Next?

*Pirates!* (UTBG 289) is another Celia Rees book set in the past, this time a swashbuckling romance.

Or for another book about outsiders, try *Chocolat* (UTBG 74) by Joanne Harris.

*The Merrybegot* (UTBG 242) by Julie Hearn is a story of superstition and witchcraft.

This is a book for readers who want believable characters, loads of emotion and a vivid insight into how prejudice and bullying have affected lives for centuries. Without doubt, an unforgettable read.

**Rosie Rushton**

# A WIZARD OF EARTHSEA
## Ursula Le Guin

Long before Harry Potter went to Hogwarts, on a faraway island an unloved boy called Ged discovered he could do magic. This is a story about how frightening magic can be, the danger and the responsibility of it. Ged's talent leads him into wonderful adventures, on marvellous islands, and you won't be able to put the book down till you finish it. And when you do finish it, you will know something important about yourself. You may not be a Harry Potter, but you are certainly a Ged. The world you live in has a deep balance, and the best magicians learn to use magic only in the greatest emergency…
**Jill Paton Walsh**

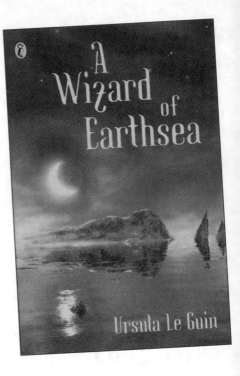

### Next?

If you love *A Wizard of Earthsea*, there's good news for you – there are sequels: *The Tombs of Atuan*, *The Farthest Shore*, *Tehanu* and *The Other Wind*.

There is also a collection of stories in *Tales from Earthsea*.

And when you've finished those you can read Le Guin's adult sci-fi. Start with *The Left Hand of Darkness* (UTBG 217). This is an author you never grow out of – you grow into her!

Frank Herbert's *Dune* (UTBG 112) and its sequels mixes science fiction and fantasy in an epic that chronicles the adventures of a young man who fulfils an ancient prophecy about his birth.

Ursula Le Guin's books sink their claws into you and don't let go. Written in simple yet powerful prose, they deal with classic themes of Good and Evil, and what it means to grow up. Her world of Earthsea is one of the great creations in fantasy: a place of many peoples, with a wild surging ocean, dragons, ancient magic and wizards both wise and foolish. This book, the first in her **Earthsea Quartet**, taught me the power of words. To me, *A Wizard of Earthsea* feels like a myth or legend, a half-remembered song. If you are looking for a grand saga, I cannot recommend it highly enough.
**Christopher Paolini**

# WOLF BROTHER  Michelle Paver

*Wolf Brother* brilliantly recreates the world of 6,000 years ago and follows a young boy, Torak, as he learns to survive in a vast and dangerous forest following the violent death of his father. There are raging rivers, hostile tribes, fever, starvation and, most frightening of all, a demon that has taken the shape of a giant bear.

Michelle Paver certainly knows her stuff – and she doesn't pull any punches. Torak is totally convincing as a primitive hero. When he kills a roe buck and cuts it up to use every bit of it either as food, clothes or weapons (he turns the stomach into a waterskin) you begin to see just how difficult it's going to be for him to survive. Paver is also a great storyteller. Just about every chapter ends on a cliffhanger, although personally I could have done without the slightly old-fashioned illustrations.
**Anthony Horowitz**

### Next?

More Michelle Paver? There will be five books in the **Chronicles of Ancient Darkness**. *Spirit Walker* is next

Jenny Nimmo's **Red King** quintet, starting with *Midnight for Charlie Bone*, is a magical thriller.

The past and our animal origins are explored in *Fish Notes and Star Songs* by Dianne Hofmeyr.

# THE WOLVES IN THE WALLS
## Neil Gaiman (illustrated by Dave McKean)

### Next?

How about John Masefield's *The Box Of Delights*, a surreal Christmas classic?

Or for slightly friendlier lupine fun, read *Wolf Brother* (UTBG 417) by Michelle Paver.

Or Neil Gaiman and Dave McKean's other collaboration, the rather less scary but no less brilliant *The Day I Swapped My Dad for Two Goldfish*. Good title, too.

Lucy knows there are wolves in the walls of her house, but nobody believes her. She can hear them creeping around, scratching and whispering, hatching their wolfish schemes. And if the wolves come out of the walls, it's all over...

Although this is intended for young children (and only recommended if you never want them to sleep again), Gaiman and McKean prove that you're never too old for a picture book. McKean's combination of traditional painting and photography lends the book an eerie feel, and Gaiman's story is deeply unsettling. Beautifully illustrated, extremely sinister and all-round good fun, it feels like reading a modern-age fairy tale. Buy this and relive every night-time terror you've ever had.
**Chris Wooding**

# SHORT AND GRIPPING BOOKS

## by Pete Johnson

Sometimes you want to read a story that doesn't hang about. You'd like to find a tale that grips you from the very first line, with strong characters and lively, realistic dialogue.

And you don't fancy a very long book, either. For life becomes extremely busy, especially in your teens. And by the time you've read all that boring stuff for school there's only a tiny bit of time – say 20 minutes before you go to sleep – to read anything for pleasure.

Well, 20 minutes is all you need to savour a short story by Paul Jennings, who's brilliant at grabbing your attention with a fantastic situation that's written in a totally believable way.

Diaries can also be great to dip into last thing at night. And if you want to fall asleep laughing, then I would strongly recommend Sue Townsend's *The Secret Diary of Adrian Mole Aged 13 ¾* (UTBG 324) (and the numerous sequels). And if you're looking for a 'fabbity fab' diary with a teenage girl at the centre, then check out *Angus, Thongs and Full-frontal Snogging* (UTBG 22) by Louise Rennison.

If you prefer a novel, how about something by Robert Swindells or Morris Gleitzman? Their books often have brief chapters with page endings, which make them impossible to put down.

And if you would like to read a shorter novel (say about 8,000 words) there's a publisher who specialises in books like that: Barrington Stoke. They even have teenagers acting as editors on their books, highlighting any words or phrases which tripped them up, or scenes which slowed the pace down too much. (Check out their website – www.barringtonstoke.co.uk – if you'd be interested in helping out!)

There's certainly not a wasted moment in *The Cold Heart of Summer* by Alan Gibbons, a heart-pounding horror tale about sightings of a girl killed 50 years ago; or Theresa Breslin's richly atmospheric *Prisoner of Alcatraz*; or Kevin Brooks' roller-coaster read *Bloodline*. Another book that sweeps

### Some easier Barrington Stoke books to try:

*Bicycle Blues* by Anthony Masters. Jamie has just got a new bike for his birthday, and someone has nicked it! Jamie is determined to find out who has taken it, but the only person helping him is Greg Dawson, and Jamie doesn't trust him.

*Sticks and Stones* by Catherine MacPhail. Greg thinks he's hilarious. He's great at making up nicknames for people, and doesn't understand why they don't find it funny too. So he's really surprised when he's accused of something he didn't do, and realises he's been set up. Surely he doesn't have any enemies? Does he?

*To Be a Millionaire* by Yvonne Coppard. Josh would do anything for fame and fortune (and to get a gorgeous girlfriend, of course). And now he thinks he's come up with a brilliant plan to get just what he wants. But it's not that simple…

# Text Game
## KATE CANN

you along is *Text Game* by Kate Cann, a love story which turns into a thriller when vicious text messages start being sent.

I've written three books for Barrington Stoke myself: *Runaway Teacher* about an over-friendly teacher; *The Best Holiday Ever* about that first holiday without parents; and *Diary of an (Un)teenager*, which is undoubtedly the most personal of the three. It concerns Spencer, who is about to hit 13 and absolutely dreading it, especially all the fuss about becoming a teenager. I've had so many letters from readers saying they felt exactly the same – but thought they were the only one.

That's another great thing about stories: they help us realise we're not on our own. So it's worth finding the time – even if it's just a few minutes at night – to read. And if you want to speed off into a pacy tale... well, now you can.

But don't just take my word for it. Check out any of the books I've mentioned. Just read the first two sentences and you'll be totally hooked...

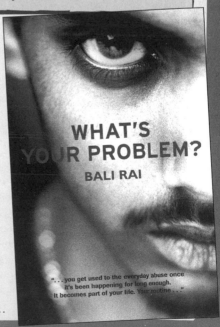

**WHAT'S YOUR PROBLEM?**
**BALI RAI**

"... you get used to the everyday abuse once it's been happening for long enough. It becomes part of your life. Your routine ..."

# THE WOMAN IN BLACK

14+

## Susan Hill

### Next?

Not as well known as *The Woman in Black*, *The Mist in the Mirror* is another atmospheric ghost story by Susan Hill.

The classic ghost stories of M.R. James (UTBG 144) haven't dated in their power to scare.

For a contemporary teenage ghost story, try *Yaxley's Cat* by Robert Westall.

There was a point in this chilling ghost story when I actually felt afraid to turn the page, so powerfully and convincingly does the author evoke the haunted atmosphere of Eel Marsh House and the bleak marshland in which it stands. This is where Arthur Kipps, a young solicitor, comes to sort out the papers left by the late Mrs Drablow. Arthur himself narrates the story – at first confident, carefree, slightly arrogant, then gradually more and more fearful. His changing voice gives the story its terrifying immediacy so that you shudder with him. And just when you think it's all over…

Compulsive and truly frightening, this is in the tradition of the very best ghost stories.
**Patricia Elliott**

# THE WOMAN IN WHITE

14+

## Wilkie Collins

You must read *The Woman in White* when you're a teenager – you'll love it, forever.

This is a Gothic story of love through richer and poorer, and there is nothing conditional about Walter Hartright's feelings for Laura Fairlie. It has an ethereal quality, a ghostliness and a sense of place that is both eerie and satisfying and gives a rich and fascinating insight into how different and difficult mid-Victorian life could be for girls. The strangeness, the madness, the ghostliness resonated for me long after I finished this book, and sent me on a journey through many other Wilkie Collins novels.
**Raffaella Barker**

### Next?

More Wilkie Collins? My favourites to go on to are *The Moonstone* (UTBG 250) (another thriller) and *No Name*.

Another great Gothic romance: *The Mysteries of Udolpho* or the parody of such things, Jane Austen's *Northanger Abbey* (UTBG 262).

Or try *The Warden* by Anthony Trollope, the first of the **Chronicles of Barsetshire**, which tell the complex stories of a cathedral town.

# THE WONDERFUL STORY OF HENRY SUGAR Roald Dahl

**12+**

**Next?**

**The Sandman** series (UTBG 320) by Neil Gaiman has a similar mixture of myth and reality.

*I Am the Cheese* (UTBG 182) tells the strange story of Adam, who is being interrogated by a psychiatrist with an ulterior motive.

*Breaktime* (UTBG 55) explores similar themes – crime, friendship, first love – and it has teasing multiple layers.

Roald Dahl isn't just the author of wickedly funny, brilliantly imagined children's books. He also wrote these surreal and disturbing stories, creating a host of different worlds, each one compelling, moving and terrifying. There's a modern-day Peter Pan, who travels the seas on the back of a giant turtle; there's a bullied boy who has a swan's wings strapped to his arms. In a third tale, the discovery of buried treasure corrupts everyone who touches it. The title story is the best of the lot, as Henry Sugar learns to stare into a flame, see through a blindfold and become a real magician. There's even the story of how Dahl himself became a writer. This is Roald Dahl as you've never read him before.

**Ariel Kahn**

# THE WORLD ACCORDING TO GARP
## John Irving

 **16+**

This is a great, big, wonderful book, and while the movie has a good stab at getting John Irving's extraordinary story up on screen (it has Robin Williams in one of his first non-comic roles), this is one you *have* to read. It'll make you laugh, possibly out loud, it'll make you sad and it will definitely stay with you long after you've put it down.

What's it about? It may sound like a big cop-out to say it's beyond description, but that's the truth, although I can tell you it has a lot to do with wrestling (with other people as well as with consciences), and that this man is one of the best writers ever. Really.

**Graham Marks**

**Next?**

More John Irving – *The Hotel New Hampshire*, *A Prayer for Owen Meany* (UTBG 293), *The Cider House Rules* – you can't go wrong.

For an odd, all-encompassing American novel with the most bizarre characters, read *Another Roadside Attraction* (UTBG 24).

Or how about a weird and sprawling mass of a novel set in a Scottish family – Iain Banks' *The Crow Road*?

# WORM IN THE BLOOD  Thomas Bloor

**12+**

### Next?

Jonathan Stroud's *Buried Fire* also has change at its crackling core but in a very different setting.

N.M. Browne's *Hunted* is about a girl who becomes a fox in an ancient world.

For spine-tingling horror, try Ann Halam's *Don't Open Your Eyes* and *The Fear Man*.

'Sam's skin has started to itch…' I've always been fascinated by the theme of metamorphosis. This is an exciting and ambitious contemporary urban horror story about transformation and the power of love, inspired by Chinese and Welsh mythology. Brief, tense episodes, like pieces of a jigsaw, finally form a picture in which past and present come together. There is a large cast of characters and enjoyable macabre humour in the scenes with the small, vulnerable Father David Lee and his formidable 'protector', Mrs Hare. Sam's transformation is convincingly described, and the atmospheric setting – the brackish canal and marshland beyond the city streets – is suitably nasty. Watch out for the sequel.

**Patricia Elliott**

# THE WORST JOURNEY IN THE WORLD

**14+**

## Apsley Cherry-Garrard

Killer whales, deadly blizzards, temperatures of minus 70 degrees – this is without a doubt the greatest adventure story ever written.

Author Cherry-Garrard was 24 when he was chosen by Scott to be part of the South Polar expedition, and this is his account of the two years that the men spent in Antarctica. The book is a mixture of personal reminiscences together with extracts from diaries and letters, and it covers far more than just Scott's doomed walk to the Pole.

The account is written by the one man who could have saved Scott, if only he'd known it – and I for one will be forever grateful that Cherry-Garrard had the courage to publish this account. Without it, men such as Captain Oates and Birdie Bowers would have remained nothing but names in a history book.

**Laura Hutchings**

### Next?

A fictional account of Scott's journey, Beryl Bainbridge's brilliant and deeply moving *The Birthday Boys*.

Or try Geraldine McCaughrean's *The White Darkness* about a girl obsessed with Captain Oates.

Once you've finished with things polar you may want to move on to the thrills of mountaineering literature. One of the best books about the perils of modern mountaineering has to be *Touching the Void* (UTBG 377).

# A WRINKLE IN TIME
## Madeleine L'Engle

Written in 1963, this award-winning book still manages to hover in the top 500 of Amazon.com – and though only slightly known in the UK, it has a fanatical American following.

It's the story of Meg Murry and her genius baby brother, children of two brilliant scientists, and their quest to rescue their father from a faraway planet overtaken by the dark shadow of evil. It's not really science fiction (phew!), though there are enough challenging scientific ideas about time travel to keep you on your toes. Instead, it's about the triumph of Meg's difficult, unruly, passionate personality where intellect alone has failed. And it's the perfect book for those of us with messy, stubborn characters, who don't always feel appreciated by the rest of the world.

**Meg Rosoff**

### Next?

This is part of the **Time** quartet; the others are: *A Swiftly Tilting Planet*, *A Wind in the Door* and *Many Waters*.

*From the Mixed-up Files of Mrs Basil E. Frankweiler* by E.L. Konigsburg has another great brother and sister relationship. This time, the siblings run away from their boring suburban life to live in the Metropolitan Museum in New York.

MADELEINE L'ENGLE
A Wrinkle in Time

Puffin | Modern | Classics

## THE DECADENT FRENCH

*Bonjour Tristesse*
by Françoise Sagan

*Gigi* by Colette

*Claudine at School* by Colette

*Le Grand Meaulnes*
by Alain-Fournier

*The Dud Avocado*
by Elaine Dundy

*Thérèse Raquin*
by Émile Zola

# THE WRONG BOY  Willy Russell

16+

Raymond Marks is a nice, normal boy from a normal, northern town, until the new headmaster at his primary school makes a scapegoat of him and Raymond becomes the Wrong Boy – a social outcast. Raymond soon discovers that being accused of one crime leads to being accused of another, and he becomes the unwitting prey of a chain of apparently well-meaning but self-seeking adults who are trying to 'help' him: Psycho The Rapist, a Lert, and the So Shall Worker. *The Wrong Boy* is both a heartrending tale of the effects of victimisation and a laugh-out-loud funny book of startling originality. It will both shock and delight you – and you won't be able to put it down.
**Sherry Ashworth**

> **Next?**
>
> Try *Strange Boy* (UTBG 358) by Paul Magrs, another funny-but-moving tale of an outsider.
>
> For a more adult read, the wonderful *The Catcher in the Rye* (UTBG 66) by J.D. Salinger, about a boy who flunks schools and drops out, spending three days alone in Manhattan.
>
> Willy Russell hasn't written any other novels, but you might like to try reading (or watching) his brilliant plays – *Educating Rita* and *Shirley Valentine* are the best-known.

# WUTHERING HEIGHTS
## Emily Brontë

14+

> **Next?**
>
> OK, fair cop: if you prefer better, mannered lovers and happier endings, then check out *Pride and Prejudice* (UTBG 294) by Jane Austen.
>
> Or if you like your love more cerebral, try *Strait is the Gate* (UTBG 357) by André Gide.
>
> If casual amorality is your thing, try 17-year-old Cécile's view of love in *Bonjour Tristesse* (UTBG 48) by Françoise Sagan.

Forget Mr Darcy – Heathcliff is the sexiest man in English literature. I first read this book when I was 13 and reread it pretty much every year for the next decade. It's a monumental love story carved of passion and brutality. In a dilemma that has resonated with women down the centuries, Cathy Earnshaw must choose between the 'good' and civilised man, Edgar Linton, and the 'bad' wild foundling of nature, Heathcliff. Linton's soul is as different from Heathcliff's as 'moonbeam from lightning, or frost from fire'. Cathy's final decision, and the revenge that follows, exact a terrible penalty on two generations of Earnshaws and Lintons.

A beautiful and savage book that makes you grateful to be alive.
**Nicky Singer**

# THE YELLOW WALLPAPER
## Charlotte Perkins Gilman

Written in the first person, this short story reads like a diary. The protagonist, a married woman with a young child, has just been relocated to the country. Her husband thinks she is tired and in need of a good long rest. Essentially he wants her to do nothing at all, and is even opposed to her writing in her diary. But she continues to write, and thus we have a story. Desperate for something to do, but not allowed to do anything, she begins to obsess about the wallpaper in her bedroom.

*The Yellow Wallpaper* was written in a time where women who were artistic, creative, or just a little different were often shunned by society. Their desire to be actively engaged was considered strange and unnatural, and they were often deemed insane; and sometimes they did, quite literally, lose their minds. This book was written in homage to these women.

**Candida Gray**

> **Next?**
>
> *The Awakening* by Kate Chopin was considered shocking when it was published.
>
> Virginia Woolf's *A Room of One's Own* (UTBG 312) set out her ideas about the role of women compared to that of men.
>
> *Daisy Miller* (UTBG 91) is the story of a young woman and her potential.

# YOU DON'T KNOW ME David Klass

14+

> **Next?**
>
> Philip Ridley's *Mighty Fizz Chilla* is another story about escaping reality. Sent away to live by the sea, Milo invents stories like no one else…
>
> The lead character in *Martyn Pig* (UTBG 236) accidentally kills his useless dad.
>
> For the strangest journey any teenager could take, dip into *Lady: My Life as a Bitch* by Melvin Burgess, in which a girl is transformed into a randy dog.
>
> Another David Klass? Try *The Braves*, about gangs, football and fitting in.

The voice of John, the narrator of this novel, is one of the best-ever achieved in fiction for teen readers. By turns incredibly funny, and then uncomfortably violent, the book tells the story of 14-year-old John and the images in his head, his life inside a life, as he tries to escape the crushing reality of his mother's abusive new boyfriend. At school he feels isolated, despite being liked by his teachers and peers. And John is a likeable character, ordinary in many ways, but his view on the absurdities of modern life make him very special indeed. In trying to make himself unknowable, he inadvertently reveals everything that he is. A powerful and moving novel.

**John McLay**

# Z FOR ZACHARIAH
## Robert C. O'Brien

14+

Every time I read this book I can't help but wonder what the author would make of its ending! Robert C. O'Brien died before he could finish the story and so his wife and daughter completed it, working from his notes.

16-year-old Ann Burden is trying to survive after a nuclear war. She lives alone but safe in a remote valley that has escaped the fallout. Then Loomis, a government scientist, arrives.

The sheer unfairness of what happens next will have you gnashing your teeth, but ultimately what stays with you is the ending. Long after you've finished the book you will find yourself wondering about Ann and her final decision. Intrigued? Read the book!

**Laura Hutchings**

**Next?**

The science-fiction novels of John Wyndham, particularly *The Day of the Triffids* (UTBG 96), offer glimpses of the end of the world as we know it.

For other post-holocaust novels, try the harrowing *Brother in the Land* by Robert Swindells, *The Postman* by David Brin or *On the Beach* by Nevil Shute.

Or the haunting *Empty World* (UTBG 115).

---

# THE ZIGZAG KID  David Grossman

14+

**Next?**

There's another David Grossman you're bound to love: *Someone to Run With* about life in modern Jerusalem.

For a story about stories, mixing fantasy and reality, try Salman Rushdie's beautiful *Haroun and the Sea of Stories*.

Or have a look at our coming of age feature on pp. 296–297.

Nonny is about to turn 13. And what a birthday it's going to be... You see, he thinks he's getting on a train to visit his Uncle Samuel, The Great Educator, who will give him an unbearable lecture on responsible behaviour. But Nonny wasn't counting on meeting Felix Glick, and he wasn't expecting what happened next...

For Nonny's father and stepmother have cooked up a magical birthday surprise, a mystery adventure tour of discovery and self-discovery. And author David Grossman has done just the same for us. His little miracle of a book is funny, thought-provoking and touching (the three most important things in a book, I reckon). It may seem like an odd thing to say, but I'm just glad this book exists; I hope you will be, too.

**Daniel Hahn**

# ZOO  Graham Marks

**Next?**

More Graham Marks? Try *Tokyo* about a boy searching for his lost sister in the seedy backstreets of Tokyo.

*Unique* (UTBG 390) also looks at the issue of cloning through the medium of a nationwide chase.

Equally addictive and unputdownable chase novels include *The Defender* (UTBG 100) by Alan Gibbons and *Jimmy Coates: Killer* by Joe Craig.

A similar psychological thriller is *Kissing the Rain* (UTBG 209).

Cam Stewart's comfortable, laid-back, American lifestyle is shattered when he is kidnapped and held up for ransom with no explanation. Escaping and killing a man on the way, Cam relies on the kindness of strangers to pick him up physically and mentally as he desperately tries to run away from the past, and starts to discover the unexpected and shocking truth of who he really is.

Edgy, hard-hitting and high-octane, Cam's disaster-ridden narrative unfolds like an episode of *24*. Cleverly timed chapters accelerate the action and maintain the momentum in this edge-of-the-seat action adventure.

**Eileen Armstrong**

# ZORBA THE GREEK  Nikos Kazantzakis

14+

'I first met him in Piraeus.' This is my comfort book. Whenever I'm ill, I read it while sipping sweet hot sage, like the narrator in the opening scene. He sits in a rain-lashed bar in the port of Athens, waiting for the ferry that will take him to his new life. But it is Zorba who leads him to a new life, and a new way of looking at things.

One of the most amazing, vibrant characters in the whole world of fiction, Zorba is childlike and warlike, gentle and sly, constantly amazed at the beauty and strangeness of this earth.

Let Zorba take you by the hand and show you his Crete, his Greece, his world.

**Caroline Lawrence**

**Next?**

Nikos Kazantzakis wrote some amazingly good and thought-provoking novels; *Christ Recrucified* sets the story of the Passion in a Greek village; while in *The Last Temptation* we're asked to believe that Jesus didn't die on the cross at all (maybe). Hugely controversial. Read it and see what you think the author meant.

*Bitter Lemons* by Lawrence Durrell is a brilliantly evocative book about Cyprus.

Or for another huge story set on a Greek island, try *Captain Corelli's Mandolin* (UTBG 63).

# About the Contributors

**DAVID ALMOND** was born in Newcastle and grew up in a big Catholic family. He has been a teacher and is now a writer, best known for the remarkable *Skellig*. He lives with his family in Northumberland, just beyond Hadrian's Wall, which for centuries marked the place where civilisation ended and the wastelands began.

**ABIGAIL ANDERSON** is a freelance theatre director who has worked on a number of plays for teenagers including an adaptation of Melvyn Burgess' *Junk*. She is also a script reader for new plays and a researcher for www.icons.org.uk

**ILIEANA ANTONOPOLOU** was born in Greece, where she first got addicted to books. Since leaving school she has lived in England where (in between books) she has studied medicine at Oxford and occasionally gone scuba diving looking for old things.

**NOGA APPLEBAUM** is up to her neck in children's science fiction, the subject of her seemingly never-ending PhD research. In 2005 she won first prize in the London Writers' Competition, in the children's books category.

**JON APPLETON** has been a reviewer of children's books, and has spent the last ten years editing them. He had lots of fun working with Danny, Leonie and Susan on the first *UBG* at A & C Black, and is now having fun being Senior Editor at Orion Children's Books.

**PHILIP ARDAGH** recently collaborated with Paul McCartney and Geoff Dunbar on Sir Paul's first children's book *High In the Clouds*, but is probably best known for his **Eddie Dickens** adventures. He regularly reviews for *The Guardian*.

**MAX AREVUO** is 13 years old. He lives in Golders Green with his parents and sister. An enthusiastic reader, he prefers autobiographies but enjoys most books that are put in front of him. As his favourite sport is cricket, he really likes cricket-based books.

**NEIL ARKSEY** writes for TV when he's not being an author. His books for teens include *Brooksie*, *MacB*, *Playing on the Edge* and *As Good as Dead in Downtown*.

**OLIVIA ARMES** is 15 and lives in London. She enjoys relaxing with friends, photography and most of all surfing. She has two Siamese cats called Coco Darling and Wooster. She has a brother, who she also likes to think of as a pet.

**EILEEN ARMSTRONG** is a high school librarian in Northumberland, a reviewer and feature writer for a variety of professional journals and author of *Fully Booked: Reader development and the Secondary School LRC*. She is currently vice chair of the national School Library Association.

**SHERRY ASHWORTH** has written many novels for teenagers, including, most recently, *Paralysed*. Her own books are reality- and character-based, but she enjoys reading everything and anything. She lives in Manchester and has a husband, two grown-up daughters and two very lazy cats.

**LYNNE REID BANKS** is one of the most respected of authors. She has written many books, but is best-known for *The L-Shaped Room* for adults and *The Indian in the Cupboard* for children. She also has the distinction of being the first-ever woman TV news reporter!

**ANDREW BARAKAT** was born in New York, NY and moved to London in 2002. He attends Arnold House School and enjoys visiting the library and reading. Academic work is a priority, though he loves sport and music, too.

**DAVID BARD** is a talkative, inquisitive, sporty and enthusiastic 13-year-old, who attends Arnold House School. Always up for a challenge, often willing to try new things and always ready for a good chat, David is great company, whatever the circumstances. Occasionally, he even reads a book.

**RAFFAELLA BARKER** lives in Norfolk. She has written seven adult novels, and one for teens called *Phosphorescence*. She was paid by her father to read as a nine-year-old and the investment yielded huge dividends in that it taught her that no price is too high to get children to read. Her sons have cost a fortune but it has been worth it.

**FELICITY-ROSE BARROW** is an aspiring writer and illustrator who left school at 15. She lives in a small colourful bubble in Warwickshire with her books and plants and is now studying art at college.

In her eight novels, **JOAN BAUER** explores difficult issues with humour and hope. A *New York Times* best-selling author, her books have won numerous awards. She lives in Brooklyn, NY with her husband.

**NINA BAWDEN** has written over 40 novels. Her best known book is perhaps *Carrie's War*, and her latest, *Dear Austen*, is about the Potter's Bar railway crash which injured her and killed her husband.

**SUSILA BAYBARS** has spent the last 13 years immersed in children's books. After a short spell at Waterstone's she's hopped around publishers, working with the good and the great, loving every minute of it.

**K.K. BECK** is the author of 21 crime thrillers. Her novels for young adult readers are *Fake* and *Snitch*, published by Scholastic.

**DAVID BELBIN** is the author of *Love Lessons*, **The Beat** series, *Denial* and many other novels for young adults. He has also written a book about eBay.co.uk and numerous short stories for both adult and younger readers.

**JULIA BELL** is a novelist and lecturer at Birkbeck, UCL. Her publications include the novels *Massive* and *Dirty Work* and the *Creative Writing Coursebook*.

**JULIE BERTAGNA**'s first-published work was a glowing review of her brother's appalling rock band for the local paper when she was a teenager, and she has been writing ever since. She is currently completing *Zenith*, the sequel to *Exodus*. She lives in Glasgow with her family.

**THOMAS BLOOR** has always lived in London. As well as writing, he also teaches adults part-time, and has worked as a library assistant, an art technician, an artificial-flower maker and a classroom assistant. He's married and has two children.

**TIM BOWLER** has written seven novels for teenagers. *Midget* and *Dragon's Rock* established him as a powerful new voice and his third novel, *River Boy*, won the Carnegie Medal. His new novel, *Frozen Fire*, is due out in 2006.

**TONY BRADMAN** decided, at the age of 13, that he wanted to be a writer. He published his first children's book in 1984, and since then has written or edited nearly 200 further titles. He is currently chair of The Children's Writers and Illustrators Group of The Society of Authors, and has recently been appointed to the PLR Advisory Committee.

**GERALDINE BRENNAN** is books editor of the *TES*, and has recently judged the Nestlé Smarties Book Prize and the Booktrust Teenage Prize.

**THERESA BRESLIN** loves reading and writing books for young people, and is prepared to talk about this to anyone who will listen! Her novel *Whispers in the Graveyard*, about a boy who struggles to read and write, won her the Carnegie Medal.

**KEVIN BROOKS** is married to Susan, a freelance editor. They have two dogs (Shaky and Jess) and live in Essex. He's had loads of horrible jobs and also spent many years involved in music (writing and recording) and art (painting and sculpture). He's been a full-time writer for the last five years.

**MELVIN BURGESS** was born in Twickenham. He did poorly at school, which he didn't much enjoy. Writing was his ambition since the age of 14, and after many rejections, his first book was published in 1990. Since then his work has been published around the world and he has won several prizes for his books.

**MEG CABOT** is the best-selling author of several series for young adults, including **The Princess Diaries**, **The Mediator**, and **Missing**, as well as *All American Girl*, *Teen Idol*, *Nicola and the Viscount*, *Victoria and the Rogue* and many books for older readers.

**JAMIE CAPLAN** is 12 years old and attends an all-boys prep school. He is passionate about sport – pretty much any sport! He reads to relax and prefers books about real-life issues.

**ALEXANDER CARN** is 13 years old and lives in London with his mother, father and sister. He prefers academic work to sport, but enjoys clay-pigeon shooting.

**ROSEMARY CASS-BEGGS**, after a degree in psychology, specialised in focus groups for consumer research and tutored in the Open University. She re-discovered literature for children in the 1960s and has read it ever since.

**ANNE CASSIDY** worked as a bank clerk and a teacher before she became a writer. She has written 20 crime novels for teenagers. She lives in east London with her husband and son. When she's not writing she is shopping or watching junk TV.

**GARY CHOW** is a 17-year-old Hong Konger living in Rugby. He has many hobbies, such as reading, reading and more reading.

**JONATHAN COE** is the author of seven novels, including *The Rotters' Club* and *The Closed Circle*, and a biography of the novelist B.S. Johnson.

**ADAM COHEN** is 13 years' old and lives in London with his parents and three brothers. He loves adventure books and is the most loyal supporter of Cardiff City and Glamorgan Cricket Club outside the Welsh borders.

**EOIN COLFER** was born and still lives in Ireland. He is the author of many books including the best-selling **Artemis Fowl**, a series which grew from his love of Irish history and legend. Its success enabled him to give up teaching and to write full time.

**WENDY COOLING** is a children's books consultant and the creator of Bookstart, which gives free books to every baby in the country. She has also edited many story and poetry collections.

**YVONNE COPPARD** was a teacher and then a child protection adviser before taking up writing full-time. She writes serious and humorous novels for children and teenagers, and some books for teachers.

**MICHAEL COX** has written over 35 children's books and is published in more than a dozen countries, including Russia, Brazil and Korea (although he says that translating 'knock-knock' jokes into Korean always gives him a headache).

**MICHAEL CRONIN** is an actor and writer. He has worked throughout the world on stage, in film and on TV. *In the Morning...*, the final title of his World War II trilogy, was published this year.

**GILLIAN CROSS** has been writing for young people for 30 years. Four of her **Demon Headmaster** books have been televised and she has won the Smarties Prize, the Whitbread Children's Book Award and the Carnegie Medal. She travels widely to speak about her work.

**BENJAMIN CUFFIN-MUNDAY** is a pupil at the King's School Chester. He plays clarinet and piano (with a special interest in jazz), and his other hobbies include rocks and fossils, pencil collecting, and of course All Things Books! In 2004 he was a judge for the Blue Peter Book Awards.

**ISSIE DARCY** is 13 and likes singing, dancing and drama. She loves reading everything from *Harry Potter* to *Lord of the Flies*. She has two dogs and seven chickens.

**JANE DARCY** taught English for years before giving it all up to go back to university where she is now studying English again and can read books all day. Sadly, not all of these are children's books.

**CHRIS D'LACEY** has written a wide variety of books for children of all ages from four to 14. He is a regular visitor to schools, libraries and book festivals throughout the land.

**BERLIE DOHERTY** has written nearly 50 books, and is translated into 21 languages. Her books and plays have won many awards. She has also written libretti for two children's operas. Her most recent titles are *Deep Secret*, *The Starburster* and *Jinnie Ghost*.

**JENNIFER DONNELLY** lives in Brooklyn, NY with her husband, daughter and two greyhounds. As a child, she loved to write and often inflicted dreadful poems and stories on her family and friends. She loved to read, too, and the high point of her week was a Saturday trip to the library. It still is.

**MALACHY DOYLE** writes picture books, young fiction and teenage novels. His work as a special needs teacher inspired his extraordinary first novel, *Georgie*. Malachy is Irish, lives in Wales, and is married to an Englishwoman.

**OSCAR DUB** is 13 and lives in North London. He likes reading because it offers an escape from life and a way to relax wherever you are, on the tube or just sitting at home.

**FLORENCE EASTOE** is 13 and lives in East Kent with her parents and younger brother. Her pastimes include reading, shopping and caring for the menagerie of household pets – mainly the cats and chickens.

**PATRICIA ELLIOTT**'s first novel *The Ice Boy* is set in Aldeburgh, where her family have a cottage. Her most recent novel is *Ambergate*, set in a parallel East Anglia. Patricia lives in London with her husband, two sons and a loopy labrador.

**ANNE FINE** has written 12 books for older readers. She was Children's Laureate from 2001–3 and has won numerous awards, including the Whitbread and the Carnegie (both twice) and the Guardian Children's Fiction Prize.

**CATHERINE FISHER** is a poet and novelist. Her best-known works include *Corbenic*, *Darkwater Hall* and the acclaimed **Book of the Crow** series. Catherine's latest publications are *The Scarab* and *Darkhenge*. She lives in Wales with her two cats, Jess and Tam.

**ANNE FLAHERTY** worked as a news journalist in Ireland, South Africa and Hong Kong before studying for an MA in children's literature. She now lives in London and is a freelance writer, in between looking after Daniel (9) and Holly Mei (2).

**CATHERINE FORDE** writes stories with young adults as her central characters. Her novels *Fat Boy Swim*, *Skarrs* and *The Drowning Pond* have contemporary settings and realistic Glaswegian dialogue.

**LINDSEY FRASER** was a children's bookseller in Cambridge before she became Executive Director of Scottish Book Trust. She is now a partner in Fraser Ross Associates, the Edinburgh-based literary agency and consultancy.

**EDDIE FRY** (a.k.a. Haggis Basher) is a small, scruffy-haired boy. He is 12, and is fanatical about rugby, jaffa cakes and Scotland. Although he is a mature head boy at his school, he still can't wait for the new *Beano* annual.

**DAVID GARDNER** is a Y11 student and National Literacy Trust accredited Reading Champion. Anyone who says teenagers don't read anymore has obviously never met David. He's made it his mission to ensure no one leaves the school library empty-handed.

**GRAHAM GARDNER** wanted to be a writer from age eight. He is now 30, and went through at least 30 jobs before he saw his first novel published. When he can find the time, he plays classical, rock and ragtime piano and listens to all kinds of music. Graham is the second-eldest of ten children and lives in West Wales.

**SUSAN GATES** lives in the north of England. She has taught in schools in Malawi, Africa and County Durham. She likes, among other things: the north of England, playing guitar (her dad is 83 and still gigging with his band) and her husband's cooking. Her latest teenage novels are *Dusk* and *Firebird*.

**JAMILA GAVIN** is known for her books reflecting her Anglo-Indian background, such as the **Surya** trilogy, though her Whitbread Children's Books' prize-winner was *Coram Boy*, set between London and Gloucestershire.

**ADÈLE GERAS** has written more than 90 books for children and two books for adults. Her latest young-adult novel is *Ithaka*.

**ALAN GIBBONS** grew up in a family of Cheshire farm labourers and went to Warwick University. His early love of reading led to a career in teaching. After 18 years at the chalkface Alan took the gamble to become a full-time writer. Since then he has never looked back. He lives in Liverpool with his wife and four children.

**MORRIS GLEITZMAN** was born in England but grew up in Australia. He always wanted to write, and after many TV comedy scripts started writing for children. Twenty-two books later, he's still doing so – and loving it!

**CANDIDA GRAY** has degrees in theatre, art history and history, but she has always wanted to have one in literature, too! Candida works in education and claims that she would never have survived adolescence without books.

**KEITH GRAY**'s first book, *Creepers*, was published when he was only 24. Now well into his 30s, he has written several award-winning novels including *The Runner* and *The Fearful*. He lives in Edinburgh with his girlfriend and their parrot.

**JULIA GREEN** writes mainly for young adults. She lives in Bath with her two teenage children, and lectures in creative writing at Bath Spa University. She is programme leader for the MA in Writing for Young People. She also runs writing workshops for young people and adults.

**ELENA GREGORIOU** is a teacher in a London prep school. She believes the best thing about the summer holidays is being able to read all day in the sun (and eating ice cream!).

**SARAH GRISTWOOD** is a former journalist and broadcaster, specialising in film interviews. She is also the author of two historical biographies – *Arabella: England's Lost Queen* and *Perdita: Royal Mistress, Writer, Romantic* – as well as of a book on women's diaries.

**HATTIE GRYLLS** is 13. She lives in Islington with her mum, dad and younger brother George, and the newest member of her household, a rescue dog called Lolly. When not playing with Lolly she reads, swims and listens to her iPod.

**MARY HOFFMAN** is the author of at least 85 books for children and teenagers. Her two most famous series are **Amazing Grace** and its sequels, and the **Stravaganza** series of teenage fantasy. She also edits the online book review magazine *Armadillo*.

**ELIZABETH HONEY** grew up on a farm in Victoria, Australia, went to art college, travelled and worked at many things before becoming an illustrator. For years she illustrated books by other people, then she tried writing and illustrating her own. Now there's no stopping her. Elizabeth and her family live in Melbourne.

**ANTONIA HONEYWELL** is taking a break from being a head of English to study for an MA. Her interest in children's literature was heightened by the birth of her first baby, Oliver, following which she will mind less if she never wins the Booker Prize.

**MARY HOOPER** has been writing for young adults for an awfully long time and enjoys the variety of being able to write historical fiction one day and funny stuff the next. She has two grown-up children and lives in Hampshire. Her hobbies are pottering about and being nosy.

**CATHY HOPKINS** lives in North London with her husband and three mad cats. She has been writing since 1987 and so far has had 34 books published. She is the author of the **Mates Dates...** teen-fiction series (set in London) and the **Truth or Dare...** series (set in Cornwall). The books are now published in 22 different countries.

**ANTHONY HOROWITZ** is the author of the best-selling **Alex Rider** series – the first of which, *Stormbreaker*, has now been filmed. He continues to live in Crouch End with his wife, his children – Nicholas and Cassian – and his dog, Loony.

**LESLEY HOWARTH** has written over 20 books for children and teenagers. Her novel *MapHead* won the Guardian Children's Fiction Prize, and she has always had a special interest in science fiction. Her latest novel *Calling the Shots* is published in April, 2006.

**LAURA HUTCHINGS** is head of English at a boys' prep school in North London. One of things that she enjoys most about her job is the fact that it gives her an excuse to read all the children's books that she'd be reading anyway!

**EVA IBBOTSON** writes for both adults and children. Many of her books for younger children are concerned with the fate of ghosts, witches and monsters, but *Journey to the River Sea* and *Star of Kazan* are about journeys to exotic places.

**BENEDICT JACKA** is half-Australian, half-Armenian, and grew up in London. Before becoming a full-time writer, he worked as a bouncer, held a job in the Civil Service and went to Cambridge University. He's now 25 and divides his time between writing, reading, martial arts and playing games.

**JULIA JARMAN** was born talking, or so her mum says. In fact she only stops talking in order to read and write. Writing, she thinks, is another way of talking, and she has written over 100 books. *Peace Weavers* is her latest for teens.

**KATIE JENNINGS** edits children's fiction and non fiction for a certain London publishing house (which

just happens to publish *The UTBG*). Like most people in children's books, she owns two cats.

**CATHERINE JINKS** was born in Brisbane, Australia in 1963. She is the author of many children's books and also writes for adults. Her fiction has been published all over the world.

**PETE JOHNSON** worked as a film critic for Radio One and as a teacher. His experiences in the classroom made him decide to write. He now writes books, some of which are funny and some of which are scary, but all of which (in the editors' opinion) are great.

**ANN JUNGMAN** was born in London of refugee parents. After taking a degree in law, Ann did some supply teaching and decided to change careers. Teaching led to writing, and Ann has published over a hundred books for children. In addition to writing, Ann runs Barn Owl Books, which reprints out-of-print quality children's books.

**ARIEL KAHN**'s cultural world is occupied with **The Sandman**, *Buffy*, and other high-brow literary figures. A fiction and poetry writer, Ariel is currently working on his first novel as well as teaching both creative writing and graphic novels at London South Bank University.

**ELIZABETH KAY** is half-Polish and half-English, and she went to art school. She wrote the **Divide** trilogy, and researches her fantasy settings in places as diverse as the jungles of Borneo, the deserts of Egypt, the volcanoes of Costa Rica and the glaciers of Iceland.

**BRIAN KEANEY** was born in London where he still lives. His parents were Irish and he grew up listening to his mother telling stories. He made up his mind at an early age that he wanted to be

a writer, and considers it the best job in the world. He has written 14 novels for young people.

**ELIZABETH LAIRD** has always been a traveller. Born in New Zealand, she has lived in Malaysia, Ethiopia, Iraq, Lebanon and Austria, and those feet still keep itching. Some of her books reflect her travels, but others are set right here in Britain.

**CAROLINE LAWRENCE** is a Californian whose obsession with ancient history and languages brought her to England to study Classics at Cambridge and Hebrew at London. She stayed on in England to teach at a London primary school. In 1999 she began writing the **Roman Mysteries**.

**MICHAEL LAWRENCE** became a writer for young people with the publication of *When the Snow Falls* in 1995. Since then he has published many more books, for all ages, including the best-selling **Jiggy McCue** series and the acclaimed trilogy about alternative realities, **The Aldous Lexicon**.

**GAIL CARSON LEVINE** grew up in New York City and has been writing all her life. Her first book for children, *Ella Enchanted*, was a 1998 Newbery Honor Book. With her husband, David, and their Airedale, Baxter, she lives in a 200-year-old farmhouse in the Hudson River Valley.

**FRANCESCA LEWIS** read English at Cambridge. She graduated in 1995 and has worked in publishing and public relations ever since. Her current role is writing features for the Department for Culture, Media and Sport.

**SUE LIMB** is a writer and broadcaster specialising in comedy. She lives in Gloucestershire in a slightly haunted cottage with her daughter

Betsy, who is an ex-teenager. Sue is a very bad cook. Her favourite animal is the toad.

**JOAN LINGARD** has published 15 adult novels and more than 40 books for young people, the best-known being her **Ulster** quintet about Catholic Kevin and Protestant Sadie in war-torn Belfast, beginning with *The Twelfth Day of July*.

**CATHERINE MACPHAIL** lives in Scotland. She always wanted to be a writer, but it was only after her children were born that she had the courage to send off her first short story. Since then she has written short stories, romantic novels and comedy series for Radio Two, but her major success has been with her teenage novels. The latest, *Roxy's Baby*, is her 21st.

**MARGARET MAHY** has written over 180 books, including picture books, middle-school books, senior and young adult books and collections of short stories. She enjoys the way language can be used in children's books to create jokes and mysteries.

**LOUISE MANNING** lives in London. She loves to read (obviously), anything from *Harry Potter* to *Pride and Prejudice*. She says she doesn't have a favourite book – she just loves all of them. In her free time she likes going out with her friends or going swimming at her local pool.

**JAN MARK**, who lives in Oxford with four cats and a houseful of books, has written many novels for all ages. She gave up teaching to become a full-time writer and, since the publication of her first novel *Thunder and Lightnings*, has twice won the Carnegie Medal.

**GRAHAM MARKS** is an ex-graphic designer turned author. When he's not writing teen / young-adult novels for Bloomsbury and

younger fiction for Usborne, he is children's books editor for the trade paper *Publishing News*, for whom he's interviewed just about every major publisher, author and illustrator in the field.

**BRENDA MARSHALL** is head of English and librarian at Port Regis, a prep school in Dorset. She is also the English co-ordinator for IAPS, an editor of *4–11*, the magazine of The English Association, and an independent schools' inspector.

**SUE MAYFIELD** was originally a teacher. Sue often leads workshops in schools and has been a youth worker and writing therapist. Born near Newcastle, she now lives in Cheltenham with her husband and three teenage sons.

**GERALDINE MCCAUGHREAN** writes for all ages. She has won the Carnegie Medal, Guardian Children's Fiction Prize, Blue Peter Book Award, four Smarties Bronzes, and three Whitbread Children's Book Awards. Perhaps because she has one teenage daughter, Ailsa, she most enjoys writing for the category '12 to adult'.

**JOHN MCLAY** is a children's books literary scout. He is also a lecturer, an anthologist and a book reviewer. He has previously worked for Puffin Books, been a children's bookseller and sold translation rights internationally.

**LIZ MCMANUS** was born in Wales, came to London to do a degree, and whilst a student secured a job as a chauffeuse during Wimbledon fortnight, driving the tennis stars around London. She stayed to teach in secondary schools around the Wimbledon area.

**ANDY MCNAB**, DCM MM, joined the army as a boy soldier and is a former member of the SAS, one of the world's elite special forces

commando units. *Bravo Two Zero*, McNab's account of the Gulf War operation that he led in 1991, is the best-selling war book of all time and launched his career as a writer.

**CLIFF MCNISH** is a fantasy writer whose first series, the **Doomspell** trilogy, won him an instant and avid readership. He has followed up the success of this series with his **Silver** sequence.

**VALERIE MENDES** knew she wanted to be a writer when she was six and her first short story was published in her school magazine. Since then she has written two picture books and four novels for teenagers, including *Girl in the Attic*, *The Drowning* and *Lost and Found*.

**LIVI MICHAEL** has written four award-winning books for adults, the **Frank** series for younger children and *The Whispering Road* for older children.

**ELEANOR MILNES-SMITH** has often been described by her friends – at least the human ones – as completely insane. She has always been an avid reader of fantasy and now, aged 13, is a fan of Terry Pratchett and Christopher Paolini.

**PHILIPPA MILNES-SMITH** is a literary agent and children's specialist at the agency LAW (Lucas Alexander Whitley). She has worked for many years in children's publishing and was previously the managing director of Puffin Books.

**NICOLA MORGAN** has written around 70 books, mostly home-learning titles based on her speciality in literacy acquisition. In 2002 she achieved her overriding ambition to be a novelist with *Mondays Are Red*. She now writes non fiction and fiction, and has a busy schedule of school talks, festivals and conferences. She lives in Edinburgh with her family.

**SAMUEL MORTIMER** lives in Devon. His hobbies include playing guitar (he's really into rock music), judo and reading.

**BEVERLEY NAIDOO** grew up in Johannesburg. As a student she joined the resistance to apartheid, ending up exiled in England. Her first book *Journey to Jo'burg* was banned in South Africa. That spurred her to keep writing! She won the Carnegie Medal for *The Other Side of Truth*.

**LINDA NEWBERY** writes fiction for all ages. Her young-adult novels, *The Shell House* and *Sisterland*, were both shortlisted for the Carnegie Medal. She also writes short stories and poems, and tutors writing courses for children, teenagers and adults.

**SARA NICKERSON** wrote for TV and film before publishing her first novel *How To Disappear Completely and Never Be Found*. When not writing, she's anxiously waiting for her two tadpoles to sprout legs.

**JENNY NIMMO** lives in Wales. She worked in the theatre before joining the BBC where she became a writer / director in children's TV. She won the Smarties Gold Award for *The Snow Spider* in 1986 and for *The Owl Tree* in 1997. She is currently writing a quintet: **Children of the Red King**.

**ANDREW NORRISS** has, over 20 years, written and co-written some 150 episodes of sit-coms and children's drama for television, and six books for children, including *Aquila*, which won the Whitbread Children's Book Award in 1997. He lives, very contentedly, in a village in Hampshire with his wife and two children.

**IAN OGILVY** is best known as an actor – in particular for his role of *The Saint*. He has also made a number of films and starred on the London stage. He has written two novels and three children's books (with more to come) all about his hero, Measle Stubbs. He lives in Southern California with his wife Kitty and two stepsons.

**KENNETH OPPEL** is the author of *Airborn*, its sequel, *Skybreaker*, as well as the **Silverwing** trilogy, which has sold over a million copies worldwide. He published his first novel at 17, after receiving encouragement from Roald Dahl.

**TERRI PADDOCK** is the author of one teen novel, *Come Clean*, and one adult novel, *Beware the Dwarfs*. Formerly a freelance journalist, she's now the editor of www.whatsonstage.com, the UK's leading theatre website, and the monthly *Theatregoer Magazine*.

**HELEN PAIBA** was born in London where she has lived most of her life. In 1974 she became the owner of The Children's Bookshop in North London and ran it for 20 years. The shop still flourishes under Lesley and Kate Agnew, whilst Helen enjoys cooking, travelling and READING.

**CHRISTOPHER PAOLINI** was born in 1983, and was home-schooled by his parents in Montana. He began writing *Eragon* as a hobby, and it was originally self-published, with all the artwork and maps being Christopher's own work. Carl Hiaasen brought the book to his publisher's attention, and the book is now on sale all over the world. On completing the trilogy, Christopher plans to take a long holiday.

**MELANIE PALMER** works as an editor in children's books, makes occasional appearances in furry mouse or spotted leopard outfits and lives in North London with seven other vagabonds.

**PHILIPPA PEARCE** is a highly acclaimed children's writer, whose most famous title is *Tom's Midnight Garden* for which she won the Carnegie Medal. Her most recent book is *The Little Gentleman*.

**MAL PEET** grew up in Norfolk and escaped to read English and American Literature at Warwick University, which threw him out a year later. He spent many years drawing cartoons while avoiding proper jobs, then settled down to write and illustrate books for children – his first novel was *Keeper*.

**HELENA PIELICHATY** won a bar of chocolate for writing a story when she was ten. She can't remember the story but she does remember the chocolate. Later, in Y9, she read *Jackie* magazine and was engrossed by 'Cathy and Clare's Problem Page'. She has been interested in chocolate and other people's problems ever since.

**CAROLINE PITCHER** writes stories for all ages. This year, *Cloud Cat* and *Sky Shifter* have been published. They are the first two books in the **Year of Changes** quartet.

**ANNA POSNER** is a sixth-form student who got to contribute to this book as she is the niece of one of the editors.

**SUSAN PRICE** was born and still lives in Dudley in the Midlands. She had her first novel published when she was 16. Since then she has written many more, including the award-winning *The Sterkarm Handshake*.

**SALLY PRUE** was rubbish at writing stories at school, but as she grew up she gradually realised she couldn't do anything else, much, either. So, as writing didn't require money or qualifications, she had a go; and, after only 15 years of toil, had her first novel, *Cold Tom*, published. She lives in

Hertfordshire with her husband and elder daughter.

**BALI RAI** is a fairly young and occasionally exciting author. He has written over ten books that deal with the realities of life in modern Britain for young adults / teens. He is also on a mission to convert all young people to his own religion – Liverpool FC. If you read his books backwards and upside down you will find that every sentence reads: You WILL support LFC.

**CELIA REES** writes for teenagers. Her novels include *Witch Child*, *Sorceress* and *Pirates!* She lives in Leamington Spa and divides her time between writing, talking to readers in schools and libraries, acting as a tutor on creative writing courses and reviewing.

**PHILIP REEVE** worked in a bookshop before becoming known as an illustrator. His first book for children, *Mortal Engines*, created one of the most intriguing worlds in fantasy fiction. The final book in the quartet, *A Darkling Plain*, will be published in 2006.

**ANTHONY REUBEN** is a BBC business journalist and television producer. He only got to contribute to this book because he is married to one of the editors, in which capacity he was also asked for his autograph for the first time at the Blue Peter Book Awards.

**JAMES REYNOLDS** is a BBC news correspondent. He is based in Jerusalem, from where he covers events in the Middle East. In his spare time he enjoys floating in the Dead Sea and translating Latin American poetry.

**JAMES RIORDAN** is Emeritus Professor at the University of Surrey and a Fellow of the Royal Society for the Arts. To keep sane in the world of academia, he also writes both picture books and

novels for young people of his own writing-age ability – 11–15.

**KATHERINE ROBERTS** graduated from Bath University with first-class honours in mathematics, but always wanted to be a fantasy writer. Her debut novel was *Song Quest*, and ten years of working as a racehorse groom led to her Alexander epic *I Am The Great Horse*. She lives in a workhouse in Stroud.

**CATHERINE ROBINSON** has been writing books for children of all ages, from pre-school to teens, for nearly 20 years. Her most recent work has been a series of one-off teenage novels for Scholastic.

**TIM ROSE** joined Walker Books in 1988 and has been designing children's books ever since. He was art director on the Scholastic fiction list for six or so years, during which he worked with many wonderful authors and illustrators. He is now art director at Orchard Books.

**KATHRYN ROSS** is a former English teacher, independent bookseller and deputy director of Scottish Book Trust. She is now a partner in Fraser Ross Associates, the Edinburgh-based literary agency.

**MEG ROSOFF** won great acclaim for her first novel, *How I Live Now*, which was published in 2004. An American, she lives in London with her husband and daughter.

**ROSIE RUSHTON** has had over 30 books published worldwide. From light-hearted series to more serious novels, her focus is always on the issues and conflicts facing young people today. She is a secondary-school governor, a lay minister in the Church of England, and has three young grandchildren.

**HUGH SCOTT** is me and time past gone I found words fun like blank jigsaws for together putting with love and meanings way beyond

usual; so write I did and rot a Book called *The Plant That Ate the World*, and chum book called *Freddie and the Enormouse*, and bigger tough chum book called *Why Weeps the Brogan?*, and three chums wow! publishers entered for Whitbread Prize thrill, and *Brogan* won, wow again.

**MARCUS SEDGWICK** is an award-winning author of children's books. He has worked in publishing for 15 years, as bookseller, editor, publisher and in sales. He currently works for Walker Books.

**DARREN SHAN** always wanted to be a writer and is now a publishing phenomenon! His **Saga of Darren Shan** has sold in huge numbers and each new volume is eagerly awaited across the globe.

**NICK SHARRATT** is the illustrator of Jacqueline Wilson's multi-million selling novels. He also illustrates picture books for writers like Julia Donaldson and Giles Andreae, as well as writing his own.

**RACHEL SHAW** is in Y9. She enjoys spending time with her friends. These are her first book reviews – and she enjoyed doing them!

**HELEN SIMMONS** works in a small independent bookshop in Bath and has specialised in children's books for most of her career. She also has a job as a school librarian and is a reviewer for Book Trust.

**NICKY SINGER**'s first novel for children, *Feather Boy,* won the Blue Peter Book Award and was made into a TV drama. Her second, *Doll,* was shortlisted for the Booktrust Teenage Prize and her latest, *The Innocent's Story*, is about terrorism and moral responsibility.

**GARETH SMITH** lives in South Wales. Like most contributors to this book, Gareth loves reading, in both English and Welsh. He was a judge for the 2004 Blue Peter Book Awards.

**JERRY SPINELLI** is the author of books, six children and 16 grandchildren. The books have been translated into many languages around the world. Jerry and his wife, fellow-author Eileen, live in Willistown, Pennsylvania.

**WILLIAM SUTCLIFFE** was born in 1971 in London. He is the author of four novels, *New Boy*, *Are You Experienced?*, *The Love Hexagon* and *Bad Influence*, which have been translated into 17 languages.

**REBECCA SWIFT** is an editor, writer and director of The Literary Consultancy. Her publications include a correspondence between Bernard Shaw and Margaret Wheeler, *Letters from Margaret*. She has also published poems and has written the libretto for the opera, *Spirit Child*, with composer Jenni Roditi.

**ROBERT SWINDELLS** was born in West Yorkshire and has lived there all his life. He's been a proofreader, a clerk, an airman, a factory worker, a security guard, a bingo checker and a teacher. He has written full time since 1980. He has retired as a visiting author, and is currently working on his 65th book. Robert says he has the best job in the world.

**MARIANNE TAYLOR** lives in North London. She is the sub-editor for *Birdwatch* magazine, and she is also a freelance writer, artist and cartoonist. In her free time she enjoys running the occasional marathon and falling over at her Aikido club.

**ALAN TEMPERLEY** lives in Scotland and can often be found on speaking tours of Scottish schools. He has written many books including *Harry and the Wrinklies*, which was made into a TV series.

**KATE THOMPSON** was born in Yorkshire but lives in Ireland. She plays Irish traditional music and

renovates old fiddles in her spare time. In 2005 she won the Guardian Children's Fiction Prize for *The New Policeman*.

**MATT THORNE** is the author of the **39 Castles** series, and six novels for adults, including *Eight Minutes Idle* and *Cherry*, which was long-listed for the Booker Prize.

**ELEANOR UPDALE**'s historical novel, *Montmorency*, won the Blue Peter Book Award for 'The Book I Couldn't Put Down'. It has two sequels. Eleanor is working on a PhD in history at the University of London, and is a patron of the Prince of Wales Arts and Kids Foundation.

**JEAN URE** had her first book published while she was still at school, and has been writing ever since. After leaving school she went to the Webber-Douglas Academy of Dramatic Art in London, where she met her husband. They now live in a 300-year-old house in South London with their family of four cats and seven dogs, all from rescue centres.

**GILL VICKERY** studied fine art and painting at college, and since then has worked as a children's librarian and English teacher.

**JILL PATON WALSH** has been a professional writer most of her working life. She has written for children and for adults. She has three children and three grandchildren and lives in Cambridge.

**ARABELLA WEIR** is a comedy writer / performer. She wrote the bestseller *Does My Bum Look Big in This?* after developing and performing the character for the BBC's *The Fast Show*.

**SARA WHEELER** writes non-fiction books, sometimes travel narratives and sometimes biographies. She

has written a travel book about the Antarctic called *Terra Incognita*, and in 2006 publishes a biography of Denys Finch Hatton, legendary white hunter and lover of Karen Blixen. It will be called *Too Close to the Sun*.

**MATT WHYMAN** is the author of several acclaimed novels, including *Boy Kills Man*, and *So Below* – the urban fantasy series. He is also known as the agony uncle for AOL UK and *Bliss* magazine.

**JEANNE WILLIS** is married with two children and lives in North London. Since 1980 she has had over 100 books published including novelty books, picture books and novels. She's won several awards and was short-listed for the Whitbread Children's Book Award for her novel, *Naked Without a Hat*.

**CHRIS WOODING** travels a lot, writes a lot, and drinks enough coffee to stun a full-grown bison every day. He writes screenplays, books for children and adults, cartoon series, graphic novels, TV shows and just about anything else he can. He lives in London, beneath an ever-increasing pile of manuscripts.

**JONNY ZUCKER** writes for children and teenagers. His work includes the **Venus Spring – Stunt Girl** series. Along the way he has worked as a stand-up comedian and a primary school teacher.

# Acknowledgements

We thought that the second book would be easier, and that we wouldn't need to depend on quite as much help from other people this time around. We were really very wrong indeed. The list of people to whom we owe a debt for helping to bring this book out is enormous. And still we're bound to have forgotten people – if we have, our apologies.

To begin with, we must give thanks to all those who made the first book a success – in particular to Jill Coleman who commissioned it, and to Jon Appleton who turned our chaotic manuscript into an exciting and special book; and then to Nicky Potter, Tabitha Pelly and Rebecca Caine, who made sure everyone in the press knew just how exciting and special it was… We were lucky enough to receive awards for the first book from Blue Peter and the National Literacy Association, for which, too, we are grateful; they helped to enhance the success of the first book, but more importantly worked wonders for our morale as we trudged through the assembling of volume two.

And so to this, the UTBG. Our most important thanks must be to our contributors, whose words make up the bulk of the book. From those who wrote single exquisite entries to those who heroically took on a dozen or more (special round of applause for Eileen Armstrong here, please): your work is – of course – what makes this book what it is. We are especially pleased that our contributors to this volume include a number of teenagers; the quality of their work, their enthusiasm, their professionalism were admirable – the rest of us could learn a great deal from them. As last time, many of our contributors have generously waived their fees, which are being donated to our chosen charity, Hope and Homes for Children (www.hopeandhomes.org) – we are delighted to have been able to raise well over £2,000 from this book to help them to continue their vital and inspiring work.

Support from publishers' publicists and authors' agents has allowed us to get hold of new titles to review and contributors to review them, without which this really wouldn't have been much of a book; so thanks to them, too.

All three of us have friends and family who have helped in any number of ways with the UTBG-ing process – some of them by writing entries or making useful suggestions, others by taking us out for drinks to take our minds off the uglier aspects of our proofreading obsessions. To Jenny Hicks for her encouragement; to Simon and Sarah and all at the Kilburn Bookshop; to Nicholas Allen and all at Arnold House School; to Noga Applebaum; to Miranda Duffy for another day spent sifting through hundreds and hundreds and hundreds of reviews sent to us by teenagers from around the country; to Sarah and David for keeping Leonie sane (not the easiest of tasks) – thanks to you all. In particular, Laura Hutchings and Anthony Reuben have shown extraordinary patience as the UTBG invaded every room of their homes and every moment of their lives – their work on the UTBG has been tireless, as has their work on other matters that have freed up the editors to get on with UTBG work when it was really their turn to do the washing-up. Laura moved house almost single-handedly on Leonie's behalf. If Anthony could possibly have carried Susan's pregnancy on her behalf, to allow her to get on with drafting her read-on suggestions, we have no doubt that he wouldn't have hesitated.

Which brings us to the latest member of the UBG team, Isaac, who very thoughtfully resisted the temptation to be born too early and throw our schedules out of kilter. His patience is more appreciated than he yet knows. In fact he turned up very efficiently a matter of hours before our deadline – before the deadline, mind, but at the last possible moment. His mother's dominant publishing gene is clearly in evidence here.

And thanks, too, to David Almond who kindly agreed to write an introduction to this book, though we did all have some doubts about whether we should invite him to write it, as on the whole we don't want him to do anything with the hours in his day but write more and more books for us to be enchanted by. Leonie and Susan disagree vigorously about the merits of almost every book they discuss – David is possibly unique in earning the highest praise from both.

Not forgetting the designers of the book, Helen Taylor and Terry Woodley, a massive thanks for making it all look so fantastic.

In the UBG we described our agent Philippa Milnes-Smith as the book's godmother, and we're delighted to say that as we graduated to book two she hasn't shirked that important rôle one bit. She and her assistants Helen Mulligan (last book) and Helen Norris (this book) have been more than generous with their time and thoughts, more than efficient in their work and – of course – a delight always. We do know how lucky we are to have them.

Finally to Susila Baybars and Katie Jennings at A & C Black, who bravely took on this project. Thanks so much for the huge amount of work you've put in. We three have enjoyed working with you on the UTBG tremendously – and just hope you have enjoyed it, too. Now on to book three…

For permission to reproduce copyright material in *The Ultimate Teen Book Guide*, the publisher thanks:

**Barrington Stoke** for permission to reproduce the covers of *Text Game* by Kate Cann and *What's Your Problem?* by Bali Rai, which appear on p. 419.

**Bloomsbury Publishing Plc** for permission to reproduce the following covers: *Girl, 15 (Charming But Insane)* by Sue Limb, which appears on p. 146; *Holes* by Louis Sachar, which appears on p. 173; *Pirates!* by Celia Rees, which appears on p. 289; *Refugee Boy* by Benjamin Zephaniah, which appears on p. 392; *Witch Child* by Celia Rees, which appears on p. 329.

**The Chicken House** for permission to reproduce the cover from *Martyn Pig* by Kevin Brooks © The Chicken House 2005, which appears on p. 236.

**HarperCollins Publishers Ltd** for permission to reproduce the following covers: *Boy Meets Boy* by David Levithan © 2003 David Levithan, which appearson p. 52; *Angus, Thongs and Full-frontal Snogging* by Louise Rennison © 1999 Louise Rennison, which appears on p. 73; *Anita and Me* by Meera Syal © 1996 Meera Syal, which appears on p. 392; *Lord Loss* by Darren Shan © 2005 Darren Shan, which appears on p. 361; *The Lord of the Rings: The Fellowship of the Ring* by J.R.R. Tolkien © George Allen & Unwin (Publishers) Ltd 1954, 1966, which appears on p. 224; *Private Peaceful* by Michael Morpurgo © 2003 Michael Morpurgo, which appears on p. 300; *Red Shift* by Alan Garner © 1973 Alan Garner, which appears on p. 39; *The Owl Service* by Alan Garner © 1967 Alan Garner, which appears on p. 281; *The Secret Adversary* by Agatha Christie © 1922 Agatha Christie, which appears on p. 104; *The Silmarillion* by J.R.R. Tolkien © George Allen & Unwin (Publishers) Ltd 1977, which appears on p. 38; *Disconnected* by Sherry Ashworth © 2002 Sherry Ashworth, which appears on p. 201.

**Hodder Children's Books** for permission to reproduce the following covers: *The Fire-Eaters* by David Almond, which appears on p. 130; *Skellig* by David Almond, which appears on p. 343; *Fleshmarket* by Nicola Morgan, which appears on p. 328.

**Macmillan Children's Books** for permission to reproduce the following covers: *Across the Nightingale Floor* by Lian Hearn © Lian Hearn Associates Pty Ltd, 2002, which appears on p. 12; *Forever* by Judy Blume © Judy Blume, 1975, Macmillan Children's Books, London, UK, which appears on p. 135; *The Princess Diaries* by Meg Cabot © Meg Cabot, 2000, Macmillan Children's Books, London UK, which appears on p. 73; *Sugar Rush* by Julie Burchill © Julie Burchill, 2004, Macmillan Children's Books, London, UK, which appears on p. 296; *The Hitchhiker's Guide to the Galaxy* by Douglas Adams © Serious Productions Ltd, 1979, cover images © Photonica/Getty Images, Macmillan Children's Books, London, UK, which appears on p. 171.

**Orion Books** for permission to reproduce the following covers: *A Child Called 'It'* by Dave Pelzer, which appears on p. 70; *The Great Dune Trilogy* by Frank Herbert, which appears on p. 232.

**Oxford University Press** for permission to reproduce the following covers: *The Merrybegot* by Julie Hearn (OUP, 2005), which appears on p. 242; *The Iliad* by Homer, translated by Robert Fitzgerald, with an introduction by G.S. Kirk, Oxford World's Classics 1998, which appears on p. 187; *The Odyssey* by Homer, translated by Walter Shewring with an introduction by G.S. Kirk, Oxford World's Classics 1998, which appears on p. 187.

**Penguin Books Ltd** for permission to reproduce the following: the front cover and the illustration that appears on p. 239 from *The Complete Maus* by Art Spiegelman (Penguin Books, 2003). Copyright © Art Spiegelman, 1973, 1980, 1981, 1982, 1983, 1984, 1985, 1986, 1989, 1990, 1991. Additional thanks for permission to reproduce the following covers: *The Chocolate War* by Robert Cormier (Gollancz, 1975, Penguin Books, 2001). Copyright © Robert Cormier, 1975, which appears on p. 75; *The Secret Diary of Adrian Mole Aged 13 3/4* by Sue Townsend (Puffin, 2002). Copyright © Sue Townsend, 1982, which appears on p. 324; *The War of the Worlds* by H.G. Wells (First published 1898, this edition first published in Penguin Classics, 2005). Copyright © the Literary Executors of the Estate of H.G. Wells, which appears on p. 233; *When the Wind Blows* by Raymond Briggs (Hamish Hamilton, 1982). Copyright © Raymond Briggs, 1982, which appears on p. 136; *How I Live Now* by Meg Rosoff (Penguin Books, 2004). Copyright © Meg Rosoff, 2004, which appears on p. 179; *Junk* by Melvin Burgess (Penguin Books, 1997). Copyright © Melvin Burgess, 1997, which appears on p. 202; *Love in the Time of Cholera* by Gabriel García Márquez (Penguin Books, 2006). Copyright © Gabriel García Márquez, 2006, which appears on p. 227; *The Beach* by Alex Garland (First published by Viking 1996, Penguin Books, 1997). Copyright © Alex Garland, 1996, which appears on p. 264; *The Big Sleep* by Raymond Chandler (Penguin, 1948). Copyright © 1939 by Raymond Chandler, which appears on p. 105; *The Catcher in the Rye* by J.D. Salinger (Penguin Books, 1958). Copyright © J.D. Salinger, 1951, which appears on p. 66; *A Wizard of Earthsea* by Ursula Le Guin (Puffin, 1971). Copyright © Ursula Le Guin, 1971, which appears on p. 416; *A Wrinkle in Time* by Madeleine L'Engle (Puffin, 1967). Copyright © Madeleine L'Engle, 1962, which appears on p. 423; *The Hound of the Baskervilles* by Sir Arthur Conan Doyle (Penguin Books, 1996), which appears on p. 336; *Wuthering Heights* by Emily Brontë (Penguin Red Classics, 2006), which appears on p. 168; *On the Road* by Jack Kerouac (Penguin Books, 2000). Copyright © Jack Kerouac, 1955, which appears on p. 264; *Hamlet* by William Shakespeare, which appears on p. 159; *Pride and Prejudice* by Jane Austen (Penguin Classics, 2003), which appears on p. 294; *Doing It* by Melvin Burgess (Penguin Books, 2004), Copyright © Melvin Burgess, 2003, which appears on p. 169.

**Piccadilly Press Ltd** for permission to reproduce the cover from *Mates Dates and Pulling Power* by Cathy Hopkins (first published by Piccadilly Press Ltd, 2003), which appears on p. 72.

**The Random House Group Ltd** for permission to reproduce the illustration that appears on p. 118 from *Ethel and Ernest* by Raymond Briggs (published by Jonathan Cape / Red Fox). Additional thanks for permission to reproduce the following covers: *Birdsong* by Sebastian Faulks, which appears on p. 329; *Catch-22* by Joseph Heller, which appears on p. 265; *Paddy Clarke Ha Ha Ha* by Roddy Doyle, which appears on p. 282; *Palestine* by Joe Sacco, which appears on p. 136; *Slaughterhouse 5* by Kurt Vonnegut, which appears on p. 232; *The Rachel Papers* by Martin Amis, which appears on p. 296; *Titus Groan* by Mervyn Peak, which appears on p. 38; *To Kill a Mockingbird* by Harper Lee, which appears on p. 375; *Trainspotting* by Irvine Welsh, which appears on p. 264; *The Curious Incident of the Dog in the Night-time* by Mark Haddon, which appears on p. 89; *Hole in My Life* by Jack Gantos, which appears on p. 200; *Noughts and Crosses* by Malorie Blackman, which appears on p. 267; *Rani and Sukh* by Bali Rai, which appears on p. 393; *The Scarecrows* by Robert Westall, which appears on p. 360; *The Shell House* by Linda Newbery, which appears on p. 235; *Eragon* by Christopher Paolini, which appears on p. 116.

**Titan Books** for permission to reproduce the following covers: *V for Vendetta* by Alan Moore and David Lloyd. Copyright © 1990, 2006 DC Comics Inc. All rights reserved, which appears on p. 137; *Watchmen* by Alan Moore and Dave Gibbons. Copyright © 1986, 1987, 2006 DC Comics Inc. All rights reserved, which appears on p. 401.

**Wordsworth Classics** for permission to reproduce the cover of *Tales of Mystery and Imagination* by Edgar Allan Poe, which appears on p. 361.

All efforts have been made to seek permission for copyright material, but in the event of any omissions, the publisher would be pleased to hear from copyright holders and to amend these acknowledgements in subsequent editions of *The Ultimate Teen Book Guide*.

# Index